THE COOK'S BOOK OF
INGREDIENTS

THE COOK'S BOOK OF
INGREDIENTS

DK PUBLISHING

LONDON, NEW YORK, MELBOURNE, MUNICH, AND DELHI

Photographers Gary Ombler, Roger Dixon, Jon Whitaker, Lorenzo Vecchia, Gary Seagraves, Petrina Tinslay, Nicki Downey, Will Heap, Chris Villano, Deepak Aggarwal
Project Editor Norma MacMillan
Editors Helena Caldon, Fiona Corbridge, Mary Scott, Belinda Wilkinson
Designer Miranda Harvey
Picture Researcher Jenny Faithful

FOR DORLING KINDERSLEY
Senior Editors Laura Nickoll, Scarlett O'Hara
Design Consultant Heather McCarry
Art Editors Kathryn Wilding, Elly King, Caroline de Souza
Editorial Assistant Kajal Mistry
Design Assistants Elma Aquino, Danaya Bunnag
Editorial Assistance
Sarah Ruddick, Alastair Laing, Andrew Roff
Senior Jackets Creative Nicola Powling
Managing Editors Dawn Henderson, Angela Wilkes
Managing Art Editors
Marianne Markham, Christine Keilty
US Editors
Nichole Morford, Margaret Parrish, Delilah Smittle
US Recipe Adaptation
Peggy Fallon
Production Editor
Maria Elia
Senior Production Controller
Alice Sykes
Creative Technical Support
Sonia Charbonnier

First American edition, 2010

Published in the United States by
DK Publishing
375 Hudson Street
New York, NY 10014

10 11 12 13 10 9 8 7 6 5 4 3 2 1
178693—October 2010

A catalog record for this book is available
from the Library of Congress
ISBN 978-0-7566-6730-6

DK books are available at special discounts when purchased in bulk for sales promotions, premiums, fund-raising, or educational use. For details, contact: DK Publishing Special Markets, 375 Hudson Street, New York, NY 10014 or SpecialSales@dk.com

Color reproduction by Colourscan, Singapore
Printed and bound by Toppan, China

Discover more at
www.dk.com

CONTENTS

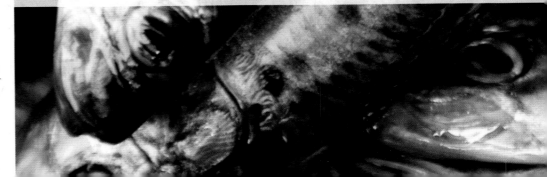

FISH & SEAFOOD

SALTWATER FISH
FRESHWATER FISH
CLAMS | SCALLOPS
MUSSELS | OYSTERS
LOBSTERS | PRAWNS
CRABS | SMOKED FISH
SALTED FISH

FISH ESSENTIALS

There are several key points to consider when choosing fish to buy. Sight, smell, and touch are needed to assess the quality of fish, and you need to know what to look for in order to determine which are the best-quality specimens. For optimum flavor, fish should be bought and cooked as fresh as possible, preferably when in season—you will find many fish species are interchangeable in recipes. Certain species are suffering from overfishing, so the sustainability of the fish should also be given consideration. If you are buying fish in advance of serving it, it is important to store it properly to keep it at its best.

BUY

Choose the freshest, best-looking fish available—one that has a bright eye and smooth, glistening skin. There are particular signs of quality all over the body of a fish, in this instance a brook trout (see page 59), that are worth knowing before you buy.

ENDANGERED FISH World fish stocks are suffering from the effects of overfishing, with some stocks near collapse and species facing extinction. Governments are imposing quotas and even outright bans to tackle the problem, but consumers can play their part, too. Check where a fish has come from and whether it has been fished sustainably; line-catching is better than nets or trawling, since it avoids unwanted by-catch and smaller fish are left behind to maintain the stocks. Instead of choosing an old favorite try something new: consider coley and pollack in place of endangered cod. And take farmed fish seriously: though it's not without issues, farms take pressure off wild stocks.

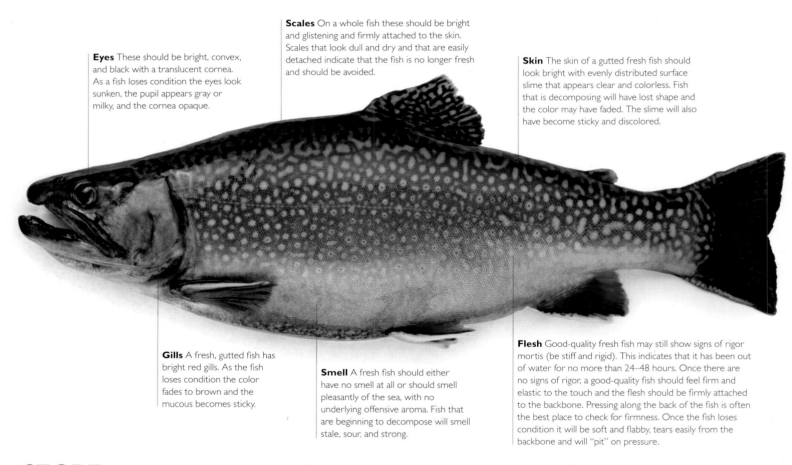

Eyes These should be bright, convex, and black with a translucent cornea. As a fish loses condition the eyes look sunken, the pupil appears gray or milky, and the cornea opaque.

Scales On a whole fish these should be bright and glistening and firmly attached to the skin. Scales that look dull and dry and that are easily detached indicate that the fish is no longer fresh and should be avoided.

Skin The skin of a gutted fresh fish should look bright with evenly distributed surface slime that appears clear and colorless. Fish that is decomposing will have lost shape and the color may have faded. The slime will also have become sticky and discolored.

Gills A fresh, gutted fish has bright red gills. As the fish loses condition the color fades to brown and the mucous becomes sticky.

Smell A fresh fish should either have no smell at all or should smell pleasantly of the sea, with no underlying offensive aroma. Fish that are beginning to decompose will smell stale, sour, and strong.

Flesh Good-quality fresh fish may still show signs of rigor mortis (be stiff and rigid). This indicates that it has been out of water for no more than 24–48 hours. Once there are no signs of rigor, a good-quality fish should feel firm and elastic to the touch and the flesh should be firmly attached to the backbone. Pressing along the back of the fish is often the best place to check for firmness. Once the fish loses condition it will be soft and flabby, tears easily from the backbone and will "pit" on pressure.

STORE

Ideally fish should be purchased on the day you intend to cook it, but if you have to store it for a short period of time, proper preparation and conditions are essential for ensuring its quality and also its safety. You can store fish in the refrigerator for up to 24 hours, but if you intend to use it after that time, it is better to freeze it on the day of purchase.

STORING FISH AT HOME The temperature of a domestic refrigerator is usually set at around 40°F (5°C), but fish should be stored at 32°F (0°C), so when storing fish in the refrigerator at home it is important to place it in the coldest part or to surround it with ice. Pack whole fish into ice and place fillets in containers set on ice. The process of commercially freezing fish is done efficiently and quickly at very low temperatures, but it is difficult to replicate this at home. Freeze fish in small quantities in double-layered freezer bags, with as much air extracted as possible and carefully sealed. Freeze the fish for no longer than 4–6 weeks.

FRESH VS. FROZEN Many fish are processed and frozen at sea for an ever-expanding market. Freezing fresh fish slows the changes that occur as spoilage takes place and, if carefully done, it can be impossible to tell the difference between fresh and frozen. Fish labeled as "frozen at sea" will have been processed and frozen within a few hours of being landed, and so the flavor is often superior to fresh fish. Fish should always be defrosted before cooking. This should be done slowly, in a refrigerator—rapid defrosting can result in loss of moisture, which will ruin the fish's texture.

PREPARE

You can buy fish already prepared, but it will not be as fresh as buying a whole fish. The amount of preparation required before cooking a fish depends on how you intend to cook it. Whole fish generally need gutting, trimming, and scaling before cooking, or you might prefer to skin and fillet it or cut it into steaks.

GUT A WHOLE ROUND FISH This essential job requires you to remove all the viscera from the stomach of the fish, usually via a cut in the belly.

1 *Place the fish on to its side and make a shallow incision into the underside of the fish. Cut along the belly, from the tail all the way up to the head.*

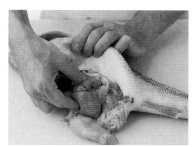

2 *Remove the guts of the fish and with the back of the knife loosen the membrane that covers the blood line located close to the back bone. Scrape this blood line away.*

3 *Rinse the inside of the fish carefully under cold running water and wipe away any gray membrane left in the belly cavity. Pat the fish dry with paper towels, inside and out.*

WHY IS MY FISH GUTTED? Some fish are gutted on landing because the guts are the first part of the fish to decompose. The belly (abdominal walls) of an ungutted fish should be smooth and show no signs of tearing. As the fish loses condition the abdomen will look blown, and as the belly tears, the guts will be visible. Some fish, including mackerel, herring, sprats, trout, and sea bass are left ungutted. Ungutted fish should be cleaned as soon as possible.

CUT STEAKS FROM A WHOLE FISH

Fish steaks are a versatile cut that are quick and easy to cook, particularly when broiled. This technique can only be used on large round fish, not small or flat specimens. Fish such as salmon, tuna, and swordfish are particularly good for cutting into steaks. The skin is left on steaks but the fish should be gutted, washed, scaled, and trimmed of any fins before being sliced.

TRIM AND SCALE If you are intending to eat the skin of the fish, you will need to trim away any fins and remove the scales for finer eating.

1 *Using scissors, remove all fins. Cut from tail to head for ease, trimming them level to the skin. Remove the tail fin after the scales, as it provides something to hold onto during scaling.*

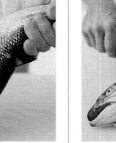

2 *Using the back of a knife or a fish scaler, scrape the scales on each side of the fish in sweeping actions from the tail to the head, against the direction in which the scales lie.*

1 *Place the prepared fish in front of you with its back toward you. Make an incision just behind the gills with a large sharp knife, and cut through to remove the head.*

SKIN A FISH FILLET Once you have deboned the fish, you can remove the skin from the fillet before cooking.

1 *Place the fish skin-side down with the thinnest part toward you. Hold the tail tip and, using a filleting knife, place the knife against your fingers, angled toward the skin.*

2 *Cut between the skin and the flesh in a firm sawing motion. Continue to move the knife along the length of the fillet, keeping the blade as close to the skin as you can.*

2 *Section the fish into steaks of even thickness using the same knife, at 1½in (4cm) intervals down to the anal vent. Fillet the tail piece, since this is too thin to steak.*

FILLET A SMALL ROUND FISH
Small round fish (such as mackerel or the red mullet shown here) can be quickly grilled, pan-fried, or poached when trimmed into two neat fillets.

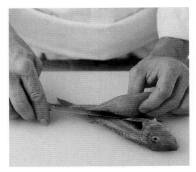

1 *With the back of the fish facing you, make a cut behind the head and the pectoral fin using a sharp filleting knife. Stop when you feel the backbone, then angle the knife to cut toward you and lift the fillet from the bone.*

2 *Remove the cut-away fillet and set aside, then turn over the fish, this time placing the head of the fish toward you. Repeat the process on the other side, but cut from the tail up to the head.*

FILLET A FLAT FISH
A flat fish can be cut up into either two fillets or, if it is a particularly large fish, like this turbot, four fillets. The fish needs scaling, the head and gills removed, and trimming before filleting.

1 *Lay the fish flat with the tail facing you. Insert the tip of a filleting knife at the top of the backbone—the top of the bone should be visible—and make a cut along the center of the fish.*

2 *Angle the knife slightly so that the tip moves over the bones of the fish, then insert it under the fillet. Carefully move the knife down to the edge of the fillet to release it at the fins.*

3 *Turn over the fish and lay it flat again, repeating the same process on the other side of the fish to create four fillets. Once you have removed the fillets, you can skin them, if you wish.*

TOOLS OF THE TRADE
Sharp knives are essential for preparing fish. Ideally, you need a large cook's knife with a 10in (25cm) blade for tougher jobs such as chopping and cutting fish steaks, whereas a flexible-bladed filleting knife makes light work of filleting fish and removing skin. A fish scaler is easier to use than a knife when removing scales. Sharp kitchen scissors are useful for trimming fish and removing fins. Fish tweezers are the most efficient tool for removing pin bones from fillets.

COOK

Fish is the ultimate fast food and most fish fillets take less than 20 minutes to cook. The muscle structure of the fish is such that quick methods of cooking suit it particularly well.

ROAST This is the most familiar way to cook fish and is best used for cooking small, prepared, and crumbed fish fillets, or larger fish, such as a whole salmon. Preheat the oven to 375°F (190°C) and lightly grease a baking tray with melted butter or oil.

1 *Arrange the fish side by side on the prepared baking tray, season the fillets and add a splash of oil or butter, or brush with oil infused with freshly chopped herbs.*

2 *Bake in the oven for 4–6 minutes, depending on the thickness of the fillets. Gently insert the tip of a sharp knife to see if the fish is cooked through—the flesh should be opaque.*

GRILL Suitable for cooking whole small fish (the fish needs to be turned halfway through cooking) or smaller fish fillets—ideally with the skin on, as this will protect the fish from drying out. Preheat the grill to its highest setting for a few minutes before cooking the fillets.

1 *Lightly score the skin of the fillets using a sharp knife. Brush the fillets with a light coating of oil (or a marinade), and season with a little salt and freshly ground black pepper.*

2 *Grill for 4–5 minutes, depending on the thickness of the fillets. Turn the fish over halfway through cooking. Remove the fish and allow to stand for 1–2 minutes before serving.*

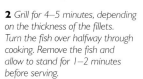

PAN-FRY This method is suitable for fillets of fish or small whole fish. The fish is fried in a smaller amount of oil than deep frying, usually using grapeseed or canola oil, and crisps up on the outside while staying moist on the inside. Pan-fried fish is especially good when coated in flour, breadcrumbs, or cornmeal before frying.

1 *Pat the fish fillet dry with paper towels to remove any excess moisture. Coat the fish with seasoned flour, breadcrumbs, or cornmeal on both sides, then shake off any excess.*

2 *Heat 1–2 tbsp of butter with a splash of oil until the butter has melted and is beginning to brown. Put the fish in the pan and cook for 1–2 minutes, until golden brown.*

3 *Turn the fish over and continue to cook on the second side for a further 1–2 minutes. Remove from the pan, drain briefly on paper towels, then serve immediately.*

HOW TO TELL WHEN FISH IS COOKED

All cuts of fish take different times to cook.
- Raw fish has a translucent appearance that turns opaque and lighter in color after cooking.
- A fish cooked whole and with its head on has various indicators: eyes turn white after cooking, the skin will pull away, and the fins can be easily pulled out.
- A fish fillet will lose its translucency and, if gently pressed, the flakes of the fish will separate. If the fish is poached in a simple, clear liquid, you can see protein released just at the point when it is cooked.

POACH Suitable for delicate fillets or steaks of fish, particularly white, textured, and smoked fish. Poached fish retains a good moisture level and the cooking liquid can then be used in a sauce, or for a stock or soup base. This method is intended for the stovetop, but fish can also be poached in the same liquid in an oven set to 350°F (180°C).

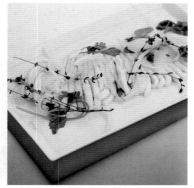

1 *Use a poaching liquid of lightly acidulated stock or infused milk. Cover the fish with the cold liquid and bring it slowly just to a boil.*

2 *Once the liquid has reached a boil, reduce the heat immediately to a gentle simmer and cook for 10–15 minutes until done.*

3 *Carefully remove the fish from the liquid in the pan; do not let it break up. Serve dressed with the poaching onions and herbs.*

STEAM This gentle, healthy method of cooking is suitable for very small whole fish, fillets, or steaks of fish. Fish for steaming can be seasoned before or after cooking and cooked with flavorings such as herbs, scallion, and citrus slices. Any liquid produced can be served with the fish or used in an accompanying sauce. All you need is a pan with a lid and a steaming rack that fits inside.

1 *Choose a saucepan with a well-fitting lid to ensure the steam is trapped. Pour in just enough water so that it doesn't touch the base of the steamer. Add any preferred aromatics to the water. Arrange the fish in a single layer in a bamboo or metal steamer basket.*

2 *Put the pan over medium heat and bring to a simmer. Place the steamer into or over the pan of liquid. Ensure that the liquid is kept at a constant boil to enable the fish to cook quickly. Don't lift the lid as this allows the steam to escape and lengthens the cooking time.*

Cooking fish en papillote—*in a parcel—is another gentle method of cooking fish fillets. Traditionally the parcel is made out of squares of parchment paper, but you can also wrap the fish in foil or banana leaves. Salmon fillets are particularly good cooked in this way, but cod and halibut are also suitable. Fish fillets can be packaged up with vegetables, herbs, a little white wine, or butter and must be tightly sealed to keep in all the flavors and the all-important steam. Cook them in an oven at 475°F (240°C) for 15 minutes, depending on the thickness of the fillets.*

COD (GADIDAE)

Fished throughout the cold waters of the Atlantic, Pacific, and, Arctic by both line and trawl, cod is one of the most important commercial fish in the northern hemisphere. Members of the cod or Gadidae family can be identified by a distinct three-fin dorsal pattern. They are "white" fish, with the main concentration of oil being found in the liver, so the flesh is low in fat. The flesh color varies, but cod is renowned for having well-flavored flesh that, when cooked, offers succulent and sweet flakes. Popular members of this group are caught to quota and a minimum size. Sustainability issues are a cause for concern, so cod farming has recently begun to develop as an industry.
CUTS Whole (gutted, with head on or off); fillet; steak. Atlantic cod: head; cheek; tongue; roe; liver; air bladder/"sounds." Some cod are also salted, dried, and smoked.
● **EAT** Cooked: Deep fry or pan fry in batter or breadcrumbs; bake; poach in stock or milk; use chopped flesh for soup or chowder; grill fillets or whole fish. **Preserved:** Cold smoked (dyed and undyed); salted; dried.
ALTERNATIVES Cod is endangered in some parts of the world. The following fish can be used interchangeably: haddock, pollack, saithe (coley or Pollock), whiting, and pouting.
FLAVOR PAIRINGS Dill, parsley, bay leaf, lemon, olive oil, tomatoes, olives, capers, garlic, breadcrumbs, butter.
CLASSIC RECIPES Deep-fried fish and chips; *brandade*; *taramasalata*; cod in parsley sauce.

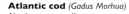

Poor cod (*Trisopterus minutus capelanus*)
Also known as capelan, this shoaling fish is a smaller member of the Gadidae family. It can grow to 16in (40cm). It is fished commercially across the eastern Atlantic as far as the Atlantic coast in the Mediterranean, and is popular in southern Europe. Much like whiting, soft, white, delicate, with a low fat content. Good pan fried, steamed, or baked.

Look for the three-fin dorsal pattern typical of the Gadidae family.

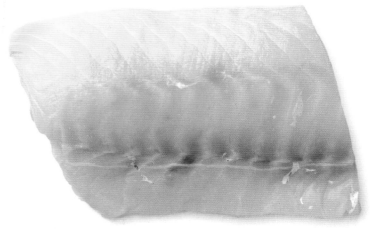

Atlantic cod (*Gadus Morhua*)
Also known as codling, sprag or scrod, Atlantic cod is one of the largest members of the Gadidae family. It is identified by a white lateral line, green/yellow marbled skin that fades to white on the belly, and a square tail. This species can grow to 5ft (1.5m). Atlantic cod is fished extensively by North America, many European countries, and Scandinavia. This fish has white, chunky flakes with a sweet seafood taste. Commonly used deep-fried in fish and chips but excellent poached for fish pie and baked with a crust.

Atlantic cod has white flesh with a firm texture that chunks and flakes well.

Arctic cod (*Boreogadus saida*)
Arctic cod is sold mostly as fillets and is most often processed at sea. It has firm, white flesh and is ideal for pan frying or baking. Arctic cod has been heavily overfished—Pacific cod is a good alternative.

Pacific cod *Gadus Macrocephalus*
Also known as Alaska cod, gray cod, true cod or treska brown, Pacific cod has dark mottled skin and a pale belly. It can grow to over 6½ft (2m) and is found in the North Pacific and Pacific Rim. It is fished by the US, China, Japan, Canada, and Korea, is exported to Europe, and is enjoyed in North and South America and also in the Caribbean. Excellent for fish and chips, poaching, and grilling.

Firm, sweet, and well flavored, Pacific cod is a popular fish.

SAITHE (COLEY) (POLLACHIUS VIRENS)

The cheeks, considered a delicacy, are sold prepared and can be poached or fried.

Saithe is also known as coley, coalfish, black cod, green cod, and sometimes as pollack. This key member of the cod family is considered an inexpensive alternative to cod and, for many years, has been viewed as good only for making cat food as it is only palatable if eaten very fresh. Young fish live in the top layers of the sea and swim deeper as they mature. Saithe is caught in the northern Atlantic, both in the US and Europe. Available all year round, though it is not at its best during the summer months.

CUTS Whole: gutted with head on or off; fillet.
● **EAT** **Cooked:** Deep fry; pan fry in batter or breadcrumbs; bake; poach in court bouillon; steam; use poached flesh for fish pie and fish cakes. Inexpensive addition to fish soups.
Preserved: Cold and hot smoked (dyed and undyed); dried; salted; cured; smoked.
FLAVOR PAIRINGS Butter, milk, beer, parsley, chives
CLASSIC RECIPES Norwegian fish soup; *Frikadeller* (fish rissoles).

If saithe is fresh it will have firm and tightly knitted flakes.

Saithe
The flesh of this fish has been described as coarse, but it has been undervalued. It looks gray pink when raw but, on cooking, whitens well and becomes flaky and well flavored. It works in a fish casserole or curry as it takes robust flavors well.

Saithe has a heavily scaled iron-gray or black back with a thick, white lateral line.

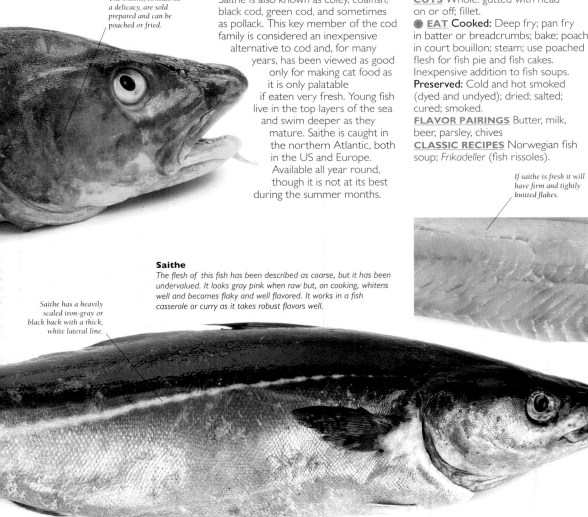

DEEP-FRIED COD AND CHIPS

An all-time classic British dish. Traditionally served with tartar sauce.

SERVES 4

4 x 6oz (170g) cod fillets, skinned

⅔ cup all-purpose flour, plus 1 tbsp

a pinch of baking powder

pinch of salt, plus extra for seasoning

1 egg yolk

1 tbsp sunflower or canola oil

½ cup equal parts milk and water

2¼lbs (1kg) Maris Piper, russet, or other floury baking potatoes, peeled and cut into wedges

oil for deep frying

freshly ground black pepper

lemon wedges, to serve

1 Remove any small bones from the cod fillets. Make the batter: sift the ⅔ cup flour into a large bowl along with the baking powder and a pinch of salt. Make a well in the center and add the egg yolk, oil, and a little of the milk-and-water mixture. Stir the flour into the liquid until smooth, adding the remaining liquid mix as needed to create a batter. Refrigerate for 10 minutes before use.

2 Soak the potatoes in cold water for 10 minutes, drain, and dry thoroughly. Heat the oil in a deep-fat fryer or large, heavy pot to 340°F (170°C). Working in batches, cook the potatoes in the oil for a few minutes until just tender; do not brown. Drain on paper towels.

3 Increase the oil temperature to 350°F (180°C). Season the remaining 1 tbsp flour with salt and pepper. Dust the cod fillets with this; then, working in batches as needed, dip them into the batter, coating all sides. Holding a cod fillet with tongs, swish it around in the hot oil, then release into the oil (this prevents the batter from sticking to the fry basket). Cook for 5-6 minutes or until the batter is a deep golden brown. Lift onto a wire rack, season lightly with salt, and keep warm. Repeat with the remaining fillets.

4 Working in batches, fry the potatoes for a second time, to allow them to brown. This will take 2-3 minutes. Lift onto clean paper towels to drain, sprinkle lightly with salt, and then serve alongside the deep-fried cod.

HADDOCK (MELANOGRAMMUS AEGLEFINUS)

Fishmongers refer to haddock, from the Gadidae family, as ping, chat, kit, gibber and jumbo (in ascending order of size). Second only to cod, it is found in the Northeast Atlantic and nearby seas. It is subject to both a quota and minimum landing size to enable the stocks to remain sustainable.

CUTS Whole (gutted, with head on or off); fillet; roe.

● **EAT** Cooked: Deep-fry or pan-fry in batter or bread crumbs (considered sweeter than cod), broil, bake, poach in a court-bouillon or milk, steam, use poached flesh for fish pie and for soup.

Preserved: Hot smoked (Arbroath smokies), cold smoked (undyed and dyed fillet), traditional Finnan haddock.

FLAVOR PAIRINGS Parsley, milk, bay leaf, dulse seaweed, Cheddar cheese.

CLASSIC RECIPES Haddock Mornay; kedgeree; haddock and chips; cullen skink.

CLASSIC RECIPE

HADDOCK MORNAY

With a layer of spinach under the poached haddock, this classic dish is a colorful one-pot meal.

SERVES 4

4 x 6oz (175g) haddock fillets, skinned

1 ¼ cups whole milk

½ cup fish stock or water

4 tbsp butter, plus extra to grease

¼ cup all-purpose flour

1 cup shredded Cheddar cheese

salt and freshly ground black pepper

8oz (250g) fresh spinach leaves, rinsed

pinch of grated nutmeg

½ cup fresh whole wheat bread crumbs

½ cup freshly grated Parmesan cheese

2 tbsp chopped parsley leaves

1 Place the haddock in a deep frying pan; add the milk and stock, and slowly bring to a boil; cover and simmer until the fish is opaque. Lift the fish from the pan and keep warm. Reserve the poaching liquid.

2 Melt the butter in a pan and whisk in the flour until smooth. Cook for 1 minute, then whisk in the poaching liquid until blended. Reduce the heat to medium-low and whisk until the sauce has thickened. Stir in the Cheddar; season to taste. Remove from the heat.

3 Put the spinach in a saucepan over medium heat with the water (from rinsing) on its leaves. Cover. Cook over low heat, stirring until wilted. Season with nutmeg; spread over the bottom of a greased baking dish. Preheat the broiler.

4 Arrange the fillets on the spinach and pour in the sauce. Mix the bread crumbs, Parmesan, and parsley, and sprinkle on top. Broil until bubbly-hot and browned.

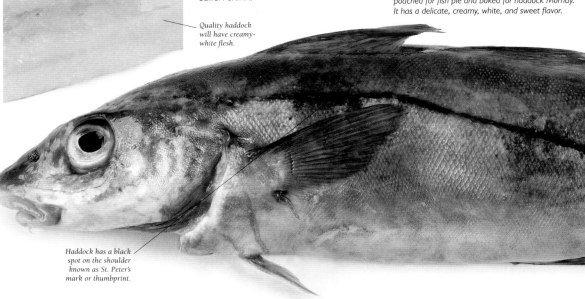

Haddock *Melanogrammus aeglefinus*
Haddock has a black lateral line on a grey back and a silver flank. Traditionally used for fish and chips, and preferred in this dish in Scotland, but also poached for fish pie and baked for haddock Mornay. It has a delicate, creamy, white, and sweet flavor.

Quality haddock will have creamy-white flesh.

Haddock has a black spot on the shoulder known as St. Peter's mark or thumbprint.

POLLOCK AND ALASKAN POLLOCK

Pollock, also known as green pollock and lythe, rivals cod in flavor and texture. Not of great importance commercially, it is a sport fish for recreational sea anglers. It is caught in the coastal waters throughout the North Atlantic, including the Newfoundland coast, and as far south as the Iberian Peninsula. It is often found in shallow inshore waters and grows up to 3ft (1m) in length. With an olive-green back fading to a silver belly, pollock has a fine lateral line that has the appearance of being stitched in place, since it is slightly puckered. Alaskan pollock, a related species, is similar to cod in color (with yellow speckles on the skin) and in the texture of the fillets (lean, snow white, and succulent). Found in the North Pacific and caught by Alaska, Russia, and Japan, it is prolific in the Bering Sea.

CUTS Whole (gutted with head on or off); fillets.

● **EAT** Cooked: Roast, deep-fry, bake, poach, steam.

Preserved: Salted; smoked.

FLAVOR PAIRINGS Tomatoes, chille, pancetta, basil.

CLASSIC RECIPE Fish and chips.

When fresh, pollock has a very firm texture and cooks to a white, delicate sweetness.

Alaskan pollock
Theragra chalcogramma
Also known as Pacific pollock and walleye pollock, this fish is the largest food-fish resource in the world and is thought to make up nearly half of all white-fish stocks. White and firm with a medium texture. Excellent for deep-frying as well as poaching to put into fish pie.

Ling *Molva molva*
Also known as common ling, this fish is excellent in fish pies, soups, and stews. This white fish cooks to an excellent firm and white-textured, sweet flesh. Salt ling is a traditional Irish feast.

The thick, scaly skin is easy to remove, but can be left on if poaching and removed afterward.

LING AND TUSK

These fish are two similar members of the Gadidae family. Ling (pictured) is a highly commercial fish found in temperate waters spanning the Northwest and Northeast Atlantic and the Northwest Mediterranean. It has a long body, reaching a maximum of 6½ft (2m). The skin can be marbled reddish-brown along the back and flanks, fading to a white belly. There is a distinct black spot at the back of the first dorsal fin. Underrated by some, ling has a long history, particularly as a salted fish to add to pies and soup. It is at its best when line caught. Tusk, also known as torsk, cusk, and moonfish, is found in the temperate waters of the Northwest and Northeast Atlantic. It can be 4ft (1.2m) long, but is mostly found at around 20in (50cm). It varies from dark red-brown to olive green along the back with a pale yellow belly.
<u>CUTS</u> Whole; fillets; steaks.
● <u>EAT</u> **Cooked:** Steam, pan-fry, broil, bake. **Preserved:** Dried, salted.
<u>CLASSIC RECIPES</u> Salted ling with mashed potatoes.

AUSTRALIAN WHITING

A wide range of important whiting from the Sillaginidae family are caught in the waters surrounding Australia, Tasmania, and New Zealand. These fish are long and tapered in shape, with two dorsal fins, each with a differing number of spines and soft rays. They are unrelated to the whiting from the Gadidae family (see page 26). Various methods of fishing are used to harvest these fish commercially, and they all have differing habitats. All members have a bony structure and white, flaky, textured flesh.
<u>CUTS</u> Whole (gutted); fillets (both single and block/butterfly fillets).

● <u>EAT</u> **Cooked:** Steam; pan-fry; broil; bake. **Preserved:** Smoked; dried; salted.
<u>FLAVOR PAIRINGS</u> Olive oil, butter, milk, parsley, chervil.
<u>CLASSIC RECIPE</u> Fish pie.

School whiting has firm flesh and a subtle flavor.

School whiting *Sillago bassensis*
There are several "school whiting" caught in waters around the Australian coast. They are similar in appearance, each with some distinguishing marks on a silver skin. A delicate, sweet flavor, similar to other whiting, low in fat with a fine texture. Best when fresh and excellent steamed, poached, and pan-fried.

If the fish is to be cooked with the skin on, the heavy layer of scales should be removed first.

Sand whiting *Sillago ciliate*
Also known as silver or summer whiting, this elegant fish is being considered for aquaculture. It is caught along the east coast of Australia by beach seine, haul nets, and gill nets and is a highly regarded angling fish.

The flesh of a sand whiting is firm, flaky, and well flavored.

ATLANTIC WHITING

Whiting is the name used to describe several species from a variety of unrelated groups of fish, including the Gadidae, Merlucciidae, and Sillaginidae families. The taste of the fish varies from one species to the next, but the flesh of whiting is always white. The Gadidae whiting is found in the North Atlantic and surrounding seas and the related southern blue whiting is caught in the Southwest Atlantic. Both these species have an easily digestible flesh. Hake (Merlucciidae family) is sometimes referred to as whiting. Whiting is undervalued by many, since it has a delicate taste (it becomes almost tasteless when the fish is past its best). It is often popular with fishmongers, since it tends to be less expensive than some other members of the cod group. The skin of a whiting

is particularly thin and care should be taken when skinning the fish, although leaving the skin on, particularly for broiling, protects the delicate flesh.
CUTS Whole (gutted); fillets (single and block/butterfly fillets).
● **EAT** **Cooked:** Steam, pan-fry, broil, bake. **Preserved:** Smoked, dried, salted.
FLAVOR PAIRINGS Olive oil, butter, milk, parsley, chervil.
CLASSIC RECIPE Fish pie.

Soft and delicate, whiting has a subtle texture and is low in fat.

Pout whiting *(Trisopterus luscus)*
Also known as bib, pout, or pouting, this fish is found as far south as the Mediterranean and up to the North Sea. It has a delicate texture and spoils easily, so should be eaten very fresh.

Pout whiting is identified by a black spot behind the pectoral fins.

Whiting flesh is delicate and should be enjoyed very fresh, as it loses condition quickly.

Whiting *(Merlangius marlangus)*
Whiting can grow up to 28in (70cm), although its usual size is around 10–12in (25–30cm). It has a light yellow-brown back, sometimes with hues of blue and green, and a gray to silvery-white belly. It has a light and delicate texture and is very low in fat.

HAKE (MERLUCCIIDAE)

Although hake is often associated with the cod and the Gadidae family, it comes from the Merlucciidae family. It is caught in many waters around the world, but particularly in the Atlantic and Northern Pacific. Silver hake (also known as Atlantic hake or New England hake) is caught in the Northwest Atlantic. European hake

is fished throughout Europe, but is particularly popular in Spain. Often regarded as a "codlike" fish, the white texture is very similar to cod, but the bone, fin pattern, and skeleton all differ. This species of fish is deceptively soft—in many other fish, soft, delicate flesh would indicate bad quality, but hake cooks to a firm and meaty texture.

ALTERNATIVES Hake is endangered in some parts of the world. Other members of the cod family can be used interchangeably.
CUTS Whole; fillets; steaks.
● **EAT** **Cooked:** Pan-fry, roast, poach, sauté, broil. **Preserved:** Dried, smoked.

FLAVOR PAIRINGS Olive oil, garlic, smoked paprika, butter, lemon.
CLASSIC RECIPES Hake in green sauce with clams (Basque recipe); *koskhera.*

Hake has a deep bluish, steel-gray back and silvery skin. Its lateral line has black edging.

MORID COD AND BLUE COD (MORIDAE, MUGILOIDIDAE)

There are a few types of morid cod, including New Zealand red cod and ribaldo, found in waters around South and Southeastern Australia and New Zealand. They have a long dorsal fin running the length of the back, and the fillet tapers toward the caudal fin. Their size ranges from 16in–5ft (40cm–1.5m). They have white, textured, soft flesh. Like whiting, these fish are best eaten very fresh. Sand-perches (from the Pinguipedidae family) are temperate marine fish found in the Atlantic and along the coasts of South America and Africa, as well as in the Indo-Pacific, from Hawaii to New Zealand, and also off Chile. New Zealand blue cod are part of this group.

ALTERNATIVE FISH Both morid cod and blue cod are endangered in some parts of the world. Use Pacific cod or hake interchangeably.

CUTS Whole fish; gutted; fillets (single or block).

● **EAT Cooked:** Steam, bake, en papillote, poach, fried, microwaved. **Preserved:** Smoked.

FLAVOR PAIRINGS Batter, capers, pickles, parsley, soft-leaf herbs.

White, sweet, and succulent, this is a popular fish.

New Zealand blue cod *(Parapercis colias)*
Other names for this fish include Boston blue cod, sand-perch, and, in Maori, rawaru or pakirikiri. It is a species that is exclusive to New Zealand and is commercially harvested by the South Island. A white-textured fish with similarities to other white fish from the true-cod group but slightly coarse in texture. Good for deep-frying, broiling, steaming, and roasting

Adult blue cod have a blue-green back, fading to white on the belly. Young fish are dappled.

ROUGHY

Roughy refers to an unusual family of fish (Trachichthyidae) that includes several roughys, slimeheads, and sawbellys. They have a wide global distribution and are landed by many countries. Orange roughy is the main species to receive international acclaim and it has been marketed intensely as an alternative to cod. Also known as sea perch or deep-sea perch, orange roughy is an important commercial fish in Australia, where it is found around the south coast of the continent, and New Zealand. Orange roughy was fished extensively until it was discovered that they mature and develop slowly and, thus, was seriously threatened. The layer of oil under the skin is routinely used in the cosmetics industry.

ALTERNATIVES Orange roughy is endangered in some parts of the world. Pacific or Atlantic cod can be used interchangeably.

CUTS Occasionally whole; commonly skinned fillets.

● **EAT Cooked:** Pan-fry, broil, deep-fry, bake.

FLAVOR PAIRINGS Olive oil, chile, lime, butter, beer batter, crème fraîche, cream.

European hake *(Merluccius merluccius)*
Also known as hake, colin, or merluche in France, this species ranges from North Africa, the Mediterranean, and as far north as Norway. A large, deep-water fish, it has been greatly affected by overfishing.

Orange roughy *(Hoplostethus atlanticus)*
The soft, moist, white, textured flesh of orange roughy has a sweet flavor. It is usually "deep skinned," to remove the skin, but also the layer of fat directly under the skin.

The flesh of this fish is soft, moist, and white, with a sweet, mild taste.

BREAM

The extensive bream family (Sparidae) is distributed globally in temperate and tropical seas. The numerous members of this group (known as porgies in the US) are important commercial fish for many countries. Most bream have a round, deep, laterally compressed body with a long, single, spiny dorsal fin. They have a good covering of large scales across the body and head. Different species are identified by the teeth as a general rule. Many are marine fish, but some dwell in estuarine brackish waters or fresh water. Most are fairly small, not growing more than 16–28in (40–70cm) in length. They require careful trimming and scaling. With white, well-textured flesh, bream are at their best simply pan-fried.

CUTS Whole; fillets, often with skin on (after scaling); thick steaks (larger species).
◉ **EAT** Cooked: Pan-fry, broil, bake, stuff.
FLAVOR PAIRINGS Fennel, Pernod, cilantro, lemon, saffron, parsley, garlic.
CLASSIC RECIPES Bream en papillote; *besugo al horno* (a classic festive Spanish dish).

Yellow fin sea bream
Acanthopagrus latus
Found in the Indo-West Pacific, yellow fin sea bream dwells in fresh, brackish, and marine waters. It is used in Chinese medicine and is popular for recreational fishing.

Firm and sweet, gilt head bream flesh is very popular in many Mediterranean counties.

The sharp points on the dorsal and anal fins should be trimmed before scaling, as they are sharp.

The cheeks (or pearls) of this fish are considered a delicacy in the Mediterranean.

Gilt head bream *Sparus aturata*
Gilt head is the most popular bream in Europe and is farmed throughout the Mediterranean. It has a lightly scaled, silvery skin with a spiny dorsal fin and a deep body with a distinctive gold band across the brow. Farmed fish has white, but firm flakes with a medium texture.

Black sea bream *Spondyliosoma cantharus*
Also known as old wife, the black sea bream is common to Northern Europe and the Mediterranean, where it is fished extensively. Like other members of the bream family, it is a shoaling fish. It is silvery in color with black markings across the body. Considered to be one of the finest of the bream family for the table. It can be cooked whole or filleted: roasting, pan-frying, or broiling the fillets are all good uses of the fish. Its firm, white-textured flesh is admired in the Mediterranean.

As with the gilt head bream, the pearls of the black sea bream are sought after.

This species is identified by a black mark around the back of the head.

Black spot bream *Pagellus bogaraveo*
Also known as red sea bream and pandora, this fish is found in the East Atlantic and the West Mediterranean. An hermaphrodite, it becomes female at between 8–12in (20–30cm) in length and can reach up to 28in (70cm), but the usual landed specimen is around 12in (30cm). Excellent flavor, slightly herbaceous with firm white fillets. Delicious roasted, broiled, and en papillote.

Golden threadfin bream *Nemipterus virgatus*
There are around 60 species in the Nemipteridae group (called false snappers or whiptail bream). This one, known as hung san in Hong Kong, is a dainty fish with pink and yellow tinges to the fins and a yellow thread to the tail. It is an important commercial fish in the East China Sea. A very delicately flavored, fine, white-textured fish. Simply pan-fried or broiled is ideal.

Red sea bream *Pagrus major*
Also known as dorade in France, and red tail or red porgy in the US, this fish has delicate bluish markings when very fresh. Red sea bream is served at special occasions, such as weddings, in Japan, and is used in Chinese medicine.

This fish has gray-blue and silver skin with a yellow tinge, and a curving lateral line.

Bogue *Boops boops*
Another member of the bream family, this species is identified by its large eyes (boops is the Latin word for Ox). It is caught in shallow inshore waters and reaches up to 14in (35cm) in length. It is particularly enjoyed in Malta, where it forms part of the Maltese soup aljotta.

Dentex *Dentex dentex*
Another member of the Sparidae group, the native range of this species is in the East Atlantic to the Black Sea. It is a predatory fish, feeding off other species of fish. Generally, it lives a solitary existence, and can grow to over 3ft (1m) in length, although the average size is 8–10in (20–25cm). Popular in the Mediterranean cooked with tomatoes, olives, olive oil, marjoram, and thyme and in North Africa with cumin, coriander, and fennel.

Young adults have a blue-black back and silvery fins, while larger fish are red-tinged.

SEA BREAM EN PAPILLOTE

A classic method of cooking fish—wrapped in paper with a selection of aromatics.

SERVES 1

1 small sea bream or porgy, trimmed, scaled, and cut into fillets

a few slices of scallion or fennel

herbs of your choice (such as dill, tarragon, rosemary, or oregano)

1 tbsp butter or a splash of olive oil

a splash of Pernod or white wine

sea salt and freshly ground black pepper

2 lemon or lime wedges, to garnish

1 Preheat the oven to 425°F (210°C). Arrange the fish fillets, skin-side down, on a large sheet of parchment paper.

2 Arrange the chosen aromatic vegetables and herbs around the fish and season lightly with salt and pepper. Add the butter; drizzle with Pernod or wine.

3 Enclose the fish securely by folding the parchment over the fish to form a "package." Fold and crimp the edges, but not too tightly, so that the steam can circulate within the package as it bakes. Bake 12–15 minutes or until cooked through. The paper will have browned and the fish will be firm and opaque.

4 Keeping the package intact, use a spatula to transfer it to a warm dinner plate. Slice open the package at the table. Squeeze the lemon juice over the fish.

EMPEROR BREAM (LETHRINUS ATKINSONI)

Known as emperor fish as well as emperor bream, these fish are also referred to as scavengers, rudderfish, and porgies. They are members of the Lethrinidae family, a relatively small group with 39 known species located in tropical reef seas of the Indian Ocean through to Australia, and also off the west coast of Africa. They are carnivorous, feeding off the bottom of the sea. Most of the species are esteemed food fish and are recognized by the two dorsal fins with 10 spines. Emperor bream has a beige back with brown lines along the flanks and an orange mark around the gill flap. The lateral line curves over along the body to the forked tail or caudal fin.

The flesh is white, full-flavored, and firm-textured.
CUTS Usually whole.
● EAT Cooked: Pan-fried, baked, or roasted; it takes robust flavors well.

Red spot bream (*Lethrinus lentjan*)
This exotic fish has a firm texture and slightly sweet flavor. It works well with regional flavors such as ginger, chili, and coriander.

The fish is densely scaled and needs trimming and scaling prior to cleaning or filleting.

GRAY MULLET (MUGILIDAE GROUP)

The dashing, sleek and silver-gray mullets of the Mugilidae family are found near the shore, in brackish and fresh water, and in tropical, subtropical, and temperate seas worldwide (in the Atlantic, Pacific, and Indian oceans). Gray mullet is very common and is a popular food fish, that is highly commercial in many countries. They are used in Chinese medicine, too. There are around 75 species, which have silvery-gray, elongated bodies with no visible lateral line. They are noted for their small mouths and, sometimes, thick lips. In Southeast Asia, gray mullet is cultivated in ponds. This fish can have a slightly earthy taste, but soaking it in a little acidulated water just before cooking helps to improve the flavor.
CUTS Whole unprepared fish; fillets (scaled, but skin on).
● EAT Cooked: Gray mullet can be pan fried, roasted, or baked. The roe is used fresh and smoked.

Preserved: Dried and salted products are available.
CLASSIC RECIPES *Taramasalata; besugo al horno.*

Common gray mullet (*Mugil cephalus*)
Its numerous names include black true, flathead or striped mullet, haarder, and, in Australia, poddies or hardgut mullet. Its olive-green back has silver shading on the sides.

The flesh is pink in color, cooking to an off-white, and it is firm and meaty.

GOATFISH AND RED MULLET (MUGILIDAE GROUP)

There are many members of the Mugilidae family, including goatfish and red mullets. Many of the 55 species are beautifully marked and brightly colored. These fish are caught in warm-temperate and tropical seas in the Atlantic, Pacific, and Indian oceans, they are sometimes found in brackish waters. They all have thick scales, forked caudal fins, and a distinct pair of chin barbells, used for detecting food and, in the case of males, attracting a female during courtship. Most are sold at around 6–8in (15–20cm), although many reach around 12in (30cm) in length. The liver of a red mullet is considered fine eating and should be left intact. The fish needs to be trimmed and scaled prior to cooking (avoid removing the liver).

CUTS Whole (gutted and scaled, with liver intact); fillets.

● **EAT** **Cooked:** Try these fish pan-fried or grilled.

CLASSIC RECIPES Provençal fish soup with *rouille*; *fritura malagueña* (Andalusian fried fish); *rougets à la provençale*.

This highly prized fish is off-white, becoming white when cooked. It has a delicate flavor.

Red mullet (*Mullus surmuletus*)
This fish is a particularly fine eating fish. It has many bones, so it is best to cook it whole so they can be easily located. Red mullet works well with citrus flavors, and herbs such as chervil and tarragon complement it nicely.

This well-flavored fish has a flaky texture, which is slightly coarser than that of red mullet.

Indian goatfish (*Mullus indicus*)
Indian goatfish is popular in Oman and East and South Africa, where it is landed. Its firm, white flesh is slightly earthier in flavor than its close relative the red mullet.

SHALLOW-FRIED RED MULLET

Pan-frying, a simple method of cooking, makes the most of the delicate sweetness of red mullet.

SERVES 4

4 red mullet, gutted, scaled, trimmed, and heads removed

salt and freshly ground black pepper

yellow cornmeal or polenta, for coating

grapeseed or canola oil, for frying

lemon juice, to finish

1 Season the fish, then coat them on both sides with cornmeal or polenta, shaking off any excess. Set a non-stick or cast-iron frying pan over medium-high heat; add enough oil to coat the bottom of the pan.

2 Put the prepared fish into the hot oil, presentation-side (the side that will show when served) face-down. Cook for 2 minutes, or until the fish is golden brown.

3 Turn the fish using tongs, and cook until the other side is golden brown. To test for doneness, insert a thin-bladed knife into the center of the fish, and then touch the tip of the knife to your thumb. If the knife is warm, the fish is ready. Drain briefly on paper towels.

BARRACUDA (SPHYRAENIDAE GROUP)

Also known as sea pike and giant pike, these members of the Sphyraenidae family are fast, aggressive predators with plenty of sharp teeth. They are found in several oceans, but are essentially warm-water marine dwellers known to frequent tropical reef areas. Species include the great barracuda of the Western Pacific, and the Eastern Pacific and Atlantic species. They vary in size, but only smaller specimens should be eaten because the toxins that can cause ciguatera poisoning affect larger fish. (This affects a handful of fish that live in some reef areas. Ciguatera poisoning has no effect on the fish, but it can cause extremely unpleasant symptoms in those who consume it, and is known to be fatal in a small number of cases.) Avoid marinating this fish for too long—particularly in an acidic juice— as the flesh will change texture and can become dry when cooked.

CUTS Both fresh and frozen: whole fish; fillets.

● **EAT** **Cooked:** Barracuda can be pan fried, grilled, deep fried, or roasted.

Preserved: Smoked barracuda is available.

FLAVOR PAIRINGS Olive oil, garlic, paprika, spices, coconut.

With a firm, meaty texture and excellent flavor, this fish takes robust flavors well.

Barracuda (*Sphyraena sphyraena*)
Its elongated body produces long fillets that are dense, meaty, and succulent. This fish works well with many flavors and makes an excellent dish when it is simply grilled with olive oil and herbs.

JOHN DORY (ZEDIAE GROUP)

There are several varieties of the dory that come from two fish groups. The six species belonging to the Zeidae family are found worldwide in temperate waters. These solitary fish have a wide, compressed body, a dramatic display of dorsal fins, and retractable jaws (so they are able to vacuum up their prey). The group from the Oreosomatidae (oreo) family include the smooth oreo and black oreo dories. With similarities to the dories of the Zeidae group, they have extremely large eyes set in a big head, a compressed body, and gray and black skin. These fish are found in waters around Australia and New Zealand, where they are fished commercially. They are thought to be slow-growing, living up to 100 years. They reach 28–35in (70–90cm) in length. Silvery John dory (*Zenopsis conchifer*) is also known as the John dory, sailfin dory or buckler dory in both the US and Australia. It is caught in the western Indian Ocean and the Atlantic, and is popular in Japan. The mirror dory (*Zenopsis nebulosa*) is a similar species found in Indian Ocean waters.

CUTS Whole (usually gutted); fillets.

⬤ **EAT** Try dories pan-fried, grilled, steamed, or baked.

CLASSIC RECIPE *Bouillabaisse*.

John dory (*Zeus faber*)
John dory is highly prized for its excellent eating quality. Sharp barbs around the fish need to be trimmed before filleting. The skin is delicate and can be left on if cooking the fish whole, or it can be skinned, revealing the fillet's three natural sections. The fish's wonderfully sweet and firm texture is often matched with rich, creamy sauces, wild mushrooms, sage, capers, lemon, and crème fraîche.

These extremely sharp barbs make filleting hazardous: trim them off with scissors.

This species bears a black mark, encircled with a gold band, on each side of the body.

The best parts of this fish are the loins (thickest parts of the fish, excellent for barbecuing and pan frying.)

GURNARD

Also known as sea robin, varieties of gurnard (from the Triglidae family) found in the Atlantic, Pacific, and Indian oceans have only recently gained a reputation as being worth cooking. However, gurnard is part of the traditional cuisine of the South of France (where *grondin* is the common name), of which the classic Provençal stew *bouillabaisse* is a fine example.

This fish has a triangular-shaped, bony head, a tapering body, and noticeable pectoral fins.

Several species are sold in Europe, including yellow, red, and gray gurnard,
and tubs. Species are available in the US and Australia. Usually 10–16in (25–40cm) long, they can reach 23⅔in (60cm). Over 40 percent of their weight is made up of bone. The head (with gills removed), bones, and skin make good fish stock. Gurnard has many pin bones and is tricky to prepare, as it has sharp dorsal spines and spiny barbs at each gill flap. The head can be removed and the fillets lifted off either side of the "tail."
CUTS Usually whole (ungutted).
⬤ **EAT** **Cooked:** Try gurnard roasted, pan fried, and grilled.

Red gurnard (*Aspitrigla cuculus*)
Also known as cuckoo gurnard and soldier, this is one of the most readily utilized of the species in Europe. It is caught around the coast of Britain and farther south to the Mediterranean. Look for brightness of color (the deep red or orange color begins to fade as the fish loses condition).

Gurnard is often best cooked on the bone; the tail is sweet and flaky.

The skin is steel gray with darker markings.

Gray gurnard (*Eutrigla gurnardus*)
This member of the group is also found in the Eastern Atlantic from Norway to Morocco, Madeira, and Iceland. Gurnard are distinctive in appearance and therefore easy to identify in the fishmonger's case. The sweetly flavored flesh can be roasted or barbecued; it requires a little olive oil or a pancetta or chorizo jacket to help prevent it drying during cooking.

TOOTHFISH

The group of fish known as toothfish and rock cod (from the Nototheniidae family) are all found in cold water, particularly in the Antarctic, but also in the southeast Pacific and southwest Atlantic. They can reach considerable lengths, but most landed fish are around 28in (70cm) long. Toothfish is often marketed under the name of sea bass, but it is not related to that group. As it is a slow-growing fish, there have been concerns over its sustainability, but the MSC (Marine Stewardship Council) has certified the South Georgia Patagonian Toothfish Longline Fishery as sustainable.
ALTERNATIVES Toothfish are endangered in some parts of the world. The white flesh has a dense texture and sweet flavor to rival other white fish, so there are no immediate alternatives, but any firm, white, textured fish, such as cod, sea bass, or pollock, can be used instead.
CUTS (Usually frozen and occasionally fresh): steaks; fillets.
⬤ **EAT** **Cooked:** Pan fried, grilled, barbecued, crusted, sautéed, roasted, and baked.
Preserved: Cold and hot smoked.

Patagonian toothfish
(*Dissostichus eleginoides*)
In recent years the popularity of some species of toothfish has grown, as they are considered fine eating. This species (also known as Chilean sea bass, Australian sea bass, and Antarctic ice fish) has become a favorite of California chefs.

Fillets are dense with a sweetness that works with soy, sesame, coriander, and chili.

The fine-quality meat has made this fish a luxury seafood in the US, Japan, and Europe.

WOLF FISH (ANARHICHADIDAE)

The wolf fish group is a small number of related species found in both Atlantic and Pacific waters. Aggressive in appearance and with a mouthful of uneven teeth, they resemble an eel in shape but have a thick-set body. Also known as seawolf, ocean catfish, and wolf eel (the common name for the Pacific species), they vary in color from a simple brown to sporting strips or spots. The flesh is firm, white, and meaty with a good flavor.

Found in marine waters, some of these fish have been subject to overfishing and there are concerns about the rapidly depleting stock.
ALTERNATIVES Wolf fish are endangered in some parts of the world. The following fish can be used interchangeably: Pacific cod, barracuda.
CUTS Available fresh and frozen; skinned; in fillets.
● **EAT** Cooked: Steam, fry, grill, poach, and bake.

RABBIT FISH AND SURGEON FISH (SIGANUS)

Also known as spinefoots or ratfish, there are around 28 species of rabbit fish. Caught in the Indian Ocean and the eastern Mediterranean, several species are fished for food. Many species are colorful and some are also very decorative, which makes them popular aquarium fish. They grow to around 16in (40cm) long and are easily identified by their small, slightly pouting lips over obvious front teeth that give the fish the appearance of a rabbit—hence the name. The dorsal fin is spiky and particularly vicious, and it needs to be trimmed away before cooking. There are around 80 species of surgeon fish found in marine tropical waters worldwide, often around a reef. The Latin name of the surgeon fish means "thorn tail," but it is also known as doctorfish and unicornfish. Each of these fish has a sharp barb, like a scalpel, on either side of the tail, that the fish can flex to protect itself from other predators.
CUTS Whole, ungutted and uncleaned; fillets.
● **EAT** Cooked: Grill, pan fry, bake, or add to curries and stews.
FLAVOR PAIRINGS Thai, African, and Caribbean flavors of coconut, cilantro, and spices.

Mild, delicate, and white, the fillets need combining with robust seasonings to lift their flavor.

The barb needs careful removal, because it is as sharp as a surgeon's scalpel.

Rabbit fish (*Siganus*)
Dark khaki-colored skin has lines running laterally along the body. The flesh is white with a subtle flavor, but dries easily and becomes quite tasteless. It is a good addition to curries and stews that have robust or Asian flavors.

The smooth skin needs little preparation, but remove the sharp spines before gutting or filleting.

Atlantic wolf fish (*Anarhichas lupus*)
Also known as rock fish, sea leopard, and sea cat, this is the largest of the wolf fish group, measuring up to 5ft (1.5m) long. The fish inhabits very cold water and is able to produce anti-freeze to keep its blood fluid.

The fish diet of spiny sea urchins and crab may account for its sweet, meaty, and succulent flesh.

Easily recognizable by its fierce appearance, it has a plain, dark brown, reddish skin with vertical black bands.

REDFISH/OCEAN PERCH (SCORPAENIDAE)

Redfish are a selection of fish that include rockfish, the spiny scorpion fish (including the rascasse, one of the key ingredients in *bouillabaisse*), some ocean perch and also rose fish. Found in temperate waters worldwide, some species are commercially significant. Norway haddock is an important member of this group; it is located along North Atlantic coasts of both Europe and North America. Younger redfish have brown skin, but as an adult, the back develops a deep red color that fades to a paler red-orange on the flanks. The fish have a large mouth and prominent eyes and can grow up to 3⅓ft (1m) in length; however, the normal market size tends to be around 12–18in (30–46cm). This fish has one long dorsal fin and a spiny, sharp front section, so it needs to be handled with care.
ALTERNATIVES Redfish are endangered in some parts of the world. The following fish can be used interchangeably: members of the cod group.
CUTS Whole, fresh, and frozen.
Prepared: head off and gutted, fillets.
◉ **EAT** Pan fried, stir fried, baked, grilled. ·

Redfish (*Sebastes marinus*)
The names redfish and Norway haddock are interchangeable. The fillets are white, flaky, and delicately flavored, and are enjoyed particularly in Scandinavia and Eastern Europe. It is harvested and frozen in fillets and exported.

As this has a heavy head and plentiful fins, only 50 per cent of this fish produces fillets.

Surgeon fish (*Acanthuridae*)
This species is particularly popular in African and Caribbean communities, where it is used in spicy dishes, including curries. The flesh is delicate and is prone to dry out and lack flavor if it is overcooked.

GROUPER/ROCK COD (SERRANIDAE GROUP)

There are several hundred members of the *Serranidae* group, including groupers, gropers, rock cod, sea perch, and some fish named as sea bass. The grouper family has some well-known members, including jewfish and the coral trout that is popular in Australia. They are often labeled by their Creole names, including *croissant* and *vieille rouge*. These diverse family members are tropical-water dwellers and are found in the Atlantic, Pacific, and Indian oceans. Many of these species are important commercial fish and have been exploited to the point of collapse in some areas of distribution. The skin of a grouper is thick and slightly rubbery, and

underneath it is a layer of fat that can cause stomach irritation. It is therefore advisable to skin the fish quite deeply prior to cooking.

CUTS Fresh and frozen; whole; fillets; steaks.

● **EAT** Cooked: Grill and pan fry. Preserved: Salted.

ALTERNATIVES Groupers are endangered in some parts of the world. The following fish can be used interchangeably: cod, dolphin fish (mahi mahi), and barramundi from sustainable sources.

Coral trout (*Plectropomus leopardus*)
Also known as leopard coral grouper, footballer cod and lunar tail rockcod (Australia), this brightly colored fish is listed as endangered but it is carefully managed in Australian waters. It has also been associated with ciguatera poisoning.

The white flesh has an excellent flavor that is popular with chefs, particularly in Australia.

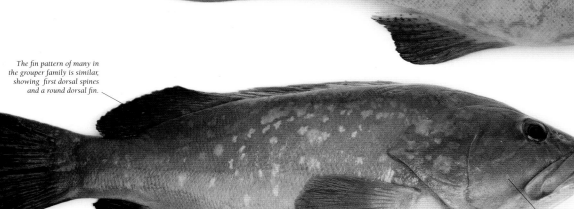

This fish is sometimes known as lunar tail rockcod.

The fin pattern of many in the grouper family is similar, showing first dorsal spines and a round dorsal fin.

All members of this group have handsome heads and prominent jaws.

Red grouper (*Epinephelus morio*)
This marine and subtropical species is often located near a reef in the Western Atlantic. It is fished to unsustainable levels in some areas. Generally the fillets of these fish are white and the flavor not dissimilar to cod, but less sweet.

Jewfish (*Epinephelus itajara*)
This important game fish is found in subtropical marine waters and close to reefs of the western and eastern Atlantic and in the East Pacific. This aggressive fish feeds on crustaceans, which may account for its firm texture and sweet flavor. Confusingly, jewfish is also the name for a member of the Sciaenidae group—see croakers.

BASS (MORONIDAE GROUP)

Confusingly, sea bass is a name used to identify several species of fish, but the group from the Moronidae family include several bass and perch, found in the temperate waters of the Eastern and Western Atlantic. They are mainly marine fish; in the wild they often locate to brackish and sometimes fresh water, specifically the American striped bass, which is a popular fish with recreational fishermen. All members have sharp spines and a thick covering of scales that need to be removed prior to cooking. Bass is often compared to sea bream, and although in northern Europe sea bass is popular, in the Mediterranean generally bream is the favorite. Its flavor is superb, and its popularity has meant that overfishing has caused stocks of these species to become threatened. There is now a legal minimum landing size in some areas for these species, while in others there is a closed season for recreational fishermen.

CUTS Whole, unprepared fish; trimmed whole fish; fillets. Fish is scaled and rarely skinned.

⊙ **EAT** Grill, bake, pan fry, and *en papillote* (baking in parchment).

ALTERNATIVES Sea bream.
FLAVOR PAIRINGS Asian flavors such as fermented black beans, sesame, dark soy sauce, tahini, and ginger. Also good with Mediterranean flavors including tomatoes, garlic, parsley, capers, rosemary, fennel, anise, olive oil, and red peppers.
CLASSIC RECIPES Sea bass in green pepper sauce; *branzino* in salt (classic northern Italian recipe with fish cooked in salt crust). This fish works particularly well with Pernod and other ingredients that have a hint of aniseed.

SEA BASS IN A SALT CRUST (*BRANZINO*)

This classic northern Italian dish is usually made using sea bass (*branzino*) and served with aïoli or mayonnaise.

SERVES 4

1 whole sea bass 3–4½lb (1.35–2kg) trimmed and gutted, but not scaled

2lb (1kg) coarse sea salt

1–2 egg whites

1 Preheat the oven to 425°F (220°C). Gut the fish, making the smallest incision possible. Clean well and rinse; do not scale.

2 Place a large piece of foil on a baking sheet, and spread a layer of salt over the top. Arrange the fish on the salt. Moisten the remaining salt with the egg whites and a splash of water, if necessary. Pack this mixture onto the fish to encase completely it.

3 Bake for 22–25 minutes. Lift the fish on to a serving dish. Take to the table and carefully chip off any remaining salt crust. Using clean utensils peel away the skin and serve the fish off the bone.

Sea bass (*Dicentrarchus labrax*)
Also known as bass, sea perch, and occasionally sea dace, this fish is found in the eastern Atlantic from Norway to Senegal, the Black Sea and the Mediterranean. It is extensively farmed in the Mediterranean, particularly Greece and the Greek Islands, to meet the high demand. Farmed fish have a good flavor and fat deposits created through the feeding process. Farming protects the fish and develops it to plate size for chefs.

Farmed sea bass have a good flavor with a slight oiliness; wild fish are savory, leaner, and meaty.

Sharp spines and scales cover its silver body, which fades to a white belly.

The cheeks of sea bass are sweet and lightly flavored, and considered a delicacy.

These fish have a thick, rough skin that requires deep-skinning before cooking.

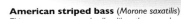

American striped bass (*Morone saxatilis*)
This temperate water dweller, like other members of the group, can be found in brackish, marine, and fresh water. A popular sport fish for recreational fishermen, this fish is found along the Atlantic Coast from St Lawrence in Canada down to the Gulf of Mexico. Some quantities are now farmed.

The fish gets its name from the black stripes on a bright silver background.

JACK, POMPANO, JACK MACKEREL, AND SCAD (CARANGIDAE GROUP)S

The Carangids are a large group of over 150 species of fish that include some very notable members. Found in the Atlantic, Indian, and Pacific oceans, most members are voracious predators. Their body shape is not dissimilar to the mackerel group, having deeply forked tails, although they have a different fin structure. Many of these species are highly commercial and are used extensively across the world, although in some species there have been reports of ciguatera poisoning in endemic areas. The flesh varies between species, but generally the fillets are a pink that lightens to white on cooking, with firm, white flakes. Exotic species have a delicate sweetness and most take robust flavors well.

CUTS Depending on the fish—but generally whole, fillets, and steaks. Fillets can be large on some species so these will be taken as a shoulder, loin, and tail cut.

● **EAT** Cooked: Broil, barbecue, or pan-fry.
FLAVOR PAIRINGS Red and green chile, ginger, soy, warm spice mixes, coconut milk, tomatoes.

The flavor and texture of this group varies, but the fillets are usually pale and delicate.

Crevalle jack
(Caranx hippos)
Crevally jack, jack, or jackfish is found in subtropical marine and brackish areas of the East and West Atlantic. The flesh dries easily so it needs carefully cooking; it is good pan-fried or broiled with flavored butter or brushed in oil.

Greater amberjack
(Seriola dumerili)
The largest member of the Carangidae fish group is found in many subtropical areas of the Mediterranean, the Atlantic, Pacific, and Indian oceans. Fast and powerful in the water, this pelagic fish is a voracious predator. It looks similar to the kingfish and has silver-blue skin with a delicate gold lateral line. Meaty steaks make excellent eating.

Laterally compressed and has a silver body and yellow fins.

DOLPHIN FISH

Also known as Lampuga (in Malta), it is more often referred to by its Polynesian name of mahi mahi, meaning "strong strong." This warm-water, marine and brackish-dwelling fish is caught in the tropical and subtropical waters of the Atlantic, Indian, and Pacific oceans. It grows rapidly, often to over 6½ft (2m), but is more commonly seen at about 3ft (1m). A striking fish, it has a domed head (particularly noticeable on a mature male) and a long, single, dorsal fin running from head to tail. Dolphin fish has a dense, meaty texture that takes robust flavors, particularly spices, very well.
CUTS Sold whole and fillets; fresh and frozen

● **EAT** Cooked: Pan-fry, barbecue, and char-broil.
FLAVOR PAIRINGS Caribbean flavors of cardamom, allspice, fennel, cilantro, curry, cayenne. and ginger. Asain flavors of chile, garlic, nam pla, and lime.
CLASSIC RECIPE Lampuga.

Dolphin fish *(Coryphaena hippurus)*
There is some aquaculture of these prized, premium fish, and there have been reports of ciguatera poisoning in endemic areas. It requires careful cooking since the flesh surprisingly takes a little longer to cook than flaky fish, and it can dry out in the process.

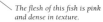

The flesh of this fish is pink and dense in texture.

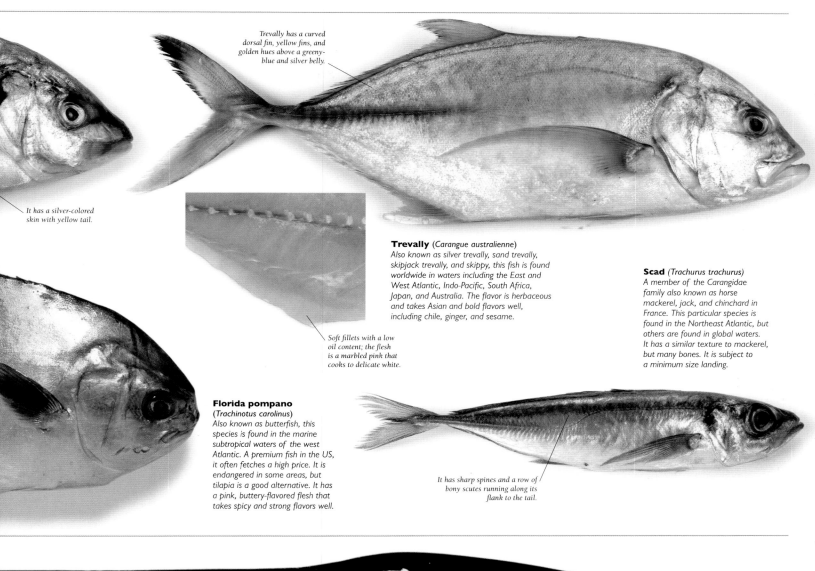

Trevally has a curved dorsal fin, yellow fins, and golden hues above a greeny-blue and silver belly.

It has a silver-colored skin with yellow tail.

Soft fillets with a low oil content; the flesh is a marbled pink that cooks to delicate white.

Trevally (*Carangue australienne*)
Also known as silver trevally, sand trevally, skipjack trevally, and skippy, this fish is found worldwide in waters including the East and West Atlantic, Indo-Pacific, South Africa, Japan, and Australia. The flavor is herbaceous and takes Asian and bold flavors well, including chile, ginger, and sesame.

Scad (*Trachurus trachurus*)
A member of the Carangidae family also known as horse mackerel, jack, and chinchard in France. This particular species is found in the Northeast Atlantic, but others are found in global waters. It has a similar texture to mackerel, but many bones. It is subject to a minimum size landing.

Florida pompano
(*Trachinotus carolinus*)
Also known as butterfish, this species is found in the marine subtropical waters of the west Atlantic. A premium fish in the US, it often fetches a high price. It is endangered in some areas, but tilapia is a good alternative. It has a pink, buttery-flavored flesh that takes spicy and strong flavors well.

It has sharp spines and a row of bony scutes running along its flank to the tail.

An iridescent metallic blue-and-green back with a golden belly.

SNAPPER (LUTJANDAE)

This group has more than 100 members, of which some are known as jobfish. Found in most tropical waters worldwide, many are key commercial fish. Some members are known to be fished beyond a sustainable level, but a level of aquaculture is developing that will support these important fish. All vary in size, from a plate-sized lane or yellowtail snapper at 10in (25cm) up to the large red snapper mostly marketed at around 1½ft (46cm). Smaller members of the group, including yellowtail and lane snappers, can be streamlined, but the larger members, specifically the Malabar, cubera, bourgeois, and true red snappers have a laterally compressed body. As with many fish of this type, they have a generous layer of thick scales and sharp spines on the fins. A fish sold whole should be trimmed, scaled, and gutted before cooking. The flesh of most is slightly off-white, lightening to white on cooking.

CUTS Whole; fillets; steaks.

● **EAT** **Cooked:** Steam, pan-fry, broil, bake, stir-fry.

ALTERNATIVES Snappers are endangered in some parts of the world. The following fish can be used interchangeably: sea bass, grouper.

FLAVOR PAIRINGS Sesame oil, soy, ginger, garlic, cilantro, palm sugar, nam pla.

CLASSIC RECIPES Blaff (Martinique fish stew); Cajun blackened snapper.

A beautifully flavored fish with sweet-tasting, white flesh when cooked.

Red snapper *(Lutjanus camperchanus)*
Many of the snapper group are a deep pink color and are mistakenly labeled as red snapper, but this one is the true red snapper. Also known as pargo, this reef marine fish is found in the Gulf of Mexico and the southeastern Atlantic coast of the US. It has a dark red back fading to a lighter red on the flank. Good cooked just with a squeeze of lemon, it also takes spices well. It can be broiled, pan-fried, roasted, and wrapped in banana leaves as en papillote.

Lane snapper *(Lutjanus synagris)*
A smaller member of the group, with fish from 6in (15cm) upward. It has a delicate pink skin with pink and yellow stripes on its side and pink tail. Caught in the West Atlantic, it is mostly exported by Brazil. It can be broiled or baked whole with coconut, lime, and lemon grass.

Its sweet, pink meat lightens to white when it's cooked.

Firm, pink flesh, excellent for eating.

Yellowtail snapper
(Ocyurus chrysurus) A striking snapper with a deep pink, scaly skin, a strong yellow stripe along the flank, and yellow tail. This is commercially caught for the table on the West Atlantic coast of the US, and it is abundant in Florida, the West Indies, and Brazil. Good marinated in warm spices such as cumin and coriander.

Deep pink scaly skin makes this a striking member of the snapper family.

VIETNAMESE CRISPY FISH

This classic crispy fish requires tiny bird's eye chiles to give it intense heat that is then tempered by the palm sugar.

SERVES 2

2 x 1lb (450g) snapper or emperor bream, trimmed, gutted, and scaled

salt

¼ cup vegetable oil

6 tomatoes, seeded and coarsely chopped

3 garlic cloves, finely chopped

2 red chile peppers (preferably Thai or bird's eye), halved, seeded, and thinly sliced

1 tbsp palm sugar or brown sugar

2 tbsp nam pla (Thai fish sauce)

1 tsp cornstarch

2 scallions, chopped

2 tbsp coarsely chopped cilantro

1 Cut the heads off the fish, slash the fillets on each side and season with salt. Working in batches, if necessary, add the fish and pan-fry on each side for 3–4 minutes, or until opaque throughout.

2 Heat the remaining oil in a large pan, add the garlic, tomatoes, and chiles, and cook over high heat until the tomatoes have softened and released their juices. Add the palm sugar, nam pla, and 6 tbsp water, and cook for a minute or two or until the mixture is well blended and slightly sticky. In a small bowl, mix a spoonful of the sauce with the cornstarch until smooth; then add it back to the sauce, along with the scallions and cilantro, and cook for 1 minute to thicken.

3 Lift the fish on to a plate and spoon the sweet, sticky sauce over the top. Serve with rice.

POMFRET (BRAMIDAE, CARANGIDAE, AND STROMATEIDAE GROUPS)

Confusingly, the name pomfret is used to describe various fish from several different fish families. Pomfrets come from the Carangidae, Stromateidae, and Bramidae groups, all of which are found in the East and West Pacific and some parts of the Atlantic. These fish share several attributes, including their deep and laterally compressed bodies.

Fillets taken from these fish are handled in much the same way as flat fish. The firm, white, and sweet-flavored flesh is good for pan-frying and broiling. The Atlantic pomfret (*Brama brama*) is a member of the Bramidae group and is also known as ray's bream, angelfish aral bream, bowfish, and carp bream. It has

a steel-colored, almost black body and a large eye, and offers a well-flavored, meaty, textured, white fillet.
CUTS Usually whole, sometimes in fillets; fresh and frozen.
● **EAT** Cooked: Pan-fry, bake, barbecue, broil. **Preserved:** Some species are dried and salted.
FLAVOR PAIRINGS Middle Eastern/North African: couscous, orange, lemon, parsley, coriander, ras el hanout spice mix, chermoula.

This laterally compressed fish is filleted in much the same way as a flat fish.

Black pomfret
(Formio niger)
A member of the Carangidae family, this fish is found in both marine and brackish tropical waters of the Indo-Pacific. It is a shoaling fish, often reaching 12in (30cm) in length. It has a sweet flavor and firm texture and is available fresh, dried, and salted.

This fish has an oval, silver body with lemon-tinted fins.

Silver pomfret *(Pampus argenteus)*
A member of the Stromateidae family, this pomfret is found in the subtropical waters of the Indo-Pacific from the Persian Gulf to Indonesia, to Japan. The usual market size is around 12in (30cm). It has sweet and dense white fillets and is excellent wrapped in foil and barbecued. It also works well with couscous and sweet, dried fruit, including apricots and almonds.

CUSKEEL (OPHIDIIDAE)

Cuskeels are distributed in shallow and deep water worldwide. They have an unusual shape similar to that of an eel, with their elongated bodies tapering to the tail. Both the dorsal and anal fins run along the fish and meet at the tail end. Cuskeels are shy marine-reef dwellers that hide during the day and appear at night to feed. There are over 200 species in the Ophidiidae group, but one particularly notable species is the fabulously flavored kingclip, whose meaty flesh is reminiscent of lobster. It is found in the Southeast Atlantic off the West African coastline from Namibia to South Africa.
<u>CUTS</u> Usually filleted, this fish produces long, slender fillets.
● <u>EAT</u> Cooked: Broil, pan-fry, roast, and barbecue.
<u>FLAVOR PAIRINGS</u> Butter, citrus, chorizo, pancetta, bay, rosemary.

Long and eel-like with a pointed head and pink-marbled skin.

CROAKER, GRUNT, AND DRUM (SCIAENIDAE GROUP)

Found extensively in freshwater, brackish, and marine waters around the globe, this large group of fish includes croakers, meagres, and drums. They take their name from the noise that they make by vibrating their swim bladders; it creates a croak or drumming noise that can be heard from some distance. A notable member is the cob, or mulloway (Aboriginal for "the greatest one"). This is a popular fish caught in around South Africa, Madagascar, and South Australia. Mulloway is considered a great catch by recreational anglers.
<u>CUTS</u> Whole and in fillets; fresh.
● <u>EAT</u> Cooked: Broil, steam, and bake. **Preserved:** Dried, smoked, and salted.
<u>FLAVOR PAIRINGS</u> Chile, lime, orange, white wine vinegar, olive oil, dill.
<u>CLASSIC RECIPES</u> Ceviche; escabeche.

Meagre (*Argyrosomus regius*)
Also known as croaker and corvina, this fish is distributed around the coasts of some subtropical waters along the East Atlantic and Mediterranean. The off-white fillets cook to a luscious and dense white. It can be broiled, roasted, and wrapped for the barbecue.

Kob or mulloway
(*Argyrosomus hololepidotus*)
Hugely popular in South Africa, kob is also known as mulloway, butterfish, kingfish, or jewfish in Australia. It is a marine, demersal fish found in coastal and estuarine waters. It is a sashimi-grade fish that is sold to the European sushi market. The pale pink flesh can be cut into steaks for baking or broiling.

A firm-textured fish, the striking scales need removing prior to cooking.

Mulloway has a stunning metallic silver-blue and bronze-colored skin with a spiny dorsal fin.

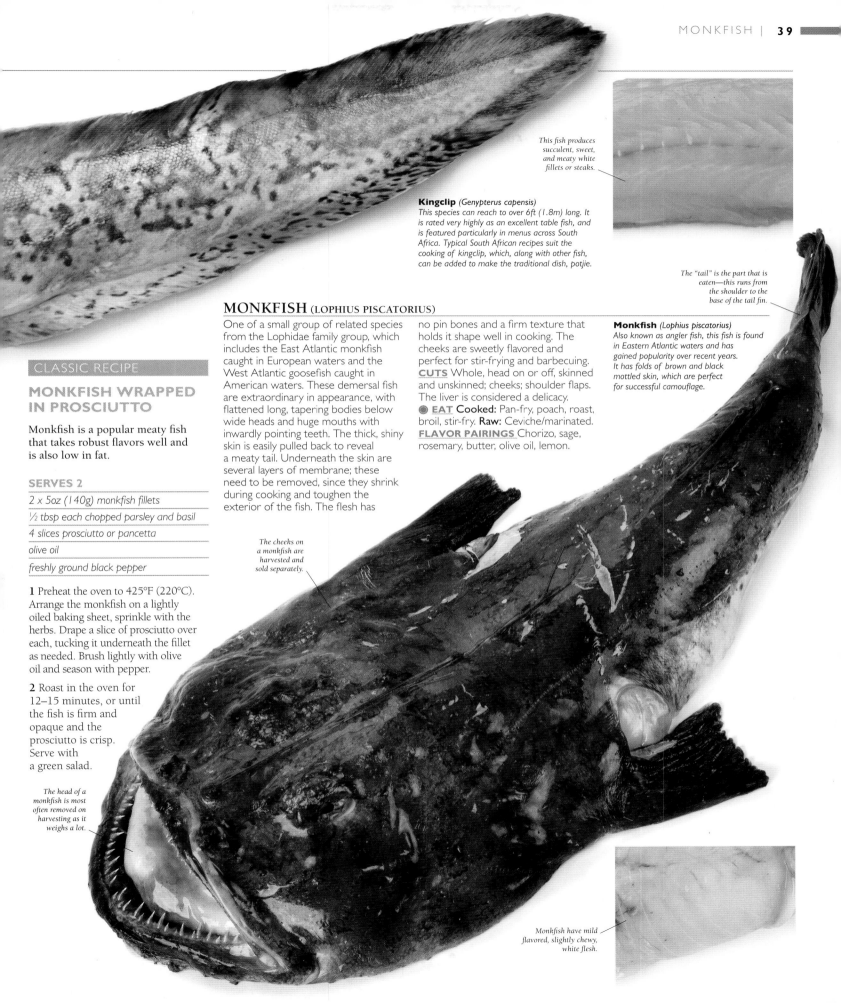

This fish produces succulent, sweet, and meaty white fillets or steaks.

Kingclip *(Genypterus capensis)*
This species can reach to over 6ft (1.8m) long. It is rated very highly as an excellent table fish, and is featured particularly in menus across South Africa. Typical South African recipes suit the cooking of kingclip, which, along with other fish, can be added to make the traditional dish, potjie.

The "tail" is the part that is eaten—this runs from the shoulder to the base of the tail fin.

MONKFISH (LOPHIUS PISCATORIUS)

One of a small group of related species from the Lophidae family group, which includes the East Atlantic monkfish caught in European waters and the West Atlantic goosefish caught in American waters. These demersal fish are extraordinary in appearance, with flattened long, tapering bodies below wide heads and huge mouths with inwardly pointing teeth. The thick, shiny skin is easily pulled back to reveal a meaty tail. Underneath the skin are several layers of membrane; these need to be removed, since they shrink during cooking and toughen the exterior of the fish. The flesh has no pin bones and a firm texture that holds it shape well in cooking. The cheeks are sweetly flavored and perfect for stir-frying and barbecuing.
CUTS Whole, head on or off, skinned and unskinned; cheeks; shoulder flaps. The liver is considered a delicacy.
◉ **EAT Cooked:** Pan-fry, poach, roast, broil, stir-fry. **Raw:** Ceviche/marinated.
FLAVOR PAIRINGS Chorizo, sage, rosemary, butter, olive oil, lemon.

Monkfish *(Lophius piscatorius)*
Also known as angler fish, this fish is found in Eastern Atlantic waters and has gained popularity over recent years. It has folds of brown and black mottled skin, which are perfect for successful camouflage.

MONKFISH WRAPPED IN PROSCIUTTO

Monkfish is a popular meaty fish that takes robust flavors well and is also low in fat.

SERVES 2

2 x 5oz (140g) monkfish fillets

½ tbsp each chopped parsley and basil

4 slices prosciutto or pancetta

olive oil

freshly ground black pepper

1 Preheat the oven to 425°F (220°C). Arrange the monkfish on a lightly oiled baking sheet, sprinkle with the herbs. Drape a slice of prosciutto over each, tucking it underneath the fillet as needed. Brush lightly with olive oil and season with pepper.

2 Roast in the oven for 12–15 minutes, or until the fish is firm and opaque and the prosciutto is crisp. Serve with a green salad.

The cheeks on a monkfish are harvested and sold separately.

The head of a monkfish is most often removed on harvesting as it weighs a lot.

Monkfish have mild flavored, slightly chewy, white flesh.

TUNA GROUP (SCOMBRIDAE)

The extensive desire for this fish has led to severe overexploitation of the species, and although some stocks globally are well managed, many are not. Choose tuna that comes from a sustainable source, and that is either pole- or line-caught. Easily identifiable by their bullet-shaped bodies that taper to a pointed snout, and their deeply forked tails, these fish can swim fast—speeds of around 43 miles per hour (70 km/hr) have been recorded. Although they come from temperate and cold waters, many are able to adapt to tropical and subtropical waters. High levels of myoglobin give the flesh a pink to deep red color, earning it the nickname the "rose of the sea." Although a deep color, the flesh has a subtle flavor and, once filleted, no bones. It is often likened to beef filet steak in texture and flavor. There are two species of bluefin tuna, both of which are critically endangered. The southern bluefin tuna (*Thunnus maccoyii*) is caught in the temperate and cold seas of the Atlantic, Indian, and Pacific oceans, but it migrates to tropical seas during spawning. These fish are particularly sought-after in Japan, where they can fetch an extremely high price. Northern bluefin tuna (or giant bluefin tuna) is native to the Western and Eastern Atlantic oceans, the Mediterranean, and the Black Sea, and are also commercially cultivated off the Japanese coast. This species is popular for the sushi trade. **CUTS** Whole and in sections; loins and steaks are usual. The loin or back is lean and popular in sushi; the belly is fatty and highly valued by the Japanese. The deep red loin is a good option for those who prefer meat to fish, as the flavor is delicate. ● **EAT** The well-managed members of this group give lean, thick loins that are suitable for chargrilling and pan-frying. Avoid simple grilling as the flesh pales to an unattractive dull brown. **Preserved:** Dried, smoked, and salted. Tuna roe is also sold dried. **Raw:** Sushi and carpaccio.

FLAVOR PAIRINGS Japanese: *shoyu*, sesame, teriyaki, shiso leaf, Japanese rice wine vinegar, wasabi. Mediterranean: tomatoes, garlic, olives.

CLASSIC RECIPES Tuna Niçoise; tuna sashimi/sushi; carpaccio of tuna with salsa verde; tuna teriyaki.

The dorsal and anal fins and finlets are bright yellow.

CLASSIC RECIPE

SALADE NIÇOISE

This well-known, classic French salad is substantial enough to be served as a main dish.

SERVES 4

6oz (150g) green beans, trimmed

4 x 6oz (150g) tuna steaks

½ cup extra virgin olive oil, plus extra for brushing

salt and freshly ground black pepper

3 tbsp white wine vinegar

juice of ½ lemon

2 tsp Dijon mustard

1 garlic clove, finely chopped

8oz (250g) ripe plum tomatoes, quartered lengthwise

2 romaine lettuce hearts, trimmed and torn into bite-size pieces

1 small red onion, thinly sliced

8 flat anchovy fillets in olive oil, drained

12 Niçoise or other black olives

8–10 basil leaves

4 eggs, hard-boiled

1 Cook the beans in a saucepan of gently boiling water for 3–4 minutes, or until crisp-tender. Drain the beans in a colander and immediately turn them into a bowl of ice water to stop the cooking.

2 Preheat a ridged grill pan over medium–high heat. Brush the tuna steaks with 1–2 tablespoons olive oil and season to taste with salt and pepper. Sear the steaks for 2 minutes on each side—the centers should still be slightly pink. Set the tuna aside. Drain the green beans again.

3 Meanwhile, make the vinaigrette. Whisk together the vinegar, lemon juice, mustard, and garlic. Whisk in the ½ cup olive oil, and season to taste.

4 Place the green beans, tomatoes, lettuce, onion, anchovies, olives, and basil in a large bowl. Drizzle with the vinaigrette and toss gently to mix.

5 Divide the salad among 4 plates. Peel and quarter each egg and add them to the plates. Cut each tuna steak in half and arrange both halves on top of each salad.

Yellowfin tuna (*Thunnus albacares*) Caught in all tropical and subtropical seas, this species is also known as yellowfin tunny and Allison's tuna. It is a big fish that can reach up to 8ft (2.5m) long. The meat taken from the back or loin of the tuna is lean, meaty, with a slight flavor of rump steak. The meat taken from the belly is much higher in fat and is popular in Japanese cuisine.

Tuna steaks are firm and meaty, almost like a rump steak.

The back is black metallic turning to dark blue.

The yellow to silver belly often has broken, practically vertical lines running along it.

Skipjack tuna (*Katsuwonus pelamis*) Also known as strip-bellied bonito, striped tuna, oceanic bonito, and watermelon in the US and Australia, this is a smaller fish, reaching a maximum of 43in (110cm). It is used extensively in the canning industry.

MACKEREL AND BONITO (SCOMBRIDAE FAMILY)

The Scombridae family of species has around 54 members, found in all oceans worldwide. It includes the mackerel, bonito, wahoo, kingfish, or king mackerel, and tuna fish groups—all extremely important commercially for many countries. These oil-rich species contain high levels of omega-3 essential fatty acids; the oil is located throughout the body and not just in the liver. All members of this group should be stored at a constant low temperature. High levels of histadine naturally occur in their flesh, and if not stored at a low-enough temperature, this converts into histamine, which can cause scombroid poisoning—upset stomach and diarrhea.

Rather confusingly, the names "mackerel" and "bonito" are used interchangeably: for example, horse mackerel and frigate mackerel are often labeled as bonito.
CUTS Usually whole and ungutted; fillets and steaks of the larger bonito, kingfish, and wahoo are available.
● **EAT** **Cooked:** Broil, bake, barbecue, and roast. **Preserved:** Canned, smoked, dried, and salted. **Raw:** Cured and used in sushi and sashimi.
FLAVOR PAIRINGS Japanese: shoyu, sesame seeds, mirin, rice vinegar, cucumber and daikon, chile and cilantro; Mediterranean: basil, olive oil, garlic.
CLASSIC RECIPES Soused mackerel; mackerel with gooseberry sauce; smoked mackerel pâté; mackerel with rhubarb; gravad mackerel; marmite (Basque fishermen's bonito dish).

The Atlantic mackerel is identified by the bar or scribble markings along its back.

Atlantic mackerel *(Scomber scombrus).* This commercially important pelagic species is the most northerly member of the family. It is found extensively in the North Atlantic, with smaller pockets in the Mediterranean. It can grow up to 2ft (60cm) long. Look for mackerel that are still stiff with rigor mortis and cook as soon as possible. Broiling, barbecuing, and roasting make the most of the creamy-textured flakes.

The fins can fold flat against the body to give a streamlined shape that enables it to swim fast.

Damage to the jaw may indicate that it has been line-caught (preferable) rather than netted.

SMOKED MACKEREL PÂTÉ

Scottish mackerel are especially suitable for smoking. This paté is traditionally served with Melba toast or vegetable crudités.

SERVES 4

4 smoked mackerel fillets, skinned

6oz (140g) cream cheese, cut into pieces, or fromage frais

1 tbsp cream style white horseradish

fresh lemon juice, to taste

salt and freshly ground black pepper

1 Put the fish fillets into a food processor. Process, pulsing the machine on and off, to chop coarsely. Add the cream cheese and horseradish, then pulse until the mixture is well blended and smooth.

2 Stir in the lemon juice to taste, and season with salt and freshly ground black pepper.

Wahoo *(Acanthocybium solandri)*
The wahoo has an iridescent bluish-green back, and silver flanks striped with cobalt blue. It can reach 8ft (2.5m), although is more commonly landed at around 5½ft (1.7m). It is found in the Atlantic, Indian, and Pacific oceans, including the Caribbean and Mediterranean seas. An often solitary fish, sometimes forming small groups rather than shoals. Superb to eat, with a firm, meaty texture and a delicate, sweet taste. In the Caribbean, slices of wahoo are cured in spices.

Wahoo steak has a dense and meaty texture.

The cheeks of many fish, including the bonito, are considered to be a delicacy.

Chub mackerel is good for sashimi, where the fillets are cured briefly to firm up the texture.

Bonito (Sarda sarda)
A selection of fish come under this heading: the belted bonito, horse mackerel, short-finned tunny, pelamid, and strip-backed pelamis. The bonito has an extensive range: it is caught in the Eastern Atlantic from Norway to South Africa; the Mediterranean and Black Sea; in the Western Atlantic, from Nova Scotia to Colombia, Venezuela, and northern Argentina. It can reach up to 35in (90cm), but is most commonly found at around 20in (50cm). Dried flakes of bonito are used in dashi, a Japanese soup stock. Bonito is perfect for broiling or barbecuing with a robust-flavored baste or marinade.

Dark, rich, and meaty, bonito has a firm texture; the flesh lightens during cooking.

Chub mackerel (Scomber colias)
Also known as Spanish mackerel, thimble-eyed mackerel, and southern mackerel. This close relation of the Atlantic mackerel has similar bar markings, but they are not so defined. The chub mackerel grows to about 50cm (20in) long; it prefers warm waters, and is found in the East and West Atlantic. Its related species in the Indo-Pacific, scomber japonicus, grows to 20–35cm (8–14in).

The chub mackerel has a lightly speckled underside.

The king mackerel is an impressive-looking fish with a slim, silver body and dark bars along its back.

King mackerel (Scomberomorus cavalla)
Also known as kingfish, The king mackerel is found in the Western Atlantic, from Canada to Massachusetts to São Paulo, Brazil; also in the eastern-central Atlantic. It reaches a maximum length of approximately 6ft (180cm), although is usually found at about 2¼ft (70cm). It lives near reefs, and in some areas may feed on plankton that cause ciguatera poisoning in humans. The meat is full-flavored and great for charbroiling or barbecuing.

ESCOLAR/SNAKE MACKEREL (GEMPYLIDAE)

The escolar, also known as the snake mackerel, is a member of the Gempylidae group that also includes gemfish, snoek, and barracouta. It has a fierce appearance, with an elongated body and head, and jaws lined with menacing sharp teeth. It is often associated with the barracuda group and is a similarly voracious predator to smaller species including mackerel, flying fish, and squid. In turn, it is hunted by tuna and marlin. Escolar are located mainly in tropical marine waters worldwide, but some are found in temperate locations. As immature fish they favor midwater depth, moving to deep water as they mature. Although Gempylidae members are found globally, most are landed as part of a catch of other more valuable species, including tuna. The oil-rich flesh of the escolar is enjoyed in Europe, the US, and Asia, where it may be served as sushi and sashimi. In the US, it is sometimes labeled as "white tuna." In Japan, escolar is often used in fishcakes and sausages; it is also popular in Hawaii and South Africa.

CUTS Whole and frozen fillets.
● **EAT** **Preserved:** Smoked and canned. **Cooked:** Broil, roast, pan-fry, deep-fry, and bake.
CLASSIC RECIPES Broiled escolar with chile dressing; teriyaki.

Escolar *(Lepidocybium flavobrunneum)*
This fish has several names: snake mackerel, black oil fish, butterfish, castor oil fish, and rudderfish in Australia. It varies in size but can grow to well over 6½ft(2m) long. It has well-flavored but very oily flesh (containing a wax ester) and can cause stomach irritation: eat only small quantities at a time. "Deep-skinning" will remove most of the wax; broiling also helps to release it. Thick, succulent, escolar steaks can be brushed with oil and pan-fried or roasted.

Steaks of escolar are thick and oily.

Once the fish has been cooked, the silver skin can be scraped away because it is so fine.

SCABBARD FISH/CUTLASS FISH (TRICHIURIDAE)

The scabbard fish or cutlass fish is closely related to the snake mackerel and shares similar characteristics. There are over 40 members of this group. It is also known as the saber fish, hairtail, ribbon fish, and frostfish. The fish gets its name from its very long, thin body. Its color varies, but most species sport a steely-blue or silver skin. They also have fanglike teeth set in a long jaw, which are coated in a powerful anticoagulant, and so need to be handled with care. Scabbard fish are found in many waters globally, and fished on both sides of the Atlantic. Black scabbard fish is a delicacy in Madeira; it has to be eaten very fresh and does not store well, so is not usually exported fresh. These fish are extremely palatable, with a delicate texture and almost buttery flavor. It may appear difficult to prepare.

CUTS Whole fish; very long and thin fillets, usually skinned. Cut into wide steaks.
● **EAT** **Cooked:** Broil, pan-fry, bake, or smoke on a barbecue.
CLASSIC RECIPES *Filetti di spatola al pane* (Italian breaded recipe); *espada Preta vinho e alos* (Madeiran recipe for cooking in wine).

PUFFER FISH/FUGU (TETRAODONTIDAE)

This highly poisonous fish must be treated with extreme care, though it is considered a great delicacy. When threatened, the puffer fish can puff itself up to many times greater than its body size. Puffer fish are found in marine, fresh, and brackish waters globally. The Japanese enjoy a delicacy, called fugu, made from puffer fish of the genus Takifugu, Sphoeroides, and Lagocephalus (they also call the fish fugu). Thousands of tons of fugu are consumed in Japan every year. The fugu is notorious, as certain parts of it contain tetrodotoxin and are extremely poisonous. The toxin causes paralysis and asphyxiation; there is currently no antidote. Despite this, it is a highly sought-after and very expensive fish. The skin may be used in salad, stewed, or pickled.

CUTS Fillets; must be prepared extremely carefully by a licensed chef.
◉ **EAT Raw:** As fugu. **Cooked:** Fry.
FLAVOR PAIRINGS Pickled ginger, soy, wasabi, sake.

The puffer fish has a rounded body. When it is prepared for sashimi, fillets are cut so thinly that the slices are almost transparent.

Puffer fish or fugu (*Takifugu, several species*). The toxin in parts of the fish causes paralysis and asphyxiation—there is no antidote; the safe preparation of fugu, by specially trained chefs, is very time-consuming. Fugu sashimi is a very popular fugu dish. Wafer-thin slices are typically arranged in a chrysanthemum pattern, which symbolizes death in Japanese culture.

The scabbard fish has long, fanglike teeth: avoid touching them.

Silver scabbard
(*Lepidopus caudatus*) *This species can grow to over 6½ft (2m). The scabbard fish is particularly popular and esteemed in Portugal and Madeira, but underrated in countries such as the US, and is often discarded from a catch. It tastes rich, nutty, and buttery.*

CHAR-GRILLED SWORDFISH

Meaty fish—including swordfish, tuna, and marlin—are best char-grilled on an indoor grill pan or barbecued outdoors, rather than simply broiled. Fish steaks need intense heat in order to char the exterior.

SERVES 2

2 x 5oz (140g) swordfish steaks (around 1in/2½cm- thick is best)

olive oil

salt and freshly ground black pepper, to serve

1 Preheat a dry, well-seasoned grill pan until it is just beginning to smoke. Meanwhile, brush the swordfish lightly with olive oil and season with salt and pepper.

2 Gently press each fish steak onto the hot grill with a metal spatula. Allow to cook for 1–2 minutes, or until the steak will lift cleanly off the grill. (If it remains stuck to the grill, leave in to cook for another few seconds and try again.) Flip the steaks over and press flat with the spatula as before. Cook for another 1–2 minutes, or until they will lift cleanly from the pan. Reduce the heat and turn the steaks back onto the first side, trying to position them so that the char-grill marks are at a perpendicular angle to those made during the first cooking. Cook for 1 minute before turning onto the second side, again at an angle.

3 Avoid turning the steaks a third time, in order to prevent disturbing the existing grill marks. Cook until the steaks are opaque and firm to the touch. Leave to rest for 1 minute before serving. Serve with a simple salad or a flavored butter.

SWORDFISH (XIPHIIDAE) AND MARLIN (ISTIOPHORIDAE)

The billfish family includes swordfish (*Xiphiidae*) and marlin (*Istiophoridae*). As the family name suggests, these fish have a long bill or spear. They produce meaty, dense steaks that are expensive to buy. Billfish are found in most warm and tropical ocean zones worldwide. These big, impressive fish have been hunted mercilessly and have become seriously endangered. Most are slow-growing species, which take many years to reach maturity. The swordfish, also known as the broadbill, resembles other members of the Istiophoridae family, but is in a group all of its own (*Xiphiidae*). It has the longest bill of the group and is known to be aggressive, often attacking before being attacked, and using its sword to slash and tear its prey. There are four main species of marlin. They can grow to over 1 ton in weight. The Atlantic sailfish (*Istiophorus albicans*) is closely related to the marlin, and is found in the Atlantic and Caribbean Sea. There has been concern about the high metal—potentially toxic—content of some billfish, particularly about traces of methylmercury. Therefore, pregnant women and small children should avoid eating it. However, it is widely argued that for the general population, the importance of eating this type of fish—which contains the important dietary omega-3 essential fatty acids, which are vital for heart health—far outweighs the possibility of consuming too much mercury.
CUTS Fresh: Steaks or whole loins, sometimes whole. **Preserved:** Smoked.
● **EAT Cooked:** Char-grill, barbecue, and pan-fry. **Raw:** Sushi, sashimi, and marinated raw.

FLAVOR PAIRINGS Basil, rosemary, cilantro, cumin, paprika, coriander, citrus, olive oil, sesame oil, mesquite smoking chips.
CLASSIC RECIPES Smoked marlin with scrambled egg (Latin American); chargrilled swordfish with salsa verde.

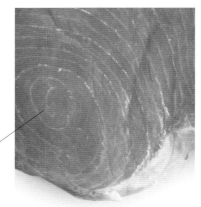

Marlin meat is very dense and meaty, with a sweet, almost gamy flavor. It is sold in steaks without bone or skin. Chargrilling and pan-frying are the best methods for cooking it. It suits just about any flavor pairing, from wild mushrooms to Japanese soy sauce.

Swordfish *(Xiphias gladius)*
The swordfish grows to a maximum of about 14ft 9in (4½m) long and is found in the Atlantic, Pacific, and Indian Oceans, and in the Mediterranean Sea. It is an important fish commercially; many are harvested from the Pacific each year, where they are now carefully managed. In the North Atlantic, systems are in place to protect juvenile fish. The color of swordfish flesh varies, according to its diet and habitat; the meaty-tasting steaks vary from white to a pinkish tinge.

MARINATED ANCHOVIES

This is a traditional Spanish recipe for curing fresh anchovies. Marinated anchovies are traditionally served as chilled tapas, along with other fish and meat dishes.

SERVES 4

8oz (250g) fresh anchovies

2 tbsp coarse sea salt

1 cup sherry vinegar

¼ cup extra virgin olive oil

finely grated zest of 1–2 lemons, to taste

sprigs of marjoram or thyme

salt and freshly ground black pepper

1 Gut and bone the anchovies. Rinse with cold water and pat dry. Lay the fish in a single layer in a shallow dish, sprinkle with salt, and pour the vinegar over them. Cover and refrigerate for 12–18 hours.

2 Drain away the salt and vinegar and pat the fish dry. Arrange on a clean serving dish and drizzle with the olive oil, sprinkle with grated lemon zest (add a squeeze of lemon juice, if you like), and garnish with the marjoram. Season with salt and pepper to serve.

ANCHOVY (ENGRAULIDAE)

Anchovies are from the *Engraulidae* family group of about 140 species, and resemble herrings in many ways. They are small, oil-rich, saltwater fish, and are found in the Atlantic, Indian, and Pacific Oceans. They are generally concentrated in temperate waters and are rare in very cold or very warm waters. Huge schools of anchovies are usually found in the shallows in estuarine waters and bays. The small, greenish fish have a hint of iridescent blue to their skin. They vary in size dramatically, from ¾in (2cm) to 16in (40cm) long. Body shape varies according to species, but on the whole it is a long, slender fish. Once landed, anchovies need to be cooked quickly—as they do not keep well—or preserved by curing in vinegar or salting. Sometimes they are available fresh from the boat.

CUTS Fresh: Whole. **Preserved:** In jars as salted, cured, or marinated/brined fish. Also made into anchovy essence.

⬤ **EAT** Raw: Traditionally marinated and enjoyed in a raw state. **Cooked:** when available fresh, pan-fry.

FLAVOR PAIRINGS Sherry vinegar, white wine vinegar, shallots, marjoram, oregano, sage, thyme, parsley, Mediterranean olive oil.

CLASSIC RECIPES *Boquerones en vinagre* (Spanish marinated anchovies); deep-fried anchovies with sage; *alici ripiene* (stuffed anchovies); *alici al limone* (marinated in lemon juice). **Dried:** *Bagna caoda* (anchovies and butter sauce); *asparagi in salsa* (asparagus with anchovy sauce); *polenta nera* (buckwheat polenta with anchovies); *puntarelle in salsa di alici* (Italy), *anchoïade* (France).

European anchovy
(Engraulis encrasicolus)
This member of the group is abundant in the Mediterranean and is caught on the coasts of Sicily, Italy, France, and Spain, where it is sold straight from the boat. It is also found along the coast of North Africa, and can extend as far north as the south of the Atlantic. It grows to a maximum of 8in (20cm). Deeply savory, salty anchovies make a classic partner to char-grilled beef steaks. They also make an excellent butter, which is delicious with grilled white fish such as brill and Dover sole.

The swordfish has a black/dark brown back, fading to gray on the flanks and belly.

A loin is taken from each side of the backbone and cut into thick, succulent steaks.

Swordfish are extremely valuable commercially: one fish can be cut to provide many steaks.

HERRING AND SARDINE (CLUPDEIDAE GROUP)

With more then 50 species, the Clupeidae group of fish includes the herring, shad, sardine/pilchard, sprat, hilsa, and menhaden. Anchovies (see page 47) are closely associated with this group. The species are mostly marine, but some are freshwater fish. These shoaling, pelagic fish feed mainly on plankton and grow rapidly. They are an important food source for large predatory fish. Herrings are an oil-rich fish, caught extensively worldwide, and form a key low-cost food for many countries; they are also widely considered to be one of the most abundant species of fish in the world. Although some stocks are threatened, others are well managed. Landed in huge quantities, the fish spoil quickly and if eaten fresh, need to be cooked while they are as close to rigor mortis as possible. This fact has led them to be processed into various products, from salted (in times past) to canned (for today's market). A whole herring, split and salted or pickled and then smoked, is called a kipper.

HERRING
CUTS Fresh: Whole, gutted or filleted, frozen, and canned. Roes, both hard and soft (milt), are popular. Female roe is a delicacy in Japan. Small, immature herring members are harvested and marketed as whitebait (but are overexploited). **Preserved:** Smoked, salted, marinated, cured, and canned. See preserved fish: kippers, bloaters, buckling, and *maatjes* herring.
⊙ **EAT Cooked:** Best is to pan-fry, but also broil, barbecue, roast, and souse.
FLAVOR PAIRINGS Sour cream, dill, oatmeal, bacon, horseradish, lemon, capers, parsley.
CLASSIC RECIPES Herrings in oatmeal; herrings with bacon; rollmops; jugged kippers; deviled whitebait.

SARDINE
CUTS Fresh: Whole, gutted, or filleted. **Preserved:** Smoked, marinated, cured, and canned (canned in olive oil, tomato sauce, etc.).
⊙ **EAT Cooked:** Pan-fry, broil, or barbecue.
FLAVOR PAIRINGS Mediterranean: olive oil, garlic, lemon, golden raisins, pine nuts, parsley, oregano, thyme.
CLASSIC RECIPES Broiled sardines with Greek salad; barbecued sardines with oregano and lemon.

SPRAT
CUTS Fresh: Whole (you will usually need to gut the fish yourself). **Preserved:** Smoked, canned, and salted.
⊙ **EAT** Broil, bake, and fry.

FLAVOR PAIRINGS Beets, white wine and red wine vinegar, flat-leaf parsley, cilantro, coriander seeds.
CLASSIC RECIPES Pan-fried sprats with lemon.

European sprat *(Sprattus sprattus)*
Also known as bristling or brisling, this small member of the herring family is found in European marine waters from the northeast Atlantic (North Sea and Baltic Sea) down to the Mediterranean, Adriatic, and Black seas. Its flesh appears gray, but changes to off-white when cooked. It has a smooth, oily texture. It can grow up to 6½in (16cm), but 5in (12cm) is more usual.

Sprats are a startlingly bright silver, with a small head and a beady black eye.

It is best to gut sardines and cook them on the bone, since the fine bones are easier to locate when the fish is cooked. The loose scales need to be removed with the back of a knife.

Atlantic herrings have a bluish-green back, bright silver flanks, and loose scales.

Sardine or Pilchard *(Sardina pilchardus)*
Pilchards are known as sardines if they are less than 6in (15cm) in length. This fast-growing fish is immensely important to many countries. It is a rounded, oil-rich fish, high in omega-3 essential fatty acids. It has a greeny-blue back, with bright, silvery sides and belly, and loose scales. The danger of overexploitation has dictated a minimum landing size (currently 4½in/11cm), although the fish can grow to 8–12in (20–30cm) in length. Sardines have a lot of bones, a coarser texture, and are meaty with a robust flavor.

Atlantic herring *(Clupea harengus)*
Also known as sild, yawling, digby, and mattie, Atlantic or sea herring is found on both sides of the Atlantic. This pelagic species forms huge schools of billions of fish. They can grow up to 18in (45cm) long, but 12in (30cm) is more usual. They were overfished during the 1990s, but today there are some well-managed, sustainable stocks. Fresh herring is at its best simply broiled with a slice of lemon. It is high in omega-3 essential fatty acids; if eaten extremely fresh, the flakes are fine and sweet and not overly oily in texture. Lots of fine bones make this fish a challenge for some to eat.

The twaite shad has a bright silver body with a covering of scales.

Twaite shad *(Alosa pseudoharengus)*
The twaite shad is found along the west coast of Europe, in the eastern Mediterranean, and in some large rivers along these coasts. It has declined in many parts of Europe over recent years. With a similar appearance to a herring, this fish is generally larger, with a more delicate taste. It produces decent-sized fillets and has a delicate, grassy, and milky taste. If cooked well, it has lovely succulent flakes, but plenty of bones.

Health-giving oily fish with naturally salted, rich-flavored meat, sardines are best cooked quickly and simply.

NILE PERCH, BARRAMUNDI, AND MURRAY COD

Several key species of freshwater fish are found in the warmer waters of Africa, Asia, and Australasia. Nile perch (*Lates niloticus*) is also known as Victoria perch and *capitaine*. It is a predatory fish living mainly in fresh, but some brackish, waters. It was introduced to Lake Victoria in Africa, where it has caused much damage by virtually wiping out other species of fish. It is an important commercial fish, harvested for export and sold at a good price. It is mostly wild, but some aquaculture has been established. The barramundi (*Lates calcarifer*) is found from the Persian Gulf to China, Asia, and Australia. It inhabits creeks, rivers, and estuarine waters. In Australia, it is farmed as a highly commercial species, and is a major export. It is very similar in taste and texture to Nile perch. The

Maccullochella genus of predatory freshwater fish is native to Australia and known as "cod." A few species are found in the river systems, including the Murray cod (*Maccullochella peelii peelii*) and the trout cod (*M. macquariensis*). Many of these species are now listed as critically endangered. Murray cod is seriously threatened, though it is farmed in Victoria, and all Murray cod on sale or served in restaurants is from this source. It is renowned for its flavor.

CUTS Whole and unprepared; fillets and steaks.

● **EAT** **Cooked:** Pan-fry, grill, barbecue, poach, and steam.

ALTERNATIVES Murray cod is only available farmed. The following fish can be used interchangeably: snapper, grouper, and coral trout.

FLAVOR PAIRINGS Nile perch and barramundi: bok choy, lime, chile, fresh herbs, white wine. Murray cod: butter, white wine, beer, white wine vinegar, orange, mild to medium spices.

Murray cod is farmed to a suitable size for individual portions.

Nile perch is usually sold ready-prepared: the neat, creamy white fillets are excellent pan-fried and battered or cooked in breadcrumbs. The fillets taste much like barramundi and can be cooked in similar ways.

Nile perch *(Lates niloticus)*
The Nile perch is native to the River Nile and other major West African freshwater rivers. It has been introduced to lakes in East Africa and North Africa, and in North America. It may grow to over 6 ft 6 in (2m) long. It is most often seen filleted, and produces firm, white, and succulent fillets. As a freshwater fish, it can have a slightly earthy taste. New-style Asian flavors complement it well, such as steamed bok choy with shiitake mushrooms.

Murray cod *(Maccullochella peelii peelii)*
Known to be the largest of Australia's freshwater fish, measured by weight, rather than length. It is a slow-developing species that lives for over 30 years. It weighs in at 44lb (20kg); the largest recorded specimen was 247lb (112kg). The flesh of this fish is considered excellent, producing large, thick, white steaks with a delicate texture. It is a versatile fish that suits many methods of cooking and flavor combinations. It can also be cooked over an open fire; good, too, for escabeche.

The firm and meaty flesh of the Murray cod works well with Asian flavors, and is equally good served as fish and chips.

To serve this fish whole, trim away fins, gut, and remove gills.

Large fish can be filleted; for small fish, scale, gut, and cook whole.

The scales of the barramundi are notoriously well attached to the flesh; the best way to remove them is with a scaler, running from tail to head.

Barramundi *(Lates calcarifer)*
Juevenile fish are brown and mottled. Adult fish grow to 3ft 11in (1.2m) long. They have a pointed head and large jaw, and light silver skin with a heavy armoring of scales. This fish has a succulent, flaky, white flesh with a low oil content, although there can be a tendency toward an earthiness, depending on where it was caught. Farmed fish are rarely much bigger than plate size; they differ in flavor from wild fish. Barramundi was popular with the native Aboriginal people, who would cook a whole large "barra" by wrapping the fish in wild ginger leaf and cooking it in the embers of a fire. The pearl (or cheek) of a barramundi is a particular treat: this is juicy and sweet-flavored. Barramundi is excellent barbecued, steamed, and grilled.

CATFISH (ICTALURIDAE AND CLARIIDAE) AND RIVER COBBLER (PANGASIIDAE)

Catfish from various families have been caught in the wild and farmed on most continents for hundreds of years. They live in fresh inland and coastal waters. Many are nocturnal, bottom-feeding, and predatory. Catfish are considered a delicacy in many parts of the world, particularly in Central Europe and Africa. Migrants from these areas took catfish to the US, where it is now a popular part of traditional Southern food. Different species are common to each continent.

Channel catfish and blue catfish (*Ictaluridae*) are native to the US, living in freshwater streams, rivers, and creeks. The "channel cat" is farmed in an industry worth millions of dollars. River cobbler or *basa* (from the *Pangasiidae* family) is native to Vietnam and Thailand, and has recently become valuable in the international market.
CUTS Live; whole; fillets; fresh or frozen portions.
● **EAT** Cooked: Pan-fry, grill, bake, poach, or deep-fry. **Preserved:**

Smoked, dried, and salted products are available.
FLAVOR PAIRINGS Cornmeal, sesame seeds, sour cream, scallion mushrooms, parsley, bay leaf, thyme.
CLASSIC RECIPES Southern deep-fried catfish with cornmeal; *pecel lele*; *ikan kele*; tuscaloosa catfish.

The skin of a catfish is like that of an eel: thick and slippery, requiring some effort with pliers to remove it.

Take care to avoid spines when preparing the fish; there are some sharp ones that can cause a nasty wound.

African sharptooth catfish (*Clarias gariepinus*)
This air-breathing freshwater catfish lives in rivers, lakes, and swamps. It is farmed in Africa, Europe, and the US. Farmed and wild catfish grow to a weight of 4½lb (2kg). It is hugely popular in the US and Africa. Catfish is moist and succulent, and as with many other freshwater species, it has a distinct taste of the river. The flesh is white and firm-textured, and suits various methods of cooking; it combines well with Asian flavors, including ginger and chile.

TILAPIA (CHICHLIDAE)

There are around 100 species in the *Chichlidae* family, and tilapia (also known as St. Peter's fish) is their common name. These fish are found in warm areas of fresh water, where they can grow to 16in (40cm) long. Tilapia is second only to carp in its production through aquaculture, and some species are extensively farmed in many areas of the world. It is omnivorous, and aquatic vegetation makes up an important part of its diet, which makes it environmentally friendly to produce, as it does not need the extensive quantity of fishmeal that other species demand. Many different hybrid species of tilapia are now farmed to produce sweet-flavored, firm-textured white flesh. Tilapia are invasive and have become problematic in some areas where they have been introduced.
CUTS Fresh: Whole (unprepared and gutted); fillets. **Preserved:** Salted, dried.
● **EAT** Cooked: Pan-fry, deep-fry, steam, bake, barbecue, or grill.
Preserved: Baked and poached products are available.
FLAVOR PAIRINGS Thai: bird's-eye chile, palm sugar, *nam pla*, shrimp paste, cilantro, coconut, chile, galangal.
CLASSIC RECIPES *Pla tub tim tod samrod.*

Tilapia (*Oreochromis niloticus*)
In Thailand, tilapia is known as pomegranate fish and is cooked in a variety of ways. This hybrid tilapia, which is gray with a darker gray banding, is underused, but becoming steadily more accepted and important. It produces very firm and white fillets with a sweet flavor, which lend themselves to various methods of cooking, and it takes many flavors well. Farmed species are usually marketed at 8–10in (20–25cm) long.

Tilapia scales are firmly attached to the body and require a scaler to remove them successfully. The skin of the fish is also cured and used for leatherwork.

Trim away the tilapia's fins prior to cooking.

River cobbler or basa is available ready processed into neat, white frozen fillets.

River cobbler *(Pangasius bocourti)*
The river cobbler is a member of the shark catfish family, and is also known as basa, bocourti, pangasius, and panga. It grows to 10–12in (25–30cm) when farmed, and is now one of the most extensively farmed species worldwide (along with carp and tilapia). Its availability takes pressure off the threatened wild stocks of some species of catfish, and it is easy and environmentally friendly to farm. The river cobbler has very little flavor, but cooks to a flaky texture; it is ideal for deep-frying or taking strong flavors to help enliven it.

DEEP-FRIED CATFISH

Catfish, particularly in this delicious dish, is a staple in the Midwestern and Southern states of the US; and is traditionally served with "slaw and ketchup". Other flavors, such as jalapeño chile and Creole seasoning, are often added to the cornmeal mix.

SERVES 4

4 x 6oz (175g) catfish fillets
1 cup whole milk
⅔ cup all-purpose flour
⅔ cup fine cornmeal or grits
salt and freshly ground black pepper
oil, for frying
lemon wedges, to garnish

1 Remove any bones from the catfish fillets and rinse in the milk. Do not pat dry. Sift the flour and cornmeal on to a plate, and mix with salt and pepper. Coat the fish on all sides.

2 Fill a frying pan one-third full with oil. Heat until very hot, then, cook the fish, turning once, until opaque on the inside and golden on the outside. Remove, blotting excess oil with paper towels. Place on a warm serving plate, and sprinkle with a little more salt.

Red tilapia *(Oreochromis niloticus)*
Tilapia varies in color from species to species, in much the same way as koi carp. Red tilapia are pinkish in hue; prepare and cook in exactly the same way as gray tilapia.

Fillets of tilapia are white and densely textured. They hold together well, so are suitable for pan-frying and grilling.

GEFILTE FISH

In the traditional Jewish preparation, the mixture was stuffed into the skin before cooking. For convenience, this recipe uses fillets, not a whole fish.

SERVES 4

2¼lb (1kg) carp or pike fillets, skinned, trimmed, cut into chunks

1 tbsp oil

1 onion, finely chopped

2 eggs

1 tsp sugar

salt and freshly ground white pepper

⅔ cup matzo meal

1 Put the fish and oil into a food processor and chop finely. Scrape the mixture into a bowl.

2 Put the onion, eggs, sugar, salt, pepper, and matzo meal into the food processor, and pulse until blended. Add to the fish and mix by hand, working into a paste. Shape the paste into balls the size of a small apple; cover; refrigerate until firm.

3 Bring a pot of fish stock to a boil. Reduce to low heat and cook the fish balls for 6–10 minutes, until cooked through. Cover; refrigerate until gelled.

CARP (CYPRINIDAE)

There are over 2,500 members of the Cyprinidae family including the carp, minnow, tench, roach, bream, dace, chub, and bitterling; also aquarium species such as the koi and goldfish. As a group, most are native to North America, Africa, and Eurasia. They have no stomach or teeth and feed mainly on vegetation and some invertebrates. The species vary in size from a few millimeters to 5ft–6½ft (1.5–2m) long. The carp, head of this family, was one of the earliest farmed species. It is still the top farmed species in the world today. Although extensively used and farmed in China, carp are not so popular in many cultures; they tend toward an earthy, slightly muddy flavor (dependent on habitat) and have lots of fine bones. Some species are farmed for the Chinese, Eastern European, and kosher markets; also in land-locked countries with no access to marine fish. Angling for coarse fish is a hugely popular recreational hobby and members of the carp family are particularly sought after. They have acute hearing, making them quite a challenge for the fisherman. Coarse fishermen work on a catch-and-release system to put the fish back in the wild.

CUTS Fresh: Usually whole, or live. **Preserved:** Carp roe, and smoked and salted.

● **EAT** Steam, roast, pan-fry, pané (dipped or rolled in breadcrumbs before frying), fry, and bake. Use carp frames for stock and soup.

FLAVOR PAIRINGS Paprika, butter, capers, dill, garlic, parsley, cornmeal, ginger, rice wine, sesame.

CLASSIC RECIPES Carp au bleu; roast Hungarian carp with paprika sauce; Gefilte fish; carp in fennel sauce (Italy).

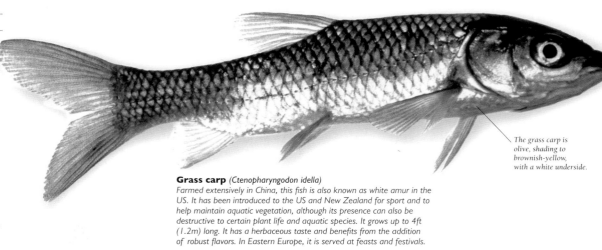

The grass carp is olive, shading to brownish-yellow, with a white underside.

Grass carp (Ctenopharyngodon idella)
Farmed extensively in China, this fish is also known as white amur in the US. It has been introduced to the US and New Zealand for sport and to help maintain aquatic vegetation, although its presence can also be destructive to certain plant life and aquatic species. It grows up to 4ft (1.2m) long. It has a herbaceous taste and benefits from the addition of robust flavors. In Eastern Europe, it is served at feasts and festivals.

STURGEON (ACIPENSERIDAE)

The sturgeon is probably best known for the exquisite delicacy of its roe, marketed as caviar. It also produces dense fillets with an excellent flavor. There are around 25 sturgeons in the Acipenseridae group, found in the northern hemisphere. Some live in brackish and fresh waters, other species are anadromous (migratory fish that enter fresh water to spawn, then return to the sea).

This unusual species looks quite prehistoric. Only some of its bones are calcified and bony; the skull and most of the vertebrae are made of cartilage. It has an elongated body with rows of scutes along the length of its back. Most species have sensitive barbels on the chin, which they use to locate food in the mud and then suck it into their mouths. Sturgeons grow slowly and can live to be 100 years old. Due to the price that caviar can reach, these fish have been relentlessly overfished and some are seriously endangered. Well-known species prized for their roe include beluga (Huso huso), osetra (A. gueldenstaedii), sevruga (A. stellastus), and sterlet (A. ruthenus). The freshwater Siberian sturgeon (A. baerii) is farmed, primarily to raise female fish for their roe, but male fish are used for their meat.

CUTS Fresh: Whole fish, steaks, and fillets; female roe. **Preserved:** Smoked.

● **EAT** Cooked: Bake, pan-fry, and steam. **Preserved:** Raw.

FLAVOR PAIRINGS Horseradish, sour cream, beets, vinegar, butter, citrus.

CLASSIC RECIPE Caviar.

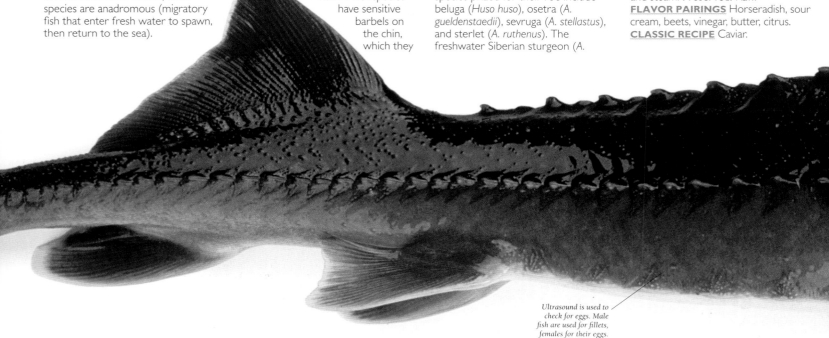

Ultrasound is used to check for eggs. Male fish are used for fillets, females for their eggs.

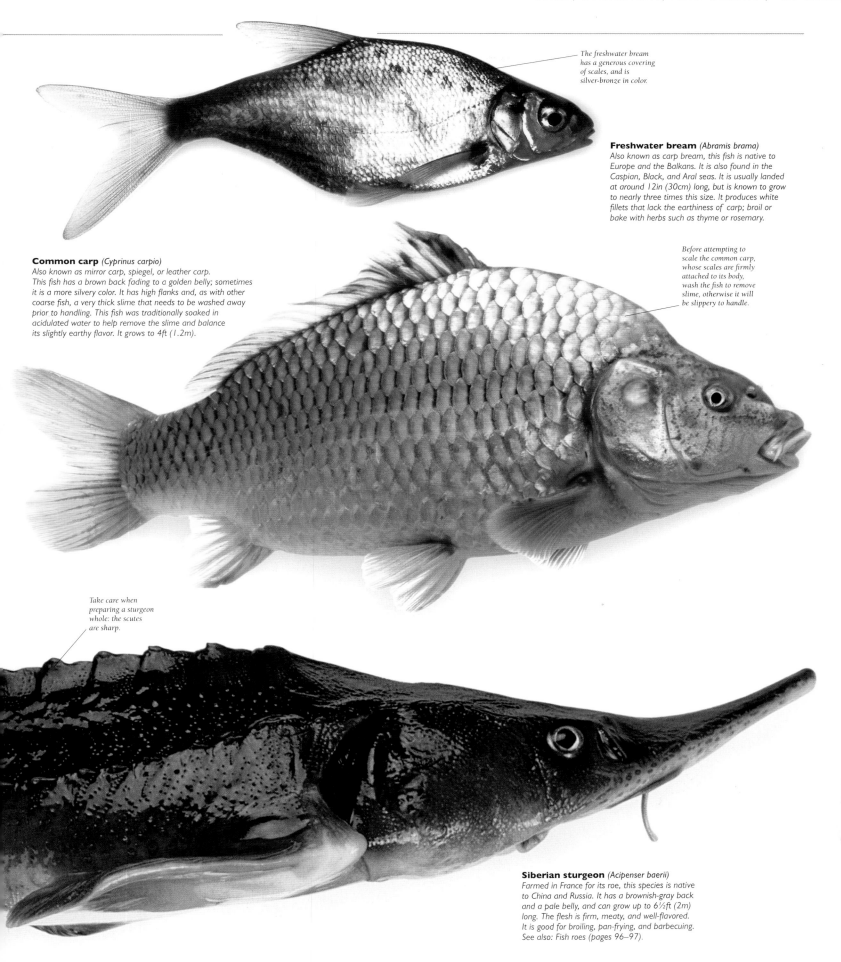

The freshwater bream has a generous covering of scales, and is silver-bronze in color.

Freshwater bream (*Abramis brama*)
Also known as carp bream, this fish is native to Europe and the Balkans. It is also found in the Caspian, Black, and Aral seas. It is usually landed at around 12in (30cm) long, but is known to grow to nearly three times this size. It produces white fillets that lack the earthiness of carp; broil or bake with herbs such as thyme or rosemary.

Common carp (*Cyprinus carpio*)
Also known as mirror carp, spiegel, or leather carp. This fish has a brown back fading to a golden belly; sometimes it is a more silvery color. It has high flanks and, as with other coarse fish, a very thick slime that needs to be washed away prior to handling. This fish was traditionally soaked in acidulated water to help remove the slime and balance its slightly earthy flavor. It grows to 4ft (1.2m).

Before attempting to scale the common carp, whose scales are firmly attached to its body, wash the fish to remove slime, otherwise it will be slippery to handle.

Take care when preparing a sturgeon whole: the scutes are sharp.

Siberian sturgeon (*Acipenser baerii*)
Farmed in France for its roe, this species is native to China and Russia. It has a brownish-gray back and a pale belly, and can grow up to 6½ft (2m) long. The flesh is firm, meaty, and well-flavored. It is good for broiling, pan-frying, and barbecuing. See also: Fish roes (pages 96–97).

PIKE (ESOCIDAE)

A member of the Esocidae family, the pike is a predator that feeds on other pike, smaller fish, birds, snakes, and mammals (including mice and rats). It is a freshwater fish, caught commercially and by recreational fishermen. The pike is also known as the pickerel (usually used to describe smaller species), snoek, and jackfish. Pike are found in the rivers of North America, Western Europe, Siberia, and Eurasia. There are several species, including the muskellunge pike (*E. masquinongy*), grass pickerel pike (*E. americanus verniculatus*), and the northern pike (*E. lucius*). It is famously used in France for *quenelles de brochet*, a *mousseline*

of sieved pike flesh with cream and egg white. Pike has a fine flavor, but contains many small bones; this recipe makes the best of the flesh, as the bones are dealt with prior to serving.

CUTS Fresh: Whole; filleted. Preserved: Smoked, salted, dried, roe.

● **EAT** Cooked: Pan fry, grill, steam, poach, roast.

FLAVOR PAIRINGS Unsalted butter, sage, lemon, cream, bay leaf, white wine.

CLASSIC RECIPES *Quenelles de brochet* (pike quenelles); traditional roast pike.

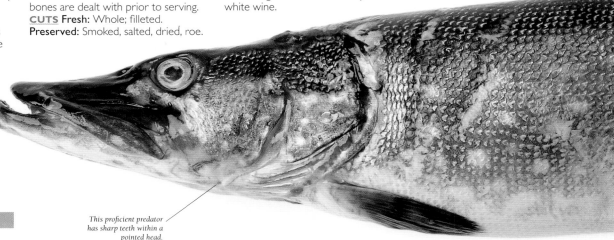

This proficient predator has sharp teeth within a pointed head.

CLASSIC RECIPE

PIKE QUENELLES

Pike fillets purée well for these delicate French dumplings.

SERVES 4

2 tbsp butter, cut into pieces, plus 4 tbsp butter, softened

2 tbsp all-purpose flour

5 tbsp whole milk

1 bay leaf

8oz (225g) pike fillet, cut into pieces

salt, freshly ground white pepper, and a dash of freshly grated nutmeg

1 egg white

2 tbsp heavy whipping cream

1 For the white sauce, melt the 2 tbsp butter in a small saucepan, stir in the flour, and cook over medium-low heat for 1–2 minutes, then whisk in the milk; add the bay leaf. Stir until it comes to a boil, and then reduce the heat to low and simmer 2 minutes. Scrape into a bowl to cool. Discard bay leaf.

2 Process fish, salt, pepper, and nutmeg until smooth. Cream in white sauce, the 4 tbsp butter, and egg white until blended.

3 Push the mixture through a fine sieve into a bowl and refrigerate, covered, for 45 minutes. Shape into small ovals using 2 tablespoons. Working in batches, gently lower the quenelles into simmering water. Cook over low heat for 8–10 minutes, turning once, until the quenelles bob to the surface and feel firm. Remove, pat dry with paper towels, and serve with beurre blanc (see page 67).

ZANDER, WALLEYE, PERCH, AND AMERICAN YELLOW PERCH (PERCIDAE)

The Percidae family of freshwater fish is found globally. At one time eaten by those with no access to the coast, many species are now less frequently used for the table. They remain popular with recreational fishermen; commercial fishing and aquaculture are still viable in some cases. Percids share the same fin pattern: the first dorsal fin is spiny (the number of spines varies), the second is soft. The family includes the zander, perch, ruffe, American yellow perch, silver perch, sauger, and walleye. The largest is the zander, a predatory fish found in fresh water; some are caught in brackish water. Native to Eastern Europe, it has also been introduced to Western Europe and the US. The perch (also known as the European perch or English perch), native to Europe and Asia, has been introduced to South Africa, New

Zealand, and Australia. It is deep green with some stripes, scaly, and has red fins. In cool European waters, it rarely reaches more than 16in (40cm); it can reach a greater size in Australia. Another sought-after species, the walleye, is closely related to zander. It is native to Canada and the northern US. The walleye is not farmed, but for decades has been used to replenish stocks in some river systems.

CUTS Usually whole fish.

● **EAT** Cooked: Pan-fry, grill, bake, roast.

FLAVOR PAIRINGS Butter, herbs including chives, sage, Rosemary, thyme, and bay, lemon and white wine vinegar, cream and eggs.

CLASSIC RECIPES Perch: *watersouchy* (fish soup). Zander: *matelote* (fish stew from the Loire). All these fish could be used for *quenelles* and *gefilte fish*.

Walleye *Sander vitreus*
Chefs often say that the walleye has the best flavor of any freshwater fish. It grows to about 3ft (92cm) long and its color depends on its habitat. The meat has few bones and is light and flaky, with a mild flavor.

Remove the generous layer of scales prior to gutting and cooking.

The pike's deep olive skin, with gold speckling, provides camouflage among river weeds.

Pike *(Esox lucius)*
This species is also known as the northern pike, or jackfish. It has an elongated body and is thought to grow to up to 6½ft (2m). It has a mild-tasting, white, and bony flesh.

American yellow perch *(Perca flavescens)*
Often thought to be a subspecies, or hybrid, of the European perch, the yellow perch is found in the US and Canada. It is paler in color than its European relative, and has a yellow tinge to its scales. It is known to have a fine flavor, and its small size; it rarely reaches more than a few inches; makes it ideal for pan-frying. In restaurants, "perch" is a name widely used to describe both this and other species of fish, which can be confusing.

The zander is a fierce and elusive game fish, known for its long, elegant body.

Zander *(Stizostedion lucioperca)*
This fish can reach a weight of 44lb (20kg) and grow to 3ft (92cm). Its flesh has a fine flavor, with an herbaceous earthiness, which is particularly admired by the French—zander features in several dishes from the Loire Valley. Good grilled.

TROUT, CHAR, AND GRAYLING (SALMONIDAE)

This group of fish is extensive and an important food globally. The species are all rich in oil. The pink color of the flesh is the result of a diet of crustaceans that have a naturally occurring caryatid pigment. Farmed fish are sometimes given a chemical substitute to replicate this. Some species of trout are used for aquaculture or to stock trout lakes. Most trout spend their lives in fresh waters around the world; others are anadromous and migrate to the sea, returning to their natal river to spawn. Trout can have an earthy flavor, because they feed over a muddy riverbed. Farmed fish may be reared with a gravel bed and then purged in clean water prior to harvest, in order to prevent this. Indigenous North American trout include the rainbow, Dolly Varden, and brook trout. Other popular species include lake trout (*S. trutta lacustris*), golden trout (*S. aguabonita*), and the cutthroat trout (*S. clarki*). The char is similar in size and appearance to trout. Lake char (*Salvelinus namaycush*) reach around 9lb (4kg) in weight; the Arctic char can reach over 13lb (6kg). The grayling (*Thymallus thymallus*) is a popular game fish in Europe and North America. It has a distinct aroma of fresh thyme when landed. It is not harvested commercially.

CUTS Whole, gutted, or fillets. Roe.
● **EAT** Cooked: Pan fry, bake, grill, roast. Preserved: Hot and cold smoked; salted roe.
FLAVOR PAIRINGS Classical French: white wine vinegar, butter, lemon, chives, almonds, hazelnuts.
CLASSIC RECIPES Trout in breadcrumbs; trout with *serrano* ham (*trucha a la Navarra*); trout with almonds (*truite aux amandes*); blue trout (poached immediately on capture in an acidulated court bouillon, and turns blue); potted char.

Once cooked, rainbow trout fillet breaks into neat flakes and has an herbaceous flavor.

Rainbow trout (*Oncorhynchus mykiss*)
The North American rainbow trout was introduced into Europe at the end of the 19ᵗʰ century. It grows quickly and is farmed extensively. In European waters, wild fish rarely grow bigger than 22lb (10kg); in the US they can be twice this size. It can be cooked whole and then gutted, or as fillets. Its very fine bones can be difficult to locate.

The rainbow trout has a bright, silvery skin with rainbow-hued speckles.

The brown trout has a pale skin with chocolate-brown and orange speckles across its flanks.

Brown trout (*Salmo trutta*)
Indigenous to the rivers of Europe, the brown trout is not fished from the wild commercially; it is farmed in small quantities, particularly organically, and can grow to up to 33lb (15kg). Wild fish are usually much smaller and are often extremely earthy in flavor. Farmed fish tend to be more delicate and sweet. Make the most of the flavor of this fish by wrapping it with bunches of mixed herbs and barbecuing it.

The Arctic char has light spots on a dark background; its color varies according to habitat and time of the year.

Arctic char *(Salvelinus alpinus)*
Also known as mountain trout and salmon trout. Some are landlocked in deep glacial lakes, specifically in the Lake District in the north of England, where they were trapped at the end of the last ice age. Farmed and harvested at about 6½lb (3kg) in weight. The flesh is less earthy than that of trout, with an aroma of thyme and cut grass. Excellent poached and potted with butter, mace, and citrus; serve on Melba toast.

Robust herbs, such as sage, rosemary, and parsley marry well with the sweet, flaky texture of Arctic char.

Brook trout
(Salvelinus fontinalis)
Also known as brook char, speckled trout, red trout, and squaretail. Its color is green to brown with a distinctive marbling. It grows up to 25½in (65cm), and its white to yellow meat is very tasty.

Sea trout *(Salmo trutta)*
Sea trout, also known as salmon trout, is the migratory form of the brown trout. It has a particularly sweet and fine flavor that is not as intense as that of salmon. Poach it whole or in fillets, and serve with hollandaise sauce and lemon.

TROUT WITH ALMONDS

Trout is a wonderfully versatile fish, but needs robust flavors to mute what is sometimes an earthy flavor.

SERVES 2

1 onion, sliced
1 carrot, sliced
1 celery rib, sliced
½ cup dry white wine
1 bay leaf
2 trout, scaled, trimmed, gutted, gills removed
4 tbsp unsalted butter
½ cup sliced almonds
lemon juice, to taste
salt and freshly ground black pepper

1 To make the court bouillon: Combine 6 cups of water, the onion, carrot, celery, wine, and bay leaf in a large sauté pan, bring to the boil, and simmer for 10 minutes. Remove from the heat to cool for a few minutes.

2 Lower the trout into the court bouillon, bring to a boil, reduce the heat and cook over low heat for 12–15 minutes. The fish will be cooked when the eyes turn white and the skin easily pulls away from the flesh. Lift onto a plate and pat dry, pull away the skin and remove any fins. Arrange on a serving platter; keep warm.

3 Melt the butter in a large frying pan, add the almonds and cook over low to medium heat, stirring, until the almonds are golden brown. Remove from the heat, add about 2 tbsp lemon juice, season lightly, and immediately pour over the trout to serve.

ATLANTIC SALMON (SALMONIDAE)

Salmon are found in both Atlantic and Pacific waters. The salmon is anadromous, spending part of its life cycle in fresh water, and part in the sea. Only one species is found in the Atlantic. The high demand for the "king of fish," the wild Atlantic salmon, has led to overexploitation and many fishing bans are now in place. Once prolific, a wild specimen of Atlantic salmon has become a rare sight and it subsequently fetches a very high price. The aquaculture of the Atlantic salmon became a big commercial enterprise during the 1980s and it caused much controversy at its inception, as there were many environmental issues to overcome. Most Atlantic salmon is now farmed in Scotland and Norway. Japan consumes one-third of the world's salmon, but it is also enjoyed in many European countries and

worldwide. Wild salmon and farmed species are quite different. Farmed fish can be of excellent quality and flavor, with a good balance of oil.
CUTS Whole, fillets, steaks, head, roe.
EAT Cooked: Pan-fry, poach, grill, bake. Head is often used as a base for soup. **Raw:** Frozen and sold for sushi and sashimi. **Preserved:** Hot- (kiln-roasted salmon) and cold-smoked (see pages 92–95). Salted roe used as keta, a caviar substitute (see pages 96–97).
FLAVOR PAIRINGS Lemon, butter, dill, samphire, tarragon, ginger, sorrel, *ketcap manis*.
CLASSIC RECIPES Poached salmon with hollandaise sauce; gravlax; coulibiac of salmon; traditional poached and dressed whole salmon.

Atlantic salmon fillets are particularly good roasted, barbecued, and pan-fried.

Atlantic salmon (*Salmo salar*)
Salmon may be described as fry, smelt, parr, grilse, or kelt, depending on the stage of its life cycle and whether in fresh water or the sea. Farmed fish are sold at 8–10lb (3.5–4.5kg). The flesh is firm, moist, and oily, with a delicate flavor. To cook a whole salmon, measure the thickest part of its girth with a piece of string. For each 1in (2.5cm), calculate 4 minutes' cooking time at 450°F (230°C). It will be sweet and succulent.

GRAVLAX

This Nordic dish was originally made by burying the salt-coated fish in the ground.

SERVES 8–10

1 cup coarse sea salt

½ cup granulated sugar

1 tbsp white peppercorns, crushed

large bunch dill, chopped

2 tbsp vodka or brandy

2 x 2¼lbs (1kg) center-cut salmon fillets with skin on, picked over to remove any small bones

3 tbsp Dijon mustard

2 tsp granulated sugar

1 egg yolk

½ cup sunflower or canola oil

1 tbsp lemon juice

3 tbsp chopped dill

1 Mix together the salt, sugar, peppercorns, dill, and vodka. Put ¼ of this cure into a shallow dish. Put in one fillet, skin-side down, cover it with most of the remaining cure, and place the other fillet on top, skin-side up. Spread the rest of the cure on top.

2 Cover with plastic wrap and weight down with a heavy plate. Refrigerate for 18 (or up to 48) hours, turning the fish once or twice during this time.

3 Wipe the cure from the salmon; slice it thinly on the diagonal. Discard the skin. The fish will keep covered in the refrigerator for 5 to 6 days.

4 To make the sauce, whisk the mustard and sugar into the egg yolk. Gradually beat in the oil. Stir in the lemon juice and dill. Use at once, or refrigerate up to 3 days.

PACIFIC SALMON (SALMONIDAE)

There are several species of Pacific salmon, including the chinook (king), sockeye, chum, coho, pink, and Japanese cherry salmon. They are prolific species and although there is some farming, they are caught commercially by many regions of the Pacific Rim, particularly Alaska and Canada. Unlike the Atlantic salmon, which can return to the river after spawning, Pacific species die. The chum salmon (*Oncorhynchus keta*) (MSC certified) is also known as dog salmon, keta salmon, *qualla*, calico salmon, *hum*, and fall salmon. It is abundant in the North Pacific, in the waters of Korea and Japan, and the Bering Sea. It is also found in Arctic Alaska and south to San Diego in California. The flesh is canned, dried, and salted; the roe is also used. Pink salmon (*O. gorbuscha*) is also known as humpback salmon and *gorbuscha*. This is the smallest Pacific salmon (it averages 5lb/2.25kg) and is found in the Arctic and northwest to eastern central Pacific Ocean.

Coho (*O. kisutch*) (MSC certified) is also known as silver salmon, blueback, medium red salmon, jack salmon, and silverside. Growing to around 43in (110cm), it is found in the North Pacific from the Anadyr river in Russia, south toward Hokkaido in Japan; from Alaska to Baja California and Mexico. It has a fine-textured flesh and full flavor. The Japanese cherry salmon (*O. masou masou*) is also known as masu. It is caught in the north-west Pacific, the Sea of Okhotsk, and the Sea of Japan.
CUTS Fresh: Whole, fillets, steaks.
Preserved: Frozen, canned.

● **EAT** Various, depending on species.
Cooked: Poach, pan-fry, microwave, grill, bake, steam.
Preserved: Smoked, roe, dried, salted.
FLAVOR PAIRINGS Asian flavors: cilantro, soy sauce, sesame, chile, and lime. Excellent for plank cooking.
CLASSIC RECIPES Coulibiac of salmon; salmon sashimi; poached and dressed salmon; squaw candy.

Chinook salmon (*Oncorhynchus tshawytscha*)
Also called the king, Pacific, spring, black, quinnat, and chub salmon. It can grow to 5ft (1.5m); the usual size is 27in (70cm). It is caught in the Arctic, and northwest to northeast Pacific, from Alaska down to California and Japan. This fish has a similar oil-rich texture and flesh to Atlantic salmon, and suits the same methods of cooking.

In the sea, the chinook salmon has a greeny-blue back with lots of small, dark spots.

A wild Atlantic salmon has well-developed fins, and iron-gray skin along the back with black specks. Farmed fish are likely to be more speckled, and they often have malformed fins.

The chinook salmon is a little leaner than the Atlantic salmon. It is succulent and sweet, and good for grilling, pan-frying, and baking.

Sockeye (Oncorhynchus nerka)
Also known as red and blueback salmon. Caught in the North Pacific, this is one of the most commercially important species and can grow up to 33in (84cm). Its lean, meaty, dense flesh is a deep orange from the crustaceans in its diet. It can take a little longer to cook than an Atlantic fish; the lack of fat also means that it can dry out: baste or use a marinade to keep it moist.

A chinook resembles the Atlantic salmon more closely than any of the other Pacific species.

CLASSIC RECIPE

BAKED SALMON WITH SALSA VERDE AND CUCUMBER

This cold dish is an excellent way to use up leftover salmon, by serving it with a piquant green sauce.

SERVES 4

1 cucumber

12oz (350g) leftover cooked salmon, sliced or flaked into chunks

For the salsa verde

handful of basil leaves

handful of mint leaves

handful of flat-leaf parsley

2 tbsp white wine vinegar

2 tsp capers, drained, rinsed, gently squeezed dry, and finely chopped

2 garlic cloves, finely chopped

8 flat anchovies in oil, drained and finely chopped

2 tsp prepared coarse-ground mustard

salt and freshly ground black pepper

6 tbsp extra virgin olive oil

1 To make the salsa verde, chop all the herbs finely and put into a bowl. Drizzle with the vinegar and stir. Add the capers, garlic, and anchovies, and stir again. Add the mustard and season well with salt and pepper. Gradually stir in the olive oil. Taste, and adjust the seasoning if needed, adding more vinegar or oil as required. Transfer to a bowl.

2 Peel the cucumber, slice in half lengthwise, and scoop out the seeds with a spoon. Dice or chop the flesh.

3 To serve, arrange the salmon on a platter or 4 plates. Spoon the salsa verde over the fish, and place the diced cucumber on the side.

NEEDLEFISH OR GARFISH (BELONIDAE) AND FLYING FISH (EXOCOETIDAE)

The billfish family of needlefish (also known as garfish) is closely related to that of the flying fish. The needlefish is a slender, elongated fish found in fresh water, brackish, and marine environments; there are around 45 species in all. For a jaw, it has a long beak containing many sharp teeth. It is found in temperate and tropical waters worldwide, and is able to make small jumps out of the water to escape predators. It is often caught at night, when it is attracted to the surface by lanterns and other sources of light. The flying fish is a marine fish with around 64 species in the family. It is found mainly in tropical and subtropical waters of the Atlantic, Pacific, and Indian oceans. It has long pectoral fins

similar to a bird's wing, which it uses to escape from predators by leaping out of the water for up to 164ft (50m) —much farther if there is updraft on a wave and it vibrates its tail. Several methods of fishing are used: one ingenious way is to hold nets in the air. These fish have long, slim fillets that are generally pale gray with a sweet taste and delicate texture.
CUTS Fresh: Whole, fillets, and roe (*tobiko*). **Preserved:** Dried.
● **EAT** Cooked: Pan-fry. **Raw:** sushi.

FLAVOR PAIRINGS Okra, cornmeal, chile, onion, garlic, peppers.
CLASSIC RECIPE *Cou cou* (national dish of flying fish from Barbados).

Atlantic needlefish
(Strongylura marina)
Caught in the Western Atlantic from Maine to the Gulf of Mexico and Brazil. It grows to 4ft (1.2m) and has a sweet, succulent white flesh.

In fresh water, eels are a deep emerald green; in brackish water they revert to dark brown and silver.

European eel *(Anguilla anguilla)*
This species usually grows to about 31½in (80cm). Eels are popular for eating at various stages in their life. Bootlace eels or elvers are usually deep-fried—a delicacy in parts of Europe. Smoked eel is also a delicacy, and the eel's very oily flesh is especially suitable for hot-smoking (see pages 92–93). For cooking fresh, eels are usually skinned as soon as they have been killed, then gutted and cut into steaks or fillets. For smoking, they are often left whole. They have a very distinctive firm, slightly rubbery, and oil-rich texture.

EEL (ANGUILLIDAE)

There are 22 known members of the eel group. They have a long, slithering, snake-like body. The eel is a catadromous fish: it is spawned in the sea and moves to fresh water to mature, then returns to the sea to spawn, after which it dies. Eels live in temperate, tropical, and subtropical waters worldwide. They have a distinct spawning ground, depending on the species. There has been a massive decline in eel populations over recent years, which is attributed not only to overfishing but also to pollution, and they are listed as critically endangered. Some species are extensively farmed in Northern Europe and Asia to try to take pressure off the wild stocks, but this has done little to halt the decline. Eels have firm and rich-tasting flesh, and an oily texture.

ALTERNATIVES Eels are endangered in some parts of the world. There is no close alternative, but you could use another oil-rich species of fish, such as mackerel.
CUTS Fresh: Live, whole. **Preserved:** Smoked whole and in fillets.
● **EAT** Cooked: Grill, pan-fry, bake, and poach (for jellied eels).
Preserved: Smoked and dried.
FLAVOR PAIRINGS Bay, vinegar, apples, red and white wine, allspice berries, cloves, mint, parsley, cream.
CLASSIC RECIPES Jellied eels; *matelote d'anguille* (classic freshwater fish stew from Burgundy, cooked in red wine); deep-fried elvers; *anguilla allo spiedo* (Italian); eel and bay leaf kebabs; *bisato sull'ara* (baked eel with bay leaves); fried eel; *capitone marinato* (marinated eel).

Garfish (Belone belone)
The garfish is also known as the garpike, hornpike, or greenbone. It is famous for its luminous green bone structure. It is widely distributed in the northeast Atlantic and the Mediterranean. (There is another group of fish found in North American waters that are considered to be "true gars"—Lepisosteidae.) Garfish grow to about 18in (46cm) long. It is used both fresh and frozen. Try it fried, grilled, and baked. It has a delicate taste and fine, flaky texture.

The Atlantic needlefish has a silvery skin; its needle-shaped body does not contain an extensive amount of meat.

Japanese flying fish (Cheilopogon agoo)
Flying fish are a popular commercial fish for Japan, Vietnam, Indonesia, India, and Barbados (where it is the national fish, though it has been overfished in this area). Japanese flying fish grow to 14in (35cm) long and have a subtle flavor; the flesh is quite meaty and firm. Best seasoned and then barbecued or fried. Their golden roe is used to garnish sushi (see pages 98–99).

MORAY EEL (MURAENIDAE)
AND CONGER EEL (CONGRIDAE)

There are over 190 known species in the conger group of eels and 200 species of moray eels, caught in many oceans worldwide. They are not particularly noted for their eating quality: most are caught as a by-catch or for sport. Some conger eels are over 10ft (3m) long and weigh well over 220lb (100kg). They are ferocious predators, with sharp, snappy teeth—so when handling live fish, extreme caution needs to be exercised. The largest and most prolific conger is the American conger (Conger oceanicus). The Japanese serve a delicacy of raw baby conger eels, called noresore, often with ponzu sauce. Unfortunately, conger eels are overfished. Moray eels are found in tropical and subtropical waters. As adults, they are usually vividly marked and have the long, slender body of other eels. They are well known for their sharp teeth, poor eyesight, and excellent sense of smell. As a fierce predator, they are known to attack humans if disturbed, causing severe physical trauma. All eels are popular in South American, Japanese, and Chinese cooking; smoked eel is a European delicacy.
CUTS Whole, or gutted and cut into steaks.
◉ **EAT** Cooked: Pan-fry or bake. **Preserved:** Smoked, dried, sometimes jellied.
ALTERNATIVES No close alternative, but monkfish has a similarly firm texture.
FLAVOR PAIRINGS Onions, paprika, smoked paprika, chile, peppers, olive oil, red wine, parsley.
CLASSIC RECIPES Caldeirada (Portugese fish stew); fried eel (Middle East).

Conger eels have a smooth, scaleless skin. The body tapers toward the tail.

Conger eel (Conger conger)
Caught in the eastern Atlantic from Norway to Senegal; also in the Mediterranean and Black Sea. It can reach over 9ft 10in (3m) long. This fish has a sweet, almost pork-like flavor and is best simply grilled with a flavored butter. It has an extremely dense texture, and is also perfect for pan-frying or casseroling. It takes strong flavors such as smoked paprika and spices well.

The tail end of a conger eel is notoriously bony, so it is best used for stock.

SKATE AND RAY (RAJIDAE)

Skates and rays are an extensive family of around 200 cartilaginous fish, found in all oceans from the Arctic to the Antarctic. Many are marine, but some are found in brackish waters. The most common genus is *Raja*. They are flat-bodied with a rhomboid shape due to their large pectoral fins (the wings), which extend from the snout to the base of the tail. The mouth and gills are located on the underside of the body. They have a long, slender tail, which in some species contains a weak electrical organ. Eggs are laid in a leathery capsule commonly known as a mermaid's purse. As a general rule, skates and rays grow slowly and have low reproductive rates. Some skates are fished commercially worldwide; many have been overexploited, and

their population levels have reduced in many areas. The species are subject to a fishing quota, and currently there is little distinction made between each species, making it very hard to make an informed choice. The skin is difficult to remove, requiring thick gloves and pliers, and it is therefore often removed prior to sale. Cartilaginous species of fish expel their urea through their gills and if incorrectly stored, a strong smell of ammonia can be obvious. If this smell is detected, do not buy the fish. The wings of skates and rays are highly regarded. They have an unusual fibrous texture and take a little longer to cook than most thin white fillets. They taste herbaceous and woody, and work well with citrus and acidic flavors. A thick piece of cartilage

at the shoulder end of the fillet comes loose when the fish is cooked.
CUTS Wings and skate "nobs" (muscles taken from the back of the fish).
● **EAT** Pan-fry, deep-fry, poach, roast.
ALTERNATIVES Responsibly sourced monkfish.
FLAVOR PAIRINGS Seasoned flour, vinegar, capers, parsley, lemon juice, butter.
CLASSIC RECIPES Skate with *beurre noisette*; skate with *beurre noir* and capers.

SKATE WITH BEURRE NOIR AND CAPERS

Skate can be cooked in a number of ways; for this French classic, poach in a lightly acidulated court bouillon.

SERVES 2

1 cup dry white wine
1 onion, sliced
1 carrot, sliced
1 celery rib, sliced
2 glasses white wine
1 bay leaf
2 x 6oz (170g) skate wings, skinned
4 tbsp butter
2 tbsp white or red wine vinegar
2 tsp capers
2 tsp chopped parsley

1 To make the court bouillon, combine 12 cups (3 quarts/3 liters) water, the wine, onion, carrot, celery, and bay leaf in a large sauté pan or flameproof casserole, bring to a boil and simmer for 10 minutes. Remove from the heat and let cool for a few minutes.

2 Lower the skate into the court bouillon, bring to a boil, reduce the heat to low, and cook for 10–12 minutes. The fish is cooked when the thick part of the cartilage at the "shoulder" of the wing will pull away easily. Lift onto a plate and pat dry with paper towels.

3 Melt the butter in a large frying pan, allow it to sizzle and then keep cooking until it has turned very dark brown, but is not smoking. Stir in the vinegar, capers, and parsley and while it is sizzling furiously, immediately pour it over the skate wings to serve.

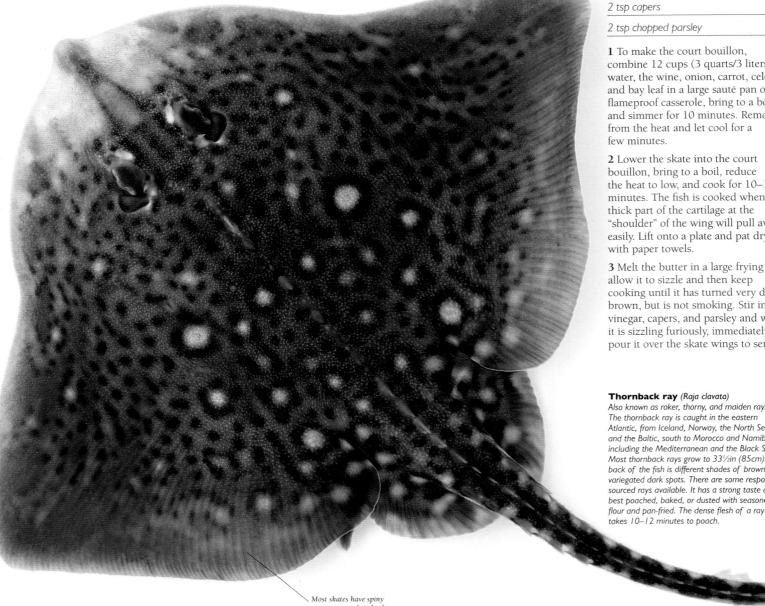

Most skates have spiny structures on their back. The thornback's back is wholly prickly.

Thornback ray *(Raja clavata)*
Also known as roker, thorny, and maiden ray. The thornback ray is caught in the eastern Atlantic, from Iceland, Norway, the North Sea, and the Baltic, south to Morocco and Namibia, including the Mediterranean and the Black Sea. Most thornback rays grow to 33½in (85cm). The back of the fish is different shades of brown with variegated dark spots. There are some responsibly sourced rays available. It has a strong taste and is best poached, baked, or dusted with seasoned flour and pan-fried. The dense flesh of a ray wing takes 10–12 minutes to poach.

PLAICE AND SOLE (PLEURONECTIDAE)

The Pleuronectidae group (the name means "side swimmers"—these are flat fish) includes plaice, some flounders, halibut, and some types of sole, such as lemon sole (*Microstomus kitt*), petrale sole, (*Eopsetta jordani*), rex sole (*Glyptocephalus zachirus*), and North Pacific sole (*Eopsetta grigorjewi*). True sole, however, belong to the Soleidae group. All are demersal fish and have white flesh; the main concentration of oil is in the liver. They are fished in Europe, North America, and in the northern Pacific. When a flat fish hatches, it is a tiny round fish; as it grows, it turns on to its left or right side and the eyes move to one side of the head. Most flat fish are dextral, with eyes on the right side. The fish use the seabed to hide and have highly camouflaged skin on the upper body to enable them to blend into their habitat. The underside of a wild fish is pearlescent white: this helps it to blend in with its environment if viewed from underneath. These fish have a delicate taste and texture. As with other species of fish, flat fish should smell fresh and be firm to the touch. They are usually gutted on landing, enabling the fish to retain quality. Most flat fish have a heavy coating of slime that in the main should be clear. As the fish loses condition, the slime becomes sticky and discolored (known as "custardy"), and this indicates that it is past its best.

CUTS Usually gutted on landing. Sold whole, head on or off. Cross-cut and quarter-cross fillets, skin on or off.
● **EAT** Cooked: pan-fry, poach, deep-fry, or bake.
FLAVOR PAIRINGS Seasoned flour, butter, lemon, parsley, breadcrumbs, sage, chestnut mushrooms, lingonberry, potato.
CLASSIC RECIPES Plaice/lemon sole: *meunière*; sole *véronique*.

Lemon sole (*Microstomus kitt*)
Also known as smear dab and Scottish sole. Lemon sole is caught in shallow seas in northern Europe. Its usual size is 10–12in (25–30cm). A very fresh fish has a heavy coating of creamy slime, unlike other fresh flat fish, which have a clear slime. It has a sweet, mild taste and delicate texture.

Lemon sole is good simply rolled in flour and pan-fired, grilled, or poached.

Lemon sole can be identified by lemon piping around the gill flap.

Plaice (*Pleuronectes platessa*)
This plaice is common in European waters, and is the most popular flat fish in Europe, with a mild taste and fine texture. It has a distinct "wrist" at the tail, and a bony ridge from the head to the gills. The underside is white with chevron markings that indicate the pattern of muscle bands. It can grow to 23½in (60cm), but this is rare today. It is regulated by a legal minimum landing size and is best from May to December/January.

A plaice has a greenish-brown skin and orange or rusty green spots.

PLAICE AND SOLE (CONTINUED)

The upper surface of the petrale sole is a uniform light to dark brown.

White, flaky fillets of petrale sole can be deep fried, pan fried, or grilled.

Petrale sole
(Eopsetta jordani)
The petrale sole is also known as Pacific Coast sole and regarded as one of the finest sole in that region. It is usually caught at around 12in (30cm). It is found in the Eastern Pacific, from the coast of Alaska to northern Baja California and Mexico. It is usually skinned and filleted for sale. It has a sweet flesh that is best pan fried.

Witch (Glyptocephalus cynoglossus)
Also known as gray flounder and occasionally marketed as Torbay sole. The witch is found in the Eastern Atlantic, from northern Spain to northern Norway, and in the western Atlantic from Canada to North Carolina in the US. It grows up to 2ft (60cm) long and has a subtle flavor. Best baked whole; or filleted, rolled in seasoned flour and pan-fried in butter and and then finish the dish with a splash of lemon.

The witch produces very slim fillets, and is best trimmed of head and fins for cooking whole.

Dab (Limanda limanda)
Dabs are found in abundance in the northeast Atlantic. It is one of the smaller flat fish and can grow to around 16in (40cm), but 12in (30cm) is more common. The white flesh of a dab is best eaten fresh, but has very little flavor. It is small, so is usually trimmed and cooked whole on the bone. Also sold dried, salted, and smoked.

Dabs are usually pale brown with darker brown blotches.

HALIBUT (PLEURONECTIDAE)

This fish is sometimes called the "Cow of the Sea" and is the largest of all the flat fish. A handful of halibut species are caught in Atlantic and Pacific waters, and are highly regarded. As with all flat fish, halibut vary in color depending on the seabed that they inhabit; the top side camouflages them so they blend in with the ocean floor. Halibut mature slowly, making them very susceptible to overfishing. Wild Atlantic halibut has been overexploited, and it is better to choose farmed or Pacific species. A wild fish can reach mammoth proportions: some very large specimens have been recorded as weighing over 700lb (330kg). However, most landed today would not exceed 24–30lb (11–13.5kg). This fish has a dense, white, firm-textured flesh and has become so sought after that it is now extensively farmed to meet high demand. The fish may be cut crosswise into steaks, or sold as fillets (also called fletches).
CUTS Large fish: steaks/cutlets. Small fish: whole, fillets.
● **EAT** **Cooked:** Steam, pan-fry, grill, poach, or bake. **Preserved:** Dried, salted, and cold-smoked.
FLAVOR PAIRINGS Butter, seasoned flour, nutmeg, pickles, capers, lemon.
CLASSIC RECIPES Poached halibut with Hollandaise sauce; grilled halibut with *beurre blanc*.

The skin of the Atlantic halibut is a uniform dark brown to black; young fish are often marbled.

Cheeks can be harvested from a halibut: they are sweet and succulent.

Atlantic halibut
(Hippoglossus hippoglossus)
This fish can reach up to 14 ¾ft (4.5m) in length. It is found in the Eastern and Western Atlantic, and is extensively farmed. A wild halibut has an even covering of clear slime; farmed fish may be covered in an inky slime, and often have dark mottling on the white underside. The fish is moist and very lean with a sweet, mild taste; the lack of fat makes it easy to over-cook, since it dries easily.

The skin of the Pacific halibut can be olive green, brown, or almost black, and it has a white underside.

Pacific halibut produces thick, white, flaky fillets with a light flavor.

Pacific halibut *(Hippoglossus stenolepis)*
The Pacific halibut is no less impressive than the Atlantic species, but with a maximum size of 8ft 2in (2.5m) long. Found in the North Pacific: the North Pacific fishery of halibut is one of the largest and most valuable fisheries for that area. Pacific halibut is noted for its dense, firm, and low-fat white fillets, which have a milder taste than Atlantic halibut. It is best served grilled or pan fried with a flavored butter.

GRILLED HALIBUT WITH BEURRE BLANC

Halibut has delicate flesh that is low in fat. Simple preparations like this suit its texture and flavor well.

SERVES 2

2 x 5oz (140g) halibut steaks

8 tbsp (1 stick) unsalted butter plus a little melted butter or oil for brushing

1 shallot, finely chopped

5 tbsp fish stock or bottled clam juice

1 tbsp white wine vinegar

salt and freshly ground black pepper

fresh lemon juice, to taste

fresh chopped dill to garnish

1 Preheat the broiler to its highest setting, or heat a grill pan over high heat. Brush the halibut steaks all over with the melted butter. Cook, turning once, for 6–8 minutes, or until the fish is lightly browned on the outside and opaque throughout

2 To make the beurre blanc, cut the unsalted butter into small chunks. Melt 2 tbsp in a small saucepan, add the shallot and cook over low heat, stirring, for 2–3 minutes, or until soft. Add the fish stock and vinegar, bring to a boil and simmer until the liquid has reduced to about 3 tbsp. Turn the heat very low and add the remaining butter, a few pieces at time, whisking vigorously between each addition. It is important to keep the stock hot, but do not allow it to boil. Once all the butter has been added, the sauce should be creamy and fairly thick. Remove from the heat, season, and add lemon juice to taste.

3 Lift the grilled halibut onto a serving plate and drizzle with the beurre blanc. Garnish with dill and serve.

THE SOLE GROUP (SOLEIDAE)

Found in waters worldwide, the "true" sole or Soleidae group includes around 165 species of fish. They all have long, slipper-shaped bodies with small eyes, mouths, and tails. Some members of the group have attractive markings and patterns; most have a unique, coarse skin texture—similar to that of a cat's tongue—if stroked from tail to head. The maximum length is usually around 27in (70cm). These species of fish are dextral, with eyes on the right side of the head. The white flesh has a subtle and distinctive flavor.

CUTS Usually gutted and sold whole, trimmed and skinned, and in fillets.

⊙ **EAT** Grill or pan-fry.

FLAVOR PAIRINGS Lemon, butter, seasoned flour, cucumber, mint, shiitake mushrooms, other mushrooms, truffle oil, capers, parsley.

CLASSIC RECIPES *Sole Colbert*; lemon sole Doria; grilled Dover sole with anchovy butter; sole *Véronique*.

Dover sole *(Solea vulgaris)*
Also known as common sole, tongue, or slip sole (a small specimen). It can be extremely expensive. Caught in the Eastern Atlantic and also farmed on a small scale. It can grow up to 27in (70cm). Very firm and slightly rubbery white flesh; full-flavored. It is also best when well past rigor mortis, as both the flavor and texture develop.

TURBOT, BRILL, AND MEGRIM (SCOPHTHALIMIDAE)

The Scophthalimidae family includes turbot, brill, megrim, and species called topknots. They are found in many temperate seas of the Atlantic and Pacific oceans. Turbot and brill are both valuable species and highly commercial. They are sinistral fish, with their eyes on the left side of the head. Turbot and brill can have a similar colored skin, but there are very distinct differences to note. Turbot is almost circular in shape and the dark eye side has no scales but large, sharp tubercles. It is extensively farmed. Turbot is exceptionally fine to eat, with firm, white, dense flesh; although it has a flaky texture, it holds its shape well and so is versatile. Brill is oval in shape. Like many other species, brill can adapt its color to its habitat. It has scales, but not the tubercles of a turbot. The megrim is particularly noted for its large mouth, which extends into a tube. Highly commercial, it is a popular food in southern Europe, particularly in Spain. Megrim is best eaten quite fresh; it needs seasoning, and butter or olive oil to prevent it from drying out.

CUTS Depending on species. Whole and head on; trimmed; fillets. Large turbots may be cut into steaks.

⊙ **EAT** Cooked: Steam, pan-fry, crust, bake, roast, and grill.

FLAVOR PAIRINGS Wild mushrooms, champagne, cream, butter, shellfish stock, lemon, Gruyère cheese, Parmesan cheese.

CLASSIC RECIPE Poached turbot with oysters and champagne.

Turbot flesh is firm, white, dense and suitable for various cooking methods.

Turbot *(Psetta maxima)*
Also known as britt, butt, breet; one of the most expensive of all the flat fish and highly sought after. It is found in the northeast Atlantic, throughout the Mediterranean and along the European coasts to the Arctic Circle. Grows up to 3½ft (1m) long. The flesh is meaty and, unlike many other white fish, holds together well enough for stir-frying; also good for poaching, pan-frying, and grilling. Often sold cut into thick steaks with the backbone running through the steak. It has a rounded and recognizable, very fine and sweet flavor.

Wild turbot varies from dark mottled brown to gray; farmed fish are light gray-green to dark gray-black.

The megrim has a glassy, light brown skin and a white underside.

Megrim *(Lepidorhombus whiffiagonis)*
Also known as meg, sale fluke, Scarborough sole, or whiff. The megrim is a deep-water fish living in the northeast Atlantic. It is commonly found at 10in (25cm) long. Best trimmed and cooked whole on the bone; it has a similar flavor to plaice and is flaky, delicate, and low in fat. Suits subtle flavors, such as butter and mild herbs.

The sand sole has yellow-brown skin with pale blotches; it looks very similar to the Dover sole.

Sand sole (Pegusa lascaris)
Also known as snouted sole, lascar, and Atlantic sole. Found in the North and southeastern Atlantic, the Mediterranean, and Black seas. It lacks the very superior flavor of the Dover sole. It is of minor commercial importance, but is available. Like Dover sole, it is skinned as a whole fish and then cooked on the bone.

Brill has a superb fine, white, flaky texture. It is best pan-fried, grilled, or roasted.

Brill (Scophthalmus rhombus)
Also known as kite and pearl. Brill reaches a maximum length of 29½in (75cm). It lives in the Eastern Atlantic, from Iceland to Morocco, throughout the Black Sea and the Mediterranean. At one time it was underrated; now it is well regarded. Has an equally fine, sweet flavor to turbot, but is more flaky.

A turbot has a lot of sharp nodules on its skin, known as turbercles.

Brill is a sandy greenish-brown; young fish are dark brown. It is often flecked with white.

SOLE MEUNIÈRE

Cooking small whole fish or fillets in clarified butter (*la meunière*) is a typically French way of preparing fish simply.

SERVES 2

2 lemon sole, filleted and skinned, or 4 sole fillets

2 tbsp all-purpose flour

salt and freshly ground black pepper

4–6 tbsp clarified butter

2 tbsp finely chopped parsley

juice of half a lemon

1 Dust the sole fillets in the flour, salt, and pepper until well coated. Arrange them in a single layer on a plate (do not stack as they will stick together and the flour will become soggy).

2 Heat half of the butter in a large frying pan until it is no longer sizzling. Working in batches if necessary, lower in the fillets and press down gently with a spatula. Cook for 1 minute. Turn the fish over and cook on the second side for another 30 seconds or so; the fish is cooked when it is firm and opaque. Transfer to a warm plate and keep warm.

3 Wipe out the frying pan with a paper towel and add the remaining 2–3 tbsp clarified butter. Allow it to cook for a few seconds until it turns golden brown, then stir in the chopped parsley and a squeeze of lemon juice, and pour, still sizzling, over the fish to serve.

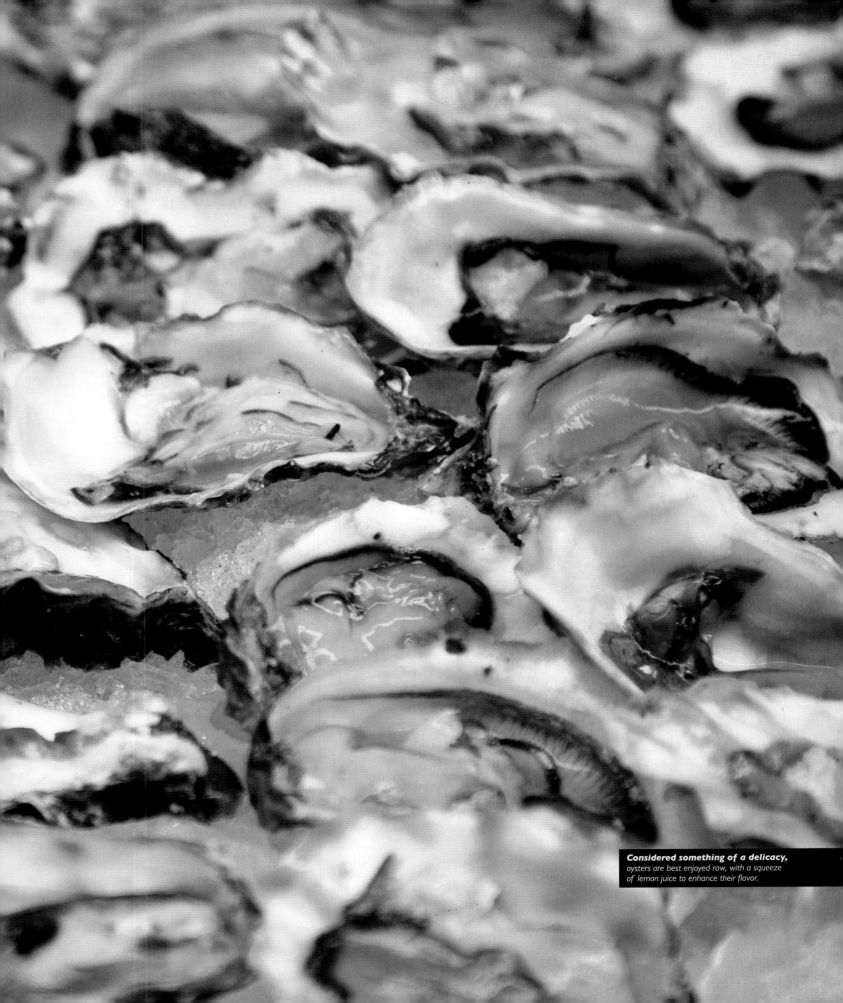

Considered something of a delicacy,
oysters are best enjoyed raw, with a squeeze
of lemon juice to enhance their flavor.

SHELLFISH ESSENTIALS

The term shellfish covers a number of edible ocean-living species that are covered by a protective shell. They are classified as follows:

Crustacean A group of mainly aquatic shellfish that can move independently. They have segmented bodies, no back bones, jointed legs/claws, and two antennae. This group includes lobsters, crabs, shrimp, and krill.

Mollusk Soft-bodied invertebrates with a hard shell. They can be subdivided into several groups:

Gastropod/univalve Typically found in one coiled shell, this group includes whelks, periwinkles, snails, and conch.

Bivalves/filter feeders Typically found in two hinged shells, these are often referred to as filter feeders, since they feed using a filter action that pumps water, extracts the nutrients from the water, and then expels it. This group includes oysters, clams, mussels, and scallops.

Cephalopods A group of invertebrate animals that have tubular heads and a number of arms with suckers. Includes octopus, squid, and cuttlefish.

Mussels are a type of bivalve mollusk *commonly cooked by steaming until they open up their shells. Often served with garlic, herbs, and a white wine or tomato sauce.*

BUY

The senses of sight, touch, and smell are vital when assessing the quality of shellfish, such as this Brown Edible crab, whether buying live, raw, or cooked creatures.

Feel When cooked or raw, the limbs of crabs and lobsters should hold firmly and snap back into position if extended. Floppy or loose limbs may indicate it is dead or dying, and so may not be safe to eat. It should feel heavy for its size and not be seeping water; a crab or lobster that feels light indicates that it has recently shed its shell, and may lack brown meat. Shells should feel crisp and dry.

Look All live shellfish should show signs of life, most obviously movement. Never buy dead, uncooked, mollusks, since decomposition begins immediately after death and they may not be safe to eat. Avoid any with cracked or damaged shells. Live bivalves should have a closed shell, or one that will close when tapped. The tubular part of octopus, cuttlefish, and squid should be white in appearance; as the flesh loses condition it will become pink and should be avoided.

Smell Good-quality cooked shellfish should have a pleasant and fresh smell with the sweet aroma of sea ozone. Avoid shellfish that smells stale, musty, and of ammonia, since it is beginning to decompose and may no longer be safe to eat.

STORE

All shellfish should be enjoyed as soon as possible after purchase. Unwrap the shellfish as soon as you get it home so that it is not sitting in any juice, arrange it on a plate and cover with plastic wrap. Live shellfish (both crustacean and mollusks) can be stored for a short period of time in the refrigerator, kept at below 37°F (3°C). They are best put in a lightly covered bowl toward the bottom of the refrigerator. Do not soak live shellfish in tap water, since this will shorten their life span.

FREEZING SHELLFISH Many prepared and cooked shellfish can be frozen if stored in appropriate thick plastic wrap. In the case of live shellfish, this should be cooked prior to freezing. The freezing process must be done carefully, since the delicate texture of shellfish can be damaged if it is not well wrapped. Frozen shellfish is frozen in much the same way as fish. Ice glazing (covering individual ingredients with a thin layer of ice) is often done to protect them from freezer burn.

COOK

Cooking shellfish requires particular care and attention for best results. When overcooked, shellfish will often end up fibrous, tough, shrunken, and dry, with little flavor; when undercooked, however, shellfish can be both unsafe to eat, as well as unpalatable.

BROIL This method of cooking uses a high heat and so it is best for prepared raw shellfish, because it is easy to overcook shellfish that has already been cooked. Suitable for scallops, split and prepared lobster, deveined and butterflied shrimp, langoustine, crayfish, clams, and squid.

I *Arrange the shellfish in a baking dish, spoon over some oil mixed with fresh herbs and seasoning, and leave to marinate for 2 hours.*

2 *Preheat the broiler to medium. Thread the scallops onto some wooden skewers that have been soaked in water for 30 minutes.*

3 *Place the skewers on a broiler pan and cook under the broiler for 2–3 minutes until they are done. They will be opaque when cooked.*

DEEP-FRY This is a popular method of cooking seafood such as shrimp, oysters, and scallops. The fish or seafood is often coated in batter, flour, or bread crumbs before being immersed in deep, hot corn or groundnut oil.

I *Heat the oil for deep-frying to 375°F (190°C). Season the shrimp then coat them with beaten egg. Shake off any excess.*

2 *Dip the shrimp into bread crumbs and roll to cover completely. Press to make sure that the crumbs adhere, then shake off any excess.*

3 *Add the shrimp, in small batches, to the hot oil. Deep-fry, turning the shrimp so they cook and color evenly; for 2 minutes or until golden.*

4 *When the shrimp are golden brown and crisp, remove with a slotted spoon, drain on paper towels, then serve immediately.*

STEAM This gentle cooking method is suitable for live bivalves such as clams and mussels, and also crab, lobster, and shrimp. The shellfish are either cooked above a liquid without touching it, or in the minimum amount of liquid, as here, so that they cook in the steam and are not poached. Any liquid left in the pan can be served with the cooked shellfish or used to make an accompanying sauce.

I *Soften some chopped shallot in oil in a pan that has a tightly fitting lid. Add a glass of wine, some herbs, and lemon juice. Bring to a boil.*

2 *Add the shellfish, cover the pan, and cook over medium-high heat for 3–4 minutes, or until the shells of the bivalves have opened.*

3 *Transfer all the shellfish that have opened to wide serving bowls, ladling the cooking liquid over them. Discard any that remain closed.*

BOIL This simple technique is suitable for cooking live gastropods, live crabs, members of the lobster group, and raw shrimp. The shellfish can be cooked simply in plain salted water or, for more flavor, a court bouillon. Prepare the raw shellfish before boiling just as you would for any other method of cooking.

Bring a large pan *of cooking liquid to a boil (enough to cover the shellfish). Add in the shellfish, cover, return to a gentle boil and simmer until done—this will vary according to the species being cooked. Once cooked, remove from the boiling liquid and submerge in ice-cold water for rapid cooling. This helps the meat shrink away from the shell and will make shelling easier.*

FLAVOR PAIRINGS

It is easy to overpower the taste of many types of shellfish, so moderation is the key to flavoring. Each country and culture has its own classic partnerships: in Europe, shellfish is usually simply cooked and served with an oil-based dressing. Cooked and cold crustaceans are matched with citrus dressings and mayonnaise. Classic herb partnerships with shellfish include parlsey, thyme, bay leaf, tarragon, chervil, and chives. Shellfish cooked in the Far East will have its own flavor matches, which include ginger, chile, soy sauce, fish sauce, and sesame.

ABALONE (HALIOTIDAE)

Abalone is considered a rare delicacy and gourmet food. It is harvested from the wild and from aquaculture in many coastal waters in oceans worldwide. There are about 100 species of this sea snail, which vary greatly in size. The well-flavored meat is found in an ear-shaped shell. Abalone is also known as ormer, sea-ear, ear-shell, Venus's ears, perlemoen (South Africa), muttonfish (Australia), and paua (New Zealand). Some abalone grow slowly; overharvesting has reduced some stocks and increased prices. Abalone attach to rocky surfaces using a very strong suction action, and ingest green algae.

AVAILABILITY **Fresh:** Sold in the shell. **Preserved:** Frozen meat/steaks (tenderized), canned, dried (used for flavoring soups), salted.

● **EAT** **Cooked:** Tenderize by pounding before cooking. Sauté or fry very briefly, as it toughens easily. **Preserved:** Add dried abalone to soup and simmer slowly to add flavor.

ABALONE WITH OYSTER SAUCE

Abalone is expensive, and often sold canned as well as fresh in the shell. It is particularly popular in China.

SERVES 2

1 x 12oz (340g) can abalone, drained and liquid reserved

2 tbsp sunflower or peanut oil

1 bunch of scallions, thinly sliced

1 tsp finely grated fresh ginger

2 tbsp oyster sauce

1 tbsp soy sauce

pinch of sugar

2 tsp cornflour

1 Slice the abalone thinly. Heat the oil in a large frying pan, add the scallions and ginger, and cook over low heat, stirring, for 1–2 minutes. Add the abalone and cook, stirring and tossing gently, until heated through.

2 In a bowl, combine 5 tbsp water with the oyster sauce, soy sauce, and sugar. Whisk in the cornstarch and the reserved abalone juices to blend well. Add to the abalone and cook over medium heat, stirring, until it just comes to a boil and the sauce has thickened. Serve.

FLAVOR PAIRINGS Chinese ear mushrooms, sesame, soy sauce, ginger, garlic, butter.

CLASSIC RECIPE Abalone with oyster sauce.

Red abalone
(Haliotis rufescens)
This species is the most generally available, and the largest of the abalone group. Found in the Pacific from Oregon to Baja California, Mexico; harvested with restrictions. Sear briefly: if overcooked, it becomes tough. It has a sweet, meaty, and strong seafood flavor.

The foot or muscle is the main part eaten. Remove the meat from the shell and pound it before searing briefly.

Small specimens can be removed from the shell, trimmed, sliced very thinly, and served raw.

CONCH (STROMBIDAE)

The queen conch (*Strombus gigas*) is one of many species of saltwater gastropods. It is also known as the pink or Caribbean conch (pronounced conk). Although this species was once abundant, commercial harvesting is now banned in the US. The main suppliers and consumers of conch are Jamaica, Honduras, and the Dominican Republic. Conch has an intense flavor.

AVAILABILITY **Wild:** frozen, chopped, or minced. **Farmed:** fresh, prepared, and frozen. Farmed conch are generally more tender.

● **EAT** Wild conch needs to be sliced thinly, then tenderized with a mallet. **Raw:** marinated in lime juice and chile as *ceviche*. **Cooked:** roast, grill, pan and stir-fry, sauté, or steam.

FLAVOR PAIRINGS Onion, garlic, peppers, tomato, jalapeño, hot sauce, cilantro, cayenne.

CLASSIC RECIPES Conch fritters; conch chowder.

The meat, which has a dark membrane, is prized from the shell as a whole piece and can be up to 12in (30cm) long. Good-quality conch is creamy white with hints of pink and orange; if it is discolored, gray, and smells strongly, do not buy it.

Once extracted from the decorative shell, conch meat can be marinated and eaten raw, or cooked by various methods.

Conch
This conch from the Strombidae group is farmed in the Calicos Islands making it more available year-round (main season is the summer). In the Caribbean, dried or minced conch is used in fritters, pan fried for salads, and as a base for chowder. The taste is sweet with a rubbery, jellied texture.

PERIWINKLE (LITTORINIDAE), WHELK (BUCCINIDAE), AND MUREX (MERICIDAE)

Sea snails in the form of periwinkles, whelks, and murex are found in waters worldwide. They are considered to be a delicacy by a small number of consumers, but the limited sales have led some to decline in availability. Periwinkles (also known as winkles) and whelks are enjoyed in northern Europe and form a part of a traditional Sunday tea in London's East End. There are around 180 species, but only a few of these are eaten. Whelks are also popular in North America, where species from the Melongenidae group are harvested. Whelks have a distinct salty, seafood taste and are often likened to clam meat. They are tough and very meaty. Murex are another family of small sea snails. They are only found in the coastal areas and specialist fish markets of Mediterranean countries. Murex taste similar to whelks but the meat is reputedly tougher.

AVAILABILITY In the shell, both raw and cooked. Winkles: fresh, frozen; shucked; pickled in vinegar and canned. In the US they are usually sold cooked, shucked, and trimmed.

● **EAT** Rinse in salt water before boiling. Cook winkles for 3–5 minutes in the shell, whelks for 12–15 minutes, murex for 10–12 minutes. Can be served in the shell. Extract the meat from the shell with a pin or a fork. The operculum (hard, corny foot) is not eaten: trim this off. If desired, coat in crumbs and pan-fry.

FLAVOR PAIRINGS Chile vinegar, malt vinegar, salt, lemon juice.

CLASSIC RECIPES Winkles in the shell with malt vinegar and salt; winkle and watercress sandwiches.

To enhance the color of the greenish-black shell, roll periwinkles in a little oil before serving to give the shell a gloss.

Periwinkle *(Littorinidae group)*
These tiny snails are popular in Europe and often harvested by hand, ensuring that little damage is done to their habitat. Traditionally served as part of a seafood platter. The intense flavor combines sweet and salty tastes. Prone to be gritty: rinse well.

Murex shells are often collected because of their beauty: they are fat and spiny, tapering to a tail-like point.

Murex *(Murex brandais)*
The Mediterranean murex has been a popular delicacy for many centuries; it was also collected to harvest a rare purple dye. The flavor is similar to that of a whelk; it needs gentle cooking since it may be tough. In the South of France, murex make a classic addition to a fruits de mer platter.

Many gastropods have a horny foot that needs to be trimmed away or removed after cooking.

Whelk *(Buccinidae group)*
The whelk group of shellfish has hundreds of members in waters worldwide. They are carnivores and scavengers. In Europe, the common northern whelk (Buccinum undatum), found in the North Atlantic, is eaten. It is 2½–5in (5–10cm) long and caught year-round in baited pots. This species is best during the summer.

CLAMS AND COCKLES (VENERIDAE, MYIDAE, MACTRIDAE, SOLENIDAE, GLYCIMERIDAE, CARDIIDAE)

There are hundreds of clam species found in waters worldwide. They are a popular food source and create an important income for many countries. Clams are particularly popular in parts of Europe, the US, and Asia. The Veneridae group has hard, tough shells and names for the species include Venus clam, carpetshell clam, hard-shell clam, and quahog. The Myidae group have a soft, thin, and brittle shell structure. Species are found in both the Pacific and Atlantic oceans. Names include steamer clam, soft-shell clam, and Ipswich clam. The geoduck (pronounced gooeyduck) clam, is also known as the piss clam (due to its long

siphon), or horse clam. It is the largest clam in the world, and is also thought to be the longest-living animal in the world. Surf clams come from the Mactridae group, and there are several related species. The Solenidae group includes razor or jackknife clams, which are harvested worldwide. They resemble a cut-throat razor and have a razor-sharp edge. The amande comes from the Glycimeridae group.

AVAILABILITY Fresh: Live in the shell, shucked as prepared meat. **Preserved:** Frozen, brined, canned.

● EAT Large clams: chopped or minced in chowder. Smaller specimens: shucked and enjoyed raw. Hard-shell: raw or steamed open to add to soups. Soft-shell: siphon sliced or minced for chowder, or thinly sliced for sushi. Body meat sliced, tenderized, and pan-fried or sautéd. In the shell: steamed. Removed from shell: served raw with lemon juice; also for chowder. Razor clams: in the shell; grilled or steamed. Removed from shell: raw in ceviche, or pan-fried.

FLAVOR PAIRINGS Cream, onion, herbs, white wine, tomatoes, garlic, parsley, bacon, chiles.
CLASSIC RECIPES Manhattan clam chowder (tomato based); New England clam chowder (cream-based); *spaghetti con vongole*; stuffed clams.

Surf clam *(Spisula solidissima)*
Also known as trough, bar, or hen clam. Found along the East Coast, where it is highly valued and used for clam chowder. Small related species are found in Europe. Surf clams are good for steamed clam dishes. Check to be sure they are alive just prior to cooking, rinse, then steam open over stock and white wine. A delicate, sweet flavor with a salty aftertaste.

Cockle *(Cerastoderma edule)*
Cockles are usually sold at around 1¼in (3cm). Wash, and then steam open over simmering stock or wine; extract from the shell to serve. Excellent in salads or as a starter with a simple dressing. They have a sweet taste of the sea; can be a little gritty, but are a real treat freshly cooked.

Check that the shells are tightly closed: this indicates that they are still alive.

The shell of a cockle is corrugated. Cockles cannot be stored long: use as soon as possible.

The glossy brown shell of the razor clam is brittle and needs careful handling as it has a razor-sharp edge.

Geoduck clam *(Panopea abrupta)*
Also known as Pacific geoduck or king clam, this clam is usually sold at 4–6in (10–15cm) in diameter. The siphon can be up to 27½in (70cm) long when fully extended. The geoduck can live 100 or more years. It can grow much bigger and weigh as much as 15½–17½lb (7–8kg). The meat can be tough, but the flavor is intense. Particularly popular in Japan.

Razor clam *(Ensis ensis)*
Usually harvested at 5in (12cm) or larger. Check that the clam is alive immediately prior to cooking: the shell should close tightly if tapped. Best steamed, or grilled (but toughens easily). Extract the sweet and tender muscle from the shell and discard the stomach contents. Slice thinly for a marinated dish, such as ceviche. The taste is not dissimilar to that of a scallop.

Hard-shell clam (*Mercenaria mercenaria*)
*Also known as quahog, round, or Venus clam.
Small, young clams may be called littleneck clams;
a half-grown clam is called a cherrystone and is
considered a delicacy (eaten raw or cooked). Small
hard-shell clams can be enjoyed raw, but the larger
ones are often used in clam chowder. The shells are
quite heavy, but open to reveal a sweet, tender, and
pleasantly salty clam meat.*

*Hard-shell clams are 3–5in
(8–2cm) wide.*

*Surf clams have a smooth beige
shell. They usually grow to
1½–in (4–5cm) in diameter, but
can reach 6in (16cm).*

Amande (*Glycymeris glycymeris*)
*Also known as the dog cockle, the amande
is caught around European coasts. Its shell
can grow up to 2¾in (7cm) across. It has a
firmer texture than most clams, so is good
for chowders and stuffing. Enjoyed raw in
Europe. Sweet, meaty, and a little chewy.*

*The siphon of the
geoduck clam is edible,
but the thick skin needs
to be removed first and
the meat cooked slowly
until tender.*

*The amande is round, with
a chocolate zigzag pattern
on a cream shell. Harvested
at about 1½in (4cm)
in diameter.*

CLASSIC RECIPE

NEW ENGLAND CLAM CHOWDER

This creamy soup is often served
with saltines or tiny oyster crackers.
Be sure to cook the clams the same
day you purchase them.

SERVES 4

36 live clams, well-scrubbed

1 tbsp oil

4oz (115g) thick-sliced bacon, chopped

2 russet or other floury baking potatoes,
peeled and cut into ½in (1cm) cubes

1 onion, finely chopped

2 tbsp all-purpose flour

2 cups whole milk

salt and freshly ground black pepper

½ cup half-and-half

2 tbsp flat-leaf parsley, finely chopped

1 Discard any open clams, then shuck
the rest, reserving the juices in a
2-cup liquid measuring cup. Add
enough water to the juices to make 2
cups. Chop the clams. Heat the oil in
a large, heavy saucepan or soup pot
and cook the bacon over medium heat
for 5 minutes, or until crisp. Remove
the bacon with a slotted spoon and
drain on paper towels.

2 Add the potatoes and onion to the
pot and cook for 5 minutes, stirring
occasionally, until the onion is soft but
not browned. Add the flour and stir
for 2 minutes. Stir in the reserved
clam juice/water mixture and milk,
and season to taste. Cover, reduce the
heat to low, and simmer for 20
minutes, or until the potatoes are
tender. Add the clams and simmer
gently, uncovered, for 5 minutes, or
until just heated through. Stir in the
half-and-half and reheat without
boiling. Serve sprinkled with the
bacon and parsley.

SCALLOPS (PECTINIDAE)

Escallops are more commonly known as scallops and are one of the most popular of all shellfish. Harvested in oceans worldwide, scallops are found in deeper water than most shellfish. There are over 500 species of scallop, coming from three groups; some are an important commercial food source, harvested from the wild or farmed. Scallops are harvested by dredging or gathered by hand. (The latter is considered to be a more responsible method; the scallops are often larger than dredged ones and fetch a high price.) Scallops are hermaphrodites and comprise a powerful adductor muscle (the white section), coral or roe containing the eggs (the orange section), and milt (the cream section). This swells and bursts in the water, mixing with the eggs for fertilization. This is the only bivalve that is sold raw in a prepared state. The sweet, succulent adductor muscle is the main part of the scallop that is eaten. The coral is also eaten in Europe; in the US

it is often discarded. The coral may be dried in a low oven and then pulverized to add to shellfish sauces, to provide a greater depth of flavor. Scallops have a sweet seafood taste and tender, succulent texture. The roe has a richer and more intense flavor.

AVAILABILITY Fresh: live in the shell, prepared on the half-shell, prepared and trimmed (processed). **Preserved:** frozen with roe both on and off, canned, smoked, some species dried.

● **EAT Cooked:** pan-fry, steam, poach, barbecue, broil; pan-fry smoked meat. **Raw:** ceviche and sushi (white meat only).

FLAVOR PAIRINGS Bacon, chorizo, red peppers, red onions, olive oil, sesame oil, black beans, scallions, ginger, chile.

CLASSIC RECIPES Scallops in bacon; scallops with black bean sauce or soy and ginger; *Coquille St. Jacques Parisienne*; scallop *gratin*.

Bay scallop
(Argopecten irradians)
This scallop is found in the western North Atlantic, and is harvested along the coast of the US. Sear in hot butter for a few seconds on both sides to make the most of the tender and sweet meat.

Do not overcook bay scallops, as they will shrink and dry out.

King scallop *(Pecten maximus)*
This scallop is caught in the deep waters of northern Europe, and enjoyed in many European countries. The shell is corrugated, which prevents it from closing very tightly, unlike other bivalves. King scallops are at their very best pan-seared, although intense heat makes the roe or coral pop. Care needs to be taken not to overcook them—cook for about a minute on each side in a hot pan.

The shell of the king scallop can reach over 8in (20cm) in diameter. It is cream with brown markings; it has a flat bottom shell and a concave top shell. The mantle and dark stomach sac are removed when a scallop is sold on the shell.

Queen scallop
(Aequipecten opercularis)
"Queenies" are rarely sold live in the shell; they are either extracted or trimmed and sold on the half-shell. They have a sweet, delicate taste. Best used in a stir-fry or in a fish stew—they overcook very easily and shrink. If served on the shell they are good with a little flavored butter and a few seconds under the broiler.

SHUCKING A SCALLOP

Open, or shuck, scallops and oysters using a small-bladed shucking knife.

1 Prize the shell open at the hinge with a shucking knife. Insert the knife into the rounded side of the shell to sever the muscle from the shell. Remove the round shell and discard.

2 Using a knife, trim away the "frill," "skirt," or "mantle" of the scallop—this contains gills and many eyes.

3 Remove the stomach sac and discard; trim away any other matter. Present a prepared scallop—coral and white muscle—on a half-shell.

Queen scallops do not usually grow to more than 2½in (6cm) across.

MUSSELS (MYTILIDAE)

Mussels live in cool waters all over the world. They are abundant and are harvested from the wild by dredging and hand-gathering; they are also farmed in large quantities. Mussels are one of the most sustainable seafoods available. There are a few different species.

AVAILABILITY **Fresh:** Live in the shell, cook fresh. **Preserved:** Frozen meat, canned in brine or vinegar, smoked. Often included in frozen seafood mix. **Green-lipped mussel:** Usually cooked on the half-shell and frozen.

⬤ **EAT** Steam, roast, and broil. Green-lipped mussel: topped and *réchauffé* as baked and broiled. Remove the shell if adding to a sauce or stew.

FLAVOR PAIRINGS White wine, butter, garlic, cream, ginger, lemongrass, spices, parsley, coriander, dill, rosemary, fennel, Pernod.

CLASSIC RECIPES Moules marinières, moules frites, paella, moules à la crème, moules farcies, mouclade.

MOULES MARINIÈRES

This classic French recipe—mussels in wine, garlic, and herbs—means "in the style of the fisherman."

SERVES 4

4 tbsp butter

2 onions, finely chopped

8lb (3.6kg) fresh mussels, well-scrubbed, beards removed (discard any opened ones)

2 garlic cloves, crushed

2 cups dry white wine

4 bay leaves

2 sprigs of thyme

salt and freshly ground black pepper

2–4 tbsp chopped parsley

1 Melt the butter in a very large, heavy pot. Add the onion and cook over medium-low heat until lightly browned. Stir in the mussels, garlic, wine, bay leaves, and thyme. Season to taste with salt and pepper. Cover, bring to a boil, and cook, shaking the pot frequently, for 5–6 minutes, or until the mussels open.

2 Remove the mussels with a slotted spoon; discard any that remain closed. Transfer to warmed bowls and cover.

3 Strain the cooking juices into a saucepan and bring to a boil. Season to taste with salt and pepper, add the parsley, pour it over the mussels, and serve at once.

PREPARING MUSSELS

Only live mussels must be used: check before preparation.

1 *Check that the mussels are alive—they should be tightly shut with an undamaged shell. Scrub the shells.*

2 *Remove any barnacles with the back of a knife. Remove the byssus thread, also known as the beard.*

Green-lipped mussel *(Perna canaliculus)*
Also known as the New Zealand mussel, or green mussel, this may grow to 9½in (24cm) long. Harvested abundantly around the New Zealand coastline, where it is of economic importance. It has a dark brown shell with a vivid green lip. It is very meaty—almost chewy—and intensely flavored.

Rope-grown mussels have little barnacle growth on the shell and are glossy. They require minimal preparation.

Common mussel *(Mytilus edulis)*
Also known as the blue mussel, the common muscle is found in temperate and polar waters worldwide. The shell varies from brown to a bluish-purple. The mussels attach themselves to rocks, or when farmed, to rope, by a strong thread called the byssus thread (or beard), a protein they secrete. They taste slightly salty, with an intense flavor of the sea.

CALDERETA ASTURIANA

This iconic fish stew from the Asturias region of Spain uses any fish that is landed on the day.

SERVES 6

2¼lb (1kg) white fish (e.g. hake, monkfish, red mullet), filleted and skinned

4 small squid, prepared

8oz (250g) shrimp, peeled and deveined

1lb (450g) each mussels and clams, prepared

⅔ cup dry white wine

3 tbsp extra virgin olive oil

1 large onion, chopped

3 cloves garlic, finely chopped

large pinch of cayenne pepper

1 heaping tablespoon all-purpose flour

1¼ cup fish stock or bottled clam juice and water, or more as needed

1 large bunch parsley, chopped (about ½ to ⅔ cup)

2 large red bell peppers, seeded and quartered lengthwise

salt and freshly ground black pepper

fresh lemon juice to taste

1 Heat the oven to 350°F (180°C). Cut the fish fillets into large pieces, and the squid into large squares. Refrigerate until needed.

2 Discard any mussels or clams that remain open when tapped. Pour the wine into a soup pot, bring to a boil and simmer for 1 minute. Add the mussels and clams and cook over medium heat for 3–4 minutes, or until they have opened. Discard any that do not open. Strain the cooking juices and reserve. Remove the cooked mussels and clams from their shells and reserve.

3 Heat the oil in a large flameproof casserole, add the onion and cook for 1–2 minutes, or until beginning to soften. Add the garlic, cayenne, and flour; stir over medium heat for 1–2 minutes. Add the reserved mussel and clam juices, fish stock, and parsley. Season lightly.

4 Add the raw seafood to the casserole, along with the peppers. The fish should be submerged in the liquid from the sauce: if it isn't, add a little extra stock or water. Cover tightly and cook in the oven for 20–25 minutes, or until all the fish is cooked through and opaque. Add the cooked mussels and clams, and return to the oven for a further 5 minutes, or until hot. Sprinkle with lemon juice and serve with chunks of warm, crusty bread.

OYSTERS ROCKEFELLER

A traditional lunch dish from New Orleans that makes an excellent first course.

SERVES 4

4 cups loosely packed baby spinach leaves, rinsed but not dried

24 live oysters, in their shells, well scrubbed

⅓ cup loosely packed flat-leaf parsley leaves

4 large shallots, chopped

1 garlic clove, chopped

8 tbsp (1 stick) butter, cut into pieces

⅓ cup all-purpose flour

2 flat anchovy fillets, drained and finely chopped

pinch of cayenne pepper

salt and freshly ground black pepper

rock salt or other coarse salt

3 tbsp Pernod (anise liqueur)

1 Put the spinach in a saucepan over medium heat with the water (from rinsing) still clinging to its leaves. Cook, stirring occasionally, for 5 minutes, or until wilted. Drain well, squeeze to remove any excess liquid, and set aside.

2 Meanwhile, discard any open oysters. Shell one oyster, reserving the liquid from the shell; then return it to its shell and refrigerate. Repeat until all the oysters have been opened. Refrigerate the oyster juices until needed.

3 Chop the spinach, parsley, shallots, garlic, and very finely with a knife, or in a food processor; then set aside.

4 Melt the butter in a small saucepan over medium heat. Add the flour, and cook for 2 minutes, stirring, without letting it brown. Gradually whisk in the reserved oyster liquid to make a smooth sauce. Then stir in the spinach mixture, anchovies, cayenne, and salt and pepper to taste (keeping in mind that the anchovies are salty). Cover the pan and leave to simmer for 15 minutes.

5 Meanwhile, preheat the oven to 400°F (200°C). Arrange a thick layer of rock salt in the serving dishes; then put in the oven to warm briefly.

6 Uncover the spinach sauce and stir in the Pernod. Taste the sauce, and adjust the seasoning, if necessary. Remove the dishes from the oven, and arrange 6 of the chilled oysters in their shells on each dish. (The salt keeps the oysters level during cooking.) Spoon the sauce over each oyster and bake for 5–10 minutes, or until the sauce is bubbly-hot. Serve immediately.

OYSTERS (OSTREIDAE GROUP)

Eating oysters is a global pastime, and a well-documented gourmet delight. Like other bivalve (two-shell) mollusks, an oyster lives inside its shell, which it opens and closes with a strong muscle. The shell is oval, either cupped or flat, and covered in frilly, rocklike crevices. Fresh oysters are tightly closed and hard to open without a shucking knife (see below). Mostly found in temperate coastal waters, oysters are harvested from both wild and farmed beds worldwide. Two main genera are gathered: *Ostrea*, native to Europe and the west coast of the US; and *Crassostrea*, native to Asia, Japan, the east coast of the US, and Australia. Once harvested, the fish are purified and graded by size. An all-time favorite is the creamy Pacific oyster (*Crassostrea gigas*), originally from the coast of Japan, but farmed in northern Europe, and the Pacific northeast, where it is famously cultivated along the coastal waters of British Columbia, Washington State, Oregon, and California.Equally popular is the small, buttery Kumamoto oyster (from Japan), widely regarded as one of the world's finest oysters. A more salty Atlantic choice is the Blue Point oyster (*C. virginica*), native to the East Atlantic coast, and Gulf States, but cultivated in beds all along the East Coast of the US. Oysters harvested in different waters differ subtly in flavor and shell color. Oyster-tasting is an art, much like wine-tasting, with many gourmet terms for the varied flavors, including tangy, metallic, nutty, grassy, ozone, sweet, cucumber, fruity, iodine, earthy, and coppery. One topic still hotly debated is whether to eat oysters cooked or raw; whether *au naturel*, or dressed.

SEASONS Wild oysters: late spring/early summer, when not spawning. Farmed oysters: year-round.

AVAILABILITY In the shell, smoked, canned.

● **EAT** Raw: In the half shell. **Cooked:** Deep-fry, pan-fry, poach, broil, and bake.
Flavor pairings Raw: Red wine vinegar, Tabasco, lemon juice. **Cooked:** Anchovy essence, butter, spinach.
CLASSIC RECIPES Oysters in the half shell with shallot vinegar; oysters Rockefeller; oyster po-boys.

Native oyster *(Ostrea edulis) Also called the European flat oyster, it is often served raw on a bed of crushed ice, dressed with lemon juice, Tabasco, and shallot vinegar. Graded by size, from 1 to 4, the largest "royals" can reach 4 in (10cm).*

Native oysters have an oval, scaly shell, intense taste, and firm texture.

The meat of the Pacific oyster is delicate beige in color, with a smooth, creamy texture.

SHUCKING AN OYSTER

Insert a shucking knife and prize open the shell, without harming the oyster, in three easy steps.

1 *Hold the oyster firmly in a thick cloth, with the shell's rounded side facing down. Insert the top of a shucking knife into the hinge of the oyster; twist the knife to get a good point of leverage.*

2 *Release pressure from the knife, then gently and firmly lever the oyster knife to break the seal between the two valves (shell halves). A "shucking" noise will be heard.*

Pacific oyster *(Crassostrea gigas) The taste of this widely cultured oyster varies enormously, depending on where it is grown. Flavors range from smoky, to grassy, and acidic, through to milky and creamy. Usually graded by weight, a fair size would be 4oz (115g), or 4½in (11cm). Store the oysters cup-side down to prevent their natural juices from escaping.*

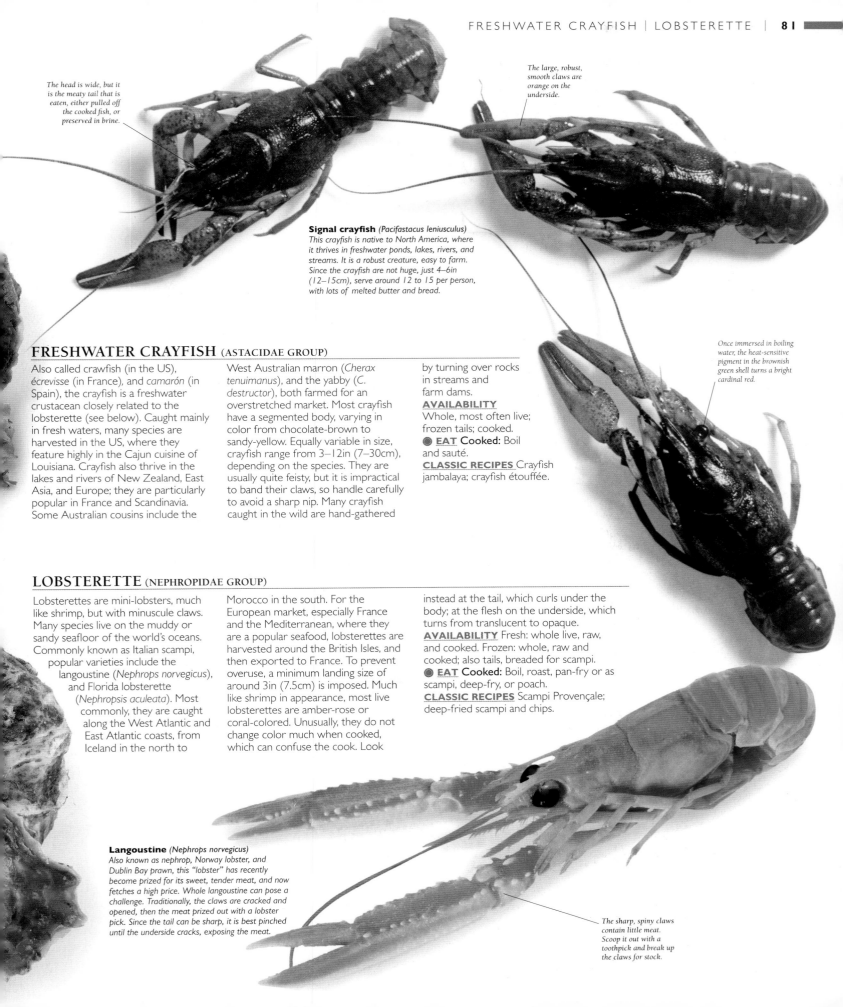

The head is wide, but it is the meaty tail that is eaten, either pulled off the cooked fish, or preserved in brine.

The large, robust, smooth claws are orange on the underside.

Signal crayfish *(Pacifastacus leniusculus)*
This crayfish is native to North America, where it thrives in freshwater ponds, lakes, rivers, and streams. It is a robust creature, easy to farm. Since the crayfish are not huge, just 4–6in (12–15cm), serve around 12 to 15 per person, with lots of melted butter and bread.

Once immersed in boiling water, the heat-sensitive pigment in the brownish green shell turns a bright cardinal red.

FRESHWATER CRAYFISH (ASTACIDAE GROUP)

Also called crawfish (in the US), *écrevisse* (in France), and *camarón* (in Spain), the crayfish is a freshwater crustacean closely related to the lobsterette (see below). Caught mainly in fresh waters, many species are harvested in the US, where they feature highly in the Cajun cuisine of Louisiana. Crayfish also thrive in the lakes and rivers of New Zealand, East Asia, and Europe; they are particularly popular in France and Scandinavia. Some Australian cousins include the West Australian marron *(Cherax tenuimanus)*, and the yabby *(C. destructor)*, both farmed for an overstretched market. Most crayfish have a segmented body, varying in color from chocolate-brown to sandy-yellow. Equally variable in size, crayfish range from 3–12in (7–30cm), depending on the species. They are usually quite feisty, but it is impractical to band their claws, so handle carefully to avoid a sharp nip. Many crayfish caught in the wild are hand-gathered by turning over rocks in streams and farm dams.

AVAILABILITY
Whole, most often live; frozen tails; cooked.
● **EAT Cooked:** Boil and sauté.
CLASSIC RECIPES Crayfish jambalaya; crayfish étouffée.

LOBSTERETTE (NEPHROPIDAE GROUP)

Lobsterettes are mini-lobsters, much like shrimp, but with minuscule claws. Many species live on the muddy or sandy seafloor of the world's oceans. Commonly known as Italian scampi, popular varieties include the langoustine *(Nephrops norvegicus)*, and Florida lobsterette *(Nephropsis aculeata)*. Most commonly, they are caught along the West Atlantic and East Atlantic coasts, from Iceland in the north to Morocco in the south. For the European market, especially France and the Mediterranean, where they are a popular seafood, lobsterettes are harvested around the British Isles, and then exported to France. To prevent overuse, a minimum landing size of around 3in (7.5cm) is imposed. Much like shrimp in appearance, most live lobsterettes are amber-rose or coral-colored. Unusually, they do not change color much when cooked, which can confuse the cook. Look instead at the tail, which curls under the body; at the flesh on the underside, which turns from translucent to opaque.

AVAILABILITY Fresh: whole live, raw, and cooked. Frozen: whole, raw and cooked; also tails, breaded for scampi.
● **EAT Cooked:** Boil, roast, pan-fry or as scampi, deep-fry, or poach.
CLASSIC RECIPES Scampi Provençale; deep-fried scampi and chips.

Langoustine *(Nephrops norvegicus)*
Also known as nephrop, Norway lobster, and Dublin Bay prawn, this "lobster" has recently become prized for its sweet, tender meat, and now fetches a high price. Whole langoustine can pose a challenge. Traditionally, the claws are cracked and opened, then the meat prized out with a lobster pick. Since the tail can be sharp, it is best pinched until the underside cracks, exposing the meat.

The sharp, spiny claws contain little meat. Scoop it out with a toothpick and break up the claws for stock.

LOBSTER BISQUE

The name "bisque" refers to a rich and luxurious shellfish soup made with cream and brandy, thought to have come from the Spanish Biscay.

SERVES 4

1 lobster, about 2¼lb (1kg), cooked
3½ tbsp butter
1 onion, finely chopped
1 carrot, finely chopped
2 celery ribs, finely chopped
1 leek, finely chopped
½ fennel bulb, finely chopped
1 bay leaf
1 sprig of tarragon
2 garlic cloves, crushed
⅓ cup tomato purée
4 tomatoes, coarsely chopped
½ cup Cognac or brandy
½ cup dry white wine or vermouth
7 cups fish stock, or a combination of bottled clam juice and water
½ cup heavy whipping cream
salt and freshly ground black pepper
pinch of cayenne
juice of ½ lemon
chopped fresh chives, to garnish

1 Split the lobster in half, remove the meat from the body, and chop the meat into small pieces. Twist off the claws and legs, breaking at the joints, and remove the meat, then crack all the shells with the back of a knife. Chop the shells into coarse pieces and refrigerate the lobster meat for later.

2 Melt the butter in a large pan over medium heat, add the onion, carrot, celery, leek, fennel, bay leaf, tarragon, and garlic and cook for 10 minutes, stirring occasionally, until softened. Add the lobster shells. Stir in the tomato purée, tomatoes, Cognac or brandy, wine or vermouth, and fish stock. Bring to a boil; then reduce the heat and simmer for 1 hour.

3 Let cool slightly, then ladle into a food processor. Process, pulsing the machine on and off, until the shell breaks into very small pieces. Strain through a coarse sieve, pushing through as much as you can, then pass it again through a fine sieve before returning to the heat.

4 Bring to a boil, add the reserved lobster meat and the cream, then season to taste, adding the cayenne and lemon juice. Serve in warm bowls, garnished with chives.

ROCK/SPINY LOBSTER (PALINURIDAE GROUP)

Unlike "true" clawed lobsters, rock, or spiny, lobsters lack claws. Instead, they have a rocky carapace (head), and short, sharp spines running the length of their bodies. Some species also have a distinctive orange-brown shell, flecked with green, yellow, and blue spots, which intensify in color when cooked. Also known as crawfish or crayfish, especially in Australasia, rock lobsters thrive along rocky coasts below the tidal zone, hiding in crevices and caverns. Typically found in the Western Atlantic, from North Carolina to Brazil, and in the Gulf of Mexico and Caribbean Sea, most are caught in the tropical and subtropical waters of the northern hemisphere and in some cold waters of the southern hemisphere. They are harvested and sold to around 90 countries worldwide, and valued as a delicacy in their own right. Although some taste less sweet than true lobster, many have particularly succulent and dense tail meat. If overcooked, though, they can become tough and fibrous.

AVAILABILITY Fresh and frozen, whole and tails.

● **EAT** Cooked: Whole tails: boiled, steamed, deep-fried, and broiled. Tail meat: diced and stir-fried, and added to soups and stews.

CLASSIC RECIPES Boiled with lemon and garlic; barbecued rock lobster.

Rock (spiny) lobster or Crawfish (*Palinurus elephas*) Although fairly large, about 16in (40cm), these shellfish lack the fleshy claws of true lobsters. Instead, the dense, sweet meat typical of the species is concentrated in the tail shell, although some meat can be extracted from the legs.

The legs of a lobster contain sweet juice that can be sucked from the shell.

The sweet, white meat in the claws can be extracted with a small lobster pick.

PREPARING COOKED LOBSTER
How to crack the shell and extract the edible parts in three easy steps.

1 Remove the head by twisting away from the body.

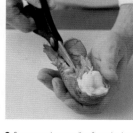

2 Scoop out the tomalley from the head shell. Then cut the tail shell on both sides to extract the meat in one piece.

3 Crack the claws with lobster crackers to take out the claw meat. Toss into salads or heat for risotto.

LOBSTER AND LOBSTER FAMILY
(NEPHROPIDAE, PALINURIDAE, SCYLLARIDAE, GALATHEIDAE, AND ASTACIDAE GROUPS)

Lobster is prized worldwide as a luxury food. Many lobster families populate the oceans of the world. Classified as invertebrates, with a hard protective shell, lobsters live in burrows, or crevices in rocks, mud, and sand, feeding on mollusks and other crustaceans. A lobster's body is made of several sections: a carapace (head), and tail shell with legs, swimlets, and, in some species, claws. Like crabs and other arthropods, lobsters molt their shells in order to grow. For the chef, lobsters come in two main types: the clawed (see below) and clawless (see opposite). Among the Nephropidae family, several members are clawed, including the European, American, and Canadian lobsters, and the Dublin Bay prawn (or *langoustine*). Both the European and American variety is extensively farmed and harvested from

the wild, to feed the appetites of Europe, the US, and Canada. Most are caught by one-way baited traps and pots. Many American lobsters are exported to Japan, where they are also prized as a delicacy. The European lobster, rather less abundant than its American cousin, is usually more expensive. It is often wondered which of the two provides the best flavor. When served in a classic dish, such as lobster Thermidor, it is hard to tell the difference. Typically, the tail meat of most lobsters is sweet, succulent, dense, and highly valued.

On harvesting, lobsters usually have their claws "banded," which makes them easier to handle and curbs their naturally aggressive and cannibalistic

behavior when captive. If banded for too long, though, the claw meat will start to atrophy.

AVAILABILITY Whole: both live and cooked. **Frozen:** cooked whole and frozen, extracted from the shell. Canned.

● **EAT Live:** freeze briefly or stun before boiling. **Cooked:** boiled—10 minutes per 1lb (450g); broiled, and baked, both extracted from the shell and in bisque.

CLASSIC RECIPES Lobster Thermidor; lobster Newburg; lobster bisque; dressed lobster.

American lobster *(Homarus americanus) Also known as the Atlantic or Maine lobster, this traditionally large and meaty shellfish can grow to at least 2ft (60cm) and take 7 years to reach 1lb (450g). An ideal weight for a main dish is 1¾lb (750g) or 2¼lb (1kg), before the shell grows too thick and heavy.*

The large and heavy crusher claw is filled with dense, sweet meat that can be extracted whole to garnish a dish.

CLASSIC RECIPE

LOBSTER THERMIDOR

This irresistibly indulgent seafood dish is thought to be named in honor of a play entitled *Thermidor.*

SERVES 4

2 lobsters, about 1½lb (675g) each, cooked

For the sauce

2 tbsp butter

2 shallots, finely chopped

½ cup dry white wine

⅔ cup heavy whipping cream

½ cup fish stock or bottled clam juice

½ tsp Dijon mustard

1 tbsp fresh lemon juice

2 tbsp chopped fresh flatleaf parsley

2 tsp chopped fresh tarragon

salt and freshly ground black pepper

½ cup shredded Gruyère cheese

paprika, for garnish

lemon wedges, to serve

1 Cut the lobsters in half lengthwise. Remove the meat from the claws and tail, along with any coral (roe) or meat from the head. Cut the meat into bite-size pieces. Clean out the shells and reserve.

2 To prepare the sauce, melt the butter in a small saucepan, add the shallots, and cook gently until softened but not browned. Add the wine and boil for 2–3 minutes, or until the liquid is reduced by half.

3 Add the cream and stock and boil rapidly, stirring, until reduced and slightly thickened. Stir in the lemon juice and mustard; then stir in herbs and season to taste with salt and pepper. Stir in half the cheese.

4 Preheat the broiler on its highest setting. Add the lobster meat to the sauce, then divide among the lobster shells. Top with the remaining cheese.

5 Place the lobsters on a foil-lined broiler pan and broil for 2–3 minutes, or until bubbling-hot and golden on top. Sprinkle with a little paprika and serve hot, with lemon wedges.

SLIPPER LOBSTER (SCYLLARIDAE GROUP)

Colorfully named the shovel-nosed lobster, Spanish lobster, sand lobster, or locust lobster, all slipper lobsters lack the meaty claws of "true" lobsters (much like the spiny lobster). Various species thrive on the sea floor in warm waters worldwide, mostly around Thailand, Singapore, and Australia. Close and commercially important cousins include the Moreton Bay bug (found in northern Australian waters), and the Balmain bug (found off the south coasts of Australia). Most slipper lobsters have a sweet but delicate, mellow taste, and medium texture, firm to the bite.

AVAILABILITY Whole and tails.

⬤ **EAT** Boil, steam, poach, deep fry, and barbecue.

FLAVOR PAIRINGS Butter, herbs, such as tarragon, chives, and dill, garlic, citrus, lemon grass, soy sauce, chile.

CLASSIC RECIPES Seafood platter; barbecued bug tails with garlic butter.

Balmain bug
(Ibacus peronii) Sometimes called a flapjack, or mud bug, this tasty Australian shellfish is especially popular in Sydney. Its meat, found only in the tail, tastes strong and sweet.

A fair-sized bug, 10in (25cm) long, should have a hard, rosy shell, and feel heavy for its size.

Moreton Bay bug
(Thenus orientalis) Named after Moreton Bay in Queensland, where it is enjoyed as a local delicacy, it looks like the Balmain bug (above), roughly 10in (25cm), but fatter, with wide-set eyes, and more of an amber hue. It is a versatile fish, with a sweet flavor, ideal for poaching and steaming, deep frying, pan frying, and stir-frying.

Slipper lobster
(Scyllarus arctus) Nicknamed the flat lobster, langosta, or cigale, this North Atlantic clawless lobster is popular in the Mediterranean. Smallish, at 6in (15cm), it traditionally forms part of a shellfish platter. Only the tail is eaten.

Once the hard, pebbly, reddish shell is removed, the tail meat is sweet and firm to the bite.

SHRIMP (PRAWN) (ALL GROUPS PENAEIDAE, ARISTEIDAE, PANALIDAE, SERGESTIDAE, ATYIDAE, PALAEMONIDAE, CRANGONIDAE, AND SOLENOCERIDAE)

Shrimps (prawns) thrive in all waters, both cold and warm, fresh and marine. Widely popular, especially in Australia, the US, Europe, and Japan, shrimps are extensively harvested and farmed. Varied use of the terms "shrimp" and "prawn" can be confusing. In the US, "shrimp" is widely used for cold- and warm-water species. In the UK and Australia, by contrast, "prawn" mostly refers to warm-water species, such as the giant black tiger prawn (*Penaeus monodon*), as well as some fair-sized cold-water species, such as the northern prawn (*Pandalus borealis*), while "shrimp" is reserved for smaller species, such as the brown shrimp (*Crangon crangon*). Generally, the larger the shrimp, the higher the price. The largest shrimps are the warm-water, or tropical variety, at least 14in (35cm), compared to cold-water shrimp, around 2in (5cm). Tropical shrimps provide more than three-quarters of the world's supply. Found mainly in the Pacific and Indian oceans, they are harvested or farmed by Latin America, Australia, China, Vietnam, Sri Lanka, and Thailand. The smaller, slower-growing, cold-water shrimps, found mainly in the Atlantic, Arctic, and Pacific oceans, are caught by the UK, US, Canada, Greenland, Denmark, and Iceland. Key species include the Atlantic white shrimp (*Penaeus setiferus*); the Pacific white shrimp (*Litopenaeus vannamei*); the brown shrimp; northern shrimp; and giant black tiger shrimp. Although taste varies with the species, cold-water shrimps often taste sweeter, but less dense and meaty.

AVAILABILTY Cold-water: fresh and frozen; cooked as *crevettes* (poached). Warm-water: cooked and frozen; peeled and soaked in brine.

⬤ **EAT** Cold-water: serve defrosted as part of a salad; or serve as potted shrimps. Use the shells for stock and flavored butters.
Warm-water: pan-fried, stir-fried, deep fried, barbecued, grilled, and baked. For a sweet, roasted flavor, pan-fry in oil with vegetables. For a subtle flavor, simmer in water.

FLAVOR PAIRINGS Mayonnaise, capers, paprika, pepper, lemon.

CLASSIC RECIPES Cold-water: shrimp cocktail; avocado pear and shrimps. Warm-water: *gambas pil pil* (garlic shrimps); shrimp *tempura*; sesame shrimp toasts.

CLASSIC RECIPE

SESAME SHRIMP TOASTS

A combination of flavors that work surprisingly well together.

SERVES 4

8oz (250g) raw tiger shrimp (prawns), peeled, deveined, and coarsely chopped
2 scallions, coarsely chopped
1⁄2in (1cm) piece of fresh ginger, peeled and finely grated
1 tsp soy sauce
1⁄2 tsp sugar
1⁄2 tsp Asian sesame oil
1 small egg white, lightly beaten
freshly ground black pepper
3 slices white bread, crusts removed
2 tbsp sesame seeds
peanut or vegetable oil, for frying
cilantro leaves, for garnish

1 Combine the shrimp and scallions in a food processor and process for a few seconds to make a paste. Transfer the paste to a bowl and stir in the ginger, soy sauce, sugar, sesame oil, and enough egg white to bind the mixture together. Season with pepper.

2 Cut each slice of bread into 4 triangles and spread each thickly with the prawn paste. Sprinkle the sesame seeds evenly over the top.

3 Heat the oil to 350°F (180°C) in a deep-fat fryer or other deep pot. Working in batches, fry the toasts, shrimp-side down, for 2 minutes. Carefully turn them over and fry for another 2 minutes, or until golden-brown and crisp.

4 Lift the toasts out of the pot with a slotted spoon and drain on paper towels. Serve warm, garnished with cilantro.

Brown shrimp *(Crangon crangon) Although measuring no more than 2in (5cm), this common shrimp is regarded as quite a delicacy, fetching a higher price than larger, warm-water species. Caught in the East Atlantic, it looks transparent when live, but turns amber-brown when cooked. Brown shrimps are traditionally served as potted shrimps. Although tedious to peel, they are absolutely delicious, sweet, and succulent.*

Crevette rose When poached, the white Central American shrimp is often called a crevette (French for "shrimp"). Wonderfully sweet and dense, it makes an appetizing addition to any platter, or an attractive rosy garnish to paella (rice and seafood).

Central American shrimp (Litopenaeus vannamei) A popular shrimp species farmed in both Latin and South American countries, these white shrimps are harvested, graded and frozen for sale. Often large, up to 10in (25cm), they are meaty and sweet. The shells provide a tasty addition to shellfish stock.

Deep-water shrimp (Pandalus borealis) Valued for its sweet, mild taste, and succulent texture, it is variously named the northern red shrimp or Alaskan pink shrimp in the US, and the northern or Greenland prawn in the UK. A fair size for a cold-water shrimp, at 2½in (6cm), it is always cooked on landing, and frozen for sale. The shells make a tasty stock, ideal for pilaf, risotto and soup; they can also be processed together with butter, and sieved to make a shrimp butter.

Giant black tiger shrimp (Penaeus monodon) A meaty tropical shrimp, which can reach 14in (35cm), it is harvested globally, and farmed extensively, raising some environmental issues; when buying, check how responsibly the fish have been sourced. To barbecue, snip off the legs and antennae; then twist and pull out the tail section. The taste is mellow, honeyed, and succulent.

SHRIMP COCKTAIL, MEXICAN-STYLE

Corn kernels and avocado give a south-of-the-border twist to this classic, perennial favorite.

SERVES 4

| 1 tbsp olive oil |
| 8oz (250g) jumbo shrimp in the shell |
| juice of 1 lime, plus extra for the avocado |
| 1 tsp hot pepper sauce, such as Tabasco |
| ¼ cup mayonnaise |
| 2 tbsp sour cream |
| 1 tbsp sun-dried tomato purée |
| 1 tbsp chopped cilantro, plus extra sprigs to garnish |
| ¼ head iceberg lettuce, shredded |
| 1 small avocado, pitted, peeled, diced, and sprinkled with lime juice to prevent browning |
| 2 tbsp canned corn kernels, drained |

1 Heat the olive oil in a large frying pan and cook the shrimp over high heat, stirring and tossing, for 1–2 minutes, or until they turn opaque and just begin to curl. Transfer to a bowl, sprinkle with the juice of 1 lime and the Tabasco, stir until the prawns are coated, and set aside to cool.

2 Combine the mayonnaise, sour cream, tomato purée and cilantro in a small bowl, and stir until combined.

3 Divide the lettuce among 4 dessert glasses.

4 Peel and devein 4 shrimp, leaving their tails on; then set aside for garnish. Peel and devein the remaining shrimp and return to the bowl. Gently stir in the avocado and corn; then spoon into the serving dishes, on top of the lettuce.

5 Top each with the mayonnaise sauce, and garnish with the reserved shrimp and cilantro sprigs.

DEVEIN AND BUTTERFLY A SHRIMP

Some warm-water, farmed shrimp do not require deveining, as they are purged (deprived of food) prior to harvesting, leaving no gritty vein.

1 Peel the shrimp by first removing the head. Keep it for stock.

2 Peel the tail shell. Keep the shell, with the head, for stock.

3 Run the tip of a knife along the back of the shrimp.

4 Pull out any visible dark vein (there may be none).

5 To butterfly, make a deeper cut through the back of the shrimp.

CRABS

Crabs come in all sizes and are a favorite crustacean on many continents. The wide availability of crab (they are found in oceans worldwide) and the variety of species, makes them popular in many countries. Crabs come from a selection of groups including the *Cancridae*, *Grapsidae*, *Portunidae*, *Lothiodiae*, and *Majidae* families. A crab has a carapace or cart as a main shell, legs, and in most cases claws, although the size of claws and legs vary from species to species. They periodically molt their shell as they grow—frequently in the first two years of life—every 1–2 years as the crab matures. Crab provides two distinct meats: the white meat, found in the claws, legs, and main body, and the brown meat found in the carapace or

THAI CRAB CAKES

These make a delicious lunch or light supper when served with rice noodles.

MAKES 20

1lb (450g) crabmeat
4oz (115g) green beans, trimmed and finely chopped
1 green or red chile pepper, seeded and very finely chopped
1 tbsp Thai fish sauce (nam pla)
1 tbsp finely chopped Chinese chives or garlic chives
1 tsp prepared lemongrass purée, or 1 tbsp finely chopped lemongrass
finely grated zest of 1 lime
1 egg white, lightly beaten
all-purpose flour, to dust
vegetable oil, for deep-frying

1 Flake the crabmeat into a bowl, picking it over carefully to remove any pieces of shell or cartilage. Mix in the green beans, chile, fish sauce, chives, lemongrass, and lime zest.

2 Add the egg white, stirring to bind the mixture together. Dust your hands with flour and shape the mixture into 20 small balls. Flatten them slightly into round patties, place on a large plate or baking sheet, spaced slightly apart so they don't stick together and refrigerate for 1 hour, or until firm.

3 In a large, deep frying pan, heat the oil to 325°F (160°C). Dust the crab cakes with flour and, working in batches, deep-fry them for 3 minutes, or until golden. Drain on a plate lined with paper towels and serve warm.

cart of the crab. As a general rule, the white is often the favored of the two and is more expensive. Brown meat from the carapace is well flavored. Some species are renowned for their white claw meat, specifically the Brown crab, Jonah, and Dungeness crab of the *Cancridae* group. Snow crabs and King crabs have valuable sweet succulent meat in their legs. Male crabs have larger claws and are therefore more valuable, hens are considered to have more intensely flavored brown meat and less white meat and are usually less expensive. Many crabs are sustainably sourced, although depending on the species and the area of capture, it can be illegal to land crabs carrying eggs (berries) and in some cases it is illegal to land female crabs.

AVAILABILITY Cooked: Whole and claws; **Prepared**: Dressed/hand-picked; Processed and pasteurized white and brown meat (usually frozen separately).

⬤ **EAT** Live: Boil—15 mins per 1lb (450g) is usual. **Cooked:** Toss into salads, rechauffé in pasta, rice dishes. Sauté. **Raw:** Sushi

FLAVOR PAIRINGS Mayonnaise, chile, lemon, parsley, dill, potato, butter, Worcestershire sauce, anchovy essence.

CLASSIC RECIPES Thai crab cakes, chile crab; dressed crab (usually brown edible crab); potted crab (crab paste); pan-fried soft shell crab; Maryland crab cakes.

Blue crab *(Callinectes sapidus)*
Native to the West Atlantic, this crab is seen in both Japanese and European waters. It is a "swimmer" crab with paddles in place of back legs. Known as "busters" or "peelers," blue crabs nearing a molting stage are held in tanks, so that once the carapace lifts away revealing the soft, delicate body underneath, they are harvested. The gills, mouth, and stomach sac are removed and frozen or sold fresh ready for the "Soft Shell Crab" season. Alternately, meat from these crabs is used for crab cakes, soups, and dips. The fresh season is usually late spring early summer. There is a minimum catch size in place.

Brown edible crab *(Cancer pagurus)*
This species is caught in baited pots around the coasts of Northern Europe. Male crabs are famed for their big claws containing sweet, succulent meat. This crab can take around 7 years to grow to just over 1lb (450g). There is a minimum catch size and the ideal size is around 2lb 4oz (1kg). There is a minimum landing size in place in many regions. It is traditionally served dressed and returned to the clean carapace, accompanied by mayonnaise, brown bread, and butter.

Red king crab *(Paralithodes camtschaticus)* King crabs from the Lithodoidae group are also called stone crabs. This is the largest crab group and most popular with particularly succulent and well flavored leg meat. Red king crab is one of the largest of the group, it can have a leg span of 6ft (1.8m).

The shiny carapace is very sharp, so discard. The legs are removed and sold in sections.

Once cooked the shell becomes a vivid red. The best meat is in the legs and claws.

Dungeness crab *(Metacarcinus magister)* A member of the Carcridae group, the Dungeness crab is found in the Pacific Ocean from Alaska to California and is the most popular crab in the Pacific Northwest and western Canada. It can measure up to 10in (25cm). Recognized for its delicate, sweet flavor, this is a popular crab for a seafood platter, served simply with melted butter.

PREPARING A CRAB

Four steps to crack open a crab's shell and extract the meat.

1 *First, remove the legs and claws by twisting them away from the shell at a point close to the body.*

2 *Once you can get inside the shell, lever the main body away from the carapace.*

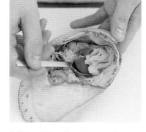

3 *Discard the gills and stomach sac. Scoop out the edible brown meat from the carapace.*

4 *Crack open the claws to remove the white meat. More meat is found in the central body section and can be removed with a lobster pick.*

CLASSIC RECIPE

DRESSED CRAB

A quintessential English classic, dressed crab is traditionally prepared using brown edible crab. Dungeness crab is a good alternative.

SERVES 2

1 large cooked crab in the shell, about 3lb (1.5kg)

splash of oil

2–3 tbsp fresh white bread crumbs

English mustard powder, such as Colman's

cayenne pepper

Worcestershire sauce

freshly ground black pepper

1 hard-boiled egg, for garnish

chopped parsley

1 Remove the meat from the crab and set aside. This is done by cracking the claws with a mallet and splitting the main body of the crab with a knife and digging out meat from the shell. Discard the claw shells, cartilage, stomach, sac, and gills.

2 Rinse the shell well and brush with a little oil. Mix the crabmeat with enough bread crumbs to allow to bind. Season with salt and pepper and add other seasonings to taste.

3 Mound the crabmeat mixture back in the cleaned shell and garnish with chopped hard-boiled egg white, sieved hard-boiled egg yolks and chopped parsley.

SQUID (CEPHALOPOD GROUP)

Although many species of squid have thrived for centuries in the world's oceans, it is only in recent years that this shellfish has become globally popular. Squid is now quite possibly the most widely consumed seafood, partly due to its availability. The common squid (*Loligo vulgaris*), popularly nicknamed "inkfish," is probably the best known. It ranges widely in size from a baby squid, measuring ¾in (2cm), to much larger specimens, some growing as long as 31–35in (80–90cm). The size of a squid is what determines the cooking method—whether fast or slow. The smaller the squid, the quicker the cooking; the larger the squid, the longer it will need to cook. Squid is made up of a long tubular body (mantle), called a "tube," once prepared. The body is flanked at one end by a pair of wing-like fins, which sometimes look like arrows, most famously on the arrow squid (*Nototodarus gouldi*). The live squid is covered in a reddish, purple, or coffee-brown membrane, sometimes with intricate brown "veins" or markings, providing camouflage. The membrane is thin, and easily pulled away, especially after the squid has been packed in ice, and jostled around in its box. Attached to the head are 10 tentacles, two long and eight smaller ones. In the center of the tentacles is the hard beak (mouth-piece). The ink, for which the inkfish is named, is contained in a small, silver ink sac in the tube. Running up the middle of the squid is an internal shell (or "pen"), which resembles plastic, and should be pulled away before cooking. The flesh of a good-quality squid is white, turning pink as it begins to decompose.

AVAILABILITY Whole: fresh, dried, smoked, and canned. Parts: frozen tubes or rings; sometimes part of a mixed seafood cocktail.

● **EAT** Raw: in sushi. **Cooked:** pan fry, stir-fry, deep fry, braise, *sauté*, or casserole. For rings or small pieces, grill or poach. Whole tubes, flattened out into a sheet and scored, taste excellent barbecued. The tube can also be stuffed with a savory breadcrumb mix, *couscous*, *quinoa*, or rice. Choose a fair-sized squid, usually with a tube that is no more than 3–4in (7.5–10cm) long. Prepare it, and cut it into rectangles or rings; or leave whole, if barbecuing.

FLAVOR PAIRINGS Chili, olive oil, breadcrumbs, lemon juice, garlic, spring onion, mayonnaise.

CLASSIC RECIPES Fried calamari; squid cooked in ink; squid stuffed with rice; *Szechuan*-fried squid.

The tough, winglike fins are best either finely sliced and stir-fried, or reserved to flavor stock.

The long, fleshy tube is often cut into rings. It is tasty and succulent—if not overcooked.

Peel off the mottled skin, and reserve it for stock, since it toughens and shrinks around the flesh when cooked.

FRIED CALAMARI

A tempting Mediterranean appetizer.

SERVES 4

2 eggs

2 tbsp cold sparkling water or seltzer

1 cup all-purpose flour

1 tsp crushed hot red pepper flakes

1 tsp salt

1 lb (500g) small squid, gutted and cleaned; tentacles halved or quartered, and bodies cut into ½in (1cm) rings

peanut or vegetable oil, for frying

lemon wedges, to garnish

1 Break the eggs into a bowl, add the sparkling water, and whisk. Combine the flour, pepper flakes, and salt in a bowl. Dip each piece of squid into the egg mixture and then into the flour, coating evenly. Dry slightly on a wire rack as you bread the remaining pieces.

2 Heat 1in (2.5cm) of oil in a deep frying pan over high heat. When the oil is hot, carefully add the squid, one piece at a time. Do not overfill the pan. Cook in batches, turning as needed, for 2–3 minutes or until golden. Remove with a slotted spoon and drain on paper towels. Serve with lemon wedges.

Common squid
(Loligo vulgaris) The "inkfish" has gained a reputation for being tough and chewy, but is only ever so if it is overcooked. In a hot pan, the meat takes no time at all. At its best, it tastes tender and mellow, with a subtle, distinctive flavor.

PREPARING SQUID

Peeling, trimming, and scoring the squid, ready for cooking.

1 Pull away the beak (mouthpiece) and eyes from the main body.

2 Trim off the eyes and the two long tentacles. Remove the fins from the head, and peel away the membrane.

3 Remove the featherlike "pen" (internal shell) from the center of the squid.

4 Open out the squid tube to reveal the roe. Score the squid for best effect; to prevent it from being overcooked, and toughening.

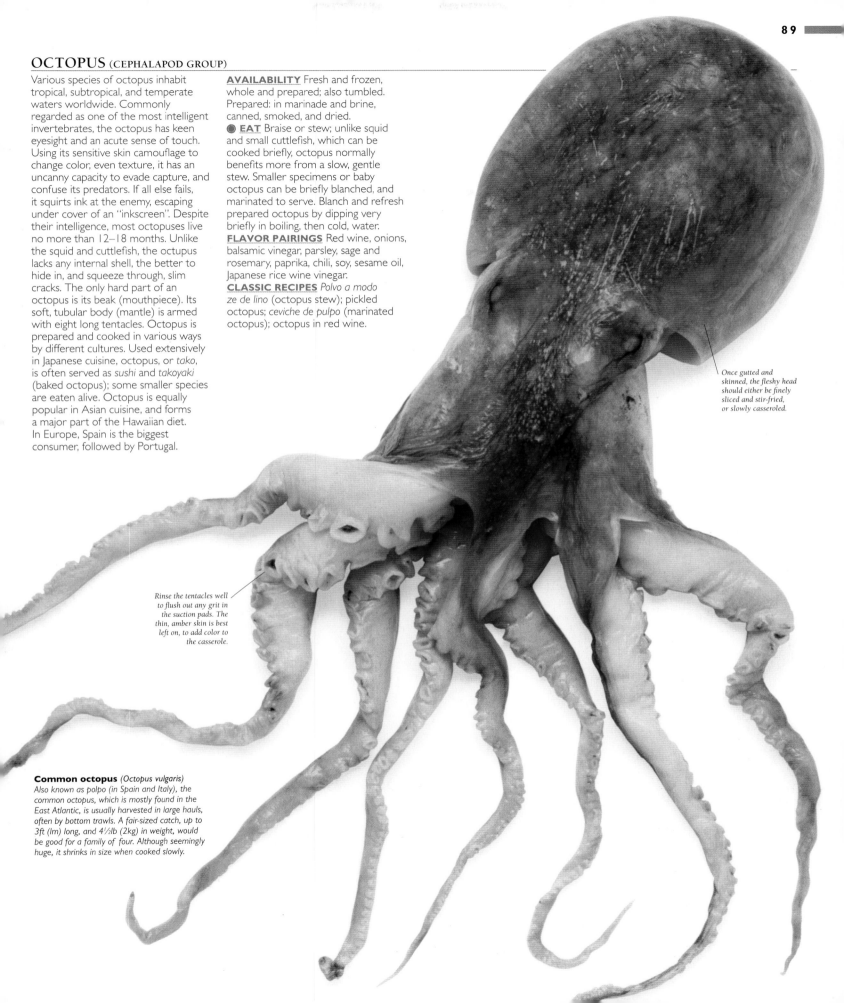

OCTOPUS (CEPHALAPOD GROUP)

Various species of octopus inhabit tropical, subtropical, and temperate waters worldwide. Commonly regarded as one of the most intelligent invertebrates, the octopus has keen eyesight and an acute sense of touch. Using its sensitive skin camouflage to change color, even texture, it has an uncanny capacity to evade capture, and confuse its predators. If all else fails, it squirts ink at the enemy, escaping under cover of an "inkscreen". Despite their intelligence, most octopuses live no more than 12–18 months. Unlike the squid and cuttlefish, the octopus lacks any internal shell, the better to hide in, and squeeze through, slim cracks. The only hard part of an octopus is its beak (mouthpiece). Its soft, tubular body (mantle) is armed with eight long tentacles. Octopus is prepared and cooked in various ways by different cultures. Used extensively in Japanese cuisine, octopus, or *tako*, is often served as *sushi* and *takoyaki* (baked octopus); some smaller species are eaten alive. Octopus is equally popular in Asian cuisine, and forms a major part of the Hawaiian diet. In Europe, Spain is the biggest consumer, followed by Portugal.

AVAILABILITY Fresh and frozen, whole and prepared; also tumbled. Prepared: in marinade and brine, canned, smoked, and dried.
● **EAT** Braise or stew; unlike squid and small cuttlefish, which can be cooked briefly, octopus normally benefits more from a slow, gentle stew. Smaller specimens or baby octopus can be briefly blanched, and marinated to serve. Blanch and refresh prepared octopus by dipping very briefly in boiling, then cold, water.
FLAVOR PAIRINGS Red wine, onions, balsamic vinegar, parsley, sage and rosemary, paprika, chili, soy, sesame oil, Japanese rice wine vinegar.
CLASSIC RECIPES *Polvo a modo ze de lino* (octopus stew); pickled octopus; *ceviche de pulpo* (marinated octopus); octopus in red wine.

Once gutted and skinned, the fleshy head should either be finely sliced and stir-fried, or slowly casseroled.

Rinse the tentacles well to flush out any grit in the suction pads. The thin, amber skin is best left on, to add color to the casserole.

Common octopus *(Octopus vulgaris)*
Also known as polpo (in Spain and Italy), the common octopus, which is mostly found in the East Atlantic, is usually harvested in large hauls, often by bottom trawls. A fair-sized catch, up to 3ft (1m) long, and 4½lb (2kg) in weight, would be good for a family of four. Although seemingly huge, it shrinks in size when cooked slowly.

CUTTLEFISH (CEPHALOPOD GROUP)

Popularly nicknamed "ink fish" for its ability to squirt ink at its enemies, the cuttlefish is often the tastiest but quite possibly the least appreciated member of the cephalopod group. Various species thrive in the depths of the world's oceans, except for North American waters. Cuttlefish are caught for their internal shell (cuttlebone) and the copious ink they produce to confuse their predators. The ink is harvested and pasteurized for commercial use, for dying pasta black, and for cooking: typically, risotto nero. Cuttlefish are mostly caught by trawl, and also as bait for recreational fishing. With a wonderfully sweet, seafood taste and firm, meaty texture, cuttlefish is enjoyed as a delicacy in many countries. If pan-fried for more than a minute, though, it will toughen and lose its translucency. The fish is particularly prized in the cuisines of China, Japan, Korea, Spain, and Italy.
AVAILABILITY Whole: unprepared. **Frozen:** ink and shell sold separately. **Preserved:** dried.
● **EAT** The head can be thinly sliced and pan-fried, deep-fried, or baked. The eight legs and two tentacles are best braised or stewed slowly.

CLASSIC RECIPES Risotto nero; chile cuttlefish; *soupies krasates* (cuttlefish in wine); Tuscan cuttlefish salad.

Peel away the outer membrane to reveal the tough, pure white body beneath.

The frilly fins of the cuttlefish peel away with the flesh. They give shellfish stock a wonderful flavor.

SEA CUCUMBER (STICHOPODIDAE)

Although commonly found in the world's oceans, sea cucumbers are something of an acquired taste, with a rather salty, savory flavor, and chewy, gelatinous texture. Reflecting their nickname "sea-slug," they shuffle slowly across the sea floor, scavenging for food. After being caught, the fish are gutted, boiled, salted, and dried, for long-term storage. To prepare, rehydrate the fish by soaking in water, and tenderize with extensive simmering. In China, the fish is a delicacy, slowly braised in rice wine and ginger. Sea cucumbers are also popular in the Philippines and parts of Europe, especially Barcelona, but they have been overfished in the Mediterranean and other seas.
AVAILABILITY Whole, usually dried.
● **EAT** Cooked: soak and simmer, or braise.
CLASSIC RECIPES Braised sea cucumber with mushrooms; braised *espardenyes*.

The skin is removed, since it is tough and rubbery. The flesh is either dried or braised from fresh.

Sea cucumber *(Stichopus regalis)* Enjoyed for centuries by fishermen, it is prized as a delicacy, eaten fresh in Japan and dried in China. Typically sluglike in shape, sloth, and size, it grows up to 8in (20cm) long.

SEA URCHIN (ECHINOIDAE)

Prickly and uninviting, sea urchins thrive on the ocean floor. More than 500 species exist, most edible. Sea urchins feature in Japanese, Italian, Spanish, and classic French cuisine. In some cultures, especially Japan and the Mediterranean, sea urchins are popular as a delicacy, which has led to overfishing. The edible part of the urchin is its roe, which needs to be carefully extracted. The entrance into a sea urchin is on its underside, through its mouth, which can be opened with a knife. First, the viscera should be removed; then the creamy orange roe (attached to the top of the shell), can be scooped out with a spoon. The resulting treat is small and relatively expensive, but offers an intense, creamy taste, much like seaweed. In Japan the urchins, or *uni*, are eaten fresh with sushi and fermented to form sea urchin paste.
AVAILABILITY Whole and, in some countries, extracted from the shell.
● **EAT** Usually raw, although they do add flavor to a creamy fish sauce.
FLAVOR PAIRINGS Lemon, seasoning.
CLASSIC RECIPES *Linguine con ricci di mare*; sea urchin omelet.

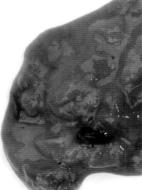

To avoid the spines, either split the urchin in half, or cut out the central beak and scoop out the middle with a teaspoon.

Sea urchin *(Echinus esculentus)* Globular, pink, and spiked, the common sea urchin found in shallow waters off the British Isles can grow up to 6in (15cm) long. Sea urchins are a challenge to prepare, but the resulting seaweed flavor is strong and creamy—never pungent or fishy.

Common cuttlefish (Sepia officinalis)
Native to the East Atlantic and Mediterranean, it is one of the largest cuttlefish, at about 16in (40cm) long. The tough tentacles need to be tenderized in a slow-cooked stew or braised.

GOOSE BARNACLE (POLLICEPES CORNUCOPIA)

The goose barnacle takes its striking name from its long gooselike neck. Like other crustaceans, it lives attached to exposed rocks in many coastal waters, except in the Arctic. Barnacle meat comes from the creature's soft protruding body, covered in thick skin. Before cooking, the tough skin needs to be removed with the help of a nail; or it can be peeled away after cooking. The barnacle has a sweet seafood taste much like crab and crayfish. Cooked to perfection, it is succulent and tender; if overcooked, it is tough and rubbery. In Portugal and Spain, goose barnacle is prized as the iconic delicacy *percebes*.
AVAILABILITY Usually whole.
● **EAT** Steamed or poached; only 2–3 minutes in boiling salted water with a bay leaf and lemon.

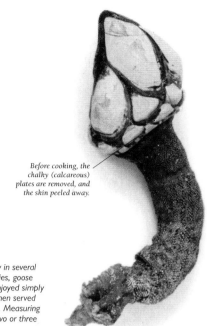

Before cooking, the chalky (calcareous) plates are removed, and the skin peeled away.

Goose barnacle
A sought-after delicacy in several Mediterranean countries, goose barnacles are often enjoyed simply steamed over stock, then served straight from the shell. Measuring about 10in (25cm), two or three make a good portion.

FROGS' LEGS (RANIDAE)

For centuries, frogs' legs have been associated with both French and Italian cuisine. In France, they were served as a meat-free treat during Lent. The frogs originally used were found in the wilds and wetlands of France, but recent commercial production has led to overuse. The species is now endangered and is protected in France. The frogs used in today's European and Asian cuisines come instead from Southeast Asia and the Americas, although concern is growing about possible overuse. The best legs are plump, about 2½in (6cm), with the texture of chicken wings, but the subtle flavor of fish.
AVAILABILITY Usually just the legs.
● **EAT** Pan-fried in lemon, garlic, and parsley in France; used in various traditional Lombard recipes in Italy.
CLASSIC RECIPES *Congee* (frogs' leg rice); *swikee* (frogs' leg soup).

The tiny morsel of flesh attached to frogs' leg bones needs to be carefully stripped off.

SNAILS (HELIX ASPERSA)

A huge variety of snails of varying sizes exist worldwide, but it is the common French garden snail (*Helix aspersa*) that is popularly eaten as *escargot* in France. Snails were originally served during Lent, but have become a traditional New Year's treat. The French manage to consume several tons per annum. It is not just in France that snails are popular, but also in Spain, where they feature in traditional recipes, such as paella (rice and seafood). Originally, wild snails would have been gathered, but these, like the frogs of French marshlands (above), have been overexploited. Instead, snails today are often imported, to be served up as a classic French dish on many a bistro table. Preparation is quite arduous. Once gathered, the snails require a period of purging to rid them of grit. This is usually achieved by withholding food for a few days. The snails are then soaked in water, blanched, and simmered. For serving, they are usually removed from the shell and arranged in a specific dish, then cooked in garlic butter. They have a rubbery, slightly gritty texture, with a vaguely savory, salty taste.
AVAILABILITY Usually preprepared and vacuum-packed in the shell, with garlic and herb butter.
● **EAT** Baked.
CLASSIC RECIPES Snails in garlic butter; *polentone con lumache* (snails with polenta).

Sea urchin roe
Prized out of its prickly shell, sea urchin roe is often enjoyed raw, but is equally delicious cooked. Add it to a cream, white wine and fish stock for the perfect addition to pan-fried fish, such as turbot.

The boiled snails are packed with garlic and herb butter to bake, then often served hot in the shell.

A stand-alone delicacy, sea urchin roe (or "tongues") is often served raw, straight from the shell. They have a umami (essence of loveliness in Japanese) that is delicately salty and rich.

CLASSIC RECIPE

SNAILS IN GARLIC BUTTER

Escargot de Bourgogne (Burgundy snails), made with big, meaty garden snails, are a classic French delicacy.

SERVES 2

4 tbsp butter, softened
2 garlic cloves, crushed
1 tbsp chopped parsley
squeeze of fresh lemon juice
salt and freshly ground black pepper
1 x 14oz (410g) can escargots with shells

1 Make the garlic butter: combine the butter, garlic, and parsley in a food processor, and process to form a green butter. Add lemon juice and seasoning to taste.

2 Drain the snails of any juice. Pack some garlic butter into each shell; place a snail on top. Press more butter on top of the snails so that they are tightly packed inside the shells. The snails should not be visible, but fully covered in butter. Chill until ready to bake.

3 Preheat the oven to 375°F (190°C). Arrange the snail shells in a snail plate that supports the shell, or lay them out in a small baking dish, ensuring that the shells cannot tip over.

4 Bake in the oven for 15 minutes until the butter has melted and the snails are piping hot. Serve with plenty of baguette.

HOT-SMOKED FISH

Hot-smoking is a technique of preservation in which fish or seafood is brined or salted for a short period, allowed to dry briefly, then smoked and cooked in a temperature-controlled kiln. An initial smoking takes place at a low temperature; the duration of this phase is dictated by the producer and the type of fish. Once the fish is impregnated with smoke, it is smoked for a second time at a higher temperature, which cooks the fish. Fish that are often treated in this way include mackerel, trout, and salmon, and shellfish including mussels and oysters. Hot-smoked fish has a lightly salted, densely smoked flavor, an opaque appearance, and a moist texture. Although products will keep for a number of days, hot-smoked fish generally has a shorter shelf life than cold smoked fish.

🔒 **BUY** Choose fish that is moist, but not slimy, and has a strong, but pleasant aroma.

🗄 **STORE** Keep refrigerated, but not directly over ice. The salt added during the smoking process automatically gives the fish a slightly extended shelf life.

⬤ **EAT** Hot-smoked products can be eaten right away or added to other dishes. Because they have already been cooked, care needs to be taken when reheating them or adding them to a hot dish. Serve them piping hot, but do not overheat, since this will toughen and change the texture.

FLAVOR PAIRINGS Horseradish, cream and crème fraîche, honey, soy sauce, sesame oil, dill, cilantro.

CLASSIC RECIPES Beef and smoked oyster pie; smoked mackerel pâté; smoked eel with beet and potato salad; smoked mackerel fish cakes.

Remove the sprat's head and peel away its skin to reveal a fillet with an excellent flavor.

Smoked sprats
A popular treat and delicacy in Germany, Sweden, Poland, Estonia, Finland, and Russia, smoked sprats are also known universally by their Swedish name of brisling. They are smoked whole and, because of their soft bones, usually eaten whole—diehard fans may eat the head, too. The smoking process dries them somewhat and gives a robust flavor.

Arbroath smokie
(hot-smoked haddock)
A product from Arbroath in Scotland. Gutted small haddock, heads removed, are tied into pairs at the tail using locally sourced jute, dry-salted for an hour, and then densely smoked. Served as they are, or used in mousses and smoked haddock pâté. Arbroath smokies have an intense flavor.

The salting process makes the texture of the herring quite dry.

Smoked mussels
The mussels are cooked, brined, and hot-smoked. Delicious as an addition to a seafood platter, or tossed into a salad. Smoked mussels are firm, sweet, and tasty. They are available freshly smoked, or canned in oil.

The process of smoking mussels gives them a firm, meaty texture and robust flavor.

Smoked eel
Firm and slightly rubbery, smoked eel is considered a delicacy, particularly in the Netherlands, so it is expensive. European and New Zealand eels are cleaned, dry-salted, and hot-smoked. The smoke cuts through the fish's oily texture.

Smoked oysters
Firm and verging on tough, brined and cooked oysters are kiln-smoked for this specialty, which is popular in Asian cooking. Most are canned in oil; also available freshly smoked or vacuum-packed. The smoking process masks a lot of their natural taste. Use in beef and smoked oyster pie, or blend with cream cheese for a dip.

Kiln-roasted salmon
The advantage of hot-smoking is that the "greasiness" associated with some cold-smoked fish is lost. Kiln-roasted salmon is excellent eaten cold, forked into salads, or substituted for cold-smoked salmon in recipes. It can also be heated and tossed into pasta and rice dishes.

Kiln-roasted salmon is usually smoked in steaks (cold-smoked salmon is smoked as a side).

The skin of smoked mackerel peels away very easily.

Smoked mackerel
Mackerel's oil-rich flesh lends itself to hot-smoking. Whole gutted fish and fillets are used. Smoked mackerel is available dyed and undyed, and as fillets encrusted in pepper or other toppings. Smoked mackerel work well with a spicy relish, or combined with creamed horseradish. Some of the best smoked mackerel comes from the UK, where Scottish-caught mackerel, which tends to have a high oil content, is used.

Smoked trout has a robust flavor and flakes easily.

Buckling
This is a herring, sometimes gutted, with the head removed. It is dry-salted for a few hours, then hot-smoked in very dense smoke for a few hours. The result is dry, salty, and smoke-flavored with an intensely fishy taste.

Smoked trout
Hot-smoking is an effective way of cooking many oil-rich species. It reduces some of the earthiness of the fish, particularly trout. You can buy it whole or as a fillet.

COLD-SMOKED FISH

This method of smoking fish takes place over a period of days. The fish is brined, and a relatively heavy salt solution is used in order to extract as much moisture from the fish as possible. Temperature is crucial: the product should not reach more than 85°F (30°C), so as not to cook the flesh or encourage bacterial growth. The fish is smoked for between 1 and 5 days, the flavor becoming richer and more intense as time goes on. Some cold-smoked fish may then be cooked (such as smoked haddock, cod, and pollack). As cold-smoked fish is essentially raw, fish that is not going to be cooked is frozen at 64°F (18°C) for around 24 hours to destroy parasites that may be present in the fish (this is a legal requirement in some countries). The flavor of smoked fish depends on how long a fish is left salted, and how long it is in the smokehouse. The taste of many fish—such as oily fish—is enhanced by smoking.

🔒 **BUY** Pick fish that looks dry, glossy, and smells smoked but not too strong.

📦 **STORE** Smoked products have a slightly longer shelf life than fresh fish.

They are never placed directly on ice, as with fresh fish, but must be chilled in the refrigerator.

● **EAT** Smoked salmon and more artisanal products (such as smoked swordfish, grouper, and tuna) can simply be sliced and served with a squeeze of lemon juice and bread, or added to more complex dishes.

FLAVOR PAIRINGS Citrus, horseradish, delicate herbs including dill and parsley.

CLASSIC RECIPES Finnan haddock with poached egg; smoked salmon with capers; kedgeree; Cullen skink.

CLASSIC RECIPE

CULLEN SKINK

Cullen Skink is named after Cullen, in northeast Scotland. "Skink" is the regional name for soup or stew. This recipe is traditionally made with Finnan haddock.

SERVES 4

2 whole finnan haddie (finnan haddock) or 4 small smoked haddock fillets

1 onion, finely chopped

1 cup whole milk

1 large russet (8oz/225g) or other floury potato, boiled, peeled, and mashed with 2 tbsp butter

salt and freshly ground black pepper

1 Put the fish into a large sauté pan. Pour in 1 cup of water and add the onion. Poach the fish for 8–10 minutes, or until opaque. Lift the fish on to a plate and pull away the flakes of flesh. Set aside. Return the bones to the water and continue to cook for another 15 minutes. Strain the stock into a container. Recover as much of the onion as possible from the sieve, and stir in the strained stock, then stir in the milk.

2 Return the stock mixture to the pan and whisk in the mashed potato to form a thick, creamy soup. Season to taste and add the flaked fish. Serve at once.

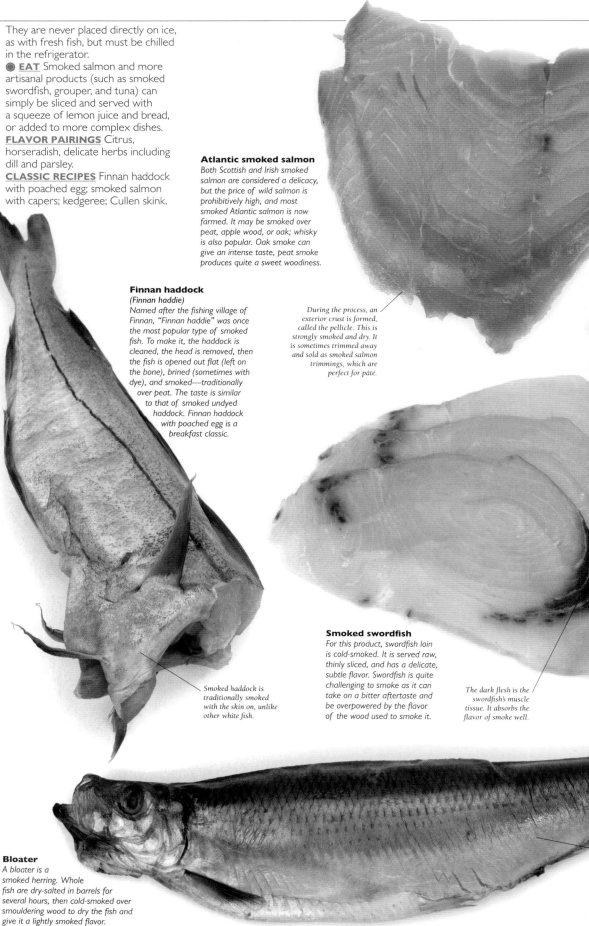

Atlantic smoked salmon
Both Scottish and Irish smoked salmon are considered a delicacy, but the price of wild salmon is prohibitively high, and most smoked Atlantic salmon is now farmed. It may be smoked over peat, apple wood, or oak; whisky is also popular. Oak smoke can give an intense taste, peat smoke produces quite a sweet woodiness.

During the process, an exterior crust is formed, called the pellicle. This is strongly smoked and dry. It is sometimes trimmed away and sold as smoked salmon trimmings, which are perfect for pâté.

Finnan haddock
(Finnan haddie)
Named after the fishing village of Finnan, "Finnan haddie" was once the most popular type of smoked fish. To make it, the haddock is cleaned, the head is removed, then the fish is opened out flat (left on the bone), brined (sometimes with dye), and smoked—traditionally over peat. The taste is similar to that of smoked undyed haddock. Finnan haddock with poached egg is a breakfast classic.

Smoked haddock is traditionally smoked with the skin on, unlike other white fish.

Smoked swordfish
For this product, swordfish loin is cold-smoked. It is served raw, thinly sliced, and has a delicate, subtle flavor. Swordfish is quite challenging to smoke as it can take on a bitter aftertaste and be overpowered by the flavor of the wood used to smoke it.

The dark flesh is the swordfish's muscle tissue. It absorbs the flavor of smoke well.

Bloater
A bloater is a smoked herring. Whole fish are dry-salted in barrels for several hours, then cold-smoked over smouldering wood to dry the fish and give it a lightly smoked flavor.

Dyed haddock fillets are excellent for kedgeree, as their color shows up well against the white rice.

Smoked haddock fillets
Dyed fillets (soaked in brine colored with tartrazine) and undyed fillets are available. A natural dye made with turmeric and annatto powder is now used by some producers. Dyed haddock can be slightly saltier than undyed, but this depends on the producer. Haddock is a sweet fish and smoking suits it well. Best poached in milk to draw out excess saltiness.

Undyed haddock is a pale straw color; avoid fish that has pink flesh and looks wet: this is a sign of deterioration.

Smoked halibut is best sliced thinly, as the fish has a slightly dry and firm-textured flesh.

The bloater's skin is easily pulled off to reveal the ready-to-eat flesh under the skin.

Traditionally, kipper is split down the back and smoked on the bone, but it is also available as a fillet.

Kipper
A kipper is a cold-smoked herring. It is split down the back and cleaned, brined, sometimes dyed, then smoked over sawdust fires. English herrings are often considered the best species of herring for smoking; Manx kippers are particularly fine. Kippers can be grilled or jugged (boiling water poured over the fish and left to stand). Kippers have a dense, intensely salty, sweet, and smoky taste—but it varies according to producer.

Smoked halibut
Halibut has a delicate taste and the process of smoking it can overpower the natural flavor of the fish. Smoked halibut is available as a fillet or sliced. Serve the raw slices with a simple garnish of dill and a wedge of lemon.

CLASSIC RECIPE

KEDGEREE

This classic Anglo-Indian recipe became a popular breakfast dish in Victorian times. It is widely considered to be Indian in origin.

SERVES 4

1 cup long gran or basmati white rice
salt and freshly ground black pepper
4 tbsp butter
1 onion, finely chopped
1 tsp Madras curry powder
8oz (225g) cooked smoked haddock, flaked with a fork
1 tbsp chopped parsley (optional)
2 hard-boiled eggs, peeled and quartered

1 Fill a large saucepan two-thirds full of water. Bring water to a boil over high heat, add ½ tsp salt; add the rice. Boil until the rice is just tender, about 10 minutes. Drain and rinse with cold water.

2 Melt the butter in the same pan. Add the onion and cook over low heat until soft and translucent. Add the curry powder and stir for 1 minute.

3 Add the rice and smoked haddock, increase the heat and toss over the heat until piping hot. Season with salt and pepper; stir in the parsley. Arrange the eggs on top and heat. Serve at once.

SALTED FISH AND DRIED FISH

The earliest form of preservation was to dry fish in the sun and wind. Other fish were preserved in brine or dry-salted. In the Mediterranean, eels, anchovies, sardines, herring, tuna, and roe were commonly salted. One of the earliest dried and salted fish, cod, was caught by boats that traveled long distances to fish it. The cod was cleaned, air-dried, and packed in brine or salt for the voyage home. The process of salting fish is influenced by the weather, the size and species of fish, and the quality of the salt used. The fish must be completely saturated with salt, or "struck through," to make sure that it will be safe to eat. There are two methods of salting—placing the fish directly in a brine or packing it in salt, which in turn creates its own brine as moisture is drawn from the fish. The amount of salt used differs from one fish and product to another. Fish may also be dried to remove moisture content but left unsalted. Stockfish is unsalted fish, usually cod, which is dried by the sun and wind on wooden racks, or in specially adapted drying houses. Other species of white fish, including ling, tusk, gray mullet, bonito, and saithe are dried, as are some shellfish, such as cuttlefish, squid, oysters, shrimp, and scallops. Some salted and dried fish are rehydrated, by soaking in several changes of water, to draw out as much of the salt as possible, and then cooked as a fresh fish (the flavor is more intense than that of a fresh fish and a gentle, lingering saltiness is evident). Some dried fish, such as Bombay duck and cuttlefish, are served dried.

CUTS Whole (gutted), split whole fish on the bone, shredded fish strips.

● **EAT** Try poaching, pan-frying, or broiling salted and dried fish.

FLAVOR PAIRINGS Olive oil, garlic, orange, capers, onion, parsley, milk, coconut.

CLASSIC RECIPES Salt fish and achee; salt fish cakes; *bacalao*; *brandade*.

Salted anchovies
One of the most popular salted fish, anchovies are also brined. Intensely salty, they are often used to top pizzas or garnish Mediterranean dishes such as salade Niçoise. They can be soaked briefly in milk before use to remove some of the saltiness; this softens and rounds the flavor.

Matjes herrings are usually eaten whole and unadorned, or simply with bread. They have a sweet, intense flavor.

Dried tuna loin
Mosciame del tonno is a delicacy in Italy and Spain (where it is called mojama). Strips of tuna loin are salted and sun-dried, to make a firm slab that resembles a dried meat. It has a rich, meaty flavor and may be grated to add to pasta or salads.

Dried tuna loin is firm and dry, and best shaved or grated. It has a strong flavor and only a little is needed to flavor a dish.

Salt mackerel is available both as whole gutted and salted fish and as fillets.

Maatjes herring
Hailing from Amsterdam, maatjes herring is also known as virgin herring, since it is made from young fish that have not produced roe. The fish, caught around Norway and Denmark, are soused (soaked in a mild brine). They are only partly gutted, as the offal is key to the success of the curing process. A similar product from Germany is made using more intense brine.

Bombay duck
The small bummaloe fish is native to Southeast Asia. It is eaten fresh in India, where it is usually fried to serve as a side dish. It may also be dried in strips and called Bombay duck. It has a strong, aromatic, fishy flavor.

Bombay duck is served in its dried state as an appetizer. It has a strong, hearty taste.

Dried shrimp

Unshelled shrimp, lightly salted and dried, are used extensively in China, Southeast Asia, and parts of Africa. They are usually added to a dish to give it a depth of flavor.

Dried shrimp have a distinctive smell that is strongly seafoodlike and also sweet. Soak prior to use, or use dry as a seasoning.

Dried scallops

Dried scallops are used extensively in the cuisine of the Far East; one popular recipe is as part of a spicy chile salsa. Used whole or grated, they add a dynamic seafood flavor and a certain sweetness to a dish.

Dried scallops have a strong flavor and very dry texture. Use dry or soak in water to rehydrate.

Salt pollock

Alaskan pollock is abundant; salted pollock is popular in the Far East and Caribbean. It requires lengthy soaking before use; excellent poached or used in fishcakes. It has a milder flavor than salt cod. Good with spices and mashed potato.

Salt pollock is usually sold as a fillet or in strips, often ready pin-boned.

Salt mackerel

This product is popular in the Far East, particularly in Korea. The fish must be soaked in cold water overnight before use. Poach for about 30 minutes and use for pâté or salad; it is also good pan-fried. After soaking, the fish still has a strong salty taste, and the flesh is a little fibrous.

Salt cod

Dried unsalted cod is called stockfish and used in several countries in soup and as an additional ingredient. Salt cod is prepared in Scandinavia, and is also a speciality in Portugal, exported globally. It requires 36–48 hours of soaking, in several changes of water, prior to use. A salty taste is present once cooked, and the flavor is strong and almost meaty, with little comparison to fresh cod.

Salt cod is sold as whole split fish, fillets, loins, and in strips. Strips are quickest to use.

CLASSIC RECIPE

BRANDADE DE MORUE

This dish of creamed salt cod is popular in Mediterranean countries, particularly in the South of France.

SERVES 4

1lb (450g) salt cod
2 garlic cloves, crushed
¾ cup olive oil
½ cup whole milk, brought to a boil and then allowed to cool

To serve

2 tbsp chopped flat-leaf parsley
olive oil, to drizzle
freshly ground black pepper
sliced bread, cut into triangles and fried in olive oil
black olives

1 Soak the fish in a bowl of cold water for 24 hours, changing the water three or four times during this period.

2 Drain the cod and place in a large, shallow pan, then cover it with cold water and bring to a gentle simmer. Cook for 10 minutes, then remove the pan from the heat and leave the cod to sit in the water for another 10 minutes before draining.

3 Remove the skin and bones from the fish, then flake the flesh into a bowl and pound to a paste with the garlic.

4 Put the fish paste in a pan over low heat. Gradually beat in enough olive oil and milk, a little at a time, to make a creamy white mixture that still holds its shape. Serve hot, sprinkled with chopped parsley, drizzled with olive oil, and seasoned with black pepper, alongside fried bread triangles and black olives.

FISH ROE

Although the roe of both male and female fish is edible, it is the "hard" roe, or eggs, of the female fish that has traditionally gained extraordinary heights as a delicacy, and often fetches a premium price. The milt or "soft" roe is the soft male roe or sperm of some species, particularly herring, and it is also sometimes valued as a delicacy, especially in Europe. Several species of fish produce excellent "hard" and "soft" roe, whether for use as a garnish or stand-alone *hors-d'oeuvre*, and many countries favor specific varieties. In Japan, *kazunoko*, the salted eggs of herring, are most popular. In Southeast Asia, a particular favorite is crab roe, harvested from female mud crabs. In Europe, "caviare" originally the name for the eggs of sturgeon, has long been prized. Traditionally the three most celebrated sturgeon caviars—beluga, oscietra and sevruga—were processed by the Russians and Iranians. But the popularity of sturgeon roe has led to overexploitation, with many species now almost extinct. As an alternative, sturgeon are now being farmed in France. Methods of preparation vary.

With most "caviar-type" products, the female roe is harvested, rinsed to remove the egg membrane, lightly salted, drained of excess liquid, then packed; many are also pasteurized to extend their shelf life by a few months. Caviar substitutes treated in a similar way include the roe of Pacific salmon (or keta), Atlantic salmon, salmon trout, trout, lumpfish, capelin, carp (or icre), and flying fish. Non-caviar roes are sold either fresh or preserved, whether salted and dried, or smoked. Most eggs are soft and translucent, with a salty taste and grainy texture.

AVAILABILITY Caviars: fresh and pasteurized. Other roes: fresh, salted, smoked.

● EAT Usually raw, except for fresh cod and haddock roes, and herring milt, which is served cooked.

FLAVOR PAIRINGS Caviars: melba toast, chopped egg white, chopped onion, parsley. Soft herring roes: butter, capers, lemon. Smoked roe: olive oil, garlic, lemon.

CLASSIC RECIPES *Taramasalata*; caviar with scrambled eggs; grated bottarga with truffle oil and linguine.

ALTERNATIVES Icre, herring roe, keta, and farmed sturgeon roe.

Sevruga caviar *After beluga and oscietra, sevruga ranks third in the line-up of popular sturgeon caviars. Of the three, sevruga eggs are the least expensive and most readily available, since the fish matures relatively early at 7 years old. Although small, the eggs are a rich metallic gray, with an intense flavor, often preferred to that of beluga or oscietra.*

Salted herring roe
A popular alternative to caviar, lightly salted herring roe is marketed under various names. It is better than lumpfish roe, as it does not run color, making it ideal as a canapé topping.

Salted herring roe has a delicate fish taste with a slightly lemony tang, and a hint of salt.

"Soft" herring roe is at its very best dipped in seasoned flour, pan-fried in butter and served with a splash of lemon. It has a rich, creamy taste.

Bottarga makes a perfect appetizer, served thinly shaved with a splash of lemon.

Bottarga di muggine
(huevas de mujol or poutargue)
The amber-colored eggs of gray mullet, sometimes called the "poor man's caviar", are a Mediterranean delicacy. Traditionally, the eggs are washed, salted, pressed, and sun-dried, then dipped in beeswax to hold their flavor. To serve, the roe can be thinly sliced, or freshly grated and tossed into pasta (but not cooked).

Herring roe *Marketed under a variety of names, female herring roe is now readily available and sold as a low-cost alternative to other caviars. It competes on the market with lumpfish roe, but is unlikely to be dyed, making it ideal as a garnish. Kazunoko, a salted variety, is a Japanese delicacy.*

Beluga caviar *Illegal in some countries, beluga is considered the grandest of caviars. The beluga (Huso huso) sturgeon is the biggest of the family and known to live for up to 20 years. The eggs are large, soft, and smoky gray in color. One of the most expensive caviars, it is traditionally served with a round-edge, mother-of-pearl spoon, to protect the eggs.*

Pan-fry the eggs of "hard" herring roe for a subtle flavor and firm, crunchy texture.

Keta *Large, translucent, and bright orange, keta eggs come from the Pacific salmon keta (or chum). The roe makes an excellent garnish for canapés or sushi. Keta caviar is often used in small quantities, as the eggs, once broken, release a rich salmon-oil taste that is quite exceptional.*

Lumpfish roe *The small eggs of this unextraordinary fish are often dyed black or orange. As the eggs taste salty and textured, they are best suited as a garnish for blinis (pancakes) or cream cheese.*

The tiny eggs of the flying fish are crisp, with a shallow flavor and vibrant coloring.

Flying fish roe *(tobiko)*
The Japanese delicacy tobiko is fast gaining global recognition. A fine-grained, crunchy, textured roe, it is naturally golden. Although flying fish roe can serve as a stand-alone dish, it is most often used as a garnish to sushi. It can be dyed black with cuttlefish ink, or turned delicate green from wasabi horseradish.

The finest smoked cod's roe comes from Icelandic cod. Its thick skin binds the roe well during smoking.

Smoked cod's roe *A popular alternative to the fresh variety, the smoked roe of cod, ling, and gray mullet is mainly used for the Turkish and Greek dish taramasalata. The intensive process of salting and smoking gives this variety a particularly dense texture and rich flavor.*

Fresh cod's roe
Both the "hard" roe from cod and the much smaller eggs of haddock are popular in the northern hemisphere. The roe is first blanched to set it hard, then sliced, panéed with flour, egg, and crumb, before being deep fried. The smaller haddock eggs are simply rolled in seasoned flour and fried.

CLASSIC RECIPE

TARAMASALATA

Tarama is Turkish for the salted and dried roe of gray mullet that is traditionally used in this recipe.

SERVES 4–6

8oz (250g) piece smoked cod roe
juice of 1 lemon
½ cup fresh white breadcrumbs, soaked in 3 tbsp cold water
¼ cup extra virgin olive oil
1 small onion, grated and patted dry with paper towels
paprika, for garnish

1 Split the roe down the center using a sharp knife, and carefully peel away and discard the skin. Place the roe in a blender with the lemon juice and soaked breadcrumbs; blend well.

2 With the motor running, very slowly add the oil in a thin steady stream until the mixture resembles smooth mayonnaise.

3 Spoon into a small serving dish and stir in the onion. Cover and refrigerate for 30 minutes, then sprinkle with paprika before serving.

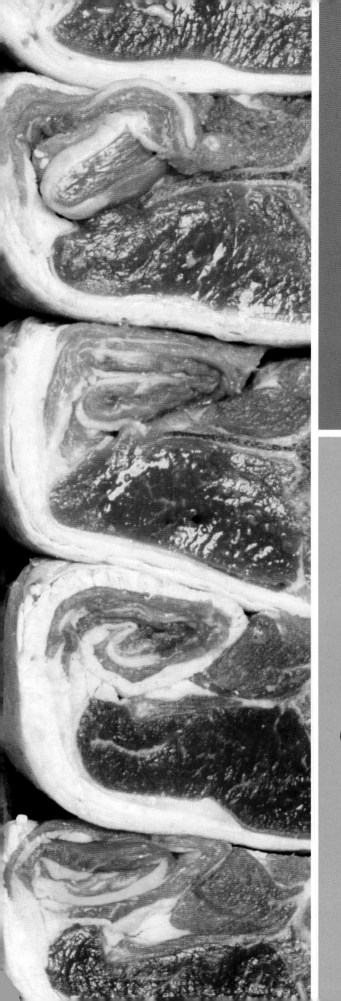

MEAT

BEEF | VEAL | PORK
LAMB | CHICKEN | TURKEY
DUCK | VENISON
RABBIT | GOOSE
LIVER | KIDNEY | HEART
CURED MEAT

MEAT ESSENTIALS

Meat is a good source of protein, vitamins, iron, and fat, and has always been a prestigious and celebratory food, in part due to the fact that it is a relatively expensive ingredient. Although some people avoid meat altogether, on the whole, more meat is being eaten now than ever before. However, we do now appreciate that smaller meat portions, combined with more vegetables, grains, and pulses, produce a healthier diet. Meat is generally younger and more tender than it used to be, and it is also often leaner. One drawback to breeding very lean animals is that it can make some meat dry and tasteless, and so, although it is advisable to remove large amounts of visible fat, the small amounts that flavor well-marbled meat so superbly are considered to be an acceptable part of a balanced diet. Regional variations in preparing and cooking meat are

enormous, but the qualities of each cut remain constant—some are most suitable for broiling or roasting, while others need slow, gently cooking to make them as tender and flavorsome as they can be.

Meat benefits *from cooking to tenderize it and to add flavor, and, more importantly, cooking also kills many harmful bacteria. Methods of cooking have evolved to suit particular cuts, and are designed to get the very best flavor and texture out of the meat. However, some meats, such as beef, can be eaten raw if they are of sufficiently good quality and flavor. These are most enjoyable when made easy to chew, by being prepared in thin slices, such as carpaccio, or finely ground or chopped, as in steak tartare.*

BUY

Good-quality meat should have little odor and the fat should look creamy (lamb and beef) or white (pork). Always use the cut most suited to your recipe.

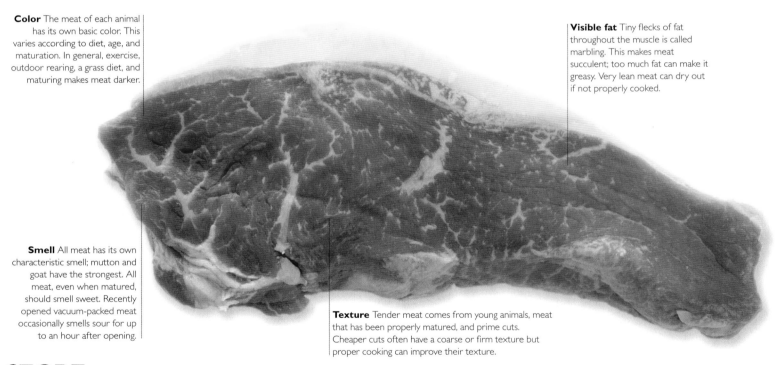

Color The meat of each animal has its own basic color. This varies according to diet, age, and maturation. In general, exercise, outdoor rearing, a grass diet, and maturing makes meat darker.

Visible fat Tiny flecks of fat throughout the muscle is called marbling. This makes meat succulent; too much fat can make it greasy. Very lean meat can dry out if not properly cooked.

Smell All meat has its own characteristic smell; mutton and goat have the strongest. All meat, even when matured, should smell sweet. Recently opened vacuum-packed meat occasionally smells sour for up to an hour after opening.

Texture Tender meat comes from young animals, meat that has been properly matured, and prime cuts. Cheaper cuts often have a coarse or firm texture but proper cooking can improve their texture.

STORE

Raw meat carries bacteria and must be stored carefully to prevent contamination. The most important consideration when storing meat is the temperature—meat should never be allowed to become too warm, or to sweat.

REFRIGERATE Domestic refrigerators should run between 32 and 41°F (0° and 5°C), which are safe temperatures in which to store meat. Remove meat from any packaging and place it in a container or on a plate and cover with a lid or plastic wrap. This prevents the meat from contaminating other products in the fridge and keeps flavors from being absorbed from other food. Store processed meat in the coldest part of the fridge. Cover and cool cooked leftovers before storing in the refrigerator, then use them within two days. Always store cooked meat above, not below, raw meat to prevent contamination.

FREEZE If meat is kept frozen and airtight it can be stored for years in the freezer without becoming harmful. However, some meat and meat products (especially fat or cooked meats) will deteriorate over time, leading to loss of flavor or texture, and so are less enjoyable. In these cases a few months of freezer life is advised. Always freeze meat before its use-by date; exclude all air, and wrap it thickly to avoid "freezer burn," which tastes unpleasant. Thaw meat in a dish in the refrigerator to prevent liquid from contaminating surfaces or other food. Make sure meat is completely defrosted before cooking.

PREPARE

Farm animals offer us a variety of meats; each of these produces both tough and tender cuts, and also fatty and lean cuts. All of these can be delicious, depending on how we butcher, cut, cook, and carve it. The amount of preparation required for cooking meat will vary, depending on the intended use of the meat and also the cut—for example, whether it is on or off the bone, or particularly fatty.

CUT Meat is made of fibers that give it a "grain". When meat is cooked, the fibers toughen. Correct cutting is important, since some meat can feel tough and stringy if it has been sliced in the wrong direction. If meat is sliced across the grain, it shortens the fibers, making it feel more tender. This is important when carving roast meat. Some meat is naturally tender, so it can be sliced with the grain, which is easier to do. Cutting into cubes—both across and with the grain—results in quick-cooking pieces.

Cut across the grain

Coarse-grained cuts, like this brisket, are often used in stews and casseroles, and need to be cut across the grain to keep them tender and palatable. Trim off the fat, then cut at right angles to the direction of the grain.

Cut with the grain

Prime cuts, like this fillet, are so tender that the direction of slicing is less important. If stir-fry strips are required, then cutting with the grain is advisable. This is not recommended for tougher cuts except when dicing.

Cube fillet steak

For cubes, cut fillet steak across the grain into pieces, then cut each piece into slices against the grain. Lay the slices flat, then cut into manageable cubes. Cubes cook quickly and are ideal for sautéing.

SCORE PORK SKIN There are four simple steps to getting crisp crackling: score the rind with a sharp knife, rub it with salt and oil, roast at a high temperature for 15 minutes, and then do not baste the joint for the rest of the cooking time.

Score the rind widthwise with a very sharp knife or a scalpel, keeping the lines parallel and close together. First work from the middle toward one edge, then turn the meat around and work from the middle toward the other edge. This is easier than scoring in a long line. Always tilt the knife blade away from your other hand and make sure the knife cannot slip toward your body.

Butterfly leg of lamb This is a leg that is boned so that the meat can be spread out in order to broil or barbecue it more quickly and evenly. The leg bones comprise the shank at the narrow end, and the thigh bone and pelvic bone at the meaty end. Take great care when cutting toward your fingers or body.

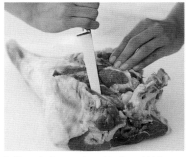

1 Place the leg meatiest side down. Holding the pelvic bone in one hand with the knife edge turned toward it, work the knife around the edge of the bone and pare away the meat.

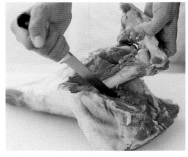

2 Once the thigh bone is exposed, cut down to the bone all the way to the knuckle side of the shank. Pull up the thigh bone and pare away the meat from all sides of the bone.

3 Once the whole thigh bone is completely exposed, pull it upward away from the shank and ease away the meat that is attached around the knuckle.

4 Pare away the meat from the shank bone (it is visible on one side) and work up toward the knuckle and thigh bone. Cut through any remaining sinews and remove all the bones.

5 Slash the thickest muscles so that all the meat is of an even thickness when laid on the work surface. Flatten out all the muscles until the meat piece is roughly square.

6 The butterflied leg is now ready for seasoning and broiling. If it is to be stuffed and rolled, cut slices off the thickest muscles and lay them in the thinnest parts to make the roll more even.

Marinades are great for flavoring meat such as beef and pork, and bringing it to life under the broiler or on the barbecue. Marinate the meat for 1–5 hours, depending on the type and density of the cut.

Asian marinade Whisk together 2 tbsp dark soy sauce, 1 tbsp Worcestershire sauce, a splash of mirin or dry sherry, 1–2 tsp Sichuan peppercorns, and a pinch each of grated fresh ginger and garlic. Add a splash of olive oil to thicken, then brush on the meat, covering it completely.

Mediterranean marinade Mix together 2 tbsp olive oil, 1 tbsp lemon juice, 1 tbsp red wine vinegar, a good pinch of oregano, a crushed garlic clove, and some salt and pepper. Brush on the meat, covering it completely.

COOK

High-temperature cooking (broiling, roasting, frying, stir-frying) uses tender cuts that are browned for flavor, cooked quickly, then removed from the heat before the inside becomes too hot. As meat heats up, it toughens and releases moisture; when it reaches 170°F (77°C) internally, the protein (blood) coagulates and loses moisture and further cooking makes the meat tougher and drier. So most fast-cooked meat benefits from being slightly undercooked, then rested to finish cooking. Slow cooking (stewing, pot-roasting, simmering) gradually softens the collagen (gristle) in tough cuts, to keep meat tender.

RESTING MEAT Fried, broiled, and roasted meat is more tender and succulent if it is slightly undercooked and left to rest. When the protein on the outside of the meat is fiercely heated it stiffens, pushing the juices toward the center. Resting meat allows the juices to be reabsorbed by the outer edge, while the heat is distributed toward the center, giving an evenly pink, moist slice. The meat continues to cook gently while it rests so the resting process finishes the cooking. The meat needs to be kept warm while it rests; also a warm plate is sufficient for steaks, small roasts should be covered with foil, medium joints need a cloth over the foil, while large joints, and pork with crisp skin are best rested uncovered in a very cool oven. Resting times depend on thickness: rest steaks for 5–10 minutes, joints for up to 40 minutes.

ROAST Joints of meat that are on the bone and have a covering of fat, such as a rib roast or the sirloin shown, need longer cooking than lean, boneless joints. For a beef joint, cook first at an oven temperature of 425°F (220°C) for 25 minutes to brown the meat, then roast at 375°F (190°C) for 15 minutes per 1lb (450g) for rare beef, 20 minutes per 1lb (450g) for medium, and 25 minutes per 1lb (450g) for well-done.

Roast sirloin

1 Place the joint, fat side uppermost, in a roasting pan. If lean, brush it with oil, melted dripping, or butter, but if there is a covering of fat, none is necessary. Put the pan in the oven.

2 Once cooked, transfer the meat to a carving board, cover loosely with foil and leave to rest for 15–30 minutes. Run a carving knife between the ribs and meat to separate them.

3 Discard the bones and set the meat fat side up. Cut downward, across the grain, into thin slices. Always use a guarded carving fork when carving toward your hand.

Roast leg of lamb

1 Preheat the oven to 400°F (200°C). Using a sharp knife, make deep slits over the joint 2in (5cm) apart. Press halved garlic cloves deep into the holes with some rosemary tips.

2 Brush the surface of the meat all over with oil or melted butter, season with black pepper and a little salt, and place the joint in a roasting pan.

3 Place the roasting pan in the middle of the oven and roast for 20 minutes per 1lb (450g) for rosy pink meat. Remove from the hot oven, cover with foil, and rest for 20–30 minutes.

4 To carve a leg, start by slicing across the grain in the center of the leg as shown. Cut even slices 1cm (½in) thick, working from the center to the edges.

Roast shoulder of pork

1 Score the skin with a very sharp knife across the grain of the meat. Make parallel cuts about ¼in (5mm) apart, cutting from the center right to the edge. Turn the joint around and score from the center to the other edge. Rub the skin thoroughly with salt and a little oil.

2 Put the joint on a rack in a roasting pan, and cook in a hot oven for 20-30 minutes, until the skin colors. Turn the oven down to 300°F (150°C) and roast for 1½ hours. Add some vegetables (onions, carrots, parsnips, lemons), to the pan. Cook for 1–2 hours more.

3 When the meat is cooked, lift it onto a carving board and rest in a warm place for 20 minutes. Remove and keep the roasted vegetables warm, too. Remove the crackling by slipping a knife just under the skin, leaving the fat on the joint.

4 Carve the meat into thick slices using a sharp carving knife, cutting downward across the grain. Cut the crackling into serving pieces with kitchen scissors and serve them with the pork on a dish with the roasted vegetables and some gravy.

FRY This cooking method is suitable for all steaks and chops. A hot, ridged griddle needs less fat than pan frying. The cooking time depends on the meat's thickness: very thin steaks of ¼in (5mm) need a very hot pan and no resting; thick steaks up to 1½in (3cm) need resting. If the meat is thicker than this, it is better oven-roasted.

1 *Heat the oil until starting to smoke, then lay the meat in the pan gently and leave to brown for 1–2 minutes. Turn and repeat.*

2 *Turn the meat and cook on the other side for 1–2 minutes. Thicker steaks may need to be cooked for 2–5 minutes more, or to taste.*

GRIDDLE A ridged cast-iron griddle pan mimics a barbecue by draining off fat and burning grid lines onto the meat. Use the technique shown below for both, though excess fat can flare on a barbecue.

Heat the griddle *on a high heat until smoking. Brush the meat with oil and cook for 1–2 minutes. Turn and repeat. Serve thin steaks at once. Turn thick steaks again, placing them at a 45° angle to create a pattern. Cook for 1–2 minutes more.*

RARE, MEDIUM, OR WELL-DONE? Knowing when meat is cooked perfectly takes practice, especially when everybody's idea of "done" is different. Looking at the color of the meat will help you to gauge doneness, however, as well as testing with your finger to judge "give."

Rare *has a 75 percent red center and is soft, with only a slight resistance.*

Medium *has a 25 percent pinkish-red center and feels fairly firm and springy.*

Well-done *is brown all through; it feels firm and springs back quickly.*

BROWN Meat is usually browned before stewing to give color and extra flavor to the sauce. Occasionally, a more delicate flavor and pale color is desired—when cooking veal, for example—then meat is simply cooked gently from raw without browning.

Cut the meat *into large chunks or slices if not being cooked whole. If you want thick gravy, roll the meat in flour before browning it. Heat some oil in a large pan and brown the meat all over; do not overcrowd the pan.*

BRAISE AND STEW Braising and stewing are slow-cooking methods that use liquids to keep the meat moist. They are excellent ways of using cheaper cuts of meat. Stewed meat is cut into smaller pieces and completely covered with liquid, while braised meat is cooked with less liquid in slices or as a whole joint.

1 *Cover the meat pieces with water, stock, wine, or another liquid. For a joint, add liquid one-third of the way up the meat.*

2 *During the cooking, check that the meat is not drying out and top up the pan with more liquid if necessary.*

3 *Add herbs, spices, and diced vegetables about 45 minutes before the end of the cooking so they will remain firm.*

MAKE STOCK Worth making in quantity and freezing, a rich stock makes many dishes, such as soups and casseroles. Meaty scraps and bones such as rib and backbone give flavor, while those with cartilage, such as knuckle bones, give a silky texture. Aim for a mixture.

1 *Brush the bones and meat trimmings with oil and place in a roasting pan. Add onions, carrots, and celery sticks, cut in quarters. Roast at 450°F (230°C) for 45 minutes.*

2 *Put everything into a stock pot, with some celery, a bay leaf, thyme, and rosemary. Cover the bones with hot water. Bring to a boil, cover the pot, then simmer for 1–2 hours.*

3 *Strain the stock through a fine sieve into a heatproof container. If completely clear stock is needed, strain again through a muslin cloth. Use immediately or freeze when cool.*

BEEF

Beef has always been a high prestige meat. Today's extensive production systems include cattle ranched in wild terrains, and cattle raised on grass pastures. Intensive systems range from barn-reared cattle to those that hold thousands of cattle in feedlots. Some countries permit the use of growth promoters in the feed. Even organic beef can be raised intensively, provided the feed is organic. Renowned beef cattle breeds include Aberdeen Angus, Belgian Blue, Charolais, Kobe, Limousin, and Murray Grey. The meat from breeds such as these is superior to that from cattle used purely for dairy production.

BUY Beef that indicates its origin and breed is likely to be of better quality than anonymous beef. A darker red indicates that the beef has been matured (3–4 weeks is ideal). Muscle meat that is marbled with fat cooks and tastes best, but avoid excessive fat around the edge of the meat.

STORE Store beef, wrapped, at the bottom of the fridge: joints up to 6 days, steaks and diced meat up to 4, and ground up to 2. Beef can be frozen, tightly wrapped, for up to 9 months.

EAT Raw: Slice thinly for carpaccio or grind as steak tartare. Cooked: Fry or grill tender steaks; roast prime leg and sirloin cuts. It is safe to eat these rare. Braise or stew tougher cuts. Use ground beef for burgers, pies, and other homestyle dishes.

FLAVOR PAIRINGS Cream, chile, garlic, mushrooms, truffle, tomatoes, shallot, tarragon, rosemary, sage, black pepper, curry, paprika, horseradish, soy sauce, oyster sauce, mustard, red wine.

CLASSIC RECIPES *Châteaubriand with béarnaise; ragù alla bolognese; chile con carne; steak au poivre; beef Wellington; beef Stroganoff; boeuf bourguignonne; bollito misto; meatloaf; bistecca all fiorentina; sauerbraten; tzimmes; matambre.*

Sirloin joint
The finest roasting joint, sirloin should have a layer of creamy fat on the outside and be well marbled. The best sirloin joint will include some fillet on the other side of the bone, as in the T-bone steak.

Ground
Forequarter (second grade) ground beef can be quite fatty but has good flavor. Ground shin needs longest cooking. Steak ground from the back or leg is leanest and most tender.

❶ FOREQUARTER CUTS
Chuck/blade; stewing steak; braising steak; diced shoulder; thick rib/leg of mutton cut; ground (second grade); neck/clod; shin; ox cheek/jowl.

❸ BREAST AND FLANK CUTS
Brisket/thin runner; rib/short rib; thin/hindquarter flank; forequarter flank; skirt/flap/diaphragm.

Shoulder
A boned and rolled shoulder makes an economical and tasty joint, but needs slow cooking by pot-roasting with plenty of vegetables, herbs, and spices.

Brisket
A braising cut full of flavor, brisket is also used to make salt beef and is good for pickling.

Brisket is sometimes very fatty and excess should be trimmed before cooking.

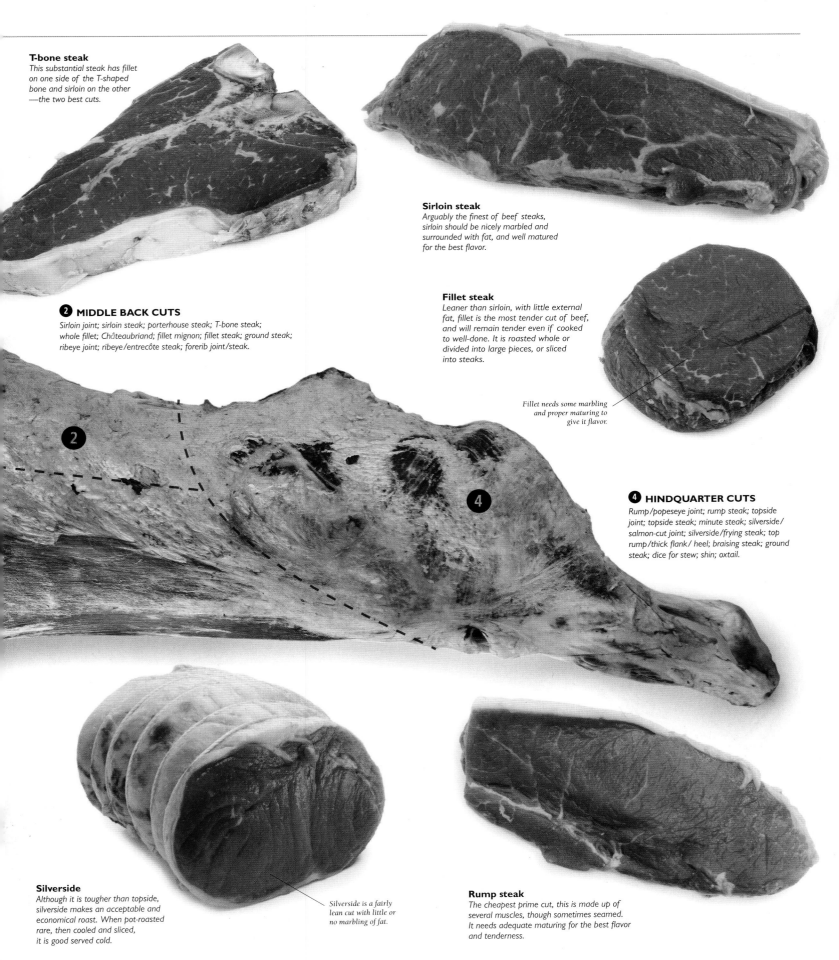

T-bone steak
This substantial steak has fillet on one side of the T-shaped bone and sirloin on the other —the two best cuts.

Sirloin steak
Arguably the finest of beef steaks, sirloin should be nicely marbled and surrounded with fat, and well matured for the best flavor.

Fillet steak
Leaner than sirloin, with little external fat, fillet is the most tender cut of beef, and will remain tender even if cooked to well-done. It is roasted whole or divided into large pieces, or sliced into steaks.

Fillet needs some marbling and proper maturing to give it flavor.

❷ MIDDLE BACK CUTS
Sirloin joint; sirloin steak; porterhouse steak; T-bone steak; whole fillet; Châteaubriand; fillet mignon; fillet steak; ground steak; ribeye joint; ribeye/entrecôte steak; forerib joint/steak.

❹ HINDQUARTER CUTS
Rump/popeseye joint; rump steak; topside joint; topside steak; minute steak; silverside/ salmon-cut joint; silverside/frying steak; top rump/thick flank/ heel; braising steak; ground steak; dice for stew; shin; oxtail.

Silverside
Although it is tougher than topside, silverside makes an acceptable and economical roast. When pot-roasted rare, then cooled and sliced, it is good served cold.

Silverside is a fairly lean cut with little or no marbling of fat.

Rump steak
The cheapest prime cut, this is made up of several muscles, though sometimes seamed. It needs adequate maturing for the best flavor and tenderness.

CHÂTEAUBRIAND WITH BÉARNAISE

This simple yet superb dish was created for the 18th-century politician Châteaubriand in Napoleonic France.

SERVES 2

1lb (450g) Châteaubriand (beef fillet, center cut)

salt and freshly ground black pepper

4 tbsp butter

2 tbsp olive oil

For the béarnaise sauce

½ cup dry white wine

2 tbsp white wine vinegar

1 shallot, finely chopped

1 tbsp chopped tarragon

2 egg yolks

8 tbsp (1 stick) butter, cubed

1 Preheat the oven to 450°F (230°C).

2 First make the sauce. Combine the wine, wine vinegar, shallot, and half of the tarragon in a small nonreactive saucepan or frying pan and boil until reduced to 2 tbsp. Pour this into a heatproof bowl set over a pan of barely simmering water. Whisk in the egg yolks, then add the butter one piece at a time, stirring constantly as it melts and before adding the next piece of butter. Continue until all the butter has been incorporated and the the sauce thickens; stir constantly. If the sauce curdles, beat in a few drops of water. Immediately remove from the heat and strain the sauce through a sieve. Add the reserved tarragon, and season lightly with salt and pepper. Keep warm.

3 Season the beef all over with the salt and pepper. Heat the butter and oil in a heavy frying pan with an ovenproof handle. When the butter stops foaming, add the beef and brown briefly but well on both sides.

4 Transfer the frying pan to the oven and roast the meat until cooked to the desired doneness, about 8–10 minutes for medium rare, depending on the thickness of the meat. Remove from the oven and allow to rest in a warm place, loosely covered, for 5 to 7 minutes.

5 Slice the beef across the grain and serve with the warm béarnaise sauce.

BEEF COOKING CHART

Choosing the correct cooking method for a cut of beef is vitally important. Use this chart to identify the best way to prepare your chosen cut.

CUT	DESCRIPTION	BROIL	
		Timings are for 1in (2.5cm) thick steaks.	
RUMP/POPESEYE	From the top of the leg, this has a coarser grain than sirloin but nevertheless yields a good roasting joint. Rump steak is preferred by many to sirloin for its fat content.	Rump steak: Preheat broiler to high. Brush meat with oil or melted butter. Broil 2½ min per side for rare; 4 min per side for medium; 6 min per side for well-done. Rest 2–3 min.	
TOPSIDE	Boneless, less expensive, and leaner than sirloin but still good for roasting and broiling/frying. When sliced very thinly it is called minute steak.	Broil topside steak as rump steak.	
SILVERSIDE	For braising, this lean joint needs moisture to prevent it from drying out. Slices are suitable for quick cooking only if served pink; sometimes sliced thinly into minute steaks.	Broil silverside slices as rump steak.	
T-BONE STEAK	A large, tender cut, including the sirloin and fillet on either side of the bone.	Broil T-bone steak as rump steak.	
SIRLOIN	Tender and marbled with fat, this yields one of the most popular steaks and the best roasting joint of beef on the bone, with a covering of fat. Without the bone, this joint cooks a little quicker.	Broil sirloin steak as rump steak.	
FILLET	Extremely tender, but can be very lean. The whole fillet, the center portion called Châteaubriand, and the tapering end or tail are usually roasted but can also be braised. Steaks are often cut thicker so adjust cooking times.	Broil fillet steak as rump steak, but 2 min per side for rare; 3 min per side for medium; 4 min per side for well-done.	
RIBEYE	The trimmed main muscle from the forerib yields a good marbled joint and a tender steak (ribeye/entrecôte).	Broil ribeye/entrecôte steak as rump steak.	
FLANK/SKIRT	Has long fibers and connective tissue so needs either slow cooking or quick frying. Cut across the grain. If flash-fried it must be served very pink or it will toughen.	Not recommended.	
BRISKET	The element of fat makes it a good braising joint. Also good for curing. Slices can be fried but must be served pink or they will toughen.	Not recommended.	
LEG OF MUTTON/ THICK RIB	A leg-shaped muscle from the shoulder. Slices can be fried but must be served pink or they will toughen.	Not recommended.	
FORERIB	From the shoulder end of the sirloin, this is a less expensive but excellent bone-in joint for roasting and braising.	Not recommended.	
TOP RUMP/THICK FLANK AND THIN FLANK	These cuts can be rolled into a joint, sliced, or diced for braising and stewing, or ground.	Not recommended.	
SHIN/HEEL AND NECK/CLOD	Sliced or diced for slow, moist cooking, the collagen in these muscles gives a silky texture to stews and casseroles.	Not recommended.	
RIB/SHORT RIB/ RUNNER	Chunks of rib bone with meat and fat attached. Stew to make a hearty, rustic dish.	Not recommended.	
CHUCK/BLADE	With a variety of marbling and connective tissue, these shoulder cuts are superb for braising, stewing, and ground.	Not recommended.	
GROUND BEEF	Top-quality ground steak has no connective tissue. Regular ground beef comes from a range of muscles, so fat and sinew content can vary greatly.	Preheat broiler to high. Press ground beef onto skewers or form into patties. Brush with oil and broil, turning occasionally, for 10–15 minutes.	

FRY	ROAST	BRAISE/STEW
Timings are for 1in (2.5cm) thick steaks.	*Thermometer internal-temperature readings: rare 140°F (60°C), medium 160°F (71°C), and well-done 170°F (75C°).*	*For timing, weight is less important than if meat is sliced/diced or a joint.*
Rump steak: Heat oil, or butter and oil, in a frying pan until very hot. Place steak in pan and do not move until turning it over. Fry 2½ min per side for rare; 4 min per side for medium; 6 min per side for well-done. Rest 2–3 min.	Rump joint: Preheat oven to 375°F (190°C). Roast 20 min per 1lb (450g) plus 20 min for rare; 25 min per 1lb (450g) plus 25 min for medium; 30 min per 1lb (450g) plus 30 min for well-done.	Rump steak (1in/2.5cm thick) and rump joint: Preheat oven to 325°F (160°C). Brown meat and add liquid. Braise steak for 1½–2 hours; braise joint for 2–3 hours.
Fry topside steak as rump steak. Fry minute steak for 1–1½ min per side and serve at once.	Roast topside joint as rump joint.	Braise topside steak and joint as rump steak and joint.
Fry silverside slices as rump steak.	Not recommended.	Braise silverside slices and joint as rump steak and joint.
Fry T-bone steak as rump steak.	Not recommended.	Braise T-bone steak as rump steak, but for 1–1½ hours.
Fry sirloin steak as rump steak.	Sirloin joint bone-in: Preheat oven to 450°F (230°C). Roast for 25 min. Reduce heat to 375°F (190°C) and roast 12–15 min per 1lb (450g) for rare; 20 min per 1lb (450g) for medium; 25 min per 1lb (450g) for well-done. Rest 20–30 min. Boneless sirloin joint: Preheat oven to 375°F (190°C). Roast 20 min per 1lb (450g) plus 20 min for rare; 25 min per 1lb (450g) plus 25 min for medium; 30 min per 1lb (450g) plus 30 min for well-done. Rest 20–30 min.	Braise sirloin steak as rump steak, but for 1–1½ hours. Braise sirloin joint for 1–2 hours.
Fry fillet steak as rump steak.	Whole fillet, Chateâubriand, and fillet tail: Preheat oven to 450°F (230°C). Brown meat in hot oil in a frying pan, then place in oven. Roast for 10–12 min per 1lb (450g) for rare; 12–15 min per 1lb (450g) for medium; 14–16 min per 1lb (450g) for well-done. Rest 10 min.	Braise fillet steak as rump steak, but for 1–1½ hours. Braise whole fillet, Chateâubriand, or fillet tail for 1–2 hours.
Fry ribeye/entrecôte steak as rump steak.	Roast ribeye joint as rump joint.	Braise ribeye/entrecôte steak as rump steak, but for 1–1½ hours. Braise ribeye joint for 1–2 hours.
Fry flank/skirt steak as rump steak, but for 2–3 min per side.	Not recommended.	Braise flank/skirt joint as rump joint.
Fry brisket slices as flank steak.	Brisket joint: Preheat oven to 350°F (180°C). Pot-roast for 30–40 min per 1lb (450g) plus 30–40 min.	Braise brisket joint as rump joint.
Fry leg of mutton/thick rib slices as flank steak.	Pot-roast leg of mutton/thick rib joint as brisket joint.	Braise leg of mutton/thick rib joint as rump joint.
Not recommended.	Roast forerib joint as bone-in sirloin joint.	Braise forerib joint as rump joint, but for 1–2 hours.
Not recommended.	Not recommended.	Braise top rump/thick flank and thin flank joints as rump joint.
Not recommended.	Not recommended.	Braise shin/heel and neck/clod as rump joint, but for 3–4 hours.
Not recommended.	Not recommended.	Braise rib/short rib/runner as rump joint, but for 3–4 hours.
Not recommended.	Not recommended.	Braise chuck/blade as rump joint.
Heat oil in a frying pan until medium—hot. Form ground beef into patties. Brush with oil and fry, turning occasionally, for 10–15 minutes.	Not recommended.	Brown ground beef, add liquid, and simmer, or braise at 325°F (160°C), for 1–1½ hours (ground steak) or 1½–2 hours (ground beef).

CLASSIC RECIPE

RAGÙ ALLA BOLOGNESE

A dark, rich, slowly cooked pasta sauce, this originated in Bologna, in the north of Italy. Serve with tagliatelle or fettuccine.

SERVES 2–4

1 tbsp olive oil

6oz (150g) pancetta, finely chopped

¼ cup finely chopped onion

¼ cup finely chopped carrot

¼ cup finely chopped celery

1 lb (300g) lean ground beef

1 tbsp tomato paste

½ cup dry red wine

¾ cup whole milk, plus extra if needed

1 Heat the oil in a heavy saucepan and cook the pancetta gently, stirring occasionally, until browned at the edges. Add the onion, carrot, and celery and cook until the onion is softened but not browned. Add the beef and cook, stirring frequently, until it is nicely browned and crumbly.

2 Stir in the tomato paste and wine until well blended, then gradually add the milk, stirring until it has been absorbed.

3 Cover and simmer very gently for 3–4 hours. Stir occasionally to prevent the sauce from sticking to the pot, and add a little more milk if it becomes too dry.

4 When the sauce is ready, it will be thick and smooth, with the meat almost disintegrated. Season to taste with salt and pepper.

VEAL

Veal is calf meat and a by-product of the dairy industry. Veal calves that are traditionally reared are removed from their mothers and fed on milk. Some are reared in stalls or crates; others are raised in housed groups. Their age at slaughter is 5–9 months, although bob veal is slaughtered at a few days old. Free-range veal calves (sometimes called rose veal) remain with their mothers and have access to grass and/or grain for feed. Milk-fed veal is pale pink and delicate in flavor, whereas grain- or grass-fed (rose) veal is darker pink. Grass-fed veal is usually leaner than milk-fed and grain-fed veal.

🔒 **BUY** Good-quality veal should be lean and firm with a little creamy-white fat (veal is not as heavily marbled as beef). Avoid veal that is watery or that has gray bones.

📦 **STORE** Store, wrapped, at the bottom of the fridge. Joints can be kept for up to 6 days, steaks and diced veal up to 4, and mince up to 2. Or freeze, tightly wrapped, for up to 9 months.

⬤ **EAT** Fry or grill steaks, chops, and escalopes; roast the prime leg and sirloin cuts. It is safe to eat all of these rare. Braise or stew forequarter, flank, and tougher leg cuts. Add ground veal to ground beef and pork for meatloaf.
FLAVOR PAIRINGS Cream, eggs, lemon, shallot, garlic, sorrel, mushrooms, pickles, capers, rosemary, tarragon, thyme, parsley, white wine, vermouth, Marsala.
CLASSIC RECIPES *Osso buco; blanquette de veau; weiner schnitzel; saltimbocca alla romana; cotoletto alla milanese; vitello tonnato.*

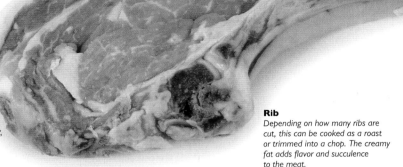

Rib
Depending on how many ribs are cut, this can be cooked as a roast or trimmed into a chop. The creamy fat adds flavor and succulence to the meat.

OSSO BUCO

This rich veal stew from Milan is always finished with a pungent fresh mixture called gremolata.

SERVES 4

3 tbsp all-purpose flour

salt and freshly ground black pepper

4 veal hind shanks, sawed crosswise into pieces about 1½in (4cm) thick and weighing about 9oz (250g) each

6 tbsp butter

12oz (350g) ripe tomatoes, chopped

1 cup dry white wine

1 cup beef stock, or more as needed

For the gremolata

¼ cup chopped flat-leaf parsley

2 garlic cloves, finely chopped

2 anchovy fillets in oil, drained and finely chopped

finely grated zest of 1 lemon

1 Season the flour with salt and pepper. Roll the veal in the flour to coat and shake off any excess.

2 Melt the butter in a large flameproof casserole pan. Add the veal and cook, turning, for 5 minutes, until browned on all sides. Remove and et aside.

3 Add the tomatoes, wine, and 1 cup of stock to the casserole pan. Season with salt and pepper. Bring to a boil, then reduce the heat to low, cover, and simmer for 1½ hours, or until the meat is very tender. If the liquid evaporates during cooking, add more stock to make a rich sauce.

4 To make the gremolata, mix together the parsley, garlic, anchovies, and lemon zest in a bowl. Sprinkle over the osso buco just before serving.

Escalope
An escalope, cut from the leg, is rolled or beaten out very thinly, then usually wrapped around a filling or coated in egg and breadcrumbs before cooking.

Diced veal
Diced shin is leaner than diced neck or shoulder, but needs longer cooking. Diced leg is lean and tender.

Loin chop
Leaner than rib chops, loin chops have a bone in between the loin and fillet muscles, similar to a T-bone steak. They weigh 9–12oz (250–350g) each. Chops from pure milk-fed veal are the palest pink in color.

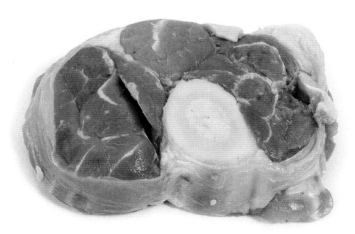

Osso buco
The sinews in these slices of shin/shank produce a succulent texture when cooked, and the marrow from the bone enriches the sauce.

VEAL COOKING CHART

Choosing the correct cooking method for a cut of veal is vitally important. Use this chart to identify the best way to prepare your chosen cut.

CUT	DESCRIPTION	GRILL	FRY	ROAST	BRAISE/STEW
		Timings depend on thickness.	*Timings depend on thickness.*	*Thermometer internal-temperature readings: medium rare 145°F (63°C), medium 150°F (65°C), and well-done 170°F (75C°).*	*For timing, weight is less important than when the meat is sliced/diced or cooked as a joint.*
LEG	The prime roasting joint is the topside, sometimes called cushion. Steaks are usually sliced from the topside or rump; escalope (schnitzel/cutlet) is a leg steak beaten out very thinly. Lean, diced leg is ideal for kebabs or a quick casserole.	Leg steak (1in/ 2.5cm thick): Preheat grill to high. Brush meat with oil or melted butter. Grill 2½ min per side for rare; 4 min per side for medium; 6 min per side for well-done. Rest 2–3 min. Escalopes: Preheat grill to high. Brush meat with oil. Grill for 2 min per side (not suitable if coated with breadcrumbs). Kebabs: Preheat grill to high. Brush meat with oil. Grill for 2–3 min on all sides.	Leg steak (1in/ 2.5cm thick): Heat oil, or butter and oil, in a frying pan until very hot. Place steak in pan and do not move until turning it over. Fry 2½ min per side for rare; 4 min per side for medium; 6 min per side for well-done. Rest 2–3 min. Escalopes: Heat ¼in (5mm) lard, oil, or butter and fry breadcrumbed escalopes for 3 min per side, or uncoated escalopes for 2 min per side. Diced leg: Heat oil, or butter and oil, and brown meat quickly on all sides, then serve; for large dice, rest for 5 min.	Leg joint: Preheat oven to 400°F (200°C). Roast for 20–35 min per 1lb (450g) plus 25 min. Rest 10–15 min.	Leg steak (1in/2.5cm thick): Brown on both sides, then add browned vegetables and liquid, and simmer gently, or braise in oven at 350°F (180°C), for 1 hour or until tender. Diced leg: Braise as steak, but for 1–1½ hours. Leg joint: Braise as steak, but for 1½–2 hours.
T-BONE STEAK	Includes the loin and fillet muscles on either side of the bone.	Grill T-bone steak as leg steak.	Fry T-bone steak as leg steak.	Not recommended.	Braise T-bone steak as leg steak.
FILLET	The most tender cut of all, and very lean. Yields boneless joints and steaks.	Grill fillet steak as leg steak.	Fry fillet steak as leg steak.	Fillet joint: Preheat oven to 400°F (200°C). Roast for 15–30 min per 1lb (450g) plus 25 min. Rest 5–10 min.	Braise fillet steak as leg steak. Braise fillet joint as diced leg.
BEST END	The fore part of the sirloin. Yields tender, marbled joints such as rack, with the bone ends neatly trimmed, and boneless ribeye, as well as cutlets cut from the rack and boneless ribeye/entrecôte steaks.	Grill cutlets and ribeye/entrecôte steaks as leg steak.	Fry cutlets and ribeye/entrecôte steaks as leg steak.	Roast best end and rack joints as leg joint. Roast ribeye joint as fillet joint.	Braise cutlets and ribeye/entrecôte steaks as leg steak. Braise best end and rack joints as leg joint. Braise ribeye joint as diced leg.
SIRLOIN/LOIN	Sirloin/loin, also called fillet or chump end, is a prime roasting joint, bone-in or boneless. Loin chops are one of the most popular veal cuts.	Grill loin chop as leg steak.	Fry loin chop as leg steak.	Roast sirloin joint as leg joint.	Braise loin chop as leg steak. Braise sirloin joint as leg joint.
BRISKET	Has some fat cover, but quite lean otherwise.	Not recommended.	Not recommended.	Roast brisket as leg joint.	Braise brisket as leg steak, but for 2–2½ hours.
BREAST	Can be fatty and needs powerful flavors in contrast.	Not recommended.	Not recommended.	Not recommended.	Preheat oven to 350°F (180°C). Brown breast joint, then add liquid and braise for 3 hours. When tender, strain off sauce and reduce.
SHOULDER	Boneless shoulder makes a tasty joint, perfect for slow cooking. Blade steak is cut from a muscle next to the shoulder blade. Diced veal can come from the shoulder, neck, or shin.	Not recommended.	Not recommended.	Not recommended.	Braise blade steak as leg steak. Braise diced shoulder as leg joint. Braise shoulder joint as leg steak, but for 2–2½ hours.
NECK/SCRAG END	Usually diced for stews, or ground for homestyle dishes.	Not recommended.	Not recommended.	Not recommended.	Braise diced neck/scrag end as leg steak, but for 2–2½ hours.
OSSO BUCO	Slices of shin and shank including the marrow bone.	Not recommended.	Not recommended.	Not recommended.	Braise osso buco as leg joint.
RIBS/SHORT RIBS	A rustic cut with a lot of bone that needs slow cooking and powerful flavors to complement the fattiness.	Not recommended.	Not recommended.	Not recommended.	Braise ribs/short ribs as breast joint.
GROUND	Good for meatballs, burgers, and all kinds of pasta dishes.	Preheat grill to high. Press mince on to skewers or form into patties. Brush with oil. Grill for 8 min to brown, turning twice. Reduce heat and grill for 8–10 min.	Heat oil, lard, or butter in a frying pan until medium—hot. Form into patties. Fry for 15–18 min, turning occasionally.	Not recommended.	Brown ground veal and vegetables in a frying pan, then add liquid and simmer gently, or cook at 350°F (180°C), for 1–1½ hours.

PORK

One of the earliest domestic animals, pigs were traditionally reared in backyard sties and fed on waste food. There is still small-scale farming of pigs outdoors, but today most pigs are reared in highly sophisticated industrial units, fed on a grain- and soy-based diet. Medication is used differently across the world, with some countries, and all organic systems, banning the prophylactic use of antibiotics. The method of rearing, diet, and the breed of pig all affect the flavor and texture of the pork produced. Intensively reared pork is the palest and generally the leanest; it sometimes exudes moisture during cooking. Outdoor reared pork has darker, firmer meat with a more pronounced flavor and tastier fat. Pork also yields lard, which is back fat, to be used fresh or rendered; it may also be salted and smoked. A popular treat in many countries is suckling pig, fed on its mother's milk until it is 2–6 weeks old. The meat is tender and delicate, and after roasting, the skin is crisp and crackling.

BUY Intensively reared pork is the cheapest to buy. All pork should be pink (pale or more deeply colored), not gray or red. The fat should be white; it is softer than other fats.

STORE Keep pork wrapped and at the bottom of the fridge for up to 3 days. Lean pork can be frozen, tightly wrapped, for up to 9 months, and fatty pork for up to 3 months.

EAT Cooked: Roast the leg and loin; if skin is left on, score it before cooking. Grill or fry leg and loin steaks and fillets; stir-fry diced meat. Braise shoulder joints and diced pork. Slow-cook pork belly joints and slices; joints are usually roasted whole but can be boned out and stuffed. Wrap thin slices of fresh lard around lean roasting joints (and birds) or dice and add to stews. Once rendered, lard can be used for making pastry and for frying. **Preserved:** Pork is one of the major meats for preserving by salting, smoking, and drying.

FLAVOR PAIRINGS Eggplants, cabbage, chile, tomatoes, leeks, garlic, onions, sage, rosemary, apples, lychees, orange, pineapple, plums, ginger, cloves, mustard, vinegar, cider, soy sauce.

CLASSIC RECIPES Swedish meatballs; *porc à la normande*; sweet and sour pork; maple-barbecued spare ribs; roast sucking pig; rostinciana.

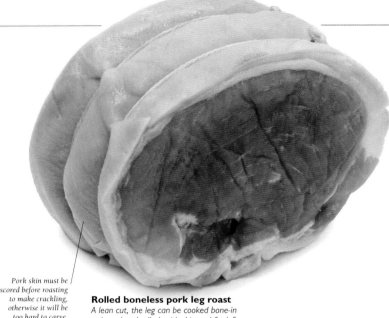

Pork skin must be scored before roasting to make crackling, otherwise it will be too hard to carve.

Rolled boneless pork leg roast
A lean cut, the leg can be cooked bone-in or boned and rolled, with skin and fat left on. It is also sold without the outer skin.

❷ MIDDLE BACK CUTS
Fillet/tenderloin/Valentine steak; loin joint; loin steak; loin chop (with and without kidney); rack; crown roast; skin; back fat.

❶ HINDQUARTER CUTS
Leg joint; leg steak; scallop (schnitzel); roasting joint; loin chop; diced leg/stir-fry; ground pork; tail; skin.

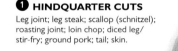

Slices of pork belly sometimes include small amounts of rib bone.

Leg steak
These are very lean and need careful cooking to prevent them from drying out. Grill or fry just until no longer pink, or braise.

To cook as a scallop (schnitzel), leg steaks are beaten out very thinly.

Belly slices
Fatty cuts of porklike belly may be grilled or fried to crisp the fat, or slowly cooked to add flavor. Belly is also minced for using in terrines.

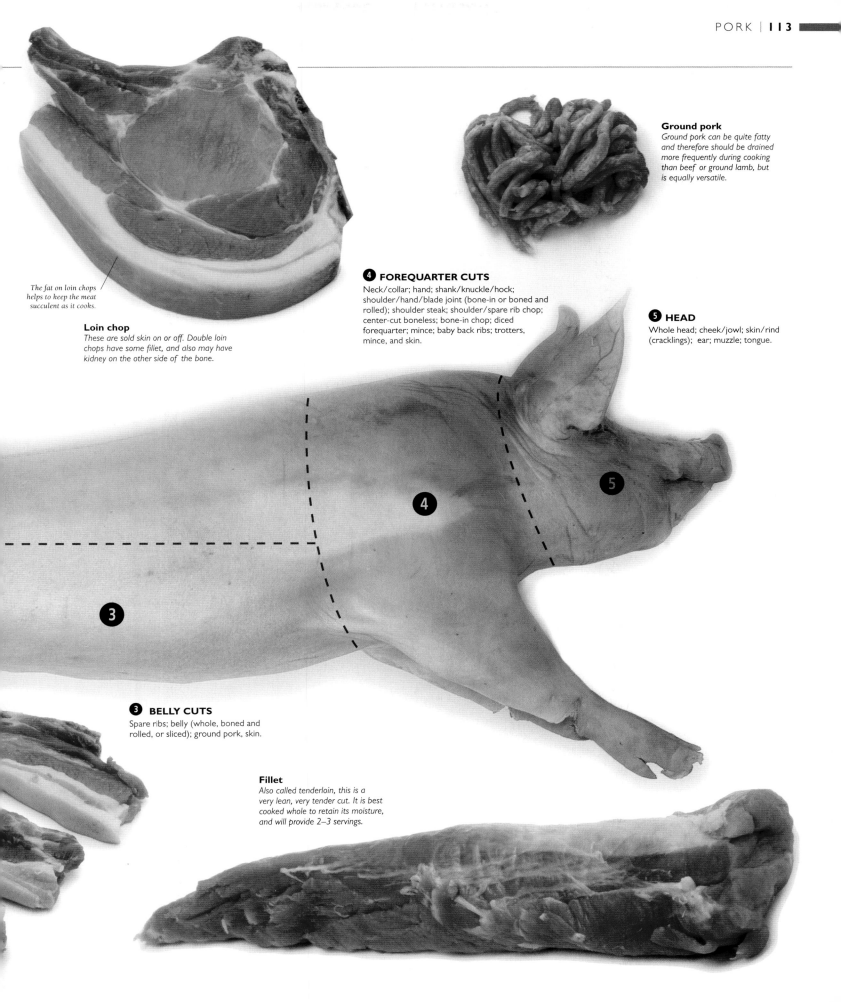

Ground pork
Ground pork can be quite fatty and therefore should be drained more frequently during cooking than beef or ground lamb, but is equally versatile.

The fat on loin chops helps to keep the meat succulent as it cooks.

Loin chop
These are sold skin on or off. Double loin chops have some fillet, and also may have kidney on the other side of the bone.

❹ FOREQUARTER CUTS
Neck/collar; hand; shank/knuckle/hock; shoulder/hand/blade joint (bone-in or boned and rolled); shoulder steak; shoulder/spare rib chop; center-cut boneless; bone-in chop; diced forequarter; mince; baby back ribs; trotters, mince, and skin.

❺ HEAD
Whole head; cheek/jowl; skin/rind (cracklings); ear; muzzle; tongue.

❸ BELLY CUTS
Spare ribs; belly (whole, boned and rolled, or sliced); ground pork, skin.

Fillet
Also called tenderloin, this is a very lean, very tender cut. It is best cooked whole to retain its moisture, and will provide 2–3 servings.

SWEDISH MEATBALLS

Regarded as a Swedish national dish, these rich pork meatballs are popular in all Scandinavian countries.

SERVES 4

½ cup fresh bread crumbs

½ cup heavy whipping cream

4 tbsp butter

1 small onion, finely chopped

1 lb (450g) lean ground pork

¼ tsp freshly grated nutmeg

1 egg, beaten

salt and freshly ground black pepper

For the sauce

½ cup beef stock

1 cup heavy whippping cream

1 Put the bread crumbs in a bowl, stir in the ½ cup cream, and set aside to soak. Meanwhile, heat 1 tbsp of the butter in a small frying pan, add the onion, and fry over low heat until soft but not browned. Remove from the heat and allow to cool.

2 Add the ground pork and nutmeg to the bread crumbs. Stir in the onion and beaten egg. Season with salt and pepper. Cover the bowl with plastic wrap and refrigerate for 1 hour.

3 With damp hands, shape the meat mixture firmly into 1in (2.5cm) balls. Place the meatballs in a single layer on a large plate or jellyroll pan, cover with plastic wrap, and refrigerate for 15 minutes.

4 Melt the remaining butter in a large frying pan over a medium heat and fry the meatballs, in batches, for about 10 minutes, or until browned on all sides and cooked through. Remove with a slotted spoon and drain on a plate lined with paper towels.

5 To make the sauce, discard any excess fat from the frying pan, then add the stock and cream. Cook over low heat, stirring with a wooden spoon to scrape up any brown residue from the bottom of the pan. When bubbles appear around the edge of the pan, cook 2 minutes longer to thicken slightly. Taste, adding salt and pepper as needed. Drizzle the sauce over the meatballs and serve.

PORK COOKING CHART

Choosing the correct cooking method for a cut of pork is vitally important. Use this chart to identify the best way to prepare your chosen cut.

CUT	DESCRIPTION	BROIL
		Timings for steaks and chops are for 1in (2.5cm) thickness.
LEG	The hind leg is a prime but lean roasting joint, bone-in or boned and rolled. If the skin is on, it can be slashed to form crisp crackling. Leg steaks are lean, boneless slices; cutlets (schnitzels) are thinner. Cubed boneless leg is suitable for kebabs and stir-frying.	Leg steaks, scallops, kebabs: Preheat broiler to high. Brush meat with oil. Broil scallops for 3 min on each side. Broil steaks for 3 min on each side, then reduce heat and cook for another 2 min per side (or longer if thicker). Broil kebabs for 2–3 min on each side.
RUMP	From the rump end of the back, this yields a roasting joint that is usually boned and rolled, as well as the largest of the pork chops.	Rump chops: Preheat broiler to high. Brush meat with oil. Broil for 2–3 min on each side, then reduce heat and cook for another 2–3 minutes per side.
FILLET/TENDERLOIN	A slim, tender, tapering muscle from the hind end of the loin that is usually cooked whole. May be sliced into medallions, which when part-sliced and opened out become Valentine steaks.	Whole fillet and slices thicker than 1¾in (4.5cm): Preheat broiler to high. Brush meat with oil. Broil for 2–3 min on each side to brown, then reduce heat and broil, turning, for another 10 min. Rest for 5–10 min. Broil medallions and Valentine steaks as leg steaks.
LOIN	Tender loin joints are sold on the bone with skin on, and also boned and skinless. Rack is a joint from the fore end of the loin, sometimes with the skin on; two racks tied together and stuffed become a crown roast. Loin is cut into chops, with bone, and into steaks, which are slices with a covering of fat on one side.	Broil loin steaks and chops as rump chops.
BELLY	A fatty cut, boned and rolled as a joint, or sliced/diced for broiling and frying or marinating and slow-cooking. Spare ribs, trimmed from inside the belly, are a popular cut for marinating and broiling or baking.	Spare ribs: Precook for 20–30 min in oven or by simmering. Then coat with marinade/sauce and broil under medium heat for 10–15 min, brushing with sauce and turning to glaze. Belly slices: Broil under medium heat for 10–15 min, turning several times, then raise heat to high to crisp skin, if necessary.
SHOULDER	Shoulder/arm/blade joint may be on the bone or boned and stuffed; slow-roast for delicious flavor. A steak is a succulent slice of shoulder; a chop includes some bone. Diced boneless forequarter meat is suitable for stews.	Broil shoulder steaks and chops as rump chops.
SUCKLING PIG	Very tender young piglet, usually whole, sometimes boned and stuffed.	Not recommended.
GROUND PORK	May be fatty. Use for satays, kebabs, burgers, and sausages as well as homestyle dishes.	Preheat broiler to high. Press ground pork onto skewers or form into patties. Brush with oil and broil for 10–15 min, turning frequently.
NECK/COLLAR	A well-marbled cut that can be sliced, diced, or cooked as a joint.	Not recommended.
SHANK/KNUCKLE/HOCK	Often sold smoked. Good for stock, rustic soups, and homestyle dishes.	Not recommended.
PIG'S FEET	Need very slow simmering; then they are cooled, stuffed, and broiled.	After cooking and cooling, split in half, brush with butter, and roll in bread crumbs. Cook under a medium broiler for 15–20 min, or until crisp and golden brown.
HEAD AND CHEEK/JOWL	Pig's head is cooked whole for buffets but mostly used to make head cheese. Cheek and jowl are fatty cuts from the head that can be used like belly, or cured into small hams.	Not recommended.

FRY	ROAST	BRAISE/STEW
Timings for steaks and chops are for 1in (2.5cm) thickness.	*Thermometer internal-temperature reading for well-done pork: 175°F (80°C).*	*For timing, weight is less important than if meat is sliced/diced or cooked as a joint.*
Leg steaks, scallops, diced leg: Heat oil in a heavy frying pan until smoking hot. Fry scallops for 2 min per side. Fry steaks for 2 min per side, then continue cooking for another 2 min per side (or longer, if thicker); rest for 2–3 min before serving. Stir-fry diced leg until well browned on all sides.	Leg joint: Preheat oven to 425°F (220°C). If there is skin, score it and rub with salt. Roast for 30 min, then reduce heat to 325°F (160°C) and cook for 23 min per 1lb (450g). Rest for 20–30 min.	Leg steaks (1in/2.5cm thick): Preheat oven to 325°F (160°C). Brown meat, add browned vegetables and liquid, and braise for 1½–2 hours. Leg joint: Braise as leg steaks, but covered and for 3–3½ hours; if skin is on, increase heat to 400°F (200°C) and cook uncovered for final 20–30 min to crisp skin.
Fry rump chops as leg steaks.	Roast rump joint as leg joint.	Braise rump chops as leg steaks. Braise rump joint as leg joint, but for 2–3 hours.
Whole fillet and slices thicker than 1¾in (4.5cm): Heat a little oil or butter in a heavy frying pan until smoking hot. Fry for 10 min, turning to brown, then reduce heat and cook for another 5 min. Rest 5–10 min. Fry medallions and Valentine steaks as leg steaks.	Not recommended.	Whole fillet: Preheat oven to 300°F (150°C). Brown meat, then add vegetables and liquid. Braise for 1–2 hours, basting from time to time to glaze.
Fry loin steaks and chops as leg steaks.	Roast loin joint and rack as leg joint.	Braise loin steaks and chops as leg steaks. Braise loin joint and rack as leg joint, but for 1½–2 hours.
Belly joint: Precook by simmering for 2 hours, then cool, slice or cut thickly, and fry in a very hot frying pan for 8–10 min to crisp and brown. Belly slices: Fry over medium heat for 15–20 min, turning several times, then increase heat to crisp fat and skin if necessary.	Spare ribs and slices: Preheat oven to 350°F (180°C). Roast for 20–30 min, then coat with marinade/sauce and roast for another 10–15 min until well glazed. Or slow-roast at 325°F (160°C) for 1–1½ hours, basting with liquid or sauce; increase heat to 400°F (200°C) and roast for 20–30 min to brown and glaze. Belly joint: Preheat oven to 425°F (220°C). Score skin and rub with salt. Roast for 20 min, then reduce heat to 300°F (150°C) and cook for 3–4 hours.	Belly joint: Simmer gently for 2–3 hours; slice thinly to serve with or without a glaze. Or brown belly, then braise at 250°F (130°C) for 4–5 hours; cool, slice, and glaze in a frying pan or hot oven.
Fry shoulder steaks and chops as leg steaks.	Shoulder/arm/blade joint: Preheat oven to 425°F (220°C). Score skin and rub with salt. Brown for 30 min, then reduce heat to 300°F (150°C) and continue roasting for 3–3½ hours.	Braise shoulder steaks and chops as leg steaks. Shoulder/arm/blade joint: Preheat oven to 300°F (150°C). Braise with vegetables for 4–4½ hours; baste from time to time to glaze. Diced shoulder: Preheat oven to 300°F (150°C). Brown meat, add vegetables and liquid, and stew for 1½ hours.
Not recommended.	Preheat oven to 450°F (230°C). Truss piglet. Score skin and rub with salt. Protect ears, snout, and tail with foil. Roast for 30 min, then reduce heat to 350°F (180°C) and roast for 10 min per 1lb (450g), or 15 min per 1lb (450g) if stuffed. Baste every half hour. Rest for 30 min.	Preheat oven to 300°F (150°C). Brown all over, then add liquid, cover, and braise for 3–4 hours. Increase heat to 400°F (200°C) and cook uncovered for the last 20–30 min to crisp the skin.
Heat oil in frying pan. Form ground pork into patties. Brush with oil and fry, turning occasionally, for 10–15 min. .	Not recommended.	Brown ground pork and vegetables, add liquid, and simmer for 1–1½ hours.
Not recommended.	Not recommended.	Braise neck/collar as shoulder/arm/blade joint.
Not recommended.	Not recommended.	Simmer for 2–3 hours or until tender.
Not recommended.	After cooking and cooling, split in half, brush with butter, and roll in bread crumbs. Roast at 400°F (200°C) for 15–20 min, or until crisp and golden brown.	Simmer gently for 1–2 hours. Then cool, split in half, roll in bread crumbs, and broil or roast.
Not recommended.	Head: Preheat oven to 375°F (190°C). After braising, protect ears with foil and roast for 30–45 min to color the skin; remove foil for the last 15 min.	Head: Brown vegetables, then add head and liquid and simmer, or cook in oven at 300°F (150°C), for 3–3½ hours. Cheeks/jowl: Brown with vegetables, then add liquid, cover, and simmer, or braise at 375°F (190°C), for 45–60 min.

PORC À LA NORMANDE

Apples, cream, and cider are the hallmarks of the cuisine of Normandy in northern France.

SERVES 8

2 tbsp olive oil

1 tbsp butter

3lb (1.35kg) lean boneless pork, cut into bite-size pieces

2 onions, finely chopped

2 tbsp Dijon mustard

6 celery ribs, finely chopped

6 carrots, finely chopped

1 tbsp finely chopped fresh rosemary

4 garlic cloves, finely chopped

3 crisp, tart eating apples, such as Granny Smith, peeled, cored, and diced

1 cup dry French cider, hard cider, or white wine

2 cups heavy whipping cream

1 cup chicken stock, heated

1 tsp black peppercorns, coarsely crushed

salt

1 Preheat the oven to 350°F (180°C). Heat the oil and butter in a large cast-iron pan or flameproof casserole, add the pork, and cook over a medium heat for 6–8 minutes, or until golden brown on all sides. Remove with a slotted spoon and set aside.

2 Add the onions and cook over low heat for 5 minutes, or until starting to soften. Stir in the mustard. Add the celery, carrots, rosemary, and garlic. Cook over low heat, stirring often, for about 10 minutes, or until the vegetables are tender. Add the apples and cook for another 5 minutes.

3 Pour in the cider, then raise the heat and boil for a couple of minutes to evaporate the alcohol. Return the pork to the pan and pour in the cream and stock. Stir in the peppercorns.

4 Bring to a boil, then cover the pan and put it into the oven to cook for 1 hour, or until the pork is tender. Check the seasoning before serving with rice or mashed potatoes.

LAMB

Sheep were originally reared for their milk and wool; meat was a by-product. Today, by contrast, many are kept solely to produce meat, being reared in grassland and upland areas. Lamb comes from sheep under 1 year old; from 3–5 months old they are called spring lamb. The meat of spring lamb is pale pink and mild; lamb from older sheep is darker pink and has a stronger flavor. Although most commercial lamb is grass-fed for good flavor, the lamb from sheep that graze on salt marshes or shorelines has a special cachet. In the Middle East and Asia, fat-tailed sheep are reared for the fat deposits on their rump, which is considered to be a delicacy.

🔒 **BUY** Native lamb cuts increase in size throughout the year; imported lamb, which arrives fresh and frozen, can be any size. All lamb should have just a thin covering of white fat. It is

not marbled, although when becoming more mature it can have quite a lot of intramuscular and external fat.

📦 **STORE** Keep wrapped, in the bottom of the refrigerator for up to 4 days. Or tightly wrap and freeze for up to 6 months; protect sharp bones before wrapping.

⬤ **EAT** Roast the leg, loin, saddle, and rack to serve rosy pink. Roast or braise the shoulder. Broil or fry leg steaks and chops. Stew diced lamb, and use ground lamb for koftas, pies, and other homestyle dishes.

FLAVOR PAIRINGS Yogurt, eggplants, turnips, garlic, dill, mint, rosemary, apricots, cherries, quince, prunes, lemon, raisins, olives, almonds, cumin, coriander, red currants, oregano.

CLASSIC RECIPES *Koftas*; shish kebab; navarin of lamb; *kibbeh*; lamb *biryani*; *mechoui*; lamb tagine; *mansaf.*

LAMB KOFTAS

Serve these spicy meatballs from the Middle East and India with a cooling yogurt and cucumber relish.

SERVES 4

1 lb (450g) ground lamb
8 fresh cilantro sprigs, leaves finely chopped
8 fresh parsley sprigs, leaves finely chopped
1 tbsp ground cumin
1 garlic clove, crushed
½ tsp salt
freshly ground black pepper, to taste

1 Put 16 wooden skewers in hot water and leave to soak.

2 Combine the ground lamb with the cilantro, parsley, cumin, garlic, salt, and pepper in a large bowl. Mix thoroughly with your hands.

3 Using wet hands, roll 2 tbsp of the mixture into an even sausage shape. Repeat with the remaining mixture for a total of 16 koftas. Carefully push a soaked skewer lengthwise through each.

4 Position the oven rack 4in (10cm) from the heat; preheat the broiler to high. Lightly brush the koftas with oil.

5 Put the koftas on a broiler pan and place under the broiler to cook, turning several times, until nicely browned and cooked to the desired doneness—about 6–8 minutes for slightly pink, and 10 minutes for well done.

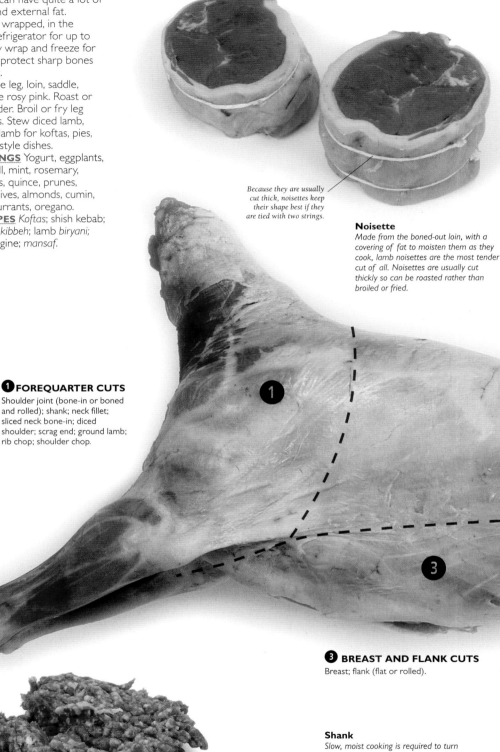

Because they are usually cut thick, noisettes keep their shape best if they are tied with two strings.

Noisette
Made from the boned-out loin, with a covering of fat to moisten them as they cook, lamb noisettes are the most tender cut of all. Noisettes are usually cut thickly so can be roasted rather than broiled or fried.

❶ FOREQUARTER CUTS
Shoulder joint (bone-in or boned and rolled); shank; neck fillet; sliced neck bone-in; diced shoulder; scrag end; ground lamb; rib chop; shoulder chop.

❸ BREAST AND FLANK CUTS
Breast; flank (flat or rolled).

Shank
Slow, moist cooking is required to turn the sinews in the shank to a succulent jelly. Allow one shank per person. Foreleg shanks are slimmer than those from the back leg.

Ground lamb
This can be quite fatty, which will add flavor and succulence to a dish. However, too much fat can make it greasy. Leg or shin will yield the leanest ground meat.

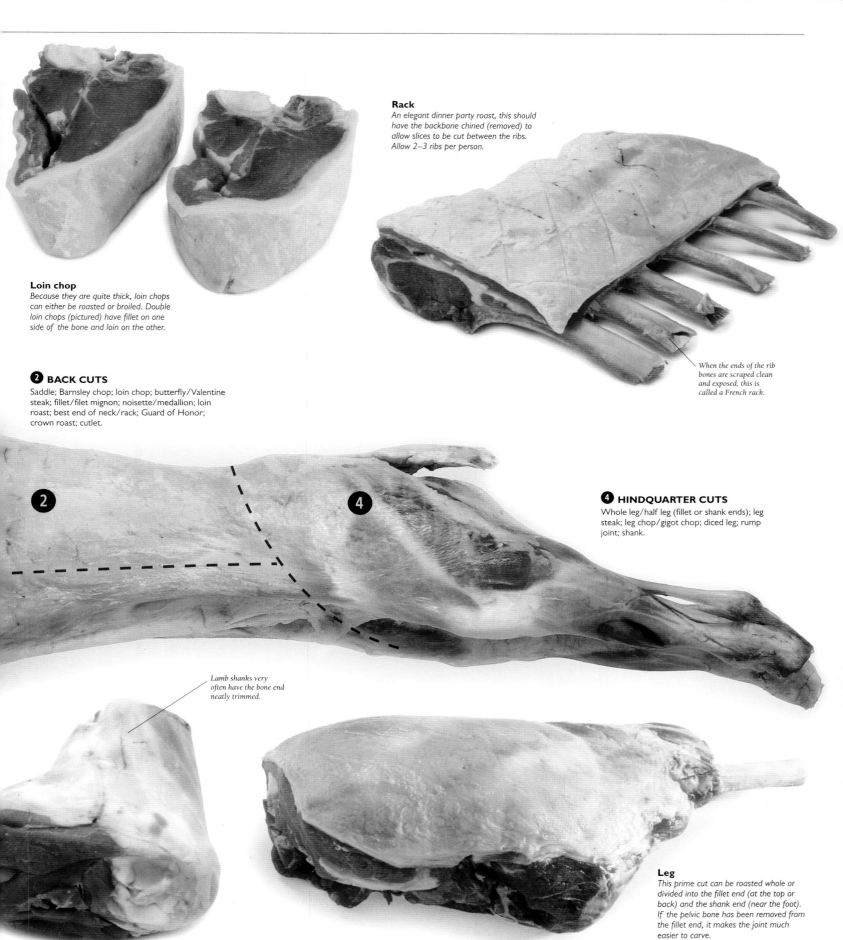

Loin chop

Because they are quite thick, loin chops can either be roasted or broiled. Double loin chops (pictured) have fillet on one side of the bone and loin on the other.

Rack

An elegant dinner party roast, this should have the backbone chined (removed) to allow slices to be cut between the ribs. Allow 2–3 ribs per person.

When the ends of the rib bones are scraped clean and exposed, this is called a French rack.

❷ BACK CUTS

Saddle; Barnsley chop; loin chop; butterfly/Valentine steak; fillet/filet mignon; noisette/medallion; loin roast; best end of neck/rack; Guard of Honor; crown roast; cutlet.

❹ HINDQUARTER CUTS

Whole leg/half leg (fillet or shank ends); leg steak; leg chop/gigot chop; diced leg; rump joint; shank.

Lamb shanks very often have the bone end neatly trimmed.

Leg

This prime cut can be roasted whole or divided into the fillet end (at the top or back) and the shank end (near the foot). If the pelvic bone has been removed from the fillet end, it makes the joint much easier to carve.

MOUSSAKA

This popular lamb and eggplant dish originated in the Balkans and eastern Mediterranean.

SERVES 6–8

| 4lb (1.8kg) eggplants |
| about ⅔ cup olive oil |
| 11 tbsp (1 stick plus 3 tbsp) butter |
| 1¼ cups all-purpose flour |
| 2 cups whole milk, heated |
| ½ tsp grated nutmeg |
| 3 egg yolks |
| salt and freshly ground black pepper |
| 3 onions, chopped |
| 2lb (900g) ground lamb |
| 1 cup lamb or beef stock |
| 1 tbsp tomato paste |
| 3 garlic cloves, chopped |
| 2 bay leaves |
| 2 tbsp chopped fresh oregano or 2 tsp dried oregano leaves |
| 1½lb (700g) ripe tomatoes, chopped |
| ¾ cup freshly grated kefalotyri or Parmesan cheese |

1 Preheat the broiler. Cut the eggplants crosswise into ½in (1cm) slices. Brush them with olive oil and broil, turning once, until soft and brown on both sides. Alternatively, cook the eggplant slices in oil in a large frying pan.

2 Melt the butter in a saucepan and stir in the flour. Cook over medium heat for 2 minutes, whisking frequently. Gradually whisk in the hot milk. Bring to a boil, then reduce the heat to low and stir until the sauce is thick and creamy. Remove from the heat and add the nutmeg and egg yolks. Mix well. Season with salt and pepper.

3 Preheat the oven to 350°F (180°C). Heat 2 tbsp oil in a large, deep frying pan and cook the onions until soft and golden. Add the lamb and cook, stirring often, until browned and crumbly. Add the stock, tomato paste, garlic, and bay leaves and stir to mix. Reduce the heat, then cook gently for 30 minutes, stirring occasionally.

4 Oil a large baking dish and lay half of the eggplant slices over the bottom. Cover with the lamb mixture and lay the remaining eggplant slices on top. Mix the oregano with the chopped tomatoes and spread over the eggplant. Whisk the sauce again briefly; pour it evenly over the surface. Sprinkle the cheese on top.

5 Bake for 45–60 minutes, or until the top is browned and the filling bubbly-hot. Let stand for 15 minutes before serving. Serve warm, not hot.

LAMB AND MUTTON COOKING CHART

Choosing the correct cooking method for a cut of lamb or mutton is vitally important. Use this chart to identify the best way to prepare your chosen cut.

CUT	DESCRIPTION	BROIL
		Timings are for 1in- (2.5cm-) thick steaks and chops.

LAMB

CUT	DESCRIPTION	BROIL
LEG	On the bone or boned and rolled, the hind leg is a prime roasting cut. Half leg joints are either fillet (rump) end or shank end. Can be boned and butterflied for barbecuing. Tender steaks and chops (gigot chops) are cut from the leg or chump (rump). Diced boneless leg meat is suitable for kebabs and stews.	Leg chops and steaks: Preheat broiler to high. Brush meat with oil. Broil for 3–4 min per side, then rest 5 min. Kebabs: Broil as steaks and chops, but for 2 min each side.
SADDLE	A prime bone-in roasting joint from the back of the lamb, consisting of both loins joined together. The fillet/filet mignon is a tiny tender muscle underneath the backbone, cooked whole.	Fillet: Preheat broiler to high. Brush meat with oil. Broil 2 min on each side, then rest for 5 min.
LOIN	The most tender muscle above the backbone. Joints can be left on the bone or boned and rolled. Loin chops include the loin eye; double loin chops include the fillet and sometimes kidney. Barnsley chops, sliced through the whole loin, include the loin eye and fillet on either side of backbone. Butterfly/Valentine steaks are nearly sliced through and opened out to form thin, heart shapes. Noisettes/medallions are small, round loin steaks.	Broil loin and Barnsley chops and noisettes as leg steaks and chops. Broil butterfly steaks as kebabs. Loin joint: Brown 1 min per side at top heat, then reduce heat to half and broil for 3–4 min per side; rest 5–10 min.
BEST END OF NECK	From the fore end of the loin, best end gives cutlets when sliced through the bone. The neck fillet makes a good mini-roast. When trimmed of fat, and the chin bone is removed, best end becomes a rack. If the rib ends are exposed it is called a French rack. Two racks leaning together form a Guard of Honor; two formed into a circle and stuffed make a crown roast.	Broil cutlets and neck fillet as leg steaks and chops.
SHOULDER	May be the whole shoulder, or halved into blade end or knuckle end, and bone-in or boned and rolled, sometimes with stuffing. Cut into chops or steaks, on or off the bone, and into boneless dice, which can be quite fatty.	Broil shoulder steaks and chops as leg steaks and chops.
SHANK	A tasty cut from the end of the fore and back legs needing long, slow cooking. Back leg shanks are the plumpest.	Not recommended.
BREAST	A cheaper cut from under the ribs. If boned, good for stuffing and rolling.	Not recommended.
FLANK	Tougher cut suitable for stuffing and slow cooking, or for ground meat.	Not recommended.
SCRAG END	Slices of neck on the bone; sometimes boned and diced.	Not recommended.
GROUND LAMB	Good for dishes like moussaka or koftas.	Preheat broiler to high. Press gound meat on to skewers or form into patties. Brush with oil and broil 2 min on each side, then rest for 5 min.

MUTTON

CUT	DESCRIPTION	BROIL
LEG	The hind leg, whole or half, either on the bone or boned and rolled. The leg chop, a slice of the leg with a round bone, is quite lean as is cubed boneless leg for kebabs or stews.	Leg chops and kebabs: Preheat broiler to high. Brush meat with oil or butter. Broil chops for 3–5 min per side, according to taste. Broil kebabs for 2–4 min per side.
LOIN	A slim muscle from the boned-out saddle, this yields a roasting joint as well as chops that include the loin eye and fillet.	Broil loin chops as leg chops.
RIB	Cutlets/rib chops are sliced through the rib and include a rib bone.	Broil cutlets as leg chops.
SADDLE	A roasting cut, including loin, fillet, backbone, and connective skin	Not recommended
SHOULDER	Joints may be the whole shoulder or half, on the bone or boned and rolled, sometimes stuffed. Good for braising although they may be fatty. Boneless cubes of shoulder are fattier than leg.	Not recommended
SHIN/SHANK	Tough cut with good flavor. Needs long, slow cooking.	Not recommended
FLANK	Tough fibrous cut suitable for stuffing and slow cooking or as ground meat.	Not recommended
NECK/SCRAG END	Slices of neck on the bone, sometimes diced for stew. Needs slow cooking.	Not recommended
GROUND MUTTON	Gives good flavor to made dishes and used for koftas and burgers.	Preheat broiler to high. Press ground meat on to skewers or form into patties. Brush with oil and broil until cooked through.

FRY	ROAST	BRAISE/STEW
Timings are for 1in- (2.5cm-) thick steaks and chops.	*Thermometer internal-temperature readings: medium-rare 145°F (63°C), medium 160°F (70°C), and well-done 170C° (75C°).*	*For timing, weight is less important than if meat is sliced/diced or cooked as a joint.*
Leg steaks and chops: Heat oil and butter in a hot frying pan. Brown meat for 2 min each side, then reduce heat and cook for 2–4 min per side. Rest before serving. Kebabs: Fry for 2 min each side, then serve immediately.	Leg steaks and chops (1in/2.5cm thick): Preheat oven to 400°F (200°C). Brush meat with butter or oil and roast for 30–45 min. Leg joint, bone-in or boneless: roast for 25–30 min per 1lb (450g), then rest 5 min per 1lb (450g).	Leg steaks and chops (1in/2.5cm thick): Brown meat, then add liquid and simmer, or cook in the oven at 375°F (190°C), for 1 hour. Diced leg: Braise as steaks and chops, but for 1–1½ hours. Leg joint, bone-in or boneless: Brown all over, then add liquid and cook in oven at 350°F (180°C) for 3–3½ hours.
Fry fillet as leg steaks and chops.	Roast saddle as leg joint.	Braise fillet as leg steaks and chops. Braise saddle as leg joint, but for 2–2½ hours.
Fry loin and Barnsley chops and noisettes as leg steaks and chops. Fry butterfly steaks as kebabs. Loin joint: Brown meat for 2 min each side, then reduce heat and cook for 3–5 min per side; rest 5–10 min.	Roast loin and Barnsley chops as leg steaks and chops. Not recommended for butterfly steaks. Loin joint: Preheat oven to 425°F (220°C). Brown joint on all sides, then roast for 8–10 min; rest for 5–10 min.	Braise loin and Barnsley chops and noisettes as leg steaks and chops. Not recommended for butterfly steaks. Braise loin joint as leg joint, but for 1–1½ hours.
Fry neck fillet, cutlets, and best end of neck joint as leg steaks and chops.	Roast neck fillet and cutlets as leg steaks and chops. Roast rack of lamb as loin joint. Roast crown roast, Guard of Honor, and best end joints as leg joint.	Braise neck fillet and cutlets as leg steaks and chops. Braise best end of neck, rack of lamb, and crown roast as leg joint, but for 1–1½ hours.
Fry shoulder steaks and chops as leg steaks and chops.	Shoulder joint, bone-in or boneless: Preheat oven to 400°F (200°C). Roast for 20–30 min per 1lb (450g) plus 30 min. Rest for 30 min.	Braise shoulder steaks and chops as leg steaks and chops. Braise diced shoulder as leg steaks and chops, but for 1½–2 hours. Braise shoulder joint as leg joint.
Not recommended.	Not recommended.	Shank: Brown, then add liquid and simmer, or cook in oven at 325°F (160°C), for 1½–2 hours.
Not recommended.	Not recommended.	Braise breast joint as shank.
Not recommended.	Not recommended.	Braise flank as shank.
Not recommended.	Not recommended.	Braise scrag end as shank.
Heat oil and butter in a hot frying pan. Form ground meat into patties or balls. Cook for 3–5 min each side.	Not recommended.	Braise ground meat as shank.
Leg chops and kebabs: Heat oil and butter in a frying pan. Fry chops for 3–5 min per side, according to taste. Fry kebabs for 2–4 min per side.	Leg joint: Preheat oven to 450°F (230°C). For pink meat, roast for 12 min per 1lb (450g), then rest for 12 min per 1lb (450g).	Leg chops and diced leg: Brown meat, then add liquid and simmer, or stew in oven at 350°F (180°C), for 1–1½ hours. Leg joint: Brown all over, then add vegetables and liquid, cover, and simmer for 1½–2 hours.
Fry loin chops as leg chops.	Roast loin joint as leg joint	Braise or stew loin chops as leg chops. Loin joint: Preheat oven to 300°F (150°C). Brown joint all over, add liquid, and cook in oven for 50 min; reduce heat to 250°F (130°C), baste well, and cook for 45 min longer.
Fry cutlets as leg chops.	Not recommended	Braise or stew cutlets as leg chops.
Not recommended	Roast saddle as leg joint.	Braise saddle as leg chops.
Not recommended	Not recommended	Braise shoulder joint, bone-in or boned and rolled, as leg chops, but for 2–2½ hours. Braise diced shoulder for 1½–2 hours.
Not recommended	Not recommended	Braise or stew shin/shank as leg chops, but for 2½–3 hours.
Not recommended	Not recommended	Braise or stew flank as leg chops but for 2–2½ hours.
Not recommended	Not recommended	Braise or stew neck/scrag end as flank.
Heat oil in a frying pan until medium hot. Form ground meat into patties. Brush with oil and fry, turning occasionally, until cooked through.	Not recommended	Brown ground meat, then add liquid and simmer gently for 1½–2 hours.

MUTTON

Mutton comes from sheep more than 2 years old, or even older if from a breeding ewe. (The meat from sheep under 1 year is lamb; between 1 and 2 years it is called hogget.) Darker, fattier, and tougher than lamb, mutton has a distinctive "sheep" smell, with yellower fat and a flavor that reflects its age and diet of wild plants. Mutton should be matured for 2 weeks before butchery. Cuts are similar to lamb, with leg and diced meat being the most popular. Sometimes goat meat is sold as mutton.

BUY Mutton is available from specialty butchers, markets, and internet sites. Allow larger portion sizes than you would for lamb, to compensate for the extra fat that may need trimming off, especially on cuts from the shoulder and back.

STORE Keep mutton, wrapped, in the bottom of the refrigerator for up to 4 days. Or freeze, tightly wrapped, for up to 4 months, or up to 6 months if all fat is removed.

EAT Slowly braise, pot-roast, or simmer joints. Use diced mutton for stews, pies, and curries, and groiund mutton for raised pies and other homestyle dishes. Broil chops slowly to serve pink. Marinated mutton tastes similar to marinated venison.

FLAVOR PAIRINGS Yogurt, carrots, onion, celery root, turnips, capers, oregano, pearl barley, black pepper, cardamom, coriander, cumin, curry powder, turmeric, red wine.

CLASSIC RECIPES Irish stew; mutton *biryani* or *rogan josh*; mutton pie; Scotch broth.

Diced mutton
Diced leg is quite lean. It makes excellent stews and curries, and if from a young animal can be broiled on skewers (do not overcook). Diced shoulder is much fattier, although it also makes good stews.

CLASSIC RECIPE

IRISH STEW

This classic Irish dish cooks lamb and potatoes long and slow for maximum flavor and tenderness.

SERVES 4

2lb (900g) blade, arm, or sirloin lamb steaks or chops, bone in, trimmed of excess fat

1¾lb (800g) onions, sliced

3 carrots, thickly sliced

1¾lb (800g) russet or other floury potatoes, peeled and thickly sliced

salt and freshly ground black pepper

large sprig of fresh thyme

1 bay leaf

2 cups lamb or beef stock

1 Preheat the oven to 325°F (160°C). Layer the chops, onions, carrots, and one-third of the potato slices in a large, heavy casserole. Season each layer with salt and pepper.

2 Tuck in the thyme and bay leaf, then top with the remaining potato slices. Pour the stock over, cover, and place in the oven to cook for 1½ to 2 hours, or until the lamb and potatoes are tender.

3 Remove the lid and return the casserole to the oven to cook for another 30–40 minutes, or until the top is browned. If the mixture appears dry during cooking, add a little more stock or water. Serve hot.

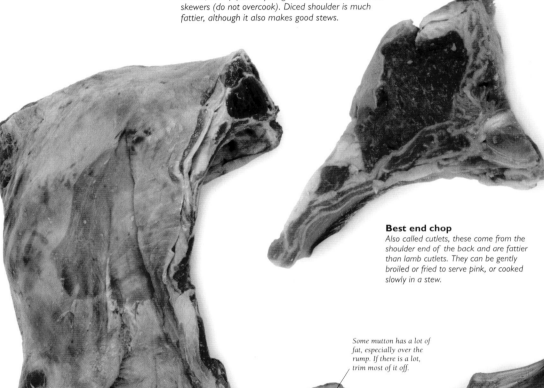

Best end chop
Also called cutlets, these come from the shoulder end of the back and are fattier than lamb cutlets. They can be gently broiled or fried to serve pink, or cooked slowly in a stew.

Some mutton has a lot of fat, especially over the rump. If there is a lot, trim most of it off.

Forequarter
This is usually parted into the shoulder (bone-in or boned and rolled), the breast (usually rolled, or stuffed and rolled), and the forequarter chops. The meat is quite fatty and includes some connective tissue. All the forequarter cuts are good for slow, flavorsome cooking.

Leg
A leg from a younger animal makes a good slow-roasting joint as long as it is served pink. From an animal older than 3 years, the leg will be a deeper red with a stronger flavor and is best braised like a lamb shank. Boneless leg can also be sliced into steaks, or diced.

GOAT

Domestic goats have been herded since Neolithic times, mostly for their milk but also for meat and their skins. But there are now breeds grown specially for producing young tender meat that tastes not unlike lamb. Kid (baby goat), which is light, mild, and lean, is often prepared as a celebratory dish. Meat from older goats is darker, while that of wild goats, which are indigenous to Asia and Europe, has a much stronger flavor.

BUY Goat meat is often available through Halal butchers. Young goat meat (often sold under names like Capra and Chevon) is cut into steaks, chops, joints, dice, and ground. Kid (or Cabrito) is usually sold as a whole carcass weighing around 32lb (15kg). Older goat is sold as stew meat or made into sausages and burgers.

STORE Keep meat, well wrapped, in the bottom of the refrigerator for up to 4 days. Or tightly wrap and freeze for up to 6 months.

EAT Roast whole kid or goat leg and saddle joints gently at 325°F (165°C) for 30 minutes per 1lb (450g) plus 30 minutes. Fry or broil steaks and chops. Stew or braise forequarter cuts and meat from older animals or wild goats.

FLAVOR PAIRINGS Yogurt, chile, garlic, onion, ginger, mint, orange, peanuts, allspice, cumin, curry powder, fenugreek, jerk seasoning, honey, vinegar, soy sauce.

CLASSIC RECIPES Goat curry; roast kid; goat tagine.

Diced goat
This is most commonly used to make curries and other spicy dishes. Meat from the leg is lean but some prefer the stronger, fattier meat from the shoulder.

Leg steak
From kid or from young goats, leg steaks are a similar color to lamb and can be broiled or fried in the same way. Leg steaks from older goats are darker and should be braised or stewed.

Whole kid
Most male goats are sold as kids because their meat toughens at a younger age than females. Often cooked whole, especially on the barbecue, kid may also be boned, stuffed, and rolled before roasting.

Kid meat has very little fat, so if cooking whole, baste frequently to prevent the outside and the thinner parts (like the flank and ribs) from drying out.

HORSE

In many countries, eating horse meat is culturally unacceptable; it is not kosher for Jews and discouraged by Muslims. But in parts of Europe, Asia, and North America it is much enjoyed. Because horses run hard, their meat is dark and lean, although surprisingly tender. The flavor is slightly sweet. Young horse meat is paler in color than that of older horses, which is similar to the color of venison. Horse fat is much prized for cooking.

BUY The cuts of horse meat are similar to beef but they are usually more limited. Buy as steaks, joints, ground meat, and dice, as well as the fat. It is a filling meat, so allow 5–6oz (150–180g) per portion. Horse meat is also available to buy smoked and made into sausages.

STORE Keep in the refrigerator, wrapped, for up to 3 days. Or remove any fat and freeze, tightly wrapped, for up to a year. Horse fat can be stored in the freezer for up to 3 months.

EAT Fresh: Horse meat can be eaten raw as carpaccio or steak tartare.
Cooked: Cook joints and steaks from the back and hindquarter like venison, to serve pink. All forequarter cuts should be cooked slowly; lard joints for braising to keep them moist. Use ground meat for burgers and koftas and as a lean substitute for ground beef in other homestyle dishes.

FLAVOR PAIRINGS Blue cheese, mushrooms, chile, horseradish, shiso, ginger, onions, arugula, olives, lemon, mustard, peppercorns, soy sauce, wine.

CLASSIC RECIPES *Pastissada; sauerbraten; basashi;* horsemeat rice vermicelli.

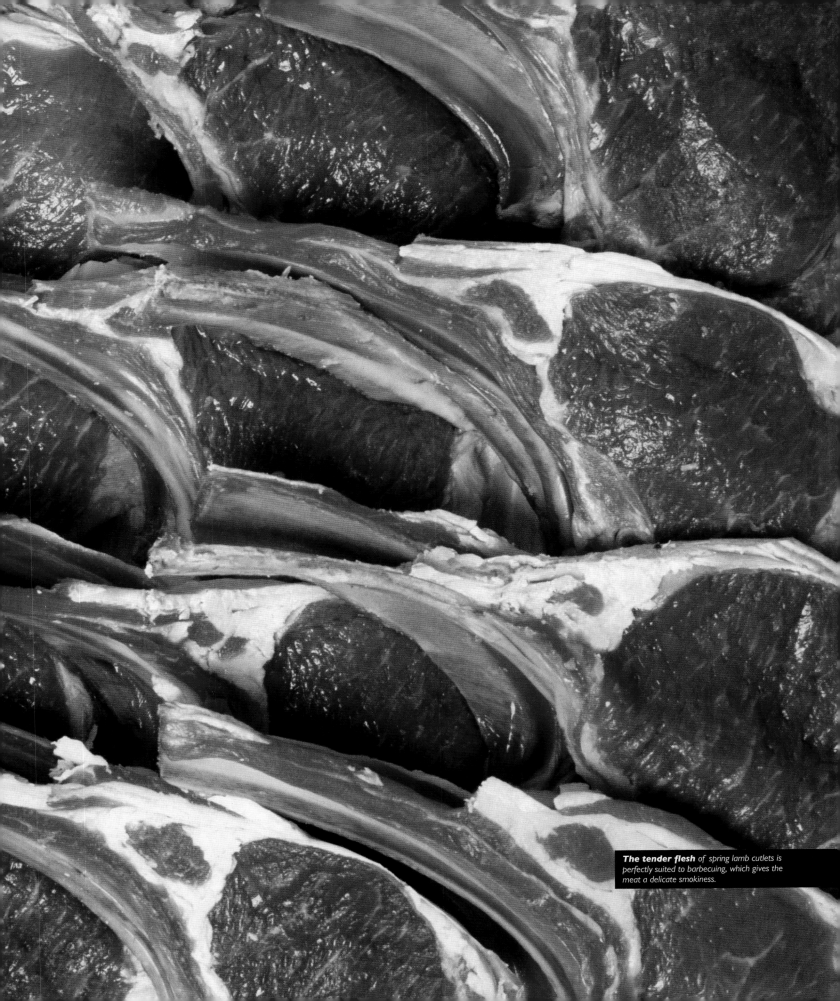

The tender flesh of spring lamb cutlets is perfectly suited to barbecuing, which gives the meat a delicate smokiness.

POULTRY ESSENTIALS

As a result of intensive farming, poultry has become a popular, everyday meat that is relatively cheap to buy and is available year-round. Whether bought as a whole bird or as breasts, legs (drumsticks), or wings, poultry is very versatile, lending itself to a multitude of styles of cuisine and cooking techniques.

BUY

Intensively farmed poultry is cheaper than organic or free-range birds, but it doesn't have the same flavor. Buy poultry from a quality source and make sure the meat is plump and the skin is not dry.

The cut Buy the cut that is most appropriate for the recipe you are cooking, or that you prefer. Buying a whole bird is often cheaper than buying portions, with the added bonus that you can use the carcass to make stock after cooking. Breasts are the most expensive cuts; thighs and legs (drumsticks) are the cheaper options.
Look for plump flesh. The meat should be plump and firm, the skin should have no dry patches, tears, or bruising.
Coloring Corn-fed chickens will have yellow skin, otherwise poultry generally should be a pale pink color with a whitish skin.
Check the bird's aroma. The bird should have a clean, fresh smell; a bad odor will indicate the bird is past its best and therefore not safe to eat.

Chicken drumsticks *are more fatty than breasts, and have darker meat. They are ideal for roasting, barbecuing, and for use in slow-cooked stews and casseroles.*

STORE

Fresh poultry should be stored in the coldest part of the fridge and cooked and eaten within a couple of days of purchase. Put the meat in a sealed container where its juices can't touch or drip on other food. If the bird has its giblets, remove them and store separately. Freeze poultry on the day of purchase, for up to three months. It should be defrosted slowly in the fridge. Cooked poultry should be cooled before storing in the fridge for up to two days.

PREPARE

Whole birds need a little preparation before roasting or braising. Some techniques, such as removing the wishbone, are optional, but do have benefits.

REMOVE THE WISHBONE

Removing the wishbone is not essential, but doing so does make the bird easier to carve into neat slices, or to dissect into joints. Each poultry species has a slightly different shape, but for all the birds, the wishbone is in the same place—just below the neck.

1 *Lift up the flap of skin at the neck end of the bird. Feel with your fingers the arched shape of the wishbone round the cavity.*

2 *With the tip of a sharp knife, pare the meat away from the wishbone (it is not attached to anything at the top).*

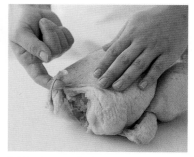

3 *After the top is freed, twist and bend the wishbone outward and downward. Then tuck the flap of skin back under the bird.*

STUFF A WHOLE BIRD Unless a bird is going to be cooked long and slow (for example, pot roasted), it is not advisable to put stuffing in the cavity because undercooked juices will drip onto it and could cause food poisoning. However, there are two alternatives. Stuffing can be made into little balls and roasted beside the bird in the roasting pan, or cooked in a separate dish in the oven. The latter is advisable with meat-based stuffings. The other alternative (shown here) is to push stuffing under the skin of the breast, where it protects the breast meat from drying out while allowing the skin to crisp and brown. It is not necessary to do this with duck and goose, which are already fatty.

Starting at the neck *end, push the back of a spoon or—better still—your fingers under the skin to part it from the breast meat. Be careful not to tear the skin, especially with small birds like Cornish game hen or quail. Gently push the stuffing in an even layer between the skin and meat, and fold the flap of neck skin back under the bird to secure it.*

STUFF A WHOLE BREAST

When stuffing poultry breasts it is important to use a stuffing that is either precooked, or one that will not require so much cooking that the meat is overcooked by the time the stuffing is safe to eat. For this reason is it better to avoid using any kind of raw meat in poultry stuffing unless the breasts are to be slowly and thoroughly cooked. Stuffings add texture as well as flavor and can range from crunchy items, such as nuts, to soft items, such as cooked rice or pearl barley. Complementary flavors include spicy ingredients, such as chilis, vegetables including sweet pepper, and fruits like raisins.

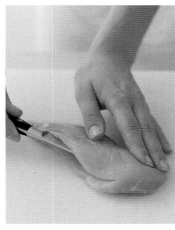

1 Lay the palm of your hand on the top of the breast meat. Using a small, sharp knife, cut horizontally through the meat, beginning in the center of the thick end. Use a stroking movement to keep the slit in the center of the meat and slightly tilt the knife away from your hand to avoid cutting yourself.

2 Pack the stuffing firmly into the cavity. If the slit has not gone far enough in, open it out a little more with the knife. Secure the stuffing with toothpicks or skewers, making sure they won't prevent the meat from touching the frying pan.

SPATCHCOCK

This flattening technique is normally used for small birds, such as Cornish game hen, squabs, quail, and small game birds. Flattening them allows the meat to cook evenly—avoiding burning sections and leaving thicker parts undercooked. It is commonly used for grilling and barbecuing and is not necessary for roasting. Spatchcocked birds can then be marinated or rubbed with spices before cooking.

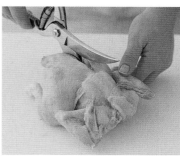

1 Using a pair of poultry shears or strong, sharp kitchen scissors, cut the bird from end to end on either side of the backbone. Remove and discard the backbone.

2 Turn the bird over, open it out and flatten it by pressing down sharply on the breast with the palm of your hand (as shown) to make it as evenly flat as possible.

3 If there is a big difference in the thickness of the muscles on the bird, such as on the thighs, slash the plumpest parts of the meat to ensure even cooking.

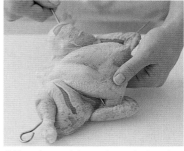

4 Thread a metal skewer diagonally through the drumstick, thigh, lower breast, and wing, making sure that the end result is flat. Repeat with another skewer on the other side.

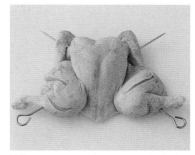

5 If necessary, press down again on the bird to make sure it is well flattened. The neatly spatchcocked bird is now ready for seasoning, marinating, and grilling.

MAKE POULTRY STOCK

Home-made stock gives genuine flavor to soups and sauces. Good-quality stock needs some meat as well as bones; if you don't have enough at first, freeze and combine them with another batch. An old boiling fowl, cut into pieces, makes excellent stock. For pale stock there is no need to brown the bones first; but for a deeper-colored stock, brush the bones with oil and roast at 400°F (200°C) for 20–30 minutes until golden brown, but no darker.

1 Pack the bones into a large pan with a selection of vegetables (onion, celery, carrot, garlic). Add a bunch of fresh herbs (parsley, coriander, thyme, bay leaf). Do not add salt.

2 Pour over enough water to cover the chicken bones and the vegetables. Bring the liquid to the boil, cover, and immediately reduce to a gentle simmer.

3 Simmer on the stove top or cook in a preheated oven at 325°F (160°C) for 1–1½ hours without letting it boil. If poultry stock is boiled, it will go cloudy.

4 Strain the cooked stock through a sieve into a clean bowl, cover, discarding the bones and vegetables. Allow to cool before putting it in a container in the fridge or freezer.

5 Poultry stock will keep for 2–3 days in the fridge. To freeze, pour into sealable storage container or thick freezerproof bags, making sure you expel the air before closing it.

MARINATE There are two main reasons to marinate poultry. One is to tenderize the meat, and the other is to add flavor to it. Most poultry sold today is relatively young and tender, so the tenderizing properties of marinating are not as important as they once were. As far as flavoring is concerned, most poultry, especially chicken, has a delicate flavor that can be drowned in a heavy, strong marinade, so flavors should be used with caution if the poultry flavor is to be preserved. Marinated poultry should always be kept in the fridge, completely covered in the marinade, as well as plastic wrap or in a sealed container. The poultry pieces should be turned in the marinade several times to distribute the flavors.

Liquid marinades

Wine, vinegar, or citrus juice combined with oil and flavorings, such as onion, garlic, herbs, spices, or fruit jelly will make a marinade that can be brushed over poultry or in which the pieces can be immersed. Acids, such as lemon and vinegar can dry out the meat, so use sparingly.

Oil-based marinades

This is the quickest and most effective way of transferring spicy flavors to the meat. These marinades include ingredients, such as lemon, lime, or orange zest, dried spices, chiles, juniper berries, crushed herbs. Rub thick mixtures thoroughly into the bird's skin.

COOK

Poultry is very versatile and can be cooked in a variety of ways, depending on the cut and the length of time you want to spend cooking. Whole birds take longer to cook than pieces, and can be roasted, or poached for a more delicate flavor. Pieces can be roasted, fried, grilled, barbecued, pot-roasted, or stewed.

ROAST All poultry can be roasted, from the smallest Cornish hen to the largest turkey. White meat needs plenty of oil or butter to prevent the meat drying out, but duck has enough fat to keep it moist. An initial high oven temperature is important to brown and caramelize the skin, but prolonged high heat will dry out the bird. Generally you should allow 20 minutes per 1lb (450g), plus 20 minutes over. Resting the cooked bird allows the heat from the outer parts to finish cooking it in the center.

1 Preheat the oven to 400°F (200°C). Smear the breast with oil or butter and sprinkle with black pepper. Larger birds will exude their own fat so a little oil will suffice. Place some aromatic flavors (spices, lemon, thyme, tarragon) in the cavity to perfume the meat.

2 Place in a pan and roast in the center of the oven for 15 minutes to brow the breast. Turn the bird over and baste it. Roast for another 30 minutes so that the legs cook without drying up the breast. Turn the chicken over onto its back, baste again, then finish the cooking.

3 Test for doneness by piercing the thickest part of the thigh right down to the bone. If there is any sign of red, or even pink, in the juices, return the bird to the oven.

4 When it is done, remove the bird to a warm carving dish, and cover loosely with foil (too tightly and the crisp skin will go soggy). Rest in a warm place for 15–20 minutes.

POACH Poaching is a gentle, slow way of cooking poultry, keeping it immersed in liquid so that it stays moist and very tender. Because it is not browned, the meat has a delicate, subtle flavor so it is worth buying a good-quality bird. Poaching is used in dishes where a particularly good stock is needed to make the accompanying sauce.

1 Choose a large pot that will comfortably accommodate the bird along with the vegetables and necessary liquid. Pour in enough boiling water to just cover it.

2 Add vegetables to taste (onions, garlic, carrots, celery), and a bunch of fresh herbs. Bring to a boil then reduce the heat and simmer for 40 minutes. Skim off foam.

3 Once cooked, lift the bird out gently in case it falls apart. Drain off any stock from the cavity. Poached poultry must be served very soon after it has been removed from its stock.

4 If serving the poached chicken as pot-au-feu, as here, season it to taste and serve the broth and vegetables in deep bowls with the sliced meat.

MAKE PAILLARDS

Chicken and turkey are the most common birds that are flattened into thin slices. They are either coated in breadcrumbs then fried like a *Weiner schnitzel*, as shown here, or wrapped around a stuffing, breadcrumbed, and fried, as in Chicken Kiev. Either the breast or the leg meat may be used; leg is more succulent but is not such a neat shape as the breast. Both may be purchased boned and skinned.

I *Place the meat between two pieces of plastic wrap, and using a rolling pin or meat tenderizer, beat out the meat until it is an even depth—just under ¼ inch (5mm) thick.*

2 *Season the meat to taste with spices, herbs, mustard, salt and pepper. In a skillet, heat 2 teaspoons of butter and enough oil to fill the skillet ¼ inch (5mm) deep.*

3 *Beat one or two eggs in a shallow bowl until well combined, and then dip the seasoned paillards in the beaten egg. Shake off any excess.*

4 *Dip the egged paillards into the breadcrumbs on both sides, pressing the meat down so it is well covered.*

5 *Quickly fry the coated paillards in the hot oil for 2–3 minutes on each side until golden brown. Drain on kitchen paper then serve.*

BARBECUE

Poultry requires a little patience on the barbecue, and it can be a tricky meat to get right. Never cook high and fast, as the skin will appear charred and cooked but the insides will not be. Choice cuts for barbecuing are wings, legs, and thighs with the bone left in. Marinate the poultry pieces in a flavored oil and roast in the oven first for 20 minutes—this will ensure that the insides are properly and safely cooked. Slash the flesh, add the pieces to the barbecue and cook over a medium heat for 5–10 minutes. Move the pieces to the edges of the grill so they cook through on a gentler heat for 15–20 minutes, turning frequently.

STEW, BRAISE, AND POT ROAST

All these methods involve browning the outside of the meat, adding liquid and vegetables, then cooking it slowly, either on the hob or in the oven. Generally speaking, stews have more liquid than braises, and pot roasts usually involve a whole bird rather than small joints or pieces of meat.

I *Heat some oil over a high heat in a heavy-bottomed pan until smoking. Brown the poultry all over. Be careful not to crowd the pan as the pieces will stew rather than brown.*

2 *After the meat is browned, add some shallots and brown these. Add garlic, mushrooms, and some chunks of carrots or celery next. Turn down the heat.*

3 *Add some water, wine, or stock and loosen any bits on the bottom of the pan into the liquid. Add some tomato purée, or herbs like tarragon, thyme, rosemary, sage for flavor.*

4 *Bring the liquid to a boil, cover the pan and reduce to a simmer. Small joints and diced poultry need 50 minutes to I hour. Do not overstew as the meat will be dry and stringy.*

MAKE GRAVY

The best gravy is that made in the roasting pan in which the bird has been cooked, because the residues will be dissolved into the gravy. Adding a little tomato paste, wine, herbs, spices, garlic or lemon zest will add another dimension to the flavors and a richness to the gravy. The thickness of the gravy is purely a matter of personal preference.

I *Skim off all the fat from the roasting pan with a large metal spoon, leaving behind the brown residue and roasting juices.*

2 *Place the roasting pan over a low heat, add I tbsp of all-purpose flour with a little of the fat and whisk it into the pan juices. Add stock or water and bring to the boil.*

3 *When the gravy has reached the desired consistency, strain it through a sieve into a hot container, discarding any solids, then serve it with the roast.*

CHICKEN

With its succulent, mild-flavored flesh that absorbs a huge variety of flavors, chicken is the most widely eaten meat in the world. Being economical and easy to rear, chickens were initially kept by small-scale farmers for their eggs; once too old to lay, the birds were only fit for boiling, and a roast chicken was an expensive treat. Today, chickens are farmed in the millions, often in highly intensive units, and chicken is the cheapest meat to buy. Broilers or roasters, about 12 weeks old, have tender meat; older boiling fowl need to be stewed, but have excellent flavor. *Capons* are castrated males that are fattened to produce especially tender, plump breasts. Corn-fed chicken has very yellow skin and fat.

BUY Free-range, corn-fed, and organic chickens are more expensive than intensively reared, but usually have better flavor and texture. Avoid chicken with bruised or broken legs, and meat that exudes a lot of liquid.

STORE Keep at the bottom of the fridge for up to 2 days, completely wrapped to avoid contaminating other foods. If there are giblets inside, remove them and use or freeze on the day of purchase. Portions can be frozen, tightly wrapped, for 6 months.

EAT Roast whole broilers. Grill, barbecue, fry, or braise joints; stir-fry *goujons*. Use ground chicken for burgers and homestyle dishes. Gently simmer boiling fowl for stews or soup.

FLAVOR PAIRINGS Bacon, cream, onion, garlic, mushrooms, tomatoes, lemon, cashews, coconut, chile, thyme, tarragon, paprika, cardamom, cumin, saffron, sesame, soy sauce, wine.

CLASSIC RECIPES Chicken Kiev; chicken korma; *coq au vin*; Circassian chicken; *poulet à l'estragon*; *pollo alla Marengo*; *waterzooi*.

Leg meat is much darker than breast meat; some people consider it to be more succulent.

Whole leg
Comprising the thigh and drumstick, a leg joint is good for the barbecue with a spicy coating, or for tasty stews like coq au vin.

Thigh
Sold skin on or skinless, bone-in or boneless, chicken thighs have particularly succulent meat. They are delicious roasted with the skin on, or marinated and simmered. When the bone is removed they can be stuffed and rolled up.

Ground chicken
Good for extra-lean burgers and meatballs, ground chicken can also be substituted for beef in many other dishes.

Drumstick
The end part of the leg, drumsticks make excellent finger food, and are popular roasted or barbecued, whether plain, marinated, or coated in sauce.

The skin around the drumstick keeps it moist during cooking; it has very little fat compared to the thigh.

Diced chicken
Lean and tender, diced chicken is useful for casseroles, and also for kebabs for the barbecue.

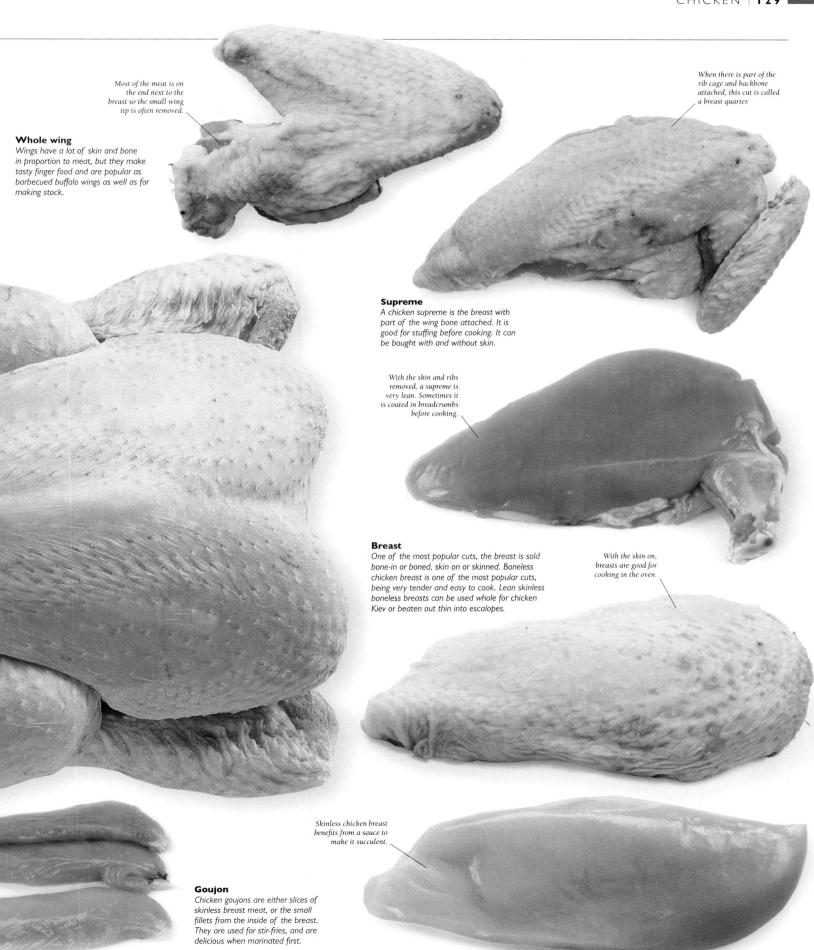

Most of the meat is on the end next to the breast so the small wing tip is often removed.

When there is part of the rib cage and backbone attached, this cut is called a breast quarter.

Whole wing
Wings have a lot of skin and bone in proportion to meat, but they make tasty finger food and are popular as barbecued buffalo wings as well as for making stock.

Supreme
A chicken supreme is the breast with part of the wing bone attached. It is good for stuffing before cooking. It can be bought with and without skin.

With the skin and ribs removed, a supreme is very lean. Sometimes it is coated in breadcrumbs before cooking.

Breast
One of the most popular cuts, the breast is sold bone-in or boned, skin on or skinned. Boneless chicken breast is one of the most popular cuts, being very tender and easy to cook. Lean skinless boneless breasts can be used whole for chicken Kiev or beaten out thin into escalopes.

With the skin on, breasts are good for cooking in the oven.

Skinless chicken breast benefits from a sauce to make it succulent.

Goujon
Chicken goujons are either slices of skinless breast meat, or the small fillets from the inside of the breast. They are used for stir-fries, and are delicious when marinated first.

CHICKEN (CONTINUED)

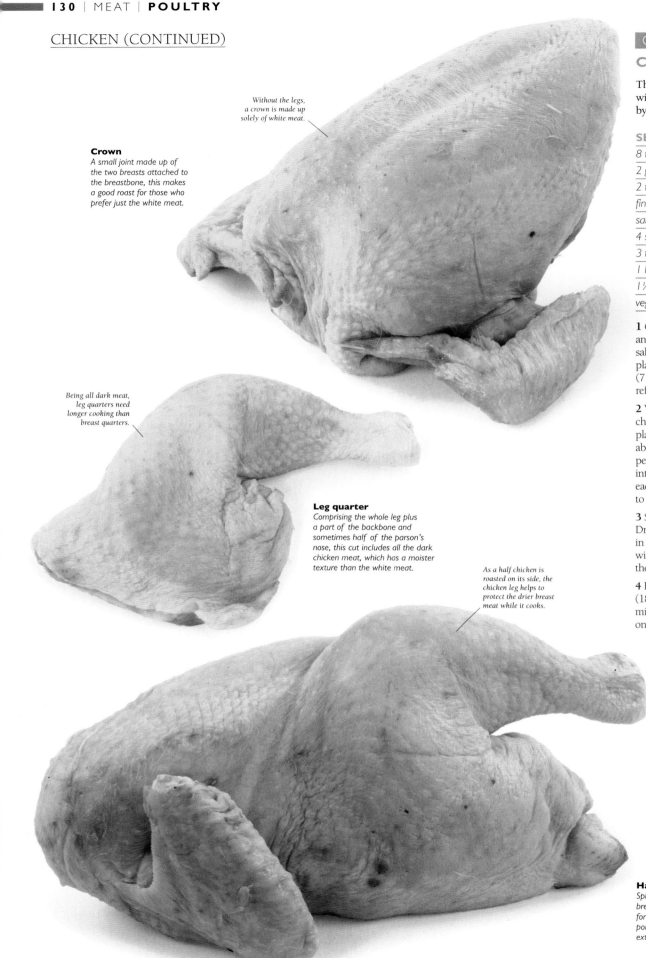

Crown
A small joint made up of the two breasts attached to the breastbone, this makes a good roast for those who prefer just the white meat.

Without the legs, a crown is made up solely of white meat.

Being all dark meat, leg quarters need longer cooking than breast quarters.

Leg quarter
Comprising the whole leg plus a part of the backbone and sometimes half of the parson's nose, this cut includes all the dark chicken meat, which has a moister texture than the white meat.

As a half chicken is roasted on its side, the chicken leg helps to protect the drier breast meat while it cooks.

Half chicken
Split lengthwise down the spine and breastbone, a half chicken is useful for serving 2 people, or if extra portions are needed and a whole extra chicken is too much.

CHICKEN KIEV

This classic dish of chicken stuffed with a garlic butter was given its name by Russian immigrants in France.

SERVES 4

8 tbsp (1 stick) butter, softened

2 garlic cloves, crushed through a press

2 tbsp chopped fresh parsley

finely grated zest of 1 lemon

salt and freshly ground black pepper

4 skinless boneless chicken breast halves

3 tbsp all-purpose flour

1 large egg, beaten

1½ cups fresh bread crumbs

vegetable oil, for deep-frying

1 Combine the butter, garlic, parsley, and lemon zest in a bowl. Season with salt and pepper. Spoon onto a sheet of plastic wrap and shape into a 3 x 2in (7 x 5cm) rectangle. Wrap and refrigerate for 2 hours, or until very firm.

2 Working with 1 at a time, pound the chicken breasts between two sheets of plastic wrap to an even thickness of about ¼in (5mm). Season with salt and pepper. Cut the garlic butter lengthwise into four equal sticks and place one on each chicken breast. Fold in 2 sides; roll to enclose the butter completely.

3 Season the flour with salt and pepper. Dredge each chicken parcel in flour; dip in beaten egg, and, finally, coat evenly with bread crumbs. Take care to keep the chicken wrapped around the butter.

4 Heat a deep pan of oil to 350°F (180°C). Cook the chicken for 6–8 minutes, or until golden brown. Drain on paper towels and serve hot.

CHICKEN COOKING CHART

Choosing the correct cooking method for a cut of chicken is vitally important. Use this chart to identify the best way to prepare your chosen cut.

CUT	DESCRIPTION	BROIL/BARBECUE	FRY	ROAST	STEW
		Thermometer internal temperature reading: 165°F (75°C).	*Thermometer internal-temperature reading: 165°F (75°C).*	*Thermometer internal temperature reading: 165°F (75°C).*	
WHOLE OR HALF	Includes all skin, bone, and fat. Remove giblets from whole bird before cooking. Split lenthwise for half chicken (often more convenient than a whole bird).	Not recommended.	Not recommended	Whole or half chicken: Preheat oven to 350°F (180°C). Roast for 20 min per 1lb (450g) plus 20 min, or until juices run clear.	Whole or half chicken: Brown if desired, then add liquid, plus vegetables, if required, and cover. Simmer, or stew at 325°F (160°C), for 1–2 hours.
QUARTER	Usually breast plus wing and rib, but also a whole leg with thigh and a little backbone.	Heat barbecue or broiler to medium-high. Brush chicken with oil and brown all over, then reduce heat to low. Cook, turning, for 35 min, or until juices run clear. Apply barbecue sauce or other baste 10 min before end.	Heat fat in deep fryer. Fry gently in deep fat for 30–40 min, or until juices run clear.	Preheat oven to 350°F (180°C). Roast for 30 min or until juices run clear.	Simmer or stew as whole or half chicken, but for 1–1½ hours.
CROWN	This is the whole of the breast: two breasts attached to the breastbone.	Not recommended.	Not recommended.	Roast crown as whole or half chicken.	Simmer or stew as whole or half chicken.
WHOLE LEG	Comprises the thigh and drumstick.	Barbecue or broil whole leg as quarter.	Fry whole leg as quarter.	Roast whole leg as quarter.	Simmer or stew whole leg as whole or half chicken, but for 1 hour. Also suitable for soup.
THIGH	May include skin and bone, or be skinned and boned.	Barbecue or broil thigh as quarter.	Fry thigh as quarter. Or, if boneless, slice and stir-fry.	Roast thigh as quarter.	Simmer or stew thigh as whole or half chicken, but for 1 hour. Also suitable for soup.
DRUM-STICK	Includes bone; may or may not be skinned.	Barbecue or broil drumstick as quarter.	Fry drumstick as quarter.	Roast drumstick as quarter.	Simmer or stew drumstick as whole or half chicken, but for 1 hour. Also suitable for soup.
WING	Contains a lot of bone in proportion to meat.	Barbecue or broil wing as quarter, but for 20–25 min.	Fry wing as quarter, but for 25–30 min.	Roast wing as quarter, but for 20 min.	Simmer or stew wing as whole or half chicken, but for 1 hour. Also suitable for soup.
BREAST FILLET	Boneless. Usually skinless but may have skin on.	Barbecue or broil breast fillet as quarter, but for 20–30 min.	Fry breast fillet as quarter, but for 10–20 min.	Not recommended.	Simmer or stew breast fillet as whole or half chicken, but for 1 hour.
GOUJONS	Thin-cut strips of breast meat ¼in (5mm) thick.	Heat barbecue or broiler to medium-high. Brush goujons with oil, thread onto skewers, and cook for 10–15 min, turning several times to brown on all sides.	Heat oil in a frying pan or wok over a high heat. Stir-fry goujons for 3–5 min, or until cooked through.	Not recommended.	Not recommended.
DICED CHICKEN	Boneless pieces of meat.	Heat barbecue or broiler to medium-high. Thread dice onto skewers and brush with oil. Brown on all sides, then continue to cook for 10–15 min, or until cooked through.	Heat oil in a frying pan over a high heat. Brown dice all over, then lower heat and continue cooking for 5–15 min, or until cooked through.	Not recommended.	Simmer or stew dice as whole or half chicken, but for 1 hour.
MINCE	Use for koftas or burgers or in made dishes.	Heat barbecue or broil to medium-high. Press mince onto skewers or shape into patties, including some fat. Cook for 10–20 min, depending on thickness, or until cooked through.	Heat oil in a frying pan over medium heat. Press mince onto skewers or shape into patties, including some fat. Fry for 10–20 min, depending on thickness, or until cooked through.	Not recommended.	Brown mince and vegetables, then add liquid and simmer, or cook at 160°C (325°F/Gas 3), for 1–1½ hours.

TURKEY

Modern turkeys are descended from the smaller wild turkey native to North America. Nowadays, they are mainly industrially reared, but there are also a number of free-range premium birds available, such as the bronze turkey, which have better texture and flavor. The average size of a whole turkey is 12lb (5.5kg); smaller birds are supplied outside the festive seasons. Turkey meat is leaner than chicken. The dark (leg) meat has more fat and is more succulent than white (breast) meat.

BUY Turkeys are sold both fresh and frozen, whole or in pieces, all year round. For roasting, look for a bird with a plump breast. Allow 12oz (350g) per person for whole birds, 5–6oz (150–180g) for boneless cuts.

STORE Keep whole birds and pieces at the bottom of the fridge for up to 2 days, completely wrapped to avoid contaminating other foods. If there are giblets inside a whole bird, remove them and use on the day of purchase. Tightly wrapped pieces can be frozen for up to 6 months, and ground turkey for up to 2 months.

EAT Thaw a frozen whole turkey thoroughly and bring to room temperature 1 hour before cooking. Roast whole birds, crowns, boneless joints and rolls, and legs, making sure they are cooked right through: the internal temperature reading should be 165°F (75°C). Grill, fry, or stir-fry breast cuts; these and legs can also be stewed. Diced turkey can be stewed or stir-fried, or grilled or fried on skewers. Use ground meat for burgers, or as a lean substitute for beef.

FLAVOR PAIRINGS Bacon, garlic, chile, mushrooms, onion, tomatoes, coriander seed, sage, cranberry, lemon, chestnuts, cardamom, chocolate.

CLASSIC RECIPES *Mole poblano*; roast stuffed turkey; turkey schnitzel; deviled turkey legs.

Leg
One of the cheapest cuts, the leg comprises the thigh and the drumstick. Turkey leg has lighter meat at the top, and becomes much darker at the drumstick end. It can be roasted, but is often better stewed, or braised.

Boneless breast joint
A tender joint for roasting. One breast makes a slim joint; both breasts together are plumper. The two boneless breasts sold joined but untied is called a butterfly.

Turkey roll
A turkey roll normally comprises both breast and leg meat, rolled together to make an easy-to-slice roast; some are made of offcuts of turkey meat molded into a roll. The two boned breasts rolled together with stuffing in between are also sold as turkey roll. Calculate cooking times as for a whole turkey.

Skin on a turkey roll will keep it moist during cooking; if sold skinless, wrap with bacon.

The large proportion of skin makes the wing crisp well.

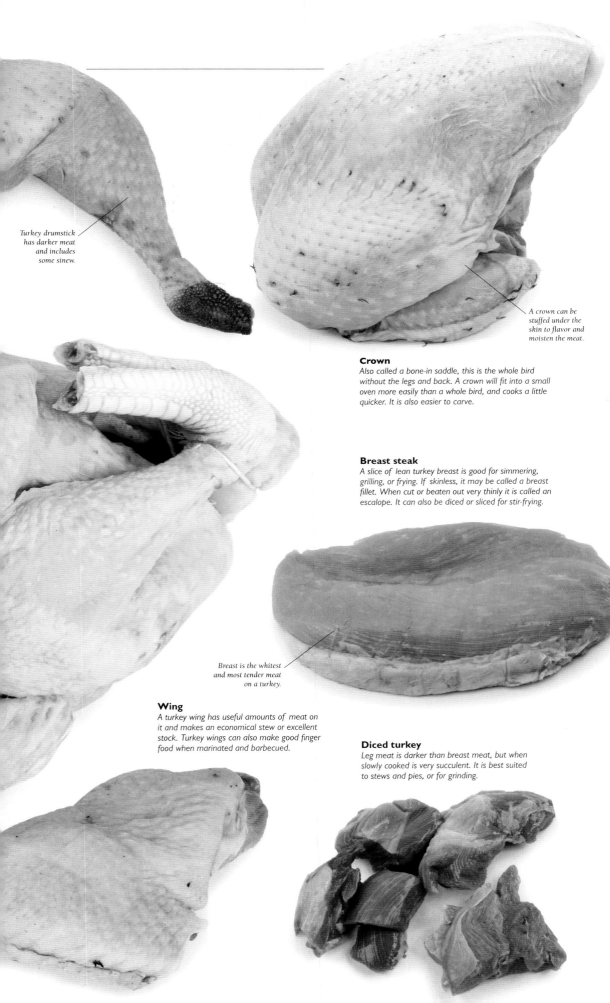

Turkey drumstick has darker meat and includes some sinew.

A crown can be stuffed under the skin to flavor and moisten the meat.

Crown
Also called a bone-in saddle, this is the whole bird without the legs and back. A crown will fit into a small oven more easily than a whole bird, and cooks a little quicker. It is also easier to carve.

Breast steak
A slice of lean turkey breast is good for simmering, grilling, or frying. If skinless, it may be called a breast fillet. When cut or beaten out very thinly it is called an escalope. It can also be diced or sliced for stir-frying.

Breast is the whitest and most tender meat on a turkey.

Wing
A turkey wing has useful amounts of meat on it and makes an economical stew or excellent stock. Turkey wings can also make good finger food when marinated and barbecued.

Diced turkey
Leg meat is darker than breast meat, but when slowly cooked is very succulent. It is best suited to stews and pies, or for grinding.

MOLE POBLANA

This complex chocolate-enriched sauce from Mexico is traditionally served with cooked turkey parts, such as legs, thighs, and wings.

SERVES 10

10 mulato or other dried chile peppers
9 ancho chile peppers (dried poblanos)
3 pasilla or other dried chile peppers
2 canned chipotle chile peppers packed in adobo sauce, drained
7oz (200g) lard or 1 cup corn oil
1 onion, chopped
3 garlic cloves, crushed
2 red bell peppers, chopped
10 tomatillos, peeled and chopped
4 tomatoes, peeled and chopped
¾ cup dark raisins
4oz (115g) sesame seeds, toasted
2oz (60g) pumpkin seeds
1 cup coarsely chopped almonds
1 cup coarsely chopped peanuts
3 corn tortillas, toasted and torn into pieces
1 bolillo or other roll, crumbled and toasted
10 allspice berries
10 anise seeds
6 coriander seeds
6 whole cloves
1 stick cinnamon
½ tsp grated nutmeg
4 cups turkey stock
3oz (85g) Mexican or dark chocolate
sugar, freshly ground black pepper, and vinegar, to taste
cooked turkey legs, thighs, and wings

1 Remove stems and seeds from the chiles. Cook the mulato, ancho, and pasilla chiles in 2 tbsp lard to soften. Transfer to a food processor. In the same pan, cook the onion, garlic, bell peppers, tomatillos, and tomatoes in 3½ tbsp lard until the onion is soft, then add along with the chipotles and raisins to the processor. Purée.

2 Gently cook the sesame seeds, pumpkin seeds, almonds, peanuts, tortillas, and bread crumbs, and 3½ tbsp lard until the nuts are golden. Process until smooth, adding a little stock. Return to the pan with the chiles and vegetables and gradually stir in the remaining stock. Stir over low heat until smooth and thick.

3 Heat the lard in a casserole and cook the turkey until browned. Lower the heat and add the sauce. Add the chocolate and, once melted, the sugar, pepper, and vinegar. Cook for 30 minutes. Serve with rice or tamales.

DUCK IN ORANGE SAUCE

A superb French classic of rich duck with a bitter orange sauce, this was originally made with wild duck, but works well with domestic duck.

SERVES 4

4 tbsp butter

½ cup all-purpose flour

4 cups game or chicken stock, heated

1 x Long Island duck, weighing about 4½ lbs (2kg)

2 Seville (bitter) oranges

¼ cup granulated sugar

3 tbsp red wine vinegar

1 Melt the butter in a large saucepan. When it turns golden brown, stir in the flour. Gradually whisk in the stock until smooth. Bring to a boil, then reduce the heat and simmer for about 1 hour or until reduced by half.

2 Meanwhile, preheat the oven to 400°F (200°C). Prick the skin of the duck all over with a fork and season with salt. Place breast-side down on a rack in a roasting pan. Roast for 30 minutes. Pour the fat from the pan, turn the duck over, and roast for another 1 hour. Remove from the oven and, when cool enough to handle, remove the legs and breasts. Set aside in a warm place.

3 Use a vegetable peeler to remove the thin orange skin off the oranges and cut it into fine strips. (Do not cut into the bitter white pith.) Blanch the orange strips in boiling water for 5 minutes, then drain; reserve the zest. Squeeze the juice from the oranges.

4 Heat the sugar in a small saucepan until it melts and begins to caramelize. Carefully add the vinegar (with caution, as it can sputter and splash) and dissolve the caramel—this takes a few minutes. Add to the thickened stock together with the orange juice and stir to mix. Add most of the strips of orange zest.

5 Warm the duck pieces gently in the orange sauce, being careful not to overcook the duck. Cut the breast meat across the grain into diagonal slices, if desired. Garnish with the remaining orange zest before serving.

DUCK

Ducks have been domesticated for over 4,000 years. Nowadays they are intensively reared. Most breeds are descended from the wild mallard and have dark meat with a thick layer of fat under the skin; those that are bred from the Muscovy duck are larger and leaner. With all duck, the ratio of meat to fat and bone is low, but the meat is very tasty and rich. Where duck is mainly reared for foie gras production, much of the rest of the carcass is made into confit (duck pieces preserved in duck fat). The fat is also sold separately for cooking.

🔒 **BUY** Free-range ducks are more expensive than intensively reared housed ducks, but have superior flavor and texture. Look for birds with plump breasts, preferably without excessive fat. Rich duck meat is filling, so a 6oz (180g) breast makes a generous portion. Allow at least 1½lb (650g) per person with whole birds.

STORE Keep whole birds and pieces, well wrapped, at the bottom of the fridge for up to 3 days. Or freeze, tightly wrapped, for up to 6 months.

EAT Roast whole duck at 350°F (180°C) for 45 minutes per 2¼lb (1kg), plus 20 minutes. Grill, fry, or barbecue duck breasts to serve pink; score or prick skin to release the fat and start cooking them fat-side to the heat. Or slice into strips for stir-fry. Grill or barbecue legs, or use them for stews and confit.

FLAVOR PAIRINGS Garlic, scallions, turnips, ginger, sage, apples, cherries, cranberries, plums, orange, olives, almonds, soy sauce, hoisin sauce, honey, vinegar, wine.

CLASSIC RECIPES Duck in orange sauce; duck confit; Peking duck; *faisinjan*; *pato con peras*; *anatra alla Bartolomeo Scappi*; *cassoulet*; *pasticcio*.

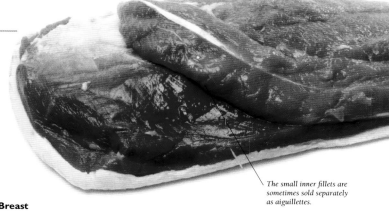

The small inner fillets are sometimes sold separately as aiguillettes.

Breast
Duck breasts have dense, rich meat. If cooking whole, score or prick through the skin and fat, then fry skin-side down, or grill skin-side up, to melt and release excess fat. Or, remove all skin and fat, and slice into goujons for stir-frying.

A whole duck leg makes one portion.

Leg
Duck legs have superb flavor. They take longer to cook than breast meat, and have a little more sinew, but can be grilled, roasted, or used to make confit. Prick or slash the skin and fat layer beneath before cooking.

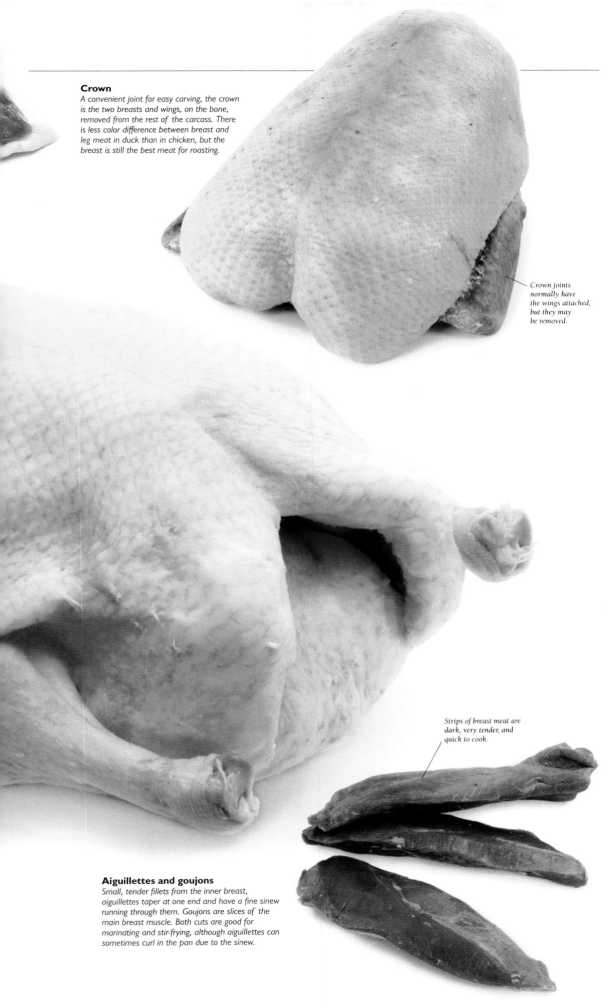

Crown

A convenient joint for easy carving, the crown is the two breasts and wings, on the bone, removed from the rest of the carcass. There is less color difference between breast and leg meat in duck than in chicken, but the breast is still the best meat for roasting.

Crown joints normally have the wings attached, but they may be removed.

Strips of breast meat are dark, very tender, and quick to cook.

Aiguillettes and goujons

Small, tender fillets from the inner breast, aiguillettes taper at one end and have a fine sinew running through them. Goujons are slices of the main breast muscle. Both cuts are good for marinating and stir-frying, although aiguillettes can sometimes curl in the pan due to the sinew.

CLASSIC RECIPE

DUCK CONFIT

From Gascony in France, this uses a time-honored method of preserving meat by salting and then cooking it in its own fat.

SERVES 4

4 duck legs
6oz (175g) coarse sea salt
4 garlic cloves, crushed
1oz (30g) white peppercorns
1 tsp coriander seeds
5 juniper berries
1 tbsp chopped fresh thyme
2¼lbs (1kg) duck or goose fat, heated until liquid and then cooled slightly

1 Dry the duck legs on paper towels. Pound the salt, garlic, peppercorns, coriander seeds, juniper berries, and thyme in a large mortar and pestle to make a coarse paste. Alternatively, process in a food processor. Rub this mixture into the skin of the duck legs, then arrange them in a single layer, skin-side down, in a non-metallic dish. Cover with plastic wrap and refrigerate for 12 hours.

2 Preheat the oven to 275°F (140°C). Rinse the duck well and pat dry, then place the pieces side by side in a baking dish just large enough to hold them in a single layer. Spoon the duck fat over the legs.

3 Place in the oven to cook for 1½ hours, or until the duck is very tender when tested in the thickest part with the pointed tip of a knife.

4 Transfer the duck legs to a plastic container. Ladle the fat over the duck through a fine sieve, being careful not to scoop up any of the juices from the bottom of the dish. Be sure the meat is covered with at least 1in (2.5cm) of fat. Leave to cool, then transfer the duck and fat to a crock, large glass jars, or freezer bags. Seal and refrigerate until needed.

5 When ready to serve, remove the duck legs from the fat and sauté or broil, turning occasionally, until well browned and heated through. Duck fat can be heated and strained, and refrigerated or frozen in an airtight container for future use.

STUFFED ROAST GOOSE

A rich goose is a traditional British treat at Michaelmas in September, or for Christmas.

SERVES 6–8

1 goose with giblets, weighing 10lbs (4.5kg)
4 onions, finely chopped
1 cup fresh breadcrumbs
4 tbsp butter, melted and cooled slightly
10 fresh sage leaves, chopped
salt and freshly ground black pepper
1 egg yolk
2 tbsp all-purpose flour
tart apple sauce, to serve

1 Preheat the oven to 450°F (230°C). Remove excess fat from inside the goose. Prick the skin all over with a fork. Chop the goose liver and set aside. Simmer the giblets in a pot of water to make stock.

2 Add the onions and chopped goose liver to a pot of boiling water; cook for 5 minutes, then drain and let cool for a few minutes. Mix with the breadcrumbs, butter, sage, salt and pepper. Stir in the egg yolk until well blended. Stuff loosely into the cavity of the goose and sew or secure closed with a skewer. Cover the wings and drumsticks with foil to prevent burning.

3 Place the goose upside down on a rack in a deep roasting pan. Roast for 30 minutes, then turn the goose over and roast for another 30 minutes. Drain off the fat in the roasting pan, reserving the fat. Cover the goose with foil, lower the heat to 375°F (190°C), and roast for 1½ hours. Drain off fat again. Remove the foil and roast for a final 30 minutes. Transfer the goose om to a warm serving platter, cover loosely, and allow to rest for 30 minutes before carving.

4 To make the gravy, heat 3 tbsp of goose fat in a saucepan, stir in the flour, and cook for 5 minutes over low heat. Gradually whisk in enough hot giblet stock until the mixture has the consistency of gravy. When the goose has been removed from the roasting pan to rest, pour off all the fat from the pan and add the gravy. Cook over low heat, using a wooden spoon to scrape up any browned bits from the bottom of the pan. Strain the gravy through a fine sieve and keep warm. Strain the gravy.

5 Carve the goose and serve with the gravy, stuffing, and tart apple sauce.

GOOSE

Domestic geese are grass-eaters and do not thrive in intensive conditions, so they are reared free-range. They are seasonal birds, traditionally eaten at Christmas. The proportion of meat to bone is low, so goose is an expensive treat; however, the light fat is superb for frying and other cooking. With its deeply colored, rich meat, domestic goose is very different from wild goose, which has darker, often very lean meat that is inclined to be tough from flying. Geese are also reared for *foie gras*.
🔒 **BUY** Green (young, grass-fed) geese are available in early fall; thereafter geese are grain-fed and fatter. They can also be found frozen year round. Usually sold as whole birds, (look for a plump breast), joints are also available. Allow at least 1½lb (650g) per person when roasting a whole, fat bird.
📦 **STORE** A large goose may not fit in some domestic fridges, but stored at 39°F (4°C) or below will keep for up to 5 days; otherwise use within 2 days of purchase. Or freeze, well wrapped, for up to 6 months; allow 2 days for thorough thawing.
● **EAT** Stuff and roast, whole young birds at 425°F (220°C) for 16 minutes per 1lb (450g); the internal temperature should be 155°F (70°C) (pour off and keep the large amount of fat produced). Stuff goose neck skin. Use older birds, legs, and wild goose for casseroles and confit, or ground breast meat for terrines, burgers, and homestyle dishes.
FLAVOR PAIRINGS Apples, onion, red cabbage, tomatoes, white beans, ginger, sage, oatmeal, almonds, apricot, prunes, soy sauce, red wine.
CLASSIC RECIPES Roast goose; *cassoulet*; stuffed goose neck.

Whole goose
Although there isn't a lot of meat on a goose, it is one of the most delicious of all roasted birds. Before cooking, check inside both ends and pull out excess fat.

Goose should have a good covering of fat, but too much is poor value. Young (green) goose has less fat than mature birds.

Breast fillet
The most tender part of the goose, a whole breast weighs around 2¼lb (1kg); the thick layer of fat means that it will reduce significantly during cooking. Because geese are grass-fed, the breast may be roasted or grilled to medium-rare safely.

Score through the thick layer of fat before cooking.

GUINEA FOWL

Originally from Africa, guinea fowl have been domesticated for hundreds of years in Europe and are now sold around the world. They have a yellow skin similar to corn-fed chicken, though proportionally less breast meat. Their flesh is darker than chicken, with a flavor halfway between chicken and pheasant. Although tender, the meat is quite lean and inclined to be dry if not cooked carefully.
🔒 **BUY** Guinea fowl are usually sold as whole birds, occasionally as boneless breasts. Allow 9–12oz (250–350g) per person on the bone.
📦 **STORE** Store whole birds or breasts, wrapped, at the bottom of the fridge for up to 3 days. Or freeze, tightly wrapped, for up to 6 months.
● **EAT** Roast whole birds like chicken, making sure they are completely cooked, through not overdone.
To prevent them from drying out, cover the breast with bacon or baste the bird regularly. Grill, fry, or poach the breasts, or dice or cut into strips for a stir-fry. Legs can be grilled, barbecued, or casseroled.
FLAVOR PAIRINGS Bacon, cream, mushrooms, shallots, sweet potatoes, cilantro, saffron, tarragon, thyme, lemon, grapes, plantains, chestnuts, soy sauce, sherry, cider, wine.

OSTRICH

The ostrich's diet is mainly vegetarian, with a few insects. Native to Africa, this big, flightless bird is now farmed in many countries for its skin and feathers, but also for meat, as is emu, the smaller Australian equivalent. Farmed ostrich is fed on commercial rations as well as grass. The lean, dark red meat from young birds tastes like mild venison. Any fat is confined to the outside and is usually trimmed off before sale; there is no marbling. Ostriches have very little breast meat; the back and thigh give the prime steaks and joints. Lower leg meat is diced or ground.

BUY Ostrich is available from supermarkets, farmers' markets, and specialist butchers. Allow 6–7oz (180–200g) per portion.

STORE Keep, wrapped, at the bottom of the fridge for up to 5 days. Store prepacked meat according to instructions. Boneless cuts can be stored in the freezer for up to a year.

EAT Grill, fry, roast, and barbecue the back and thigh cuts. Because ostrich is very lean, roasting joints and steaks should be served pink. Braise or stew tougher leg meat, and use ground meat for burgers and other homestyle dishes.

FLAVOR PAIRINGS Bacon, anchovy, shrimp, cream, bulb fennel, garlic, lemongrass, prunes, red berries, peanuts, curry paste, ginger, honey, soy sauce, wine.

Thigh fan fillet
A triangular-shaped piece of meat, this is the largest of the thigh muscles. It is tender enough to roast, or can be sliced into steaks.

When cutting steaks, it is important to slice against the grain.

Because of its shape, this cut is also called tenderloin.

Back fillet
This comes from the back, and the meat is dark and lean. The most tender cut of ostrich, it can be cooked like a venison loin –– roasted whole or sliced into medallions.

Neck
Neck meat is good for braising and stewing, or for grinding. If making burgers, add some fat to lubricate this very lean meat.

POUSSIN

Poussin is the French name for a young chicken sold at 4–6 weeks old. Rock Cornish game hens, popular in North America, are a slightly heavier type of chicken, but are also 4–6 weeks old (despite their name, they are neither game birds nor necessarily female). Because both of these birds are immature, there is a high proportion of bone to meat, but they are very tender and succulent.

BUY Although most commonly sold whole, these birds are also available boned and stuffed or spatchcocked. A whole poussin weighs about 1lb (450g) and makes one portion. A Cornish game hen (sometimes called a double poussin) weighs up to 2¼lb (1kg) and will feed 2–3 people.

STORE Keep fresh birds, wrapped, at the bottom of the fridge for up to 3 days. Or, tightly wrap and freeze for up to 6 months.

EAT Roast, bake, or simmer whole and stuffed birds. If roasting, rub all over with butter or oil and sprinkle with sea salt for a crisp skin. Allow 40–60 minutes, plus extra cooking time if stuffed; the internal temperature reading should be 165°F (75°C). Grill, fry, or barbecue spatchcocked birds.

FLAVOR PAIRINGS Bacon, garlic, shallots, tomatoes, mushrooms, lemon, saffron, lemongrass, rosemary, thyme, tarragon, bay leaf, Makrut lime, soy sauce, white wine.

CLASSIC RECIPE Roast poussin.

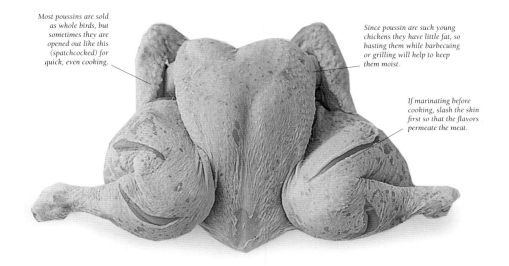

Most poussins are sold as whole birds, but sometimes they are opened out like this (spatchcocked) for quick, even cooking.

Since poussin are such young chickens they have little fat, so basting them while barbecuing or grilling will help to keep them moist.

If marinating before cooking, slash the skin first so that the flavors permeate the meat.

GAME ESSENTIALS

The term "game meat" covers a large number of species, roughly divided into furred game (animals), and feathered game (birds), which are further divided into land birds and waterfowl. Their common feature is that they are wild and hunted for both sport and food. In a global context, therefore, the list of possible species is huge, since nearly every animal has been hunted for food at some stage. So, for the purposes of this book, the species covered here are those that are most popularly sold across the world. Availability varies between countries, of course; in some, such as the US, it is illegal to sell indigenous wild game, although it is eaten in large quantities. Much game is farmed; some in free-ranging conditions, so they are similar to the young of wild species, others semi-intensively.

BUY

Wild game is best bought in season when it is fresh and in best condition. Game that has no season is generally best in late summer and fall. Farmed game is sold all year round.

Small game birds, such as quail, can be quickly cooked on a barbecue, or under a grill. A glaze adds flavor, but be careful not to mask the delicate flavor of the meat.

PREPARE

Game birds were traditionally sold with their feathers on and undrawn; very often a "brace" (a male and a female) was sold. Nowadays most are sold plucked and drawn, ready for cooking. Male birds are bigger than females, and although a brace was traditional, it is actually better to cook two or more of the same size together, regardless of sex, so that they cook evenly. Game birds are most commonly cooked whole, though increasingly just the deboned breasts are sold to be cooked as steaks. Occasionally the "crown" of a bird (the two breasts attached to the breastbone) is sold roasted on its own. Crowns are usually skinned, in which case the meat needs to be protected with bacon or some other lubricating substance during cooking. Small game birds are sometimes spatchcocked, that is, split down the middle and opened out flat so that they will cook evenly when grilled or barbecued. Small game animals, such as hare and rabbit, are usually sold as whole skinned carcasses, although occasionally they will be sold jointed into pieces. Large game animals, such as deer and boar, are butchered as for domestic meats, although sometimes there is less variety in cuts. If you prefer not to prepare your game from scratch, a good butcher will do some or all the work for you.

JOINT A RABBIT Rabbit is best skinned as soon as it is shot. If sold in fur, wash carcass after skinning. Wild rabbit varies in size and tenderness. Young and farmed rabbit has firm, meaty flesh that is tender and so can be roasted, but it is just as good slow-cooked in casseroles or stews. Stew or simmer old rabbit. Allow 12oz–1lb (350-450g) per person to account for the bonier parts.

1 Place the rabbit on its back on the work surface. Using kitchen scissors, cut away the liver from the cavity and set aside.

2 Next, remove the leg by cutting through the ball and socket joint in the direction of the backbone, with a very sharp boning knife.

3 Repeat this with the other leg and set it aside. Turn the rabbit over and cut off each foreleg as close to the rib cage as possible.

4 Once all the legs have been removed, use a sharp chef's knife to cut away the backbone that is now visible. Press hard on the knife in order to make a clean cut through the bone.

5 Flip the rabbit over onto its back again, and cut right up through the breastbone using sharp kitchen scissors. The breast meat should separate into two even sections.

6 Turn the rabbit over once more, tucking the breast sections neatly underneath. Make a clean cut with a chef's knife, so that there are just four ribs attached to the loin.

7 The saddle may be grilled or roasted, and the rest casseroled, while the bones can be cooked up for stock. The liver and kidneys can be fried or grilled, or added to stews or pies.

BUYING AND HANDLING GAME
Although you can buy oven-ready game from supermarkets, a specialist game dealer will be able to give you more advice on your meat.

GAME SEASONS In most countries, game animals and birds have a "close season"; or a period of the year during which the animal may not be killed or its meat sold. Close seasons are designed to protect animals while they breed and rear their young; however, species that have become pests due to overpopulation have no close seasons. Each country has its own laws regarding killing game, though as a general ruled the spring and summer are the periods during which close seasons often apply.

SHOT When game meats have been shot with guns there is always the possibility of finding fragments of shot or bullets in the meat. (This rarely applies to farmed game.) This is particularly true of small animals, like rabbits and birds, which are dispatched with shotguns that fire a dose of pellets, unlike large animals such as deer or boar that are shot with rifles that fire a single bullet. Some waterfowl guns now use steel pellets, which are even harder than lead. Pellets and bullet fragments can damage teeth if they are bitten into, so examine the meat when purchasing to see if pellets have entered the flesh, then remove them where possible. Removing the breasts from game birds makes it easier to see any lurking pellets.

HANGING AND STORING In some countries it is customary to mature game meat by hanging it in a cold, airy environment to enhance the subtle characteristics of the meat. The amount of hanging time required varies according to the size of the animal or bird, the surrounding temperature, the humidity, and the air circulation. Cold, dry conditions are ideal, and the larger the animal, the longer the time it needs. Boneless meat is sometimes matured in a vacuum pack, which gives very different results to open hanging of a carcass. Vacuum-packed meat should always be opened at least one hour before cooking. In all storage instructions, it is assumed that the temperature of a domestic fridge is 40°F (4°C) or less.

COOK

A feature of many game meats is that they have very little fat and no marbling. From a culinary point of view, as a general rule, the darker and leaner the meat, the more dense it is and the more carefully it needs to be cooked—overcooking at high temperatures can make it dry and hard. Young, tender game can be roasted, but tougher, more mature specimens are better braised.

FAST COOK Roasting, grilling, and frying are excellent ways of cooking game, but as it is lean, it should be served pink to prevent it becoming dry and tough. Brown the meat first, then part-cook it to an internal temperature of 115°F (45°C). Let the meat rest to distribute the heat and juices. (Thicker pieces need longer to rest.) Small or thin pieces ½in (1cm) or less (thin steaks or stir-fry) should be served as soon as they are browned. If you don't want pink meat, cook it slowly at a low temperature, unless the meat is a prime cut from a very young animal or bird.

Fast-cooked *game meat should be browned on the outside, but pink in the middle. Leave larger cuts of meat to rest before slicing to ensure the juices are evenly distributed.*

MARINATE This essentially means soaking meat in a mixture of wine, acids, oils, spices, and herbs. It is not necessary to marinate game, as it masks its elegant flavor. However, some countries like to marinate game because they believe it gives a richness to the meat, and over-strong or bruised game can benefit from this treatment. An hour or two is sufficient for steaks, 24 hours for roasts. It is worth noting that many children do not like the taste of wine in stews or casseroles, so the rich natural flavor of unmarinated game meats are a good substitute.

Game *soaked in a strong marinade can have a dry surface, so brushing it with oil and spices will keep it moist and impart flavor. Take care not to overcook it.*

SLOW COOK Tough cuts and older game animals and birds are best cooked gently in a liquid over several hours. The breasts of large game birds and joints of lean meat benefit from larding before cooking in this way; the meat should be browned first to add flavor and then immersed in a large pan of liquid to keep them moist. Other flavors may also be added to taste. Food can be slow-cooked by being simmered on top of the stove, or by being baked in the oven at the lowest temperature. Once cooked, it is important that the meat is kept completely submerged in liquid, or it can dry out very quickly.

Place game birds *upside down in the liquid to keep the breast meat moist, then turn right-side up and baste with the sauce.*

LARD AND BARD Larding is the technique of inserting fat deep into meat. This is completely unnecessary when serving game pink; it is only necessary if you want to cook the meat past that stage, for example when braising. To lard, cut the fat into strips and insert the strips deep into the meat with a larding needle or sharp knife. This task is much easier if the fat has been frozen beforehand. Barding means wrapping the meat in fat before cooking it. However, this does not help to lubricate the inside of the meat, and so it is now deemed unnecessary unless you are spit-cooking a large joint over an open fire.

Wrapping game *in fatty meat is another method of barding. Here quails are wrapped in vine leaves and bacon before roasting.*

VENISON

Venison is the meat of all species of deer. Every continent has its own wild species (sometimes introduced), which can vary greatly in size. Deer are also farmed in many countries, and the meat of some African antelopes (which are bovids, not deer) is also sold as venison. Dark red, venison is extremely lean, although it can have much more fat if from mature deer after the summer. The delicate, but distinctly meaty flavor can be strengthened by hanging the carcass. It also acquires a strong, gamy taste when hung in the fur or marinated.

BUY Wild venison is restricted to seasons; farmed is not. Buy from game dealers, butchers, and supermarkets. It should already have been hung before butchering. Avoid any excessively dark, bruised meat. Prime cuts come from the haunch and saddle. Venison is filling, so allow about 6oz (175g) of boneless meat per portion.

STORE If pre-packed, follow the storage instructions. Otherwise, keep, covered, in the fridge for up to 4 days, or remove any fat and freeze, tightly wrapped, for up to a year.

EAT Open vacuum-packed meat an hour before cooking. Prime cuts can be eaten raw as carpaccio. Roast prime joints and fry steaks to serve pink (if overcooked they will be dry).

Shoulder from young and small deer can also be roasted. Braise or stew venison from older deer and all forequarter cuts; joints to be braised should be larded. Use ground venison for burgers and meatballs, pasta sauces, pies, and other homestyle dishes.

FLAVOR PAIRINGS Bacon, cream, bulb fennel, red cabbage, pears, pomegranate, prunes, red berries, pine nuts, juniper berries, curry spices, ginger, chocolate, red wine.

CLASSIC RECIPES *Viltgryta*; venison *Baden-Baden*; civet of venison; roast haunch with sauce *Grand Veneur*; *ragoût de chevreuil chasseur*; *gebratener rehrucken*; *radjurssler*.

Fillet or tenderloin
The boned-out saddle (back) yields the loin and fillet muscles. These two prime cuts are often confused in recipes, with the loin erroneously called fillet, but cooking times are very different, as loin is at least twice as thick as fillet; also, the cuts from different species vary in size.

The fillet muscle tapers at one end; the other end (not shown) sometimes has a thicker muscle attached. The loin muscle (sometimes called loin fillet) does not taper.

Rolled haunch (leg)
The haunch from small species of deer may be roasted whole or boned, or sliced into steaks. Larger haunches can be cooked on the bone, but are usually parted into individual muscles or pavés. These may be rolled and tied for roasting, or sliced into steaks.

Venison haunch is as lean as skinless chicken. Roasts should be served pink or they will be dry.

Diced venison
Stir-fry, grill, or stew diced haunch. Diced shoulder and shin are best stewed, but should not be mixed together as they cook differently.

VILTGRYTA

This venison stew with chanterelles is a Swedish favorite. Serve with boiled potatoes and lingonberry jelly.

SERVES 6

2¼lbs (1kg) venison stew meat, or boned haunch of venison, cut into bite-size chunks

oil or butter, for frying

about 1¼ cups venison or beef stock, or as needed

2 onions, chopped

12oz (350g) fresh chanterelles or other wild mushrooms

1 tbsp red wine vinegar

2 tsp granulated sugar

salt and freshly ground black pepper

½ cup heavy whipping cream

2 tbsp all-purpose flour

For the marinade

1¼ cups red wine

2 tbsp olive oil

2 tsp juniper berries, crushed

½ tsp dried thyme

¼ tsp cracked black pepper

¼ tsp ground cloves

2 bay leaves

1 Mix together all the marinade ingredients in a deep bowl. Add the venison, cover, and leave to marinate for 24 hours, turning once or twice.

2 Drain off the marinade and reserve. Pat the meat dry and brown in a large casserole. Add the marinade and stock to cover. Bring to a rolling boil, then cover and simmer for 1½ hours.

3 Cook the onions in butter until softened. Add the chanterelles and cook until they release their juices. Stir in the vinegar and sugar, then add to the stew. Simmer for 30–45 minutes, until the meat is just tender. Season with salt and pepper. Whisk the cream and flour together, and mix into the stew. Simmer for 20 minutes.

VENISON COOKING CHART

Choosing the correct cooking method for a cut of venison is vitally important. Use this chart to identify the best way to prepare your chosen cut. Be aware that the different species of deer are very different in size, so the size of their cuts will vary accordingly.

CUT	DESCRIPTION	BROIL	FRY	ROAST	BRAISE/STEW
		Timings vary according to thickness.	Timings vary according to thickness.	Thermometer internal-temperature readings: rare 140°F (60°C), medium 150°F (65°C).	
HAUNCH/ BACK LEG	From small deer, this may be the whole leg, whereas from larger deer it is usually cut into smaller joints. Bone-in or boneless, rolled, and tied. Also single muscles may be rolled and tied or seamed into smaller muscle blocks or pavés. If the joint is on the bone, the "H" bone should be removed for easier carving. Boneless haunch is sliced for steaks or cut into cubes (excluding shin).	Haunch steak (only from young deer): Preheat broiler to high. Brush meat with butter or oil. Broil to brown on both sides, then reduce heat and continue broil, turning once: 1½ min per ½in (1cm) for rare; 2 min per ½in (1cm) for medium. Do not overcook; undercook steaks thicker than 1in (2.5cm), then rest for 3–5 min. Diced haunch (only from young deer): Thread on to skewers and brown on all sides.	Haunch steak (only from young deer): Heat pan with butter and/ or oil and brown steak on both sides, then reduce heat and continue frying, turning once; rest to finish cooking. For rare: brown 3 min, cook 1 min per ½in (1cm), and rest 1 min per ½in (1cm). For medium: brown 4 min, cook 1½ min per ½in (1cm), and rest 1½ min per ½in (1cm). Diced haunch (only from young deer): Cook loose or thread meat on to skewers. Brush with butter or oil. Brown on all sides in a very hot pan, then serve immediately.	Haunch joint (only from young deer): Preheat oven to 450°F (230°C). Brown joint all over. For rare bone-in joint: roast for 2½ min per ½in (1cm), then reduce heat to 170°F (80°C) and rest in oven 2 min per ½in (1cm). For medium bone-in joint, roast for 3 min per ½in (1cm), then rest for 3 min per ½in (1cm). For rare boneless joint: roast for 2 min per ½in (1cm), then rest for 2–3 min per ½in (1cm). For medium boneless joint: roast for 3 min per ½in (1cm), then rest for 2–3 min per ½in (1cm).	Bone-in and boneless haunch joints (only from young deer): Preheat oven to 375°F (190°C). Brown meat, then braise for 1½–2 hours. Haunch steaks (only from young deer): braise as joints, but for 1½ hours. If joints or steaks are from older deer braise at 350°F (180°C) for 2–3 hours. Diced haunch: Preheat oven to 325°F (160°C). Brown meat, then braise for 1½ hours, or 2–3 hours for older deer.
SADDLE	The supreme bone-in joint from the back of the deer comprising the loins, fillets, the backbone, and the surrounding skin.	Not recommended.	Not recommended.	Roast saddle as bone-in haunch joint.	Braise saddle as haunch joint from young deer.
LOIN/LOIN FILLET	The boneless, trimmed top muscle from the saddle (back). Do not confuse with the fillet. Loin is sliced for steaks, which may be partially cut through and opened out for butterfly steaks.	Broil loin joint and steaks as haunch steak.	Fry loin joint and steaks as haunch steak.	Roast loin joint as boneless haunch joint.	Braise loin joint as haunch joint from young deer. Braise loin steaks as diced haunch from young deer.
RACK	The fore end of loin with all skin and sinew removed, and with trimmed and chined rib bones still attached.	Broil rack as haunch steak.	Not recommended.	Roast rack as boneless haunch joint.	Braise rack as haunch joint from young deer.
FILLET/ TENDERLOIN	The tapering muscle from the underside of the saddle. Significantly smaller than loin. Not often used from very small deer, as it is too tiny.	Broil fillet as haunch steak.	Fry fillet as haunch steak.	Roast fillet as boneless haunch joint.	Braise fillet as haunch joint from young deer.
T-BONE STEAK	A slice through the rump end of the saddle comprising a piece of loin and a piece of fillet separated by a T-shaped bone.	Broil T-bone steak as haunch steak.	Fry T-bone steak as haunch steak.	Not recommended	Braise T-bone steak as haunch joint from young deer.
CHOPS/ CUTLETS	Slices through the saddle and shoulder with chine and/or rib bone still attached.	Broil chops/cutlets as haunch steak.	Fry chops/cutlets as haunch steak.	Not recommended	Braise chops/cutlets as diced haunch from young deer.
SHOULDER	The whole shoulder with shank removed. Cut into 2–3 pieces on large deer. Bone-in or boneless, usually rolled and tied. Shoulder fillet is the fore end of loin; it consists of two muscles. For dice, boneless shoulder has major sinews and fat removed.	Broil shoulder fillet (only from young deer) as haunch steak.	Fry shoulder fillet (only from young deer) as haunch steak.	Roast shoulder joints (only from young deer) as bone-in and boneless haunch joints.	Braise shoulder fillet and diced shoulder as diced haunch. Shoulder joint: Preheat oven to 325°F (160°C). Brown meat, then braise for 2–3 hours, or for at least 4 hours if from older deer.
SHIN/SHANK	The lower part of the fore or hind leg. May be sold whole with a length of marrow bone exposed, or boned and diced. Osso buco are thick slices that vary in diameter.	Not recommended.	Not recommended.	Not recommended.	Simmer, or stew at 325°F (160°C), for 4 hours, or 4–5 hours if from older deer.
NECK	May be cut into thick slices, or boned and diced or ground.	Not recommended.	Not recommended.	Not recommended.	Preheat oven to 325°F (160°C). Brown meat, then braise/stew for 2–3 hours, or 3–4 hours if from older deer.
GROUND	Lean trimmings with fat and sinew removed before being ground.	Preheat broiler to high. Press on to skewers or form into patties. Brush with oil and broil, turning occasionally, for 8–10 min.	Press onto skewers, or form in to patties. Heat oil to medium—hot. Fry, turning occasionally, for 8–10 min.	Not recommended.	Brown, then simmer, or braise at 325°F (160°C), for 1–2 hours.

BOAR

These fierce game animals are found in the wild throughout the world; they are also farmed for meat and crossed with domestic pigs. In addition, feral pigs are hunted and their meat sold as wild boar. Wild boar meat is dark and lean. Young wild boar (marcassin), with paler meat, make the best eating, since meat from older wild boar can be very tough. The meat from farmed boar is milder and more tender than wild boar and may be fattier.

BUY Buy wild boar from game dealers and specialty butchers in season, in fall and winter; farmed boar has no season and is sold as roasting joints, steaks (scallops), stew, or ground meat. Marcassin is often sold whole. Allow about 6oz (175g) of boneless meat per portion.

STORE If pre-packaged, follow storage instructions. Otherwise, keep covered in the refrigerator for up to 4 days, or remove any fat and freeze, tightly wrapped, for up to 6 months.

EAT Cooked: Roast haunch and saddle and serve pink; broil or fry leg or saddle steaks. If the meat is from older animals, braise or stew it; lard joints to be braised. All forequarter cuts should be cooked slowly or ground for pasta sauces, pies, and other dishes.

FLAVOR PAIRINGS Cream, chile, garlic, bulb fennel, apple, pomegranate, orange, cranberry, walnuts, juniper berries, curry paste, ginger, soy sauce, red wine, vinegar.

CLASSIC RECIPES Roast leg of wild boar with berry compote; *cinghiale in dolceforte; cinghiale alla cacciatora; filet de marcassin au cidre.*

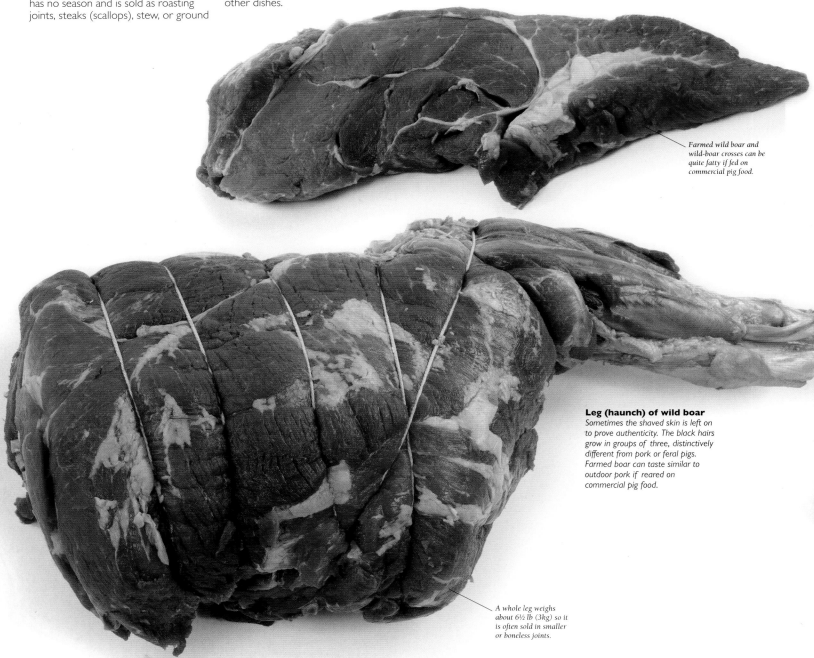

Wild boar steak
Leg steaks are suitable for frying and broiling; shoulder steaks should be braised.

Farmed wild boar and wild-boar crosses can be quite fatty if fed on commercial pig food.

Leg (haunch) of wild boar
Sometimes the shaved skin is left on to prove authenticity. The black hairs grow in groups of three, distinctively different from pork or feral pigs. Farmed boar can taste similar to outdoor pork if reared on commercial pig food.

A whole leg weighs about 6½ lb (3kg) so it is often sold in smaller or boneless joints.

KANGAROO

Because in their native Australia kangaroo were once culled in great numbers as a pest, their meat used to have a poor reputation. However, today, culling has been carried out far more carefully under license and the meat is exported from Australia. Being grass-fed, very lean, and full of iron, it is not unlike venison in both taste and texture, and like venison it is a naturally dark meat. Wallaby meat is very similar.

BUY Kangaroo meat is available in larger supermarkets and from specialty butchers, both vacuum packed and frozen. It is usually sold as steak, diced cubes for stewing, or ground.

STORE Vacuum-packed kangaroo meat can be kept in the refrigerator for up to 2 weeks, or according to the package instructions. Tightly wrapped, it will freeze very well for up to a year.

EAT Soak the meat in oil for about 15 minutes before cooking. Fry steaks to serve pink (overcooked meat will be dry). Stew or braise diced meat or add to soup. Use ground meat for burgers, meatballs, curries, pies, and other homemade dishes.

FLAVOR PAIRINGS Bacon, scallions, carrots, chile, bulb fennel, mushrooms, red cabbage, cranberry, peanuts, ginger, coriander, cumin, chocolate, wine, coconut milk.

CLASSIC RECIPES Outback kangaroo; kangaroo tail soup; kangaroo stew.

Kangaroo steaks are extremely lean, and those from old kangaroo can be tough, so cook carefully.

BISON AND BUFFALO

Bison are found in Europe and North America, where they are sometimes called buffalo (although they are not true buffalo). Bison are also farmed and can interbreed with cattle to become beefalo. A similar species to bison is the water buffalo, native to Asia, which is farmed to be eaten and used for milk production for mozzarella cheese. The meat of all these animals is much like beef, although darker and leaner, with a larger proportion of forequarter meat. In common with other furred game, the meat from farmed animals is normally more tender than wild, which is usually older, although that from old breeding water buffalo can be tough.

BUY Buy from specialty butchers, fresh and frozen. The cuts are similar to those of beef, with the same cuts (from the hind leg and back) designated the prime ones.

STORE Keep in the refrigerator, covered, for up to 4 days, or wrap tightly and freeze for up to 9 months (up to a year if very lean).

EAT Roast, fry, or broil the prime cuts (sirloin, fillet, and topside); as bison and water buffalo are generally leaner than beef, overcooking will make them dry. Braise or stew other cuts, using almost any beef recipe.

Bison and water buffalo can also be ground to make burgers, pasta sauces, pies, and other homemade dishes.

FLAVOR PAIRINGS Smoked ham, cream, celery, onion, garlic, ginger, mushrooms, tomatoes, chile, mustard, horseradish, beer, soy sauce, red wine.

CLASSIC RECIPES Buffalo stew; buffalo burgers; roast bison.

Even if there is some external fat, wild bison and some buffalo have little or no marbling so should be cooked like venison.

Bison sirloin roast
Encased in fat and very moist and tender, this is an extremely versatile cut of meat.

RABBIT

Wild rabbits exist in many parts of the world and are also widely reared, both commercially and privately. Most countries have no closed season. Rabbit flesh is lean, pale, and mild in flavor. Wild rabbits can be quite tough unless they are young, and often have a stronger flavor than farmed ones, due to the way they are handled. Farmed rabbits are bigger than wild rabbits and are more tender, with a flavor that is similar to free-range chicken.

🔒 **BUY** Wild rabbits are usually sold whole, skinned, or in fur, and are not hung; females or small, plump males make the best eating. Farmed rabbits are available preprepared: whole, disjointed, and as boneless chunks. The back legs and saddle have the most meat, while the shoulder has comparatively less. Allow 9–12oz (250–350g) bone-in rabbit per person, or 6–9oz (175–250g) if boneless.

📦 **STORE** If in fur, skin and remove bruised parts, then cut whole the rabbit into joints. Both wild and farmed rabbit joints (bone-in or boneless) can be kept, covered, in the refrigerator for up to 3 days, or frozen, tightly wrapped, for up to 9 months.

⬤ **EAT** Broil, roast, or braise young wild rabbit joints and farmed rabbit; the saddle and legs are the best cuts for roasting. Older wild rabbit is best slowly stewed or made into a pie. The liver and kidney can be fried.

FLAVOR PAIRINGS Bacon, carrots, fennel, garlic, mushrooms, tomatoes, olives, coriander, parsley, rosemary, thyme, lemon, prunes, mustard, soy sauce, cider, white wine.

CLASSIC RECIPES Rabbit pie; *lapin en gibelotte; coniglio all'ischitana; conejo en pepitoria.*

Saddle
Although the saddle has the most tender meat, the proportion of bone to meat is high so allow one whole saddle per person, or two if the rabbits are small.

On older, wild rabbits, the silvery skin over the saddle is very tough so needs to be carefully removed with a sharp knife before cooking.

On a farmed rabbit the saddle is large enough to be boned out and stuffed.

On wild rabbit, the forequarter has very little meat on it; farmed rabbit shoulders are more meaty and tender.

When marinated in oil and fragrant herbs, diced farmed rabbit meat can be threaded on skewers and charcoal-grilled.

Diced rabbit
Diced rabbit meat usually comes from the leg. If there is a lot of white/silvery sinew attached, this indicates that it is from an older animal and will be tougher.

Diced wild rabbit meat is most commonly stewed or made into pies, often mixed with other game meats for a game pie.

GUINEA PIG

In many countries, guinea pigs are farmed for food. In Peru, where they are called *cuy*, they are esteemed as a delicacy—the tradition goes back at least 2,500 years. They are eaten in other countries in South America and also in parts of Asia. Their flavor is not unlike rabbit or dark chicken meat.

🔒 **BUY** Guinea pigs are sold in the fur and also skinned; it is preferable to buy them preprepared (skinned and cleaned, with the intestines already prepared for cooking). For a main dish, allow one guinea pig per person.

📦 **STORE** If possible, eat guinea pig on the day of purchase. Preprepar ed, it can be kept, covered, for 2–3 days in the refrigerator, or frozen, tightly wrapped, for up to 6 months.

⬤ **EAT** Either cut into quarters or split the carcass and open it out flat, then broil, fry, or barbecue and serve with a hot, spicy sauce. Whole guinea pig can also be roasted, stuffed with a mixture that includes the intestines and herbs.

FLAVOR PAIRINGS Sweet peppers, chiles, manioc root, potatoes, rice, tomatoes, onions, garlic, parsley, mint, oregano, *huacatay*, lime, peanuts, walnuts, cumin, paprika.

HARE

Originating in Europe, wild hares are found all over the world, both in open grassland and on the mountains and moors. In some countries they are farmed. Not to be confused with rabbit, their meat is dark and rich, somewhat like venison. In common with other game, the meat of a young hare (leveret) is more tender than that of an older animal.

🔒 **BUY** Hares are usually not available in the spring breeding season. They are sold whole, in fur, or skinned, and sometimes disjointed; avoid very dark, bruised meat. The back legs and saddle are the meatiest cuts. A leveret will feed 4–5 people, an older hare 6–8. A saddle will feed 2. If making a civet, ask for the blood.

🗄 **STORE** If in fur, hang for up to a week, then skin and disjoint (reserving the blood). Joints can be kept, covered, in the refrigerator for up to 3 days or frozen, tightly wrapped, for up to 9 months.

⚫ **EAT** Roast the saddle, whole or boned and stuffed, and serve pink. Roast or broil the back legs of leverets or farmed hare. Or cook all cuts slowly in a liquid, using the blood to thicken the sauce for a civet.

FLAVOR PAIRINGS Bacon, cream, garlic, ginger, mushrooms, juniper berries, cloves, chocolate, red currant jelly, raisins, grapes, soy sauce, port, wine, wine vinegar.

CLASSIC RECIPES Jugged hare; *lepre in agrodolce; lasen-braten; civet de lièvre à la lyonnaise.*

Saddle
If the saddle is to be roasted, remove the tough outer skin and replace with bacon or fat to keep the outside of the meat moist.

The dark patch on the front corner indicates a small area of bruising; trim this off.

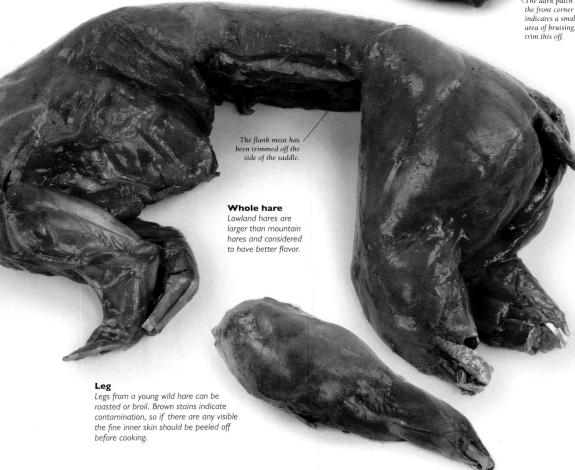

The flank meat has been trimmed off the side of the saddle.

Whole hare
Lowland hares are larger than mountain hares and considered to have better flavor.

Leg
Legs from a young wild hare can be roasted or broil. Brown stains indicate contamination, so if there are any visible the fine inner skin should be peeled off before cooking.

SQUIRREL

Squirrels live in temperate woods, both deciduous and coniferous. The red squirrel is a protected species in most countries, whereas the larger gray squirrel is humanely trapped or shot to be eaten. There is no season, but the flavor is better when squirrels are fat from feeding on nuts and berries. They are not hung before eating.

🔒 **BUY** Squirrel is most commonly sold from mid-fall to mid-spring although it is available year-round. If possible, buy squirrel ready skinned, since it is difficult to skin. The back legs and saddle have most of the meat, although if using for a stew it is worth cooking the whole carcass.

🗄 **STORE** Keep in the refrigerator, covered, and use within 2 days of purchase; if prepacked follow the instructions. Ready-skinned squirrel can also be frozen, well wrapped: if f atty for up to 3 months, if lean for up to 6 months.

⚫ **EAT** Stew or simmer boneless meat and use in fricassees, pies, and pasties. Roast, broil, or fry back legs and saddle (do not overcook them or the meat will toughen).

FLAVOR PAIRINGS Bacon, cream, onions, mushrooms, tomatoes, sweet peppers, chiles, sage, tarragon, coriander, apples, lemon, walnuts, honey, soy sauce, cider, wine.

CLASSIC RECIPES Brunswick stew; Southern-fried squirrel.

CLASSIC RECIPE

JUGGED HARE

A rich, blood-thickened stew like this is traditional in both Britain and in France, where it is called a civet. It can also be made with venison.

SERVES 6–8

1 hare, 4½–6½lb (2–3kg) in weight, prepared and jointed (liver and blood reserved)

3 tbsp red wine vinegar

4 tbsp butter

8oz (250g) unsmoked bacon, cut into strips 1in (2.5cm) long and ¼in (5mm) wide; or diced salt pork

15 baby onions or small shallots, peeled

2 tbsp all-purpose flour

1 cup dry red wine

2 cups beef stock

salt and freshly ground black pepper

6–8 bread triangles, fried in oil

for the marinade

1 onion, sliced

bunch of assorted fresh herbs, such as thyme, rosemary, sage, and parsley

¼ cup dry white wine

¼ cup red wine vinegar

¼ cup cup olive oil

1 Stir the wine vinegar into the blood and set aside in a covered dish with the liver; refrigerate until needed. Put the hare pieces in a bowl. Mix together the marinade ingredients and pour over the hare. Cover and leave to marinate in the refrigerator for 12–24 hours, turning the pieces over once or twice.

2 Lift the hare from the marinade and pat dry. Melt the butter in a flameproof casserole dish or other large pot and gently cook the bacon or diced salt pork and onions or shallots over medium-low heat, stirring occasionally, until lightly browned. Add the hare pieces and brown them gently all over.

3 Add the flour and stir into the fat. Pour in the red wine and enough stock to almost cover the meat. Season, then cover and simmer gently for 2–3 hours, or until tender.

4 Meanwhile, mash the liver into the blood and vinegar. Pass this through a fine sieve.

5 Add the liver and blood mixture to the hare and stir constantly as the sauce thickens. Do not allow it to boil. Taste and add more salt, pepper, and wine vinegar, if needed.

6 Serve the jugged hare hot, garnished with the bread triangles.

GROUSE

Grouse inhabit forests and mountains of the northern hemisphere, where they are shot for sport. There are several species, including willow and hazel grouse, and the larger black grouse and capercaillie. These plump birds are not farmed and their diet of vegetation, especially heather, gives them dark flesh with a unique gamy flavor that is world renowned. Capercaillie, which live on pine shoots, have a strong flavor of turpentine.

🔒 **BUY** The red grouse, unique to Britain, is available from the "Glorious Twelfth" of August; it is widely exported. Other grouse are usually shot from the late summer until the season ends in winter. Grouse are sold whole, in feather or oven ready, or as boned breasts. Avoid badly shot birds with torn skin. Allow one grouse or 2 breasts per person.

📦 **STORE** Hang in-feather birds for up to a week, then pluck and draw. Oven-ready birds and breasts can be kept, well wrapped, in the refrigerator for up to 4 days, or frozen for 9 months.

● **EAT** Soak capercaillie in milk overnight to remove its strong piney flavor. Roast whole birds or crowns if young (protect the breast with strips of fat or bacon); braise older birds. Fry, broil, braise, or stew breasts. Use the legs for soup and stock, or braise and serve with the breasts.

FLAVOR PAIRINGS Bacon, ham, celery, shallots, watercress, wild mushrooms, game fries, orange, honey, juniper berries, red currants, cranberries, whisky, wine.

CLASSIC RECIPES Roast grouse with game fries and watercress; *salmis* of grouse.

If there are a lot of feathers remaining on the breast and legs, pluck these out before cooking.

Traditionally, red grouse are served with the feet on. Pull them out of the cavity, then clean and truss before cooking.

When roasting, cover the breast with fat or bacon strips to keep it moist.

PARTRIDGE

Partridges are small, seed-eating birds found in most parts of the northern hemisphere on grassland and agricultural margins. Gray partridge and chukar partridge have a better flavor than red-legged partridge, which is widely reared for release into the wild for shooting. Young partridges have paler, more delicately flavored flesh and are more tender than the larger older birds.

🔒 **BUY** Available in the fall and winter, partridges are sold whole, either in feather or oven ready, or sometimes as boned breasts. Avoid birds with bruised, badly shot breasts. An oven-ready partridge weighs about 10oz (300g), so allow one per person or 2–4 breasts.

📦 **STORE** Hang in-feather partridges for 4–7 days, then pluck and draw. Oven-ready birds and breasts can be kept, well wrapped, in the refrigerator for 3 days, or frozen for up to 9 months.

● **EAT** Roast whole birds if young (protect the breast with strips of fat or bacon); braise older birds. Fry, broil, braise, or stew partridge breasts. Use the legs for soup and stock, or braise and serve with the roasted breasts.

FLAVOR PAIRINGS Bacon, cream, cabbage, watercress, lentils, shallots, wild mushrooms, grapes, lemon, pear, quince, red currants, chestnuts, juniper berries, sage, chocolate, wine.

CLASSIC RECIPES Roast partridge; partridge with lentils; *perdrix au choux; perdrix en chartreuse; perdices con chocolate.*

The wings of small game birds such as partridge are often removed by the game dealer, since there is so little meat on them.

PHEASANT

One of the most popular game birds in the world, pheasants now exist in the wild in most continents. They are also widely reared and released into the wild for shooting: the season is usually during the fall and winter. Unless bruised, pheasant flesh is paler than that of many game birds, similar to a free-range chicken. And, unless bruised, it has a mild flavor. To produce a more gamy flavor, pheasant is hung in feather.

🔒 **BUY** Pheasant is sometimes available in feather and traditionally as a brace (pair). Normally, though, it is sold plucked and drawn or as crowns or boned breasts. Buy fresh in season, or frozen out of season. A hen pheasant weighs about 1lb 10oz (750g), a rooster about 2lb (900g). Allow one bird for 2–3 people, or one breast per person.

📦 **STORE** Hang in-feather birds for up to a week, then pluck and draw them. Store oven-ready birds and breasts, well wrapped, in the refrigerator for 3 days, or in the freezer for 9 months.

Pheasant drumsticks contain many fine, bony sinews. The thighs make better eating.

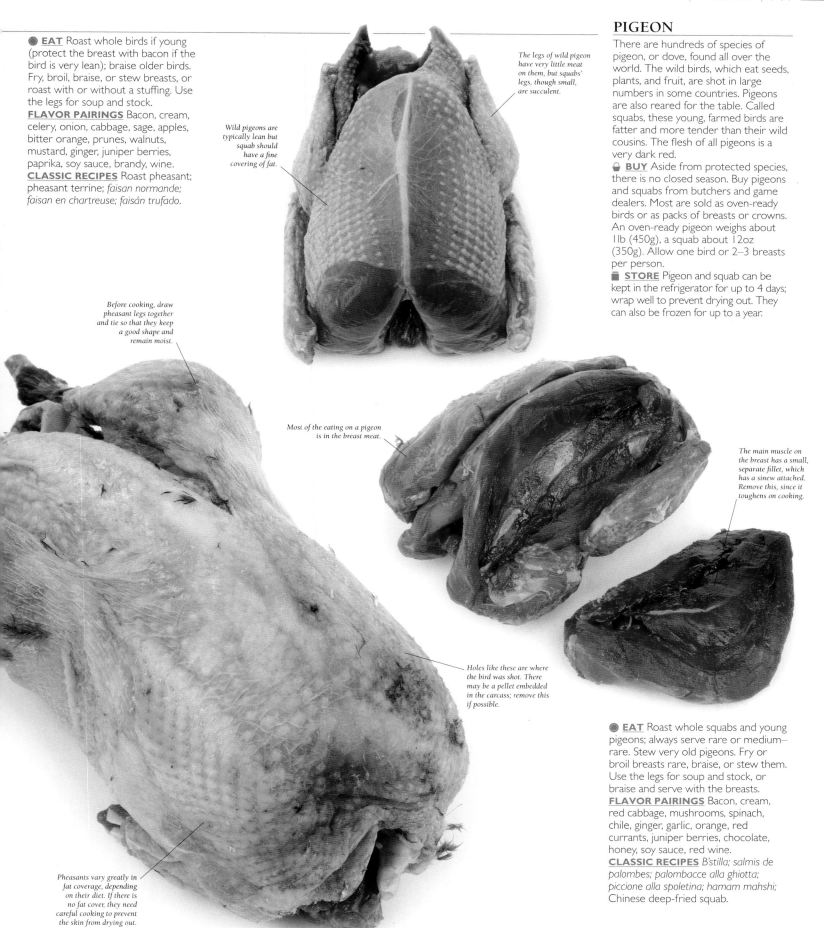

● **EAT** Roast whole birds if young (protect the breast with bacon if the bird is very lean); braise older birds. Fry, broil, braise, or stew breasts, or roast with or without a stuffing. Use the legs for soup and stock.
FLAVOR PAIRINGS Bacon, cream, celery, onion, cabbage, sage, apples, bitter orange, prunes, walnuts, mustard, ginger, juniper berries, paprika, soy sauce, brandy, wine.
CLASSIC RECIPES Roast pheasant; pheasant terrine; *faisan normande; faisan en chartreuse; faisán trufado.*

The legs of wild pigeon have very little meat on them, but squabs' legs, though small, are succulent.

Wild pigeons are typically lean but squab should have a fine covering of fat.

Before cooking, draw pheasant legs together and tie so that they keep a good shape and remain moist.

Most of the eating on a pigeon is in the breast meat.

Holes like these are where the bird was shot. There may be a pellet embedded in the carcass; remove this if possible.

Pheasants vary greatly in fat coverage, depending on their diet. If there is no fat cover, they need careful cooking to prevent the skin from drying out.

PIGEON

There are hundreds of species of pigeon, or dove, found all over the world. The wild birds, which eat seeds, plants, and fruit, are shot in large numbers in some countries. Pigeons are also reared for the table. Called squabs, these young, farmed birds are fatter and more tender than their wild cousins. The flesh of all pigeons is a very dark red.

🔒 **BUY** Aside from protected species, there is no closed season. Buy pigeons and squabs from butchers and game dealers. Most are sold as oven-ready birds or as packs of breasts or crowns. An oven-ready pigeon weighs about 1lb (450g), a squab about 12oz (350g). Allow one bird or 2–3 breasts per person.

📦 **STORE** Pigeon and squab can be kept in the refrigerator for up to 4 days; wrap well to prevent drying out. They can also be frozen for up to a year.

The main muscle on the breast has a small, separate fillet, which has a sinew attached. Remove this, since it toughens on cooking.

● **EAT** Roast whole squabs and young pigeons; always serve rare or medium—rare. Stew very old pigeons. Fry or broil breasts rare, braise, or stew them. Use the legs for soup and stock, or braise and serve with the breasts.
FLAVOR PAIRINGS Bacon, cream, red cabbage, mushrooms, spinach, chile, ginger, garlic, orange, red currants, juniper berries, chocolate, honey, soy sauce, red wine.
CLASSIC RECIPES B'stilla; *salmis de palombes; palombacce alla ghiotta; piccione alla spoletina; hamam mahshi;* Chinese deep-fried squab.

WOODCOCK

The woodcock is largely a northern-hemisphere bird with a few southern populations. Living in deciduous or mixed coniferous woodland, large numbers migrate out of northern Scandinavia and Russia into Europe and North America. Notoriously difficult to shoot, they are considered to be one of the most delicious game birds, especially when cooked with the entrails ("trail") intact and head on.

BUY Woodcock is not often available commercially, so needs to be ordered through a game dealer during the winter months. Ask for them in feather if the entrails are wanted for cooking, otherwise they will be plucked and drawn. Allow 1 bird per person.

STORE If in feather, hang for 1 day maximum, then pluck and draw. If retaining the trail, only remove the gizzard. Once drawn, keep, covered, in the fridge for up to 2 days, or wrap tightly and freeze for up to 9 months.

EAT Cooked: Roast, boned and stuffed or whole, or spatchcock to broil or fry. If the trail is intact, braise gently, then make the trail into a pâté; spread this on a crouton to place under the bird.

FLAVOR PAIRINGS Bacon, cream, shallots, celery root, watercress, garlic, ginger, apples, grapes, bay, parsley, thyme, nutmeg, soy sauce, Madeira.

CLASSIC RECIPES Woodcock on toast; *woodcock à la fine champagne*; braised woodcock.

Look for woodcock with a fine layer of fat, and unbroken skin.

SNIPE

About half the size of a woodcock, snipe live on marshy uplands and fields, using their long beaks to forage for invertebrates. There are species in all continents of the world. Very difficult to shoot, snipe are usually protected during the breeding season. Like woodcock, they are often eaten with their entrails ("trail") intact and prepared like this are considered a great delicacy.

BUY Not commonly seen for sale, snipe will need to be ordered from a game dealer during the winter months. Ask for them in feather if the entrails are wanted for cooking, otherwise they will be plucked and drawn. Allow 1–2 birds per person.

STORE If in feather, hang for 1 day, then pluck and draw. If retaining the trail, remove just the gizzard. Once drawn, keep, covered, in the refrigerator for up to 2 days, or freeze, wrapped tightly, for up to 9 months.

EAT Cooked: Roast, whole or boned and stuffed, or spatchcock to broil, grill, or fry. If the trail is intact, braise gently, then make the trail into a pâté; spread this on a crouton to place under the bird.

FLAVOR PAIRINGS Bacon, butter, cream, shallots, celery root, potatoes, watercress, garlic, ginger, bay, parsley, thyme, nutmeg, soy sauce, Madeira, white wine.

CLASSIC RECIPES Snipe on toast; broiled snipe.

MALLARD

Of all waterfowl, the mallard is the best known and most widespread species of wild duck, occurring in all continents of the world as it migrates long distances. It is the ancestor of the domestic duck. Mallard are dabbling ducks so their diet is mainly vegetation and seeds with some crustaceans, although they also eat grain crops. Usually shot in the winter months in large numbers, they can be long-lived birds. The young ones are the best for the table. Their flesh is

The fat covering on mallard varies according to condition. A thin covering of fat greatly enhances the eating quality.

QUAIL

The common quail is a native bird of the Middle East and Mediterranean but there are species found in most countries of the world. Some quail migrate in huge numbers, and they are usually protected during their spring breeding season. However, quail are also widely farmed, both for their meat and for their tiny eggs, and most that are available for sale will be farmed.

BUY Quail is not hung. Farmed quail (and quail eggs) are sold all year round, sometimes boned and stuffed. They are tiny birds (5–7oz/140–200g), so allow 1 per person for an appetizer, 2 per person for a main course.

STORE Keep fresh quail, wrapped, in the fridge for up to 3 days, or freeze, tightly wrapped, for up to 6 months.

EAT Cooked: Quail are usually roasted whole, sometimes boned and stuffed and often barded with bacon to keep the breast moist. They are also split in half or spatchcocked, to be broiled or sautéed, and they can be braised.

FLAVOR PAIRINGS Bacon, cream, bell peppers, mushrooms, truffle, grapes, quince, cherries, prunes, almonds, honey, cumin, cinnamon, brandy, white and red wine.

CLASSIC RECIPES Stuffed quail; spatchcocked quail.

Most quail are now farmed, and their tender flesh is among the palest of the game birds.

OTHER WILD DUCK

The variety of duck species (some of which interbreed) is enormous and spans the world, ranging from the large Muscovy, whose carcass can weigh 11lb (5kg) or more, down to teal weighing only 5oz (140g). The meat of diving ducks (which live in rivers, estuaries, and the sea) can sometimes taste fishy, so the better-flavored dabbling ducks (such as mallard, widgeon, and teal) are generally preferred for the table. Wild ducks have at best only a thin covering of fat—sometimes none at all—and the meat is dark, so cooking techniques for other dark-fleshed game birds are more suitable than those for domestic duck.

BUY Buy wild duck oven ready if small (it takes a long time to pluck); it is also available as pairs of breasts. Wild ducks are in season in the winter but can be bought frozen at other times. Allow 1lb (450g) per person if cooking a whole bird, or 7oz (200g) of breast meat.

STORE It is not usual to hang wild ducks for more than a day or so, and diving ducks not at all. Keep oven-ready duck and duck breasts,

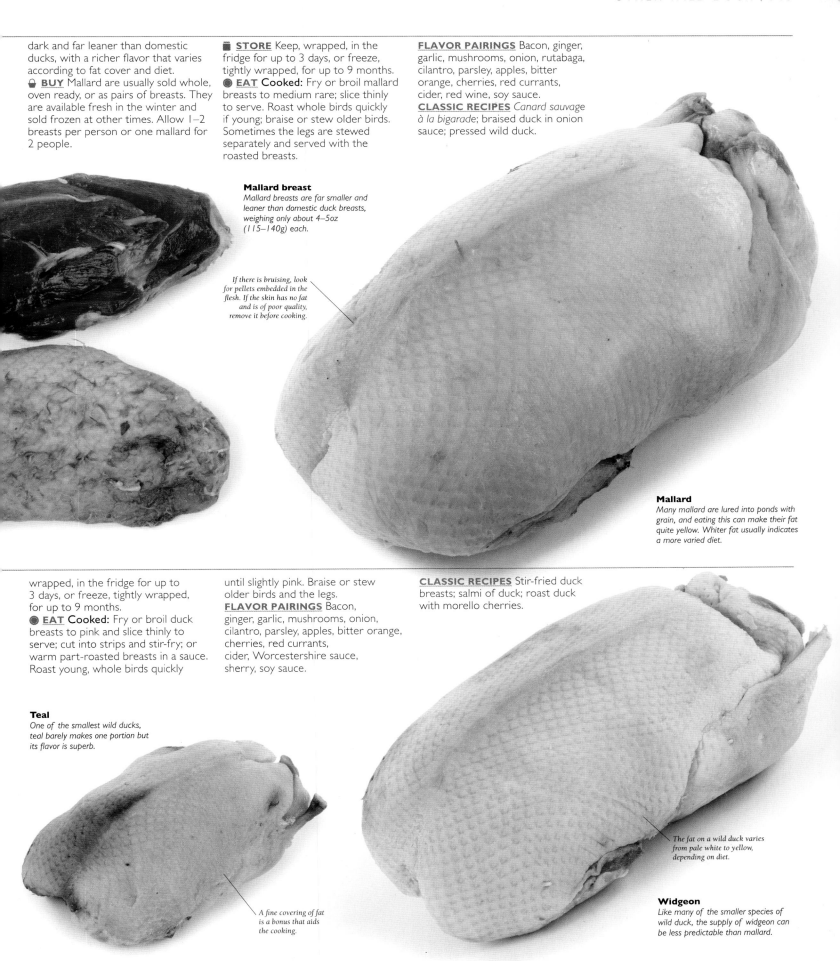

dark and far leaner than domestic ducks, with a richer flavor that varies according to fat cover and diet.

🔒 **BUY** Mallard are usually sold whole, oven ready, or as pairs of breasts. They are available fresh in the winter and sold frozen at other times. Allow 1–2 breasts per person or one mallard for 2 people.

📦 **STORE** Keep, wrapped, in the fridge for up to 3 days, or freeze, tightly wrapped, for up to 9 months.
⦿ **EAT** Cooked: Fry or broil mallard breasts to medium rare; slice thinly to serve. Roast whole birds quickly if young; braise or stew older birds. Sometimes the legs are stewed separately and served with the roasted breasts.

FLAVOR PAIRINGS Bacon, ginger, garlic, mushrooms, onion, rutabaga, cilantro, parsley, apples, bitter orange, cherries, red currants, cider, red wine, soy sauce.
CLASSIC RECIPES *Canard sauvage à la bigarade*; braised duck in onion sauce; pressed wild duck.

Mallard breast
Mallard breasts are far smaller and leaner than domestic duck breasts, weighing only about 4–5oz (115–140g) each.

If there is bruising, look for pellets embedded in the flesh. If the skin has no fat and is of poor quality, remove it before cooking.

Mallard
Many mallard are lured into ponds with grain, and eating this can make their fat quite yellow. Whiter fat usually indicates a more varied diet.

wrapped, in the fridge for up to 3 days, or freeze, tightly wrapped, for up to 9 months.
⦿ **EAT** Cooked: Fry or broil duck breasts to pink and slice thinly to serve; cut into strips and stir-fry; or warm part-roasted breasts in a sauce. Roast young, whole birds quickly

until slightly pink. Braise or stew older birds and the legs.
FLAVOR PAIRINGS Bacon, ginger, garlic, mushrooms, onion, cilantro, parsley, apples, bitter orange, cherries, red currants, cider, Worcestershire sauce, sherry, soy sauce.

CLASSIC RECIPES Stir-fried duck breasts; salmi of duck; roast duck with morello cherries.

Teal
One of the smallest wild ducks, teal barely makes one portion but its flavor is superb.

A fine covering of fat is a bonus that aids the cooking.

The fat on a wild duck varies from pale white to yellow, depending on diet.

Widgeon
Like many of the smaller species of wild duck, the supply of widgeon can be less predictable than mallard.

OFFAL ESSENTIALS

Offal, sometimes known as "variety meats" or "organ meats," comprises a collection of animal parts, of which some are organs (liver, kidney, heart, sweetbreads, etc.), some are extremities (head, feet, tails, etc.), and others are off-cuts from the main carcass (bones, fat, membranes, etc.). The world of offal includes the firm bite of kidneys, the gelatinous silkiness of oxtail, the creaminess of brains, and the crunchiness of cartilage—while the fuzzy texture of tripe is unlike that of any other meat. Intestines and stomachs are put to use as casings for sausages, salamis, and puddings. Most offal is rich in nutrients and essential fatty acids, and low in fat.

BUY

You can buy some of the most popular types of offal in supermarkets, but for the best variety and quality, make friends with your butcher. Purchase only clean-looking offal that smells fresh, with no strong odor.

STORE

Generally, organ meat has a much shorter shelf life than other cuts of meat and should be cooked or frozen immediately after purchase.

PREPARE

Many kinds of offal require thorough preparation, whether by washing, removing hair, membranes, or extraneous blood vessels, or, in some cases, salting. You can ask your butcher to do this, or buy them ready prepared.

PREPARE KIDNEYS FOR FRYING If you buy a whole, unprepared kidney, you need to remove the suet casing before chopping.

1 Pull away and discard the fat (suet) that is encasing the kidneys, then rinse them in cold water. Pat the kidneys dry using paper towels.

2 With the kidney upside down, cut around the fatty core and pull it away—this will release the membrane that covers the kidney.

3 Discard the core and peel off the membrane covering the kidney. Discard. Trim away any bits of membrane that are still attached.

4 Cut into bite-sized pieces according to the kidney's natural divisions, then cut off the fatty cores from each piece.

PREPARE CHICKEN LIVER These livers need cleaning, and any bits of sinew or membrane should be removed before frying.

Rinse the livers in cold, running water, then pick over them before you start cleaning them to identify any green patches, membranes, and fibers. Cut these away carefully using a sharp knife, and discard. Pat the livers dry with a paper towel.

PREPARE CALF'S LIVER Slices of this large piece of offal are considered a delicacy in many restaurants. Calf's liver is perfect for frying because it will cook very quickly over a high heat.

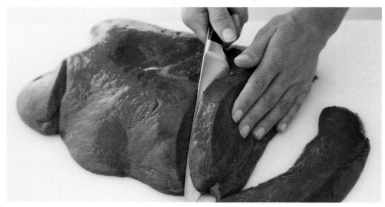

Prepare the liver by first trimming it of any membranes and arteries, and discard. Cut the liver into even, thick slices using a large, sharp knife.

COOK

Many delicious traditional dishes are made from combinations of offal, sometimes from different animals. Some types of offal are viewed as delicacies, either because of their superior flavor or because a carcass yields so little of a particular cut. One such is foie gras, the fattened liver of duck and geese, which is one of the world's most refined and expensive foods. With a few exceptions (such as raw liver), offal is cooked thoroughly, either by gentle simmering or slow stewing. However, in recent years, cuts that were once traditionally stewed or baked (such as heart) are now enjoyed quickly fried and served pink, rather like steak.

Chicken liver should be fried quickly (about 2 minutes) in a pan of very hot oil. They are done when brown on the outside and pink in the center.

MEAT LIVER

Liver is probably the most popular of all the meat offal cuts. Delicate and mild calf's (veal) and lamb's livers are generally more sought after than the more strongly flavored pig's and beef (ox) livers. Venison liver, although dark in color, is very sweet and tender.

🔒 **BUY** Available from butchers, farmers' markets, and supermarkets, liver is usually sold sliced. Calf's and lamb's liver is paler than beef or pig's liver. All liver should smell fresh and sweet. For Jewish cuisine, liver is bought koshered (cooked completely).

🗄 **STORE** Keep liver in the fridge and cover it to prevent the surface drying out. Store whole for 2–3 days, or sliced for 1–2 days. Liver freezes well as it has no fat; store it for up to a year.

⦿ **EAT** **Cooked:** Before cooking, soak strong pig's or beef liver in milk to sweeten it. Remove any large tubes, which toughen on cooking. Sauté, grill, or braise calf's, lamb's, and venison livers; braise pig's and beef livers, or stuff and roast. Use for pâtés.

FLAVOR PAIRINGS Bacon, cream, onions, garlic, thyme, parsley, lemon, raisins, brandy, soy sauce, wine vinegar.

CLASSIC RECIPES Fegato alla veneziana; lamb's liver and bacon; liver pâté.

The liver from a lamb should be a deep, rich red color.

Lamb's liver
With its mild flavor and tender texture, sliced lamb's liver is delicious with crisp bacon. A whole liver, which weighs 1–1½ lb (450–675g), is excellent braised.

Calf's liver
Milk-fed calf's liver is the palest and most tender of all meat livers. It has a smooth texture and delicate flavor, ideal for quickly sautéeing with herbs, such as sage or softened onions.

Slice calf's liver thinly for frying, so that it will cook quickly and evenly.

Pig's liver
As it has a strong flavor, pig's liver is usually braised or used in pâtés rather than fried. A whole liver will weigh about 2lb (900g).

Remove the central white tissue and any side membranes before cooking.

FEGATO ALLA VENEZIANA

Here is a Venetian favorite: tender calf's liver with a vinegar-enhanced, caramelized onion sauce.

SERVES 4

¼ cup olive oil

4 tbsp butter

1 large onion, very thinly sliced

1lb (450g) calf's liver, cut into ½in (1cm) slices

salt and freshly ground black pepper

3 tbsp all-purpose flour

½ cup dry red wine

1 tbsp white wine vinegar

1 Heat the oil and butter in a frying pan, add the onion, and cook gently for 30–40 minutes, or until they are soft and golden brown. Remove to a dish using a slotted spoon, leaving the buttery oil in the frying pan.

2 Turn up the heat. Season the slices of liver with salt and pepper, and dust them in the flour, then cook for 2 minutes on each side. Remove from the pan to a warm dish. Add the wine and vinegar to the pan and stir with a spoon to scrape up any brown residue from the bottom of the pan.

3 Return the onions and liver to the pan and reheat them very gently. Serve hot, with polenta.

POULTRY LIVER

Although the livers of other poultry, such as turkey, are eaten, chicken livers are by far the best known, being found in every country and every cuisine. In Europe, the larger duck and goose livers are fattened to make *foie gras*, which is a highly prized delicacy.

🔒 **BUY** Fresh and frozen chicken livers, and to a lesser extent duck and turkey livers, are sold whole, by weight. Avoid livers that are dark or strong-smelling. Fresh or frozen *foie gras*, which should be a pale, flesh color, can be found in speciality shops; preserved foie gras in delicatessens.

🗄 **STORE** Fresh chicken, turkey, and duck livers can be kept in the fridge for up to 3 days. Wrap well to avoid contaminating other food. Fresh *foie gras* will keep in the fridge for 10 days, preserved *foie gras* in a cool place for at least a year.

⦿ **EAT** **Cooked:** Chicken, turkey, and duck livers should be thoroughly cooked. Chop and fry them with a variety of flavorings, and also use them in soups and stuffings and to add richness to pâtés. Quickly fry fresh *foie gras*; serve preserved foie gras chilled and sliced.

FLAVOR PAIRINGS Bacon, eggs, onions, garlic, truffles, figs, grapes, raisins, prunes, chutney, Sauternes.

CLASSIC RECIPES Chicken liver pâté; chopped liver and onions; foie gras with Sauternes; pâté de foie gras.

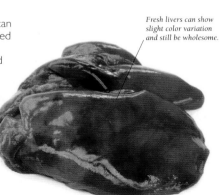

Fresh livers can show slight color variation and still be wholesome.

LIGHTS (LUNGS)

The lungs, commonly known as lights, of all animals have traditionally been used in peasant cooking. These days, perhaps because of the spongy texture, lights are generally used only in commercially manufactured products like sausage, although a few regional specialities, such as Scottish *haggis*, exist.

🔒 **BUY** Lights are unlikely to be available from supermarkets and usually have to be ordered in advance, either direct from the slaughterhouse or from a specialist butcher.

📦 **STORE** It is difficult to vacuum pack lights, so they are normally sold in sealed plastic bags. Keep them in the bag in the fridge and cook within 2 days of purchase. Or wrap tightly and freeze for up to 6 months.

● **EAT** First remove the windpipe and any gristle, then simmer lights for 1-2 hours. Once tender, dice or mince and add to soups, savory casseroles, and sausages. Lights can also be sliced, seasoned, and grilled.

FLAVOR PAIRINGS Onions, garlic, tomatoes, lemon, almonds, oatmeal, cinnamon, allspice, pepper, ginger.

CLASSIC RECIPES *Haggis*; pig's fry; lung soup.

Remove the tough, gristly membrane between the lobes before cooking.

HEART

The heart has a texture like very fine-grained meat. Since it is a well-used muscle, it needs careful, slow cooking to avoid toughness. Calf's and lamb's hearts are more tender and smaller than beef (ox) heart. Poultry hearts, usually included in giblets, are enjoyed in South America. In Scandinavia, deer hearts are smoked and dried.

🔒 **BUY** Fresh and frozen hearts, usually whole, but sometimes sliced or diced, are available from farmers' markets, supermarkets, and butchers. Whole, untrimmed heart can have considerable amounts of fat around the top, but this is often trimmed off before sale.

📦 **STORE** Seal fresh heart in a zip-close bag and store in the fridge for up to a week. Or trim off all fat, seal tightly, and freeze for up to 6 months.

● **EAT** Sauté small hearts (rabbit and poultry) or preserve as a *confit*. Halve or slice larger hearts to grill or fry. They can also be stuffed and roasted or braised whole, or diced and stewed.

FLAVOR PAIRINGS Suet, fennel, onions, carrots, sage, lime, oatmeal, pepper, red wine.

CLASSIC RECIPES *Faggots*; *haggis*; *gefühltes kalbsherz*; *coeur de veau à la bonne femme*; scrapple.

KIDNEY

Meat kidneys have a distinctive flavor that is much enjoyed. As with other offal, calf's and lamb's kidneys are paler and more delicate tasting than those of other animals. When kidneys are cooked, the texture is firm yet creamy.

🔒 **BUY** Kidneys are available from farmers' markets, supermarkets, and butchers. Beef (ox) and calf's kidneys, which are made up of a cluster of lobes, can be bought sliced or diced. The smaller, smooth kidneys of other animals are usually sold whole, often in pairs. Occasionally lamb's kidneys are sold embedded in their suet fat.

📦 **STORE** Kidneys do not keep well, so store in the fridge, well wrapped to prevent them from drying out, and cook within 1-2 days of purchase. Or wrap tightly and freeze for up to a year.

● **EAT** Remove any silvery membrane and internal gristle. Slice small kidneys lengthwise and grill or fry. Dice larger kidneys to sauté and serve with a sauce, or add to stews to enrich them. Braise whole kidneys or roast in their fat. Cooked, grated pig's kidney is used to lend body to some French cakes and sweet dishes. Poultry and rabbit kidneys can be fried or added to stews.

FLAVOR PAIRINGS Cream, mushrooms, shallots, lemon, brandy, mustard, white wine.

CLASSIC RECIPES Deviled kidneys; steak and kidney pudding or pie; *rognoncini trifolati*.

The fine, silvery-white membrane must be removed before cooking because it will burst.

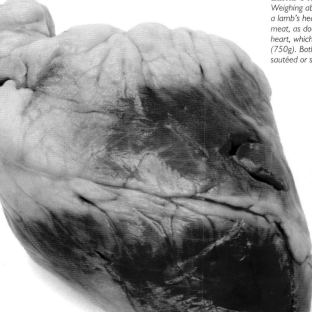

Lamb's heart
Weighing about 6oz (175g), a lamb's heart has very tender meat, as does the larger calf's heart, which weighs about 1lb 10oz (750g). Both can be sliced and sautéed or stuffed and roasted.

TRIPE (STOMACH)

While pigs and horses have just one stomach, all ruminants (eg cattle, sheep, goats, and deer) have four. The lining of the first two stomachs yields tripe. Blanket tripe is smoother than the more deeply textured honeycomb tripe; both have a soft, chewy texture when cooked slowly. The fourth stomach (paunch) is most commonly used as a casing for savory puddings, such as *haggis*. Lacy caul fat from the stomach is used to wrap meat patties and line terrine molds.

BUY Look for precleaned tripe in a butcher's shop. It should be moist and have a delicate scent and creamy white color. It may be sold raw (blanched) or partially cooked to reduce final cooking times.

STORE Keep tripe in the coldest part of the fridge, tightly covered to avoid contaminating other foods, and use within 2 days of purchase. Or seal tightly and freeze for up to 6 months.

EAT Mince or finely chop tripe for sausages and puddings. To stew, chop or slice, then simmer for 1-2 hours, either in a well-flavored broth or, for a more delicate dish, in milk. Tripe can also be grilled or fried.

FLAVOR PAIRINGS Ham, milk, egg, onions, sweet peppers, breadcrumbs, mace, bay leaf, sage, mustard, cloves, ginger, tamarind, coriander, cumin, wine, cider.

CLASSIC RECIPES Tripe and onions; *tripes à la mode (de Caen)*; pepperpot soup; *menudo*; *haggis*; *trippa verde*.

Recognizable by its honeycomb appearance, this type of tripe needs less cooking than the smoother blanket tripe.

SKIRT AND DIAPHRAGM

Also called flap or plate steak, the skirt or diaphragm is a thick membrane with a small amount of muscle meat that is attached to the inside of the ribs. Although it is a tough, coarse-grained cut, with lengthy cooking it becomes tender and gives a good, strong meaty flavor to many dishes.

BUY Trimmed of excess fat and any bone fragments, the skirt or diaphragm is available from most butchers as a boiling cut. If the thick membrane is removed by the butcher, and the meat is pounded to a thin sheet, it is sometimes sold as skirt steak for frying.

STORE Keep in the fridge and use within a week of purchase, or wrap tightly and freeze for up to 6 months.

EAT Slice across the grain to maximize tenderness. Skirt steak can be marinated if wished and then quickly grilled, fried, or stir-fried.

More commonly, it is sliced and stewed very gently for a long time. It can also be stuffed and rolled up for roasting or braising.

FLAVOR PAIRINGS Sour cream, carrots, avocado, onions, sweet peppers, chillies, tomatoes, cumin, oregano, pepper.

CLASSIC RECIPES Fajitas; Cornish pasties.

Intestines in brine are easier to handle than those that have been dry salted.

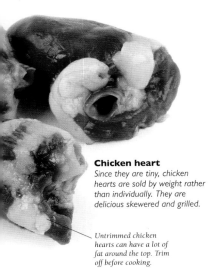

Chicken heart
Since they are tiny, chicken hearts are sold by weight rather than individually. They are delicious skewered and grilled.

Untrimmed chicken hearts can have a lot of fat around the top. Trim off before cooking.

INTESTINES

The traditional cuisine in many countries includes dishes of slowly cooked pork intestines (chitterlings), as well as a few recipes that use the intestines of young, milk-fed animals, such as calf and lamb. Large intestines also make casings for meat puddings while the medium and smaller ones are used as casings for sausages and salamis.

BUY Fresh intestines need to be specially ordered (cleaning them is a lengthy job best left to specialists). Dry salted or brined intestines to be used as sausage casings can be ordered from a butcher or butchers' suppliers, or by mail order via the internet.

STORE Keep fresh intestines in the fridge and use within 2 days. Brined or dry salted intestines will keep for up to 6 months in the fridge.

EAT Thoroughly wash the fresh intestines of young, milk-fed animals, then grill on skewers or stew. Soak dry salted and brined intestines overnight before stuffing with minced or chopped meat and fat to make sausages, which can then be smoked or dried. (Use within 1 day of soaking, or they may disintegrate.)

FLAVOR PAIRINGS Pork fat, chicken, beef fat, cream, tomatoes, mushrooms, truffle, garlic, chili, sage, thyme, pepper, cumin, oatmeal.

CLASSIC RECIPES Chitterlings; *andouillette*; *kishke*.

BRAIN

The delicate yet rich flavor and creamy texture of brain is highly prized in many cuisines. Calf's brain is considered to be the best, followed by lamb's. There is little difference between brain from other animals.

BUY Brain can be bought from specialist butchers and some large supermarkets; it may need to be ordered in advance. (Beef (ox) and lamb's brain is not sold in countries affected by BSE/mad cow disease.)

Normally sold fresh and whole, brain should smell fresh and have little blood or discoloration.

STORE Keep covered in the fridge and use on the day of purchase. Or seal tightly and store in the freezer for up to 4 months.

EAT Soak brain in salty water for 1-2 hours to whiten it, then poach for 15-20 minutes; drain and press until cool. After this it can be sliced and sautéed, or deep-fried as fritters.

FLAVOR PAIRINGS Bacon, butter, eggs, capers, lemon, lime, coconut milk, parsley, mace.
CLASSIC RECIPES Brains with black butter; *fritte alla fiorentina; cervelles à la génoise.*

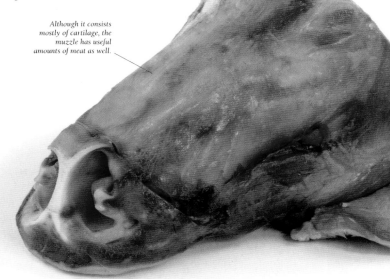

Although it consists mostly of cartilage, the muzzle has useful amounts of meat as well.

Trim off the spinal cord, extraneous parts, and any greenish bits to leave the two lobes.

MUZZLE

Like the ears, the muzzle of an animal is cartilaginous so its primary use in the kitchen is to add a crunchy texture to rustic preparations of meat in jelly.

BUY Muzzle can be bought from specialist butchers (it may need to be ordered in advance). Lamb's muzzle is usually sold skinned. Pig's, calf's, and beef (ox) muzzle may be skinned or blanched to remove hair.

STORE Keep covered in the fridge for up to 2 days. To freeze, seal tightly and store for up to 6 months.

EAT Sometimes the muzzle is brined before cooking. The cartilage needs long, slow simmering to soften it. Once cooked, it is either served in the flavored broth, or sliced or chopped and set in the rich jelly. In some countries, muzzle is stewed with other parts of the head, such as tongue or ears, and sometimes with the feet.
FLAVOR PAIRINGS Salad leaves, parsley, celery, pickles, capers, cloves, ginger, mustard, nutmeg, wine vinegar.
CLASSIC RECIPES *Museau de boeuf à la vinaigrette; feijoada.*

There may be two small bones left at this end. Remove them after cooking.

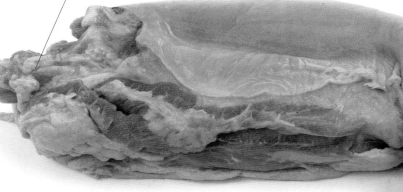

The cheeks or jowl provides the largest piece of meat from a head.

TONGUE

Tongue is highly nutritious and has long been considered a delicacy due to its soft, melting texture. Tongues of all animals are cooked, even down to the tiny tongues of rabbit and songbirds. Lamb's, calf's, and deer tongues are the most tender and delicate; beef (ox) has the strongest flavor. Beef and reindeer tongues are often pickled and smoked after being skinned.

BUY Tongue is sold fresh, when it should look moist and pink or reddish, as well as cured in a brine, when it is

deeper in color. It is also available cooked and sliced as a delicatessen item, and canned, ready for slicing.

STORE Fresh tongue can be kept in the fridge for 2 days, brined tongue for up to a week. Or you can freeze fresh or brined tongue for up to 6 months.

EAT Brined tongue needs to be soaked before cooking. Simmer tongue until tender, then peel off the tough skin and serve hot with a sauce; or press and cool to serve cold in slices with its jellied savory stock.

FLAVOR PAIRINGS Onions, celery, capers, pickles, parsley, chestnuts, nutmeg, mustard, horseradish, chutney, white wine.
CLASSIC RECIPES Pressed tongue; *bollito misto;* tongue in onion sauce; sweet and sour tongue.

EAR

The most commonly eaten ears are those of pig and calf, although lamb's ears are also enjoyed. Ears need gentle simmering to tenderize their cartilage. However, it never completely softens and the crunchy texture forms part of their appeal.

🔒 **BUY** Fresh ears are available from butchers (they may need to be ordered in advance). They should be well cleaned inside and out, and have all the hair removed. Sometimes you can buy brined ears or precooked ears that are ready to grill or fry.

🗄 **STORE** Keep fresh ears tightly covered in the fridge for up to 3 days or in the freezer for up to 6 months. Cooked ears will keep for up to 3 days in the fridge.

⬤ **EAT** Poach or braise, either whole, stuffed, or sliced, and then serve hot in a spicy sauce; or cool and coat in breadcrumbs to bake, fry, or grill.

FLAVOR PAIRINGS Anchovies, onions, capers, salad leaves, thyme, lemon, mustard, nutmeg, cloves, mace, chutney, vinegar.

Ears should be clean, with hair removed, and the fine outer membrane has been peeled off.

HEAD

The head is cooked as a celebration dish in many cuisines and is presented whole or boned, sometimes with the feet of the animal, or the eyeballs served as a separate delicacy. Since the head contains muscle, fat, and cartilage, as well as brain and tongue, it offers crunchy, creamy, and fibrous textures, as well as a mixture of flavors.

🔒 **BUY** A whole head will need to be ordered from a butcher. Pig's and calf's heads are sometimes sold with the skin on, but scalded to remove the hair. Otherwise they are sold like sheep's head: skinned and sometimes split in two. Calf's head is also sold precooked.

🗄 **STORE** If possible, cook on the day of purchase, or keep for no more than 1 day in the fridge. A head can also be cured in a brine for up to a week.

⬤ **EAT** Soak heads overnight, then slowly simmer to cook the meat thoroughly. Once cooled, the head can be roasted for a decorative glaze. Alternatively, take the meat off the bone and serve in a sauce or make into brawn, or head cheese, with the jellied cooking liquid.

FLAVOR PAIRINGS Egg, onions, kale, garlic, orange, pickles, capers, cloves, nutmeg, cumin, allspice, mustard, molasses, vinegar.

CLASSIC RECIPES *Tête de veau;* brawn or head cheese; roast boar's head; scrapple; *powsowdie.*

CHEEK OR JOWL

The cheek or jowl is a choice morsel of rich, dense meat from the head of any animal, although because it is a muscle used for chewing, it is quite tough and needs long, gentle cooking to tenderize it.

🔒 **BUY** Cheek is available from some traditional butchers, but normally needs to be ordered in advance. Beef (ox) and calf's cheeks are usually sold fresh and skinned. Pig's cheek may be sold smoked and cured, ready to cook; it sometimes includes the skin.

🗄 **STORE** Keep fresh or raw cured cheek in the fridge, covered, for up to 4 days, or in the freezer for 6 months.

⬤ **EAT** Beef cheeks are usually gently stewed for a rich dish, or used in head cheese or savory pies. Cured pork cheeks can be cooked, then rolled in breadcrumbs to make Bath chaps, a kind of ham, or used in rustic soups.

FLAVOR PAIRINGS Bacon, carrots, celery, onions, garlic, sage, bay leaf, allspice, red wine, soy sauce.

CLASSIC RECIPES Baths chaps; *feijoada.*

If the whole head is to be roasted, protect the tip of the snout and the ears with foil to prevent them from burning.

SWEETBREAD

Considered a delicacy, sweetbread includes several glands: the thymus, also called throat or neck sweetbreads (only present in young animals since the glands shrink with age), and the pancreas. The testicles (fries) are sometimes also included as a type of sweetbread.

🔒 **BUY** Sweetbreads are available from specialist butchers (they may need to be ordered). They should be pale flesh-pink, with no dark discoloration. Throat sweetbreads are sold in pairs connected by a duct.

🗄 **STORE** Keep wrapped in the fridge and use within 24 hours of purchase, since they deteriorate quickly. Or seal tightly to freeze for up to 6 months.

⏺ **EAT** Soak in cold, acidulated water for 2-3 hours, then blanch. Remove membranes and tubes, and then either poach or braise to serve with a sauce, or slice and sauté, grill, or deep-fry.

FLAVOR PAIRINGS Cream, butter, celery, capers, chanterelles, lemon, *béchamel sauce*, nutmeg, mustard.

CLASSIC RECIPES *Ris de veau forestière; mollejas a la pollensina.*

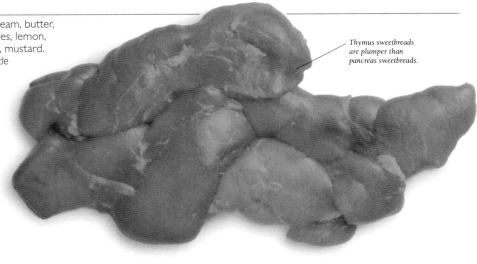

Thymus sweetbreads are plumper than pancreas sweetbreads.

Thymus sweetbreads
The type most commonly sold, calf's thymus sweetbreads are considered to be the best because of their delicate flavor and soft, creamy texture.

Pancreas sweetbreads
Beef pancreas is larger than calf's and has a slightly less delicate flavor.

The membranes surrounding the pancreas need to be removed before cooking, as shown here.

MELT (SPLEEN)

The spleen is a spongy organ located near the intestines. Culinarily called melt, or milt, it tastes a bit like kidney. Most often from beef (ox), calf, or pig, melt is not widely eaten other than in manufactured products, but there are some traditional dishes that use it.

🔒 **BUY** Melt needs to be ordered from a traditional or specialist butcher.

🗄 **STORE** Store in the fridge, covered, and use within 24 hours of purchase. Or seal tightly to freeze for 6 months.

⏺ **EAT** Melt can be simmered, alone or with other offal, and served with a rich wine sauce, or used to enrich stews. Stuff and braise, or make into a pâté, faggots, or sausages. In Sicily slices are deep fried and served with cheese in soft rolls.

FLAVOR PAIRINGS Ricotta cheese, garlic, coriander, lemon, allspice, cinnamon, cumin, Madeira, wine vinegar.

CLASSIC RECIPE *Guastelle.*

Melt is dark red in color, with pig's and beef melt being darker than calf's.

GIZZARD

Along with the neck, heart, liver, and feet, the gizzard makes up a bird's giblets. Since the gizzard is used to grind up the bird's food, it is a very tough muscle indeed, but has a good flavor that is useful in stocks and soups.

🔒 **BUY** The gizzard is usually included with the other components of giblets, but may also be sold separately. A gizzard is only slightly larger than the heart, so several are needed to make up a portion. Duck and goose gizzards are available preserved in cans or jars.

📦 **STORE** Fresh gizzards can be kept, wrapped, in the fridge for up to 3 days. If they have not been cleaned, slice in half, remove the grit and thick inner membrane, and wash thoroughly.

⊙ **EAT** Simmer to make soup stock. To preserve as *confit*, salt overnight, then cook very slowly in poultry fat. Simmer or braise in flavored broth to use in a filling for pies and stews.

FLAVOR PAIRINGS Eggs, cilantro, garlic, scallions, orange peel, ginger, star anise, white wine, rice wine, soy sauce.

CLASSIC RECIPES *Confit de gésiers*; stuffed goose neck; giblet soup; braised giblets.

POULTRY NECK

Poultry necks are usually sold skinned as part of the giblets (with the heart, liver, gizzard, and sometimes the feet), although the skin is also used. There is a useful amount of meat on the neck, but it is not easily accessible, so necks are usually added to the stockpot.

🔒 **BUY** When you buy a bird, the neck will normally be included in the giblets, but you can buy necks separately from Chinese and kosher suppliers. Fresh duck and goose necks are sold in the area where the birds are reared. Canned, stuffed duck and goose necks are sold in delicatessens.

📦 **STORE** Keep fresh necks covered in the fridge and use within 2 days of purchase, or freeze for 6 months.

⊙ **EAT** To improve flavor, first roast or grill skinned necks to brown them, and then simmer to make soup stock.

FLAVOR PAIRINGS Foie gras, garlic, shallot, thyme, bay leaf, paprika, chili, coriander, corn meal, noodles, brandy.

CLASSIC RECIPES Stuffed goose neck; chicken noodle soup.

The hard outer gristle of the gizzard softens to a jelly when cooked slowly.

The skin of poultry neck is sometimes taken off and stuffed to make a kind of sausage.

Pig's trotters are usually brined before cooking. They should be thoroughly cleaned between the toes.

FEET

Animals' feet—the most popular being pig's trotters and calf's feet—and also their tendons are an excellent source of gelatin, and so they are commonly added to stocks and stews to give a better flavor and silky texture. They are also used to make clear jellies and aspic. But there is enough meat on them to make dishes in their own right.

🔒 **BUY** Available from traditional butchers (although they may need to be ordered in advance), pig's trotters and calf's feet are sold scalded and cleaned; lamb's, sheep's, and beeg (ox) feet are skinned. Some are sold precooked. Feet from the hind legs have more meat than those from the forelegs.

📦 **STORE** If not already done, clean raw feet thoroughly. They can be kept covered in the fridge for 3 days or in the freezer, tightly wrapped, for up to a year. Wrapped, precooked feet can be kept in the fridge for 3 days.

⊙ **EAT** All feet and tendons need lengthy simmering to release their gelatin and soften the cartilage. After simmering, roll in breadcrumbs and grill; or bone, stuff, and reform; or chop and serve with the jellied cooking liquid.

FLAVOR PAIRINGS Onions, garlic, celery, carrots, bay leaf, parsley, truffle, capers, lemon, mustard, ginger, lentils, tartare sauce, vinegar.

CLASSIC RECIPES Grilled pig's trotters; *pied de cochon à la Sainte-Ménehould*; *zampone*; *magiritsa*; calf's foot jelly.

POULTRY FEET

Poultry feet (chicken, duck, and goose) are not traditionally used in Western cooking, but their crunchy, gelatinous texture makes them much appreciated in Chinese cuisine. They are also used in Middle Eastern cooking.

🔒 **BUY** Chicken feet are the most easily found, followed by duck. They are available fresh and frozen from butchers (included in packs of giblets and sometimes separately) and Chinese food suppliers. Goose feet are not common, except where geese are reared. If possible, avoid buying unwashed feet since they could be a source of contamination.

📦 **STORE** If not already cleaned, scrub thoroughly, and then blanch in boiling water to sterilize before storing covered in the fridge for up to 3 days.

⊙ **EAT** Poultry feet need lengthy simmering to soften the cartilage. Once cooked, the skin and bones may be removed, although feet are sometimes soft enough to eat in their entirety. They may be served stewed, refried, or chopped and set in their jellied cooking liquid.

FLAVOR PAIRINGS Garlic, spring onion, capers, parsley, lemon, orange zest, ginger, star anise, soy sauce, rice wine.

CLASSIC RECIPES Potted chicken feet; Phoenix claws.

The cartilage in poultry feet produces gelatin to set their cooking liquid.

Meat attached to bones adds rich color to stock if it is browned before simmering.

BONE

The bones of animals and poultry carcasses yield gelatin to enrich stocks, soups, stews, and sauces as well as providing wonderful flavor. Beef and calf bones also contain marrow, which is a prized delicacy in many countries.

BUY Poultry carcasses are sold by butchers, sometimes along with the giblets. Beef, lamb, and pig bones are also available from butchers, and from farmers' markets, although they may need to be ordered in advance. All fresh bones should smell sweet. Pork knuckle bones are also sold smoked.

STORE Keep all bones in the fridge. Use poultry carcasses on the day of purchase. Use knuckle and marrow bones within 2 days, or seal tightly and freeze for up to 4 months.

EAT For stocks, soups, and savory jellies, first brown bones, then simmer slowly to extract the gelatin (cook poultry carcasses very gently to avoid cloudiness). Roast or poach leg bones to cook the marrow, which can then be scooped out.

FLAVOR PAIRINGS Bacon, celery, onions, carrots, capers, parsley, bay leaf, thyme, lemon.

CLASSIC RECIPES *Consommé; osso buco; risotto alla milanese.*

TAIL

In the West the most popular of this animal extremity is strong-flavored, meaty oxtail. Smaller tails from pigs are also eaten, although they have little meat on them. The tails of fat-tailed sheep are highly prized in the Middle East for their distinctive brown fat, while in Asia, deer tails are used in a form of broth in Chinese medicine.

BUY Oxtail is widely available, sold in bundles of pieces varying from ¾in (2cm) to 5in (12cm) in diameter. Pig's tail has to be ordered from a specialist butcher. Fat lamb tails can be bought from butchers in the Middle East and Asia, and from specialist *halal* shops.

STORE Keep oxtail or pig's tail well wrapped in the fridge for up to 4 days, or freeze for up to 6 months. Fat lamb tail can be frozen for up to 4 months.

EAT Since they need to be cooked slowly to break down the cartilage, which gives a silky texture, use oxtail and pig's tail in hearty stews and soups. Cooked pig's tail can be rolled in breadcrumbs and grilled until crisp. Fat lamb tail fat is eaten raw or cooked to flavor dishes.

FLAVOR PAIRINGS Bacon, celery, parsnips, carrots, turnip, onions, peppercorns, nutmeg, cumin, allspice, mustard, red wine, soy sauce.

CLASSIC RECIPES Braised oxtail; oxtail soup; *feijoada.*

Oxtail is surrounded by yellowish fat that lends its distinctive flavor to dishes when stewed.

BRAISED OXTAIL

This traditional British dish is rich and hearty. For the best flavor, make it a day in advance.

SERVES 4

3lbs 3oz (1.5kg) oxtails, cut into large pieces by a butcher

all-purpose flour, to dust and toss

salt and freshly ground black pepper, to season

3–4 tbsp beef drippings or vegetable oil

1 large onion, coarsely chopped

1 large carrot, cut into chunks

1 large celery rib, cut into thick slices

1 large parsnip, cut into chunks

1 small rutabaga, cut into chunks

3 cups beef stock or water

⅔ cup red wine or port

bouquet garni (a bundle of mixed fresh herbs, such as bay leaf, thyme, and rosemary, tied together with cotton string)

1 Preheat the oven to 325°F (160°C). Dust the pieces of oxtail lightly with the flour and season with pepper. Melt the drippings in a heavy, flameproof casserole and, in batches, brown the oxtails. Remove to a dish.

2 Toss the vegetables in flour, then brown (add more drippings if needed). Pour in 2 cups of stock and, with a wooden spoon, scrape up and dissolve brown residue from the bottom of the pan.

3 Return the oxtails to the casserole. Pour in the wine and tuck in the *bouquet garni.* Cover the pan tightly. Bring to a boil, and then transfer to the oven to cook for 2½-3 hours. Remove from the oven and cool, then refrigerate overnight.

4 Next day, remove solid fat from the surface and pour in the remaining stock. Reheat in a 350°F (180°C) oven for 30 minutes. Add salt and pepper.

SKIN AND FAT

Meat and poultry skin is enjoyed for its texture, whether boiled to add succulence, or fried or roasted to a crisp finish, such as the "crackling" on roast pork in Britain. The fat from animals keeps lean meat and birds moist during cooking, and is rendered to provide frying and baking fat such as lard, dripping, and kosher *schmaltz.*

BUY Pork skin, sheets of back fat, and caul, as well as poultry neck skin for stuffing, may need to be specially ordered from a butcher.

STORE If no meat is attached, fresh fat can be stored in the fridge, well sealed, for 1-2 months or frozen for up to 4 months. Fat with some meat

attached as well as fresh skin can be kept in the fridge for up to a week.

EAT Fry or bake chopped skin until crisp, or simmer and add to head cheese or other cold-meat preparations. Render fat by cooking in a slow oven. Wrap lean meat and birds with sheets of fat, or thread (lard) with strips of fat, before roasting. Use caul fat to wrap meat patties or line terrine molds.

FLAVOR PAIRINGS Scallions, coriander, lemon, lime, salt, chili, pepper, ginger, soy sauce, rice wine.

CLASSIC RECIPES Pork scratchings; *crépinettes;* fried chicken skin; *chicharrón.*

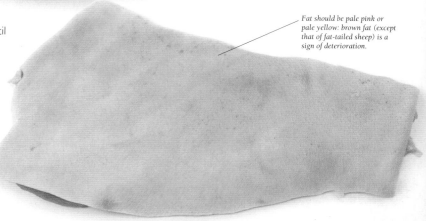

Fat should be pale pink or pale yellow: brown fat (except that of fat-tailed sheep) is a sign of deterioration.

The natural oils and marinated spices in cured sausages are released when the sausages are cooked, to give a rich, exotic flavor.

BACON

Bacon is pork that has been cured with salt (dry or as a brine) and then often smoked. Long used as a means of preserving pork, regional and national variations have developed in the breeds of pigs and the cuts used—from the belly, side, and loin—and in the salting techniques. Unsmoked or "green" bacon has pale pink flesh and white fat; smoked bacon is deeper in color. Chicken, turkey, duck, goat, lamb, and beef are also sometimes salted and then sold as "bacon."

🔒 **BUY** Normally sold sliced, and by weight, bacon can be bought from butchers or from supermarkets, when it is usually vacuum packed.

📦 **STORE** Unopened packs can be kept in the fridge for several weeks or frozen for up to 2 months. Once opened, keep in the fridge and use within a week.

● **EAT** Grill, fry, or bake strips to serve alongside eggs, offal such as liver, poultry, or fish; use in sandwiches; or scatter over salads. Or dice and cook with other ingredients to make pasta sauces, stuffings, soups and casseroles, and savory pastries.

FLAVOR PAIRINGS Chicken, kidneys, liver, oily and white fish, scallops, shrimp, cheese, cauliflower, potatoes, tomatoes, avocado.

CLASSIC RECIPES Quiche Lorraine; BLT; liver and bacon; bacon baked beans; *omelette bonne femme*.

Back bacon
From the loin, back is the leanest cut of bacon and is often grilled or fried to accompany eggs for breakfast or to use in a sandwich. Middle bacon, from the side of the pig, also has a good eye of lean meat.

Smoked bacon
The belly yields streaky bacon strips, which have a good balance of fat and lean, making them ideal for laying over the breast of a chicken or turkey to be roasted, to prevent it from drying out.

Streaky bacon
Taken from the fatty belly, streaky bacon is the most commonly sold type of bacon in the US, and is normally smoked. When cooked, its fat melts readily and the bacon becomes very crisp. So-called "Canadian" bacon from the eye of the loin is considerably leaner.

Lardo
Made in Italy by brine-curing pork back fat with herbs and spices in wooden barrels—or, in Carrara, in marble containers—lardo has a silky-smooth texture and wonderful flavor. It is traditionally served on toast as an antipasto.

Wiltshire cure bacon *This is the usual, commercial brine cure for bacon in the United Kingdom, entailing immersion and injection of the brine into the meat. Depending on the brine, this may create a milder flavor than dry-cured bacon.*

Wiltshire cure bacon is normally sold with the rind attached. When cooking, the fat should melt away to leave a crisp remnant with a delicate flavor.

Marinating and long drying give Chinese bacon a mahogany color.

Lap yuk
Literally translated as "wax meat," this strongly flavored Chinese bacon is made from pork belly marinated in Chinese spices and then slowly dried. It is normally chopped to add flavor to other dishes.

Ayrshire cure bacon *Unusually, with this Scottish method the pork is skinned to give a rind-free bacon. This permits the dry cure to enter the meat and, depending on the cure, can produce a strongly flavored bacon.*

Dry-cured bacon
Bacon cured in a dry salt mixture contains less liquid than brine-cured bacon, so does not exude a milky liquid as it cooks. Some dry salt cures include herbs, spices, sugar, and other seasonings.

The meat of dry-cured bacon is usually harder and darker than brine-cured bacon.

QUICHE LORRAINE

This famous French savory tart has a smooth, rich custard filling with pieces of crisp, salty bacon.

SERVES 4–6

For the pastry

| 1½ cups all-purpose flour |
| 8 tbsp (1 stick) butter, cut into cubes |
| 1 egg yolk |

For the filling

| 8oz (200g) sliced bacon, cut crosswise into ½in (1cm) pieces |
| 1 small onion, finely chopped |
| ½ cup shredded Gruyère cheese |
| 4 large eggs, lightly beaten |
| ½ cup heavy whipping cream |
| ½ cup whole milk |
| freshly ground black pepper |

1 To make the pastry, combine the flour and butter in a food processor, and process until it resembles fine crumbs. Add the egg yolk and 3–4 tbsp ice water and process briefly to make a smooth dough. Turn out on to a floured surface and knead briefly. Refrigerate for at least 30 minutes. Preheat the oven to 375°F (190°C).

2 On a lightly floured surface, roll out the pastry and use to line a 9in (23cm) tart pan or pie plate that is at least 1¾in (4cm) deep. Prick the bottom of the pastry with a fork; then line with parchment paper and fill with pie weights. Bake for 12 minutes. Remove the paper and pie weights, and bake for 10 minutes, until golden.

3 Heat a frying pan and cook the bacon for 3–4 minutes. Add the onion and cook for another 2–3 minutes, stirring occasionally, until the bacon is crisp and the onion soft. Drain, and spread the mixture across the pastry shell. Top with a layer of cheese.

4 Whisk together the eggs, cream, milk, and pepper. Pour into the pastry shell. Set the pan on a baking sheet and bake for 25–30 minutes, or until the filling is golden and just set. Cool slightly, then slice and serve.

PANCETTA

Pancetta is pork belly that has been dry-salted and then air-dried for about 12 weeks. It is not usually smoked, but herbs, spices, and garlic are often used to augment the salting. It may be cured flat (*stesa*) or rolled up (*arrotolata*). Originally Italian, with many regional variations, pancetta is now produced in other parts of the world and valued by cooks everywhere.

🔒 **BUY** Pancetta is available as slices or dice in packs in supermarkets. Or buy it freshly cut from Italian delicatessens.

📦 **STORE** Packs can be kept in the fridge for several weeks. If purchased fresh from a delicatessen, store in the fridge, loosely wrapped, for up to a week.

🔵 **EAT** Use pancetta in pasta sauces, to top pizzas, in bean casseroles and risottos, in soups, and to wrap fish and poultry for grilling. Thinly sliced rolled pancetta can be served as antipasti.

FLAVOR PAIRINGS Parmesan, asparagus, tomatoes, chile.
CLASSIC RECIPES *Spaghetti alla carbonara*; *bucatini all'Amatriciana*.

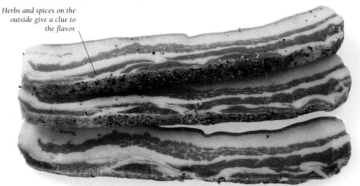

Herbs and spices on the outside give a clue to the flavor.

HAM OR GAMMON

In many parts of the world, the hind leg of a pig is salted (traditionally dry-salted, but now more commonly brine-cured) and matured, then sometimes smoked. In Britain, the term gammon is used for this type of cured pork, although it is also widely known as ham.

🔒 **BUY** Uncooked gammon can be bought prepacked or from a butcher as thick strips or steaks, or as a joint with or without the bone. It is also sold cooked and ready to eat hot or cold.

📦 **STORE** Unopened packs can be kept in the fridge for several weeks or frozen for up to 2 months. Once opened, keep in the fridge and use within a week.

🔵 **EAT** If heavily salted, soak in several changes of water before cooking. Bake or simmer joints to eat hot with a sauce or cold with salad or in sandwiches. Fry, grill, or braise thick strips and steaks.

FLAVOR PAIRINGS Eggs, pineapple, dried fruits, mustard, cloves.

Jambon de Paris
Also known as jambon blanc, the common French brine-cured, boned ham is usually sold already boiled. Slice and serve with mustard.

Prosciutto cotto
This Italian brine-cured, boned ham is sold ready to eat as antipasti. It can also be diced and added to sauces.

Jamón cocido
In Spain, boned, brine-cured ham is sometimes baked in a mold or boiled before sale. Slice to eat as a first course or in a bread roll.

Smithfield ham
Considered to be the best North American "country" ham, from Smithfield, Virginia, this is dry-salted and heavily smoked. It is usually baked or boiled.

Jambon de Paris is tender and pale in color.

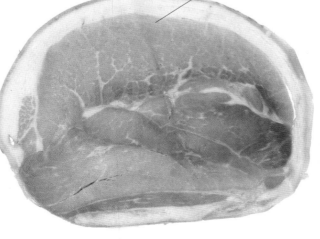

HAM OR GAMMON (CONTINUED)

Virginia ham
Traditionally dry-salted, then usually smoked and matured for 2–3 years, this ham is often sweetened with sugar or honey. It may be sold as an entire ham or sliced, almost always cooked and ready to eat.

The best long matured hams have deeply colored meat.

York ham
Although traditionally dry salted, most York ham is now brine cured and then normally smoked. Tender and mild, it is sold both precooked and for home boiling or baking, bone-in or boned.

The best jambonneau has a good quantity of meat but the presence of cartilage is also essential for good texture.

Jambonneau
For French jambonneau, lightly brine-cured pork hocks are boiled and often sold coated in breadcrumbs with the bone removed. The mild flavor works well in cold meat starters or as picnic fare.

HONEY-ROAST HAM

A British favorite, serve this hot for one meal and use the leftovers in salads, sandwiches, and soups.

SERVES 10—12

6½lb (3kg) smoked half-ham on the bone, skin-on

2 celery ribs, coarsely chopped

2 carrots, coarsely chopped

1 onion, coarsely chopped

bouquet garni of 8 black peppercorns, 2 bay leaves, 4 fresh thyme sprigs, a few parsley stems, and 12–16 cloves, all tied in a piece of muslin or cheesecloth

a handful of extra cloves

4 tbsp runny honey

1½ tbsp prepared hot or Dijon mustard

1 Place the ham, celery, carrots, onion, and bouquet garni in a large pot, and cover with cold water. Bring to a boil, then reduce the heat and simmer uncovered for about 1¾ hours.

2 Lift the ham onto a board and discard the vegetables and cooking liquid. Preheat the oven to 350°F (180°C).

3 Cut the skin off the ham, leaving a smooth layer of fat. Score the fat with a sharp knife, first in one direction and then in the opposite direction, to make a diamond pattern.

4 Stud the fat with cloves, placing one in the center of each diamond shape. Set the ham in a roasting pan. Mix together the honey and mustard and drizzle this glaze evenly over the fat.

5 Roast for about 45 minutes, basting with the glaze a couple of times, until ham is covered with a dark golden glaze. Serve warm, or allow to cool and refrigerate, covered, for up to 1 week.

OTHER SALT-CURED MEATS

Most cured meats are made from pork but other meats are also cured in many regions of the world, either by using a dry, salt-based cure or by brine-curing, which is commonly known as pickling. Dry-cured meats may be described as salted, pickled, or "corned," which is a reference to the crystals of salt used in the original dry-cure process.

🔒 **BUY** Cured meats are often sold sliced, either freshly cut from deli counters in supermarkets or commercially packaged. Canned corned beef is easily found in supermarkets.

🗄 **STORE** Freshly cut slices can be kept, loosely wrapped, in the fridge, for up to a week. Store commercially packaged slices according to instructions.

◉ **EAT** Use in sandwiches, serve as a starter, or with salad.

FLAVOR PAIRINGS Mustard, pickles, pickled onions.

CLASSIC RECIPES Reuben sandwich; corned beef hash.

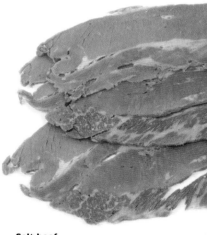

Salt beef
As the name suggests, this is beef preserved by soaking in a very salty, seasoned brine; historically it was the staple meat for sailors on long voyages. It is often served hot, piled high in sandwiches.

Eisbein
In Germany, this salt-cured and sometimes smoked hock or knuckle of pork is simmered slowly to serve with potatoes or sauerkraut.

Eisbein is normally well covered with soft fat, which enhances flavor.

Cured venison

Best prepared from a single muscle in the haunch, or less frequently the saddle, venison is cured by dry salting or in brine. Each producer creates his own recipe, often adding sugar or molasses as well as herbs and spices. Serve thinly sliced.

Corned beef

Sold in rectangular cans, the chopped and pressed form of salt beef is less popular today than it once was, but is still a convenient pantry standby. Use it for hash.

There is normally a significant amount of fat, which contributes to the flavor and texture of corned beef.

Salt beef is tender and well supplied with fat. It is sometimes bright red due to the addition of saltpeter (potassium nitrate, a food preservative) to the brine.

Pastrami

For this popular American sandwich meat, beef, such as brisket, is dry cured with a highly seasoned salt mixture, then smoked and cooked. It can be eaten hot or cold, usually with rye bread and mustard.

Smoked venison

Lean venison, usually haunch, is either dry cured or wet cured with a salt-based brine that may contain juniper or other herbs, then hot-smoked to cook it thoroughly. Eat cold.

Kassler

Kassler or Kasseler is a salt-cured and smoked pork popular in Germany, Denmark, and Poland. Usually the neck or loin, other cuts may be used including rib cutlets.

Smoked duck and goose

In France, boneless meat from ducks (left) and geese (right) is lightly brine cured and then smoked for eating raw.

Cured tongue

Tongue is normally soaked for a few days in brine, then boiled until the skin can easily be removed. It is then pressed until cold and served in thin slices.

Goose fat should be thick but restricted to the outside and it should have a slightly smoked taste.

DRY-CURED HAMS

Hams described as dry-cured—first salted and then air-dried or dry-aged, sometimes smoked—are traditionally found in southern regions of Europe or mountainous areas that are windy enough to permit drying. Such hams are generally eaten raw. Regional variations in the breed and diet of the pig, the cut used (normally the hind leg, but occasionally other parts), the length and method of salting and subsequent drying, and then whether the ham is smoked all contribute to the flavors in the huge range of dry-cured hams available.

🔒 **BUY** Slices can be cut from whole bone-in hams in delicatessens, or bought in packs from supermarkets.

📦 **STORE** Packs of sliced ham can be kept in the fridge for several weeks; once opened use within a week.

⬤ **EAT** Sliced very thinly, dry-cured ham is enjoyed as tapas in Spain, hors d'oeuvres in France, and antipasti in Italy. It can also be used in sandwiches and salads, and added at the last minute to cooked dishes.

FLAVOR PAIRINGS Parmesan, pickles, figs, melon, asparagus.

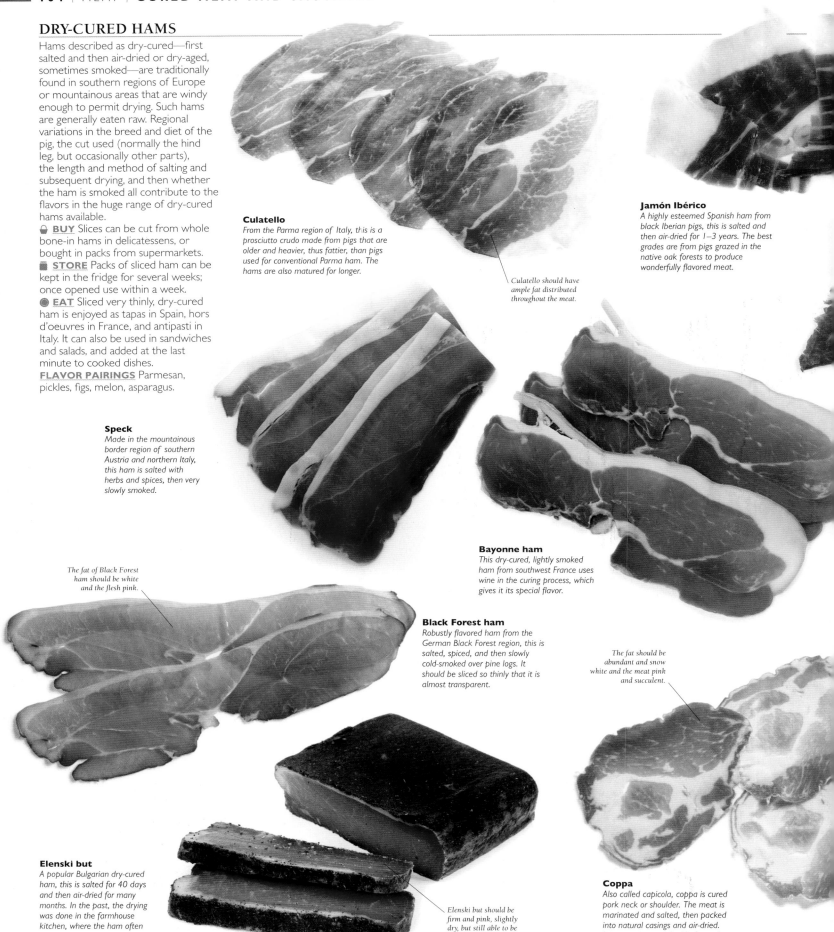

Culatello
From the Parma region of Italy, this is a prosciutto crudo made from pigs that are older and heavier, thus fattier, than pigs used for conventional Parma ham. The hams are also matured for longer.

Culatello should have ample fat distributed throughout the meat.

Jamón Ibérico
A highly esteemed Spanish ham from black Iberian pigs, this is salted and then air-dried for 1–3 years. The best grades are from pigs grazed in the native oak forests to produce wonderfully flavored meat.

Speck
Made in the mountainous border region of southern Austria and northern Italy, this ham is salted with herbs and spices, then very slowly smoked.

Bayonne ham
This dry-cured, lightly smoked ham from southwest France uses wine in the curing process, which gives it its special flavor.

The fat of Black Forest ham should be white and the flesh pink.

Black Forest ham
Robustly flavored ham from the German Black Forest region, this is salted, spiced, and then slowly cold-smoked over pine logs. It should be sliced so thinly that it is almost transparent.

The fat should be abundant and snow white and the meat pink and succulent.

Elenski but
A popular Bulgarian dry-cured ham, this is salted for 40 days and then air-dried for many months. In the past, the drying was done in the farmhouse kitchen, where the ham often acquired a smoky flavor.

Elenski but should be firm and pink, slightly dry, but still able to be cut with a sharp knife.

Coppa
Also called capicola, coppa is cured pork neck or shoulder. The meat is marinated and salted, then packed into natural casings and air-dried. It is sometimes cooked before sale.

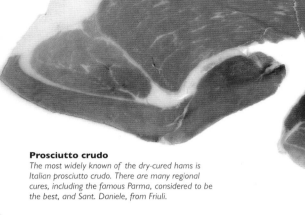

Prosciutto crudo

The most widely known of the dry-cured hams is Italian prosciutto crudo. There are many regional cures, including the famous Parma, considered to be the best, and Sant. Daniele, from Friuli.

Jamón serrano

Meaning "mountain ham" in Spanish, these salted and air-dried hams have many regional variations, such as jamón de Teruel and de Huelva. They are sweet with a chewy texture.

Jamón bellota

One of the most expensive dry-cured hams in the world, this is the highest-quality jamón Ibérico, prepared from pigs that have fed on acorns. The creamy-yellow fat has an exquisite, sweet flavor.

Westphalian ham

Made in the Westphalian forest of Germany from pigs raised on acorns, this air-dried ham is smoked over beech and juniper. The aromatic flavor is complemented by pumpernickel bread.

Jinhua ham

Much loved in China, this is made from the hind legs of a particular breed of pig, which are dry-salted and then soaked before drying for several months to develop a distinctive flavor.

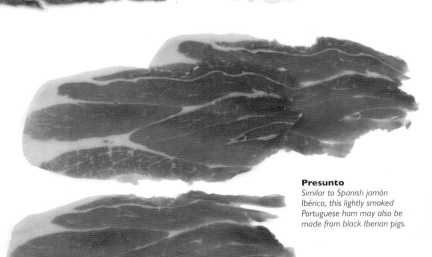

Presunto

Similar to Spanish jamón Ibérico, this lightly smoked Portuguese ham may also be made from black Iberian pigs.

Jinhua should have abundant, cream-colored fat and dark red meat.

AIR-DRIED MEAT

Being simple and easily transportable, meat preserved by air-drying has a long history associated with man's survival. While hams are the best-known dried-meat products, other meats are also preserved in this way—normally by initial salting, followed by washing, and then drying in the wind or heat of the sun. Flavorings of hot spices, herbs, and smoke are commonly applied. The meat is usually boned beforehand and may be sliced or ground to speed up the drying process.

🔒 **BUY** Air-dried meats should in general be firm and not too dried out.

▪ **STORE** Dried meats have a very long shelf life of many months, as long as conditions are not humid. Keep unwrapped in a dry, well-ventilated place, or wrapped in the fridge.

● **EAT** Dried meats are usually eaten raw, as snacks or as antipasti and hors d'oeuvres. Less commonly they may be cooked by grilling or lightly frying in oil, or be used in baking.

FLAVOR PAIRINGS Hard cheeses, cream, pickles, fresh figs, white beans, red onions, olive oil.

Bakkwa
Known also as rougan or long yok, Chinese bakkwa is pork cured with salt and sugar, flattened, and dried.

Bresaola
To make this well-known antipasta, boned beef from the hind legs is salted, with juniper berries and other herbs, for a few days and then air-dried. Valtellina in the Italian Alps is the center of production.

Pastirma
This and similarly named products exist throughout the Middle East, Balkans, and Turkey, prepared from salted pork, lamb, goat, water buffalo, and camel. Once dried, they are pressed, covered in a paste of hot spices, and further dried.

Once it is dried, bündnerfleisch is pressed into a rectangular shape, so yields very uniform, thin slices.

Carne de sol
A speciality from northeastern Brazil, where it is also known as jabá, this is beef that is salted and then left to dry in the sun (the name means "meat of the sun").

Cecina de Leon is often served with a mild dressing and shavings of cheese.

Bündnerfleisch
Also called viande des Grisons, this is dried beef made in Switzerland's Grisons region. The meat is boned, marinated in wine with salt and spices, and then air-dried. It is not normally smoked.

Often studded with spices, the outside of biltong is quite hard. The interior is less hard and should be able to be cut with a sharp knife.

Biltong
Of South African origin, the thick strips or slices of beef or game meat are marinated in vinegar-based liquid, then salted and dried.

Jerky
This is a popular North American dried-meat snack. The thin slices of wild or domestic meat (usually beef) are often marinated in spicy dressings before drying, and are sometimes then smoked.

The meat should be a rich, dark color, and not too hard.

Charqui
This South American salted and wind-dried meat is usually made from llama, beef, or horse.

Slinzega
Like bresaola, this is also made in Valtellina, but using smaller strips of meat, traditionally horse, but increasingly venison or pork.

Pemmican
Made from pounding dried game meats with melted fat and often berries, pemmican is traditional to Native Americans, and is still marketed.

Kuivaliha
To make kuivaliha, strips of meat, often reindeer or venison, are dried over a few weeks in Finland when the spring weather is appropriate. It is also called kapaliha.

Cecina
Often beef from the hind legs, but also traditionally made with horse meat, cecina is salted, flattened, sometimes sun-dried, and usually smoked. Cecina de Leon (pictured) is a famous Spanish variety, normally served as a first course, or added to a variety of cooked dishes as a final garnish.

Lomo embuchado
Lomo embuchado is a Spanish dry-cured and air-dried loin of pork. It is usually served in thin slices in cold collations, and as a snack in bars.

FRESH SAUSAGES

Fresh sausages are generally made by forcing seasoned, minced, or chopped uncured meat (sausage meat) into a natural casing (such as intestine or neck skin) or an artificial casing, although there are also sausages prepared without casing. Recipes vary widely in the meat and seasonings used, and whether some sort of starchy filler is added (which is common in the UK), as well in as the proportion of lean to fat; however, sausages tend to be high in fat so they can be fried or grilled successfully. Some fresh sausages are sold lightly smoked.

BUY Available from butchers and supermarkets, sausages are normally sold by weight, loose or prepacked.

STORE Keep in the fridge and use within a few days of purchase. Or freeze for up to 6 months.

EAT Fresh sausages are always cooked, normally by frying, grilling, or barbecuing, and roasting, to caramelize the casing.

FLAVOR PAIRINGS
Potatoes; white beans; onions; apples; goose fat; sage; mustard; tomato ketchup, eggs.

CLASSIC RECIPES
Toad-in-the-hole; *cassoulet; lenticchie con salsiccie; medister;* mixed grill.

Cumberland sausage
The high meat content of this English chopped pork sausage gives it a firm, dense texture. Fry or grill like other fresh sausages.

Cumberland sausage is sold in a continuous coil or as individual long, curved sausages.

Pork sausage
Sausages are made up of meat, fat, plus fillers and seasonings, such as herbs and spices. Generally the higher the meat content the better the sausage.

Beef sausages should be quite dark in color, reflecting their high meat content.

Beef sausage
Beef sausages are generally leaner than pork sausages and with a drier texture. Better quality sausages are high in meat content but still need sufficient fat content so that they can be fried or grilled.

German Bratwurst
A spicy, fine-textured sausage made from veal, beef, or pork, this is probably the most popular sausage in Germany. Almost always sold fresh, occasionally smoked. Fry or poach and then grill. Delicious with stewed apples.

Merguez sausage
Made from lamb, beef, or both, in lamb casings, this highly spiced North African sausage is often eaten with couscous. Its red color is due to chile.

There are many regional variations of bratwurst in Germany, with different sizes and ingredients.

Saucisse de Toulouse
Made from pork shoulder and belly, this coarse-textured French sausage is a classic ingredient in cassoulets.

Saucisse de Morteau
Like saucisse de Montbéliard, this fresh, French pork sausage is cold-smoked before sale.

Cotechino
A speciality of Modena, cotechino (or cotecchino or coteghino) is a large pork sausage flavored with white wine and garlic. It is often served with lentils or cannellini beans to celebrate the New Year.

Wild boar sausage
Wild boar are among the fattier game species so they can readily be made into sausages, usually with the addition of a little pork fat. They have a meaty flavor and quite a dense texture.

Andouillette
These popular French sausages have a unique flavor and texture, crumbling into separate morsels when eaten. They are usually fried to serve with French-fried potatoes and mustard.

Chorizo fresco
The uncooked version of the well-known Spanish sausage is normally made with finely minced pork, but other meats may be used. It is usually removed from the casing before cooking, lending its spice and color to Mexican and Spanish dishes.

Venison sausage
Venison sausages are often low in fat with a consequent meaty flavor and dense texture. Most have pork fat added to the mixture. They are normally fried, grilled, or baked.

Venison sausages can replace pork or beef sausages in many recipes.

Andouillettes are made of pork or veal tripe and intestine.

FRESH SAUSAGES (CONTINUED)

Chipolata
These small, thin sausages are popular in France and Britain. Normally pork, they may also be made from other meats such as beef and venison.

Being thin, chipolatas cook more quickly than regular fresh sausages.

Crépinette
French crépinettes (sometimes called fricandeaux) are small, flat sausages wrapped in caul fat. They may be sold ready cooked to eat cold, or raw for roasting and eating hot.

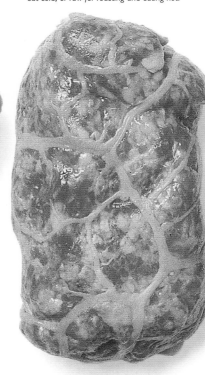

Chair à saucisse
This is the meat used for stuffing sausages. It may be made from any meat but should be coarsely minced or chopped and with enough fat to permit frying or grilling. It can be made into patties or meatballs, or used to stuff poultry.

COOKED AND PART-COOKED SAUSAGES

There is a great variety of sausages sold part-cooked or part-cured, which need to be further cooked before eating, as well as those sold fully cooked or cured and ready to eat. The processing may entail boiling, blanching, smoking, or drying. In Europe, where sausages are boiled or poached before being sold, they are sometimes called puddings; it is customary to reheat these for eating.

🔒 **BUY** Both part-cooked and cooked sausages should look moist, not wet, and smell fresh and pleasant.

🗄 **STORE** Keep part-cooked sausages in the fridge for no more than a week, unless prepacked; cooked sausages can be kept for up to 2 weeks. Or freeze for up to 6 months.

⬤ **EAT** Poach part-cooked sausages or, if they have a high enough fat content, fry, grill, or bake. Add to other dishes such as hearty soups and casseroles. Depending on their type and texture, fully cooked sausages can be used in antipasti, salads, sandwiches, soups, stews, and many other dishes.

FLAVOR PAIRINGS Turnips, onions, potatoes, red cabbage, white beans, tomatoes, apples, dried fruits, mustard.

CLASSIC RECIPES *Fabada*; haggis and neeps; black pudding with apple; *himmel und erde*; *bigos polski*; *bollito misto*.

Saucisse de Montbéliard
Meaty and dense saucisse de Montbéliard is a fresh pork sausage that is cold-smoked. Cooked either by grilling or boiling, it is often eaten with sauerkraut.

Lorne sausage is molded into a loaf and sliced into squares for frying.

Lorne sausage
Also know as slicing sausage, this Scottish skinless sausage may be made from beef or pork. It is often quite strongly peppered and is served fried for breakfast, sometimes on a bread roll.

Boudin noir
The French version of black pudding contains little or no cereals, but usually has cubes of pork fat and sometimes meat, as well as apple, onion, chestnut, or other ingredients. Boudin noir is normally sliced and fried before serving.

Boudin noir is richly colored with pig's blood.

Boudin blanc
Like other puddings, boudins blancs are sold pre-cooked by poaching, and are then usually further cooked by frying. They are made with pork, chicken, veal, or rabbit, and often enriched with cream and eggs.

The speckled appearance of a white pudding is due to black pepper and toasted oatmeal.

White pudding
White puddings contain animal fats but no meat. In Scotland, a white pudding is known as mealie pudding; the mixture without the casing is called skirlie. Battered and deep-fried, they are often sold in fish and chip shops.

Modern black puddings are often sold in black synthetic skins rather than the authentic intestine.

Saveloy
Similar to a frankfurter, the saveloy is prepared with lightly cured pork, cereal filler, and seasonings and then smoked. It is popular as a take-out snack in the UK, as well as in Australia and New Zealand.

Black or blood pudding
Rich British black pudding is made from blood, usually pig's, plus a filler like breadcrumbs or oatmeal, cubes of pork fat, and seasonings. It is simmered and sold cooked. Sauté slices to serve with mashed potatoes.

FABADA

From Spain, this is a rich and spicy bean stew with lots of meaty sausage and bacon. Serve with crusty bread.

SERVES 4

8oz (250g) morcilla (Spanish black pudding) or blood sausage

8oz (250g) Spanish chorizo or Portuguese linguica

8oz (250g) thick-cut tocino, bacon, or pancetta

1 tbsp olive oil

¼ cup dry red wine

2 x 15oz (400g) cans white beans, drained

pinch of saffron powder

1 bay leaf

2 cups chicken stock, or as needed

1 Cut the morcilla, chorizo or linguica, and tocino, bacon, or pancetta into large chunks. Heat the oil in a large saucepan, add the sausages and tocino, and cook, stirring, over medium–low heat for 2 minutes. Increase the heat, add the wine, and then allow it to boil and reduce for 2–3 minutes.

2 Stir in the beans, saffron, bay leaf, and just enough chicken stock to cover. Bring to a boil, then reduce the heat, cover the pan, and simmer for 30 minutes. Serve hot.

COOKED AND PART-COOKED SAUSAGES (CONTINUED)

The color of a kishka is influenced by the quantity of paprika used.

Kishka
From Eastern Europe, kishka can be made with a great variety of fillings, usually including blood, sometimes liver. The vegetable base is normally buckwheat, but may also be barley or even potato. Sold cooked, they are normally further cooked before eating.

Chouriço de sangue
This Portuguese black pudding can be made entirely from blood, but is usually made from similar ingredients to Spanish morcilla and other blood puddings: rice, cereals, onions, pieces of pork fat, and so on. It may be eaten cold with other meats, or cooked and used in casseroles.

When sliced, the pieces of foie gras can be seen surrounded by the goose-meat stuffing.

Stuffed goose neck
For this French delicacy (cou d'oie farci), the skin of the goose neck is stuffed with goose or duck meat, foie gras, truffles, morel, and so on. It is sold cooked and ready to slice and eat.

Morcilla is an essential ingredient in the Spanish bean stew fabada.

Morcilla de Burgos
Perhaps the most renowned of the Spanish black puddings, this uses rice as the filler. Other varieties include onions, pine nuts, or almonds, as well as pig's blood, pork fat, and seasonings. Like other black puddings, morcilla is sold cooked, but is normally further cooked before eating.

Like crépinettes, faggots are small sausage parcels wrapped in caul fat.

Haslet
Traditional English recipes for haslet wrap a mixture of seasoned pork, minced onions, and a cereal-based filler in pig's caul, then bake. Serve slices with a salad or use in sandwiches.

Mortadella di Bologna
This very large sausage is traditionally made from finely minced, seasoned pork, often studded with cubes of fat, peppercorns, or pistachio nuts. That from Bologna is considered to be the best. Sold sliced and ready to eat, it is usually served as an antipasto.

Some chouriço de sangue is colored a rich red by the addition of paprika.

Haggis
Loved by Scots everywhere, haggis is made by coarsely mincing sheep's liver, heart, and lungs with onions, beef suet, oatmeal, and seasonings; stuffing this into a sheep's stomach; then boiling. Bought cooked, haggis only needs to be heated through.

The skin containing the haggis may still be the stomach of a sheep, but is more often now the large intestine of cattle.

Blutwurst
The best-known German black pudding, this has many regional variations, some of which are smoked. All contain pig's blood, plus meats such as bacon and calf's or pig's offal. Blutwurst is often served hot with boiled potatoes.

Faggots
English faggots are made from minced pig's offal, salt pork, or bacon, and a cereal filler, plus seasonings such as nutmeg and onion. Delicious when homemade and slowly baked.

COOKED AND PART-COOKED SAUSAGES (CONTINUED)

Unlike American frankfurters, the German variety are normally sold in a casing.

Bologna
Sold ready to eat, this large sausage is made from highly seasoned, finely minced meat and fat. The meat is usually pork but can be poultry or beef. Unlike the American version, Italian bologna sausage (pictured) has visible pieces of fat.

Braunschweiger
Braunschweiger is a smoked pork, liver sausage, sometimes incorporating beef that is enriched with eggs. The texture is soft and it is usually eaten spread on bread.

Diots
These Savoyard sausages, usually made of pork and vegetables including beets, are either grilled or poached in wine. Diots are also sold smoked or dried.

The color of knackwurst is influenced by the extent of the smoking.

German Knackwurst
This fat, stumpy beef and pork sausage is flavored with cumin and garlic—often highly spiced. Cold smoked, it needs to be cooked before eating.

American bratwurst
Nicknamed "brats," these were originally made from minced pork and veal, but they now have a smoother texture. Usually fresh, they are sometimes sold precooked or smoked.

A guide to quality is the finely minced texture of the filling: it should not be a paste.

German frankfurter
Made from finely ground mixed pork and beef, this is a slim, lightly smoked sausage. Simmer gently to serve with potato salad and sweet German mustard.

American knackwurst
Like its German counterpart, this is a short, fat, garlicky sausage made from highly seasoned beef and/or pork, and smoked.

Kielbasa
A large variety of Eastern European sausages take this name. They are usually garlicky, and may be smoked or fresh. In Poland, lightly smoked kielbasa is eaten with braised cabbage or used in the hearty stew called bigos.

Cajun andouille
This American version of pork andouille is heavily spiced and smoked, and used in traditional Cajun dishes, such as jambalaya.

American frankfurter
Also known as hot dog and weiner, this smoked sausage may be made from pork, beef, veal, or poultry, and comes in all sizes. Although precooked, it must be reheated for serving.

In the US, the frankfurter is usually sold skinless.

COOKED AND PART-COOKED SAUSAGES (CONTINUED)

German Bockwurst
Traditionally made in the spring from minced veal and pork, this now uses lamb, poultry, or even horse meat. It is often smoked.

Cervelas
A meaty Swiss or German smoked sausage, cervelas is made from finely minced beef, pork, pork rind, and bacon in natural casings. There is also a pure pork French version.

The skin color of Swiss cervelas is a result of the smoking process.

German Mettwurst
Made from minced pork, cured and smoked, this sausage may be soft enough to spread or coarse in texture, and can be eaten raw.

Leberwurst
A creamy-textured liver sausage, this incorporates pork liver, lean meat, offal, bacon, and spices. Occasionally, chicken or veal replace the pork. It is sometimes smoked.

Teewurst
Because of its high fat content, this spicy, smoked pork or beef and bacon sausage is easy to spread.

Saucisse de Strasbourg
Also known as "knack," this smoked pork sausage from Alsace is similar to the frankfurter. It is poached before eating.

American Bockwurst
With a smoother texture than the German original, this herb-flavored sausage is sometimes known as a "white hot dog". It is sold partially cooked or smoked, as well as fresh.

Like the similar German weisswurst American bockwurst is very white.

American Mettwurst
Usually made of pork and sometimes beef, this cured, smoked sausage has a soft, spreadable texture. It is sold ready to eat.

DRIED AND SEMI-DRIED SAUSAGES

Usually made from cured meats and fat packed in casings, sausages preserved by drying do not need to be cooked before eating. Those dried completely, such as salami-type sausages, have a very firm, even hard texture. Before or after drying, sausages may be smoked to add extra flavor.

BUY They are sold both whole and sliced in packs. White powder on the exterior of the casing improves flavor.

STORE Hang whole sausages in a cool, dry, well-ventilated place where they will keep for a long time. Keep packed slices in the fridge.

EAT The casing is normally not eaten. Slice thinly for appetizers; add to salads; or scatter over pizzas. Use to flavor sauces, rice dishes, stews, and savory pastries.

FLAVOR PAIRINGS Cheese, tomatoes, pickles, black olives.

CLASSIC RECIPES Pepperoni pizza; *fabada*; *paella valenciana*.

Genoa salami can be recognized by the rippled edge, made by a cord wrapping.

Salame di Genoa
Made from pork and veal and moistened with red wine, this is a garlicky air-dried sausage with a high fat content.

Fuet catalan
Delicious as tapas, this is a long, thin, cured pork sausage from Catalonia, Spain.

Salame di Felino
Handmade near Parma from pure pork and pork fat, this is seasoned with white wine, garlic, and peppercorns.

Cacciatorini
This small, dried, pork and beef sausage is so-named ("hunter salami") because hunters could carry it in their pockets for snacks.

Salame di Milano
Milan's traditional dried sausage is made with fat and lean pork with beef or veal, seasoned with garlic, pepper, and wine. It is one of the best-known of the Italian salami.

Salami secchi
Most types of Italian dried sausages contain pork and pork fat, with other meats including beef, horse, turkey, and venison. The meats are cured before packing into casings.

Whole peppercorns are often included.

The fat should be in small pieces and evenly distributed throughout the sausage.

DRIED AND SEMI-DRIED SAUSAGES (CONTINUED)

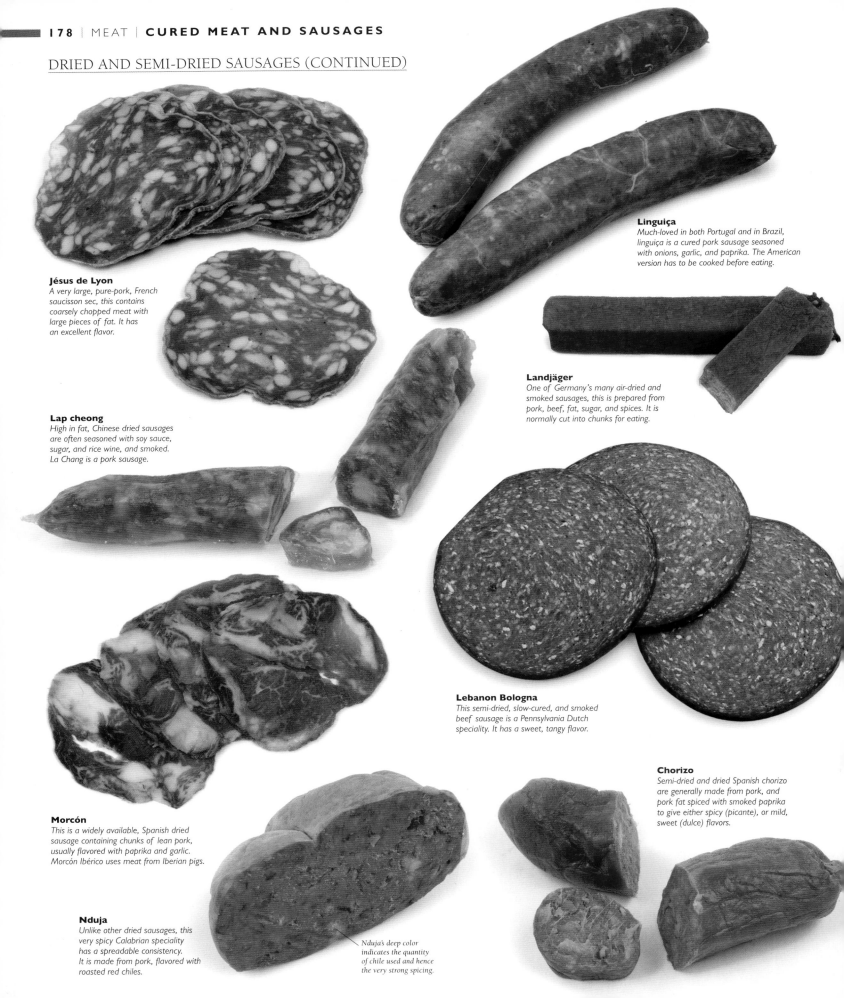

Jésus de Lyon
A very large, pure-pork, French saucisson sec, this contains coarsely chopped meat with large pieces of fat. It has an excellent flavor.

Lap cheong
High in fat, Chinese dried sausages are often seasoned with soy sauce, sugar, and rice wine, and smoked. La Chang is a pork sausage.

Morcón
This is a widely available, Spanish dried sausage containing chunks of lean pork, usually flavored with paprika and garlic. Morcón Ibérico uses meat from Iberian pigs.

Nduja
Unlike other dried sausages, this very spicy Calabrian speciality has a spreadable consistency. It is made from pork, flavored with roasted red chiles.

Nduja's deep color indicates the quantity of chile used and hence the very strong spicing.

Linguiça
Much-loved in both Portugal and in Brazil, linguiça is a cured pork sausage seasoned with onions, garlic, and paprika. The American version has to be cooked before eating.

Landjäger
One of Germany's many air-dried and smoked sausages, this is prepared from pork, beef, fat, sugar, and spices. It is normally cut into chunks for eating.

Lebanon Bologna
This semi-dried, slow-cured, and smoked beef sausage is a Pennsylvania Dutch speciality. It has a sweet, tangy flavor.

Chorizo
Semi-dried and dried Spanish chorizo are generally made from pork, and pork fat spiced with smoked paprika to give either spicy (picante), or mild, sweet (dulce) flavors.

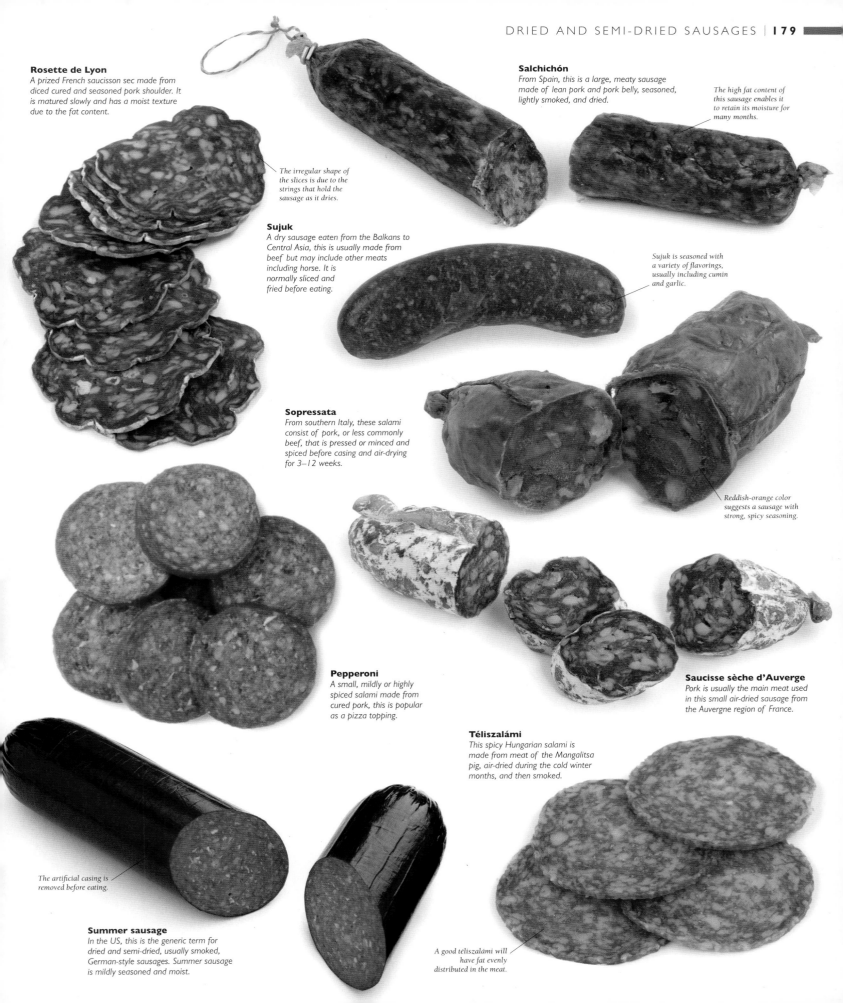

Rosette de Lyon
A prized French saucisson sec made from diced cured and seasoned pork shoulder. It is matured slowly and has a moist texture due to the fat content.

The irregular shape of the slices is due to the strings that hold the sausage as it dries.

Salchichón
From Spain, this is a large, meaty sausage made of lean pork and pork belly, seasoned, lightly smoked, and dried.

The high fat content of this sausage enables it to retain its moisture for many months.

Sujuk
A dry sausage eaten from the Balkans to Central Asia, this is usually made from beef but may include other meats including horse. It is normally sliced and fried before eating.

Sujuk is seasoned with a variety of flavorings, usually including cumin and garlic.

Sopressata
From southern Italy, these salami consist of pork, or less commonly beef, that is pressed or minced and spiced before casing and air-drying for 3–12 weeks.

Reddish-orange color suggests a sausage with strong, spicy seasoning.

Pepperoni
A small, mildly or highly spiced salami made from cured pork, this is popular as a pizza topping.

Saucisse sèche d'Auverge
Pork is usually the main meat used in this small air-dried sausage from the Auvergne region of France.

Téliszalámi
This spicy Hungarian salami is made from meat of the Mangalitsa pig, air-dried during the cold winter months, and then smoked.

Summer sausage
In the US, this is the generic term for dried and semi-dried, usually smoked, German-style sausages. Summer sausage is mildly seasoned and moist.

The artificial casing is removed before eating.

A good téliszalámi will have fat evenly distributed in the meat.

VEGETABLES

CABBAGES | LEAFY GREENS | ROOTS AND POTATOES | SHOOTS AND STEMS | BULBS PODS | MUSHROOMS SEA VEGETABLES

VEGETABLE ESSENTIALS

Vegetables are the foundation of a healthy diet, and they are at their freshest, tastiest, and most nutritious when they are in season and locally grown by sustainable methods. In season, vegetables reach their flavor peak. That's also when they are most abundant and most economical. Local farmers are likely to grow the most flavorful varieties, including heritage varieties that have been selected by generations of farmers and gardeners for their superior qualities. Local growers often use organic or sustainable methods too, choosing to protect the environment and preserve the soil's natural fertility without the use of agricultural chemicals.

BUY

Good color Buy vegetables that have bright, vibrant colors with no yellowing—especially in cauliflowers and leafy greens. There should be no bruising, discoloration, blemishes, soft spots, cuts, or pits, and no suggestion of mold growth.
Firmness The vegetable should feel firm and heavy in the hand; lighter vegetables may be drying out.
Tight skin Loose skin indicates that the vegetable is drying out, so look for taut, firm skin.
Fresh ends To ensure freshness and the quality it implies, check the cut ends of vegetables that have been harvested from a root or mother plant. The cut should look fresh and moist, not dried out. Leaves should be glossy and mid-ribs stiff.
Smell The vegetable should have a clean, fresh fragrance.

STORE

Different vegetables store for varying lengths of time, depending on their type. Delicate leafy vegetables store best wrapped loosely in a moist paper towel inside a closed plastic bag or refrigerator storage container. Root vegetables, such as carrots and parsnips, keep well in an open plastic bag in the crisper of the refrigerator. Vegetables, such as bell peppers and cabbage, store well in paper bags rolled shut and placed in the crisper. Some vegetables store best at room temperature in the dark, such as potatoes; while others, such as onions, need a basket to contain them. Tomatoes will continue to ripen when placed on a windowsill. All vegetables begin to lose freshness as soon as they are harvested, but this happens more or less rapidly depending on their type. If you can only use part of a vegetable, store the remainder sealed snugly in plastic wrap in the refrigerator.

Choose vibrant-colored tomatoes *with firm flesh and tight skin that have that distinctive aroma of the tomato plant.*

Select green leafy vegetables *that have crisp, fresh-looking, green leaves, with no yellow coloring, and firm mid-ribs.*

PREPARE

Some vegetables need to be peeled to remove the skin, because it is tough, tastes bitter, may contain traces of pesticides, or purely for personal preference. With other vegetables, it is often sufficient to wash them well. Delay washing and peeling until just before use, since exposure to air and moisture will cause the vegetables to deteriorate and lose their vitamins.

PEEL Vegetable peels range from tough to tender, and they often contain more nutrients and flavor compounds than the flesh inside. To preserve flavor and conserve nutrients, cook vegetables with the skin on. If you need to peel the vegetable, remove the skin after the food has cooled. One of the chief reasons people peel their vegetables is to remove impurities or agricultural chemical residues.

Squash has *a particularly tough skin that needs removing before the flesh is sliced into chunks. Use a vegetable peeler to do this.*

WASH Wash most vegetables with lukewarm tap water and a soft-bristled brush. Where brushing isn't appropriate, swish vegetables in a pan of water. Some markets sell food-safe cleansers to remove oil-based pesticides, waxy preservatives, and oil from the hands of employees and customers who have handled the vegetables.

Leeks collect *soil between the layers, so it is important to wash the inside thoroughly before use. Shake off any excess water.*

CUTTING Vegetables are not produced in a uniform shape, so cutting them up is not the same for every variety either. The size and shape of cut pieces depends on how you are going to use the vegetables in recipes—whether as chunks, as elegant side dishes, or as a garnish.

Cut batonnets

1 *Cut vegetables into ¼in (5mm) thick slices, then cut into ¼in (5mm) wide strips.*

2 *Cut across the width of the strips to make batonnets 1½–2in (4–5cm) long.*

Cut diamonds

1 *Slice the vegetable in half down the length and lay each piece flat side down on the board.*

2 *Start at the white root and cut diagonally along the length into diamond-shaped pieces.*

Shred

Rub the vegetable *down the length of a grater, choosing the hole size that gives you the size you prefer, or shred in a food processor.*

Dice

Cut vegetables into strips *of equal width and thickness, then cut them into dice the same length as the width and thickness.*

Slice greens

1 *Using a sharp chef's knife, cut out the tough mid-rib by slicing along the length on each side.*

2 *Roll up the leaves into a sausage shape and slice across the roll to make even strips.*

Julienne

Making juliennes *is similar to cutting batonnets, but slices should be ⅛in (3mm) thick, then cut into strips ⅛in (3mm) wide.*

Slice with a mandolin

Mandolins *will produce very thin slices or batons. Use one with adjustable blades to cut at any thickness. The blades are very sharp.*

Turn carrots

1 *Use a turning knife to start shaving off the sides of 2in (5cm) pieces of carrot.*

2 *Continue to turn the carrot in your hands while cutting, to create a seven-sided football.*

COOK

Some vegetables can be eaten raw, but many need to be cooked to break down the starch and cellulose they contain, thereby making them digestible. Any form of cooking—boiling, grilling, frying, steaming—will achieve this, but texture and nutrients are best preserved if the cooking is as brief as possible.

BOIL Do not boil vegetables for too long, to avoid color and nutrients leaching into the cooking water. Generally, starchy vegetables should be started in cold water, green ones should be added to boiling water.

1 While the pan of water is heating, rinse the vegetables to be boiled in a colander. Shake off any excess water.

2 When the water is boiling, add the vegetables in small handfuls, bring the water back to the boil, then simmer until cooked.

3 Once cooked to the desired doneness, drain the vegetables and rinse them under cold running water to stop the cooking process.

DEEP FRY This is a great way to cook wafer-thin slices of vegetables, such as potatoes, carrots, and beets. More delicate vegetables may cook better when coated in a tempura batter to protect them from the hot fat. If the ingredients are cooked very quickly, they will absorb the minimum amount of fat.

1 Heat the oil until a small vegetable piece dropped into it sizzles, then add the vegetables.

2 Cook until the desired doneness is reached—the vegetables should be crisp and golden-brown.

3 Remove from the pan with a slotted spoon, drain on paper towels, and sprinkle with salt.

GRILL A delicious and healthy way to eat vegetables. Most are suitable for grilling, but some, such as carrots and potato, may need to be parboiled first.

Heat a griddle or a barbecue grill to a high heat for 15–20 minutes, scrub it with a wire brush, then brush with vegetable oil. Reduce the heat to the desired level then add the vegetables, brushed with a little oil on each side. Grill for 4–5 minutes, turning them over halfway through. They should be crisp but just tender when done.

STIR-FRY A delicious and healthy way to get the best out of ingredients, the secret to successful stir-frying is speed. Cooking fast at a high heat ensures that the texture, flavor, and nutrients of food are preserved, and that minimum oil is needed to cook them.

1 Heat a tablespoon or two of vegetable oil in a wok or stir-fry pan until the oil is hot but not smoking. Add the vegetables that take longest to cook first, then keep adding the others.

2 Stir the vegetables often, moving them up the sides of the pan to reduce their exposure to the heat. When all the vegetables are added, stir constantly until all are lightly cooked.

SAUTÉ Another quick method of cooking in which vegetables are fried in a small amount of oil in a large frying pan. The fat should be at a high heat as you add the vegetables, which should be moved around continually during cooking. For best results, do not crowd the pan.

1 Set the pan over a high heat and add some vegetable oil or butter. Once the fat is heated, toss in the vegetables.

2 Cook the vegetables in batches, if necessary, and stir them around the pan often. Sauté until the vegetables are browned and tender.

STEAM This is one of the healthiest methods of cooking vegetables. Since the ingredients do not touch the water in the pan, there is no loss of nutrients and the vegetables retain more of their flavor and texture.

ROAST Roasting vegetables allows them to retain all their delicious flavors and to take on a new texture. This method uses the dry heat of the oven and gives the vegetables a delicious golden-brown exterior.

1 *Place 1in (2.5cm) of water and a steaming basket in a large pot with a lid. Add the vegetables, cover, and turn the heat to high.*

2 *Allow the vegetables to steam to the desired doneness—test them with the sharp point of a knife. Be careful not to overcook them.*

Roasting in a pan
with a little vegetable oil in the bottom improves the flavor of diced root vegetables and winter squashes, among other vegetables. You can add extra flavor by tossing in some fresh herbs.

PRESERVE

Vegetables taste much better when they are in season, so it is worth preserving them and their flavors for the months when they are not available fresh. Some vegetables are best dried, others pickled, and many can be frozen. Preserve vegetables only at the peak of freshness.

FREEZE Hard vegetables, such as carrots, beans, broccoli, peas, and corn, can all be frozen. Freeze cut and prepared vegetables on the day of purchase to retain all their flavors, textures, and nutrients.

PICKLE As well as a method of preservation, pickling is popularly used to add a sweet–sour tang to vegetables. It is important when pickling to use clean, sterilized jars. Most soft vegetables can be pickled raw, but hard roots need to be cooked to soften them. Place vegetables in a jar with a tight-fitting lid and fill the jar with a vinegar-based pickling solution.

DRY This method involves drying vegetables, such as tomatoes, mushrooms, and squash, as well as some fruits to help retain their nutrients and intensify their flavors. To do this you need a dehydrator, which will keep the vegetables at the recommended temperature of below 118°F (48°C).

1 *Slice the prepared vegetables to the desired thickness. Thinner slices dry faster.*

2 *Arrange the slices on the drying tray, allowing no overlap. Brush lightly with olive oil.*

3 *The slices are ready when they are crisp, not flexible. Cool, then store in airtight containers.*

Blanch or cook vegetables *before freezing them on covered trays, well spaced out. Once frozen, divide them into meal-sized portions and return to the freezer in freezer bags or other containers.*

CABBAGE

Native to the Atlantic coast of Europe and the shores of the Mediterranean, today cabbages are grown around the world in temperate zones. The leaves of some varieties are loose, but most have compact heads of various sizes and shapes, with smooth or crinkled leaves of different colors. When properly cooked, cabbage has a sweet flavor.

🔒 **BUY** Although cabbage is available year-round, it is at its best in winter. Look for solid heads with a clean, fresh smell and no yellowed outer leaves. The cut end should be moist, not dry.

📦 **STORE** Whole heads can be kept for a month or two in plastic bags in the crisper of the fridge.

🍽 **EAT** Fresh: Shred red, green, or white cabbage for salads. **Cooked:** Boiling releases sulphurous compounds that many people find unpleasant, yet this is probably the most common way of cooking cabbage. Cook until just tender: cabbage smells "cabbagey" when it has been overcooked. Alternatively, steam, stir-fry, sauté, bake, or braise; stuff and roll leaves, or stuff whole heads, then simmer or steam. **Preserved:** Sauerkraut is the classic way to preserve cabbage.

FLAVOR PAIRINGS Bacon, sausage, salt beef, ham, poultry, pork, garlic, horseradish, juniper berries, potatoes, caraway seeds, almonds, nutmeg, cilantro, sugar, mustard.

CLASSIC RECIPES Braised red cabbage; coleslaw; New England boiled dinner; colcannon; bubble and squeak; *choucroute garnie*; stuffed cabbage rolls; corned beef with cabbage; ribollita soup; *zuppa di pane e cavolo*; stuffed cabbage.

Celery cabbage
The tender, sweet leaves of these cabbages (Hispi, shown here) form a long, pointed head.

White cabbage
Also known as Dutch cabbage, this makes a firm head of tightly packed leaves with a solid core. It has a sweet taste, and keeps particularly well.

PREPARING LOOSE-LEAVED CABBAGE

Suitable for all looser-leaved varieties.

1 *Discard any limp or discolored leaves. Wash well in cold water, and pat dry with a paper towel.* **2** *Using a sharp knife, slash each leaf at an angle on either side of the rib. Remove and discard the rib.* **3** *Roll up large leaves and cut across into shreds of the desired width. Leave smaller, tender leaves whole.*

Round cabbage
Also known as ball-head cabbage, this can be eaten raw and cooked, as most varieties of cabbage can, but it is best for stir-frying and braising.

CLASSIC RECIPE

BRAISED RED CABBAGE

A traditional sweet-and-sour German accompaniment, often served with sausages, duck, goose, and game.

SERVES 4

2 smoked bacon slices, chopped

1 onion, finely chopped

1 tbsp sugar

1 large tart apple, peeled, cored, and chopped

2lb (900g) red cabbage, quartered, cored, and shredded crosswise

¼ cup red wine vinegar

salt

1 In a large frying pan or flameproof casserole, cook the bacon over low heat until it renders its fat. Add the onion and cook for about 5 minutes, or until softened. Stir in the sugar and cook for another 5 minutes, or until the mixture is golden. Add the apple. Cover and cook for 3–4 minutes, stirring occasionally.

2 Add the cabbage to the pan. Toss to coat with the bacon fat, then stir in the vinegar. Cover again and cook over low heat for 10 minutes.

3 Add a little salt and ½ cup water. Cover and simmer over medium—low heat, stirring occasionally, for 1–1¼ hours, or until the cabbage is tender. Season to taste and serve hot.

Flat cabbage
Widely popular in the Middle East, the flattened, white heads of this type have a mild, sweet flavor.

Red cabbage
Known for its beautiful, vibrant color, red cabbage is sweeter than white, but the leaves are tougher, so they take longer to cook.

Color will turn blue unless acid fruit, vinegar, or wine are used when cooking.

The steamed leaves make excellent wrappers for stuffed cabbage rolls.

Savoy cabbage
The attractively crinkled leaves are more loosely wrapped around the head than those of other cabbages, and are more full-bodied in flavor.

BRUSSELS SPROUTS

The Brussels sprout was bred from a cabbage, selected for its habit of producing small side heads when the main head is harvested. Brussels sprouts produce, in effect, miniature heads of cabbage along a tall stalk. Although a biennial, it is grown everywhere in cool, temperate climates as an annual. It has the flavor of a sweet cabbage.

BUY Peak season for quality is winter, as frosts sweeten up sprouts. Usually they are sold loose, but if you can find sprouts still on the stalk, these will be the best. Look for tight, small heads, slightly smaller than a golf ball: the smaller the sprout, the better the flavor. Yellowed outer leaves are a sign that the sprouts are old. The cut ends should look fresh and moist, and there should be no noticeable odor.

STORE Like other members of the cabbage family, sprouts start turning bitter as soon as they are harvested. Use on the day of purchase, or store for no more than a week in a closed plastic bag in the fridge. They will freeze well.

EAT Fresh: Slice very thinly and add to coleslaw or a green salad. Cooked: Take care only to cook them until tender (test them with the point of a knife). Overcooked sprouts develop an off-putting smell and will eventually disintegrate. Steam, bake, boil, sauté, and braise whole sprouts; or shred and stir-fry.

FLAVOR PAIRINGS Bacon and pancetta, cream, cheese, apples, lemon, chestnuts, pine nuts, almonds, thyme.
CLASSIC RECIPES Brussels sprouts with bacon; Brussels sprouts with chestnuts.

Look for tight, small heads, with no yellow outer leaves.

CAULIFLOWER

This relative of the cabbage is grown in tropical and temperate climates throughout the world. While some varieties are green, purple, and orange, and sometimes pointed in shape, the most familiar type of cauliflower is a round, white head of densely packed curds, or florets. The curds are, in fact, the compacted tips of branching, unopened flowerheads. Cauliflower has a mild flavor when raw, becoming nutty when it is cooked.

BUY Fall is the season for the choicest cauliflower. Choose snow-white rather than creamy or yellowish heads. Reject any with brown spots or green leaves protruding through the curds, both signs of declining quality. Make sure the cut ends are fresh.

STORE Try to use cauliflower soon after you buy it, although it can be kept, loosely wrapped in a paper bag, in the refrigerator for 3–4 days.

EAT Fresh: Separate into small florets for salads and crudités. **Cooked:** Boil or steam whole or in florets; florets can also be roasted, baked in sauce, coated in batter and deep-fried, or sautéed. **Preserved:** Pickle with other vegetables or use in chutney.

FLAVOR PAIRINGS Brown butter, Gruyère cheese, wheatgerm, garlic, hollandaise sauce, olive oil, parsley, lemon juice.

CLASSIC RECIPES Moroccan lamb and cauliflower stew; Pennsylvania Dutch chow-chow; cauliflower cheese; *cavolfiore stracciato*; *gefüllte blumenkohl*; fried cauliflower; *choufleur à la polonaise*.

Common cauliflower
Cauliflower has a mild cabbagelike flavor when raw, becoming rich and savory when roasted. The tight crunchy curds add pleasing texture to curry dishes and stir-fries.

When dividing into florets, slice any thick ones lengthwise through the stem so they will cook in the same time as smaller florets.

Romanesco
Admired for its intriguing spirals, Romanesco is one of the best-tasting cauliflowers—nutty, meaty, and slightly sweet. The texture is soft and creamy.

The tender and delicate curds are best lightly steamed or roasted, since they disintegrate easily.

BROCCOLI

Broccoli, a relative of the cabbage, is widely grown in temperate climates in many parts of the world, particularly in the cooler regions. Like its cousin the cauliflower, it is made up of the unopened flower heads of the plant. In the familiar dark green broccoli, also called calabrese, the buds are tightly packed in large, pebbly heads, whereas in sprouting species the buds, which may be purple, white, or green, are in groups on individual long, slender stems. Very similar, although more leafy, is broccoli raab, also called broccoli di rape, or cime di rapa in Italy. Dark green broccoli has a fine texture and a light cabbagelike flavor with a hint of sweetness; sprouting broccoli is sweeter and more tender. Broccoli raab is the least sweet of the types, with a pleasant, zesty bite.

🛒 **BUY** Although available year-round, the best broccoli is in the markets in fall through winter to spring. With dark green broccoli, the heads should be dense, with no separation between the green buds and no yellow flowers showing: the presence of even one flower means the plant is turning fibrous and woody. Sprouting-broccoli types should have firm stems and fresh leaves. Cut ends should look moist, not split and dried out.

📦 **STORE** Broccoli will keep well in a plastic bag in the crisper of the refrigerator for 3–4 days.

⊙ **EAT** Fresh: Brocolli can be separated into small florets and peeled strips of stem to eat raw, in salads or as crudités. **Cooked:** Boil or steam, bake in sauce, braise, coat in batter and deep-fry, stir-fry, or sauté.

FLAVOR PAIRINGS Bacon, anchovies, cheese, pesto, hollandaise sauce, lemon, garlic, pine nuts, olive oil.

CLASSIC RECIPES Chinese stir-fried broccoli; *broccoli alla Romana; à la crème, à la polonaise; al burro e formaggio.*

CHINESE STIR-FRIED BROCCOLI

Serve this easy Chinese vegetable dish with grilled meats, poultry, or fish, and some steamed sticky rice.

SERVES 4

1 large head of broccoli
1 tbsp sesame seeds
1 tbsp vegetable oil
1 tbsp soy sauce
⅛ tsp crushed hot red pepper
¼ cup vegetable stock or water
salt and freshly ground black pepper

1 Cut the broccoli into florets. Peel the stems and cut them crosswise into thin slices.

2 Heat a large frying pan or wok over medium heat. Add the sesame seeds and cook, stirring almost constantly, about 1–2 minutes, or until lightly toasted. Transfer to a plate.

3 Add the oil, soy sauce, and hot pepper flakes to the hot pan and stir to combine. Add the broccoli and stir-fry for about 2 minutes.

4 Pour in the stock and cover. Cook for about 2 minutes longer, or until crisp-tender. Stir in the sesame seeds and season with salt and pepper. Serve hot.

Baby cauliflower
The same variety as full-sized cauliflower, baby heads are kept small by crowding their growing conditions. They make a fine addition to trays of crudités, stir-fries, and steamed vegetable mixtures.

Broccoli (calabrese)
The most common variety of broccoli, this is rich green with a meaty flavor and, if not overcooked, a crunchy texture. It is packed with nutrients that are best retained by steaming.

Purple cauliflower
Purple varieties tend to be milder than the white. Cooked with care by light steaming, the curds will retain some of their attractive color.

Purple sprouting broccoli
The elegant spears have a chewy texture and full-bodied flavor. In Italy, sprouting broccoli is served in the same way as asparagus—with olive oil, melted butter, or hollandaise sauce.

Remove flowerheads with some stem and leaves attached. Peel the central stem if it is fibrous and halve lengthwise if thick.

ASIAN LEAFY GREENS

Hundreds of kinds of Asian leafy greens are grown in temperate and tropical climates around the world—so many that even botanists have a hard time classifying them. However, most are brassicas, or members of the cabbage and mustard family. Some of them are open, leafy plants, while others are tight heads of wrapped leaves, with colors from red and purple through green to white. They range in flavor from peppery-hot to mildly sweet. Many have the Chinese word *choy* or *choi*, meaning vegetable, in their names. All are highly nutritious.

BUY Where winters are fierce, these vegetables are best in the cool weather of spring and fall; in milder climates, their season is winter. Light frosts sweeten them. When buying, check the cut ends: they should look moist and freshly cut. The stalks should snap when bent and the leaves show a bright color.

STORE Wrap in moist paper towels, place in a plastic bag, and keep in the crisper of the fridge. Because freshness is so essential to Asian cooking, store for just 1–2 days.

EAT Shred, cut, or use leaves whole. **Fresh:** Some varieties can be eaten raw in salads. **Cooked:** Braise them, stir-fry, use as wrappers for meaty fillings, steam, or sauté, either by themselves or with other vegetables and meats. **Preserved:** Some Asian leafy greens—cabbages and mustard greens, for example—can be pickled. Spicy Korean *kim chee*, made with Chinese cabbage, is probably the most popular pickle.
FLAVOR PAIRINGS Shrimp, garlic, ginger, scallion, snow peas, soy sauce, oyster sauce, toasted sesame oil, vinegar, mushrooms, five-spice powder, star anise, cilantro.
CLASSIC RECIPES *Kim chee;* spring rolls.

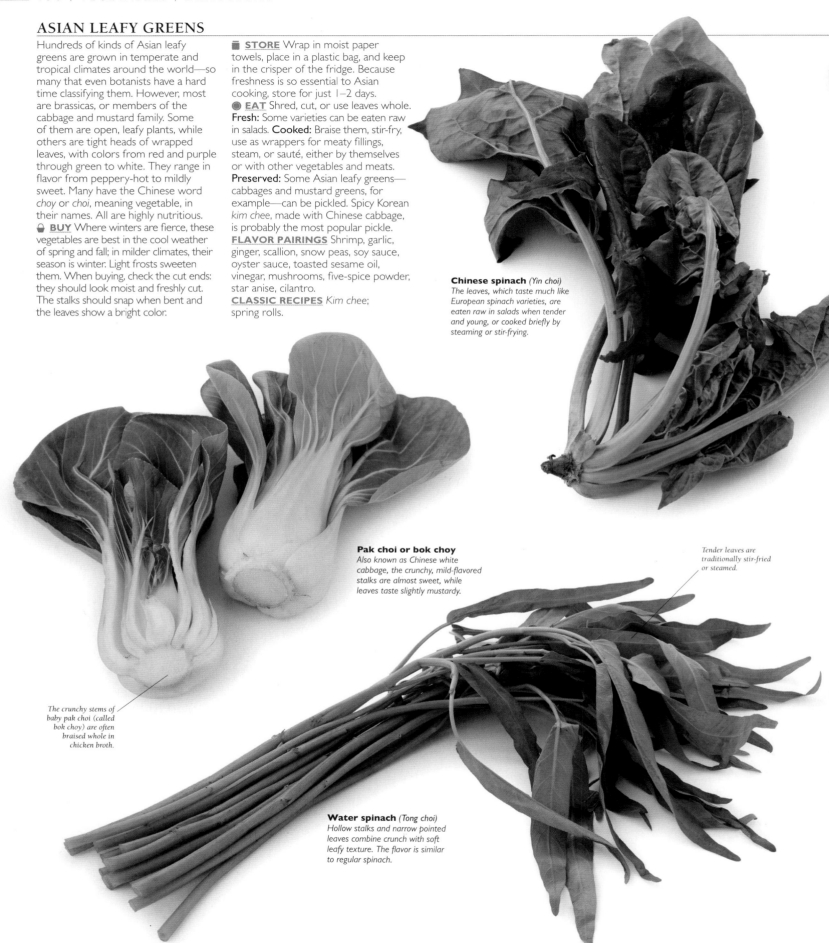

Chinese spinach *(Yin choi)*
The leaves, which taste much like European spinach varieties, are eaten raw in salads when tender and young, or cooked briefly by steaming or stir-frying.

Pak choi or bok choy
Also known as Chinese white cabbage, the crunchy, mild-flavored stalks are almost sweet, while leaves taste slightly mustardy.

Tender leaves are traditionally stir-fried or steamed.

The crunchy stems of baby pak choi (called bok choy) are often braised whole in chicken broth.

Water spinach *(Tong choi)*
Hollow stalks and narrow pointed leaves combine crunch with soft leafy texture. The flavor is similar to regular spinach.

Use the pretty leaves as edible plates to hold rice or grain-based salads.

Japanese mustard spinach
(Komatsu-na)
Eaten raw as a salad green when young, the flavor gets stronger and hotter in older leaves, which can be cooked in stir-fries and soups, or salt-pickled.

Chinese leaf or leaves
Also called Napa cabbage, celery cabbage, and Peking cabbage, the large, mild leaves are pulled away from the stalk to use raw in salads, or in soups and stews.

Chinese broccoli *(Gai lan)*
Also called Chinese kale, this sometimes has small white flowers. The stalk, thick leaf, and buds can all be eaten, traditionally in stir-fries, or braised and served with oyster sauce.

Edible rape *(Yu choy, choi sum)*
This variety has tender, crunchy stalks and, when they appear, the little flowers and buds all have a mustard-like bite.

Chinese mustard greens or mustard cabbage *(Gai choi)*
There are many types in various colors, textures, and sizes. A common reddish variety is peppery-hot.

ASIAN LEAFY GREENS (CONTINUED)

Edible chrysanthemum
(Shungiku, Tong ho) Leaves have a slightly sour flavor and chewy texture, best suited to meat-based stir-fries and soups. If lightly blanched, young leaves can be used in salads.

Chinese flat cabbage
(Tatsoi) This grows in a flattened rosette shape. Young leaves are mildly pungent and add crisp, juicy crunch to a salad. Mature leaves are chewier and best stir-fried.

MUSTARD GREENS

Mustard greens or leaf mustard are catch-all names for a number of different brassicas with a distinctive peppery taste. Popular in Asia, Italy, and the American South, they range from light green to dark burgundy in color, from tender to chewy in texture, and from mild to ferociously pungent in flavor. All types grow well in cool weather in temperate zones.

🛒 **BUY** Mustard greens are found in markets year-round, but they are at their best from late fall to spring. Look for spritely, freshly cut leaves, and avoid any that show yellowing or limpness.

🗄 **STORE** Store unwashed mustard greens wrapped in damp paper towels in an open plastic bag in the fridge crisper for 3–4 days.

⦿ **EAT** Fresh: Add a few small, tender leaves to a salad to give a spicy bite.
Cooked: Young leaves can be steamed or stir-fried; when large and mature, mustard greens are best stewed or braised until very tender.

FLAVOR PAIRINGS Seafood, butter, garlic, soy sauce, vinegar.

CLASSIC RECIPE Boiled greens with ham hocks.

COLLARDS

Collards or collard greens look much like the wild, primitive form of non-hearting cabbage from which modern cabbage plants derive, except that their spatulate leaves are larger. Particularly popular in the Southern United States, they range in color from flat green to a slightly hazy bluish-green, and have an intense cabbagey flavor. British spring greens are similar in appearance, although they are actually young cabbages and have a milder flavor.

🛒 **BUY** Collards can be found year-round, but are at their best in the cold months. Choose compact, small, very fresh leaves that show no browning, yellowing, or excessive limpness. Check the stem ends for fresh-cut moisture.

🗄 **STORE** They will keep in an open plastic bag in the crisper of the fridge for 4–5 days. Store them away from apples, which give off ethylene gas, because this will turn the collards yellow.

⦿ **EAT** Boil or steam, braise, sauté, or stir-fry; use in soups and stews. They need lengthy cooking to make them soft.

FLAVOR PAIRINGS Bacon, ham, lemon, onions, potatoes, salt pork.

CLASSIC RECIPE
Greasy greens.

Check the cut ends to be sure they are moist.

Leaves should look fresh and have a lively color.

KALE

Descended from the wild cabbages of southern Europe, modern varieties of kale have a cold-hardy nature and are now grown around the world in cold to warm temperate climates. The curly-leaved Scottish variety is the most familiar. Frosts sweeten up its leaves, which have a chewy texture and slightly bitter, cabbagey flavor.

BUY Fall and winter are the peak seasons. Like any leafy green vegetable, kale should be as freshly picked as possible, with no brown spots or yellowed leaves.

STORE In a plastic bag, kale can be kept for a week in the crisper of the fridge. Don't store kale with any fruits that give off ethylene gas, such as apples, or the leaves will quickly yellow.

EAT Fresh: Tender leaves of baby kale will pep up winter salads. The juice makes a fine addition to raw carrot-juice drinks. **Cooked:** Boil or steam, braise, sauté, or stir-fry, or simmer in soups and stews.
FLAVOR PAIRINGS Sausage, bacon, cheese, garlic, onions, potatoes, olive oil.
CLASSIC RECIPES *Caldo verde;* clams in white wine with kale; *zuppa toscana; couve à mineira; ribollita.*

Cavalo Nero
Also known as Tuscan Black cabbage or Dinosaur Kale, this member of the kale family is widely used in Tuscan cooking. The deeply puckered leaves are tender and mildly flavored. Lightly steam, or sauté.

Strip leaves from tough stems by folding in half so upper surfaces touch, then pull the stem firmly toward the tip.

Trim the stem ends if they are fibrous, then slice leaves across into broad ribbons.

Curly kale
Exceptionally nutritious, the leaves of curly kale have a rich, meaty flavor and robust texture. Boil or steam until tender-crisp, then toss with butter or olive oil.

Red kale
The red variety is softer-textured than curly kale and slightly sweeter with a satisfying buttery flavor. For a pleasing color contrast, try cooking with the green.

HUAZONTLE

Huazontle is a native Mexican plant related to quinoa, whose use as a vegetable is primarily confined to Mexico and Central America. There are no cultivated varieties. It resembles sorghum, with a dense flowering seedhead atop a stiff stem. Flower clusters taste similar to spinach with an earthy, acidic, somewhat bitter flavor, but have a texture similar to sprouting broccoli. Seeds are mildly bitter in flavor.

BUY The flower clusters on their stems should be freshly cut.

STORE Use the flowering stems the same day they are purchased.
EAT Cooked: boil or steam small leaves, but eat in small quantities. Steam flower clusters, or coat in batter and deep-fry.
FLAVOR PAIRINGS Cheese, lemon, garlic, ginger, tomatoes.
CLASSIC RECIPE
Tortas de huazontles.

CLASSIC RECIPE

CALDO VERDE

A traditional Portuguese soup, this is made from kale (in Portugal called galega cabbage) and potatoes.

SERVES 4

4 medium russet or other floury baking potatoes, peeled and cut into chunks

salt and freshly ground black pepper

1 lb (500g) kale, leaves trimmed from the thick stems, rinsed, and very finely sliced

2 tbsp olive oil

1 Put the potatoes in a saucepan with 8 cups water and add a little salt. Bring to a boil and simmer gently for about 15 minutes, or until tender. Mash the potatoes lightly with a fork, leaving them in the water.

2 Cook the kale in a pan of boiling water for 3–4 minutes. Drain and stir into the potato broth with the olive oil. Simmer for 1–2 minutes. Season to taste and serve hot.

SPANAKOPITA

A Greek dish of spinach and dill layered with filo pastry. Crumble some feta cheese over the spinach filling, if you like.

SERVES 6

2½lb (1.1kg) spinach leaves, washed well to remove any dirt or grit, then chopped

salt and freshly ground black pepper

1 bunch of scallions, trimmed and finely chopped

½ cup finely chopped fresh dill weed

pinch of freshly grated nutmeg

1 egg, lightly beaten

10 sheets fresh or thawed frozen filo dough

3–4 tbsp olive oil

melted butter to glaze

1 Preheat the oven to 375°F (190°C). First, cook the spinach: put it into a large, heavy saucepan, sprinkle in a little water, and add a pinch of salt. Cook gently for a few minutes until the spinach starts to wilt. Drain, then squeeze as much water as possible from the spinach. Put it in a bowl, add the scallions and dill, and stir to combine. Season with the nutmeg, and salt and pepper to taste. Mix in the egg.

2 Keep the filo covered with plastic wrap to prevent it from drying out, removing the sheets one at a time, as needed. Oil a 9in (23cm) square baking pan. Layer 5 sheets in the pan, brushing each one with oil before you lay it in the pan (fold the excess pastry back into the pan). Spoon the spinach mixture on top and spread out to cover the pastry. Top with 5 more sheets of filo, brushing each with oil as before. Finally, brush the top generously with melted butter.

3 With a sharp knife, mark the pie into 6 squares. Bake for 30–35 minutes, or until the pastry is golden. Allow to cool slightly before cutting into squares to serve, or let cool and serve at room temperature.

SPINACH

Spinach still grows wild in its native Iran, but it has long since spread to temperate zones world wide. The Asian varieties of spinach, which are small-leaved, smooth, and tender, are usually sold as "baby" or salad leaves to eat raw, while the larger, more crinkly leaves of Western types are better cooked. The flavor of spinach is sweet, with an appealing hint of bitterness; the deep green of the leaves can color dishes and foods such as pasta beautifully. New Zealand spinach, an unrelated plant, has a flavor similar to spinach and is used in the same way; unlike spinach, it does not reduce much in bulk when cooked.

BUY Spinach is available year-round, and is best in late spring to fall.

Look for glossy leaves with freshly cut stem ends. Avoid leaves that are broken or slimy.

STORE Store spinach in the fridge in an open plastic bag for 3–4 days.

EAT Fresh: Add small, tender leaves to salads or scatter over a hot pizza. **Cooked:** The volume of fresh spinach reduces dramatically after cooking.

Boil, steam, wilt in hot butter, or dressing, sauté, stir-fry, or braise.
FLAVOR PAIRINGS Bacon, fish, anchovy, egg, cheese, cream, butter, yogurt, olive oil, garlic, onions, avocado, mushrooms, lemon, nutmeg, curry.
CLASSIC RECIPES Spanakopita; wilted spinach salad; épinards à la crème; saag paneer; a wide range of dishes à la florentine; erbazzone; fatayer.

Tear coarse midribs and stems from large spinach leaves before cooking.

Spinach
Spinach has juicy, tender leaves with a distinctly earthy, acidic flavor. Since they are composed mostly of water, they dramatically reduce in bulk once cooked.

Stems and midribs are undeveloped in baby spinach, so the leaves do not need trimming.

Baby spinach
The mildy flavored leaves are brittle but soft. They are good in a salad with bacon and avocado, or wilted in an omelet or frittata.

CHARD

While its cousin the beet was bred to yield large roots, chard (or Swiss chard) was developed to produce large leaves and fleshy stems—two different vegetables in one. Today, chard is widely grown around the world in temperate climates. Its leaves are dark green and crinkly, with a texture between soft and chewy. Depending on the variety, stems and leaf veins may be white, bright scarlet, fuschia, lavender, yellow, or orange. The flavor is pleasantly tangy and earthy, like beets or strong spinach. A close relative is sea kale beet, similar in appearance and cooked in the same way.

BUY Chard is at its best in early summer and again in early fall. Look for bunches with leaves that are glossy and fresh-looking; the central midribs should be crisp, not pliable. Stems should be firm with no brown marks.

STORE Wrap the bunch in moist paper towels and keep in a plastic bag in the crisper of the fridge for 3–5 days.

EAT Fresh: If very young and tender, chard can be added to salads. **Cooked:** Young leaves can be cooked whole; otherwise, take the leaves from the stems and cook them separately. Steam, braise, sauté, and stir-fry stems; boil, steam, or pan-fry leaves, or use them as wrappers.

FLAVOR PAIRINGS Ham, garlic, onion, chiles, olive oil.

CLASSIC RECIPE Blitva and potatoes; *Adass bil hamud.*

Colored-stemmed chard
These colorful varieties have a typically earthy, acidic flavor. Use raw in salads when very young; otherwise, steam, boil, or sauté like spinach.

The stems are slimmer than those of Swiss chard. Cook lightly to preserve their color.

Wash the leaves in several changes of water to remove grit trapped in the crevices.

Swiss chard
Notable for its fleshy, edible stems, Swiss chard has huge, deeply crinkled leaves with a complex earthy flavor and slightly chewy texture.

Stems need to be cooked longer than leaves, so are usually separated, sliced, and added to the pot first.

CLASSIC RECIPE

BLITVA AND POTATOES

This rustic Croatian side dish of chard and potatoes cooked with garlic is simple yet delicious.

SERVES 4

1½ lb (700g) Swiss chard, well rinsed
4 medium potatoes, peeled and cut into 1in (2.5cm) cubes
2–3 tbsp olive oil
2 garlic cloves, finely chopped
salt and freshly ground black pepper

1 First, prepare the chard. Separate the stems from the leaves. Trim any tough ends from the stems, then cut crosswise into 1in (2.5cm) pieces. Coursely chop the leaves. Set aside.

2 Drop the potatoes into a pot of boiling salted water and cook for 10 minutes. Add the chard stems and cook for another 5 minutes, or until the potatoes are just beginning to soften. Drain well.

3 Heat a little of the oil in a large frying pan over medium heat. Add the potato and chard mixture and the garlic. Cook for a couple of minutes, stirring, then add the chard leaves. Cook 10 minutes longer, or until the leaves are wilted and the vegetables are tender, adding more olive oil as needed. Season to taste with salt and pepper before serving.

CHICORY AND ENDIVE

Native to the Mediterranean, chicories and endives grow in temperate climates around the world. These two very closely related plants are commonly and confusingly mixed. Chicories include the blanched witloof type (what the Americans call Belgian endive and the British call chicory) and the red-leaved type (radicchio). Endives include curly endive, sometimes known as frisée, and batavian endive, also called batavia or escarole. While chicories and endives vary in appearance, all are crisp in texture and have an icy-sweet, slightly bitter edge. Escarole has a stronger bite than the other types.

BUY The best season for chicories and endives is winter. Look for fresh leaves with no browned edges and no browning at the cut end. The leaves of Belgian endive heads, or "chicons," should be tightly wrapped around; the cut end should be fresh and moist.

STORE Try to use as quickly as possible, because they lose freshness fast. Store in moist paper towels in plastic bags in the fridge for a day or two at most.

EAT Fresh: Add to salads, or use whole Belgian endive leaves as crudités. Cooked: Sauté, stir-fry, grill, braise, or bake in a gratin.
FLAVOR PAIRINGS Bacon, ham, blue cheese, nuts, garlic, watercress, olive oil.
CLASSIC RECIPES *Chicorée mornay; gestoofde andijvie; insalata di puntarelle con alici; radicchio di Treviso al forno; endives au jambon.*

Curly endive or frisée
The frizzy leaves have a crisp texture; the flavor is pleasantly sweet with a distinct, though mild, bitterness. They are best mixed with other leaves, or used as a garnish.

The slightly coarse leaves are best torn into bite-sized pieces.

Break the leaves from the head and use whole for scooping up dips.

Belgian endive
Also known as Witloof chicory, this has crisp, tightly furled, spear-shaped leaves that may be tipped with yellow-green or red. Both types are sweet and nutty, with a slightly bitter bite. They add welcome crunch to leafy green salads.

Red chicory is delicious grilled: halve whole heads lengthwise, brush with olive oil, and cook cut-side up.

The darker outer leaves have a stronger flavor than those in the paler heart.

This variety is recognizable by the pale yellowy-green background to the red flecks; more bitter varieties are deeper green.

Batavian endive or escarole
Less bitter than curly endive, batavian endive has a well-rounded flavor and softer, pleasantly chewy leaves.

Loose-headed chicory
One of the least bitter chicories, Variegata di Castelfranco has slightly chewy, red-flecked leaves with a well-rounded flavor. An attractive addition to winter salads.

Radicchio Treviso
Radicchio Rossa Trevigiana Tardiva is a sought-after, late-harvested variety. The handsome, spear-shaped leaves are pleasingly bitter, delicious dressed in olive oil, lemon juice, and garlic.

The thick, elongated, white root can be thinly sliced and added to salads along with the leaves.

Radicchio Rosso
Radicchio Palla Rossa is a common variety of hearted chicory, with snugly folded leaves and a bittersweet flavor. The leaves have a chewy texture and are best sliced for salads.

ARUGULA

Native to Asia and southern Europe, arugula grows well in all temperate zones around the world, where it is variously known as rocket, rucola, and roquette. Other similar plants are also sold as arugula: *Diplotaxis erucoides* and *D. muralis* are called "wall rocket" in the US and Europe, and *Bunias orientalis* is a pungent Turkish variety known as "rokka". Arugula and wall rocket are salad greens with an earthy, nutty flavor that is only slightly bitter when the leaves are tender and young; as hot weather arrives, it develops aggressive, peppery heat. Rokka is sharper and more coarse in texture, and is better cooked.

BUY Arugula is at its best when young and grown in cool weather, so late spring and fall are its choice seasons. Look for small leaves no more than 3–5in (7.5–12cm) long, without blemishes and with a fresh, green color. Check the cut ends for freshness. Avoid leaves that are limp or beginning to curl.

STORE Wrap leaves in moist paper towels in a plastic bag or closed container, and keep in the fridge for up to 3 days.

EAT Fresh: Young spring leaves, with an attractive peppery quality and a bit of bitterness, make a good complement to sweet lettuces in a salad mix, and an excellent substitute for lettuce in a sandwich. Purée peppery summer leaves to make a dipping sauce or pesto to dress pasta, or to stir into soups. **Cooked:** Use Turkish rokka in a vegetable frittata or other cooked dish.

FLAVOR PAIRINGS Blue cheese, Parmesan cheese, potatoes, tomatoes, lemon, olive oil, garlic, pears, fresh thyme, toasted nuts.

Though tender, the leaves of arugula can become intensely pungent in late summer. Combine with milder-tasting leaves to counteract the heat.

DANDELION

The dandelion is native to the northern temperate regions of Europe and Asia, but over centuries has virtually conquered the world's lawns and meadows. Luckily for us, this familiar plant is entirely edible—from the roots to the attractively serrated leaves and bright yellow flowers. Leaves (dandelion greens) can be picked from the wild for the kitchen when they are young and tender; they have a pleasing, light bitterness. Cultivated varieties offer larger leaves that may be strongly bitter or mild, depending on variety.

BUY Spring is the season for tender, young dandelion greens. Usually only the young leaves are sold in markets, but whole crowns or clumps and roots can sometimes be found. Check to be sure the leaves are very fresh and that the cut leaf ends are still moist to indicate freshness.

STORE Dandelion greens and crowns can be kept for 2–3 days in a plastic bag in the crisper of the fridge. Roots wrapped in moist paper towels in a plastic bag in the fridge will keep for 1 week.

EAT Fresh: Use young leaves in mixed green salads, or alone, wilted with a hot dressing. Roots can be sliced and eaten raw. **Cooked:** Boil, steam, braise, sauté, or stir-fry. Unopened flower buds that are still inside the crown can be added to pancakes, omelets, fritters, and frittatas. Bake, or roast roots. **Preserved:** Slice and pickle roots.

FLAVOR PAIRINGS Bacon, cheese, garlic, onion, lemon, mustard, olive oil, vinegar.

CLASSIC RECIPE *Salade de pissenlit aux lardons.*

If milky sap shows when a stalk is nicked with a thumbnail the leaves are not fresh.

BORAGE

Borage is a native European annual that is grown around the world, mostly in temperate climates. It is often found in herb gardens. Both the leaves and the flowers are edible and have a refreshing, mild cucumber flavor. Young, tender leaves can be used in salads or as a vegetable; tough, older leaves acquire bristly hairs, so are best cooked as a pot herb, which softens the bristles.

🔒 **BUY** Fresh borage is found most often at farmers' markets, and is at its best in spring and summer months. The plants should be just picked, and the pretty blue flowers should show pretty, bright blue or pink petals around a clutch of dark anthers. If using as a vegetable, choose stems with many young leaves.

📦 **STORE** Use the same day you buy, or store wrapped in damp paper towels in a plastic bag for 1 day in the crisper of the fridge.

⬤ **EAT Fresh:** Add finely shredded young leaves to salads. Use borage flowers as a pretty garnish for cold drinks, salads, and other cold dishes. **Cooked:** Boil or sauté leaves and eat as a vegetable like spinach. In Italy, borage is added to stuffings for ravioli and cannelloni; in Turkey, it flavors a pea soup. Germans make a green sauce of borage leaves. **Preserved:** Crystalized (candied) borage flowers are used to decorate cakes and pastries.

FLAVOR PAIRINGS Eel and other oily fish, white cheeses, yogurt, potato salad, chives, dill, mint.

CLASSIC RECIPES Pimm's Cup; *Borraja à la navarra.*

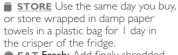

Borage flowers
The fragile, exceptionally pretty flowers can be added to salads and summer drinks.

Remove the stamens and black pistils from the center of the flower before eating.

Borage leaves
Although thought of as a herb, borage is also used as a vegetable. The cucumber-flavored leaves are tender when young, becoming chewier as they grow larger.

The stems take slightly longer to cook than the leaves, so separate and add them to the pot first.

MIZUNA

A member of the mustard family, mizuna originated in China but has been cultivated for centuries in Japan: today, it is considered to be a Japanese vegetable. It has also made its way into Western cuisines, primarily as a salad herb. The finely cut, feathery leaves are slightly bittersweet when young, developing a peppery quality when they are older.

🔒 **BUY** The best season for mizuna is spring. As with most salad greens, look for snapping fresh leaves with a healthy green color, no limpness or yellowing, and cut ends that are still moist.

📦 **STORE** Wrapped in damp paper towels in a plastic bag in the crisper of the fridge, it will keep for up to 5 days.

⬤ **EAT Fresh:** Mizuna appears in salad mixes with other leaves such as Chinese red mustard. It is also good in sandwiches, as a bed for seafood or meat dishes, and as a garnish. **Cooked:** Steam or stir-fry briefly; use in soups, and noodle or pasta dishes.

FLAVOR PAIRINGS Pork, fish, shellfish, ginger, lemon, sesame oil, olive oil, tamari.

Baby mizuna leaves are far less pungent than larger ones.

NETTLES

Nettles, or stinging nettles, are edible wild plants that grow along the edges of moist woods and shady spots in temperate climates. In many parts of the world, they are gathered when young and tender, to be cooked as a leafy green vegetable; cooking destroys their "sting." Nettles have a herbaceous, earthy flavor, a bit like sorrel.

🔒 **BUY** Nettles are rarely seen in markets. When gathering them from the wild (and preparing them), it is a good idea to wear rubber gloves.

They are at their best in mid-spring when just emerging from the ground.

📦 **STORE** For best results, prepare and cook nettles as soon as you get them home.

⬤ **EAT** Use only the tender tops of the plants. Cook like spinach—boil, steam, braise, or stir-fry; or use to make a soup.

FLAVOR PAIRINGS Eggs, cheese, cream, lemon.

CLASSIC RECIPE Nettle soup.

Remove stems before cooking, using scissors to avoid being stung.

LETTUCE

An annual or biennial herbaceous plant, lettuce probably originated in the eastern Mediterranean and Near East. It has been cultivated for centuries and today is grown in temperate climates around the world. The milky fluid that it exudes gives it its genus name, Lactuca (*lac* means "milk"). Early lettuces were bitter, but most modern varieties are mild, with just different shapes, sizes, textures, and colors. Some form heads, while others are loose clusters of leaves.

BUY Lettuce likes mild, moist weather and is at its best in late spring and early fall. Freshness is the whole point with lettuce, since it forms the base for salads. Check the core on tall head lettuce like romaine; it should be crisp, not flabby and bendable. If buying loose leaves, make sure they are crisp and snap-break when bent.

STORE Wrap head lettuce with moist paper towels and keep in a plastic bag in the fridge crisper for up to 5 days. Store loose-leaf lettuce in a bowl topped with moist paper towels and covered with plastic wrap. Head lettuce will keep better than leaf lettuce, but use within a few days.

EAT Fresh: Use in salads (ideally, make a salad the same day the lettuce is purchased or harvested from the garden). Soft lettuce leaves make fine wrappers for cold mixtures of shrimp or avocado, and jicama sticks; crisp leaves are used as wraps for Chinese shredded duck and other meats. **Cooked:** Braise, steam, or shred and cook with vegetables such as peas. Use in summer soups.

FLAVOR PAIRINGS Anchovies, cheese, mayonnaise, avocado, lemon, garlic, onions, tomatoes, bitter or pungent greens, pomegrante seeds, olive or nut oils.

CLASSIC RECIPES Caesar salad; *petits pois à la française; fattush.*

Tear the leaves into pieces rather than slicing them: a knife blade can cause bruising.

Loose-leaf or Red "Picking" lettuce
Bred for continual picking of young leaves, this loose-leaf Mediterranean variety does not form a heart. The attractive, bronze-tinged leaves are tasty and crisp.

Don't discard the flavorsome outer leaves. Tear them into bite-sized pieces and mix with the heart.

Butterhead
Perhaps the most popular of all lettuce types, butterheads have thick, soft, tender leaves with a mild, sweet flavor.

The red-splattered leaves make Freckles a stylish addition to a salad.

Cut away the thick stems from outer leaves, since they can be bitter and slightly fibrous.

Freckles
A high-quality, heirloom, cos variety with thin, tender leaves, this is appreciated for its buttery texture and sweet flavor.

Cos or Romaine
One of the best-tasting varieties of all, cos is valued for its crunch and full-bodied flavor. The succulent leaves are ideal for burgers, salads, sandwiches, and wraps.

LETTUCE (CONTINUED)

*The tender, flavorful leaves
are often used in
a typical mesclun mix of
young leaves and shoots.*

Merveille de Quatre Saisons
*An heirloom variety from France, with
a fresh, sweet flavor, a touch of
bitterness, and crisp, succulent leaves.*

*The loose outer leaves
conceal a compact heart
of delicious, creamy
yellow leaves.*

Red Oak
*An attractive loose-leaf lettuce with
a well-rounded sweet, earthy flavor, this
has thin, soft leaves and crunchy stems.*

Iceberg (crisphead)
*Low in flavor but high in crunch, iceberg is the
lettuce for sandwiches and burgers. The capacious
leaves can also be stuffed with meat or fish, rolled
up, and then steamed.*

Little Gem
*A deliciously sweet cos variety with tightly
packed, buttery leaves and crisp, fleshy
stems. Invaluable in salads and sandwiches.*

Lamb's Lettuce
Also known as mâche or corn salad, lamb's lettuce has soft, buttery leaves and tender stems. The mild flavor contrasts well with peppery arugula or watercress in a mixed-leaf salad.

The frilly leaves can harbor dust and soil, so need to be washed and dried carefully.

The delicate little leaves grow in sprigs that can be added whole to salads.

Lollo Rosso
A mildly flavored, slightly coarse-textured lettuce admired for its striking leaves. A few added to a mixed-leaf salad add contrasting texture and color.

WATERCRESS

A Eurasian native, watercress has spread around the world's temperate regions and often naturalizes where there's a steady supply of running water. The crunchy stems and crisp leaves have a pungent, peppery bite and clean, refreshing flavor. There are many plants that resemble watercress or are used in the same way, including land cress, garden cress, and nasturtium. Although not related to watercress, their leaves have a similar taste.

🔒 **BUY** Fresh watercress is available year-round, at its best from fall to spring. Snap a stem—it should break rather than bend. Look for glossy, deep green leaves, avoiding any watercress that is limp or yellow.

📦 **STORE** Wrapped unwashed in moist paper towels in a plastic bag,

watercress can be kept in the fridge for up to 2 days.

◉ **EAT** Fresh: Use in salads and sandwiches, or as a garnish. **Cooked:** Stir-fry, or make into a soup or a sauce.

The pungency of the leaves will increase as the weather warms up in summer.

FLAVOR PAIRINGS Cucumber, beets, salmon, chicken, oranges, potatoes.
CLASSIC RECIPE Watercress soup.

PURSLANE

This sprawling annual grows wild throughout much of the world. Purslane has been used as a food plant for centuries in southern Europe and the Middle East. The fleshy, paddle-shaped leaves and stems have a refreshing, astringent, lemony taste, and a crunchy, juicy texture.

🔒 **BUY** In Mexico, you find purslane readily in markets; elsewhere, look for it in Greek and Turkish stores. Select bunches of young leaves because older leaves can be tough. The leaves and stems should be pliable and succulently juicy, the color a lively golden green.

📦 **STORE** Unwashed purslane will keep for 2–3 days wrapped in damp

paper towels in a plastic bag in the crisper of the fridge.

◉ **EAT** Fresh: Young leaves and shoots make an agreeable addition to a salad. The flowers can also be added to salads. **Cooked:** Cooking emphasizes the mucilaginous content, which provides a good thickening for soups and stews. Stir-fry, sauté, bake, fry, or stew. **Preserved:** Pickle purslane in a brine made with white wine vinegar.
FLAVOR PAIRINGS Beets, fava beans, cucumber, spinach, potatoes, tomatoes, eggs, feta cheese, yogurt.
CLASSIC RECIPES Lebanese fattoush; *domatesli semizotu*; braised pork with tomatillos and chipotles.

The fleshy leaves of purslane are slightly mucilaginous, and can be used to thicken soups and stews in the same way as okra.

WATERCRESS AND PEAR SOUP

One of the oldest-known vegetables, watercress became a popular soup in England in the 1700s.

SERVES 4

2 tbsp butter
1 onion, finely chopped
6oz (175g) watercress
3 ripe pears, cored, and coarsely chopped
4 cups vegetable stock
salt and freshly ground black pepper
1 cup heavy cream
juice of ½ lemon
freshly shaved Parmesan cheese, to garnish
olive oil, to drizzle

1 Melt the butter in a saucepan and cook the onion over low heat, stirring occasionally, for 5 to 7 minutes, or until soft but not brown.

2 Meanwhile, trim the watercress and pick off the leaves. Add the watercress stems to the onion with the pears and stock. Season with salt and pepper.

3 Bring to a boil, then cover and simmer gently for 15 minutes. Working in batches, if needed, pour into a blender. Add the watercress leaves and blend until very smooth.

4 Stir in the cream and lemon juice, and check the seasoning. If necessary, reheat the soup, taking care not to boil. Serve topped with Parmesan shavings and drizzled with oil.

HEART OF PALM

The edible centers, or hearts, of emerging palm shoots are a favorite food in tropical regions where they are grown, as well as in other parts of the world. While many of the hundreds of species of palms will yield hearts, most are provided by varieties that produce multiple new shoots after harvesting, such as the peach palm (*Bactris gasipaes*). Hearts of palm have a smooth and tender yet crunchy texture, and a flavor that combines the sweetness of water chestnuts with the herbaceousness of artichoke and the nuttiness of soybean.

🔒 **BUY** Fresh palm hearts are found year-round in markets specializing in tropical produce. In supermarkets everywhere, they are widely available canned. Fresh hearts should be an appealing light, whitish-beige color. The cut ends should look fresh, with no dry spots.

📦 **STORE** Fresh hearts can be kept for 1–2 days in water in a covered container in the fridge. Store opened canned hearts in the same way.
⬤ **EAT** Fresh: In thin slices, they are wonderful in salads, or with charcuterie or fruit. **Cooked:** Steam, grill, sauté, stir-fry, or stew. **Preserved:** Pickle.
FLAVOR PAIRINGS Bacon, shrimp, crab, lime, vinaigrette.
CLASSIC RECIPE Ceviche.

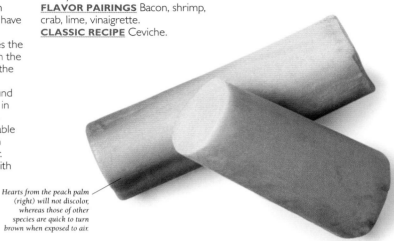

Hearts from the peach palm (right) will not discolor, whereas those of other species are quick to turn brown when exposed to air.

CACTUS PAD

Commonly called prickly pear, cactus pads are native to North and South America, but have spread around the world. Various species and varieties now grow in tropical and warm, temperate climates. The thick, fleshy leaves, or pads, are an important vegetable in Mexican cuisine, where they are known as *nopales*. They have a tender crunch, and a taste reminiscent of green beans, with a citrus tang.

🔒 **BUY** Pads can be harvested any time, but spring is their best season. Most have "eyes" with small, stinging spines emerging from them, but there are spineless types; choose these if you find them. Pads should be fresh looking, without pits or soft spots. Look at the scar where the pad was attached to the mother plant; it should be freshly cut, not browned or dried out.

📦 **STORE** Wrapped in dry paper towels in a plastic bag, pads will keep in the fridge for up to 4 days.
⬤ **EAT** Remove any prickles and eyes with a swivel peeler (wear rubber gloves), then shave the rim off each pad. The pads can then be boiled or steamed, braised, sautéed, or coated with batter and deep-fried. Once cooked, use in salads, egg dishes, tortilla fillings, soups, and other dishes. The sticky juice cactus pads exude will thicken liquid slightly, as okra does.
FLAVOR PAIRINGS Eggs, cheese, onions, tomatoes, chiles, cilantro, oregano, thyme.
CLASSIC RECIPE *Mostaccioli di fichi d'India.*

After shaving off prickles and eyes, and the rim of the pad, rinse well to remove excess sticky fluid.

STEAMED ARTICHOKES

This simple, traditional French way of preparing artichokes is a true classic and needs no embellishment.

SERVES 1

1 artichoke

4 tbsp butter

juice of ½ lemon

salt and freshly ground black pepper

bay leaves and fresh rosemary stalks, to serve (optional)

1 Break off any tough outer leaves from the artichoke and trim the stem level with the base. Snip off the pointed tips from the remaining leaves.

2 Set the artichoke in a vegetable steamer (you can flavor the steaming water with bay and rosemary sprigs, if you wish). Cover and steam for about 30 minutes, or until you can pull away an outer leaf with complete ease.

3 Melt the butter in a small pan, then add the lemon juice and season with salt and pepper. Pour the warm lemon butter into a ramekin and serve alongside the hot artichoke.

4 To eat, pluck off the leaves, one by one, dip the fleshy end in the melted butter, and scrape off the flesh with your teeth; discard the leaf. When you get to the little cone of pale inner leaves, pull this out to reveal the hairy choke; scoop all of this out with a spoon and discard. Then enjoy eating the succulent heart with the rest of the melted butter.

ARTICHOKE

The globe artichoke, which looks like an unopened flower bud, finds a home in Mediterranean climates around the world. Commercially, Italy and North Africa produce many varieties, ranging from tiny buds to large heads, while North America's big, green globes come almost exclusively from cool, coastal California. Very small artichokes can be eaten in their entirety, while only the heart, or bottom, and fleshy bases of the leaves (bracts) of large heads are edible. The choke, which is the bunch of hairy fibers above the heart, is inedible. Artichokes have an earthy, nutty flavor with a slight astringency.

🔒 **BUY** The artichoke season runs from late spring to mid-fall. Look for heads with tightly closed leaves and firm stalks. Cold weather will produce brown discolorations, but these don't negatively affect flavor.

📦 **STORE** For the best flavor, use artichokes as soon as you get them home. If you must keep them, cut a fresh end on the stalk, wrap in moist paper towels, and place in a plastic bag in the fridge; use within 1–2 days.

⚫ **EAT** When preparing artichokes, prevent browning by rubbing all cut surfaces with lemon, or dropping the heads into water acidulated with lemon juice. The choke is easier

to remove from large artichokes after cooking. **Fresh:** Hearts and the tender, fleshy part of leaves can be eaten raw in a salad or antipasto. **Cooked:** Coat small, whole artichokes in batter, or egg and crumbs, and deep-fry. In Italy, the leaf tips are trimmed and a mixture of breadcrumbs, olive oil, and cheese is stuffed behind the leaves, then the artichokes are roasted. Large heads can be braised, grilled, stuffed and roasted, pressure-cooked, or steamed until a skewer will slide easily into the heart. **Preserved:** Pickle hearts and tender inner portions of leaves, or preserve in olive oil.

FLAVOR PAIRINGS Sausage, prosciutto, pancetta, anchovies, hollandaise sauce, Parmesan cheese, cream, garlic, lemon, olive oil, white truffles, white wine.

CLASSIC RECIPES Steamed artichokes; *artichauts à la grecque*; *alcachofas con jamón*; artichokes braised with white wine and garlic; tagine of lamb and artichokes; *carciofi alla giudia*; *artichauts à la barigoule*; *torta di carciofi*.

Before cooking whole, use scissors to snip off the spiny leaf tips.

Green Globe
Widely available, this popular large-headed variety has succulent, fleshy leaves with a meaty flavor.

Baby purple artichoke
This immature variety has a mild artichoke flavor, with a hint of sweetness. Once trimmed, it is tender enough to be deep-fried, either whole or sliced into wedges.

Benicarló
From Valencia in Spain, this highly prized variety has achieved PDO (Protected Designation of Origin) status. It has an exceptionally full, meaty flavor.

Violetta di Chioggia
Smaller and more elongated than the green-globe type, this handsome purple variety has an unobtrusive choke and a strong artichoke flavor.

CARDOON

The cardoon looks like an overgrown thistle, because that is what it is—a descendant of a Mediterranean weed that also gave us the globe artichoke. Both cardoons and artichokes like warm, mild-winter climates. Whereas with artichokes we eat the unopened flower buds, from the cardoon we take the long, central leaf stalks. These are wide, flat, and silver-white, with a succulent but crunchy texture and a delicate flavor that combines artichoke, celery, and salsify, with a hint of anise. Look for cardoon in farmers' markets, Italian groceries, or specialty produce markets from mid-winter to spring.

BAKED CARDOONS WITH CHEESE

The delicate flavor of cardoon is enhanced when baked and topped with a delicious cheese sauce in this Italian classic.

SERVES 4

2 lb (1kg) cardoons

salt and freshly ground black pepper

juice of 1 lemon

2 tbsp butter

1½ tbsp all-purpose flour

1 cup milk, heated

¼ cup freshly grated Parmesan cheese

1 Trim the cardoons, discarding the tough outer ribs. Remove and discard any strings. Cut crosswise into 3in (7.5cm) pieces. Put the cardoons in a pot of salted water and add the lemon juice. Bring to a boil, then reduce the heat and simmer for 30 minutes or until just tender. Drain well and arrange in a greased baking dish.

2 Preheat the oven to 350°F (180°C). Melt the butter in a small saucepan, then remove from the heat and stir in the flour. Return to the heat and cook, stirring, for 1 minute. Gradually stir in the milk. Cook, stirring, until smooth and thickened. Remove from the heat, season with salt and pepper, and stir in half the Parmesan. Pour evenly over the cardoons and sprinkle with the remaining Parmesan.

3 Bake uncovered for 20–25 minutes, or until golden and bubbling. Serve hot, with crusty bread.

BUY Large stalks are tough, so choose those that are small to medium, 3–4in (7.5–10cm) wide. The cut ends will be discolored—that's natural. If stalks are hollow, they will be fibrous.

STORE Use the same day you buy them, if possible. Or keep in a paper bag in the fridge for a day or two.

EAT Peel stalks to remove strings, then use like celery or fennel. **Fresh:** Very young, tender stalks can be eaten raw: the Italians dip peeled sticks in a garlic and anchovy *bagna cauda*. **Cooked:** Boil, steam, braise, stew, or sauté; purée to add to soups and stews. **Preserved:** Pickle.

FLAVOR PAIRINGS Veal, anchovies, Parmesan cheese, cream, lemon.
CLASSIC RECIPES Baked cardoons with cheese; cardoon with almond sauce; *sformato di cardoni*; *cardons aux anchois*.

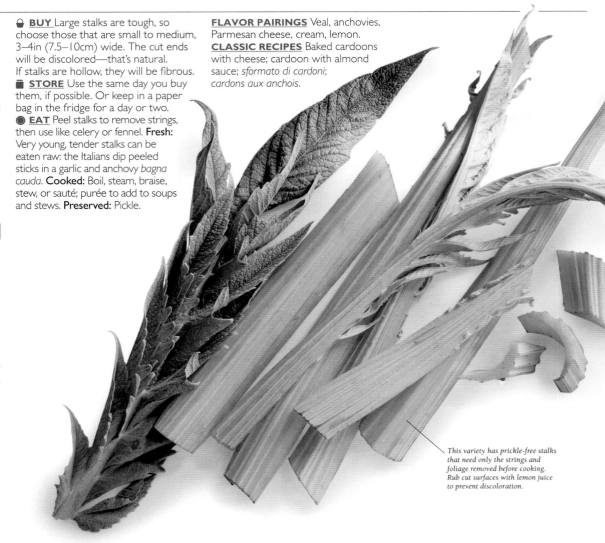

This variety has prickle-free stalks that need only the strings and foliage removed before cooking. Rub cut surfaces with lemon juice to prevent discoloration.

BAMBOO SHOOTS

In the milder regions of the temperate zones and in semi-tropical areas of China and Japan, tender young shoots of certain varieties of bamboo that emerge in the spring are highly prized as a vegetable. Shoots of different species look very similar—pointed spears or cones that are harvested when the tips just appear above ground. Their flavor is mild, their texture crunchy.

BUY Bamboo shoots are sometimes found fresh in Asian markets in late winter or early spring; some species are available year-round. They should be firm and smell sweet, never sour. The outer layers should be blemish-free and tightly held to the creamy white core. Check the cut ends for freshness. In the West, bamboo shoots are most often sold canned, but can also be found dried or pickled.

STORE Unpeeled fresh bamboo shoots will keep for at least a week in the crisper of the fridge. Peeled and parboiled shoots, as well as leftover canned shoots, can be kept for 4–5

days in a container of water in the fridge.

EAT Due to the presence of hydrocyanic acid, fresh bamboo shoots must be cooked before use; they will retain most of their crisp texture after cooking. First, trim off the roots and peel the outer leaves to reveal the homogenous, creamy core. Boil in salted water for 20 minutes. Taste and, if still acrid or bitter, boil in new water or 5 more minutes. Then cut into shapes or shred to use as you would any crunchy vegetable, such as radishes, water chestnuts, or jicama.

FLAVOR PAIRINGS Fish sauce, eggs, dill, miso, seaweed, sherry, toasted sesame oil, soy sauce.

Pare away any tough, fibrous sections from the inner core before cooking.

CELERY

Wild celery, or smallage, is native to marshy areas along seashores in the temperate regions of the world. It likes sun, but also the plentiful water found at those sites. From it, our modern celery has been bred and is grown in temperate climates around the world. The intense bitterness in smallage has been transformed into a mild, sweet, crunchy vegetable.

🔒 **BUY** In markets year-round, the peak season is fall through winter to spring. The stalks should be stiff and any leaves fresh looking.

🗄 **STORE** Celery can be kept for up to 10 days in a perforated plastic bag in the crisper of the fridge. Wrap in damp paper towels, if necessary, to keep it from drying out.

⬤ **EAT Fresh:** Raw celery sticks make excellent crudités, or fill small pieces with blue or creamy cheese and other savory mixtures for hors-d'oeuvres. Dice for salads and sandwich fillings. Use stalks to garnish tall drinks or a cheese plate. **Cooked:** Steam, braise, bake in a gratin, sauté or stir-fry, or add to stuffings.

FLAVOR PAIRINGS Blue cheese, béchamel and hollandaise sauces, mayonnaise, onions, lemon.

CLASSIC RECIPES Waldorf salad; _minestra di sedano e riso; mirepoix._

Green celery
A kitchen staple, green celery is delicious both raw and cooked. The crisp stalks have a slightly astringent flavor, while the heart is creamy and nutty.

Giant Pascal
This French heirloom variety has noticeably thick, fleshy, white stalks and a nutty flavor.

Trim the leaves, but keep a few to use as a garnish, or to add flavor to stocks and stews.

FENNEL

Looking like a bulbous celery heart, Florence fennel, or _finocchio_, is in fact the swollen base of the stem of the plant. It grows best in Mediterranean or mild, temperate climates around the world. The herb fennel and fennel seed do not come from the same plant, although they are close relations.

🔒 **BUY** Florence fennel is at its best in fall. Look for clean, freshly cut bulbs with the long stems and fronds attached, if possible. Old fennel will look dull with brown patches and the fronds, if any, will be limp.

🗄 **STORE** Bulbs can be kept in a plastic bag in the crisper of the fridge for a week, but will be crispest the day that you buy them.

⬤ **EAT Fresh:** Slice or shred for salads. It is great for crudités, too.

Cooked: Boil or steam whole or in wedges; braise, roast, or sauté; boil thick slices until tender, then grill.

FLAVOR PAIRINGS
Pancetta, parmesan cheese, fish, veal, chicken, dill.

CLASSIC RECIPE Fennel gratin.

Chop the fronds finely and use to give a subtle anise flavor to soups, salads, and fish dishes.

Florence fennel
With its sweet, warm, anise flavor and crisp texture, fennel makes a tasty salad ingredient. The flavor is subtler when cooked, but the texture remains pleasingly crunchy.

Baby fennel
More tender than the large bulbs of Florence fennel, baby fennel can be eaten whole. It's delicious brushed with oil and grilled on the barbecue.

CLASSIC RECIPE

FENNEL GRATIN

This rich, creamy topping works perfectly with the subtle anise flavor of fennel.

SERVES 4

2 fennel bulbs, trimmed and cut lengthwise into 6 slices or wedges

salt and freshly ground black pepper

1 teaspoon finely chopped fresh rosemary (optional)

½ cup heavy cream

¼ cup freshly grated Parmesan cheese

1 Preheat the oven to 350°F (180°C). Add the fennel to a pan of salted boiling water and simmer gently for about 5 minutes, until only barely tender. Drain well.

2 Arrange the fennel in a greased shallow baking dish. Sprinkle with the rosemary, if using, and season with salt and pepper. Pour the cream over the top and sprinkle with half of the Parmesan. Cover the dish with foil and bake for 30 minutes.

3 Remove the foil. Top with the remaining Parmesan and return to the oven, uncovered, to bake for another 5 minutes, or until the top is lightly browned. Serve hot.

Sweetly flavored with a crisp and crunchy texture, cherry radishes are a colorful addition to salads.

ASPARAGUS

Asparagus grows in temperate zones worldwide where there is regular summer water from either rain or irrigation. Spears can range in thickness from pencil thin to the size of your thumb. All asparagus is either green or purple: white asparagus, so prized in Europe, is simply green asparagus that has been grown away from light and has not manufactured chlorophyll. Green and purple asparagus have the most pronounced flavor, while white is milder and sweeter.

BUY Asparagus is naturally a spring crop, but growers have learned how to force spears throughout the summer and early fall. Choose fresh, spritely spears with a clean-looking cut end. The growing tips should be tightly closed.

STORE Asparagus should be used as soon as possible, preferably on the day of purchase. If necessary, it can be stored, unpeeled, for up to 2 days in the fridge, in a jug of water loosely covered with a plastic bag.

EAT Snap off the tough ends of the stalks. Then, if you like, you can peel stalks to below the tips just before cooking: the tough fibers are very near the surface so you will only need to remove a thin layer of skin. **Fresh:** Tender, young asparagus can be eaten raw, although it does not agree with some people. **Cooked:** Steam, simmer, stir-fry, roast, grill, or barbecue.

FLAVOR PAIRINGS Bacon, anchovies, salmon, hollandaise sauce, mornay sauce, cream, Parmesan cheese, lemon, orange, pesto, mustard, vinaigrette.

CLASSIC RECIPES Asparagus with hollandaise; risotto primavera; *asparagi alla milanese*.

Sprue asparagus
These very slender spears are the first "thinnings" of the crop, usually sold loose. Tender and mildly flavored, they are best used in stir-fries or soups.

Spears should be straight and plump.

Spears bought in a bunch should be of similar thickness, so that they cook evenly.

PREPARING ASPARAGUS

Peeling large spears removes any woody strings and gives a professional finish.

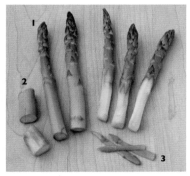

1 Rinse under cold running water. **2** Snap off the coarse, woody ends where they naturally break when the spear is bent. **3** If you want to peel the lower part of the stalks, use a swivel vegetable peeler and run it down the stalk away from the tip.

Purple asparagus
Purple varieties tend to be sweeter and less fibrous than green ones.

Green asparagus
Of all the asparagus types, green asparagus has the most pronounced flavor. Slender spears are best briefly steamed; fatter ones can be brushed with oil and grilled until slightly charred.

The skin of white asparagus can be tough, so it should be peeled off.

White asparagus
The fat, white spears are milder in flavor than the green type. They are deprived of light as they emerge from the ground, which prevents them from becoming green.

PAN-GRILLED ASPARAGUS WITH HOLLANDAISE

Rich and tangy hollandaise sauce and fresh asparagus is a time-honored partnership.

SERVES 4

1 lb (450g) fresh asparagus

1 tbsp olive oil

For the sauce

2 tbsp white wine vinegar

4 large egg yolks

8 tbsp (1 stick) butter, melted

1 tbsp lemon juice

salt and freshly ground black pepper

1 Snap off the woody ends from the asparagus spears. Brush a ridged grill pan with the oil and heat over medium-high heat until the pan is very hot. Cook the asparagus, turning once, for 4 to 6 minutes, until it has grill marks and is crisp-tender (thick spears may take longer, so reduce the temperature as needed so the asparagus cooks without charring).

2 Meanwhile, make the sauce. Boil the vinegar until reduced by half. Remove from the heat, and add 2 tbsp water. One at a time, whisk in the egg yolks.

3 Return the saucepan to very low heat and whisk until thick and pale. Remove from the heat and gradually whisk in the melted butter. Stir in the lemon juice. Season with salt and pepper.

4 Divide the asparagus between serving plates. Spoon the sauce over the asparagus, and serve at once.

RADISH

Thought to be native to Western Asia, radishes are now grown in temperate climates worldwide. They vary greatly in size, shape, color, and pepperiness —from small, spicy, red balls, to large, mild, white cylinders and extra-pungent, black-skinned, turnip shapes. Radishes may be classified into three groups: western or small, which include the familiar red, round, or oval varieties; winter; and Chinese. There are also varieties grown for leaves and pods.

🔒 **BUY** Although available year-round, western radishes are best from late spring to fall. They should be firm with no splits or cracks. If they have tops, these should be fresh and green.

📦 **STORE** Remove the leaves, then wrap in damp paper towels, unwashed, and keep in a plastic bag in the fridge crisper. Western and Chinese radishes should be used within 3–4 days, whereas winter radishes can be kept for up to 2 weeks.

⬤ **EAT Fresh:** Add to salads and salsas. Radishes make fine crudités, although winter radishes may need salting to reduce their heat. In Japan, grated Chinese radish, or *daikon*, is the traditional garnish for sashimi. **Cooked:** Chinese and winter radishes are excellent stir-fried, steamed, or sautéed, or can be added to soups and stews. **Preserved:** Use Chinese radishes in pickles; salt and dry.

FLAVOR PAIRINGS Smoked fish, cheese, potatoes, spring onions, chives, parsley, citrus, vinegar.

CLASSIC RECIPE *Kim chee.*

Red Icicle
Growing up to 6in (15cm) long, Red Icicle, a Western variety, has more bite than the white variety. The crunchy flesh is good finely chopped in a salsa.

White Icicle
This tapered western variety has dense, mildly flavored flesh that rarely becomes pithy. It is delicious finely sliced and mixed with red varieties in a salad.

Peel black winter radishes, as the skin is tough.

French Breakfast
Widely available in supermarkets, French Breakfast has a milder flavor than other western varieties. It is good served with sea salt as a crudité.

Cherry radish
This small, round western radish, which is at its best in summer, has a mildly peppery flavor and crisp, white flesh.

Winter radish
Popular in mainland Europe, this black winter radish has white, strongly pungent flesh that is dense and slightly dry. It is good in pickles, or grated and mixed with mayonnaise.

The uniform cylindrical shape makes Chinese radish easy to slice into neat rounds.

Chinese radish
Usually known as daikon or mooli, this pure white variety grows up to 18in (46cm) long. The crisp, juicy flesh is very mildly flavored. Use daikon to add texture to raw pickles and salsas.

KOHLRABI

Most loved in Germany, through Eastern Europe down to Hungary and the Middle East, kohlrabi is gaining popularity in other parts of the world. The swollen stem, which grows just above ground, may be pale green or purple. Its crisp flesh combines flavors of the cabbage family with a turnip-like taste, albeit sweeter and more delicate. The leaves are also very palatable.

BUY Summer and fall are the peak seasons for kohlrabi. If you find it with the leaves intact, their freshness will tell you about the quality of the bulb; without leaves, make sure the bulb is firm and unblemished, with a bright, light green or purple color. Bulbs larger than a tennis ball are more likely to be tough.

STORE Don't wash the bulb, just trim off the leaf stalks, then keep in a plastic bag in the crisper of the fridge for up to a week. The leaves and stalks are more perishable, so use as soon as possible.

EAT Fresh: You can crunch on peeled wedges of kohlrabi as you would an apple. Use for crudités or grate into salads and coleslaw. **Cooked:** Both the bulb, leaves and long leaf stalks can be cooked. Cooking intensifies the turnip-like flavor of the bulb. Bake (good in a gratin), roast, boil, steam, sauté, or stir-fry it. Or, chop and add to soups and stews. A traditional way to cook larger kohlrabi is to hollow it out for stuffing and then to braise it. Cook the leaves like cabbage. **Preserved:** Pickle sliced kohlrabi.

FLAVOR PAIRINGS Butter, cream, lemon, parsley.

CLASSIC RECIPES Hungarian kohlrabi soup; kohlrabi coleslaw.

Kohlrabi
Though similar to the turnip in flavor, kohlrabi's crisp, clean-tasting flesh is juicier and at its best eaten raw. It can also be lightly cooked. Peel before use.

Purple kohlrabi
Once peeled, purple kohlrabi is identical to the green, although it is often more mildly flavored.

RUTABAGA

This root-like member of the cabbage family is widely grown in the cooler parts of temperate zones around the world. Also called Swede, Swedish or Russian turnip, and, in Scotland, "neeps," it has a deep, rich, sweet flavor. The flesh is yellowish-orange to yellowish-beige and darkens a little when cooked.

BUY Fall and winter are the prime seasons for rutabagas. Look for medium-sized roots without any rot, pits, or scars. Avoid those that have been waxed to preserve moisture—they are invariably old and the wax can seal in mold spots that hasten loss of quality.

STORE Rutabaga will keep well in the crisper of the fridge for 3–4 weeks; it will lose moisture and quality after that.

EAT Fresh: Cut sticks of sweet, crunchy rutabega for crudités, or grate into salads.

Cooked: Boil, steam, bake, roast, deep-fry as fries, or add to soups and stews. **Preserved:** Include in a pickled vegetable medley or chutney.

FLAVOR PAIRINGS Bacon, onions, carrots, cream, lemon, nutmeg, thyme.

CLASSIC RECIPE Haggis and neeps.

Yellow rutabaga
Very similar in flavor to the purple rutabaga, this has fine, yellow flesh. Coarsely grated raw, it adds color to a winter salad. It is also good for roasting.

Purple rutabaga
This is a fine-textured variety with a mild flavor—slightly sweet with a hint of bitterness. Roasting caramelizes the juices and intensifies sweetness; boiling makes the flavor milder.

PARSNIP

Parsnips grew wild across Europe and Asia, and have been cultivated since Greek and Roman times. Today's modern parsnips are grown throughout the world's temperate zones. The flavor of the creamy-beige root has hints of parsley and carrot, but with a slight sweetness and nuttiness.

BUY Winter parsnips are the sweetest. Make sure the roots are firm, without any pitting. Look for signs of freshness: a pleasant aroma and no regrowth of green tops.

STORE Do not wash parsnips before storage; simply wrap them in dry paper towels and put them in a plastic bag in the fridge crisper, where they will keep for several weeks.

EAT If peeling, peel thinly. Remove the core from large, old parsnips, as it can be woody. **Fresh:** Cut sticks for crudités. **Cooked:** Parsnips are versatile, but unless you intend to purée them, take care not to overcook as this quickly turns them unpalatably soft and mushy. Steam or boil, deep-fry as french fries, grill, roast to a glazed crispness, braise, or sauté. Use in soups and stews, too.
FLAVOR PAIRINGS Curry powder, nutmeg, garlic, parsley, thyme, potatoes, tarragon.
CLASSIC RECIPES Curried parsnip soup; parsnip gratin.

Use the scrubbed peel with other vegetable trimmings to make a winter vegetable stock.

HAMBURG PARSLEY

As its name suggests, the large-rooted form of this versatile herb is mostly cultivated in eastern and northern Europe, where it is a popular vegetable. The flavor of Hamburg parsley (also called turnip-rooted parsley or parsley root) is herbaceous and slightly sweet, like a combination of parsley and celery root. The aromatic leaves are also edible, mainly used as a garnish.

BUY The best season for this root is winter: it becomes much sweeter after enduring several hard frosts. The tops are usually trimmed at the market, but if you can find roots with green tops, you will get two vegetables in one. Make sure the roots have no mold, are firm, and have a clean, pleasant aroma. A lot of small rootlets indicate that the root is old or has been stored too long.

STORE Hamburg parsley will keep well in a plastic bag in the crisper of the fridge for at least 3 weeks, but will start to lose firmness and sweetness after this.

EAT Fresh: Grate into salads, or slice for crudités. **Cooked:** Bake or roast, braise, boil or steam, pan-fry, or stir-fry. Or add to soups, stews, and root-vegetable mixtures. Use leaves like parsley. **Preserved:** Pickle.
FLAVOR PAIRINGS Chicken, fish, game, eggs, mushrooms, carrots, potatoes, turnips, thyme.
CLASSIC RECIPE *Supa de chimen.*

CELERY ROOT

Celery root, or celeriac, grows best in cool, temperate regions. The thick, rough skin of the bulbous root conceals crisp, white flesh that has a refreshing, lightly herbal flavor, combining the tastes of parsley and parsnip with celery.

BUY The peak season for celery root is late fall through winter. Choose roots that are at least the size of a small grapefruit. They should feel heavy for their size and be firm to the touch, especially at the top where the leaves emerged.

STORE Celery root can be kept for up to 2 weeks in the fridge, unpeeled in a paper bag in the crisper, but is best used as fresh as possible.

EAT Fresh: Cut sticks for crudités, or grate for a salad. **Cooked:** Steam, boil, braise, roast, deep-fry, or sauté. Or use in soups and stews. After boiling until tender, purée and mix with an equal amount of mashed potato. Add diced celery root with celery to poultry stuffings. **Preserved:** Pickle alone or with other vegetables.
FLAVOR PAIRINGS Bacon, Parmesan, garlic, potatoes, parsley, dill, olive oil, mustard.
CLASSIC RECIPE *Céleri rémoulade.*

PREPARING CELERY ROOT
You have to peel away a lot of the outer part to get to the crisp, white flesh beneath.

1 *Trim the top and bottom with a sharp knife. With a smaller knife, remove the tough skin.* **2** *Cut up the flesh, dropping the pieces into a bowl of water with a piece of lemon to prevent discoloration.*

TURNIP

A swollen-rooted member of the cabbage family, turnips hail from northern Europe and Scandinavia, thus preferring cool to cold weather, which keeps them sweet and crisp. Grown as a farm crop for at least 4,000 years, this delicious vegetable has long been disdained as cattle fodder. There are dozens of varieties sold around the world, from white, mild globes that may be as small as radishes or as large as oranges, through to roots shaped like spinning tops with purple or green shoulders, to sizeable, cylinder-like, deep-red roots. Turnips have a fresh, slightly pungent, sweet, and pleasant taste. The coarsely textured turnip tops or greens are pungently peppery.

BUY With all turnips, the younger the better, so look for small roots not much bigger than golf balls, ideally sold in bunches with their tops on, from fall through winter into spring.

If the tops are fresh, the turnips will be, too. The roots should be firm, not wrinkled or soft to the touch. Avoid extra large turnips, which can have a coarse, even woody, texture and very overpowering taste.

STORE Keep for no more than a week in the crisper of the fridge. Store them in a plastic bag to conserve moisture, which they are prone to lose quickly in storage.

EAT Small, young turnips can just be scrubbed; older turnips are best peeled. **Fresh:** Cut into sticks for crudités, or grate into salads. **Cooked:** Turnips retain their freshness if cooked gently until just tender; overcooking turns them tasteless and flabby. Boil (especially with potatoes), steam, roast, sauté, or stir-fry, or use in stews. **Preserved:** Turnips can be pickled whole or sliced.

FLAVOR PAIRINGS Lamb, bacon, duck, cheese, apples, mushrooms, potatoes, sherry.

CLASSIC RECIPES Irish stew; glazed turnips; *canard aux navets; torshi.*

White turnip
Pure white, round turnips such as this Tokyo Cross (above) have a mild flavor and a crunchy, juicy texture, much like a radish.

Turnip tops
Some turnip varieties are grown for their flavorful green leaves, which can be cooked like other hearty greens or pickled.

The roots of turnips grown specifically for their leaves stay small and are too bitter to eat.

Purple turnip
The familiar top-shaped turnip is usually purple fading to white at the root. When small, the flavor is sweet and delicate.

JICAMA

Native to Central America, jicama is now cultivated in every tropical corner of the globe. It is a popular vegetable in Mexico, as well as in China and other parts of East Asia. The ivory flesh has a pleasant, mild flavor—somewhat similar to pear or apple—and a juicy texture that stays crunchy whether it is used fresh or cooked. It pairs well with other foods.

BUY Jicama is available year-round, but is especially fresh in Asian or Latin American markets from fall to spring. Choose unblemished tubers with a fresh-looking sheen. Dull, older tubers will be dried out and full of tough fibers.

STORE Keep the whole tuber, without bagging, in the crisper of the fridge for up to 2 weeks. If you use just a piece, seal the cut side of the unused portion with plastic wrap.

EAT Jicama, like Jerusalem artichoke, can be difficult for some people to digest, so it is best to add it to your diet slowly at first. **Fresh:** Grate, dice, or julienne to add crunchy texture to salads. Good in fruit salads, too. Cut into slices or sticks for crudités—try sprinkling them with lime juice, salt, and hot chili powder, as they do in Mexico. **Cooked:** Steam, boil, bake, stir-fry, sauté, or braise. **Preserved:** Pickle sticks of jicama.

FLAVOR PAIRINGS Chile, lime, avocado, mango.

CLASSIC RECIPE Green papaya salad.

Just before using jicama, peel off the skin and fibrous layer beneath to reveal the crisp flesh.

TARO

As corn or maize, potatoes, and wheat are staples for people who live in the temperate regions of the world, so taro is a staple in the tropics around the globe. Although called a root, it is actually a corm, or swollen stem base. There are many varieties, ranging widely in size and shape, and its numerous names include dasheen, eddo, and colocasia. Large taros have a dense texture; smaller varieties tend to be smoother and creamier when cooked. Taro has a unique aroma and flavor, like a cross between chestnuts, coconut, and white potato. Large varieties are strongly flavored; small ones are more bland.

BUY Taro is available year-round. Choose corms that are very hard, with no splitting, softness, pits, or mold.

STORE Keep at room temperature in a well-ventilated, cool place for no more than 2 days, because taro loses quality quickly.

EAT **Cooked:** Steam, boil, fry, or deep-fry, or add to soups and stews. Once cooked, purée taro to use as the base for soufflés or croquettes. **Preserved:** Candy pieces in syrup like *marrons glacés*.

FLAVOR PAIRINGS Sweet potatoes, chile, star anise, cinnamon, cardamom, toasted sesame oil.

CLASSIC RECIPE Hawaiian poi.

Small taro can be boiled or baked in their skin.

PREPARING TARO

Raw taro can cause skin and eye irritation, so wear rubber gloves when preparing it.

1 Hold the taro under cold, running water and use a sharp knife or vegetable peeler to remove the skin. **2** Cut out any soft spots or discolored patches from the firm, moist flesh, then cut into slices or cubes.

YAM

There are dozens of species of yams and hundreds of common names for them. They come in a wide range of shapes, from lumpy to round and elongated, as well as varying widely in size and color. In the tropics—and increasingly in temperate zones where they are imported—they are a staple, like potatoes, corn, or beans. Cooked, yams have a mild and starchy flavor and a fluffy or pasty texture that readily accepts savory sauces, and they are the foundation of many meals.

BUY Yams appear year-round in markets, depending on supply. They should be firm and feel heavy in the hand, with no soft spots or evidence of mold or pitting. The size of the yam is not an indication of quality. Solidity is. They should smell clean and fresh.

STORE Keep at room temperature for up to a week.

EAT Yams must never be eaten raw and need to be peeled before cooking. Some types will irritate skin, so wear rubber gloves when preparing. Boil, steam, bake, roast, fry, or deep-fry, or add to meat stews.

FLAVOR PAIRINGS Eggs, cheese, cream, curry powder, coconut.

CLASSIC RECIPE Fufu.

When cut, the flesh forms a sticky coating which should be removed. Rinse well before cooking.

BEET

Although beets with miniature edible roots were eaten by the ancient Greeks, our modern beet wasn't developed until the 16th century. Beets now grow in temperate climates around the world. They vary widely in color, shape, and flavor, but the most common are globe-shaped and red, with intensely colored juice. One of the chief features of this vegetable is its sweetness.

BUY Beets are available all year, but are at their best from midsummer to late fall. Any leaves should be glossy and fresh, and the roots themselves should feel hard, with no mold, cuts, or abrasions on their surface. Small to medium roots are likely to be more tender than older, larger ones, which may be woody. Beets are also available pre-cooked and vacuum-packed.

STORE Fresh beets will keep well for up to 2 weeks in a paper bag in the crisper of the fridge. Remove leafy tops before storing.

EAT If they have their leafy tops, trim these off to cook as a separate vegetable, just as you do for the leaves of their close relative, chard. **Fresh:** Raw beet, which has a very earthy flavor, is sometimes grated as a salad ingredient. **Cooked:** Don't peel beets before cooking or they will bleed. Bake, roast, or boil whole; beets are done when they feel tender when pierced with the tip of a knife. Slices can be steamed. **Preserved:** Pickled beets are easy to make and keep for weeks in the fridge.

FLAVOR PAIRINGS Bacon, smoked salmon, sour cream, goat cheese and other cheeses, orange, brown sugar, nutmeg, horseradish.

CLASSIC RECIPES Borscht; coleslaw.

PREPARING RAW BEETS

Wear rubber gloves to protect your hands from being stained by the beet juice.

1 *Trim off the top and bottom. Using a vegetable peeler, thinly peel away the skin.* **2** *Grate the flesh coarsely for salads and to add to soups, or slice thinly with a mandolin slicer or with a sharp knife.*

PREPARING COOKED BEETS

After cooking beets whole, the skin will slip off easily in your fingers.

1 *Wash under cold-running water. Trim off the tops, being careful not to pierce the skin, then boil, steam, or roast in the skin until tender. Once cool, pull off the thin skin.* **2** *The beets are now ready to be sliced, chopped, or diced.*

Stalks and leaves are edible, but more perishable. Separate from the bulb and use within 1–2 days.

Red beet
The firm, juicy flesh of the common red beet has a uniquely earthy, sweet flavor. They are best cooked with other red vegetables or those that will absorb the seeping crimson juices.

Yellow beet
Burpee's Golden is an exceptionally tasty beet with fine-textured, tender flesh. It is best when no bigger than a golf ball. Great as a contrast in a red and yellow beet salad.

This beet keeps its startlingly bright color when cooked and does not bleed when cut.

Thinly sliced and used raw, the colorful striped flesh can be shown off in a salad.

Striped beet
Grown for looks rather than flavor, the striped variety, or Chiogga, is much milder than the red beet. When cooked, the stripes fade and the flesh becomes a uniform pink.

The cylindrical shape makes these beets ideal for slicing into rounds of equal size for sandwiches and salads.

Elongated beet
The narrow, cylindrical variety, or Forono, is mildly flavored, with deep crimson, smooth flesh. The roots are slow to become fibrous, even when allowed to grow large.

BORSCHT

Thickly textured and satisfying, versions of this peasant soup come from all over Eastern Europe.

SERVES 4

2 large red beets
1 onion
1 carrot
1 celery rib
3 tbsp butter or goose fat
1 x 14.5oz (400g) can chopped tomatoes
1 garlic clove, crushed (optional)
7 cups vegetable stock
2 bay leaves
4 whole cloves
2 tbsp fresh lemon juice
salt and freshly ground black pepper
¾ cup sour cream

1 Roughly grate the beets, onion, carrot, and celery.

2 Melt the butter or goose fat in a large saucepan over medium heat. Add the grated vegetables and cook, stirring, for 5 minutes, or until just softened.

3 Add the tomatoes and crushed garlic, if using, and cook for another 2–3 minutes, stirring frequently. Stir in the stock.

4 Tie the bay leaves and cloves in a small piece of muslin or cheesecloth and add to the pan. Bring the soup to a boil, then reduce the heat, cover, and simmer for 1 hour 20 minutes.

5 Discard the muslin bag. Stir in the lemon juice and season to taste with salt and pepper.

6 Ladle the soup into warm bowls and add a swirl of sour cream to each Serve hot, with dark rye bread.

Choose young, slim, highly colored carrots to add sweetness and texture to salads.

CARROTS

Our modern carrots are descended from wild progenitors that grew—and still grow—in Afghanistan. Carrots as we know them were developed in Holland in the 17th century, and are now cultivated in temperate climates around the world. In addition to the familiar long, tapered orange carrots, they may be cylindrical, stubby, round, or finger-size, and in color purple, yellow, dark red, or white. All carrots have a refreshing taste and aroma when very fresh, and their natural sugars make them delightfully sweet.

🔒 **BUY** Although available year-round, carrots are never better than in the late spring when they are young and tender. If you buy them with the feathery green tops on, make sure these are fresh-looking and bright; if trimmed there should be no mold on the top. The carrots should be firm, not limp. Avoid those sprouting thin white rootlets.

📦 **STORE** Carrots can be kept for 2–3 weeks in a plastic bag in the crisper of the fridge, but will lose their fresh aromas and flavors as the days pass. Remove the feathery green tops.

◉ **EAT** For best flavour, just rinse, scrub, or scrape if possible, rather than peeling; older carrots usually need sto be peeled.

Fresh: Cut into slender sticks for crudités. Grate or shave into ribbons for salads. Run through a juicer for fresh, creamy-sweet carrot juice.

Cooked: Carrots are versatile in the kitchen, and can be roasted, boiled, braised, steamed, sautéed, or stir-fried. When their sugars are caramelized during cooking they add deep flavor to savory dishes. This natural sweetness has also long been put to good use in sweet cakes and desserts. **Preserved:** Pickle with other vegetables such as onions and peppers, or use to make a sweet jam or conserve.

FLAVOR PAIRINGS Beef, lemon, orange, ginger, celery, chervil, fennel, parsley, cumin, peas, pine nuts, thyme.

CLASSIC RECIPES Carrot cake; mirepoix; potage Crécy; carottes Vichy.

Nantes
Shaped like a sausage rather than tapered, this carrot is prized for its superior crisp and extra sweet flesh.

Chantenay
When full-grown these carrots are short and stubby. Their flavor is extraordinarily rich and there is no need to peel them before use.

Red carrot
Actually a very deep orange, this variety was bred in Australia. It has a rich flavor, perfect for raw uses like crudités and salads.

The vibrant color is due to a high level of carotenoids and other antioxidants that help to prevent disease.

Little finger carrot
Finger carrots stay slender and small. They are often used whole for crudités and salads, rather than in cooked dishes.

Imperator
A large, long, straight carrot commonly found in supermarkets. It is sweet and flavorful, and perfect for raw or cooked use.

Yellow carrot
Bred in the United States and believed to be extra rich in lutein, a substance that enhances eye health.

Remove the leafy tops before storing, as they draw moisture from the roots.

Purple carrot
The original wild carrots of Afghanistan were purple, and new strains have regained the color that supplies beneficial anthocyanin and lycopene along with rich carrot flavor.

CLASSIC RECIPE

CARROT CAKE

Top this moist cake with a traditional cream cheese frosting, or simply dust it with powdered sugar.

SERVES 8 OR MORE

1 ½ cups all-purpose flour
1 cup granulated sugar
1 ½ tsp baking soda
1 tsp baking powder
1 tsp ground cinnamon
½ tsp each ground cloves, nutmeg, allspice, and salt
½ cup canola or corn oil
3 eggs
2 cups peeled, grated carrots
1 cup chopped walnuts
1 cup golden raisins

For the frosting

8oz (225g) cream cheese
5 tbsp unsalted butter, at room temperature
2 tsp vanilla extract
1 lb (450g) confectioners' sugar, sifted
finely grated zest of 1 orange

1 Preheat the oven to 350°F (180°C). Grease a 13 x 9in (30 x 23cm) baking pan and line with parchment paper. Stir together the flour, sugar, baking soda, baking powder, spices, and salt.

2 Beat together the oil and eggs, then stir them into the flour mixture until just combined. Add the carrots, walnuts, and raisins and mix well.

3 Pour the mixture into the pan and spread evenly. Bake for 30–35 minutes or until a knife inserted in the center comes out clean. Cool in the pan.

4 To make the frosting, beat the cream cheese, butter, and vanilla together with an electric mixer until smooth. Gradually beat in the sugar. Fold in the orange zest with a spatula. Spread the frosting over the top of the cooled cake. Cut into squares to serve.

SALSIFY AND SCORZONERA

Native to the Mediterranean region, salsify, also called goatsbeard, has thin, light brown skin sprouting thin, tangled rootlets. Often confused with salsify is another root, scorzonera, which has sepia, bark-like skin and very few rootlets. Salsify tapers to a point, whereas scorzonera is a uniform thickness. Despite the differences, both have similar creamy-white flesh, with a flavor that recalls artichoke, and they can be used interchangeably in recipes.

BUY Salsify and scorzonera can be hard to find in the US; farmer's markets are your best bet. Look for firm, fresh-looking roots from fall to spring. If flabby or wizened, they are too old. Their tops, if attached, should be a fresh-looking green. Avoid roots that are pocked or blemished.

STORE Both salsify and scorzonera can be stored, unwashed, in a paper bag in the crisper of the fridge for up to a week. Roots can be blanched and then frozen.

EAT After peeling and slicing, drop into water acidulated with lemon juice to prevent discoloration.
Fresh: Salsify and scorzonera can be eaten raw. If leaves are young and tender, add to salads. **Cooked:** Both roots are best either boiled or steamed, then briefly sautéed in butter. Also bake, roast, sauté, or deep-fry, or add to soups and stews.
Preserved: Pickle flowers and buds, as well as roots.
FLAVOR PAIRINGS Parmesan cheese, béchamel sauce, onions, shallots, olive oil, lemon, nutmeg.
CLASSIC RECIPES Salsify fritters; *salsifis à la crème*; salsify gnocchi; scallops with salsify.

Choose roots with as few whiskers as possible. Trim well before peeling.

Salsify
Said to resemble oysters in flavor, salsify has creamy-white flesh with a slightly dense, waxy texture.

Scorzonera
The smooth, cream-colored flesh of scorzonera is softer and more delicately flavored than salsify. The skin exudes a milky latex when cut. To avoid sticky hands, boil unpeeled and strip away the skin once cooked.

Scorzonera is recognizable by its bark-like skin and even, cylindrical shape.

SALSIFY FRITTERS

Serve these tasty Mediterranean fritters as an easy side dish with meat or fish.

MAKES 4

1lb (400g) salsify, peeled and cut into small, equal-size pieces

4 tbsp butter

1 garlic clove, crushed

freshly ground black pepper

1 tbsp all-purpose flour

1 tbsp olive oil

1 Add the salsify to a pan of boiling salted water and cook for about 20 minutes, or until beginning to soften. Do not overcook. Drain well.

2 Mash the salsify, then add half the butter, the garlic, and some pepper and mash again. Divide into four equal portions and then shape each portion into a patty.

3 Dust both sides of the patties with flour to coat lightly. Heat the olive oil with the remaining butter in a non-stick pan, add the patties, and cook for about 2 minutes, or until the bottoms are golden. Turn the patties and cook the other sides for about 2 minutes. Serve hot.

PREPARING SALSIFY AND SCORZONERA

Both roots discolor quickly when peeled and cut, so rub with lemon or drop into acidulated water right away.

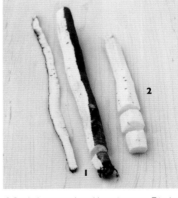

1 *Scrub the root under cold running water. Trim both ends, then peel with a sharp knife.* **2** *Cut across into bite-size pieces or thinner slices.*

WATER CHESTNUT

Water chestnuts are the corms (swollen bases of the leaf stalks) of a tropical plant cultivated primarily in southern China and Southeast Asia. They are sold canned in many countries, but are much better fresh and raw, when they have a sweet, intriguing flavor and a satisfying, crunchy texture. About the size and shape of a chestnut, their white flesh is covered with a tough brown skin.

BUY Fresh water chestnuts are most likely to be found in Asian markets. The corms should be firm, with no soft spots or shriveling, and they should smell clean. Buy a generous amount because much will be lost when peeling.

STORE They can be kept, unpeeled, for 1–2 weeks in a paper bag in the crisper of the fridge. Once peeled, they will keep for up to 1 week immersed in slightly salted water in a covered container in the fridge. Peeled water chestnuts can be frozen.

EAT Fresh: Slice raw into salads (even fruit salads) and Asian dishes. Thin slices also make fine crudités. **Cooked:** Peeling is easier after an initial five minutes' blanching. Boil, steam, or stir-fry, or add to soups and rice and noodle dishes for texture.

Once cut, immerse the crisp white flesh in lightly salted water to prevent discoloration.

Preserved: Dry or pickle. In China, fresh water chestnuts are candied in a sugar syrup.
FLAVOR PAIRINGS Shrimp, beef, chicken, pork, oyster sauce, soy sauce, ginger, sesame oil.
CLASSIC RECIPES Chop suey; *rumaki*.

BURDOCK

Burdock is native to China, from where it traveled east to Japan and west to Europe. It is now grown in temperate to tropical climates, most frequently in east Asia. While popular in Japanese cuisine, burdock has never found much favor in Western cultures, although it is used to flavor a soft drink in Great Britain. The Japanese, who call it *gobo*, have selected strains that grow very long. It has a fine, crunchy texture, and an earthy flavor similar to salsify.

BUY Burdock roots store in the soil, so it shows up in markets in any season, but current year plantings are harvested in fall and winter. Look for roots that are firm rather than limp.

STORE The roots will keep for about a week in a paper bag in the fridge crisper.

EAT Scrub well, then soak in water acidulated with lemon juice for about 30 minutes to remove bitterness. **Fresh:** Use very young roots like radishes in salads. **Cooked:** Braise, boil, steam, or stir-fry. Add to soups and stews, as you would other root vegetables. The Japanese make a traditional dish of carrots and burdock seasoned with soy and sesame. **Preserved:** Pickle.
FLAVOR PAIRINGS Shellfish, cheese, béchamel sauce, hollandaise sauce, vinegar, soy sauce.
CLASSIC RECIPE *Kinpira gobo*.

LOTUS ROOT

The imposing and beautiful lotus grows in water in warm climates throughout Asia. The "root," which looks like large, linked sausages, is really a *rhizome*—an underground runner from which true roots grow. The flavor is mild and earthy, similar to artichoke, and the crisp texture recalls jicama or water chestnut. Lotus seeds and young leaves are also eaten.

BUY Lotus root can show up in markets, especially Asian shops, at any time. Look for roots whose cut ends are moist and sticky, not dried out. Avoid roots with dark, sunken, or soft spots. Pale beige roots are best.

STORE Uncut whole roots can be kept in a paper bag in the crisper of the fridge for 2–3 weeks. Once sliced, blanch, cool under cold water, and sprinkle with lemon juice before storing in a covered container in the fridge for 3–5 days.

EAT Peel, removing the fibrous sections between the links, then slice or cut into chunks. **Cooked:** When cooked, lotus root retains much of its texture. Blanch, then use slices in salads. Boil, steam, or braise to serve as a vegetable; add to soups, stews, and stir-fries. **Preserved:** Blanched slices can be candied (this is a special treat in China). The seeds are also candied and used in sweets in Thailand. In Japan, lotus root is pickled.
FLAVOR PAIRINGS Citrus, garlic, onion, cilantro, chervil, star anise.
CLASSIC RECIPE *Lotus root kinpira*.

The long, slender roots do not need to be peeled.

When sliced across, lotus root reveals a pretty pattern of air channels.

Choose the type and variety of potato best suited to your dish—whether you need to bake it, slice it, or mash it.

POTATO

Potatoes originated in the South American Andes 8,000 years ago. Today, they are a staple food of people all around the world, with the chief producers located in temperate regions of China, Russia, India, and the United States. Potatoes vary in size from tiny balls to large, handful-sized spuds, and in color from tan to pink, red, blue, and purple. Their cooked flavor is rich in umami: the fifth taste, described as "yummy."

ALL-AROUND POTATOES are midway between waxy and floury in texture, making them good for many uses in the kitchen.

WAXY POTATOES keep their shape when cooked.

BAKING POTATOES usually have a soft, fluffy texture when cooked; if boiled they tend to disintegrate.

WAXY POTATOES

BUY Fall and winter are a good time for potatoes—then they have had a full growing season and time to cure in the soil before being dug up. Choose firm potatoes with unbroken skins, no patches of green color, and no mold or pitting. The potato's "eyes" should be tightly closed.

STORE Cold turns the potato's starch to sugar and light creates toxins such as solanine, which turns potatoes green, so store them in the dark at cool room temperature, for example in a paper bag or closed basket in a dark cupboard. They can be kept for 1–2 weeks.

EAT All-around potato varieties can be cooked all ways—boiling, steaming, baking, deep-frying, sautéing, roasting —while others suit particular methods. Waxy types are ideal for boiling and steaming, and in stews. Baking types are the best for baking or mashing, but not boiling.

FLAVOR PAIRINGS Bacon, ham, cheese, crème fraîche, sour cream, mushrooms, celery root, garlic, onions, turnips, dill, fennel, nutmeg, thyme, olive oil.

CLASSIC RECIPES Spanish omelet; *gratin dauphinois*; potato gnocchi; German potato salad; twice-baked potatoes; *latkes*; *Himmel und Erde*; *boxty*; *rösti*; *colcannon*; Parmentier potatoes; *pommes Anna*; chips; French fries.

Marfona
A large, smooth-fleshed variety, this has a slightly sharp flavor. It is best baked or boiled.

French Fingerling
Like many fingerlings, this French variety is low in starch. The creamy, dense flesh has a buttery flavor, and is ideal boiled or steamed, or in potato salads.

International Kidneys are delicious cooked in their skins. A quick scrub will remove any soil.

Bintje is easily recognized by its pale, silky skin.

Bintje
A Dutch heirloom variety, Bintje has a unique nutty flavor and a creamy texture. It excels in the kitchen, and is recommended for making Italian gnocchi.

International Kidney
Also known as the Jersey Royal, this famous heritage variety from the UK Channel Islands is one of the first to arrive in the spring. The smooth, waxy flesh has a distinctive rich, buttery flavor.

SPANISH OMELET

The traditional flat omelet, known as *tortilla* in Spain, is made with just potatoes, onions, and eggs.

SERVES 4

5 medium potatoes (any type)

1 cup olive oil

3 medium onions, quartered and sliced into thin crescents

salt and freshly ground black pepper

5 eggs

1 Peel the potatoes and cut into slices about ¼in (5mm) thick. Heat the olive oil in a deep-sided ovenproof frying pan (preferably non-stick). Add the potatoes, and cook at a gentle simmer for about 15 minutes, or until the potatoes are soft when you test them with a sharp knife. Remove the potatoes with a slotted spoon and put them in a large bowl to cool.

2 Pour most of the oil out of the pan (you can strain it and re-use in step 4). Add the onions and a pinch of salt. Cook over low heat until the onions are soft and beginning to caramelize. Add to the potatoes and leave to cool.

3 Whisk the eggs with a fork, then pour into the cooled potato and onion mixture. Season with salt and pepper. Fold together gently so all the potato slices are coated, trying not to break them up too much.

4 Preheat the oven to 400°F (200°C). Heat 1 tbsp of the strained olive oil in the frying pan until hot, then carefully slide in the potato mixture, spreading it evenly in the pan. Reduce the heat to medium-low and cook for 6–10 minutes, or until almost set.

5 Transfer the pan to the oven and bake for 10 minutes, or until set and golden. Alternatively, after cooking the first side of the omelet, invert it on to a plate and slide it back into the pan to cook the other side.

6 Remove from the pan and allow to cool slightly (or completely), then slice into wedges. Serve warm, at room temperature, or cold.

POTATO GNOCCHI

These light-as-air potato dumplings, served with a simple sage and butter sauce, make a good supper dish.

SERVES 4

1lb 10oz (750g) russet or other floury baking potatoes

2 large eggs, beaten

1⅓ cups all-purpose flour, as needed

For the sauce

10 tbsp butter

about 20 sage leaves

juice of ½ lemon

salt and freshly ground black pepper

1 Cook the whole, unpeeled potatoes in a pot of boiling water for about 25 minutes, or until just tender. Drain and let cool. Peel the potatoes and mash finely with a potato ricer or rub through a wire sieve.

2 Place the warm mashed potatoes on a work surface. Make a well in the center. Add the eggs and ⅓ cup of the flour into the well. Mix the ingredients, using your hands, adding more flour as needed, to make a soft but not sticky dough that can be shaped. Do not add too much flour or the gnocchi will be heavy.

3 Divide the dough into 4 equal portions. Roll each portion of dough on a lightly floured work surface into a rope about ¾in (2cm) thick. Cut into pieces 1¼in (3cm) long. Press each piece lightly with the back of a fork to give the traditional concave shape. Transfer the gnocchi to a floured baking sheet.

4 Bring a large saucepan of lightly salted water to a gentle boil. Add the gnocchi and cook for 2 minutes, or until they float to the surface.

5 Meanwhile, make the sauce. Heat the butter and sage in a frying pan over medium heat until the butter has melted. Add the lemon juice, and salt and pepper to taste.

6 Drain the gnocchi and toss in the sauce. Serve immediately, garnished with sage leaves.

BAKING AND ALL-PURPOSE POTATOES

Maris Piper
A popular, main-crop potato grown in the UK, this has a full flavor and fluffy texture. It is excellent for mashing, baking, roasting, and making French fries.

King Edward
A famous British variety, King Edward has a full flavor and fluffy texture. It is an excellent all-around potato in the kitchen due to its texture being midway between floury and waxy.

The particularly deep-set eyes should be carefully brushed clean of any soil before baking.

Edzell Blue
Bred in Scotland in the 1900s, both the skin and flesh are a deep blue. It is good sautéed, or fried (as fries or potato chips), but can also be roasted or baked. It doesn't boil well, as the flesh disintegrates.

Desiree
A Dutch all-purpose variety, Desiree has a nice flavor and a texture midway between floury and waxy. It is good baked, mashed, roasted, boiled, or fried.

Rooster is best boiled or steamed in its skin to help prevent the floury flesh from disintegrating.

Kennebec
American variety named after a mountain in Maine, Kennebec has a moderately floury texture and a good flavor. It is excellent baked, mashed, or fried.

Rooster
Ireland's favorite potato, the Rooster's floury texture makes it ideal for baking, mashing, roasting, and frying.

Scrubbed and baked, the skin is pleasantly crisp and chewy, and full of flavor.

Vivaldi
A multi-purpose variety with smooth flesh and a distinct buttery flavor. Known as the "butterless" potato, it is lower in calories than other varieties.

Red Duke of York
This sought-after heritage variety is noted for its full-bodied flavor. It is ideal for roasting and baking, but should be boiled with care as the flesh tends to disintegrate.

WAXY POTATOES (CONTINUED)

Linda
This German variety is prized for its exceptional flavor and melting, creamy texture. It is popular with organic farmers.

La Ratte
A small variety widely grown in France, where it is renowned for its superior, chestnut-like flavor, and smooth, firm flesh. Excellent for boiling and salads.

Pink Roseval
A prized French variety with smooth, firm flesh and an appetizing, earthy flavor. It is good boiled or fried, and is ideal for salads.

Nicola
A German variety, Nicola is an ideal salad potato with firm, yellow flesh and a buttery flavor. It is also good in gratins and casseroles.

Bamberger
Unique to northern Bavaria, this acclaimed heritage variety has a nutty flavor and smooth flesh that stays firm after boiling. It is ideal for potato salads and gratins.

Charlotte
A high-quality French variety with smooth, slightly sticky flesh and a fresh, mild flavor. It is best plainly boiled, or steamed in its skin.

Red LaSoda
A mild-flavored variety grown in the US, with a firm, smooth texture. It keeps its shape when boiled, making it ideal for potato salads and gratins.

Congo Blue
This striking heirloom variety has a full-bodied, chestnut-like flavor, and flesh that is waxy but slightly dry. It makes an unusual, colorful addition to a salad.

Recognizable by lavender-flecked purple flesh, Congo Blue keeps its color best when it is steamed rather than boiled.

Anya
A cross between Pink Fir Apple and Désirée, Anya has a nice, earthy flavor and fine-textured flesh. Best boiled, or steamed in its skin, it can also be fried.

GRATIN DAUPHINOIS

A great French regional dish, this gratin is rich with cream and fragrant with garlic and nutmeg.

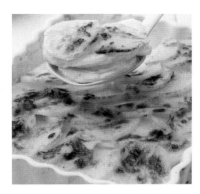

SERVES 4–6

2lb (900g) waxy potatoes

salt and freshly ground black pepper

2 cups heavy cream

1 garlic clove, cut in half

fresh nutmeg

3 tbsp butter, cut into small pieces

1 Preheat the oven to 350°F (180°C). Butter a gratin dish.

2 Peel the potatoes and slice into even rounds about ⅛in (3mm) thick—use a mandolin or a food processor fitted with a slicing blade, if you have one. Rinse the potato slices in cold water, drain, and pat dry with paper towels or a clean kitchen towel.

3 Arrange the potato slices in layers in the prepared dish, seasoning each layer well with salt and pepper.

4 Pour the cream into a saucepan, add the garlic and a good grating of nutmeg, and bring just to a boil. Pour the cream over the potatoes and dot the top with butter.

5 Cover with foil and bake for 1 hour. Remove the foil and continue baking for 30 minutes, or until the potatoes are tender when pierced with a knife and the top is golden. Let stand 10 minutes before serving.

BAKING AND ALL-PURPOSE POTATOES (CONTINUED)

Yukon Gold
*This yellow-fleshed, Canadian
variety is renowned for its
buttery flavor. It has a
starchy, fine-grained texture
and is suitable for mashing,
frying, and roasting.*

Vitelotte Noire
*Also called Truffe de Chine,
this is an ancient variety from
Peru with slightly floury,
purple-and-white marbled
flesh, and a mild flavor.
It keeps its color when
cooked, and is best lightly
boiled or steamed.*

*The smooth, thin skin
adds to the flavor, and
can be left in place when
boiling or roasting.*

Primura
*A large, mild-flavored Dutch variety
that is ideal for baking and roasting.
It keeps its shape when boiled, and
is firm enough for salads.*

CASSAVA

Cassava, also known as manioc and yuca (no relation to yucca), is a thick, club-shaped tropical root with a hairy brown bark or skin and white flesh. Thought to originate in Brazil, it is now grown around the world in many tropical countries—its production in metric tons is only one-third less than that of potatoes. Although mainly used to produce a starch in various forms (e.g. cassava or tapioca flour and pearl tapioca), cassava root can be eaten as a vegetable; it has a bland and buttery flavor. The fresh leaves are also edible.

BUY Being a tropical root, cassava is available year-round. The roots should be hard and the bark clean, with no cracking. Avoid roots with dark interior streaks or dark areas under the skin, or any with soft spots. Look for young, fresh leaves.

STORE Cassava is highly perishable, so ideally should be used right away. If you have to keep it, store the whole root in a cool, dark place for just a few days at most. Once cut, wrap it in plastic wrap and store in the fridge just for a day. Should any darkening occur, cut that part of the root away.

EAT Some varieties contain cyanogenic glucosides, so it is best never to eat cassava root or leaves raw; the glucosides are destroyed by cooking. **Cooked:** After peeling the root, bake, boil, roast, use in a stew, stir-fry, or deep-fry as fries. Boil the leaves as greens, or use as wrappers for food to be baked, or roasted. Use cassava flour as a thickening agent, and pearl tapioca in puddings and other sweet dishes. **Preserved:** Cassava is used in some parts of the world to make beer, and in the Caribbean it is boiled to make a potent dark syrup called "cassareep," which is the basis for the West Indian dish pepperpot.
FLAVOR PAIRINGS Butter, garlic, citrus, cilantro, chile.
CLASSIC RECIPES Tapioca pudding; *sancocho*; pepperpot.

*The flesh starts to shred if boiled
vigorously, so to cook, put peeled
chunks or slices into cold water,
slowly bring to a boil, and
simmer gently.*

SWEET POTATO

Sweet potatoes are not related to ordinary potatoes, nor to yams, with which they are sometimes confused. Native to Central America, they have become a staple carbohydrate food source all over the world, and are now widely cultivated in the tropics and warm, temperate regions. There are many varieties of sweet potato, with varying skin and flesh color. After cooking, orange-fleshed varieties are sweet, moist, and creamy; those with white or pale yellow flesh have a drier, firmer texture.

🛒 **BUY** Late summer and fall are the peak season for sweet potatoes in temperate regions; in the tropics, they are available year-round. The best tubers are firm, fat, and unblemished. They should feel heavy for their size.

📦 **STORE** They can be kept for up to 10 days at cool room temperature, never in the fridge where the cold will hasten their loss of quality.

⦿ **EAT** Cooked: Boil, steam, bake, roast, deep-fry as French fries, or tempura, or sauté. Puréed orange-fleshed sweet potatoes are also widely used in cakes, breads, and muffins, as well as in pies, puddings, and custards. White-fleshed varieties of sweet potato are particularly favored in Asia, where they are used like white potatoes. Preserved: Slices are dried or candied in many parts of the world.

FLAVOR PAIRINGS Apples, brown sugar, molasses, ginger, maple syrup, honey, citrus, chile, hickory nuts, nutmeg, thyme.

CLASSIC RECIPES Sweet potato chips; sweet potato pie; *dulce de camote*.

Boniato
Popular in the Caribbean, Boniato, also known as Cuban sweet potato, is less sweet and moist than other varieties. The flesh has a nice, fluffy texture that mashes and bakes well.

Scrubbed and baked, the skin is pleasantly crunchy.

Jewel
With typically sweet, moist flesh, this orange-fleshed variety lends itself to baking, boiling, mashing, and roasting. It can also be used in cakes and pies.

SWEET POTATO CHIPS

Potato chips were invented in 1850s New York. Those made with sweet potatoes and other root vegetables are now becoming modern classics.

oil for deep-frying

1 lb (450g) sweet potatoes

sea salt (optional)

1 Heat the oil in a deep pan or deep-fryer to 350°F (180°C). Meanwhile, peel the sweet potatoes and slice very thinly using a mandolin or food processor fitted with a fine slicing blade.

2 When the oil is hot (you can test the temperature by dropping in a slice of potato: it should rise to the surface and start sizzling immediately), add a small batch of the potato slices, using a slotted spoon or frying basket to lower them into the oil.

3 Fry for 1–2 minutes, or until crisp and lightly golden brown on both sides. Do not overcook. Lift the sweet potato chips out of the oil and drain on paper towels. Repeat with the remaining sweet potato slices. Before serving, sprinkle with salt, if you like.

JERUSALEM ARTICHOKE

Despite the name, the Jerusalem artichoke is not an artichoke: it is a species of sunflower native to North America (the first European explorers found the Native Americans cultivating these tubers, which had a taste of artichoke). And they have nothing to do with Jerusalem—in Italian they are called *girasole*, which seems to have sounded enough like Jerusalem to have donated the moniker. To add to the confusion, the often knobby, bulbous tubers are sometimes also known as sunchoke in the US and *topinambour* in France. Jerusalem artichokes grow easily in temperate zones around the world. Their flavor is mildly sweet, nutty, and earthy; when raw the texture is crunchy, softening when cooked.

🛒 **BUY** Winter and early spring are the peak seasons for these tubers. They should be firm and fresh-looking, without tears or pitting.

📦 **STORE** They will store well in a paper bag in the crisper of the fridge for 2–3 weeks.

⦿ **EAT** These tubers, raw or cooked, can be hard to digest. Fresh: Slice raw for crudités, or grate or chop into salads. Cooked: Boil, steam, bake (like potatoes) or use in a gratin. Roast, stir-fry, sauté, or deep-fry as fries or chips. Purée for soup. Preserved: Pickle.

FLAVOR PAIRINGS Béchamel and hollandaise sauces, butter, cream, ginger, lemon, scallions.

CLASSIC RECIPES Palestine soup; *topinambours en daube*.

The skin does not need peeling except for aesthetic reasons. Scrub well under running water and remove any small knobs.

SQUASH

Native to Mexico and Central America, squashes were cultivated for at least 7,000 years before the European discovery of the New World. Now grown in tropical and warm, temperate regions around the world, squashes come in many different colors, shapes, and sizes. SUMMER SQUASH are harvested young, before their skins harden and seeds mature. They have a moist texture and mild flavor.
WINTER SQUASH are harvested in the fall and because of their maturity can be stored through the winter. The flesh is more dense and can have a rich, robust sweetness.

BUY Although many varieties are available year-round, as the names indicate summer squash is best in summer, winter squash in fall and winter. For preference, choose small, young summer squash, such as 6–8in (15–20cm) zucchini, as they will be less watery. Avoid squash with gouges, nicks, soft spots, or cuts.
Make sure the hard skin of winter squash has no mold.

STORE Summer squash should be used as soon as possible; keep it in a plastic bag in the fridge for no more than 2 days. Whole winter squash will store well for several weeks in a cool room on a bed of newspaper; if cut, wrap and store it in the fridge.

EAT Summer squashes can be eaten in their entirety, unless the seeds have hardened. Remove the tough skin of winter squash before or after cooking, as well as the central seeds and fibers. **Fresh:** Tender summer squash can be grated or shaved into ribbons for a salad. **Cooked:** Steam, sauté, deep-fry as tempura, stuff and bake, roast, or use in soups and stews; winter squash can also be boiled. Grated summer squash is added to cake and muffin batters; puréed winter squash to pie fillings and custards.

The flowers of summer squash, in particular those of zucchini, are also eaten; they are a delicacy when stuffed, coated in a light batter, and deep-fried.
Preserved: Pickle summer squash. Roast and salt hulled seeds from winter squash such as pumpkin and butternut. Pumpkin is also candied to be eaten as a sweetmeat.
FLAVOR PAIRINGS (summer squash) Bacon, Parmesan, basil, curry, cinnamon, and olive oil; (winter squash) Cheddar, Gruyère, apples, pears, garlic, ginger, maple syrup, sage, thyme.
CLASSIC RECIPES Ratatouille; pumpkin pie; *tortino di zucchine; tortelli di zucca;* pumpkin tart; stuffed zuccini flowers; *zuccini escabeche; Basque talos; Asturian tortos.*

SUMMER SQUASH

Yellow zucchini
Like the green varieties, yellow zucchini has a mild, faintly mushroomy flavor, with tender flesh and skin. Mix it with green zucchini for a colorful summer dish.

Choose firm, young fruit with glossy skin. The skin adds flavor and texture, and does not need peeling.

Green zucchini
Often called green squash, zucchini is identical in flavor and texture to yellow varieties. Small zucchini are superior to large ones, which tend to be fibrous and bland.

The edible flowers are fragile, so handle with care when preparing. Snip off the internal stamen before stuffing.

Round summer squash
Related to the elongated zucchini, round squash have a similar mild flavor. Their shape makes them ideal for halving and stuffing. Small ones can be stir-fried or steamed whole.

If the skin is slightly fuzzy, a quick dip in cold water will remove any clinging dirt.

Pattypan squash
These flattened, scallop-edged squash, which come in yellow, green, or white, have thin skin and tender flesh. The greater ratio of skin to flesh improves the overall flavor and texture.

Cocozelle
This Italian striped heirloom squash has a stronger flavor than most, and an almost buttery, smooth texture. It holds its shape well when sliced and sautéed.

Tondo di Nizza
Identifiable by its mottled pale green stripes, this round variety of summer squash has a subtle but satisfyingly meaty flavor. It is at its best when only slightly larger than a golf ball.

Check the cut ends: they should be moist and freshly cut. Trim the stalk before cooking.

Crookneck summer squash
Crookneck squash has tender skin, a firm texture, and a clean, lemony flavor. If the bulbous end is large, halve lengthwise before cutting into chunks, so that it cooks evenly.

CLASSIC RECIPE

RATATOUILLE

This popular Southern Mediterranean dish is delicious hot or cold, drizzled with fruity olive oil.

SERVES 4

4 tbsp olive oil
1 onion, chopped
1 garlic clove, chopped
1 zucchini, sliced
1 small eggplant, about 8oz (225g), cut into 1in (2.5cm) cubes
1 red bell pepper, cored, seeded, and cut into 1in (2.5cm) pieces
½ cup vegetable stock
2 ripe beefsteak tomatoes, peeled and chopped, or 1 x 14.5 oz (400g) can chopped tomatoes
2 tsp chopped fresh oregano, plus 2–3 sprigs of leaves to garnish
salt and freshly ground black pepper

1 Heat the oil in a large flameproof casserole over medium heat. Add the onion and cook for 5 minutes, or until soft and translucent. Stir in the garlic, zucchini, eggplant, and red pepper. Cook for another 5 minutes, stirring frequently.

2 Add the stock, tomatoes with their juice, and the chopped oregano. Bring to a boil, then reduce the heat to low and partially cover the pan. Cook, stirring occasionally, until the vegetables are tender.

3 Season to taste with salt and pepper. Spoon the ratatouille into a serving dish and serve immediately, garnished with oregano sprigs; or allow to cool and then refrigerate to serve cold.

WINTER SQUASH

Pumpkin
Pumpkins are usually more fibrous and watery than other squash. If sold in pieces, use within a few days—the flesh is more perishable once cut.

Spaghetti squash
A mellow-tasting squash that can be orange or yellow` in color, with the orange variety commonly referred to as orangetti. The flesh separates into long spaghetti-like strands as it cooks. Use as spaghetti, or in salads, soups, and casseroles.

Delicata squash
Also known as sweet potato squash, this variety is renowned for its exceptionally smooth, moist, honey-flavored flesh. Ideal for pumpkin pie and cakes.

Turban squash
A distinctively shaped variety with bland, slightly dry, yellow-orange flesh. The internal cavity is larger than most winter squash, so there is correspondingly less flesh.

Red Kuri squash
This Japanese variety has smooth, buttery flesh and a rich, sweet flavor reminiscent of chestnuts. It is very good in soups, and in sweet dishes, too.

Make sure winter squashes have 2in (5cm) of dried stalk attached, or they won't keep for more than a few weeks before turning soft.

The bottom half can be cut off and hollowed out for stuffing, or used as a striking bowl for soup.

Bitter melon
The juicy but bitter flesh of this winter squash is made more palatable by lightly blanching, then sprinkling with salt and leaving for 30 minutes before cooking. Discard the pulp and seeds first.

Crown Prince
A renowned variety of winter squash with tender, smooth-textured, sweet flesh. It is ideal roasted and puréed, then used in soups and cakes, or as a ravioli filling.

It is easier to scoop out the flesh after roasting, because the tough, pale blue-grey skin is hard to peel off.

Calabash
This tropical variety, also known as bottle gourd squash, has a nutty flavor and a firmer texture than other winter squash. Sliced or chopped, it is good in curries and stir-fries.

Winter melon
When young, the squash has fuzzy, green skin, and thick, white, sweetish flesh. It is traditionally used in China to make a popular soup.

As winter melon matures, the skin develops a waxy coating that enables it to be kept for several months.

The vibrantly colored pumpkin's nutty sweetness is ideal for warming soups, curries, and stews.

PUMPKIN PIE

Butternut squash makes a pie filling with a richer flavor and smoother texture than pumpkin. Serve with vanilla ice cream or brandy butter.

SERVES 8

1 large or 2 small butternut squash (about 4lb/1.8kg total)
3 eggs, separated
1½ cups heavy cream
6 tbsp light soft brown sugar
2 tbsp granulated sugar
⅔ cup golden syrup, or light corn syrup
2 tbsp molasses or black treacle
1 tsp ground cinnamon
¼ tsp each ground cloves, nutmeg, allspice, and ginger
1 tsp vanilla extract
½ tsp salt
1 x 9in (23cm) unbaked pie pastry shell, 2in (5cm) deep

1 Preheat the oven to 350°F (180°C). Cut the squash in half and remove the seeds. Place cut-side up in a shallow roasting pan with a little water in the bottom. Bake for 1–1½ hours, or until the squash is soft and breaking apart.

2 Remove the squash from the oven and reduce the temperature to 325°F (160°C). Scoop out the flesh, discarding the skin and any burnt spots, and measure 1lb (450g) into a large bowl.

3 Add the egg yolks, cream, sugars, syrup, molasses or treacle, spices, vanilla, and salt. Beat well with a whisk, or blend in a food processor, until smooth.

4 In another bowl, beat the egg whites until they form soft peaks. Fold gently into the squash mixture. Spoon into the pie shell, then bake for about 1½ hours or until a knife inserted in the center of the filling comes out clean. Allow the pie to cool before serving with the ice cream or brandy butter.

WINTER SQUASH (CONTINUED)

PREPARING WINTER SQUASH

The seeds and fibers need to be removed, as well as the hard skin.

1 Holding the squash firmly on the chopping board, cut in half, cutting from the stalk end directly through the core end. You will need a large, sharp knife to do this. **2** With a spoon or a small ice cream scoop, remove the seeds and fibers from each squash half; discard these. **3** If removing the skin before cooking, cut the squash into sections, then peel the sections using a vegetable peeler or sharp knife. To remove the skin after cooking, peel it off with the help of a small knife, or just scrape the flesh from the skin with a large spoon.

Butternut squash

One of the more common varieties of winter squash, butternut has smooth, dense flesh that becomes sweet and nutty when baked or steamed. The cavity can be stuffed.

The tough skin is hard to remove. It is best to cut the squash into chunks before peeling with a small knife.

Gourds

These small, hard squashes come in attractive shapes and sizes. They are mostly used for decoration since the flesh is sparse and of varying quality.

Slice off the top third and use as a lid to protect the contents when baking stuffed.

Jack Be Little

An attractive miniature pumpkin, the Jack Be Little has yellow-orange, very sweet flesh with an agreeably sticky texture. It is good hollowed out for stuffing and baking whole.

Acorn squash
A mild-flavored squash, lightly sweet, with firm, yellow-orange flesh, this is best baked with a few tablespoons of butter and some brown sugar in the cavity.

Broad ribs running from stalk to tip make this squash easy to recognize.

The skin is thick and hard to cut through. It's easier to remove after roasting the squash in large segments.

Kabocha
Native to New Zealand, the kabocha squash has dense, smooth-textured, slightly dry flesh. The flavor is reminiscent of chestnuts, with just a hint of sweetness.

The flesh is dense enough to be sliced thinly or cut into small cubes without disintegrating during cooking.

Vegetable marrow
An oversized, mature zucchini, the vegetable marrow—also called marrow squash—has a rather watery texture and bland flavor that is improved by savory stuffings and spicy seasonings.

CUCUMBER

There is evidence that cucumbers, thought to be native to southern India, were cultivated in prehistoric times. The wild ones are small and bitter, and people have been trying—successfully of late—to make them bigger and sweeter ever since. Cucumbers will thrive wherever there's plenty of hot weather and water, from the tropics to the temperate regions around the world, varying in their length and girth, and the color and texture of their skin. Because of their high water content, the pleasantly crisp flesh is refreshing.

🔒 **BUY** The heat of midsummer is the best season for cucumbers. Young cucumbers with soft, easy-to-eat seeds are firm when squeezed, and green all over with no yellow patches.

📦 **STORE** Keep in a plastic bag in the crisper of the fridge for no more than a week. Once cut, wrap tightly in plastic wrap, including the cut end, and use within 2–3 days.

⚫ **EAT** Garden cucumbers need to be peeled, as do pickling cucumbers if eaten fresh (the skin is left on for pickling). Smooth-skinned varieties do not. **Fresh:** Cut into sticks for crudités and dipping, or use in salads. **Cooked:** Steam, simmer, or sauté; or hollow out, stuff, and bake. **Preserved:** Pickle or preserve in salt.

FLAVOR PAIRINGS Anchovies, cream cheese, feta cheese, yogurt, sour cream, dill, fennel, mint, tomatoes.

CLASSIC RECIPES *Raita*; Greek salad; *tzatziki*; dill pickled cucumbers; gazpacho; cucumber finger sandwiches.

PREPARING CUCUMBER

You can hollow out halves to fill with a savory mixture and bake. Or cut into small, neat pieces.

1 *Trim top and bottom.* **2** *Using a vegetable peeler, peel away the green skin.* **3** *Cut the cucumber in half and scoop out the watery seeds.* **4** *Slice or dice as required.*

Armenian cucumber
Technically a melon, this extra-long variety, also known as the Snake cucumber, has very thin, edible skin with no trace of bitterness. It is at its best when no more than 12–15in (30–38cm) in length.

Pickling cucumber
Pickling cucumbers are typically stubby in shape with solid, crisp flesh that keeps its texture when pickled. They are also good eaten raw.

Remove the peel if eating pickling cucumbers raw. It is bitter and indigestible.

Garden cucumber
Shorter and fatter in shape, garden cucumbers have a mild flavor and crisp, slightly dry, pristine white flesh. Peel before use.

Carosello Barese
This rare heirloom variety from Puglia in Italy has a peach-like, fuzzy skin, which is best peeled. The flesh is crisp with a mild cucumber flavor.

Garden cucumbers contain small seeds that sometimes taste bitter. It is best to remove them before eating.

Burpless cucumber
Reputed not to cause digestive upsets, this British slicing cucumber is valued for its thin, edible skin and mildly flavored, crisp flesh.

Instead of seeds, English cucumbers have a jelly-like structure in the middle.

Lebanese cucumber
These typically small Middle Eastern fruits have thin, edible skin, undeveloped seeds, and dense, crisp flesh with a distinctive cucumber flavor.

Removing evenly spaced strips of peel along the length will create an attractive profile to cucumber slices.

English cucumber
Slicing cucumbers have typically thin, non-bitter skin, and undeveloped seeds. The crisp, mildly flavored flesh is ideal for sandwiches and salads.

RAITA

A cooling, yogurt-based dipping sauce, traditionally served with most Indian meals.

MAKES 1¼ CUPS

1 English (hothouse) cucumber, peeled
½ tsp salt
½ tsp cumin seeds, lightly toasted
½ cup full-fat plain yogurt
½ tsp sugar
1 garlic clove, crushed through a press
1 tbsp chopped mint
1 tbsp chopped cilantro

1 Grate the cucumber into a bowl. Add the salt and set aside for 1 hour.

2 Squeeze out as much liquid from the cucumber as possible.

3 Crush the cumin seeds into a fine powder. Transfer to a bowl and stir in the cucumber, yogurt, sugar, garlic, mint, and cilantro. Refrigerate for at least 1 hour, or up to 24 hours.

CHAYOTE

This pear-shaped member of the gourd family, native to Mexico and Central America, has many names, including mirliton, christophene, choco, pepinella, and custard marrow. It is grown and used around the world, from the Caribbean to Europe to Asia to North and South America. Its usefulness in widely varying cuisines derives from its mild flavor and texture, combining elements of summer squash, cucumber, and kohlrabi. The smooth skin is most commonly light green and cream, with several clearly defined grooves down its length; the flesh is creamy white.

BUY Chayotes are found in markets throughout the year, coming, as they do, from tropical farms. Look for small, firm fruits that feel heavy in the hand, with no cuts, pits, or soft, brown areas.

STORE Place in paper bags rolled up tightly and store in the crisper of the fridge; they will keep for several weeks.

EAT You can eat the skin of tender, young chayotes; peel older ones before or after cooking. When cut, the flesh exudes a slippery substance that can cause irritation. **Fresh:** Chayote is usually cooked, but can be grated raw into salads and salsas. **Cooked:** All methods suitable for summer squash will work well for chayote. Steam, sauté, fry, grill, bake (in chunks or halved and stuffed), or use for soup. Young shoots and flowers and starchy tuberous roots are also eaten. **Preserved:** Pickle or use in chutneys. **FLAVOR PAIRINGS** Fish, shellfish, cheese, garlic, onion, chiles. **CLASSIC RECIPE** Chayotes con natas.

The seed has a nutty flavor and can be cooked with the flesh.

FRENCH ONION SOUP

This Parisian classic is given extra punch with a spoonful of brandy in every bowl. Serve it piping hot.

SERVES 4

2 tbsp butter

1 tbsp sunflower or vegetable oil

1½lb (675g) yellow onions, thinly sliced

1 tsp sugar

salt and freshly ground black pepper

½ cup dry red wine

2 tbsp all-purpose flour

6 cups hot beef stock

4 tbsp brandy

8 baguette slices, toasted

1 garlic clove, cut in half

1 cup shredded Gruyère or Emmental cheese

1 In a large, heavy pot or flameproof casserole, melt the butter in the oil over low heat. Add the onions and sugar and stir to coat well. Season with salt and freshly ground black pepper, then press a piece of damp parchment or wax paper on top of the onions. Cook, uncovered, lifting the paper occasionally to stir, for 40 minutes or until they are a deep golden brown color. Watch carefully to be sure the onions do not burn.

2 Discard the paper and stir in the wine. Increase the heat to medium and stir for 5 minutes to glaze the onions. Add the flour and stir for 2 minutes. Pour in the stock and bring to a boil. Reduce the heat to low, cover, and simmer for 30 minutes. Taste and season with salt and freshly ground black pepper, if necessary.

3 Preheat the broiler to its highest setting. Divide the hot soup among 4 flameproof bowls and stir 1 tbsp of brandy into each. Rub the toasted baguette with the cut garlic and place 2 slices in each bowl. Sprinkle with the cheese and broil on the upper rack of the oven for 2–3 minutes, until the cheese is golden. Serve at once.

ONION

The onion evolved across a broad swath of Central or Western Asia and the Middle East. From the cold north to the warm south, the world's temperate zones are still home to much of the world's onion cultivation. Types range in color from white through yellow and green to red and purple, from globe-shaped to narrow and pencil thin, and from sweet to pungent. Eaten raw, onions vary from mild to very pungent and biting; when cooked they may be gently savory or pleasantly sweet. Wild onions, ubiquitous in the temperate zones, are usually small and pungent in both aroma and flavor.

🛒 **BUY** Onions are available year-round, but late summer through winter into spring are their best seasons. They should be firm when squeezed, with their papery outer leaves still on, even if they are broken. Pungent yellow, white, and red onions should have small, tight necks; sweet onions have looser necks and do not store as well. Scallions, which are young onions usually grown as a spring crop and variously known as green onions, spring onions, bunching onions, salad onions, cebolleta, calçots, and other names, should have bright green tops. Avoid white onions with green shoulders— they are old. All onions should smell clean.

🗄 **STORE** Pungent yellow, white, and red onions, also called storage onions, keep well in a mesh bag in a cool, dark place. Both sweet onions and scallion varieties should be used as soon as possible, but can be stored in the fridge for a week or two—wrap sweet onions individually in paper towels inside a paper bag; keep scallions in an open plastic bag.

🍽 **EAT** Fresh: Add scallion to salads or use as a garnish. Both pungent and sweet onion slices can top a sandwich or hamburger, or add texture to a salad. **Cooked:** Savvy cooks know that every good meal begins by chopping an onion. With slight variations, onions

can be boiled, steamed, baked, fried, braised, barbecued, roasted, sautéed, deep-fried, or stir-fried. **Preserved:** Onions, especially small white onions, make good pickles.

FLAVOR PAIRINGS Bacon, liver, lamb, cheese, Parmesan cheese, eggs, mushrooms, tomatoes, peas, thyme, parsley, bay leaves, oranges, balsamic vinegar.

CLASSIC RECIPES French onion soup; stuffed onion; onion bhajis; soubise; pissaladière; liver and onions; fried onion rings; Alsatian onion tart.

PREPARING ONIONS

You can dice all round onion varieties in the same way. Keep the root end on, so you have something to hold while slicing.

1 Trim the stalk end and peel the onion, then cut in half lengthwise. Place one half cut-side down and make cuts vertically toward and almost through the root end. Make a couple of horizontal slices toward the root end. **2** Cut vertically again, at right angles to the original slices, which will result in perfect dice.

Yellow onion
The workhorse of the kitchen, the pungent yellow onion is used in numerous savory dishes, either raw, fried, braised, stewed, boiled, or roasted.

White onion
White onions are often intensely pungent eaten raw, but become milder once cooked. With their crisp, juicy texture, they are ideal for batter-dipped, fried onion rings.

Sweet red onion
The juicy crimson and white flesh is noticeably sweet, although pungent when raw. Roasting caramelizes the juices and mellows the flavor.

Scallion
Harvested while young and slender, scallions have crisp, straight stems and a mildly pungent flavor. They add zest to salads and stir-fries.

Green onion
Resembling a clump of miniature leeks, these are mildly flavored and delicious raw as a crudité or in salads. The hollow green stems can be sliced and used as a garnish.

Torpedo onion
A spindle-shaped variety, torpedo onions are mildly flavored and juicy. They contain more water than regular yellow onions, and therefore cannot be stored as long.

Calçot
A speciality from the Catalan region of Spain, calçots resemble young leeks. They are traditionally grilled until blackened and served with a piquant sauce.

CLASSIC RECIPE

ONION BHAJIS

These crisp vegetable fritters are made with chickpea flour, also known as gram flour or besan, which can be found in many Indian food shops and Middle Eastern markets.

SERVES 4

1 ½ cups chopped onions

¾ cup chickpea flour

2 tsp cumin seeds

1 tsp ground coriander

½ tsp turmeric

1 green or red jalapeño or other hot chile pepper, seeded and minced

vegetable oil, for frying

1 In a large bowl, mix together the onions, chickpea flour, cumin seeds, coriander, turmeric, and chile. Add enough cold water (about ½ cup) to make a thick batter.

2 Pour enough oil into a large, deep saucepan to reach 2in (5cm) up the sides, and heat to 350°F (180°C). Working in batches, add spoonfuls of batter (about the size of golf balls) to the oil. Deep-fry about 3 minutes, turning occasionally, until just golden.

3 Using a slotted spoon, transfer the bhajis to paper towels to drain.

4 Just before serving, return the bhajis to the hot oil and deep-fry again until crisp and golden-brown. Drain briefly on paper towels and serve hot.

ONION (CONTINUED)

Tree onion
Named after its habit of producing bulblets from the top of a tall stem, tree onions, also called top onions, are remarkably pungent. They make a flavorful addition to salads, soups, or the pickle jar.

Finely chopped bulblets come in handy when only a small amount of onion is needed to add flavor to a dish.

Ramp
Also known as ramps, wild garlic, or wild onion, this is found in the wild in parts of North America. The leaves smell strongly of garlic when crushed, and are used in the same way as garlic or scallions.

Pearl onion
Harvested when tiny, pearl onions have a mildly sweet flavor and crunchy texture. They are often used as a garnish or added to stews, or pickled for use as a cocktail onion.

Lampascioni
These slightly bitter, tiny wild onions are considered a delicacy in southern Italy. They are good pickled in vinegar, or added to omelets and salads.

Ramsons
Found in the wild in Britain in late spring, ramsons, also known as rampion, give off a strong garlic smell when crushed, hence their other names, wild garlic and bear's garlic. The leaves make a verdant soup or tasty pesto, and are also good added to salads and stir-fries.

SHALLOT

Like its cousin, the onion, the shallot originated in Western or Central Asia. Shallots are grown almost everywhere now, across Southeast Asia and Western Europe. Rather than being one bulb, like the onion, a shallot consists of a head of two or three individual bulbs or cloves. Their ski is generally coppery and the fine flesh flushed with fuchsia or bluish grey. In flavor, they are onion-like, although sweeter and more complex, but still pungent.

BUY Fall and winter are the peak seasons for shallots. They should be firm and dry, with no soft spots, sprouting, or oniony smell.

STORE Keep shallots in a cool, dark, dry basket with air circulation, never in the fridge, for up to 2 months.

EAT Fresh: Grate into salads, or finely slice to top sandwiches. Serve diced with pickled or creamed fish. **Cooked:** Roast whole, peeled shallots; braise for sauces; bake in a gratin; or sauté to glaze. **Preserved:** Pickle whole.

FLAVOR PAIRINGS Mushrooms, red wine, parsley, sorrel, thyme.
CLASSIC RECIPES Béarnaise sauce; bordelaise sauce; *beurre blanc.*

French grey shallot
Beloved of chefs, the bulbs have an exceptional flavor—full-bodied, sweet, and piquant. They impart a rich, pervasive flavor to many classic French dishes.

Banana shallot
These juicy, single-cloved shallots, also called echalion shallots, provide sweet, subtle flavor to stews, braises, and soups. They are good halved lengthwise, then roasted or sautéed until golden.

LEEK

Leeks are probably descendants of the wild onion found all over Europe. They grow well in temperate zones around the world, particularly in the cooler regions of the north. The long, cylindrical stems, consisting of many layers of tightly wrapped leaves, are white where they have been earthed up and green where exposed to light. When cooked, leeks have a mild flavor, more restrained than other members of the onion family, but they are just as pungent raw.

BUY The best season is from early fall to the end of winter. Look for leeks with a long run of white between the roots and the green tops. Roots should not be dried out. Quality leeks will have some "give" when bent: stiff leeks are tough leeks. Choose straight, cylindrical leeks rather than those starting to form a bulbous base.

STORE Leeks need isolation in the fridge, so store them unwashed and wrapped in a sealed plastic bag in the crisper for up to a week.

EAT Fresh: Cut crosswise into very thin rings for salads. **Cooked:** Boil, steam, sauté, or stir-fry slices; braise or grill whole or split. Use in soups, stews, and savory pie fillings.

FLAVOR PAIRINGS Fish, cream, butter, cheese, peas, parsley, potatoes, lemon, olive oil.

CLASSIC RECIPES Vichyssoise; cock-a-leekie; cawl mamigu; frittata de prasa.

Baby leek
A delicacy in early fall, baby leeks are tender enough to eat thinly sliced in a salad. They also make a tasty topping for pizzas and savory tarts, and are good grilled.

The coarse outer leaves need not be wasted. Chop them roughly and add to the pot.

Round red shallot
Though they resemble miniature onions, these shallots have a deliciously sweet, flowery flavor that does not overwhelm. They form a rich flavor base for numerous sauces.

Leek
Leeks range from pencil thin to fat-shanked giants. They add meaty texture and flavor to all kinds of dishes. Unlike the onion, they do not cause tears when sliced.

VICHYSSOISE

Despite its French name, this silky smooth, cold soup actually comes from the US. It is also delicious served hot— simply add the cream and chives at the end of cooking.

SERVES 4

2 tbsp butter

3 large leeks (white parts only), thinly sliced

2 russet or other floury baking potatoes, about 6oz (175g) in total, peeled and chopped

1 celery rib, coarsely chopped

4 cups hot vegetable stock

salt and freshly ground black pepper

½ cup heavy cream, plus extra to garnish

2 tbsp finely chopped chives

1 Melt the butter in a heavy pot over medium heat, add the leeks, and stir to coat well. Press a circle of damp parchment or wax paper on top of them, cover with a lid, and cook, shaking the pan gently from time to time, for 15 minutes or until they are soft and golden. Discard the paper.

2 Stir in the potatoes, celery, and stock; then season with salt and pepper. Bring to a boil, stirring all the time, then cover with a lid and simmer for 30 minutes or until the vegetables are tender. Stir in the ½ cup cream and cook over low heat for 1 minute.

3 Remove the pan from the heat and leave to cool slightly, then, working in batches, process the soup in a blender until very smooth. Season to taste with salt and pepper, then chill for at least 3 hours. To serve, pour into bowls, stir a little cream into each, then sprinkle with the chives and more freshly ground black pepper.

FRESH BEANS

Before the discovery of the New World, the only pulses available to people in Europe were broad or fava beans. It didn't take long for New World beans to be accepted. Today they are grown in temperate zones everywhere and there are hundreds of types, some with edible pods that are eaten in their entirety and others that are removed from the pods for eating. The latter—so-called shell or shelling beans—are in fact fresh versions of beans commonly available dried.

⊙ **BUY** Early summer through fall is the best season for buying fresh beans. Those with edible pods should be bright green and firm: bend one and it should snap cleanly in half. Older beans, which will be dull and limp, are more likely to be tough.

▣ **STORE** Fresh, edible-podded beans and shell beans should be used as soon after purchase as possible, but if you need to store them, keep them in a plastic bag in the fridge for 1–2 days at most. Fresh beans freeze well.

⊙ **EAT** Cooked: Steam or boil edible-podded beans and shell beans. Preserved: Pickle.
FLAVOR PAIRINGS Bacon, quail, béchamel sauce, anchovies, almonds, mushrooms, tomatoes, onions, garlic, Parmesan cheese, oregano, parsley.
CLASSIC RECIPES Fava bean dip; succotash; *loubieh bizeit*; *haricots verts à la lyonnaise*; *birnen*; *bohnen und speck*.

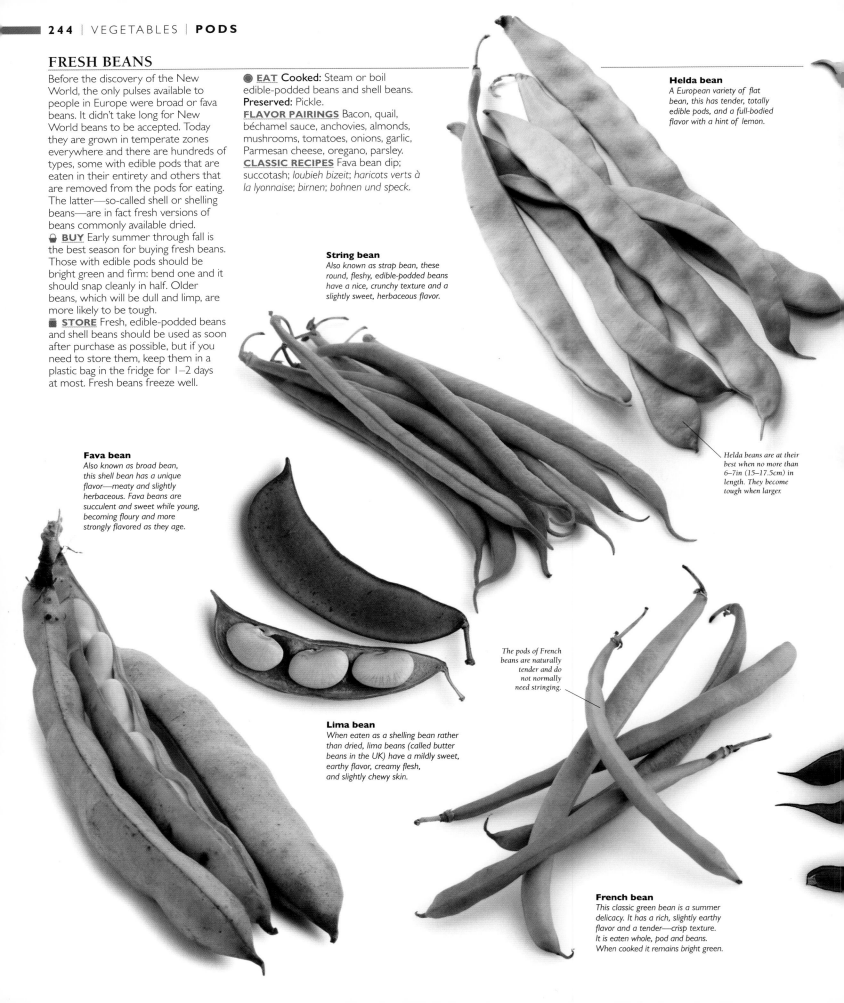

Helda bean
A European variety of flat bean, this has tender, totally edible pods, and a full-bodied flavor with a hint of lemon.

Helda beans are at their best when no more than 6–7in (15–17.5cm) in length. They become tough when larger.

String bean
Also known as strap bean, these round, fleshy, edible-podded beans have a nice, crunchy texture and a slightly sweet, herbaceous flavor.

Fava bean
Also known as broad bean, this shell bean has a unique flavor—meaty and slightly herbaceous. Fava beans are succulent and sweet while young, becoming floury and more strongly flavored as they age.

Lima bean
When eaten as a shelling bean rather than dried, lima beans (called butter beans in the UK) have a mildly sweet, earthy flavor, creamy flesh, and slightly chewy skin.

The pods of French beans are naturally tender and do not normally need stringing.

French bean
This classic green bean is a summer delicacy. It has a rich, slightly earthy flavor and a tender—crisp texture. It is eaten whole, pod and beans. When cooked it remains bright green.

Yellow Wax bean
The edible-podded variety Nugget has an exceptionally rich, buttery flavor and a tender—crisp texture.

The tips of the four winged edges should be shaved off with a swivel peeler, as they can be tough.

Flageolet bean
A well-known shelling variety from southern France, flageolets are normally dried. When cooked while still fresh, they have a mild flavor and creamy texture.

Winged bean
A tropical variety, the winged bean, or asparagus pea, has completely edible pods and seeds. It has a slightly chewy texture and a delicious, asparagus-like flavor.

FAVA BEAN DIP

This Greek dip is great picnic food. Serve with flatbread and hard-boiled eggs, or on bruschetta.

SERVES 8

| 1½lbs (750g) fresh fava beans |
| 3 tbsp olive oil |
| 1 small yellow onion, finely chopped |
| salt and freshly ground black pepper |
| 1 x 15oz (400g) can cannellini beans, drained and rinsed |
| 1 tbsp chopped fresh dill |
| 2 scallions, thinly sliced |

1 Remove the fava beans from their pods, then slip off the skins. Set aside.

2 Heat the oil in a heavy saucepan over low heat. Add the chopped onion and cook gently for about 5 minutes, or until soft and translucent.

3 Add the fava beans and cook for 10–15 minutes, stirring occasionally. Add 2 cups water, season with salt and pepper, and partially cover the pan with a lid. Bring to a gentle simmer and cook for 25 minutes, mashing the beans a little during this time. Drain and allow to cool.

4 Put the cooled fava bean mixture in a blender or food processor. Add the cannellini beans, dill, and scallions, and process to a chunky purée. Season with salt and pepper.

There is no need to trim off the tender tips.

Purple haricot bean
These edible-podded, stringless beans are smooth-textured and crisp, with a pleasantly earthy, flavor. They become dark green once cooked.

Purple bean
A purple variety of French bean, this has a pleasant, tender—crisp texture and a fresh, lemony flavor. The beans lose their purple color when cooked, reverting to a deep green.

FRESH BEANS (CONTINUED)

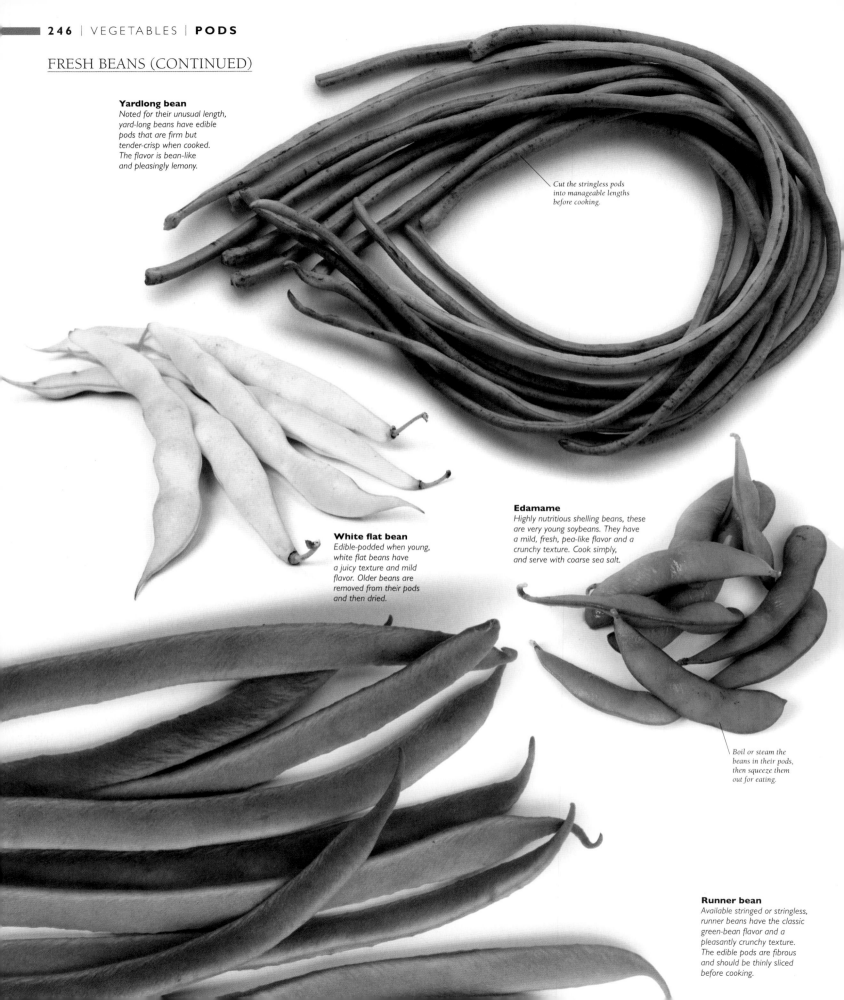

Yardlong bean
Noted for their unusual length,
yard-long beans have edible
pods that are firm but
tender-crisp when cooked.
The flavor is bean-like
and pleasingly lemony.

*Cut the stringless pods
into manageable lengths
before cooking.*

White flat bean
Edible-podded when young,
white flat beans have
a juicy texture and mild
flavor. Older beans are
removed from their pods
and then dried.

Edamame
Highly nutritious shelling beans, these
are very young soybeans. They have
a mild, fresh, pea-like flavor and a
crunchy texture. Cook simply,
and serve with coarse sea salt.

*Boil or steam the
beans in their pods,
then squeeze them
out for eating.*

Runner bean
Available stringed or stringless,
runner beans have the classic
green-bean flavor and a
pleasantly crunchy texture.
The edible pods are fibrous
and should be thinly sliced
before cooking.

...

PEAS

Native to Turkey, Syria, and Jordan, garden or green peas are now grown in temperate regions around the world. From the garden pea, which is removed from its pod for eating, have been bred two varieties with tender edible pods: snow peas and sugar snap peas. Picked straight from the vine, garden peas are wonderfully sweet, although they lose sweetness rapidly as they are stored. Sugar snap peas and snow peas have a more herbaceous flavor than garden peas; sugar snaps are also deliciously sweet.

BUY All peas are sweetest and most prolific in late spring, although cool-weather fall crops are also grown. Freshness is of the essence. Pods should be an even green, with no brown, yellow, or decaying spots. With garden peas, look for plump peas that are not quite touching in the pod; avoid fat pods with oversized peas.

Snow peas and sugar snap peas should be crisp and moist.

STORE Fresh peas should be used as soon as possible to preserve their sweetness. Keep them in a closed plastic bag in the fridge for no more than 1–2 days. For longer storage, blanch and freeze.

EAT Fresh: Garden peas from just picked pods make great eating out of hand. Use snow peas and sugar snap peas as crudités or in salads. **Cooked:** Boil or steam until just tender. Also stir-fry or tempura-fry snow peas and sugar snaps.

FLAVOR PAIRINGS (Garden and sugar snap peas) bacon, ham, onions, mushrooms, mint; (snow peas) almonds, chicken, mushrooms, sage.

CLASSIC RECIPES *Petit pois à la française; risi e bisi; menestra de guisantes;* pea and mint soup.

Sugar snap peas
Rounder and fatter than snow peas, the edible, fleshy pods and seeds are crunchy and wonderfully sweet. Eat them whole or thickly sliced.

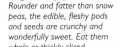

Snow peas
The flat, edible pods and minuscule seeds have a sweet, herbaceous flavor. They add crisp texture and brilliant color to stir-fries.

Garden peas
Plump, juicy garden peas have a uniquely sweet, grassy flavor and a tender—crisp texture. They should be only lightly cooked to prevent them from becoming starchy.

Pea shoots
The tender leaves and tips of the pea vine are edible, with an intense, pea-like flavor. They are delicious steamed or stir-fried, or added raw to salads.

The tiny peas need only a minute or two in boiling water.

Petits pois
A naturally small-seeded variety, petits pois are the sweetest of all peas. They are delicious eaten raw or lightly cooked.

CLASSIC RECIPE

PETITS POIS À LA FRANÇAISE

This traditional French dish can be made with canned petits pois when fresh baby peas are not available.

SERVES 4–6

8oz (250g) pearl onions

5 tbsp butter, at room temperature

3 cups shelled baby peas, or frozen or canned petits pois

½ cup ham stock or water

1 tsp granulated sugar

salt and freshly ground black pepper

1 tbsp all-purpose flour

2 tbsp chopped fresh mint or parsley

2 hearts of lettuce, such as Little Gem, trimmed and finely shredded

1 Cut an X into the root end of each onion, drop into a pan of boiling water, and cook until the water returns to a boil; then rinse and drain the onions. Peel the onions. Melt 2 tbsp of the butter in a saucepan. Add the onions and cook over medium heat for 2 minutes.

2 Add the peas and stock and bring to a boil. Skim off any foam, and add the sugar and season with salt and pepper. Reduce the heat to low and simmer gently for 5–8 minutes. Mix the remaining butter with the flour to make a paste.

3 In small pieces add the paste to the pan, stirring constantly, thickening the liquid. Stir in the mint or parsely and lettuce and serve hot.

For maximum freshness and sweetness, red peppers should have firm, shiny skins, and green beans should snap when broken.

CLASSIC RECIPE

HUMMUS

This thick garbanzo bean purée, made in the Middle East for centuries, is now known everywhere.

SERVES 6

1 cup dried garbanzo beans (chickpeas), soaked overnight, then drained, or 2 x 15.5oz (400g) cans garbanzo beans

2 large garlic cloves, crushed

juice of 2 lemons

5 tbsp olive oil, plus extra to garnish

½ cup tahini (Middle Eastern sesame seed paste)

salt

cayenne pepper, to dust

2 tbsp chopped flat-leaf parsley, to garnish

warm pita bread, cut into strips or wedges, to serve

1 Put the soaked dried garbanzo beans in a saucepan and cover with cold water. Bring to a boil. Partially cover and simmer for 2–3 hours, until tender. Drain, reserving the liquid.

2 Set aside 2–3 tbsp garbanzo beans. Put the remainder in a blender or food processor. Add the garlic, lemon juice, olive oil, and ½ cup of the reserved cooking liquid. (If using canned garbanzo beans, add ½ cup warm water or as much as needed to achieve a thick, creamy consistency.) Add the tahini and process briefly until smooth. Season with salt and cayenne pepper, then transfer to a bowl.

3 Drizzle with a little olive oil. Garnish with the parsley, a dusting of cayenne, and the reserved whole garbanzo beans. Serve with pita bread.

DRIED BEANS, PEAS, AND LENTILS

Grown all around the world in the tropics and the temperate zones, leguminous plants provide one of mankind's staple foods: the edible seeds inside their fruiting pods, which are sometimes eaten fresh, but more often dried. These dried beans, peas, and lentils (often collectively called pulses) vary in size and shape as well as in color, from black through browns, greens, reds, and yellows to white, sometimes speckled or blotchy. When they are cooked, their flavors range from mild to savory, identifiably "beany" and meaty.

BUY If buying a bag of pulses, inspect it for any signs of tearing where animals may have been at work. If buying in bulk, pulses should be clean and unbroken, and free of dust or grit, or any signs of spoilage.

STORE In a tightly closed container, pulses can be kept indefinitely in a cool, dry place, but as they age and dry out further, they will need a longer cooking time. Most kinds of pulses are sold pre-cooked in cans.

 EAT First, soak pulses in several changes of water for at least 2 hours, or preferably overnight. Start the cooking with a 10-minute rapid boil, then simmer briskly until tender. Lentils and split peas usually do not need to be soaked before cooking, nor do they require an initial 10 minutes of boiling. Add salt, sugar, or acidic ingredients such as tomatoes near the end of the cooking time as these can slow the softening. Once tender, use pulses in salads and pasta dishes, or purée them for soups and dips.

FLAVOR PAIRINGS Bacon, ham, cheese, cream, chiles, peppers, epazote, garlic, onions, oregano, rice, tomatoes. **CLASSIC RECIPES** Falafel; Tuscan bean soup; hummus; red beans and rice; *pasta e fagioli*; *dhansak*; African bean cake; chili con carne; *cassoulet*; Boston baked beans; refried beans; *feijoada*; *ful medames*; *minestra*; *farinata*; *mujaddarah*; *cocido madrileño*; *lentilles au jarret de porc*.

Flageolet bean
Integral to French cuisine, flageolet beans have an exceptionally creamy texture and delicate flavor. They are traditionally served as a vegetable with roast or braised lamb.

Flageolets are recognizable by their flat oval shape and unique greenish-gray color.

Cannellini bean
This classic Italian white bean is a member of the haricot-bean family. It has an elusive, nutty flavor and a very smooth texture when mashed.

Lima bean
These large, white beans have a rich flavor, and a soft, floury texture that is ideal for soaking up savory meat juices.

European Soldier bean
With their fruity flavor and floury texture, soldier beans are ideal for soups and purées. They plump up well after soaking and cooking.

Mung bean
Best known in their sprouted form, mung beans have a robust flavor and a creamy texture. They do not need to be soaked before cooking.

Pinto bean
A member of the kidney-bean family, pinto beans have a satisfying, earthy flavor and a powdery texture. They are commonly used for Mexican refried beans (frijoles refritos).

Red kidney bean
Best known as an essential ingredient in chili con carne, red kidney beans have a robust, full-bodied flavor and a soft, floury texture.

Soybean
These silky-textured beans have little flavor, although they contain the most protein and fat of all beans. They are good in stews and are also used for making soy products such as tofu, miso, soy sauce, and soy milk. They require lengthy soaking and cooking before they become tender.

Kidney beans contain toxins, which will be destroyed by the initial 10 minutes' boiling.

Baby lima bean
Although not quite as buttery as large lima beans, this small variety is creamy and tender, with a mild chestnut flavor.

Adzuki bean
Valued for their nutty, slightly sweet flavor, adzuki beans are particularly popular in China and Japan, where they are used to make sweet bean desserts. They hold their shape extremely well, even when cooked until soft.

Garbanzo beans
With their nutty flavor and smooth, buttery texture, garbanzo beans, also known as chickpeas, are ideal for dips and sauces. They are also good in stews and curries, as they hold their shape well when cooked.

Adzuki beans are small enough to cook without soaking.

FALAFEL

Popular Middle Eastern street food, these can be made with garbanzo beans or dried fava beans, or a combination of the two.

MAKES 12

1 ⅓ cups dried garbanzo beans, soaked overnight in cold water, then drained, or 2 x 15.5oz (400g) cans garbanzo beans

1 tbsp tahini (Middle Eastern sesame seed paste)

1 garlic clove, crushed

1 tsp salt

1 tsp ground cumin

1 tsp turmeric

1 tsp ground coriander

½ tsp cayenne pepper

2 tbsp finely chopped fresh parsley

juice of 1 small lemon

vegetable oil, for frying

pita or other flatbreads, cut in half, and salad greens, to serve

1 Put the soaked dried garbanzo beans in a large saucepan and cover with cold water. Bring to a boil, then partially cover and simmer for 2–3 hours, or until tender. Drain. Put the garbanzo beans in a food processor. Add the tahini, garlic, salt, spices, parsley, and lemon juice. Process, pulsing the machine on and off, until finely chopped but not puréed.

2 Transfer the mixture to a bowl, cover, and refrigerate for at least 30 minutes, or up to 8 hours.

3 Moisten your hands with water and shape the mixture into 12 balls. Press the tops down slightly to flatten.

4 Heat 2in (5cm) of oil in a deep frying pan. Working in batches, fry the balls, turning once, for 3–4 minutes, or until lightly golden all over. Drain on paper towels and serve hot, tucked inside halved flatbreads, with salad greens.

DRIED BEANS, PEAS, AND LENTILS (CONTINUED)

Black-eyed pea
Native to Africa, these beans—variously known as black-eyed peas and cowpeas—are quick to cook, and they blend well with other ingredients. They have a robust, fruity flavor and a creamy texture.

The beans have thick, leathery skins and need lengthy soaking and cooking to make them palatable.

Cranberry bean
With its meaty flavor and creamy texture, this classic Italian bean, also called borlotti bean, is invaluable for soups and pasta dishes. It holds its shape well when cooked.

Pigeon pea
Popular in Caribbean cuisine, pigeon peas are a small, round variety of bean with a sweet, meaty flavor and powdery texture. They benefit from long, slow cooking.

Egyptian Brown bean
An everyday staple in Egypt, where they are known as ful medames, these have a rich, meaty flavor and a creamy texture. They are typically stewed very slowly and served with hard-boiled eggs.

TUSCAN BEAN SOUP

Dried beans feature prominently in Tuscan cooking. This soup is a classic peasant dish from the region.

SERVES 4

¼ cup extra virgin olive oil, plus extra for drizzling

1 onion, chopped

2 carrots, sliced

1 leek, sliced

2 garlic cloves, chopped

1 x 14.5oz (400g) can chopped tomatoes

1 tbsp tomato purée

3 cups chicken stock

salt and freshly ground black pepper

1 x 15oz (400g) can cannellini or cranberry (borlotti) beans, drained and rinsed

8oz (250g) cavolo nero or other kale, cored and thinly sliced

8 slices ciabatta or other crusty Italian bread

freshly grated Parmesan cheese, to garnish

1 Heat the oil in a large soup pot or saucepan and cook the onion, carrots, and leek over low heat, stirring, for 10 minutes, or until softened but not browned. Add the garlic and cook for 1 more minute. Stir in the tomatoes with their juice, the tomato purée, and stock. Season with salt and pepper.

2 Mash half of the beans with a fork and add to the pot. Bring to a boil, then lower the heat and simmer for about 30 minutes. Add the remaining whole beans and the cavolo nero to the pan. Simmer for another 30 minutes, stirring occasionally. Taste and add more seasoning, if necessary.

3 When ready to serve, toast the bread until golden. Place 2 slices in each soup bowl and drizzle with olive oil. Ladle the soup into the bowls, top with a sprinkling of Parmesan, and drizzle with a little more olive oil.

Black Turtle bean
A favorite in Central and South America, turtle beans have an exceptionally rich, nutty flavor, and a meaty texture. They are particularly good in soups and casseroles.

Spanish Pardina lentil
Valued for their savory, nutty flavor, pardina lentils do not turn mushy when cooked, so are good in a salad. They can also be puréed to make a rich, thick soup.

Fava bean
Dried fava or broad beans have a distinctive, earthy flavor and a floury texture. They are good in a spicy stew, or mashed to make falafel, a popular Middle Eastern street snack.

French green lentil (Puy)
Considered a delicacy in France, speckled Puy lentils have a rich, earthy flavor and a firm yet tender texture when cooked. They are usually served as a salad or as a separate side dish.

The attractive magenta streaks fade to a uniform brownish-pink once boiled.

Brown lentil
Readily available, brown lentils have a nutty flavor and a soft texture. They will hold their shape when cooked, but can disintegrate if simmered for too long.

Split pea
Split peas have a sweet, earthy flavor. They need no soaking and cook very quickly, but do not keep their shape, which makes them ideal for purées, soups, vegetarian bakes, and pâtés.

Castelluccio lentil
Native to Umbria in Italy, these lentils are prized for their rich, earthy flavor and creamy texture. Although they have thin skin and cook very quickly, they remain intact.

Split Red lentil
The most common variety, split red lentils have a mild flavor. They cook very quickly, as the husk has been removed, and the inner seed split. They also soften and break down readily, making them good for smooth soups.

SPROUTED BEANS AND SEEDS

Most whole beans and lentils, and seeds such as fenugreek, pumpkin, and mustard, as well as grains such as wheat, corn, and rye, can be sprouted (germinated) to yield highly nutritious seedlings, or sprouts—a technique that has been applied in Asia for thousands of years. One of the most popular commercially cultivated sprouts is grown from mung beans. These have a fresh, clean, herbaceous flavor and a refreshing, crunchy texture. Other sprouts offer different flavors and textures: alfalfa sprouts are spicy, while sprouted wheat berries are sweet and earthy.

🔒 **BUY** Commercially cultivated sprouts are available year-round. Be sure they are fresh and crisp, with no brown tips or wilting. It is also easy to grow your own sprouts.

📦 **STORE** Fresh sprouts can be kept for 1–2 days in a closed plastic bag in the fridge.

⦿ **EAT** Sprouts grown from soybeans should be cooked for a few minutes to make them digestible. **Fresh:** Use in salads or sandwiches. **Cooked:** Add to stir-fries, or fillings for spring rolls or omelets. Incorporate wheat sprouts into hearty breads.
FLAVOR PAIRINGS Soy sauce, ginger, fish sauce, toasted sesame oil.
CLASSIC RECIPE *Kong gul na muk.*

Adzuki bean sprouts
Nutty, sweet, and redolent of peas, adzuki sprouts are ideal for vegetarian pâté, stir-fries, and casseroles.

Mung bean sprouts
Sweet and nutty with a pleasantly crisp texture, mung bean sprouts are perfect for stir-frying. They are also good raw in salads and sandwiches.

Garbanzo bean sprouts
Crisp and crunchy garbanzo bean sprouts have a nutty, earthy flavor. They are good blended with cooked garbanzo beans to make a nutritious hummus.

Soybean sprouts
These sturdy, juicy sprouts have a distinct bean-like flavor, but can quickly become sour after sprouting. Use while still very fresh.

Alfalfa sprouts
Crisp and mildly flavored, alfafa sprouts are particularly nutritious. They are ideal for sandwiches or sprinkling over omelets and soups.

Wheat grass
A complete food in itself, wheat grass should be juiced for consumption. Once processed, it produces dark green, chlorophyll-rich juice, with a potent flavor.

Lentil sprouts
These delicate sprouts have an earthy flavor, redolent of the lentil itself. Add them to a lentil salad for extra flavor, or use in soups, nut roasts, or vegetarian pâté.

GARLIC

Originating in Central Asia, garlic has conquered the world. Its delicious pungency and ability to enrich all kinds of dishes have made it indispensable in almost every kitchen on the planet. Like a shallot, garlic grows in a head consisting of individual cloves, each in its own papery wrap. Depending on how it is prepared, it can be mild and sweet or sharply hot and odiferous. There are two sub-species: softneck garlic has a pliable, papery stem, while hardneck produces a long, woody stalk, at the end of which is a seedpod that produces flowers and bulblets.

BUY Midsummer is peak season for quality dried garlic. ("Green" or "wet" garlic is harvested earlier and is sold before drying.) Heads should be firm, with papery husks. In the cold-weather months, avoid heads whose cloves are sprouting bitter little green shoots.

STORE Garlic can be kept for several weeks in a cool, dark place where there is some air circulation.

EAT The more that garlic is cut, the more pungent its flavor: crushed or pounded garlic is far stronger than whole, halved, or sliced cloves. **Fresh:** A little of garlic's pungency goes a long way. Use in salad dressings, sauces, and marinades, or rub over bread. **Cooked:** Never let garlic burn, or it will taste acrid and bitter. Roast whole heads; braise whole cloves; sauté, or stir-fry, or incorporate in sauces, soups, and stews. Crush as a rub on meat, or under skin. **Preserved:** Pickle.

FLAVOR PAIRINGS Lamb, beef, chicken, pork, fish, shellfish, pulses, pasta, potatoes, tomatoes, eggplants, mushrooms, zucchini, potatoes.

CLASSIC RECIPES Aioli; *skordalia; rouille;* pesto; *tarator; gremolata;* chicken with 40 cloves of garlic; *thum;* garlic bread.

Hardneck garlic
With a reputation as France's very best garlic, this hardneck variety, Rosé de Lautrec, has a distinctive, full-bodied flavor, with a subtle hint of sweetness.

Softneck garlic
A classic, white-skinned garlic, California Early is one of the most commonly grown varieties in the US. It has a pleasantly mild flavor and stores well.

Green garlic
Highly prized by chefs, green garlic, also known as "wet" garlic, has moist, pliable skin and soft, juicy cloves. The flavor is milder than mature garlic, and leaves hardly a trace on the breath.

The tender cloves are best in light, summery dishes. They are also delicious thinly sliced and used raw in sandwiches.

To appreciate the powerful flavor, crush the cloves with the flat of a knife, or grind with a pinch of salt.

The fat, meaty cloves can be thickly sliced and sautéed in butter to serve as a side dish.

Elephant garlic
Not a true garlic, but related to the leek, elephant garlic has excessively large cloves. The flavor is surprisingly mild, with a hint of onion.

AIOLI

This rich, garlicky sauce from Provençe is perfect with fish, cooked vegetables, and crudités.

MAKES ABOUT 1¾ CUPS

2 tbsp white wine vinegar
1 whole egg, at room temperature
2 egg yolks, at room temperature
1 tbsp Dijon mustard
1 tbsp light brown sugar
salt and freshly ground black pepper
1¼ cups olive oil (or half olive oil and half sunflower or vegetable oil)
3 garlic cloves, crushed through a press
2 tbsp fresh lemon juice

1 Place the vinegar, whole egg, egg yolks, mustard, sugar, and some salt and pepper in a small bowl set on a folded kitchen towel. Using a balloon whisk, beat until thick. Start adding the oil, drop by drop, whisking constantly after each addition.

2 When the sauce is thick and creamy, the oil can be added more quickly, about 1 tbsp at a time. Once all the oil is incorporated, whisk in the garlic and lemon juice. Refrigerate in a screw-topped jar for up to 4 days.

CORN CHOWDER

There are recipes for this thick, rich, and chunky North American soup dating back to the 1880s.

SERVES 4–6

4 fresh corn (corn on the cob)

salt and freshly ground black pepper

2 bay leaves

2 tbsp olive oil

1 large onion, chopped

4 fresh sage leaves, chopped, or ½ tsp dried sage

1 tsp chopped fresh thyme leaves, or ½ tsp dried thyme

1 carrot, chopped

2 celery ribs, chopped

1 large russet or other floury baking potato, peeled and chopped

½ cup milk

half-and-half and paprika, to garnish

1 Remove the husk and silk from the ears of corn, then shave off the kernels and scrape the "milk" from the cob into a bowl. Set the kernels and "milk" aside. Place the cobs in a large saucepan and add 2 cups water, a good pinch of salt, and the bay leaves. Bring to a boil, then reduce the heat, cover, and simmer for 15 minutes. Remove and discard the cobs and bay leaves. Reserve the stock.

2 Heat the olive oil in the rinsed-out saucepan and cook the onion until soft and translucent. Stir in the sage, thyme, carrot, celery, and potato. Cook for about 5 minutes, or until the vegetables are starting to soften. Add the reserved stock and continue to simmer for about 10 minutes, or until the potato is falling apart.

3 Meanwhile, put the corn kernels in another saucepan and add just enough cold water to cover. Bring to a boil and cook for 2 minutes. Set aside.

4 Add the milk to the soup mixture, then puree until smooth using a hand (immersion) blender; or in batches in a standard blender or food processor. Add the corn kernels with their cooking liquid and the corn "milk." If you like, quickly process the chowder one more time with the blender to break up the kernels slightly.

5 Reheat the chowder, and adjust the seasonings if necessary. Ladle into warm bowls, drizzle with half-and-half, and dust with a little paprika. Serve hot.

CORN

The vegetable we call corn is the seed head, or ear, of a type of maize, which is a grass grown all over the world, from the tropics to any northern region with a sufficient growing season. Other products from maize include cornstarch, cornmeal and polenta, and popcorn. In the corn ear, the tender grains, or kernels, are set in rows along the central cob ("corn on the cob"); the ear is wrapped in long, silky threads inside a papery husk. Corn, also called sweetcorn, may be classified according to sugar levels: "supersweets" have four-to-ten times more sugar than "standard" or "normal sugary."

🛒 **BUY** High summer is the season for corn. Check the cut end of the stalk to be sure it is not dry. The leaves of the husk should be moist and bright green, with a fresh tassel of silk. If you can, puncture a kernel with a thumbnail; look for a milky fluid, rather than a clear fluid or a paste-like mass.

📦 **STORE** All corn starts to lose its sweetness as soon as it's picked, so try to use it the same day you buy it. If you must keep it for a day or so, store in the husk, wrapped in damp paper towels, in the fridge. Kernels removed from the cob can be frozen.

◉ **EAT** Roast whole in the husk, or shuck (remove husk and silk) and then boil, roast, or grill. Boil, braise, bake, or sauté kernels.
FLAVOR PAIRINGS Bacon, butter, cheese, cream, chiles, lime, black pepper.
CLASSIC RECIPES Corn chowder; corn on the cob; succotash; corn fritters; sopa de elote.

White corn
One of the most popular types of corn in the US is the normal sugary variety Silver Queen. It has a good flavor and juicy, slightly chewy kernels.

PREPARING CORN

Ears of corn can be cooked whole as corn on the cob, or the kernels can be shaved off to use in soups or casseroles.

1 *Pull off the husk and all of the silk.* **2** *Hold the ear upright on a cutting board and, using a sharp knife, slice straight down the sides to cut off the kernels.* **3** *Hold the cob upright but at a slight angle in a bowl, and scrape down the length of the cob with the knife to extract the rest of the corn "milk."*

Baby corn
Unlike full-grown ears, baby corn is completely edible, including the central cob. With its mild flavor and crunchy texture, it is a useful ingredient in stir-fries.

Bicolor corn
The ornamental supersweet variety Honey 'n' Pearl has an exceptionally sweet flavor and tender, juicy kernels.

OKRA

Okra, also known as lady's fingers or *bhindi* outside the US, is the pretty pod of an annual grown in tropical and sub-tropical regions around the world. It originated in Ethiopia, from where it spread to the rest of Africa and then around the world; it voyaged to the New World on slave ships, with its alternative name, gumbo, which it gave to the local spicy soup—stews. Okra has a mild, sweet, vegetal flavor. When the pod is cut, a sticky juice is released; this helps to thicken cooked dishes in the same way as cornstarch.

BUY Okra is at its best in the heat of high summer. Look for small pods about 3–4in (7.5–10cm) long and appearing freshly picked, with a bright green color. Red okra may be slightly longer at 4–5in (10–12cm). Avoid dry, flaccid pods, as they will have lost their sweetness.

STORE Okra doesn't keep well, so use the day you buy it, or store for no more than 1–2 days in a cool spot, not in the fridge.

EAT Fresh: Red okra can be eaten as a crudité or sliced in salads. **Cooked:** Steam, stew, or bake in a sauce; coat in batter or cornmeal and deep-fry; stir-fry; or sauté. **Preserved:** Pickle fresh, sweet, little okra pods.

FLAVOR PAIRINGS Butter, garlic, chiles, curry spices, coconut, green peppers, tomatoes.

CLASSIC RECIPES Gumbo; *bil-zeyt; bil-lahmeh.*

Yellow corn
Golden Bantam is an early-ripening, normal-sugary variety, with a superior sweet flavor. The broad kernels have a creamy texture.

Okra
Known for its slippery texture, okra is tender and sweet tasting, with a mild flavor similar to runner beans.

Red okra
Red okra is similar in texture and flavor to the green type. It reverts to green when cooked.

PEPPERS

Peppers, both sweet and hot, are members of the *Capsicum* genus and native to the tropical regions of the Americas. The milder types of peppers vary in size from 1in (2.5cm) round cherry types to the lantern-shaped bell variety; in color from green when unripe to red, yellow, orange, purple, brown, and near black when ripened; in flavor from sweet to mildly hot. Mature peppers have thicker walls and sweeter flesh than unripe green peppers. See page 342–3 for hot pepper varieties.

🔒 **BUY** Summer and early fall are the best seasons for peppers. Choose fruits that are glossy and firm, with no soft spots or mold; they should have some heft to them, rather than feel light. The stalk end should look freshly cut and moist.

🗄 **STORE** Kept in paper bags or open-topped plastic bags, peppers will store well in the fridge for up to 2 weeks. Once cut, they should be used within 24 hours.

⊙ **EAT** Fresh: Cut sticks for crudités, or add to salads. **Cooked:** Stuff and bake, roast, grill, barbecue or chargrill, or stew; slice to sauté, stir-fry, or coat in batter and deep-fry. **Preserved:** Pickle in vinegar or in oil.

FLAVOR PAIRINGS Chicken, lamb, anchovies, garlic, sweet corn, onions, tomatoes, olives, capers, cheese.

CLASSIC RECIPES Peperonata; stuffed peppers; *lesco*; *pipérade*; ratatouille.

Red bell pepper
As they ripen, bell peppers turn from green to red, and become sweeter and fleshier. With their boxy shape, they are ideal for stuffing or roasting whole.

Green bell pepper
Unripe green bell peppers have thinner walls than ripe bell peppers, and a distinct herbaceous flavor that mellows as they mature.

Pimentos de Padrón
These thin-fleshed peppers are a delicacy in Spain, where they are fried and served with coarse sea salt. The flavor varies from mild to hot.

Blushing Beauty
This sweet, flavorful pepper starts green, pales to light yellow or ivory, and then acquires areas of red blush when ripe.

PREPARING PEPPERS

All peppers have white ribs and seeds that should be removed before eating or cooking.

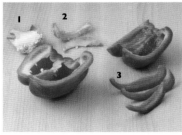

1 *Wash under cold, running water. Using a small knife, cut around the stalk and pull gently to remove it.* **2** *Cut the pepper in half lengthwise. Remove the ribs and seeds from each half.* **3** *Cut into strips or dice, ready for eating raw or cooking.*

PEELING PEPPERS

Charring and removing the skin makes peppers softer and gives them a slightly smoky flavor.

1 *Using long-handled tongs, hold the pepper over a flame (or place under a hot grill) until the skin is blackened and blistered on all sides.* **2** *Put the charred pepper in a plastic or paper bag, seal, and leave for 5–10 minutes, to allow it to steam, which will loosen the skin. Remove from the bag and use your fingers to peel away the charred skin.* **3** *Pull off the stalk, taking the core with it, and remove the seeds from the inside.* **4** *Tear the peeled pepper into sections and cut lengthwise into strips.*

Yellow wax pepper
This variety has medium-thick flesh that is not overly hot. Use in the same way as sweet bell peppers—in salads, stir-fries, braises, and pickles.

Wax peppers are usually eaten while the skin is still yellow, though they change to red once ripe.

Anaheim
A pepper with mild heat and medium-thick flesh, this is usually eaten fresh while green, or dried when red. It is excellent stuffed with cheese, dipped in batter, and deep-fried.

The thin, tender skin does not need to be removed, which makes this pepper perfect for speedy frying.

Peperoncino
The sweetish flavor and mild heat of this thin-fleshed pepper are good in tomato-based dishes. It is usually sold pickled in cans or glass jars.

Italian sweet pepper
The Italian heirloom variety, Nardello, has a mild flavor when green, becoming intensely sweet when red. It is ideal fried with slices of Italian sausage and served on a soft bread roll.

Spanish dried red pepper
The variety shown, called Ñora, is pleasantly earthy and mildly hot. It is used to flavor rice dishes, and is essential for romesco sauce and making sweet paprika.

CLASSIC RECIPE

PEPERONATA

Enjoy this Italian pepper stew hot or cold, with crusty bread and a green salad, with hot pasta or served alongside grilled meat.

SERVES 4

2 tbsp olive oil

1 onion, sliced

2 garlic cloves, finely chopped

2 red bell peppers, halved, seeded, and cut into strips

2 green bell peppers, halved, seeded, and cut into strips

6 ripe tomatoes, peeled, seeded, and chopped

salt and freshly ground black pepper

small handful of fresh basil leaves

1 Heat the oil in a large frying pan or flameproof casserole, add the onion, and cook for about 5 minutes, or until soft and translucent. Stir in the garlic and cook for a few more seconds.

2 Add the peppers and stir them into the onion mixture. Cook over very low heat for 5 minutes; then cover and cook gently for 5–10 minutes, stirring occasionally to prevent burning.

3 Add the tomatoes and season well with salt and pepper. Partially cover the pan and cook for about 20 minutes, or until the peppers are very soft. Stir in the fresh basil leaves just before serving.

EGGPLANT

Native to tropical Asia, this vegetable has a long history and many names, including eggplant, aubergine, eggfruit, and brinjal. Ancient Romans thought it was poisonous and called it *mala insana* (apple of insanity), from which is derived the Italian melanzana and Greek melitzana. Today, eggplants are grown worldwide. They may be large and round or elongated, egg-shaped, or resembling a bunch of grapes; they vary in color from the familiar deep purple to lavender, green, and white. The meltingly tender flesh is slightly bitter with a light herbaceous note, and it easily absorbs other flavors.

BUY High summer and fall are the best seasons. Look for relatively small, firm eggplants with glossy skin and bright green cap and stalk. A thumb indentation will stay indented on an old eggplant, which will be bitter and soggy.

STORE An eggplant should be used the day you bring it home, or at least by the next day. Don't put it in the fridge; keep in a cool spot until needed.

EAT Although with modern varieties salting to draw out bitterness is not necessary, this initial preparation will reduce the amount of oil that eggplants soak up during cooking.
Cooked: Bake or roast, braise, broil, barbecue or charbroil, stir-fry, sauté, coat in batter and deep-fry, or stew.
Preserved: Pickle.

FLAVOR PAIRINGS Ham, lamb, cheese, garlic, mushrooms, tomatoes, sweet peppers, lemon, mint, olive oil.
CLASSIC RECIPES Baba ghanoush; moussaka; *melanzane parmigiana*; Imam bayildi; *salna*; *ratatouille*; *ikra iz baklazhan*; *kahrmus*; *caponata*.

Italian long white eggplant
This white variety has a chewy texture and pleasing flavor, redolent of mushrooms. It contains few seeds and little trace of bitterness.

The pristine white skin and flesh become particularly soft when cooked.

Thai long green eggplant
The creamy flesh has a firm, chewy texture and a pleasantly meaty flavor, but with some bitterness. It is best sliced and stir-fried with spices or used in a curry dish.

Thai green eggplant
Small but intensely flavored, these crisp, firm eggplants are a key ingredient in the traditional Thai green chicken curry.

Oval deep-purple eggplant
The familiar, fat, elongated eggplant develops a complex flavor and silky texture when cooked. It is good thickly sliced and broiled, or roasted whole and then puréed with spices.

The skin keeps its attractive mottled stripes even when cooked.

Italian striped eggplant
Rosa Bianca, an heirloom variety, has firm, creamy flesh, which makes it a choice ingredient for melanzana alla parmigiana.

Thai pea eggplant
A miniature green variety, this has a slightly bitter flavor and crisp texture. The high seed-to-flesh ratio makes the eggplants pleasantly crunchy, and they do not soften with cooking.

East Asian purple eggplant
The long, narrow, purple-green eggplant is mild-flavored and sweet and uniform in size.

Round green eggplant
Sometimes called apple eggplant, this has a firm, crisp texture and agreeable mildly bitter flavor. Slice into segments and use in curry dishes or raw in Asian-style salads.

As with most varieties of eggplant, the edible skin adds to the flavor of the finished dish.

Italian round eggplant
Prosperosa, a widely available variety, has non-bitter, smooth-textured flesh that retains its shape when cooked. The squat, round shape lends itself to stuffing and baking.

BABA GANOUSH

No Middle Eastern mezze table is complete without this creamy dip. Serve with warm strips of pita bread.

SERVES 6

2lb (900g) eggplants, cut in half lengthwise
2 large garlic cloves, crushed
2 tbsp extra virgin olive oil
2 tbsp plain yogurt
3–4 tbsp tahini*
2–3 tbsp fresh lemon juice
salt and freshly ground black pepper
coarsely chopped cilantro, for garnish

1 Preheat the oven to 425°F (220°C) and lightly grease a baking sheet. Score the flesh of each eggplant half, without cutting through the skin, then place cut-side down on the baking sheet. Bake for 25–30 minutes, or until the flesh is softened and collapsing.

2 Transfer the eggplant halves to a colander and leave to cool for about 15 minutes.

3 Scoop the eggplant flesh into a food processor or blender; discard the skin. Add the garlic, olive oil, yogurt, 3 tbsp tahini, and 2 tbsp lemon juice, and process until smooth. Taste and add more tahini and lemon juice, if you like, then season with salt and pepper.

4 Scoop into a bowl and sprinkle with cilantro before serving.

* Middle Eastern sesame seed paste. Available at Middle Eastern markets and many well-stocked supermarkets.

Whether you are making a salad, a soup, or a sauce, choose the type and variety of tomato best suited to your needs.

AVOCADO

Originally native to Central America and the Caribbean, this tropical fruit today has over 500 cultivars planted around the world. Fruits of different species range from the lumpy-skinned, small Hass to smooth-skinned, large Mexican and Guatemalan types. Most commercial varieties today are hybrids of the latter two, and have a mild, somewhat nutty flavor and a smooth, oily texture. Avocados, which are sometimes called avocado pears because of their shape, contain exceptional levels of monounsaturated fat (the good kind), about the same amount of potassium as bananas, and nearly twice the amount of soluble fiber found in apples.

BUY Since avocados ripen off the tree, you can buy them firm and let them ripen at home. Or look for ripe ones: under gentle thumb pressure these will have a slight "give" on the shoulder near the stalk end.

STORE Allow avocados to ripen on a windowsill or kitchen counter (not in the fridge), then eat when ripe. If using only half a ripe avocado, coat the cut surface of the unused half with lemon juice and wrap it in plastic wrap to prevent it from turning black, then store in the fridge for 2–3 days.

EAT Avocado is best used fresh, although it is sometimes baked or cooked in a soup. Slice for sandwiches; add to salads, especially seafood salads; mix it with sugar and pineapple; or purée to make ice cream.

FLAVOR PAIRINGS Parma ham, dried beef, shrimp, tomatoes, grapefruit, lime, mango, pineapple, sugar, balsamic vinegar.

CLASSIC RECIPES Guacamole; *insalata tricolore.*

The area just above the widest part is the place to test for ripeness. It should give under gentle pressure.

Sharwil
A medium, small-stoned variety, this has a nutty flavor and oil-rich flesh with an easily spreadable texture.

The pebbly skin becomes almost black as the fruit ripens.

PREPARING AVOCADO

Avocado goes brown quickly, so prepare just before use, or sprinkle well with lemon juice.

1 *Insert a sharp knife at the stalk end and cut all the way around the stone, through the skin and flesh. Twist the cut halves in opposite directions to separate them and reveal the stone.* **2** *Carefully but firmly press the blade of the knife into the stone, then twist the knife to pull the stone free from the avocado. Alternatively, scoop out the stone with a teaspoon.* **3** *To remove the flesh from the skin, cut each half lengthways in half again, and gently peel the skin away from the flesh.*

Hass
The only year-round avocado, the Hass is a good choice for dips and spreads. The creamy flesh is silky smooth and the flavor is wonderfully rich and nutty.

Unlike the Hass variety, the skin of the Fuerte is smooth and remains green when ripe.

Fuerte
An easy-peeling variety with a mild flavor and pale yellow flesh that slices well. It is ideal for salads and salsas.

GUACAMOLE

This popular dip, which has its origins in Mexico, can also be used as a condiment for grilled meats and seafood.

SERVES 6

3 large, ripe avocados (preferably the Hass variety)

juice of ½ lime

½ onion, finely chopped

1 medium tomato, seeded and minced

1 or 2 fresh hot red chiles, seeded and finely chopped

2 tbsp chopped cilantro, plus a few sprigs to garnish

salt

2 tbsp sour cream (optional)

1 Pit and skin the avocados. Place the flesh in a bowl and combine with a fork or potato masher until the mixture is mashed but still chunky.

2 Add the lime juice then the onion, tomato, and chiles. Mix well, then stir in the cilantro. Season with salt to taste.

3 Fold in the sour cream, if using. Mound the guacamole into a bowl, garnish with cilantro sprigs, and serve immediately. If you cannot serve immediately, cover with plastic wrap, pressing it directly onto the surface.

TOMATO

This fruit of a tropical plant—grown in almost all temperate climates, even Siberia—is an essential ingredient in all of the world's cuisines. Modern varieties range in color from near black through yellow, orange, and red to near white; in size and shape from that of a pea to a huge sphere, and in flavor from sweet to spritely acid. GLOBE TOMATOES are the classic, more or less globe-shaped, and available in a rainbow of colors. CHERRY TOMATOES are small and round, with a high sugar content. BEEFSTEAK TOMATOES are large, usually with a slightly flattened shape, and have a meaty texture. PLUM TOMATOES, more oval in shape, make the best sauces because their flesh has a high solid content.

BUY High tomato season is summer through to early fall. Look for vine-ripened fruit, which may be turning soft but has the best flavor. Out of season tomatoes should be firm and blemish-free.

They will continue ripening at home over several days.

STORE Keep at room temperature, not in the fridge unless they are very ripe. Arrange so tomatoes don't touch each other as they continue to ripen on a counter or windowsill.

EAT Tomatoes are wonderfully versatile. **Fresh:** Enjoy small tomatoes whole; cut larger ones any way you like. **Cooked:** Bake whole (with or without stuffing), roast, grill, fry, sauté, or stew. Make into sauce or soup. Add to casseroles and stews. **Preserved:** Oven-dry and pack in olive oil. Make ketchup or chutney. Pickle green (unripe) tomatoes.

FLAVOR PAIRINGS Parmesan cheese, mozzarella, basil, garlic, onions, shallots, parsley, olives, balsamic vinegar, oregano, thyme, marjoram.

CLASSIC RECIPES Tomato sauce; gazpacho; *insalata caprese*; BLT sandwich; cream of tomato soup; *gestegen tomaten*; *tomates farcies à la provençale*; *pappa al pomodoro*; *panzanella*; *pomodori ripreni*; tomato and red onion salad; *penne arrabbiata*; *tiella di verdure*.

GLOBE TOMATOES

Golden Queen
An heirloom variety with a mild flavor and juicy, yellow flesh, this is best in a salad, mixed with more strongly flavored varieties.

Black Zebra
The solid, juicy flesh has a complex tomato flavor typical of black varieties. With a high flesh-to-seed ratio it is a good variety for sauces, as well as slicing for salads.

Cindel
A popular variety in Ireland, this is noted for its sweet juiciness. It has firm flesh and a mild flavor.

Moneymaker
A British heirloom variety, Moneymaker has a rich tomato flavor, a fine balance of sweetness and acidity, and juicy flesh.

Stupice
A variety bred in the Czech Republic, with well-balanced sweetness and acidity, and juicy texture. Good for snacking on whole and in salads.

TOMATO SAUCE

An Italian chef, Francesco Leonardi, is said to have created the first tomato sauce for pasta in 1790.

MAKES 2 CUPS

4 tbsp sunflower or canola oil

1 onion, chopped

1 garlic clove, chopped

4 tbsp tomato purée

4 ripe beefsteak tomatoes, peeled and chopped, or 2 x 14.5oz (411g) cans chopped tomatoes

8 fresh basil leaves, torn

salt and freshly ground black pepper

1 Heat the oil in a large saucepan over medium heat. Add the onion and cook, stirring occasionally, until soft and golden. Stir in the garlic and cook for a few more minutes.

2 Add the tomato purée, the tomatoes with their juice, half the basil, and salt and pepper to taste. Lower the heat and simmer, uncovered, stirring occasionally for about 20 minutes, or until thickened, stirring occasionally. Stir in the remaining basil just before serving.

CHERRY TOMATOES

This bite-sized variety is best bought with the calyx still attached.

Sungold
Many consider this the best-tasting variety of cherry tomato. It has an exceptionally good balance of sweetness and acidity, thin tender skin, and juicy flesh—perfect for salads or snacking on whole.

The Yellow Pear tapers at the top, making it stand out from other cherry varieties.

Yellow Pear
One of the oldest varieties, this grows to about 1in (2.5cm) long and is sometimes sold as a spray. Its flavor is mild but sweet, ideal for those who find other tomatoes too acidic.

With thicker flesh than most cherry varieties, grape tomatoes cook down into a quickly made sauce or salsa.

Grape tomatoes
The attractive elongated fruits are intensely sweet and juicy with firm but tender skin. Being bite-sized, they are popular with children and ideal for a lunchbox.

Both the skin and flesh of this variety are a dark purple-reds.

Black Cherry
Like many of the dark-colored varieties, Black Cherry has a deep, rich, satisfying tomato flavor. Combined with red and yellow tomatoes, it makes a dramatic contrast in a salad.

Cherry tomatoes
These small-fruited varieties are usually more flavorsome than larger ones. Handy to eat whole as a snack, or when lightly crushed and warmed in oil, they make a colorful pizza topping.

BEEFSTEAK TOMATOES

The skin will slip off easily after a 30-second plunge into boiling water.

Costoluto Fiorentino
An old-fashioned, all-purpose variety of Italian tomato from Florence, this has a fine flavor.

With its generous diameter, Brandywine is ideal for slicing, to use in salads and sandwiches.

Brandywine
A gourmet-quality tomato, Brandywine is highly praised for its distinctive, well-balanced acidity and sweetness.

Cuor di Bue
From Liguria, Italy, this fleshy, heart-shaped tomato is renowned for the quality of the sauce it makes.

Pantano Romanesco
A Roman variety much used for sauces. Its flesh bursts with rich, complex tomato flavors.

Montserrat
A large Spanish variety with thick, sweet flesh, low acidity, viscous juice, and an enticing fragrance. Slowly simmered with onion and garlic, it makes a richly flavored sauce.

BEEFSTEAK TOMATOES (CONTINUED)

The tomato keeps its beautiful lime-green color even when ripe.

Costoluto Genovese
This deeply ribbed Italian heirloom variety from Genoa has a concentrated, sharp tomato flavor and thick flesh, making it perfect for rich sauces rather than eating fresh.

Like many beefsteak varieties, this one reveals an intricate thick core when sliced. Together with the flesh, the core gives body to a sauce.

Evergreen
Exceptional both in flavor and looks, this beefsteak tomato variety has a perfect balance of sweetness and acidity. The firm flesh is ideal for salads, sandwiches, and frying.

PLUM TOMATOES

The tomatoes keep their shape when halved or sliced for broiling or roasting.

Roma
A commonly available plum variety, with dense meaty flesh and a rich flavor, this is one of the best tomatoes for sauces and soups.

Most of the flavor is in the jelly surrounding the seeds, so do not discard them.

Olivade
The high flesh-to-juice ratio of this attractive plum tomato makes it a good choice for sauces, as well as for using raw in salads and sandwiches.

San Marzano
With its superior, rich tomato flavor and meaty interior, this is the classic variety for canning and paste-making. Many consider it to be the best sauce tomato in the world.

GAZPACHO

This chilled, no-cook Spanish soup from Andalucia is always popular when the weather gets hot.

SERVES 4–6

2 thick slices white bread, crusts removed

2lb (1 kg) tomatoes, plus extra to serve

½ cucumber, peeled and finely chopped, plus extra to serve

1 small red pepper, seeded and chopped, plus extra to serve

2 garlic cloves, crushed

4 tbsp sherry vinegar

salt and freshly ground black pepper

½ cup extra virgin olive oil, plus extra to serve

1 hard-boiled egg, white and yolk separated and chopped, to serve

1 Place the bread in a bowl, and cover with cold water. Leave to soak while you prepare the tomatoes. Place the tomatoes in a heatproof bowl, pour over enough boiling water to cover, and leave for 20 seconds, or until the skins split. Drain and cool under cold running water, then gently peel off the skins. Cut the tomatoes in half, remove the seeds, and roughly chop the flesh.

2 Put the tomato flesh, cucumber, red pepper, garlic, and vinegar in a food processor or blender. Drain off the water from the bread, and squeeze it dry. Add to the tomato mixture. Season to taste with salt and pepper, and process until smooth. Pour in the olive oil and process again to mix. Dilute with a little water if the soup is too thick. Transfer to a serving bowl, cover with plastic wrap, and chill for at least 1 hour.

3 When ready to serve, finely chop the extra tomato, cucumber, and red pepper. Place these and the chopped egg yolk and egg white in individual bowls. Ladle the soup into bowls and serve, letting each diner add their own garnish, including a drizzle of oil, if desired.

TOMATILLO

Native to Mexico and the highlands of Central America, tomatillos are still essential to the cuisines of those regions. More recently, they have become popular in much of North and South America, although they haven't made much headway in the rest of the world. Although distantly related to tomatoes, and sometimes called Mexican green tomatoes, the tomatillo is closer to its cousins, the physalis or Cape gooseberry and the ground cherry, which also have papery husks. Tomatillos range from cherry to plum size. They may ripen to bright yellow even shading to purple and the flesh can sweeten, but they are most often used green, when their flavor is tangy and acidic, with a hint of citrus.

BUY Tomatillos are available summer through fall. They should be firm and slightly sticky to the touch, with no bruises, scratches, or soft spots. Their papery husks should be golden-beige, not dark brown.

STORE In a plastic bag in the fridge, they will keep well for up to 2 weeks.

EAT Fresh: Chop into salads, salsas, and guacamole. Use as a substitute for tomatoes in gazpacho. **Cooked:** Stew into a sauce, poach, fry, bake or roast, or braise. **Preserved:** Make into chutney.

FLAVOR PAIRINGS Chicken, salmon, halibut, chiles, corn, onion, cilantro.
CLASSIC RECIPES Salsa verde; mole verde.

Under their papery husks, tomatillo skins are thin and need no peeling.

BREADFRUIT

Breadfruit originated in the area extending from Malaysia to the South Pacific islands and West Indies. This large, round, starchy fruit is now also cultivated in other tropical climes. Cooked when slightly ripe but still green, it resembles a slightly fruity bread in texture and taste. As it ripens, it changes texture—becoming more pulpy, sticky, and eventually runny—and develops a fruitier flavor, although it is still bland even when fully ripe.

BUY Available year round, look for sound green fruit that you can ripen to the desired degree over a few days at home. Avoid fruit with soft spots or cuts, since these will disintegrate quickly.

STORE In a sealed, heavy-duty plastic bag in the vegetable crisper of the fridge, or other cool place, it can be kept for 7–10 days. Avoid excessive chilling, since this can damage the flesh.

EAT Cooked: Cook in the same way as potatoes: boil or steam, roast or bake, or deep-fry as fries or chips. Purée cooked flesh for soups or to use in sweet desserts, tea breads, cakes, and pie fillings.

FLAVOR PAIRINGS Chiles, sweet peppers, tomatoes, garlic, onions, cilantro, cumin, nutmeg, lime.

The flesh of young breadfruit is hard and starchy, becoming softer and slightly sticky as the fruit ripens.

MUSHROOMS AND FUNGI

What we call mushrooms are the fruiting bodies of soil-borne fungi that live from nutrients they take from plants living and dead. They flourish throughout the world's temperate zones and add varying levels of earthiness and savory flavor to foods. Their flavor character and intensity depend almost entirely on the type of mushroom they are, rather than whether they are cultivated, what color they are, or their size. Most culinary fungi have a cap and stalk, but not all: for example, the puffball is spherical and stalkless.

🔒 **BUY** The mushroom season lasts from late summer to early winter, although some varieties, such as the morel, appear in spring. No matter what type of mushroom you are buying, it should have been freshly harvested: check the cut end, which should not be stiffly dried out. Smell them, too—their aroma should be earthy and sweet, not sour. If you are foraging for wild mushrooms, do not eat any unless you are absolutely sure they are edible. Wild mushrooms can be delicious, or deadly.

🗄 **STORE** Fresh mushrooms can be kept in the fridge in a closed paper bag for up to a week. They dry well and can be stored for months; reconstitute by soaking in warm water.

⬤ **EAT Fresh:** Slice thinly to add a bass note to a salad. Some, like enoki, are eaten whole and raw in sandwiches. **Cooked:** Mushrooms take to just about any type of cooking. Fry, bake, broil, barbecue, sauté, or steam. **Preserved:** They are sometimes preserved in oil, and some varieties lend themselves to pickling and making into a ketchup, but the most common way of preserving mushrooms is by drying.

FLAVOR PAIRINGS Beef, pork, poultry, eggs, garlic, onions, peas, tomatoes, sherry, lemon juice, oregano, parsley.

CLASSIC RECIPES Mushroom soup; beef stroganoff; duxelles; veal scaloppine with mushrooms; mushrooms à la grecque.

PREPARING MUSHROOMS

There is no need to peel cultivated mushrooms before use. Everything is edible.

1 *Using a small, sharp knife, trim the end of the stalk, or cut it off level with the cap.* **2** *With damp paper towel or a brush, clean soil off the caps and remaining stalk. If the mushrooms are very dirty or sandy, rinse briefly in a colander and pat dry.* **3** *Cut into slices, or as required.*

Chestnut or Crimini mushroom
A young version of the portobello, this all-purpose mushroom has a nutty flavor and meaty texture. It can be sliced raw into salads, but is better sautéed or stir-fried.

Portobello mushroom
A large, meaty mushroom with firm flesh and a full-bodied flavor. The generous size makes it perfect as a meat replacement in burgers.

Mushroom peel contains much of the flavor, so just wipe cultivated mushrooms clean with a damp paper towel.

Cut off and discard the woody stems after soaking. Only the caps are used.

Chinese dried mushroom
Valued for a concentrated savory flavor and intense aroma, Chinese dried mushrooms (which are, in fact, shiitakes) are soaked until pliable, then used in the same way as fresh mushrooms.

Shiitake mushroom
Shiitakes are widely available in the West and prized in Japan. They have a faintly woody flavor and chewy texture, ideal for stir-frying or adding to soups.

Enoki mushroom
Cultivated in clumps, enoki have a crisp texture and mild mushroomy flavor. They are good in soups and stir-fries, or used raw in salads and sandwiches.

St. George's mushroom resembles several highly poisonous mushrooms, so be careful when gathering from the wild.

St. George's mushroom
A spring mushroom, St. George's has a mealy texture and smells vaguely of cucumber. It is usually fried in butter, which enhances the flavor.

Flat white mushroom
These are full-grown button mushrooms, with a firm texture and earthy flavor. They can be broiled, pan-fried, stuffed, or roasted.

Look for shiny caps with no stains or cracks. They should feel slippery when touched.

Button mushroom
Widely available year-round, button mushrooms have a very mild flavor, which is improved by sautéing in butter. They can also be used raw in salads and as crudités.

Nameko mushroom
Popular in Japan and widely exported, namekos develop an interesting jellylike texture when cooked. They are ideal for Japanese-style soups and stir-fries.

Take advantage of the wide variety of edible mushrooms, each with a different aesthetic, texture, and flavor profile.

MUSHROOMS CONTINUED

The trumpet shape and concave cap make chanterelles easy to recognize. The striking yellow color fades as the mushrooms mature.

Straw mushroom
Native to China, these cone-shaped mushrooms have a neutral flavor that combines well with other ingredients. They are highly perishable and usually sold canned.

Chanterelle or Girolle
Highly prized chanterelles have smooth tender flesh and a noticeably nutty, fruity flavor that complements egg dishes, chicken, veal, and pork. They are best sautéed.

Porcini or Cep
Also known as penny bun, this is one of the most revered of all mushrooms, valued for its smooth, creamy flesh, rich, savory flavor, and distinguished shape. Delicious sautéed, or added to risotto and pasta dishes.

Field mushroom
Recognizable by its thick white flesh and pleasant earthy aroma, the field mushroom has pink or brown gills—never white, as you find in the deadly amanita. Ideal for broiling and frying.

Dried Cep or Porcini
Dried slices of cep (usually labeled porcini) are available in delis and better supermarkets. The flavor is intensely concentrated—ideal for fortifying sauces and soups. They reconstitute easily in warm water.

The smooth, brown, gleaming cap has pores on the underside instead of gills.

Bay bolete
This has a milder flavor than its relative the cep, although the flesh has a similar creamy texture. It is improved by sautéing with garlic and parsley.

Buna-Shimeji
These attractive Japanese clumping mushrooms have a nutty flavor and crisp texture. They are noticeably bitter when raw, so should always be cooked.

Trim and discard the base of the clusters, leaving the stems intact. Then separate into individual mushrooms.

These mushrooms are at their best when the cap is about 3in (7.5cm) in diameter. The cap exudes a milky substance when cut.

Before cooking with morels, just shake their intricate heads free of insects and brush off any traces of dirt.

Morel
One of the most sought-after wild mushrooms, morels have a unique, steaklike flavor, best appreciated when simply sautéed. Morels should never be eaten raw.

Saffron Milk Cap
Much loved in Europe, this variety has a nutty flavor and faintly crunchy texture, which it keeps when cooked. It is good in rich creamy sauces.

Look for beige to cream gills, extending down the stalk from the outer edge of the cap.

Oyster mushroom
Young oyster mushrooms are tender and mildly flavored, with a hint of anise, becoming acrid and tough as they age. Use in stir-fries and Asian-style soups.

CLASSIC RECIPE

MUSHROOM SOUP

This smooth soup captures an intense, true mushroom flavor. Serve with warm crusty bread.

SERVES 4

1 tbsp olive oil
2 tbsp butter
1 onion, finely chopped
salt and freshly ground black pepper
2 garlic cloves, finely chopped
4 fresh thyme sprigs, leaves stripped
1 1b (450g) mixed cremini and white mushrooms, half of them grated and half finely chopped
3 cups vegetable or chicken stock
finely chopped parsley, to garnish

1 Heat the oil and butter in a large pot. When the butter has melted add the onion and season with salt and pepper. Cook on low heat for about 5 minutes, or until the onion is soft and translucent; do not brown. Stir in the garlic and thyme and cook for a few more seconds.

2 Now add the grated mushrooms and cook them over low heat for about 5 minutes, or until they begin to release their juices. Add the chopped mushrooms and cook for another 5 minutes. Pour in a little of the stock and bring to a boil, then add the remaining stock. Simmer gently for 20–30 minutes, or until the mushrooms are very tender.

3 Working in batches, purée the soup in a blender until smooth. As each batch is puréed, pour it into a clean pot. Reheat the soup, adding a little hot water if it is too thick, then taste for seasoning. Ladle into soup bowls, sprinkle with parsley, and serve.

MUSHROOMS (CONTINUED)

Black Trumpet
Also called Black Chanterelle, this has an intense, earthy flavor. The thin flesh makes it particularly suitable for drying and grinding to a powder, which can be used as a tasty seasoning.

The Black Trumpet is recognizable by its fragile, wavy edges, leathery stalks, and absence of gills.

The fleshy cap has tooth-like spines on the underside, which add to its interesting texture.

Hedgehog fungus
Also called Sweet Tooth, this is appreciated for its hearty flavor and slightly crisp, meaty texture, which remains firm even when cooked. It is especially good in a cream sauce.

Matsutake or Pine mushroom
This sought-after variety is prized for its smooth, creamy texture and rich, complex— though not overpowering— flavor. It is hard to harvest, therefore expensive.

The dried flesh is reconstituted by soaking in warm water until pliable.

Cloud Ears
These Chinese dried mushrooms are relatively tasteless, but readily take on the flavors of other ingredients. They become gelatinous when cooked.

Dried maitake
Good to keep in the pantry, dried maitake adds a concentrated mushroomy flavor to soups, stews, and stir-fries.

Maitake or Hen of the Woods
Meaty and richly flavored, maitakes often measure more than 2ft (61cm) across. When fresh, the substantial flesh is best cut into chunks for use in braises and stews, or to make pickles.

TRUFFLES

Truffles are the aromatic, fruiting bodies of fungi that grow underground on tree roots (in particular those of oak, but also beech, poplar, birch, hornbeam, hazel, and pine), in well-watered, temperate regions. There was a time when truffles meant just black ones from Périgord in France or white ones from Alba in Italy, but that has changed with advances in truffle culture and the development of a truffle industry in various places such as China, the Pacific Northwest of the US, and European countries other than France and Italy. Black Périgord types

have a charcoal-colored interior with white veins, while Italian white truffles are beige outside and tan inside with white veins. All truffles have an intense aroma and flavor of earth, with floral and fruity overtones.

🔒 **BUY** Different types appear in various seasons: black truffles are best in midwinter; white in fall. Because of their rarity, truffles are expensive, so when buying, be sure your truffle is firm, not soft, with a clean, earthy—fruity aroma. Shrunken, dry truffles will have lost their intensity.

🗄 **STORE** Fresh truffles quickly lose quality. Store just for a day or two wrapped in dry paper towels in a paper bag in the fridge.

◉ **EAT** Fresh: Grate or shave on top of hot food, particularly pasta or risotto, just before serving. **Cooked:** Warm butter or duck fat will carry the aroma and flavor of truffles throughout a dish. Insert slices under the skin of poultry breast before roasting. Add to eggs for an omelet or to scramble. Extravagantly, bake whole in pastry with foie gras or braise in Madeira.
FLAVOR PAIRINGS Poultry and game birds, eggs, cheese, foie gras, potatoes, pasta, rice.
CLASSIC RECIPES Spaghetti tartufi; *fonduta*; sauce Périgueux; *pâté de foie gras truffé*; risotto with truffles; *poulet aux truffes*.

White or Alba truffle
White truffles exude outstandingly complex, earthy aromas and flavors, redolent of garlic and compost among others. The texture is firm, making them easy to shave for serving.

Black or Périgord truffle
With aromas of fresh earth, the forest floor, and chocolate, the black truffle is subtler than the white, though it is still pervasive. It has a firm, corky texture.

Raw shavings add robust flavor to all kinds of dishes. The skin is left on, so as not to waste a single part.

SPAGHETTI TARTUFI

A simple yet superb dish of pasta and sliced black truffles. This can also be made using white truffles, if you're lucky enough to have some.

SERVES 4

2 fresh black truffles, brushed clean and sliced very thinly (or use dried from a jar)

about 6 tbsp extra virgin olive oil

12oz (350g) spaghetti

1 garlic clove, crushed through a press

freshly grated Parmesan cheese or pecorino, to garnish (optional)

1 Put the truffles in a small bowl and add enough olive oil to cover. Cover the bowl and leave to infusefor about 1 hour.

2 Bring a large pot of salted water to a boil. Add the spaghetti and cook until tender yet still firm to the bite, 8 to 10 minutes (or according to the package instructions).

3 Meanwhile, pour about 1 tbsp of the infused truffle oil into a small saucepan and warm gently over low heat. Add the garlic and cook for a few seconds until soft and fragrant.

4 Drain the spaghetti, reserving a little of the cooking water. Return the spaghetti to the empty pot, along with the reserved cooking water. Add the garlic and the truffles with the remaining oil, and toss gently to mix. Serve immediately, sprinkled with cheese, if you wish.

SEA VEGETABLES

The world's oceans are a bath of minerals in which the algae called seaweeds grow. Because many of these are edible, and wonderfully nutritious, they can accurately be described as sea vegetables. Other plants that grow around the sea, along coasts and marshes, are also included in this group of foods. Sea vegetables are harvested wherever the ocean waters are clean —especially in northern Japan, where they are an important and normal part of the diet, but also along the Pacific Northwest coast of the US, Canada's east coast, and the countries bordering the North Atlantic. Sea vegetables come in myriad shapes, sizes, and colors, and range in flavor from mild to tasting strongly of the sea. Those such as samphire and sea-kale stems are tender and pleasantly salty.

🛒 **BUY** Sea vegetables are available fresh all year round; according to type; they should be moist and pliable, with no decay. Most seaweeds are sold dried, to be reconstituted, or used as flakes or powder in the kitchen.

📦 **STORE** Fresh sea vegetables should be packed moist in a plastic bag and will keep in the fridge for up to a week. Dried seaweeds can be stored in the kitchen pantry.

⬤ **EAT** Fresh: Use kelp and samphire in salads. Fishermen and women in Ireland and Scotland and around the North Atlantic eat *dulse* raw, using it like chewing gum because it is rubbery and slowly yields its flavor. Dried sheets of *nori* are used to wrap sushi. **Cooked:** Depending on the type of sea vegetable, boil, steam, braise, or stew. Use to make stock (such as *kombu*, a type of kelp, used for *dashi*) or to flavor soups. **Preserved:** Dry or pickle.
FLAVOR PAIRINGS Seafood, potatoes, onions, soy sauce, miso, eggs, ginger.

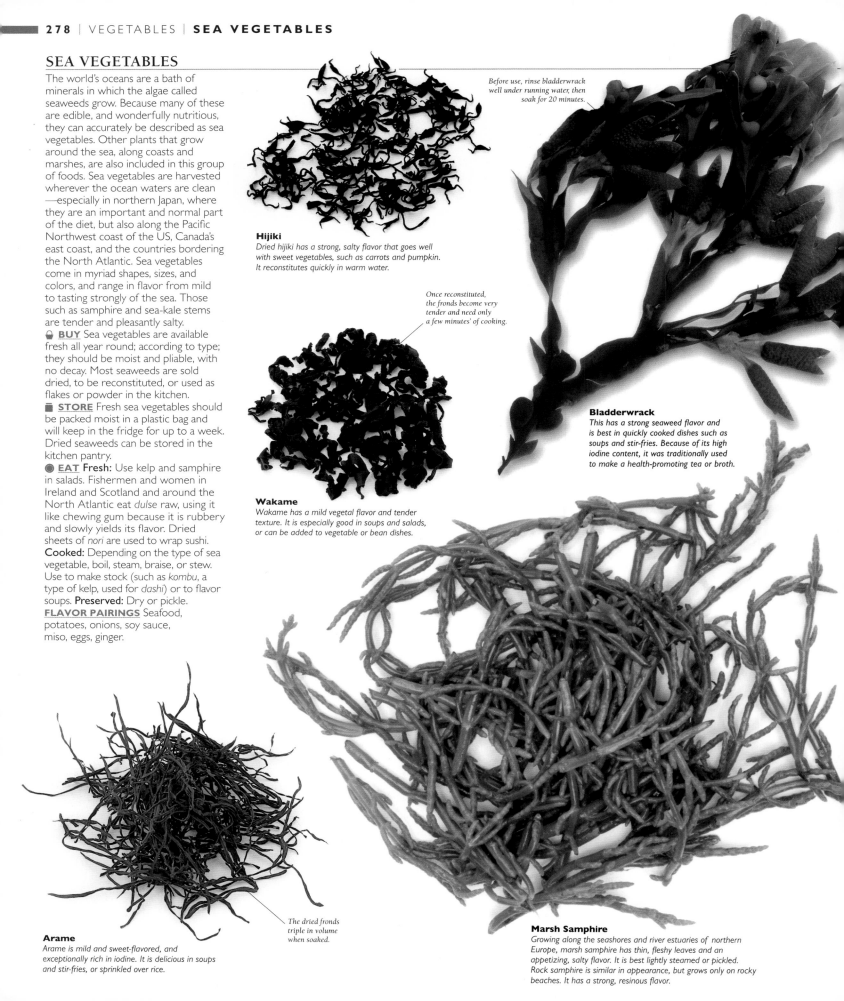

Hijiki
Dried hijiki has a strong, salty flavor that goes well with sweet vegetables, such as carrots and pumpkin. It reconstitutes quickly in warm water.

Once reconstituted, the fronds become very tender and need only a few minutes' cooking.

Wakame
Wakame has a mild vegetal flavor and tender texture. It is especially good in soups and salads, or can be added to vegetable or bean dishes.

Before use, rinse bladderwrack well under running water, then soak for 20 minutes.

Bladderwrack
This has a strong seaweed flavor and is best in quickly cooked dishes such as soups and stir-fries. Because of its high iodine content, it was traditionally used to make a health-promoting tea or broth.

Arame
Arame is mild and sweet-flavored, and exceptionally rich in iodine. It is delicious in soups and stir-fries, or sprinkled over rice.

The dried fronds triple in volume when soaked.

Marsh Samphire
Growing along the seashores and river estuaries of northern Europe, marsh samphire has thin, fleshy leaves and an appetizing, salty flavor. It is best lightly steamed or pickled. Rock samphire is similar in appearance, but grows only on rocky beaches. It has a strong, resinous flavor.

Dulse
Popular in Ireland and Scotland, dulse has a rich/meaty flavor and a gelatinous texture. It is good in long-simmered stews and soups, or mixed with fried potatoes.

Lightly toast nori sheets over a gas flame or electric burner before use. It is ready when crisp and fragrant.

Kelp
Found along North Atlantic shores, kelp is valued for its rich/meaty flavor. It makes tasty and nutritious stock, or can be boiled and served as a vegetable.

Nori
Cultivated in Japan, nori is dried and pressed into tissue-thin sheets. Tasting mildly of the sea, the sheets make a tender wrapper for sushi, or for morsels of fish or meat.

Agar-agar
This flavorless, colorless, gelatinous substance extracted from various sea vegetables is a useful vegetarian alternative to gelatine. The form used for jelly making is sometimes colored red (pictured left).

Sea Lettuce
The large, wavy-edged leaves have a mildly salty flavor. They are tender enough to use raw in salads. Alternatively, add them to clear soups or fry in butter until crisp.

HERBS

CHERVIL | TARRAGON
FENNEL | LAVENDER
BAY | BASIL | OREGANO
PARSLEY | ROSEMARY
SORREL | SAGE | THYME

HERB ESSENTIALS

Herbs are usually used to add fragrance and flavor to a dish, rather than to provide the dominant taste. The light flavors of dill, parsley, and chervil are good with fish and seafood; the more pungent rosemary, oregano, and garlic will flavor braised or baked lamb or roast pork beautifully. Root vegetables respond well to thyme and rosemary, eggplant to Provençal herbs, green peas to chives, tomatoes to basil and parsley. It is important always to balance delicate and hearty flavors in recipes, and to use herbs judiciously so they do not overpower the flavors of the other ingredients.

A fresh herb butter *is a deliciously simple accompaniment to pasta. Freshly chopped flat-leaf parsley, basil, oregano, thyme, or other Mediterranean herbs perfectly complement fresh pasta.*

BUY

The wealth of fresh herbs now available has had the beneficial effect of banishing from many kitchens a lot of small packages of stale, dried herbs. Some herbs that are sold dried, such as basil and parsley, are never worth having; their aroma is musty at best and their taste insipid. Such herbs are meant to be eaten fresh. The clean, herbaceous notes of fresh parsley, and the complex, sweet scent of anise and clove wafting from a bunch of basil beguile first the sense of smell, and, later, also the tastebuds. Unlike many herbs, these two are not overwhelming if used in large quantities—as they are in basil sauce pesto and parsley salad tabbouleh. Robust herbs, such as oregano, thyme, sage, savory, mint, and rosemary, respond well to drying, which preserves and often concentrates their flavor. Whether fresh or dried, these herbs should be used sparingly, or they will overwhelm the other flavors in the food instead of complementing them.

STORE

Ideally, use herbs when they are freshly picked, as this is when they have the most fragrance and flavor, but there are several techniques that can be used in order to store them for a little longer without compromising their flavors. Whether storing them in the fridge, freezer, or drying them for later use, you achieve the best results by doing this as soon as possible after picking.

Store fresh herbs

The refrigerator *is the best place to store freshly cut herbs, either with their stems in water or on a damp paper towel.*

Freeze chopped herbs

Make herb ice cubes *by washing and drying the herbs well, then chop and freeze them in small pots or ice-cube trays with a little water or oil. Place in plastic bags to store.*

Freeze puréed herbs

Purée and pot *herbs in individual pots by blending them in a food processor with a little olive oil. Pack the puréed herbs into bags or plastic containers and freeze.*

Dry in a jar

Dry freshly cut *herbs by spacing them out on muslin and leaving them in a cool, dry room until the leaves feel brittle. Crumble large leaves or strip smaller leaves whole from their stems. Store in airtight containers.*

Microwave herbs

Herbs can also *be quickly and easily dried in the microwave. Scatter cleaned leaves and sprigs evenly on a double layer of paper towels and microwave at 100 percent for 2½ minutes. Store in an airtight container.*

Soft, fresh mixed herbs *lift the flavor of vegetable dishes, salads, and meat or poultry stews. Chop or tear over your finished dish.*

PREPARE

Herbs can be used whole, chopped, or pounded into a purée, depending on the requirements of the recipe. Softer-leaved herbs are better used raw, or added in the last minutes of cooking.

CHOP Herbs are chopped according to what suits the dish. Finely chopped herbs integrate well with other ingredients and add immediate flavor because much of their surface is exposed. They also allow essential oils to blend into the food quickly, but they may lose flavor in cooking. Coarsely chopped herbs keep their flavor and texture longer and survive cooking better, but are less attractive in a smooth-textured dish.

Using a mezzaluna

Some cooks like to use the curved mezzaluna when chopping large amounts of herbs. This implement is rocked backward and forward to great effect.

Using a knife

Use a large, sharp knife or you will bruise the herbs. Hold the point of the blade with the fingers of your non-cutting hand and chop up and down briskly in a rocking motion.

SLICE Any finely shredded vegetable used as a garnish is termed a *chiffonade*. Shredded herb leaves make an attractive garnish and also keep their texture well.

If shredding leaves such as sorrel, remove the thick vein from each one beforehand. Stack a few similar-sized leaves one on top of the other and roll them up tightly. Using a sharp knife, cut the roll of leaves into very fine slices.

POUND Herbs can be pounded to a paste using a pestle and mortar, and garlic is easily puréed in a mortar with a little salt. A smoother result is achieved more quickly by chopping them in a food processor. Some herb sauces, such as pesto, are made in this way.

I Pesto is the classic pounded-herb sauce. Start by pounding some basil and garlic in a large mortar to a rough purée.

2 Gradually work in some pine nuts, grated Parmesan cheese, and olive oil, and pound further until it produces a smooth paste.

HERB MIXTURES

Dried or fresh herbs can be used in many combinations. The composition of even the classic mixes is usually determined by the kind of dish they are to accompany—this is a principle to guide you for European *bouquet garnis*, Middle Eastern blends, or South American mixtures, which may all include spices along with the herbs.

STRIP AND PLUCK Some herbs—chives, chervil, cilantro—have soft stalks, but in most cases leaves must be stripped from the stalks before being used. Small leaves and sprigs are used whole in salads or as a garnish, but most leaves are chopped, sliced, or pounded depending on the dish being prepared. Keep leaves whole until just before you need them, or their flavors will dissipate.

Strip herb leaves

Hold the stalk firmly in one hand, and pull upward with the thumb and forefinger of the other hand to strip the leaves.

Pluck herb leaves

Pluck fennel leaves from the stalk, pulling the leaf sprays upward with one hand. Remove any thick stalks that remain.

Bouquet garni This little bundle of herbs is used in French cooking to impart flavor to slow-cooked dishes. The muslin cloth tied with string holds the herbs together and should be removed before serving. A classic bouquet garni contains a bay leaf, 2–3 fresh parsley stalks, and 2–3 sprigs of thyme.

COOK

Adding herbs to cooking early on will enable them to release their flavors into the dish. Dried herbs should always be put in at the beginning, and herbs with tough leaves, such as rosemary, lavender, winter savory, thyme, and bay, withstand long cooking well. If you add sprigs of herbs to a dish, remove them before serving. To restore the aroma of herbs used in a slow-cooked dish, stir a few finely chopped leaves into the pan toward the end of cooking. Strongly flavored herbs, such as mint, tarragon, fennel, marjoram, and lovage, can be added at any stage during cooking. The essential oils of delicate herbs such as basil, chervil, chives, dill, cilantro, perilla, and lemon balm soon dissipate when heated. To keep them fresh in taste, texture, and color, add them just before serving the dish.

AGASTACHE (AGASTACHE SPECIES)

Agastaches are handsome, hardy perennials of the mint family. Two are particularly worth the cook's attention —anise hyssop, *A. foeniculum*, native to North America, and Korean mint, *A. rugosa*, native to eastern Asia. The two herbs can be used interchangeably in the kitchen. A third species, Mexican giant hyssop, *A. mexicana*, grows wild in Mexico, where the leaves and flowers are used to make an infusion.

🔒 **BUY** Some specialist nurseries stock plants, although both can be grown from seed. Harvest leaves when young; they are most aromatic just before the plant flowers.

🗄 **STORE** Leaves are sturdy and will keep for 4–5 days in a plastic bag in the crisper of the fridge. They are best used fresh. Use dry leaves only to make infusions.

⬤ **EAT** Use as a garnish, or add to a hot dish just before serving. A few leaves in a salad will add an anise note; mix with other summery herbs to add to pancake batter or an omelet, or in an herb sauce for pasta. Common in teas or summer drinks, chopped leaves can also be used in marinades and sauces for fish and seafood, in chicken or pork dishes, or in plain rice. Their natural sweetness complements the sweetness in many vegetables, and they are also good with fruit.

FLAVOR PAIRINGS Fava beans, zucchini, root vegetables, winter squashes, tomatoes, summer berries, stone fruits.

Korean Mint
Although this smells of eucalyptus and mint, it has a taste that resembles anise hyssop, with a lingering anise aftertaste.

Anise Hyssop
Also called licorice mint, this has a sweet, anise aroma and flavor. The flowers resemble those of hyssop, but it is not related to either anise or hyssop.

GARLIC CHIVES
(ALLIUM TUBEROSUM)

Native to central and northern Asia, garlic chives, also known as Chinese chives, also grow in subtropical China, India, and Indonesia. The plants have flat leaves rather than the hollow stems of ordinary chives. Sometimes plants are cut back and kept in the dark: the pale yellow shoots produced by this blanching are a prized delicacy.

🔒 **BUY** Asian markets sell green and blanched chives all year round. Leaves can be cut for use at any time; flowers are harvested as buds, on the stalks.

🗄 **STORE** Once cut, they wilt quickly —blanched chives the fastest of all. Green chives will keep for a few days in a plastic bag in the fridge, but the smell is strong.

⬤ **EAT** Fresh: Cut green leaves into short lengths, then quickly blanch in boiling water to accompany pork or poultry. Add at the last minute for pungency to stir-fried dishes of beef, shrimp, tofu, and many vegetables; use in spring rolls; or dip little bunches of leaves in batter and deep-fry. Pale yellow chives can be stirred into soups, noodle dishes, and steamed vegetables at the last minute. The flower buds are a much prized vegetable, used in salads and egg, fish, and cheese dishes.
Preserved: In China and Japan, the flowers are ground and salted to make a spice.

FLAVOR PAIRINGS Noodles, green vegetables, pork, seafood, chicken, ginger, Chinese five spice.

Leaves and flowers of garlic chives have a stronger, more garlicky taste than ordinary chives.

CHIVES (ALLIUM SCHOENOPRASUM)

This smallest and most delicately flavored member of the onion family originated in northern temperate zones and has long grown wild all over Europe and North America. Now widely cultivated, chives grow as grass-like clumps of hollow, bright green stalks that have a crunchy texture. All parts of the plant have a light oniony flavor and aroma.

🔒 **BUY** If buying cut chives, they should be crisp, not floppy, but it is far better to grow them yourself.

🗄 **STORE** Ideally use quickly after cutting. Drying chives is pointless, but chopped and frozen they retain their flavor tolerably well and can be used straight from the freezer.

⬤ **EAT** Chives should never be cooked, since heat quickly dissipates their taste. Chop or snip and add in generous measure to soups, salads (in particular potato salad), sauces (stir into thick yogurt to make a fresh relish for grilled fish, or mix with sour cream to dress baked potatoes).

FLAVOR PAIRINGS Avocados, zucchini, potatoes, root vegetables, cream cheese, egg dishes, fish and seafood, smoked salmon.

CLASSIC RECIPE Fines herbes.

CHOPPING CHIVES
Because of their shape, chives are easily chopped with scissors or a knife.

1 *Gather the chives together into a bunch, gently tapping one end of the bunch on the board, so that the chive stalks are leveled.* **2** *Use kitchen scissors to snip across the bunch into pieces of the desired length. Or, cut with a large, sharp knife.*

The bright flowers have a light, oniony taste, and look good scattered over herb salads or omelets.

LEMON VERBENA (ALOYSIA CITRIODORA)

Lemon verbena is native to Chile and Argentina. When it was taken to Europe, it gained favor with fragrance manufacturers in France for its aromatic oils. The taste echoes the intoxicating aroma, but is less strong; it is more lemony than a lemon, but lacks the tartness. Leaves keep their fragrance quite well when cooked or dried.

BUY Specialist herb nurseries stock plants. Leaves can be harvested throughout the growing season.

STORE Keep fresh leaves for a day or two in the fridge; sprigs can also be put in a glass of water and kept in a cool place for 24 hours. Freeze chopped leaves in small pots or in ice cubes. Dried, the leaves retain aroma for up to a year.

EAT Fresh: Add sprigs to iced tea or summer coolers, or make an infusion of fresh leaves. Scent a syrup for poaching fruit, chop finely for a fruit salad or tart, or infuse in cream to make ice cream. A cake pan lined with leaves gives a lemon scent to a sponge or pound cake. **Cooked:** Put some sprigs into the cavity of fish or poultry, or chop and use in a stuffing or marinade. The vibrant, clean taste is also good with fatty meats such as pork and duck, in vegetable soups, and in a rice pilaf.

FLAVOR PAIRINGS Apricots, carrots, zucchini, mushrooms, rice, fish, chicken, pork, duck.

The leaves have an aromatic scent, intensified when crushed or rubbed.

ANGELICA (ANGELICA ARCHANGELICA)

A statuesque biennial—flower stalks may be over 6½ft (2m) high—angelica does best in cool climates and is hardy enough to grow in northern parts of Scandinavia and Russia. The whole plant is sweetly aromatic. Young stalks and leaves taste musky, warm, and bittersweet, slightly earthy, with notes of celery, anise, and juniper. Flowers have a honeyed fragrance.

BUY Plants are available from herb nurseries; it can also be grown from seed. Young stalks and leaves are best cut during the first summer or early the following spring.

STORE Leaves will keep in a plastic bag in the fridge for 2–3 days; young stalks for up to a week.

EAT Cooked: Add young leaves and stalks to marinades and poaching liquids for fish and seafood, or cook as a vegetable—boiled or steamed angelica is very popular in Iceland and northerly parts of Scandinavia. Add leaves to salads, stuffings, sauces,and salsas. Sliced young stalks or chopped leaves combine well with rhubarb in compotes, pies, and jams, and can also be infused in milk or cream to make ice cream or custard. **Preserved:** Candy young stalks. Essential oil distilled from seeds and roots is used to flavor vermouths and liqueurs.

FLAVOR PAIRINGS Almonds, hazelnuts, apricots, oranges, rhubarb, plums, strawberries, fish, seafood.

When rubbed, young leaves and stalks have a sweet, musky scent.

DILL (ANETHUM GRAVEOLEN)

An annual plant, native to southern Russia, western Asia, and the eastern Mediterranean, dill is widely grown for its feathery leaves (often called dill weed) and its seed. Dill leaves have a clean, fragrant aroma of anise and lemon. The taste is of anise and parsley, mild but sustained. The oval, flattish seeds smell like a sweet caraway; the taste is of anise with a touch of sharpness and a lingering warmth. Indian dill, *A. g.* subsp. *sowa*, is grown primarily for its seed, which is lighter in color, longer, and narrower than European dill seed. Its more pungent taste is preferred for curry mixtures.

BUY At the market, choose a bunch that looks crisp and fresh.

STORE Use fresh dill quickly; after 2–3 days in a plastic bag in the fridge it will droop. Freezing preserves the flavor of dill better than drying. Seed has a shelf life of 2 years.

EAT Fresh dill loses flavor if it is overheated, so use in cold dishes or add to hot dishes at the end of cooking. Mix chopped dill into salad dressings and creamy sauces for vegetables and meat, and into seafood dishes. In Greece, dill flavors stuffed vine leaves; it is added to rice in Iran. Use dill seeds for slow-cooked foods and in pickling. In Scandinavia, dill seeds are added to breads and cakes.

FLAVOR PAIRINGS (Leaves) beets, green beans, carrots, celery root, zucchini, cucumber, potatoes, spinach, eggs, fish and seafood, rice; (seeds) cabbage, onion, potatoes, pumpkin, vinegar.

CLASSIC RECIPES *Gravad lax*; dill-pickled cucumbers; spinach with dill and shallots; dill potato salad.

The feathery fronds resemble fennel, but the dill plant is much smaller.

Use the oval, flattish seeds for slow-cooked dishes and pickling.

The delicate, feathery leaves make a pretty and tasty salad garnish.

CELERY (APIUM GRAVEOLENS)

Wild celery, or smallage, is an ancient European plant from which garden celery and celery root were bred in the 17th century. Cutting or leaf celery resembles the original wild celery, with dark green, glossy leaves, similar to flat-leaf parsley. It produces an abundance of leaves on erect stalks to form a bushy plant. Chinese celery (*kun choi*) is mid-green with leaves like those of garden celery. The unrelated water or Vietnamese celery (*Oenanthe javanica*) has upright stalks with small, serrated leaves. Water celery has a fresh taste; parsley notes are more dominant than the characteristic warm bitterness of celery.

🔖 **BUY** Celery's natural habitat is marshland, but it is easily grown from seed in moisture-retentive soil.

🗄 **STORE** Cutting celery will keep for 4–5 days; Chinese celery is often sold with its roots and will last for a week if kept whole; water celery keeps for 1–2 days. Store them all in plastic bags in the fridge.

⏺ **EAT** Cooking will temper the bitterness of all types of celery, but they retain their other aromatic properties. Cutting celery is useful because you can pick leaves to add to *bouquets garnis*, soups, and stews instead of having to use a celery stick. In Holland and Belgium, the leaves are used like parsley, as a garnish or stirred into dishes just before serving. In France, cutting celery is sold as a soup herb; in Greece, it is popular in fish and meat casseroles.

Chinese celery is used as a flavoring and as a vegetable; it is rarely eaten raw. Stalks are sliced and used in stir-fried dishes; leaves and stalks flavor soups, braised dishes, rice, and noodles throughout Southeast Asia. Water celery, with its mild taste, is very popular in Vietnam as a salad herb, or lightly cooked and added to soups and fish and chicken dishes. Thais use it in a similar way and serve it raw with larp or blanched with *nam prik*. The Japanese use it for *sukiyaki*. Celery seed flavors soups and stews, dressings for vegetable salads, and breads.

FLAVOR PAIRINGS Cabbage, potatoes, cucumber, tomatoes, chicken, fish, rice, soy sauce, tofu.

CLASSIC RECIPE Eel in green sauce.

CHERVIL
(ANTHRISCUS CEREFOLIUM)

Chervil is native to southern Russia, the Caucasus, and southeastern Europe. A traditional symbol of new life, the arrival of chervil in markets signals springtime, when chervil sauces and soups appear on menus in France, Germany, and Holland. Often seen in restaurants as a garnish, chervil deserves to be more widely used in domestic cooking, too. It is sweetly aromatic, and the taste is subtle and soothing, with light anise notes and hints of parsley, caraway, and pepper.

🔖 **BUY** Chervil is easy to grow from seed. Avoid plants with flowers.

🗄 **STORE** In a plastic bag or in damp paper towels it will keep for 2–3 days in the crisper of the fridge.

⏺ **EAT** Scatter over vegetables or add to salads (try it in a warm potato salad or a beet salad with shallots or chives). Stir *fines herbes*, or chervil alone, into eggs for an omelet or scrambled-egg dish. Add to a soup based on potato or a richer version that uses cream and egg yolks, or to consommés. Chervil gives a delicate flavor to vinaigrettes and to butter or cream sauces to serve with fish, poultry, and vegetables.

FLAVOR PAIRINGS Asparagus, fava beans, green beans, beets, carrots, fennel, lettuce, peas, potatoes, tomatoes, mushrooms, cream cheese, eggs, fish and seafood, poultry, veal.

CLASSIC RECIPES *Fines herbes*; Frankfurt green sauce; chervil soup.

Celery seeds
The seed has a much stronger aroma and taste than the parent plant. It is penetrating and spicy, and leaves a somewhat bitter, burning aftertaste. Use sparingly.

Cutting celery
The leaves of cutting or leaf celery have a herbaceous, parsley-like aroma and taste, combined with warmth and a bitter note.

Chinese celery
When sold whole, with its roots on, Chinese celery looks like a small head of green garden celery, although the stalks are hollow and much thinner.

Chinese celery leaves have a slightly bitter, parsley-like flavor.

TARRAGON (ARTEMISIA DRACUNCULUS)

Native to Siberia and western Asia, tarragon was unknown in Europe until the 16th and 17th centuries, when the development of classic French cooking extended the use of tarragon in the kitchen. Indeed, the best cultivated variety is usually called French tarragon (or, in Germany, German tarragon) to distinguish it from the inferior, bitter Russian variety. French tarragon, *A. d. var. sativa*, has mid-green leaves that are sweetly aromatic, with hints of pine, anise, or licorice; the flavor is strong yet subtle, with spicy anise and basil notes and a sweetish aftertaste.

BUY Supermarkets sell tarragon in minute quantities, so it is better to grow your own. The leaves can be harvested when required, and whole stalks removed for drying in midsummer. When buying a tarragon plant, check that the label says French tarragon; if the type of tarragon is not specified, it may be the Russian variety.

STORE Fresh young sprigs can be kept for 4–5 days in a plastic bag in the crisper of the fridge. When dried, tarragon loses much of its aroma. Freezing the leaves, whole or chopped, retains more of their flavor.

EAT Use tarragon in moderation and it will enhance the flavor of other herbs. **Fresh:** A discreet addition lends a pleasant, deep note to green salads. It is very good in marinades for meat and game, to flavor goat cheeses and feta cheese preserved in olive oil, and to make a versatile herb vinegar and flavored butter.

Cooked: Long cooking diminishes tarragon's aroma, but the flavor is not lost. It is an essential ingredient in many French fish, poultry, and egg dishes. It adds a fresh, herbal fragrance to mushrooms, artichokes, and ragouts of summer vegetables; with tomatoes, it is almost as good as basil. Make a bed of tarragon stalks for roasting fish, chicken, or rabbit.

FLAVOR PAIRINGS Artichokes, asparagus, zucchini, tomatoes, potatoes, salsify, fish and seafood, poultry, eggs.

CLASSIC RECIPES Béarnaise, *ravigote*, and tartare sauces; *fines herbes*.

Keep the leaves and stalks intact, and use as a bed for roasting fish, game, and poultry.

CLASSIC RECIPE

BÉARNAISE SAUCE

This tangy sauce is the classic French accompaniment to broiled or grilled steak.

½ cup dry white wine

3 tbsp white wine or tarragon vinegar

3 shallots, finely chopped

5 sprigs of fresh tarragon, plus 1 tbsp finely chopped fresh tarragon leaves or a mixture of tarragon and chervil

freshly ground white pepper

12 tbsp (1½ sticks) unsalted butter

3 large egg yolks

salt

1 Combine the wine, vinegar, shallots, tarragon sprigs, and a good grinding of pepper in a small, heavy, nonreactive saucepan. Cook over low heat, uncovered, until the liquid has reduced to 2–3 tbsp. Strain through a fine sieve, pressing the shallots and tarragon well to extract maximum flavor. Discard the shallots and tarragon.

2 Return the liquid to the pan. Melt the butter gently and set aside. When the butter has cooled to lukewarm, discard the white residue on top. Set the melted butter aside.

3 Set the pan with the wine and vinegar reduction over very low heat and whisk in the egg yolks and a little salt. Add the melted butter, a tablespoon or so at a time, whisking continuously. Wait until each spoonful is absorbed before adding more butter. Remove the pan from the heat before adding the final spoonful. Add the tarragon leaves and taste, adding more salt and pepper if needed. The sauce can be kept warm for about 15 minutes in a bowl placed over a pan of hot (but not boiling) water.

HORSERADISH (ARMORACIA RUSTICANA)

Native to eastern Europe and western Asia, horseradish still grows wild in the steppes of Russia and the Ukraine, and its culinary use probably originated there. The taste of the root is acrid, sharp, and hot.

BUY Fresh roots are hard to find except before Passover—horseradish is one of the five bitter herbs of the Seder. Dried roots can be bought powdered or flaked.

STORE Fresh roots taken from the garden will keep for months in dry sand; bought ones remain good for 2–3 weeks in a plastic bag in the fridge, even after being cut and partially used. Grated horseradish can be frozen.

EAT Grating releases the highly pungent, volatile oil, but this dissipates very quickly and does not survive cooking. Once grated, sprinkle with lemon juice to preserve the white color and pungency. Horseradish is good in salads of potatoes or other root vegetables, and aids the digestion of oily fish. Mix with apricot preserves and mustard and use to glaze ham.

A few tender, young leaves will give a pleasant, sharp taste to a green salad.

FLAVOR PAIRINGS Apple, beef, baked gammon or ham, sausages, oily or smoked fish, seafood, avocado, beets, potatoes, sausages.

CLASSIC RECIPES Horseradish cream; *Apfelkren*.

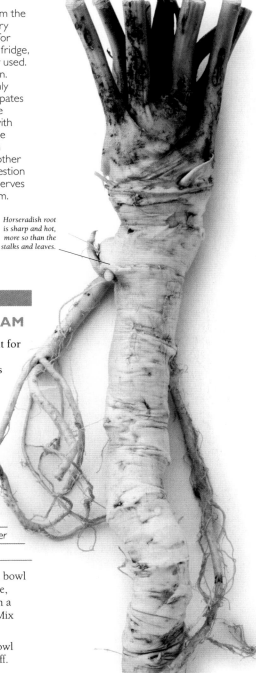

Horseradish root is sharp and hot, more so than the stalks and leaves.

CLASSIC RECIPE

HORSERADISH CREAM

The traditional accompaniment for roast and braised beef, this is also great with oily fish such as trout, mackerel, or salmon.

SERVES 4–6

3 tbsp finely grated fresh horseradish root

1 tsp white wine vinegar or cider vinegar

juice of ½ lemon

1 tsp Dijon mustard

1 tsp sugar

salt and freshly ground black pepper

1 cup heavy cream, well chilled

1 Put the horseradish in a small bowl and add the vinegar, lemon juice, mustard, and sugar. Season with a pinch each of salt and pepper. Mix well to combine.

2 Pour the cream into a large bowl and whip until thick but not stiff.

3 Fold the horseradish mixture into the lightly whipped cream. Taste, adding more salt and pepper, if needed. Cover and refrigerate for up to 2 days.

MUGWORT (ARTEMISIA VULGARIS)

Mugwort grows wild in many habitats throughout most of Europe, Asia, and North and South America. The aroma is of juniper and pepper, lightly pungent with a hint of mint and sweetness. The flavor is similar, with a mild, bitter aftertaste.

BUY In Germany, mugwort is available fresh and dried; elsewhere it is necessary to grow your own if you want fresh mugwort. Harvest young leaves just before the flower buds open: the flowers can get unpleasantly bitter. Dried mugwort is available from some Japanese shops.

STORE Fresh leaves can be kept for a few days in the fridge. Store dried buds and leaves in an airtight container for up to a year.

EAT Fresh: Shred young leaves over a green salad.

Cooked: Mugwort's aroma develops with cooking, so it should be added early. It suits fatty fish, meat, and poultry, and helps in their digestion. It is good in stuffings and marinades, and also flavors stock quite well. Called *yomogi* in Japan, it is used there as a vegetable, and as a seasoning for soba noodles. Throughout Asia, young leaves are boiled or stir-fried.

FLAVOR PAIRINGS Beans, onions, duck, game, goose, pork, eel, rice.

CLASSIC RECIPE *Mochi* (Japanese rice cakes).

Mugwort leaves are smooth on top, downy white underneath.

ORACH (ATRIPLEX HORTENSIS)

Orach grows wild in Europe and much of temperate Asia. Its old popular name was mountain spinach, and it was once gathered, and also cultivated, for use as a vegetable. Out of fashion for a long time, it has been rediscovered as an attractive salad herb. Green orach may have red-tinged stems; red orach has deep plum-colored leaves and stems. Orach has a mild, agreeable, spinach-like flavor, and is not aromatic.

BUY Orach is sometimes included in bags of gourmet salad greens. Seeds and plants are available from specialist nurseries; harvest leaves in summer and early fall.

STORE It is best to use leaves straight after picking, but they will keep for a day or two in a plastic bag in the fridge crisper.

EAT Fresh: The small, triangular leaves, particularly of red orach, make an attractive addition to the salad bowl.

Cooked: Steam or sauté green or red orach with spinach or sorrel (it alleviates the acidity of the latter).

FLAVOR PAIRINGS Salad greens such as catalogna, corn salad, lettuce, mizuna, and mustard greens.

The heart-shaped leaves make orach an attractive addition to a salad bowl.

CALAMINT (CALAMINTHA SPECIES)

These aromatic, perennial plants deserve to be better known. For the cook, lesser calamint, *C. nepeta*, also called nepitella or mountain balm, is the most rewarding. It is a bushy plant with downy, greyish foliage, and bears small, lilac or white flowers throughout the summer. The whole plant smells warm and minty, with notes of thyme and camphor; the taste is pleasantly pungent, warm, minty, and peppery, with a light bitterness in the aftertaste. Common or woodland calamint, *C. sylvatica*, is less fragrant, but can be used in the same way. Large-flowered calamint, *C. grandiflora*, is a showy garden plant whose leaves are used for infusions.

BUY Calamint is not available as a cut herb, but specialist nurseries stock plants. Leaves can be harvested from spring to late summer.

STORE Fresh sprigs will be good for 1–2 days if kept in a plastic bag in the fridge. For longer storage, dry and store in an airtight container.

EAT Lesser calamint is a favorite flavoring in Sicily and Sardinia, and also in Tuscany, where it is used with vegetables, especially in mushroom dishes. The Turks use it as a mild form of mint. It is good with roasts, stews, game, and grilled fish; in stuffings for vegetables and meat; in marinades and

When crushed, calamint leaves have a wonderful warm, minty aroma.

sauces. Use dried leaves for infusions.

FLAVOR PAIRINGS Eggplant, beans, fish, green vegetables, lentils, mushrooms, pork, potatoes, rabbit.

EPAZOTE (CHENOPODIUM AMBROSIOIDES)

Native to central and southern Mexico, epazote was long an essential ingredient of Mayan cuisine in the Yucatán and Guatemala. It is now widely cultivated and used in southern Mexico, the northern countries of South America, and the Caribbean islands. Its use is spreading in North America. The name refers to a disagreeable odor—*epatl* means "skunk" and *tzotl*, "sweat". Those who dislike it describe the aroma as that of turpentine or putty, while others are reminded of savory, mint, and citrus. The taste is pungent and refreshing, bitterish with lingering citrus notes.

BUY In regions where it is grown, fresh epazote is available in markets. Elsewhere in the world, it is almost impossible to obtain unless you grow it yourself. Use dried leaves only when fresh are unavailable: dried epazote has much less taste. Make sure you get the leaves, not the stalks, which are also sold dried—these are fine for tea, but less good in cooking.

STORE Fresh epazote can be kept in the fridge, wrapped in damp paper towels, or with the stalks immersed in water.

EAT Use epazote lightly: it easily overwhelms other flavors, and in larger doses it is somewhat toxic and can cause dizziness. Although used raw in salsas, its flavor works best in cooking; add for the last 15 minutes or so

to avoid bitterness. In Mexico, it is commonly added to bean dishes, partly for its flavor and partly because it aids digestion.

FLAVOR PAIRINGS White cheese, chorizo, pork, fish and shellfish, lime, mushrooms, onion, peppers, squash, sweetcorn, green vegetables, rice.

CLASSIC RECIPE *Mole verde*.

Only use the leaves in cooking, not the stalks.

MARIGOLD (CALENDULA OFFICINALIS AND TAGETES SPECIES)

The bright yellow to deep orange flowers of marigolds have long been used to color food and give it a slightly pungent flavor. In the Republic of Georgia, the petals of pot marigold (*C. officinalis*) and French marigold (*T. patula*) are dried and ground to make a highly prized spice with a sweet, musky aroma and hints of citrus peel. Fresh marigold petals are used in Europe and North America as a garnish and in salads along with the slightly peppery leaves. The leaves of Mexican mint marigold (*T. lucida*) are a tarragon substitute in Mexico and the southern US. In Peru, *huacatay* (*T. minuta*), also called black mint, which is strongly aromatic with citrus and eucalyptus notes and a bitter aftertaste, is an essential flavoring in traditional dishes.

🔒 **BUY** Fresh marigold flowers are available from supermarkets. Pot and French marigold plants can be bought from garden centers, or you can grow from seed. Mexican mint marigold may be found at specialist herb nurseries. Huacatay is hard to find fresh outside South America, but is sold as a paste in jars in the US.

📦 **STORE** The petals and young leaves of pot and French marigolds should be used immediately after picking. Leaves of Mexican mint marigold will keep for a day or two in a plastic bag in the fridge. Dry marigold petals in a low oven and then grind; store dried petals and powder in airtight containers.

● **EAT** Marigold petals and young leaves add a lively note to salads. Add petals to cookies and small cakes, and to custards, savory butters, and soups. Use mint marigold leaves with fish, chicken, and other foods that marry well with tarragon; mix huacatay with chiles to season grilled meats, soups, and stews. Dried petals were once used to adulterate saffron, and can still be an inexpensive coloring for rice.

FLAVOR PAIRINGS Dried marigold petals, Georgia: chiles, garlic, walnuts. Mint marigold, Mexico: avocado, sweetcorn, squash, tomatoes, melon, summer berries, stone fruits.

Dried, ground French marigold petals are a prized spice in Georgia.

French marigold
The aroma of French marigolds has a distinctive muskiness with light citrus notes, reminiscent of coriander seeds.

Mexican Mint marigold
The leaves smell more of anise than mint, with light notes of hay and some spicy warmth. The plant's other English names, winter or Mexican tarragon, refer to its tarragon-like taste.

A few pot marigold leaves add a gentle peppery note to salads.

Pot marigold
This marigold has both single and double flowers. Fresh petals have a delicate, aromatic bitterness and an earthy taste.

CLAYTONIA (CLAYTONIA PERFOLIATA)

Also called winter purslane and miner's lettuce, claytonia is a delicate-looking yet hardy annual, native to North America. It makes an excellent salad herb. The name miner's lettuce came about because miners in the California Gold Rush ate the wild plant to avoid scurvy (it is high in vitamin C). The leaves completely encircle the smooth stems, and the tiny, white flowers are borne on thin stalks from early summer. Although not aromatic, claytonia has a pleasantly mild, clean, and fresh flavor.

🌱 **BUY** Claytonia can be gathered from the wild in shady grasslands in North America, but it is less commonly found elsewhere. Herb nurseries stock plants, or you can grow it from seed.

📦 **STORE** It is best picked and used at once, but can be kept in a plastic bag in the crisper of the fridge for 1–2 days.

◉ **EAT** Fresh: Leaves, young stems, and flowers make a useful and pretty contribution to the salad bowl, particularly in winter when other salad greens can be dreary. **Cooked:** Stir-fry leaves and young stems—alone, or combined with other greens— flavoring with a little oyster sauce.

FLAVOR PAIRINGS Arugula, sorrel, and other salad greens; lightly spiced dressings.

The pretty flowers are edible. Add to a salad bowl along with the leaves and stems.

THAI DIPPING SAUCE

A staple in Thailand, this spicy sauce is good served with almost anything. The flavor actually improves after a day or two.

SERVES 4

1 tsp palm sugar, raw sugar, or brown sugar, plus extra if needed

3 garlic cloves, crushed through a press

3–4 small red chile peppers, seeded and finely chopped (leave in the seeds if you prefer a fiery-hot sauce)

2 tbsp Thai fish sauce (nam pla)

1 tbsp soy sauce

juice of 1 lime, plus extra if needed

2 tbsp chopped fresh cilantro

salt, to taste

1 This can be made with a pestle and mortar, or in a small food processor. If using a pestle and mortar, pound the sugar, garlic, and chiles to a smooth paste, then stir in the rest of the ingredients. Taste, adding salt, sugar, or lime juice, if needed.

2 If using a processor, pulse together all the ingredients except the lime juice, cilantro, and salt. Add lime juice and salt to taste, then stir in the cilantro.

3 Let the sauce sit for a few minutes to allow the flavors to develop, then taste again and add more lime juice, salt, or sugar as needed. Refrigerate in an airtight container.

CILANTRO (CORIANDRUM SATIVUM)

Native to the Mediterranean and western Asia, cilantro is now grown worldwide. The plant yields both herb and spice (called coriander), and is a staple in many cuisines. The fresh leaves are essential to Asian, Latin American, and Portuguese cooking. Thai cooks also use the thin, spindly root. In Western cooking, the coriander seed is used as a spice; in the Middle East and India, both seeds and leaves are common in the kitchen. In North America, the fresh leaves are sometimes known as Chinese parsley; in Europe, both leaves and spice are called coriander. Leaves, roots, and unripe seeds all have the same aroma: refreshing, lemony-ginger, with notes of sage; the roots are more pungent and musky than the leaves. The flavor is delicate yet complex, with hints of pepper, mint, and lemon.

🌱 **BUY** Fresh cilantro is available from markets; bunches are sold with roots intact in Southeast Asian shops.

📦 **STORE** Keep in a plastic bag in the fridge crisper for 3–4 days. For longer storage, chop and freeze in ice-cube trays (drying cilantro is not worthwhile, as flavor is lost).

◉ **EAT** Except when used in a curry or similar paste, add cilantro at the end of cooking: high or prolonged heat reduces the flavor. Both the herb and the spice are used prolifically throughout most of Asia, in soups, stir-fried dishes, curries, and braised dishes. Thai cooks use the roots for curry pastes. India and Mexico share a liking for cilantro with green chiles in chutneys, relishes, and salsas. In the Middle East, the spice and the herb are used for pungent spice pastes and mixtures. The Portuguese pair cilantro with potatoes, fava beans, and clams.

FLAVOR PAIRINGS Avocados, cucumber, root vegetables, sweetcorn, coconut milk, fish and seafood, lemons and limes, beans, rice.

CLASSIC RECIPES Thai dipping sauce; *zhug*; *chermoula*; ceviche; guacamole.

MITSUBA
(CRYPTOTAENIA JAPONICA)

This cool-climate perennial grows wild in Japan and is used extensively in Japanese cooking. It is now cultivated elsewhere. Also known as Japanese parsley, Japanese chervil, and trefoil, mitsuba has little aroma, but a distinctive mild and agreeable taste, with elements of chervil, angelica, and celery, something of the astringency of sorrel, and a hint of clove.

🌱 **BUY** You may find mitsuba in a Japanese or Asian market. Otherwise, buy a plant from an herb nursery and harvest leaves and slender stalks from spring to fall.

📦 **STORE** Leaves keep for 5–6 days if wrapped in damp paper towels, or in a plastic bag, in the crisper of the fridge.

◉ **EAT** Fresh: The cress-like, sprouted seedlings and young leaves are good in salads. **Cooked:** Blanch mitsuba quickly to tenderize, or add to stir-fried food at the last moment; overcooking destroys the delicate flavor.

FLAVOR PAIRINGS Eggs, fish and seafood, poultry, rice, mushrooms, carrots, parsnips.

CLASSIC RECIPES *Matsutake no dobinmushi*; tempura.

The thin leaves are delicate, and best added to dishes at the end of cooking, in order to retain their flavor.

Mitsuba means "three leaves" in Japanese, which is echoed in the English name trefoil.

VIETNAMESE MINT (ELSHOLTZIA CILIATA)

Native to temperate eastern and central Asia, Vietnamese mint, also called Vietnamese balm or *rau kinh gio'i*, has been used in Southeast Asia as a culinary and medicinal plant for many years. Today, this bushy plant with light green, serrated leaves and lavender flower spikes is cultivated in Germany and in those parts of the US where there are large Vietnamese populations, but as yet is little known to Western cooks. Vietnamese mint has a clear, lemon aroma with floral undertones; the flavor is similar.

🔒 **BUY** Outside its native region, Vietnamese mint is grown mostly by nurseries that supply herbs to Southeast Asian restaurants. Leaves are harvested from spring to early fall, and are sold at Asian markets.

▣ **STORE** Leaves keep for 3–4 days in a plastic bag in the fridge crisper. Sprigs from an Asian market can be encouraged to root by standing them in water, then planting.

◉ **EAT** Fresh: Add to the platter of fresh herbs that accompanies many Vietnamese meals. **Cooked:** In Thailand, leaves are most frequently cooked and served as a vegetable, but they are also used in Southeast Asian cuisine to flavor vegetable, egg, and fish dishes, in soups, and with noodles and rice.

FLAVOR PAIRINGS Eggplant, cucumber, lettuce, mushrooms, scallion, starfruit, fish, seafood.

Leaves have a flavor reminiscent of lemon balm, but more concentrated, somewhat like lemongrass.

WASABI (EUTREMA WASABI)

This herbaceous perennial grows primarily in cold mountain streams in Japan; cultivation has also started in California and New Zealand. Wasabi has a fierce, burning smell that makes the nose prickle, and a bitingly sharp, but fresh and cleansing, taste.

🔒 **BUY** Outside Japan, wasabi is seldom available fresh, but you might look for it in the freezer section of a Japanese food store. More often, it is sold either in tubes as a paste or in cans as powder. Because wasabi is so expensive, harsher-tasting horseradish mixed with mustard and green coloring is frequently passed off as wasabi paste or powder. Real paste costs twice as much as fake, and has a shorter "use by" date.

▣ **STORE** Fresh wasabi will keep for a week wrapped in plastic in the fridge. Powdered wasabi has a shelf life of several months. Tubes of paste lose potency more quickly than the powder.

◉ **EAT** Wasabi does not retain its flavor when cooked, so it is generally served with or added to cold food. In Japan, it accompanies most raw fish dishes: sashimi and sushi plates always have a tiny mound of grated wasabi or wasabi paste, which is then mixed to individual taste with a soy dipping sauce. With *dashi* (soup stock) and soy sauce, wasabi makes the popular wasabi-joyu sauce. Use wasabi to give a sharp piquancy to marinades and dressings, or make a flavored butter for steak. When using wasabi powder, mix with water and steep for about 10 minutes, to allow it to develop its penetrating aroma and flavor.

FLAVOR PAIRINGS Avocado, beef, raw fish, rice, seafood.

The knobbly root is sometimes called Japanese horseradish because of its pungency.

CULANTRO (ERYNGIUM FOETIDUM)

This tender biennial grows wild on many Caribbean islands, and is variously called *shado beni* (Trinidad), *chadron benee* (Dominica), and *recao* (Puerto Rico). Also grown in Southeast Asia, it reaches other parts of the world with names like long or spiny coriander, sawleaf herb, and Chinese or Thai parsley, as well as its Spanish name, culantro. As the Latin name indicates, it has an intense aroma with a fetid element. The taste is earthy, pungent, and quite sharp—like a concentrated version of cilantro with a bitter note at the finish.

🔒 **BUY** Bunches of leaves, sometimes with rootlets attached, are sold in Asian markets. Plants are available at some herb nurseries; leaves can be picked throughout the growing season by cutting off at soil level.

▣ **STORE** Fresh leaves can be kept for 3–4 days in the fridge. For longer storage, remove the thick central rib and purée the leaves with a little water or sunflower oil, then freeze in ice-cube trays.

◉ **EAT** Culantro can be used in dishes calling for cilantro, but reduce the amount. In its indigenous regions, it flavors soups, stews, and curries, rice and noodle dishes, and meat and fish dishes. It is a key ingredient in Trinidadian fish and meat marinades. In Asia, it is often used to temper the smell of beef, which many people find too pungent. In Vietnam, young leaves are always included in the bowl of herbs put on the table to accompany the meal.

FLAVOR PAIRINGS Beef, fish and seafood, rice, noodles.

CLASSIC RECIPES *Larp*; salsa.

If the serrated edges of the leaves are very spiny, remove the spines or use the leaves in a cooked dish.

FENNEL (FOENICULUM VULGARE)

This tall, graceful perennial, indigenous to the Mediterranean and now naturalized in many parts of the world, is one of the oldest cultivated plants. Fennel leaves and stalks have a mild taste and are best used soon after picking, although they keep their flavor well when dried. Fennel seed has a stronger flavor than the leaves. Do not confuse with the bulbous sweet or Florence fennel, *F. v.* var. *dulce*, which is used as a vegetable.

🔒 **BUY** Plants are available at garden centers. Harvest the leaves spring to fall. Wild fennel pollen, an intensely flavored, golden-green dust, can be bought via the internet.

📦 **STORE** Fresh fennel fronds will keep in a plastic bag in the fridge for 2–3 days. Cut off the seedheads for drying when the seeds are yellowy green; dried seeds will keep for up to 2 years in an airtight container. It is best to grind seed as needed.

⬤ **EAT** In spring, fresh fennel adds a lively note to salads and sauces. Later in the season, a garnish of flowers or a sprinkling of pollen will give an anise fragrance to cold soups, chowders, and grilled fish. Fennel is an excellent foil for oily fish: the Sicilians use it liberally in their pasta with sardines; in Provence, whole red mullet, bass, and bream are baked or grilled on a bed of fresh or dried fennel stalks. Fennel seed can be added to pickles, soups, and breads: try combining ground fennel and nigella to flavor bread, as is done in Iraq. In Greece, leaves or seeds are combined with feta cheese and olives to make a flavorful bread. Fennel seeds flavor sauerkraut in Alsace and Germany, and Italians use them when roasting pork. In the Indian subcontinent, fennel seeds appears in *garam masala*, in spiced gravies for vegetables or lamb, and in some sweet dishes. Indians also chew fennel seeds after a meal as a breath freshener and digestive aid. Pollen gives amore heady flavor to seafood, grilled vegetables, pork chops, and Italian breads.

FLAVOR PAIRINGS Beets, beans, cabbage, leeks, cucumber, tomatoes, potatoes, duck, fish and seafood, pork, lentils, rice.

CLASSIC RECIPES Chinese five spice powder; *panch phoron*.

Only young fennel leaves and stalks are suitable for use in the kitchen.

Green fennel
All parts of the fennel plant are edible, although the roots are no longer eaten. The aroma is warm and anise like; the taste is similar: pleasantly fresh, slightly sweet, with a hint of camphor.

Bronze fennel
A less vigorous plant than green fennel, the bronze variety has a similar, although milder, aroma and flavor.

Fennel seed
The flavor of fennel seed is less pungent than dill and more astringent than anise, with a bittersweet aftertaste. Dry-roasting the seeds before use brings out the sweetness.

WOODRUFF (GALIUM ODORATUM)

As its name suggests, woodlands are the natural habitat of this low, creeping, perennial herb. Native to Europe and western Asia, woodruff is now also found in temperate North America. Its small, white flowers and neat ruffs of narrow, shiny leaves make it an attractive garden plant in spring. Fresh woodruff has a faint scent, but cutting it releases the smell of freshly mown hay and vanilla. Flowers are more lightly scented than leaves, and the flavor echoes the scent.

BUY Plants are available from garden centers and herb nurseries. Leaves and flowers can be picked in spring and early summer; later in the year the fragrance is less pronounced.

STORE Sprigs are best picked and kept for a day or two before using: the aroma strengthens when the leaves are wilted or when they are dried, and they keep their aroma when frozen.

EAT Since woodruff contains coumarin, a substance that may cause liver damage if used in excess and which is thought to be carcinogenic, it should be used in very small amounts. Luckily just one or two stems will impart the herb's pleasant aroma. Infuse in marinades for chicken and rabbit, in dressings for salads, in wine to make a sabayon or sorbet; remove before serving or using the liquid.
FLAVOR PAIRINGS Apples, melons, pears, strawberries.
CLASSIC RECIPE *Waldmeisterbowle* or *Maibowle* (a wine punch made to celebrate May Day and other occasions in Germany).

Decorate salads with the pretty, star-like woodruff flowers.

HOUTTUYNIA (HOUTTUYNIA CORDATA)

This perennial, water-loving plant is not much appreciated as an herb by cooks in the West, but it is widely used in Southeast Asia. Native to Japan, houttuynia now grows wild across much of eastern Asia. The dark green-leaved variety is the most common in the kitchen, although the striking cultivated variety *H. c.* 'Chameleon', with multi-colored leaves, is also used. The flavor is sourish and astringent, with similarities to rau ram and cilantro, but with fishy undertones; it is aptly known as fish plant and Vietnamese fish mint. People either love or hate this herb.

BUY Nurseries and garden centers sell plants as decorative ground cover. Crush leaves to smell them before buying—some plants smell rank, while others are pungent but pleasing. Harvest leaves from spring to fall.

STORE Leaves will keep for 2–3 days in a plastic bag in the crisper of the fridge.

EAT Fresh: Houttuynia is most often eaten raw, to accompany beef and duck, or with raw vegetables to dip in fiery *nam prik*. For a salad, combine it with lettuce, mint, and young nasturtium leaves and flowers.
Cooked: In Japan, houttuynia is used as a vegetable rather than an herb, and simmered with fish and pork dishes. In Vietnam, where it is very popular, it is chopped and steamed with fish and chicken. Leaves can also be shredded into a clear soup, stir-fried vegetables, and seafood dishes.
FLAVOR PAIRINGS Fish, chicken, duck, pork, beef, chiles.

When crushed, the leaves have a cilantro aroma, with citrus and somewhat fishy notes.

HYSSOP (HYSSOPUS OFFICINALIS)

Native to northern Africa, southern Europe, and western Asia, hyssop is a handsome plant that has long been naturalized in central and western Europe. It has a strong and pleasant aroma of camphor and mint. The taste of the dark green leaves is refreshing but potent, hot, minty, and bitterish—reminiscent of rosemary, savory, and thyme. The tiny flowers have a more delicate flavor than the leaves.

BUY Hyssop grows well from seed. As it is virtually evergreen, its leaves can be picked even in winter.

STORE Fresh leaves will keep for about a week in a plastic bag in the crisper of the fridge. Both leaves and flowers retain much of their strength when dried.

EAT Toss a few leaves and young shoots into salads (to which the flowers can make a robust garnish), or add to soups and to rabbit, kid, and game stews. Rubbing it on to fatty meats such as lamb can make them easier to digest. Hyssop is very good in fruit pies and compotes, and with sherbets and desserts made using assertively flavored fruits such as apricots, morello cherries, peaches, and raspberries. It has long been used to flavor non-alcoholic summer drinks, digestives, and liqueurs.
FLAVOR PAIRINGS Apricots, peaches, beets, cabbage, carrots, winter squashes, mushrooms, egg dishes, game, beans.

Hyssop should be used sparingly or it will overwhelm other flavors.

LAVENDER (LAVANDULA SPECIES)

Native to the Mediterranean region, lavender is grown commercially on a large scale in many parts of the world, mainly to be distilled for its aromatic oils. It is slowly making a comeback as a versatile flavoring in both savory and sweet dishes. The penetrating, sweetly floral, and spicy aroma, with lemon and mint notes, is echoed in the flavor, with undertones of camphor and a touch of bitterness in the aftertaste. The flowers have the strongest fragrance.

BUY Garden centers and herb nurseries offer a variety of lavenders. Flowers are best picked just before they are fully open, when the essential oils are most potent. Harvest leaves at any time during the growing season.

STORE Fresh lavender flowers and leaves will keep in a plastic bag in the fridge for up to a week. Dried flowers can be stored for a year or more.

EAT Lavender is very potent, so use sparingly. **Fresh:** Grind fresh flowers with sugar to a powder; use the sugar for baking and desserts. Add flowers to jam or jelly toward the end of the cooking time, or to fruit compotes for a sweetly spiced note. Infuse them in cream, milk, syrup, or wine to flavor sorbets, ice creams, mousses, and other desserts. Scatter petals over a dessert or cake to decorate. Chop a few leaves for a salad. **Cooked:** Add chopped flowers to rice, or to a cake, shortbread, or sweet-pastry mixture before baking. Use chopped flowers and leaves to flavor roast leg of lamb, or roast, or casseroled rabbit, chicken, or pheasant. Add to marinades and rubs. It also makes an excellent vinegar.

FLAVOR PAIRINGS Berries, plums, cherries, rhubarb, chicken, lamb, pheasant, rabbit, chocolate.

CLASSIC RECIPES Lavender ice cream; lavender shortbread; lavender jelly.

CLASSIC RECIPE

LAVENDER ICE CREAM

The simple custard base of this ice cream is infused with the delicate, floral fragrance of lavender.

SERVES 6–8

| 1 cup whole milk |
| 4 dried lavender heads (to yield about 1 tsp petals) |
| 4 large egg yolks |
| ½ cup superfine sugar |
| 1 cup heavy cream, lightly whipped |

1 Pour the milk into a small nonreactive saucepan. Pull off lavender flowers and shake the petals into the milk. Heat until bubbles begin to appear around the edge of the pan. Remove from the heat, cover, and set aside to infuse for 30 minutes.

2 Strain the milk through a nylon sieve and pour back into the clean pan. Combine the egg yolks and sugar in a bowl and whisk until well blended. Warm the milk again as before, then gradually whisk it into the egg mixture. Return to the pan and simmer over low heat, stirring constantly, for 15–20 minutes, or until the custard mixture thickens enough to coat the back of a spoon. Do not allow it to boil. Leave to cool, or cover and refrigerate up to 24 hours.

3 Stir the cream into the custard, then pour into an ice-cream maker and process according to manufacturer's directions. Once softly set, transfer the ice cream to a covered container and freeze until firm enough to scoop, at least 3 hours or overnight. This ice cream is best eaten within a week.

French lavender
The floral spiciness of this bushy shrub, also known as Spanish lavender, has a more pungent camphor note than English lavender.

Flowers have a firm base, but petals can be plucked out.

Leaves are tough, like rosemary leaves, and need to be chopped finely before use.

English lavender
Also called common lavender, this is the best variety for the cook because of its lower camphor content. The fragrant flowers may be lilac, purple, or white.

RICE PADDY HERB (LIMNOPHILA AROMATICA)

Rice paddy herb is native to tropical Asia. It grows wild in ponds and is cultivated in flooded rice fields. Taken to other countries by Southeast Asian immigrants in the 1970s and 1980s, it is also known by its Vietnamese names, *rau om* and *ran om*. The small, trailing herb has an attractive floral—citrus, musky aroma and flavor, with a hint of the pungent earthiness of cumin.

BUY Buy plants from nurseries and harvest leaves throughout the growing season. Or, look for the cut herb in shops in Vietnamese neighborhoods.

STORE Keep stems for a few days in a plastic bag in the fridge crisper.

EAT Fresh: The Vietnamese chop it into vegetable and sour soups just before serving them, include it in fish dishes, and frequently add it to the platter of herbs provided with most Vietnamese meals. In northern Thailand it is served with fermented fish and chile sauce, and in curries made with coconut milk. Its lemony fragrance also makes it suitable for sweet dishes. **Cooked:** Malay cooks use it as a vegetable, rather like spinach.

FLAVOR PAIRINGS Coconut milk, fish and seafood, lime juice, noodles, rice, green and root vegetables.

BAY (LAURUS NOBILIS)

The bay tree is native to the eastern Mediterranean, but has long been cultivated in northern Europe and North and South America. Although it does best in warm regions, it will survive in a sheltered, sunny position in cooler climates. Leaves from the tree have a sweet, balsamic aroma with notes of nutmeg and camphor and a cooling astringency. Fresh leaves are slightly bitter; fully dried leaves have a potent flavor. The purple berries that follow the flowers are not edible.

BUY Fresh leaves can be used from a tree year-round. Dried leaves are widely available in supermarkets.

STORE To dry leaves fully, lay them flat in a dark, well-aired place until brittle, then store them in an airtight container in a dry, dark place.

EAT Two or three bay leaves will flavor a dish for 4—6 people; if you put in too many, the flavor will be too strong. The leaves yield their flavor slowly, so they are useful in stocks, soups, stews, sauces, marinades, and pickles. Crush fresh leaves to release their aromatic compounds; crumble or grind dried leaves only when you need them. Put a leaf or two on top of a homemade pâté or terrine before baking it; add bay to a fish stew or combine with lemon and fennel when filling the cavity of a fish to be baked; thread leaves on to kebab skewers (soak dried leaves in water first); or add them to a pilaf. Use bay to give a pleasantly unusual, spicy fragrance to custards and rice pudding, and to poached fruit dishes. The Turks use bay in steamed and slow-cooked lamb dishes; the Moroccans add it to chicken and lamb tagines; the French partner it with beef in *Provençal daubes*. In Turkish spice bazaars, boxes of dried figs are often lined with bay leaves.

FLAVOR PAIRINGS Beef, chicken, game, lamb, fish, chestnuts, citrus fruits, haricots beans, lentils, rice, tomatoes.

CLASSIC RECIPES *Bouquet garni*; béchamel sauce.

Fresh leaves
Bay leaves can be picked from the tree throughout the year. When fresh, they are slightly bitter, but the bitterness will fade if you keep them for a day or two, until wilted.

Dried leaves
Dried bay leaves will retain their aroma and flavor for at least a year, although they are best when only recently dried (they will be a matte, sage green). If they have turned yellow or brown, they will be stale and have no flavor.

Use the aromatic seeds of lovage in pickles, sauces, marinades, breads, and biscuits.

The ridged, hollow stalks can be blanched and used as a vegetable.

LOVAGE (LEVISTICUM OFFICINALE)

Lovage is native to western Asia and southern Europe. Wild and cultivated forms are indistinguishable, and the herb has long been naturalized elsewhere, although outside Europe its use has never become popular. Lovage leaves are strongly aromatic, somewhat similar to celery (in French it is called *céleri bâtard*, or "false celery"), but more pungent, with musky overtones and notes of anise, lemon, and yeast. The tiny, ridged seeds are aromatic and have a taste similar to the leaves, but with added warmth and a hint of clove.

BUY Cut lovage is seldom sold, but it is easy to grow your own: buy seeds or plants from an herb nursery and pick leaves at any time. Seeds and ground, dried roots can be bought from some spice merchants.

STORE Wrapped in a plastic bag, leaves will keep for 3—4 days in the fridge. They can also be dried or frozen and will retain most of their strength; dried leaves are more yeasty and celery-like than fresh ones. Seeds will keep in an airtight container for a year or two.

EAT Lovage can be used as celery or parsley in almost any dish, but is much stronger than either of these, so should be treated with caution. The pungency diminishes in cooking. **Fresh:** A few young leaves are good in green salads. **Cooked:** Use leaves, chopped stalks, and roots in casseroles and stews. Young leaves can make a soup, on their own or with potato, carrot, or Jerusalem artichoke, and are often used in seafood chowders; older leaves are good in stuffings for poultry, and liven up bean or potato dishes, such as potato cakes with Cheddar or Gruyère. Whole or ground seeds can be used in pickles, sauces, marinades, breads, and biscuits.

FLAVOR PAIRINGS Apples, carrots, zucchini, mushrooms, potatoes and other root vegetables, tomatoes, corn, onions, cream cheese, egg dishes, ham, lamb, pork, beans and pulses, rice, smoked fish, tuna.

MINT (MENTHA SPECIES)

One of the most popular flavors in the world, mint is at once cooling and warming, with a sweet fragrance. Native to southern Europe and the Mediterranean, mints have long naturalized throughout the temperate world. They hybridize easily, leading to some confusion in their naming, but for the cook they broadly divide into two groups: spearmint and peppermint. Spearmint and its relatives are mellow and refreshing, with a sweet—sharp, pleasantly pungent flavor backed by hints of lemon. Peppermint and its related varieties, which have strong menthol notes and a fiery bite, are too pungent for most culinary uses and are used primarily to flavor confectionery and toothpaste.

BUY Choose cut mint in large bunches from a market. Or buy plants from a garden center; leaves can be picked throughout the growing season. Spearmint is the dried mint most commonly found commercially.

STORE Bunches of fresh mint will keep for 2 days in a glass of water in the kitchen, or in the fridge. Store dried mint in an airtight container.

EAT Fresh mint flavors a variety of vegetables, and it goes well with meat and grilled fish, whether in a marinade, sauce, or salsa. In the Middle East, mint is part of the accompaniment for *mezze*. In Vietnam, it is added to salads. Mint also finds its way into Southeast Asian dipping sauces and sambals: the cooling notes counter the warmth of spices in curries. The herb's refreshing effect enhances fruit salads and ices, and minty notes can be a welcome addition to chocolate desserts and cakes. In Arab countries and the eastern Mediterranean, dried mint is often preferred to fresh.

FLAVOR PAIRINGS Lamb, potatoes, carrots, tomatoes, chocolate, yogurt.

CLASSIC RECIPES Moroccan mint tea; mint sauce and jelly; sauce paloise; *tabbouleh; raita; cacik;* mint julep.

When crushed, young lemon balm leaves have a fresh, lingering, lemon scent.

LEMON BALM
(MELISSA OFFICINALIS)

Lemon balm is a perennial of the mint family, native to southern Europe and western Asia, and now cultivated widely in all temperate regions. Young leaves have a mild lemon-mint flavor; large, older leaves are more musty in taste. Always cook with fresh leaves, and use generous amounts because the aroma is delicate. The variegated form, *M. o.* 'Aurea', can also be used.

BUY Seeds and plants can be bought from herb nurseries. Leaves should be harvested early in the season —they can become musty later on.

STORE Fresh leaves will keep for 3–4 days in a plastic bag in the fridge crisper. Leaves can also be dried and stored in an airtight container, where they should keep their flavor for 5–6 months.

EAT Fresh: Lemon balm's principal use is as a soothing, calming tea, made from fresh or dried leaves. A strong balm tea, well sweetened, will make the basis for a good sorbet. Infuse young leaves in summer coolers or blend in smoothies; tear for green or tomato salads; chop to scatter over steamed or sautéed vegetables, or into rice or cracked wheat. Lemon balm also makes a delicate herb butter and fragrant vinegar, and it is good in fruit desserts and creams. **Cooked:** Use in sauces, stuffings, marinades, and salsas for fish and poultry.

FLAVOR PAIRINGS Apples, figs, apricots, melons, nectarines, peaches, summer berries, carrots, mushrooms, zucchini, tomatoes, soft white cheeses, chicken, fish.

Spearmint
The most widely grown mint, this suits all recipes calling for mint. When dried, the aroma is pungent and concentrated, although it lacks the sweetness of the fresh herb.

Leaves are best harvested shortly before flowering, when the essential oils are at their strongest.

Moroccan mint
Prized for its fine, spicy aroma, this is less sweet than spearmint. It can be used in all minted dishes, and works particularly well in mint tea.

Bowles' mint
This mint has a fine flavor and can be used for all dishes requiring mint. The leaves have a soft, furry texture, so need to be chopped finely.

Mountain mint
This graceful plant is not a true mint, but young leaves and buds can be used as a mint substitute. Native to the eastern US, it smells and tastes of mint, but is more bitter.

MOROCCAN MINT TEA

This sweet mint tea accompanies most meals all across North Africa, not just in Morocco. Its ubiquity doesn't detract from its delicacy.

SERVES 8

3 tbsp loose green tea leaves or 5 green tea bags

bunch Moroccan mint or spearmint

water

1 cup superfine sugar

1 Fill a large teapot with boiling water to warm it; then discard the water. Place the green tea and fresh mint inside the teapot.

2 Pour 6 cups of water into a large pot. Bring to a boil over high heat, then carefully pour it over the tea and mint in the teapot. Steep for 5 minutes, stirring gently once or twice. Add the sugar and stir until it dissolves.

3 Pour the hot tea through a strainer into small serving cups, or cool and pour over ice cubes in glasses for iced mint tea.

Black peppermint is recognizable by its purple-tinged, dark green leaves and deep purple stalks.

Apple mint
So-called because it smells subtly of mint combined with ripe apple, this variety has a good flavor. The whole plant is downy. Leaves have a somewhat unattractive texture, so are best shredded for use.

Use the pretty leaves of chocolate mint to garnish ice creams and sorbets.

Black peppermint
A hybrid, this is attractively colored with a fine, if pungent, aroma. The taste is also pungent, so it is best used sparingly for desserts and cooling drinks, and fresh or dried for teas.

Chocolate mint
With its delightful scent of after-dinner chocolate mints, this mint variety is ideal for chocolate desserts and cakes.

MICROMERIA (MICROMERIA SPECIES)

Micromerias are perennial herbs or dwarf shrubs native to southern Europe, the Caucasus, southwestern China, and the western US and Canada. In these regions they are regularly used as a culinary herb and to make infusions. In Europe, they thrive particularly in the Balkan peninsula. Flavors of some micromerias tend toward mint, others toward thyme and savory. The species *M. thymifolia* has the finest flavor: warmly aromatic with delicate notes of thyme and savory. It is also rich in unsaturated fatty acids.

🔒 **BUY** Micromerias are not available as cut herbs, but plants are stocked by some specialist nurseries. They can also be picked from the wild. Harvest leaves from spring to late summer.

📦 **STORE** Sprigs will keep for a few days in a plastic bag in the crisper of the fridge.

⚫ **EAT** Italian cooks use young leaves with thyme—savory aromas to flavor soups, marinades, and frittate; in stuffings for meat and vegetables; with roast chicken or pigeon. Finely chopped leaves are added to pasta sauces or sprinkled over meat or poultry before grilling. In Balkan cooking, the leaves are used like thyme. Micromeria brings out the flavor of ripe tomatoes and soft, fresh cheeses. A few chopped leaves will give a depth of flavor to summer berry desserts.

FLAVOR PAIRINGS Tomatoes, chicken, pigeon, soft cheeses, summer berries.

If you grow micromeria in a rock garden you can harvest leaves from spring to late fall.

Pick small, young leaves and fully open flowers for use in the kitchen.

BERGAMOT (MONARDA DIDYMA)

The name bergamot probably derives from the similarity of the plant's aroma to that of the bergamot orange; another name is bee balm, because the flowers attract bees. Bergamot is also known as Oswego tea—from the Oswego valley near Lake Ontario, where Native American tribes made an infusion from it. Native to North America, the cultivated varieties of bergamot, with their showy whorls of different-colored flowers and slightly different scents, can be used in the same way. The whole plant has a distinctive citrus aroma. The flavor is citrus with an added warm, spicy note. Flowers are more delicately flavored than the leaves.

🔒 **BUY** Plants are sold at herb nurseries and garden centers. Pick flowers when fully open, and leaves throughout the summer.

📦 **STORE** Flowers and leaves wilt quickly and are best used soon after picking. Or they can be chopped and frozen, or dried.

⚫ **EAT** Add shredded young leaves and petals to green and fruit salads. Chop leaves into yogurt or cream for a sauce, or mix with parsley and orange for a salsa with pork kebabs or barbecued fish. Flowers are good in sandwiches with cream cheese and cucumber. Dried leaves are used for infusions: in North America, dried bergamot can be bought as an herbal tea. Try adding a few fresh or dried flowers or leaves to a pot of Indian tea, or to jugs of homemade lemonade or summer coolers for a lightly scented taste.

FLAVOR PAIRINGS Apples, citrus fruits, kiwi, melons, strawberries, papayas, chicken, duck, pork, tomatoes.

SWEET CICELY (MYRRHIS ODORATA)

Sweet cicely is an under-rated herb, a natural sweetener with a fine flavor. A hardy perennial indigenous to upland pastures from the far west of Europe to the Caucasus, it is long naturalized in northern Europe and is now cultivated in other temperate zones. By late spring, the large, feathery plant bears sweetly scented, lacy, white flowers, followed by large, attractive seedheads. The whole plant is aromatic: it has an attractive, musky aroma with notes of lovage and anise. The flavor tends more to anise, with a hint of celery and a pleasing sweetness. Unripe seeds have the strongest flavor and a nutty texture; the glossy, black ripe seeds have less flavor and are fibrous and chewy.

BUY Plants are available from herb nurseries, and can also be grown from seed. Cut leaves between spring and fall. Harvest the flowers in spring, and the green unripe seeds in summer.

STORE The leaves are best used soon after picking, but they will keep for 2–3 days in damp paper towels or a plastic bag in the fridge.

EAT Fresh: Young leaf tips give a subtle flavor to green salads and cucumber, and to cream and yogurt sauces made to accompany fish or seafood. Chop leaves into omelets and clear soups, and stir them into a purée of carrot, parsnip, or pumpkin to enhance the sweetness. Flavor fruit salads and cream-cheese desserts with leaves and seeds. Use flowers to decorate salads. **Cooked:** Use in savory dishes (add at the end of the cooking time to retain the flavor) and in cakes, breads, and fruit pies to give sweetness and a hint of spice. Cook leaves and green seeds with gooseberries and rhubarb to reduce the tartness of the fruits.

FLAVOR PAIRINGS Apricots, gooseberries, nectarines, peaches, rhubarb, strawberries, chicken, shrimp, scallops, root vegetables.

The feathery leaves remain green and edible from early spring to late fall.

MYRTLE (MYRTUS COMMUNIS)

Myrtle is native to the hilly regions of the Mediterranean basin and the Middle East. The shrub has small, shiny, oval leaves, bearing white flowers in summer and purple-black fruit in fall. The whole plant is aromatic. The leaves smell slightly resinous, with a sweet, orange-blossom note; they taste juniper-like and astringent. The berries are sweet with notes of juniper, allspice, and rosemary. The flowers are more delicately scented.

BUY Myrtle plants can be bought at specialist nurseries. Harvest leaves throughout the year, and buds and berries when they appear.

STORE Use fresh from the plant, or dry and keep in an airtight container. Once dried, buds and berries aren't as brittle as the leaves. Crush dried buds and berries to use as a spice.

EAT Fresh: Use myrtle flowers picked straight from the plant in salads or as a garnish. **Cooked:** Add leaves —very sparingly—toward the end of cooking if you are making a stew. Combine with thyme or savory to flavor meat and game, or with fennel to flavor fish. Place myrtle berries and a clove of garlic in the cavity of pigeon or quail to be roasted or fried, or use them as you would juniper berries. In southern Italy, myrtle leaves are used to wrap small, newly made cheeses, to give a subtle flavor as they mature.

FLAVOR PAIRINGS Pork, wild boar, venison, hare, chicken, pigeon, quail.

CATNIP (NEPETA CATARIA)

Native to the Caucasus and southern Europe, this attractive plant is now widely cultivated in many temperate regions, as well as being found in the wild. The names catnip and catmint are used interchangeably—it is so-called because the odor released from the bruised leaves induces a state of bliss in cats. Catnip's grey-green, heart-shaped leaves are covered by a white down; the flowers are white to lavender, dotted with red spots. When crushed, the leaves release a sweet, minty, camphorous aroma; the taste is also pungently mint like, with an acrid, bitter note.

BUY Plants are available at garden centers and specialist nurseries, or it can be grown from seed. Leaves can be harvested throughout the spring and summer.

STORE Sprigs will keep for a day or two in a plastic bag in the crisper of the fridge.

EAT Catnip was a more important culinary herb in the past than it is today, although it is still used in Italy in salads, soups, egg dishes, and stuffings for vegetables. A few of the sharply flavored leaves will give zest to a green or mixed herb salad. The robust flavor also goes well with fatty meats. It is widely used as an herbal tea.

FLAVOR PAIRINGS Duck, pork.

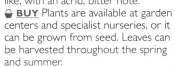

Use catnip leaves sparingly, as they are pungent.

BASIL (OCIMUM SPECIES)

Native to tropical Asia, basil is now grown almost everywhere where the climate is warm enough. There are many varieties, some with names that indicate their aroma or appearance. Sweet basil has a complex, sweet, spicy aroma with notes of clove and anise. The flavor is warm, peppery, and clovelike with underlying mint and anise tones. Purple (opal) basil, bush basil, lettuce basil, and "Ruffles" basils have rather similar flavors and aromas. The flavor of Asian basils, namely Thai, liquorice, holy, Thai lemon, lemon, and lime, differs from that of Western basils due to the different essential oils.

🔒 **BUY** Most basil leaves bruise and wilt easily, so when buying bunches of cut, fresh leaves avoid those with drooping or blackened leaves. Herb nurseries supply many varieties of basil, including Asian basils; leaves can be harvested until the first frost.

▪ **STORE** Store cut basil for 2–3 days in damp paper towels or a plastic bag in the refrigerator; the more sturdy Thai basil will keep for 5–6 days. Basil leaves will freeze well for up to 3 months; purée them with a little water or olive oil and freeze in ice cube trays. Alternatively, put the leaves in an airtight jar, layer lightly with salt, and cover with olive oil. Keep in the refrigerator: the leaves turn black, but will flavor the oil beautifully.

● **EAT** Basil quickly loses its aroma when cooked, so use it in a hot dish for depth of flavor, then stir in a little more to add fragrance when the cooking is finished. The leaves can be torn, or chopped or shredded with a knife, but cutting bruises them and they darken quickly. In Western cooking, basil is best known as a companion of tomatoes, whether in salad, sauce, or soup. Its natural partners are garlic, olive oil, lemon, and tomato. It is the key ingredient of Genoese pesto and the related *pistou* of the south of France. Basil is a good flavoring for poultry stuffings, for fish and seafood, especially lobster and scallops, and for roast veal and lamb. It also has an affinity with

raspberries. In Asian cooking, basil flavors salads, stir-fried dishes, soups, and curries. It is added at the end of cooking so that the aromatic leaves balance the spices in the dish. It is also used in Thai green curry paste.

FLAVOR PAIRINGS Western basils: mozzarella and other cheeses, eggs, cream cheese, eggplants, green beans, zucchini, lemon, olives, peas, pizza, potatoes, raspberries, rice, corn, tomatoes. Asian basils: beef, chicken, pork, fish and seafood, coconut milk, noodles, rice.

CLASSIC RECIPES Pesto; *pistou*; Thai green curry paste.

PREPARING BASIL

A quick way to chop basil leaves is to roll them up into a tight bundle before cutting.

1 *Remove the basil leaves from their stems and bunch a few together at a time into a tight roll.* **2** *Cut the rolled-up leaves into thin slices using a sharp knife.*

Sweet basil *(O. basilicum)*
Also called Genoese basil, this plant has large leaves and small, white flowers. Good for all Western cooking, it is the best basil for pesto, pistou, and tomato salads.

The sweet basil plant has distinctive large, bright green, silky leaves.

Purple basil
(O. b. var. purpurascens)
This handsome plant, also called opal basil, has purple or almost black leaves and pink flowers. It is highly aromatic, with clear notes of mint and clove. Use with rice and grains, and to add a splash of color to salads.

O. b. "Purple Ruffles"
This is an ornamental plant with large, shiny, purple-maroon leaves with a ruffled edge and pink flowers. Its flavor is warm and liquoricelike. "Green Ruffles" has big, lime-green leaves with a frilly edge and white flowers. Use both as sweet basil.

Holy basil *(O. sanctum)*
Holy basil, or bai gaprow, is intensely aromatic with a spicy, sweet pungency, hints of mint and camphor, and a touch of muskiness. The flavor is enhanced by cooking; when raw, the taste is slightly bitter. It is the essential ingredient in a Thai dish of stir-fried chicken with chiles and basil, and is extensively used in meat curries.

Lemon basil
(O. b. citriodorum)
This bushy, compact basil has a clean, lemon fragrance. In Indonesia, where it is called kemangie, it is fried with fish and seafood. Add it to salads, and scatter on scallops, broiled fish, or pork kebabs.

Bush basil *(O. b. var. minimum)*
Also called Greek basil, this makes a compact bush with small leaves, white flowers, and a peppery aroma. It is easy to grow in a pot. Use as sweet basil; add whole leaves to salads.

O. "African Blue"

This variety has a striking appearance and excellent flavor. The leaves are mottled green—purple, the flowers purple. It is strongly scented with peppery, clove, and mint notes and a hint of camphor in the background. Use it with rice, vegetables, and meats; it is very good in potato salad and makes an outstanding pesto.

Liquorice basil
(O. b. anise)
This decorative plant, also called anise basil, has purple-veined leaves, reddish stalks, pink flower spikes, and an agreeable, anise-liquorice aroma. Use as Thai basil.

Thai basil *(O. b. horapa)*
Thai basil has a heady, sweet, peppery aroma backed by pronounced anise notes, and a warming, anise—licorice flavor.

Lime basil *(O. americanum)*
This basil is similar to lemon basil, but the leaves are slightly darker and the aroma is decidedly of lime, not lemon. Use in salads and with fish and seafood.

O. b. "Cinnamon"

This variety is native to Mexico. The leaves are flushed purple and the flowers pink. It has a pronounced, sweet scent with clear cinnamon notes rising above hints of camphor. Serve it with bean and pulse dishes and with spicy, stir-fried vegetables.

Lettuce basil *(O. b. var. crispum)*
This basil has large, floppy, wrinkled leaves with a soft texture. It is excellent in salads, or chopped and mixed with diced tomato and extra virgin olive oil to make a pasta dressing. Lettuce basil is much prized in southern Italy.

Thai lemon basil *(O. canum)*
Also called hairy basil, or bai manglak, this plant has an attractive lemon—camphor aroma and a peppery, lemony flavor. Thai cooks stir it into noodles or fish curry just before serving. The seeds are soaked and used in a coconut-milk dessert and in cooling drinks. It is sometimes sold as green holy basil.

CLASSIC RECIPE

PESTO

This Genoese sauce for pasta also goes well with vegetables and as a dip or spread for bruschetta.

SERVES 4–6

4 handfuls of fresh basil leaves

¼ cup pine nuts

¼ cup freshly grated Parmesan or Pecorino cheese

1 large garlic clove, crushed

5–6 tbsp extra virgin olive oil

1 Combine the basil, pine nuts, cheese, and garlic in a food processor or blender and blend, pulsing the machine on and off, until finely chopped.

2 Scrape down the sides of the bowl. With the machine running, add the oil through the feed tube in a slow, steady stream until a thick sauce is formed. For a thinner sauce, add more olive oil.

3 If you don't have a processor, put the basil and garlic in a mortar and pound with a pestle. Add the pine nuts, a few at a time, then the cheese and oil alternately until you have a thick paste. Add more oil if desired.

OREGANO AND MARJORAM (ORIGANUM SPECIES)

Low, bushy perennials of the mint family, the marjorams and oreganos are native to the Mediterranean and western Asia. The plants are often confused, and unrelated plants with a similar aromatic profile may also be called oregano. The basic taste is warm, slightly sharp, and bitterish with a note of camphor. To this, marjoram adds a sweet, subtle spiciness, even in temperate climates. Oregano is more robust and peppery, with a bite and often a lemony note, qualities that diminish in colder climates. The flavor of oregano is generally highest in Greek and some Mexican oreganos.

● **BUY** Supermarkets sell dried oregano and marjoram and fresh-cut herbs or plants. Several varieties of oregano are sold dried under the Greek name *rígani*. It is easy to grow your own from seed or plants bought from herb nurseries. Pick leaves freely at any time; harvest for drying just after the flower buds form.

● **STORE** Keep fresh-cut herbs in a plastic bag in the refrigerator for 2–3 days. To dry, hang bunches of stalks in a well-ventilated, dry place; rub the leaves off and store them in an airtight container for up to a year. Dried marjoram and oregano are more intensely aromatic and have a stronger flavor than fresh.

● **EAT** Oregano has become an essential ingredient in much Italian cooking, especially pasta sauces, pizza, and roasted vegetables. For the Greeks it is the favorite herb for souvlaki, baked fish, and Greek salad. Throughout Spain and Latin America, it is used for meat stews and roasts, soups, and baked vegetables. In Mexico, it is a key flavoring for bean dishes, burritos, taco fillings, and salsas. While oregano stands up well to heat, the more delicate flavor of marjoram is easily lost in cooking: it should be added only at the last moment. Marjoram is good in salads (leaves and flower knots), in egg dishes, and mushroom sauces, and with fish and poultry. It makes a great sorbet. Use it with mozzarella and other young cheeses, too.

FLAVOR PAIRINGS Duck, lamb, poultry, veal, venison, fish and shellfish, cheese, eggs, eggplants, beans, carrots, zucchini, peppers, squashes.

Mexican oregano
(Lippia graveolens)
This is an attractive plant with gray-green, oval leaves and creamy-white flowers. Related to lemon verbena, it has a high volatile-oil content.

Sweet marjoram (O. majorana)
This pretty plant, also called knotted marjoram, has gray-green, slightly hairy leaves and clusters of white flowers. Its taste is more delicate and somewhat sweeter than that of common oregano, and it does not lend itself to long cooking.

Cretan dittany
(O. dictamnus)
Also called hop marjoram and native only to Crete and southern Greece, this plant is shorter than most other varieties and has deep pink flowers. Its flavor is very similar to that of sweet marjoram. It goes well with broiled fish.

Thick, silvery foliage distinguinshes the Cretan dittany plant from other types of marjoram.

Pot marjoram
(O. onites)
Sometimes called Sicilian marjoram but native to Greece and Asia Minor, this is a dwarf shrub with light green, downy leaves and white or pink flowers. A close relative of sweet marjoram, it is less sweet and more pungent.

Greek or Turkish oregano
(O. heracleoticum; O. v. hirtum)
Also called winter marjoram, this plant is native to southeastern Europe and western Asia. It has small, white flowers and a distinctive peppery note. It is the species most widely cultivated in Greece and Turkey and the most important economically, being the source for much of the dried oregano sold in Europe and North America.

Golden-leaved oregano
(O. v. "Aureum")
This oregano is a handsome ground-cover plant with dense foliage. It can be used in the same way as ordinary oregano but has a much milder flavor.

Common oregano
(O. vulgare)
The strong flavor of oregano works well with broiled meats and in stuffings, hearty soups, marinades, vegetable stews, and even hamburgers.

Common oregano has reddish stalks, with mid-green leaves that are hairy underneath.

Syrian oregano
(O. syriacum)
This oregano is cultivated for culinary use in the Middle East. Its flavor is pungent, reminiscent of thyme, marjoram, and oregano but sharper. It is sometimes sold as za'atar.

PANDAN (PANDANUS AMARYLLIFOLIUS, P. TECTORIUS)

Pandan or screwpine species grow in the tropics from India to Southeast Asia, northern Australia, and the Pacific islands. The shiny, swordlike leaves of *P. amaryllifolius* are used as a flavoring and a wrapping for food. The leaf smells sweetly fresh and floral, lightly musky, with notes of freshly mown grass. The taste is pleasantly grassy and floral. Kewra essence, a favorite flavoring of the Moghul emperors, is extracted from *P. tectorius* flowers, and has a sweet, delicate musk and rose aroma.

BUY Fresh pandan leaves may be found in Asian supermarkets. Neither frozen nor dried pandan can match fresh leaves for fragrance.

STORE Fresh leaves keep well in a plastic bag in the refrigerator for 2–3 weeks. Kewra essence or kewra water (essence mixed with water) will keep for 2–3 years if tightly closed and stored away from strong light.

EAT Leaves have to be bruised or cooked to release their flavor. To bruise, pound or scrape them with the tines of a fork, then tie in a loose knot so that the fibers do not escape. Add a knotted leaf or two to rice before cooking to give it a light fragrance, as they do in Malaysia and Singapore. Cooks there also use pandan leaf as a flavoring for pancakes, cakes, and creamy desserts made with sticky rice or tapioca, and for a soup or curry. Thai cooks steam or fry parcels of pandan-wrapped chicken or weave leaves as containers for desserts. Dilute kewra essence with a little water and sprinkle into a dish just before serving. In India kewra essence is used to flavor pilafs and meat dishes as well as sweets and kulfi.

FLAVOR PAIRINGS Chicken, coconut, curried dishes, palm sugar.

SCENTED GERANIUM (PELARGONIUM SPECIES)

Scented geraniums offer a profusion of perfumes that echo the scents of other plants. There are hundreds of varieties, smelling of apple or citrus fruits, cinnamon, clove, nutmeg or mint, roses, or pine, and they show great diversity of form and color: leaves may be sculpted, lacy, fern like, or frilled, and colors vary from deep to pale green, velvety grey-green, green and silver, or green and cream. The best for cooking are the lemon- and rose-scented plants.

BUY Nurseries stock scented geraniums each spring. Leaves can be cut throughout the summer.

STORE Cut leaves are sturdy and will keep in a plastic bag in the fridge crisper for 4–5 days. When dried, leaves retain their aroma, but they are not good for cooking. Flowers are best picked just before they are to be used.

EAT Leaves release their fragrance when they are lightly crushed. Add them to a sugar syrup and use this to make sorbets or to macerate or poach fruits, or dilute for a refreshing drink. Infuse leaves in cream or milk for ice creams and custards. Add a couple of leaves to the pan when cooking blackberries or mixed berries for a summer pudding or preserves. Bury a handful of leaves in a jar of sugar and leave for 2 weeks, then use the scented sugar for desserts and cakes. Line a cake pan with rose geranium leaves to give a subtle flavor to a sponge cake or pound cake. Flowers have little fragrance, but make a pretty garnish for desserts.

FLAVOR PAIRINGS
(Lemon geranium) peaches, apricots, plums; (Rose geranium) apples, blackberries, raspberries.

Fragrans
Commonly called the nutmeg geranium, this variety has frilly, notched leaves with a distinct nutmeg fragrance.

Lemon geranium
One of the best varieties for cooking, lemon geranium is a stiff plant with small, rough leaves. The leaves have a refreshing lemon scent.

Gently rub the leaves to enjoy the lemony fragrance.

Lady Plymouth
The deep-cut leaves of this attractive variegated variety have a scent that combines lemon, mint, and rose.

Rose geranium
The wonderful fragrance of this geranium is a blend of rose and spice, reminiscent of Turkish delight. The essential oil from the plant has been used in perfume.

Scent sugar with rose geranium leaves, to use in sweet baking.

Prince of Orange
A low, compact plant with slightly wrinkled leaves, this variety has pale pink flowers with deeper pink veins and a sweet, orange scent.

PERILLA (PERILLA FRUTESCENS)

An annual herb related to mint and basil, perilla—or *shiso*, to give the plant its Japanese name—is native to China. The aromatic leaves are widely used in Japan, Korea, and Vietnam. More recently they have been discovered by cooks in Australia, the US, and Europe.

BUY Fresh perilla leaves are sold in Asian markets, where you can also find pickled red leaves in vacuum packs and dried perilla leaves (the flavor only palely reflects that of the fresh leaves). Sprouted perilla seeds are now available from some supermarkets. They are sold as growing shoots, similar to those of mustard and cress.

STORE The fresh leaves and sprouts will keep for 3–4 days in a plastic bag in the crisper of the fridge. Store dried leaves in an airtight container for 6–8 months.

EAT Fresh: Use the red leaves in salads and as a garnish. Chopped green perilla gives a wonderful flavor stirred into cooked rice. In Japan, green leaves are served with sushi and sashimi. **Cooked:** The Japanese use green perilla leaves in soups and salads and to wrap rice cakes; coated with batter on one side they are deep-fried for tempura. The Vietnamese grill meat, shrimp, and fish wrapped in green perilla leaves and serve with a spicy dipping sauce. Add green leaves to slices of lemon or lime in the cavity of fish to be roasted or steamed, to sauces for fish and chicken, and to salsa verde instead of basil. Dried leaves can be added to rice as it cooks. **Preserved:** In Japan, red perilla is mostly used for coloring and pickling *umeboshi* (salted and dried "plums").

FLAVOR PAIRINGS Beef, chicken, fish, zucchini, *mooli*, tomatoes, noodles and pasta, potatoes, rice.

Red perilla is sometimes called beefsteak plant because of the color of its leaves.

Red perilla
This variety is less aromatic than green perilla and has a more subdued flavor—faintly musty and woody, with cumin, cilantro, and cinnamon overtones.

Green perilla
The soft, downy leaves are sweetly yet strongly aromatic, with notes of cinnamon, cumin, citrus, and anise basil, and are pleasantly warm on the palate.

PARSLEY (PETROSELINUM CRISPUM)

Probably the only herb considered indispensable by most Western cooks, parsley is a versatile, hardy biennial, native to the eastern Mediterranean region. Today it is cultivated throughout most of the temperate world. Parsley has a lightly spicy aroma with hints of anise and lemon; its clean, fresh taste is herbaceous with a light, peppery note. There are two types: flat-leaf parsley and curly parsley. Both bring out the flavors of other seasonings and are essential to a number of traditional flavoring mixtures, such as *fines herbes* and *bouquet garni*.

BUY Parsley is available all year-round in most places. Choose in large bunches or plants rather than in small packets, as this will be cheaper.

STORE Discard any sprigs that look slimy before wrapping parsley in plastic; keep in the fridge for 4–5 days. For longer storage, parsley can be chopped and frozen in small containers or in ice-cube trays with a little water.

EAT Fresh: Good for garnishes, curly parsley also gives a light, herbaceous flavor and attractive green color to mayonnaise and other sauces. Cooked: Flat-leaf parsley has the better flavor for cooking. Add it chopped at the end of the cooking time to retain the fresh flavor. Parsley stalks are good for flavoring stocks and long-cooked stews.

FLAVOR PAIRINGS Eggs, fish, lentils, rice, lemon, tomatoes, most vegetables.

CLASSIC RECIPES Chimichurri; *persillade*; *gremolata*; salsa verde; *tabbouleh*; parsley sauce; *bouquet garni*; *fines herbes*; parsley and tahini salad.

Curly parsley
Use finely chopped in cold sauces and dressings. Deep-fried sprigs of curly parsley make an excellent garnish for fried fish.

Flat-leaf parsley
Also called French or Italian parsley, this has a more persistent and finer flavor than curly parsley, and a finer texture. It retains its flavor when used in a cooked dish.

CHIMICHURRI

This fresh herb sauce is served with grilled meats in Argentina. Try it also with savory pies and vegetables, or stir into soup just before serving.

MAKES 1 CUP

4 garlic cloves, finely chopped

1 tsp ground black pepper

½ tsp crushed hot red pepper flakes

1 tsp smoked paprika

2 tsp finely chopped fresh oregano

large handful of fresh parsley sprigs, finely chopped

½ cup olive oil

5 tbsp red wine vinegar

salt

1 Mix all the ingredients together in a covered jar and shake well.

2 Refrigerate for 3–4 hours.

RAU RAM (POLYGONUM ODORATUM)

Rau ram is increasingly the accepted name for this popular tropical Asian herb, but it is also sold as Vietnamese coriander, Vietnamese mint, *daun kesom* (its Malay name), and *laksa leaf*. Vietnamese emigrants took it to France in the 1950s and the US in the 1970s, where it has built up a very enthusiastic following. The herb smells a little like a more penetrating version of cilantro with a clear, citrus note; the taste is similar—refreshing with a hot, biting, peppery aftertaste.

BUY Bunches of rau ram are sold in Asian markets. Plants are available from specialist nurseries and will grow well in rich, moist soil. Harvest leaves in summer and fall.

STORE If bought in good condition, stems of fresh rau ram will keep in a plastic bag in the crisper of the fridge for 4–5 days.

EAT Fresh: The leaves can be a component of a salad platter: the Vietnamese make an excellent chicken and cabbage salad, flavored with rau ram, chiles, and lime juice. Thai cooks also serve the leaves raw with *nam prik*, or shred them and add to larp and curries. One of its most popular uses in Singapore and Malaysia is as an aromatic garnish for *laksa*, a spicy soup made with fish, seafood, and coconut milk. Cooked: Rau ram withstands heat better than cilantro, and will impart a subtle flavor to a dish if added partway through cooking.

FLAVOR PAIRINGS Poultry, pork, fish and seafood, eggs, noodles, chiles, coconut milk, beansprouts, red and green peppers, herbs, water chestnuts.

Rau ram can be identified by the chestnut-colored marks on its leaves.

Rosemary's tough, hardy leaves retain their aromatic flavor well, making them ideal for slow cooking.

ROSEMARY (ROSMARINUS OFFICINALIS)

Native to the Mediterranean, but long cultivated in temperate regions throughout Europe and North America, rosemary is hardy enough for all but the most northern zones. It is strongly aromatic, warm and peppery, resinous, and slightly bitter, with notes of pine and camphor. The flavor dissipates after leaves are cut. Flowers have a milder flavor than leaves.

BUY Fresh sprigs are available from markets. Or buy plants or grow from cuttings; leaves and sprigs can be cut at any time of the year.

STORE Fresh sprigs will keep for several days in the fridge or in a glass of water. When dried, the herb retains most of its flavor and the leaves can easily be crumbled for use.

EAT The flavor of rosemary is strong and is not diminished by long cooking, so use it judiciously, even in slow stews. Chop the tough leaves before adding to any dish in which they will be eaten. Use with vegetables fried in olive oil and in marinades, especially for lamb; place sprigs under meat or poultry before barbecuing or roasting. Use older, stronger stalks as skewers for kebabs, or as basting brushes, and young sprigs to infuse milk, cream, or syrup for desserts, or to steep in summer drinks such as lemonade. Flowers frozen in ice cubes make a pretty garnish for cold drinks. Rosemary is also very good in biscuits, both sweet and savory, and in focaccia and other breads.

FLAVOR PAIRINGS Poultry, rabbit, pork, lamb, veal, fish, eggs, lentils, squash, eggplant, cabbage, tomatoes, mushrooms, parsnips, potatoes, onions, oranges, apricots, cream cheese.

CLASSIC RECIPE *Herbes de Provence.*

SORREL (RUMEX ACETOSA, R. SCUTATUS)

Sorrel grows wild in meadowlands throughout much of Europe and western Asia. It has been appreciated since ancient Egyptian times for the tartness it imparts to rich foods.

BUY Sorrel will grow well from seed, or you can buy plants from an herb nursery. Leaves can be harvested from spring until the plant dies down in winter. Sorrel is not often seen in markets because the leaves wilt quickly.

STORE Leaves are best used within a day or two of picking; keep them in a plastic bag in the crisper of the fridge. Sorrel does not dry well, but leaves can be frozen.

EAT Because of its sour taste, sorrel is best used in combination with other foods. **Fresh:** Shredded leaves make a nice addition to salads, but whisk a little honey or sugar into the dressing to counter the herb's acidity. Shred and add to omelets, to baked and scrambled eggs, and to creamy dishes and sauces, or use to garnish fish. **Cooked:** Sorrel cooks very quickly and reduces greatly in volume; it turns a drab khaki color, which you can mask by using in a soup or sauce, or by cooking it with spinach.

FLAVOR PAIRINGS Chicken, pork, veal, fish (especially salmon), mussels, eggs, lentils, leeks, lettuce, cucumber, tomatoes, spinach, watercress.

CLASSIC RECIPES Frankfurt green sauce; French sorrel sauce; Lithuanian creamed sorrel soup with smoked sausage; Ukrainian green borscht.

Buckler Leaf sorrel
(Rumex scutatus)
Also called French sorrel, this has a milder, more lemony, and more succulent flavor than garden sorrel.

Garden sorrel has a spinach-like appearance and texture.

Garden or common sorrel
(Rumex acetosa)
The common variety, this has a taste that ranges from refreshingly tangy and sharp to astringent; large leaves may be slightly bitter.

SAGE (SALVIA SPECIES)

The sages are native to the north Mediterranean. The great variety of their textured, velvety foliage—from pale gray-green to green splashed with silver or gold, as well as the dark leaves of purple sage—makes them attractive garden plants as well as an invaluable addition to the cook's repertoire of seasonings. Sage can be mild, musky, and balsamic, or strongly camphorous with astringent notes and a warm spiciness. Generally, variegated species are milder than common sage and some have distinctly fruity fragrances: pineapple sage and black currant sage smell like their eponymous fruits, while clary sage has a delicate scent of muscat grapes.

BUY Cut fresh sage, as well as dried, is available in supermarkets. If you grow your own, leaves can be harvested from spring to fall.

STORE Ideally, pick sage leaves and use as soon as possible. If you buy them, wrap in paper towels and keep in the crisper of the refrigerator for no more than a few days. Dried sage, which will keep for up to 6 months if stored away from light, is more potent than fresh and can be acrid and musty; it is best avoided, except for tea.

● EAT Sage is not a subtle herb, so use sparingly. Because it aids the digestion of fatty and oily foods, sage is traditionally used as a partner for them, for example, in stuffings for pork, goose, and duck. Sage also makes an excellent flavoring for pork sausages, and in Germany it accompanies eel. The Greeks use it in meat stews and with poultry, and also in a tea. Italians use sage with liver and veal to make *saltimbocca alla romana*, and to flavor focaccia and polenta. They also make a simple pasta sauce by gently heating a few sage leaves in butter. All sages have attractive, hooded flowers that make pretty garnishes.

FLAVOR PAIRINGS Cheese, dried beans, apples, onions, tomatoes, bay, caraway, celery leaf, garlic, dried ground ginger, lovage, marjoram, paprika, parsley, savory, thyme.

CLASSIC RECIPES Sage and onion stuffing; sage butter; *saltimbocca alla romana*.

S. o. "Icterina"
This cultivated variety has pretty gold-and-green foliage, but it rarely flowers. The flavor is considerably milder than that of common sage.

Purple sage
(S. o. Purpurascens Group)
This sage has musky, spicy tones and has a slightly less pungent taste than common sage. It rarely flowers, but when it does the blue flowers are stunning against the purple-green foliage.

S. o. "Tricolor"
Perhaps the most striking of all the sages, this has mottled green, cream, and pink leaves, and blue flowers. The flavor is quite gentle and mild.

Clary sage
(S. sclarea)
This aromatic biennial has a scent reminiscent of muscat grapes; the taste is slightly bitter and balsamlike. The leaves can be used for fritters, while the flowers make a beautiful, edible garnish.

Common sage
(S. officinalis)
There are broad- and narrow-leaved varieties of common sage. Young, green leaves are less pungent than the older, gray ones. Narrow-leaved sage has pretty, lilac, blue, or white flowers. The broad-leaved sage seldom flowers.

Pineapple sage
(S. elegans)
Overwintered indoors, this sage grows into a large shrub. The long leaves have a clear, pineapple scent but the flavor is less marked. Leaves can be placed in a cake pan to scent a sponge cake.

Greek sage
(S. fruticosa)
The large, gray-green, downy leaves of this species are intensely aromatic, with dominant resinous notes. Use very sparingly in cooking, or as a tisane.

CLASSIC RECIPE

SIZZLING SAGE BUTTER

This sauce is delicious drizzled over filled pasta such as ravioli, but is equally good with spaghetti and other pasta.

SERVES 4

1lb (450g) dried pasta

6 tbsp butter

2 garlic cloves, peeled and halved

16 fresh sage leaves

freshly grated Parmesan, for serving

1 Cook the pasta in a large pot of boiling, salted water, until tender yet firm to the bite, about 10 minutes or as the package directs. While the pasta is cooking, heat the butter and garlic in a small frying pan over medium heat until just golden. Add the sage leaves and cook, stirring, until fragrant, for about 30 seconds. Add salt and pepper to taste. Remove from the heat; discard the garlic.

2 Drain the pasta and return it to the warm pasta pot. Add the hot butter and sage mixture. Toss well to coat. Serve immediately with plenty of Parmesan.

Perfect with meat and poultry dishes, fresh sage should be gently flexible and slightly furry.

SALAD BURNET (SANGUISORBA MINOR)

Salad burnet is a graceful, bushy, perennial plant with sharply toothed, deep green leaves. Delicate in appearance, it is actually sturdy and hardy, its evergreen leaves often pushing up through a light covering of snow. Native to Europe and western Asia, salad burnet was taken to North America by early European colonists and is now naturalized there. The tender, young leaves have the best flavor—older leaves become bitter and are best cooked. Salad burnet is not aromatic and has a mild, lightly astringent flavor reminiscent of cucumber, with a hint of nuttiness.

BUY In some parts of Europe you can buy fresh salad burnet in the market, alongside other herbs and salad leaves, from late spring to fall. It is easy to grow from seed, and will survive any but the most frosty winter.

STORE Salad burnet will keep for a day or two in a plastic bag in the crisper of the refrigerator.

EAT Fresh: The subtle flavor of young, feathery leaves is best appreciated by eating them raw. Add them to salads—they are particularly good in fall and winter, when interesting salad leaves can be in short supply. Scatter the leaves over soups and casseroles, or chop as a garnish for vegetables or egg dishes. Combine with tarragon, chives, and chervil for fines herbes, and make into herb butters. Cooked: Older leaves are best steamed or sautéed with other greens (such as spinach), or added to casseroles or soups toward the end of the cooking time, to preserve flavor.

FLAVOR PAIRINGS Fish, eggs, cream cheese, fava beans, cucumber, salad leaves, tomatoes, chervil, chives, claytonia, mint, parsley, rosemary, tarragon.

SAVORY (SATUREJA SPECIES)

As the name suggests, savory is highly aromatic, and was one of the strongest flavorings available before spices reached Europe. Summer savory is native to the eastern Mediterranean and the Caucasus, winter savory to southern Europe, Turkey, and North Africa. Both were taken to northern Europe by the Romans and to the North Americas by early settlers. All savories have a peppery bite. Summer savory has a subtle, herbaceous scent and flavor, is agreeably pungent, slightly resinous, and reminiscent of thyme, mint, and marjoram. Winter savory has the more assertive, penetrating aroma and flavor, with notes of sage and pine. Summer savory leaves are tender, whereas those of winter savory are tough. The genus *Satureja* encompasses many other plants with pungent, spicy aromas in the mint—thyme—oregano spectrum, with a variety of common names. Many are used as flavorings in their native habitat.

BUY Savory is not available as a cut herb, but plants can be bought from nurseries or you can grow from seed.

STORE In a plastic bag in the refrigerator, savory will keep for around 6 days. Savory retains its flavor well if frozen, either chopped or as sprigs.

EAT Although the savories can be used interchangeably to some extent, both should be added judiciously, and winter savory in much smaller amounts than summer savory. Fresh: Chop summer savory finely and add to salads, especially potato, bean, and lentil salads. Cooked: Because they are pungent, both savories are good flavorings for long-cooked meat and vegetable dishes and stuffings. Savory is frequently associated with beans, as its German name *Bohnenkraut* (bean herb) indicates: summer savory is best with green and fave beans, whereas either could be used with green beans and other pulses.

FLAVOR PAIRINGS Rabbit, fish, cheese, eggs, beans, beets, cabbage.

Winter savory
(S. montana)
This is a woody, compact shrub with stiff, glossy, dark green leaves. It is called "poivre d'âne" or "pebre d'aï"—donkey pepper—in Provence and is used more widely than summer savory around the Mediterranean.

SASSAFRAS (SASSAFRAS ALBIDUM)

Sassafras is an aromatic, ornamental tree native to the eastern US, from Maine to Florida. Native Americans showed early settlers how to make tea from the leaves, bark, and roots; in modern times, the roots were one of the essential ingredients of root beer. The French-speaking Canadians who settled in Louisiana adopted a Choctaw method of using dried, ground sassafras leaves (filé powder) to flavor and thicken stews. Young leaves have an astringent, citrus—fennel aroma; the roots smell camphorous. Filé powder tastes sourish, a little like lemony sorrel with woody notes. Its flavor can be brought out by brief heating.

BUY Leaves for making commercial filé powder are harvested in spring, then dried and ground. It is best not to use fresh sassafras because in its natural form it contains safrole, a carcinogen. Root bark and leaves are now treated to remove safrole before they are sold or used commercially. Buy prepared filé powder, sassafras tea, or tea concentrate only if marked "safrole free." Some brands of filé

powder contain other ground herbs, such as bay, oregano, sage, or thyme, in addition to ground sassafras leaf.

STORE Filé powder keeps for 6 months, and sassafras tea for a year.

EAT Filé powder, or gumbo filé, is only used in the cooking of Louisiana, but it is key to the texture and flavor of many Cajun and Creole soups and stews. In particular, it is used in gumbo, a substantial, spicy soup made with a variety of vegetables, meat, or seafood, and served with rice. The mucilaginous quality of filé helps thicken the dish, provided it is stirred in when the pan is removed from the heat; cooking makes filé tough and stringy.

FLAVOR PAIRINGS Meat, seafood, rice.

CLASSIC RECIPE Gumbo filé.

The large, bright green leaves of the sassafras may have one, two, or three lobes at the apex.

Summer savory
(S. hortensis)
This savory has soft, grayish leaves. Savory is good with oily fish like eel and mackerel.

MANAQISH

A classic Middle Eastern bread
served warm with yogurt and olives.

For the dough

*3 cups unbleached all-purpose flour, plus
extra if needed*

*1⅛ tsp quick-rising active dry yeast
(about half of a 1/4oz (7g) envelope)*

2 tsp salt

*¼ cup extra virgin olive oil, plus extra for
greasing the bowl and brushing the edges
of the dough*

For the topping

6 tbsp za'atar (see page 213)

½ cup extra virgin olive oil

1 Mix the flour, yeast, and salt in
a large mixing bowl. Make a well
in the center. Add the oil to the well
and, using the tips of your fingers,
rub the ¼ cup oil into the flour until
well incorporated. Gradually add 1
cup of lukewarm water, bringing in
the flour as you go. Knead until you
have a rough, sticky ball of dough.

2 Preheat the oven to the highest
temperature. Put the dough on a
floured work surface. Knead for 2-3
minutes, sprinkling with flour if the
dough sticks. Place a bowl over the
dough and let it rest for 15 minutes.
Continue kneading until the dough
is smooth and elastic. Shape the
dough into a ball, coating it with oil,
and place in an oiled bowl. Cover
with plastic wrap and let it rise in
a warm, draft-free place for 2 hours.
Fold after the first hour.

3 Divide the dough into 10 equal
parts. Roll each piece into a ball and
cover with a damp towel to let rise
for 45 minutes. Roll out each ball
of dough into a circle about 6-7 in
(15-17.5 cm) in diameter, flouring
both the work surface and the dough
every now and then, and making sure
to form even circles. Cover the dough
with floured parchment paper and let
rest for 15-20 minutes.

4 To make the topping, mix the
za'atar and ½ cup olive oil in a bowl.
Raise the edges of the disks of dough
by pinching them, and use your
fingertips to make dimples all over the
surface of the dough. Spread ⅛th of
the mixture over each circle of dough.
Brush the edges with oil and let rest
for 15-20 minutes.

5 Bake in the preheated oven for 6-8
minutes, or until nicely puffed and
barely golden. Serve immediately.

THYME (THYMUS SPECIES)

Thyme grows wild on the hot, arid
hillsides of the Mediterranean basin,
where it has infinitely more flavor than
it ever achieves in cooler regions. Wild
thyme tends to be woody and straggly.
Cultivated varieties have more tender
stalks and a bushy form; there are
hundreds of them, each with a slightly
different aroma. The whole plant has
a warm, earthy, and peppery fragrance
when it is lightly brushed. The taste is
spicy, with notes of cloves and mint, a
hint of camphor, and a mouth-cleansing
aftertaste. The many varieties of thyme
offer a wealth of different flavors to
the cook.

BUY Common and lemon thyme
are available fresh from supermarkets.
Many varieties of thyme are sold by
nurseries, but make sure they smell
when brushed lightly by hand. Pick
leaves when needed—the more often
the better, or the plant may become
straggly and woody. Harvest thyme for
drying just before it flowers.

STORE Cut fresh thyme will keep
for up to a week stored in a plastic bag
in the fridge. Dried thyme will retain its
flavor through the winter.

EAT Unlike most herbs, thyme
withstands long, slow cooking; used
with discretion it enhances other herbs
without overpowering them.
It is indispensable in French stews,
from *pot-au-feu* to cassoulet, Spanish
stews, and those of Mexico and Latin
America, where it is often used in
combination with chiles. In Britain,
it is used in stuffings, pies, and jugged
hare, a classic dish made with cut
pieces of hare soaked in a red
wine-juniper berry marinade. It is
also a common flavoring in Middle
Eastern cooking. The dried herb
is essential in Creole and Cajun
cooking, where it appears in gumbos
and jambalayas. Use thyme to flavor
pâtés and terrines, thick vegetable
soups, tomato and wine-based
sauces, stews and casseroles, and
in marinades for pork and game.
Lemon thyme can also be used
in biscuits, bread, and fruit salads.

FLAVOR PAIRINGS Lamb,
rabbit, pulses, eggplant,
cabbage, carrots, leeks,
wild mushrooms, tomatoes,
onions, potatoes, corn.

CLASSIC RECIPES
Manakeish; bouquet
garni; za'atar
spice mix.

Common thyme
(Thymus vulgaris)
*Also called garden thyme, this
is a cultivated variety of wild
Mediterranean thyme, with
grey-green leaves and white or pale
lilac flowers. There are a number of
garden thymes, including English
"broad-leaved" and French
"narrow-leaved" varieties. It is
the basic thyme for cooking.*

Creeping thyme
(Thymus serpyllum)
*Milder than common thyme, this grows
throughout the Mediterranean region, as
well as in central and northern Europe.
It should only be used fresh: scatter the tiny
leaves over salads or grilled vegetables.
It combines well with hyssop.*

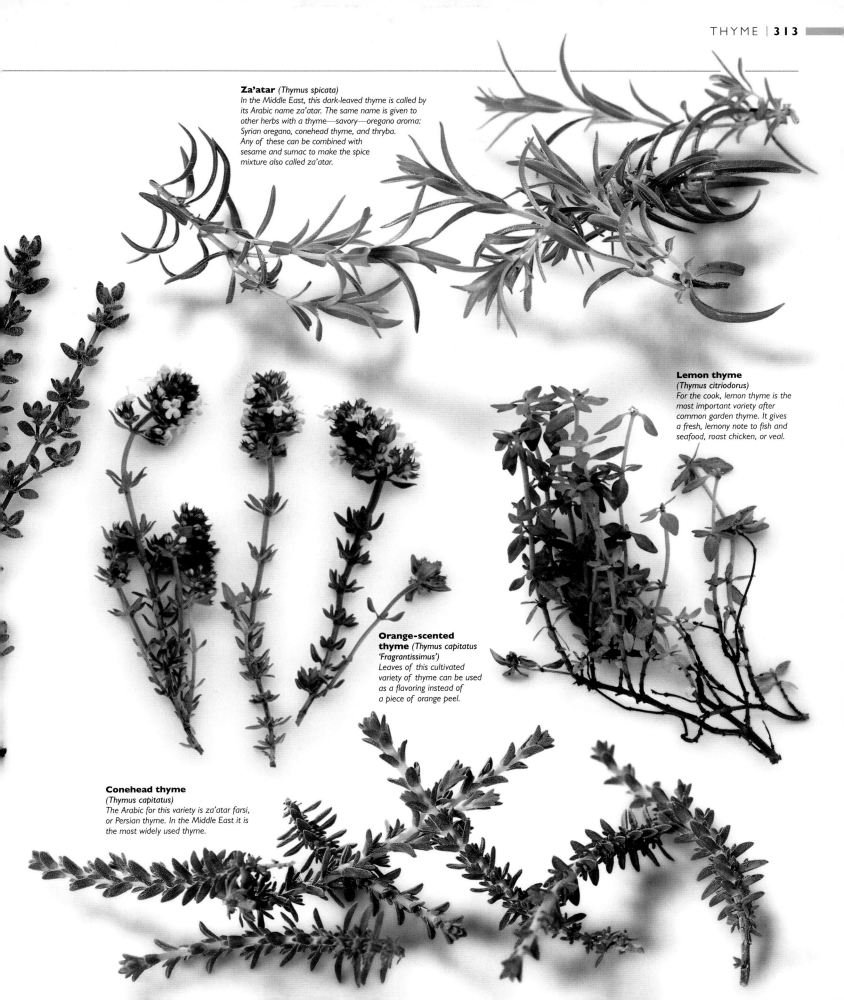

Za'atar *(Thymus spicata)*
In the Middle East, this dark-leaved thyme is called by its Arabic name za'atar. The same name is given to other herbs with a thyme—savory—oregano aroma: Syrian oregano, conehead thyme, and thryba. Any of these can be combined with sesame and sumac to make the spice mixture also called za'atar.

Lemon thyme
(Thymus citriodorus)
For the cook, lemon thyme is the most important variety after common garden thyme. It gives a fresh, lemony note to fish and seafood, roast chicken, or veal.

Orange-scented thyme *(Thymus capitatus 'Fragrantissimus')*
Leaves of this cultivated variety of thyme can be used as a flavoring instead of a piece of orange peel.

Conehead thyme
(Thymus capitatus)
The Arabic for this variety is za'atar farsi, or Persian thyme. In the Middle East it is the most widely used thyme.

NUTS
& SEEDS

ALMONDS | MACADAMIAS
HAZELNUTS | PISTACHIOS
FLAXSEED | SESAME SEEDS
PUMPKIN SEEDS

NUT AND SEED ESSENTIALS

Packed with protein, nuts and seeds are a valuable and nutritious ingredient. Although nuts and seeds are rarely served on their own (apart from as a snack), they are very versatile; used in both savory and sweet dishes. They frequently feature in confectionery, with nuts such as hazelnuts and almonds, in particular, having a special affinity with chocolate. In baking, nuts and seeds are used both for decorative purposes—placed or sprinkled on the surface of bread, cakes, cookies, and pastries—and as a flavoring within. Ground nuts and seeds are traditionally used as a thickening agent in many cuisines, from Mexican pumpkin seed sauces or Italian pesto (made from pine nuts) to African groundnut (peanut) soups and stews. Many nuts are also cultivated and used to make oils for cooking, such as groundnut, or for dressings, such as walnut oil. Sunflower seeds can be scattered over cereals to give a boost to the mineral content, pumpkin seeds over salads, and sesame seeds in dips.

BUY

Nuts can be bought either with their shells on or shelled; whole, flaked, or ground. In what form you buy them depends on how you intend to use them in cooking, and what the recipe dictates. Both nuts and seeds are sold fresh, but they are mostly available dried. Nuts and seeds are generally available year-round and are not a seasonal ingredient—with the exception of autumnal chestnuts and cobnuts. Buy fresh nuts in small quantities as they will go bad after a few weeks, and keep an eye on the use-by date.

STORE

Due to their high oil content, most nuts and seeds turn rancid very quickly and should be stored in a cool, dry place and consumed as soon as possible. One way of extending the shelf life of many seeds and shelled nuts is to store them in plastic, airtight containers or glass jars in the refrigerator.

Storing nuts

Nuts with their shells on *last longer than shelled nuts, as they have a natural protective coat. You can keep nuts such as almonds in a fabric bag at room temperature.*

Storing seeds

Seeds *such as pumpkin seeds are best kept in clean, dry, airtight plastic containers or jars in a cool, dark place to prevent them deteriorating and absorbing odors from other foods.*

PREPARE

Seeds generally need no preparation and can be eaten as they are, or can be toasted. However, nuts bought with their shells on need to have them removed in order to get to the ingredient beneath. Some nuts have thin shells that are easily cracked with a nutcracker, but larger nuts, such as coconuts, require a little more force to get to the flesh.

PEEL A COCONUT This large nut has a very thick, hard skin that needs to be broken to reveal the flesh beneath. When buying a coconut, choose one that feels heavy, and that is full of water (shake it gently to check)—the heavier the coconut, the more flesh it will contain. When preparing to break the nut, have a clean bowl handy to catch the liquid as it leaks out, which can then be used in Thai sauces.

WHOLE NUTS OR SHELLED? There are advantages and disadvantages to buying nuts with shells or without, so ultimately it is down to personal preference. Fresh shelled nuts need less preparation before use, but they do deteriorate more quickly unless stored in an airtight container in the fridge or freezer, as the released oils can turn rancid at room temperature. Dried shelled nuts, however, will keep for several weeks at room temperature. Nuts with their shells on are often cheaper to buy because they need shelling before use. They will keep for longer at room temperature, up to six months, but their condition will still deteriorate after a period of time as they lose moisture.

1 Use a metal skewer to pierce the eyes of the coconut in order to allow the liquid inside to drain out before you open the nut.

2 Strike the coconut with force using a hammer or mallet to crack its shell, then break the nut open into two halves.

3 Pry the flesh away from the shell carefully using a blunt knife. Cutting the flesh into segments first will make this job easier.

4 Peel away and discard the brown inner skin using a sharp knife or vegetable peeler, before roughly chopping the flesh.

CRACK Many nuts, such as pecans and walnuts, have thick, hard shells that require cracking, so it is worth investing in a decent nutcracker for this job. The inner skin of these nuts can be eaten—it is too difficult to peel off.

CHOP Using a large, sharp knife, chop the nuts into pieces of the required size—coarse or fine—guiding the knife with your knuckles. Larger, flatter nuts, such as almonds, can be chopped in this way.

FLAKE Hold each nut flat on the cutting board, and, using a large, sharp knife, cut it into slices of the required thickness. Larger, smooth nuts such as almonds can be slivered—cut each slice lengthwise into fine sticks.

GRIND Grind shelled nuts to the consistency of fine breadcrumbs. If using a food processor, take care not to overprocess. Nuts release their natural oils during grinding, and you could end up with a nut butter.

COOK

Nuts and seeds are delicious eaten raw, but cooking adds another dimension to them; heat brings out their flavor and oils, and also enhances their texture, making them crunchier. Roasted, blanched, and toasted nuts can be used in both sweet and savory dishes, and toasted seeds are delicious scattered over salads or used in homemade granola bars.

ROAST All around the world, nuts and seeds are most often eaten simply roasted and seasoned with salt. Although commercially roasted and salted seeds are widely available, roasting nuts or seeds yourself at home is both easy and satisfying. Furthermore, it has the advantage of allowing you to add as much or as little salt as you wish, and to season the nuts with your own choice of spices or flavorings.

1 *Preheat the oven to 325°F (160°C). Toss the nuts in oil (use 1 teaspoon per 7oz/200g) and some seasoning and spread them evenly in a roasting tin. Roast for 20 minutes, turning halfway through the roasting time.*

2 *Remove the cooked nuts from the oven, then tip them into a clean cloth or dish towel, wrap them up, then open the package and rub off the skins using your fingers. Cool completely, then store in airtight containers.*

BLANCH Some recipes require that nuts such as almonds are blanched; this is a simple job that involves removing their brown skins.

1 *Place the nuts in a heatproof bowl and pour over enough boiling water to cover them. Set aside for 3 minutes, then drain.*

2 *Once the nuts are cool enough to handle, simply rub off the skins between your fingers, leaving the blanched kernels.*

TOAST This is a quick and excellent way of enhancing the flavor of most nuts and seeds before using them in a recipe. Do not leave them unattended during cooking, though, and stir them often, because they can burn very quickly.

Heat a frying pan *over medium heat. Cook the nuts or seeds for a few minutes until they are light brown and smell fragrant.*

ALMONDS

The almond is cultivated in many Mediterranean-type climates. There are two types: bitter almonds, which are not eaten but provide oils and extracts used to flavor foods, and sweet almonds, which are wonderfully versatile for both sweet and savory cooking. Sweet almonds have a delicate yet distinctive flavor.

BUY Almonds are harvested from summer to fall, so this is the time when the new season's nuts in shell arrive in the shops. Look for firm nuts that do not rattle when shaken. Shelled almonds are available in a variety of forms, including unblanched, blanched, slivered, chopped, and ground.

STORE Unshelled almonds can be kept in a cool, dry place for a year. Store shelled almonds in an airtight container in a cool, dry, dark place and consume as soon as possible. Or keep in the fridge for up to 6 months or in the freezer for up to a year.

EAT Fresh: Enjoy as a snack or add to cereal. **Cooked:** Use in cakes, cookies, pastries, petits fours, meringues, and other desserts. Make praline and almond paste (marzipan). Add to stir-fries, sauces, stews, and curries.
FLAVOR PAIRINGS Lamb, chicken, trout, cinnamon, honey, chocolate.
CLASSIC RECIPES Almond macaroons; *cantucci*; chicken korma; trout with almonds; *panforte*; Bakewell tart; *blancmange*.

Sweet almond
The heart-shaped Marcona is a Spanish variety of sweet almond, prized for its flavor and often eaten roasted as a nibble with drinks.

When buying shelled almonds, avoid any that are split, moldy, or discolored.

Bitter almond
The oil extracted from bitter almonds is used for flavoring cakes and confectionery such as amaretti biscuits, as well as Amaretto di Saronno liqueur.

BRAZIL NUTS

Native to South America, the brazil nut is the seed of a tall tree that grows in the Amazon rainforest and can live for over 500 years. The tree has not been successfully cultivated commercially, and the nuts are gathered mainly from the wild in Brazil and Bolivia for export. The creamy-white, waxy-textured nuts have a mild, sweet flavor.

BUY Brazil nuts are harvested during the rainy season (December to March). If buying them unshelled, look for heavy nuts that do not rattle in their shells when you shake them.

STORE Because of their high polyunsaturated fat content, shelled brazil nuts can quickly become rancid. If you are going to eat them soon after purchasing, you can keep them in a sealed container in a cool, dry place. Alternatively, store in an airtight, plastic container in the fridge for 6 months or in the freezer for up to a year. Nuts in their shell can be stored in a cool, dry place for 2 months.

EAT Brazil nuts are hard to shell, so if you want whole nuts, buy them already shelled. Being rich in fat, they make a delicious snack as well as a good addition to stuffings, cookies, cakes, and confectionery.
FLAVOR PAIRINGS Bananas, dried fruits, chocolate, toffee, maple syrup.
CLASSIC RECIPES Chocolate-coated brazil nuts; brazil nut cake.

The formidably thick shell can be hard to crack without crushing the nut inside.

MACADAMIAS

Native to Australia, the macadamia tree is now cultivated in other countries including Hawaii and South Africa—a rare example of a native Australian plant becoming a worldwide commercial food crop. Inside its thick, hard shell, the nut has a waxy texture and a buttery, sweet taste.

BUY Instead of being picked from the tree, macadamia nuts are harvested when they ripen fully in late spring and summer and naturally fall to the ground. Because of their extremely hard shells, the nuts are usually sold already shelled and whole, either raw or roasted. Look for light-colored nuts without blemish or discoloration.

STORE If still in their shells, macadamia nuts can be kept in a cool, dark place for several months. Shelled macadamia nuts should be stored in an airtight container in a cool, dark place and consumed as soon as possible after purchase. For longer storage, keep them in an airtight plastic container in the fridge for up to 6 months, or the freezer for up to a year.

EAT Enjoy roasted and salted or spiced macadamia nuts as a snack with drinks. Use unsalted nuts in cookies, cakes, pastries, confectionery, and ice cream, as well as in salads, stuffings for poultry, and other savory dishes.
FLAVOR PAIRINGS Chicken, bananas, toffee, coconut, chocolate, maple syrup.
CLASSIC RECIPES Macadamia-crusted chicken; Hawaiian macadamia nut pie.

Shelled macadamia nuts are large, round, and a pale gold color.

ALMOND MACAROONS

These dainty almond cookies trace their origin back to 18th-century Italy. Serve after dinner with coffee.

MAKES 12–20

115g (4oz) blanched almonds

75g (2½oz) caster sugar

1–2 drops of almond extract

1 egg white

1 Preheat the oven to 350°F (180°C). Line one or two baking sheets with parchment paper.

2 Put the almonds in a food processor and pulse the machine on and off, just until finely ground. (Do not over-mix.) Add the sugar and process again until well mixed. Add the almond extract and egg white and pulse until the mixture forms a soft, sticky paste. (Or, finely grind the almonds using a pestle and mortar, then transfer to a bowl and mix in the sugar, almond extract, and egg white.)

3 Wet your hands and form teaspoons of the almond paste into small, evenly-sized balls. Place these, not touching, on the baking sheet(s).

4 Bake for 10–12 minutes, until pale golden. Remove from the oven and transfer to a wire rack to cool. The macaroons should be slightly soft inside. Store in an airtight container.

CANDLENUTS

Widely grown throughout the tropical regions, from India to the Pacific Islands, candlenuts are so-named because they were historically used as rudimentary lights: their very high oil content means they burn readily. These soft, cream-colored, rounded nuts have a notably waxy texture and a distinctive, bitter flavor.

🔒 BUY It is quite difficult to remove candlenuts successfully from their hard shells, so they are sold shelled. They are available in this form throughout the year. Look for candlenuts that are whole, rather than broken, as a sign of careful handling during processing. Because they turn rancid quickly, buy them in small quantities.

▤ STORE Keep in a cool, dry, dark place and use as soon as possible.

◉ EAT Cooked: Candlenuts are toxic when raw, so must be cooked before eating. They are usually lightly roasted and then crushed or finely ground before being used as a flavoring or thickening agent in many cuisines, primarily those of Southeast Asia, such as Indonesian and Malaysian, but also Hawaiian.

FLAVOR PAIRINGS Shrimp paste (*blachan*), dried shrimp, chiles, garlic, *galangal*.

CLASSIC RECIPES *Beef rendang*; *laksa lemak*; *poke*; *satay*.

CASHEWS

Native to South America, the cashew tree was introduced to India by the Portuguese and is now grown in many other tropical parts of the world, including Africa, Central America, and the West Indies. As the cashew nut is difficult to extract from its hard shell, and the shell contains powerful irritant substances, the nut is commonly sold shelled. Cashews have a mild, nutty flavor and tender texture.

🔒 BUY Shelled cashews can be bought year-round raw or roasted and salted. Look for large, whole cashews; avoid those that are small or broken.

▤ STORE Shelled, unroasted cashew nuts can be kept in a sealed container in a cool, dry place for a few weeks. For longer storage, keep them in an airtight plastic container in the fridge for up to 6 months, or in the freezer for up to a year.

◉ EAT Fresh: Prized for their flavor, salted or spiced cashews are a popular nibble with drinks. **Cooked:** In cooking, unsalted cashews are added whole or finely ground to both savory and sweet dishes ranging from stir-fries and curries to biscuits and sweets.

FLAVOR PAIRINGS Chicken, corn, black pepper, chiles, smoked paprika.

CLASSIC RECIPES Spiced cashews; stir-fried chicken with cashews; chicken korma with cashewnuts; cashew nut fudge.

Cashews are recognizable by their slender, curved shape.

You may not be able to tell whether the candle nut is raw or cooked when purchasing. They are toxic when raw, so if in doubt, roast before using.

Their thin, brittle shell means that peanuts can be cracked by hand, rather than needing a nutcracker.

SPICED CASHEWS

A popular Indian nibble, spiced cashews are very simple to make and taste particularly good freshly cooked.

MAKES 1½ CUPS

1 green cardamom pod	
½ tsp ground cumin	
½ tsp ground coriander	
¼ tsp chili powder	
1 tsp salt	
1 tsp superfine or granulated sugar	
1½ cups raw cashews	
1 tsp sunflower oil	

1 Preheat the oven to 325°F (160°C).

2 Crack the cardamom pod and remove the seeds from inside. Using a pestle and mortar, finely grind the seeds. Mix the ground cardamom with the cumin, coriander, chili, salt, and sugar.

3 Place the cashews in a large bowl, add the oil, and stir to coat well. Add the spice mixture and mix until the nuts are evenly coated.

4 Spread out on a rimmed baking sheet and bake for 20 minutes, stirring once, until the nuts are golden brown. Remove from the oven and leave to cool completely. Store in an airtight tin.

PEANUTS

This seed of a plant in the legume family originated in Central and South America, but is now cultivated in many countries including China, Indonesia, North America, and Nigeria. Because peanuts grow underground, they are also known as groundnuts and earth nuts. Each wrinkled shell contains one to four peanuts, individually wrapped in a thin, papery skin.

🔒 BUY Both unshelled and shelled peanuts are available all year round. Shelled peanuts come in a number of forms, including raw (the most useful for the cook) and roasted and salted or sweetened. When buying peanuts in their shells, choose nuts that feel heavy. Avoid blemished or shriveled nuts.

▤ STORE Shelled peanuts are best eaten as soon as possible after buying, but can be kept in an airtight container in a cool, dark, dry place for a short time, the fridge for 3 months, or the freezer for a year. Throw away any rancid or moldy nuts because they may be toxic. Unshelled peanuts will keep in a cool place for 6–9 months.

◉ EAT Peanuts, in or out of the shell, are a popular snack. Purée to make your own peanut butter, or use in curries, stews, sauces, and baking.

FLAVOR PAIRINGS Onions, wasabi, chocolate, caramel, brown sugar.

CLASSIC RECIPES *Gado gado*; Ghanaian groundnut stew; peanut butter cookies; satay sauce.

HAZELNUTS

Over a hundred varieties of hazelnut are cultivated in many temperate countries, with Turkey being the world's largest producer. The rounded nut, which may also be called cobnut or filbert, has a sweet flavor and a pleasantly crunchy texture. Fresh "green" hazelnuts are juicier and milder in taste than the mature, ripe hazelnuts.

🔒 **BUY** Fresh hazelnuts are available in the late summer months. The common mature nuts are sold either in their brittle brown shells or shelled, when they may be raw, blanched to remove their skins, or roasted. If buying in shell, choose unblemished nuts that feel heavy.

📦 **STORE** Keep both unshelled and shelled hazelnuts in a cool, dry place; eat shelled nuts as soon as possible. Or store shelled nuts in an airtight plastic container in the fridge for 6 months, or the freezer for a year.

⦿ **EAT** Roasting hazelnuts enhances their flavor and makes it easy to remove their papery skins. Eat as a snack. Use in cakes, cookies, and desserts, as well as in savory dishes.

FLAVOR PAIRINGS Fish, apples, plums, cinnamon, coffee, chocolate.
CLASSIC RECIPES Romesco sauce; nougat; *lokum*.

Tonda Gentile Romana
This small, flavorful Italian variety is associated with the Piedmont region of Italy, noted for the quality of its hazelnuts. It is the nut used in much Italian confectionery.

Kentish cobnut
This variety of cultivated hazelnut is harvested and eaten both when green (when its flavor is very mild) and when brown and mature.

The thin skin is slightly bitter, so is often removed.

If the soft husk is green and fresh, this indicates that the cobnut is young and juicy.

San Giovanni
Traditionally sold in its thick, shiny shell, this Italian variety is excellent for biscotti and pastries.

PISTACHIOS

The wild pistachio tree is indigenous to the Middle East: for centuries the Iranians have prized pistachios and cultivated the trees for the valued nuts. Today, the pistachio is also grown commercially in other temperate countries. Inside its hard shell and thin skin, the edible kernel is a striking green color and has a subtle, unique flavor.

🔒 **BUY** Once ripe, pistachios naturally split open at one end: when choosing unshelled pistachios, look for nuts open in this way. Fresh pistachios, in soft, pinkish hulls, are briefly available just after harvesting in fall; dried nuts can be found year-round. Shelled nuts are sold whole, nibbed, and chopped; blanched, unsalted nuts with a deep green color are the most useful for the cook.

📦 **STORE** Pistachios can be kept in a covered container in a cool, dry, dark place for a week or so. For longer storage, keep in a sealed plastic container in the fridge for 4–6 weeks, or the freezer for up to a year.

⦿ **EAT** Both unshelled and shelled pistachios (often roasted and salted in shell) are a popular nibble. Use blanched, unsalted pistachios in desserts, cakes, cookies, and sweet pastries; in ice cream; in sweet sauces; in rice and couscous dishes; in pâtés, terrines, and sausages; and as a pretty garnish for sweet and savory dishes.
FLAVOR PAIRINGS Chicken, fish, chocolate, vanilla, basmati rice.
CLASSIC RECIPES Baklava; *cassata*; pilaf; *pistachio burfi*.

The papery skin is usually eaten when pistachios are roasted and salted in shell.

ROMESCO SAUCE

There are a great many versions of this traditional Catalan sauce, which is served with grilled seafood or vegetables such as asparagus.

SERVES 4

1 Romano or red bell pepper

¼ cup blanched almonds

¼ cup skinned hazelnuts (filberts)

5 tbsp olive oil

3 garlic cloves, peeled

1 oz (30g) stale baguette, cubed (about ¼ cup)

1 medium tomato, coarsely chopped

1 ñora or other dried mild red chile pepper, soaked in cold water for 15–20 minutes, then drained and chopped, discarding the stem and most of the seeds

1 tsp tomato purée

½ tsp sweet smoked Spanish paprika

2 tbsp sherry vinegar or white wine vinegar

salt and freshly ground pepper

1 Preheat the oven to 350°F (180°C).

2 Under a broiler or over a gas flame, roast the red pepper, turning frequently, until charred on all sides. Seal the pepper in a paper or plastic bag and leave to cool, then peel off and discard as much of the blackened skin as possible. Chop the pepper, discarding the seeds and stem. Set aside.

3 Spread out the almonds and hazelnuts on a rimmed baking sheet and bake for about 15 minutes, shaking the pan once or twice, until golden and fragrant. Allow to cool.

4 Heat the olive oil in a heavy-bottomed medium frying pan. Add the whole garlic cloves and cook, stirring, just until golden. Remove with a slotted spoon and reserve. Add the cubed bread and cook, stirring, until golden brown. Remove from the pan and reserve. Add the tomatoes and cook, stirring, until slightly charred at the edges. Remove the pan from the heat.

5 In a food processor, pulse together the almonds, hazelnuts, garlic, and bread cubes until finely ground. Add the tomatoes, red pepper, chile, tomato purée, and paprika. Process until the mixture forms a thick purée.

6 Stir in the vinegar and season to taste with salt and pepper. Serve at room temperature.

CHESTNUTS

Long valued for its edible seeds (nuts), the sweet chestnut tree has been cultivated for centuries. There are many varieties grown in temperate climates around the world. Inside its protective prickly casing, the chestnut itself is a rounded, glossy brown nut with a rich, sweetly nutty flavor and starchy texture.

BUY Harvesting chestnuts takes place in the fall, with the fresh nuts in shops for only a few months afterward. When buying them fresh in shell, choose firm, heavy, unblemished nuts that do not rattle when you shake them. Shelled and peeled chestnuts are widely available vaccum-packed, frozen, and dried.

STORE Keep fresh chestnuts in a cool, dry place and eat as soon as possible after purchase, because they dry out and deteriorate very quickly. Store unshelled, fresh chestnuts in a sealed plastic container in the fridge for up to 1 month, or the freezer for 2–3 months.

EAT Because of their high tannin content, chestnuts must not be eaten raw. **Cooked:** They are traditionally enjoyed roasted in their shells, then peeled and eaten as a snack. In the kitchen, they are used in both savory and sweet dishes, from soups, stuffings, and braises to pastries and desserts.

FLAVOR PAIRINGS Chicken, sausage, Brussels sprouts, onion, nutmeg, vanilla, cinnamon, chocolate.

CLASSIC RECIPES *Castagnaccio; marrons glacés;* Nesselrode pudding; Peking dust; *gâteau Lyonnaise.*

PREPARING CHESTNUTS

Fresh sweet chestnuts need to be cooked before you remove their shells and skins. Do this as soon as the nuts are cool enough to handle.

1 *Make sure the chestnut shells are free of holes, cracks, and other damage. With a small, sharp knife, score an "x" on the flat side of each nut.* **2** *Soften in boiling water, or in a hot oven, for 15–25 minutes, or until the "x'"opens up a little.* **3** *While the nuts are still warm, use the small, sharp knife to remove the shell and papery inner skin.*

Sweet chestnut
The European chestnut, thought to have actually originated in west Asia, is noted for its sweet flavor.

When shopping for chestnuts in their shells, choose smooth, glossy nuts without insect holes.

Marrone del Mugello
Prized for its sweet taste, the Marrone del Mugello is a traditional chestnut variety that grows in Tuscany.

PINE NUTS

There are various species of pine tree growing in warm, temperate regions that yield these delicious nuts, including the Stone pine in Europe; the Korean pine in China, Japan, and Korea; and the piñon in North America and Mexico. Being time-consuming to harvest from the scales of pine cones, the nuts, also called pine kernels and pignolia, are costly to buy. But with their delicate, subtle, sweet flavor and soft, oily texture, they are much appreciated by cooks everywhere.

BUY Pine nuts are usually sold shelled and blanched. Look for smooth, unblemished, pale nuts. They will vary in size and shape, according to the tree from which they come: Stone pine nuts are long and slender, while Korean pine nuts are short and stubby.

STORE Because of their high oil content, pine nuts turn rancid quite quickly, so keep shelled nuts in a cool, dark, dry place for only a short time; nuts still in shell can be kept longer. Alternatively, store shelled pine nuts in an airtight plastic container in the fridge for 3 months or in the freezer for 9 months.

EAT Toasting improves their flavor. Use pine nuts in all kinds of savory and sweet dishes, ranging from sauces for pasta and fish, stews, stuffings, salads, and soups to cookies, cakes, pastries, and desserts.

FLAVOR PAIRINGS Chicken, fish, spinach, basil, mint, cinnamon, vanilla, chocolate, honey.

CLASSIC RECIPES *Biscotti con pignoli;* ice cream; *kibbeh; pesto genovese.*

Pine nuts grow lodged between the scales of cones from pine trees.

PECANS

This native American nut is cultivated commercially in temperate climates, primarily in the US. Unlike its close relative, the walnut, pecans have thin, smooth, hard shells, but like the walnut, the nut itself comes in two halves. The flavor is mild, buttery, and sweet, the texture delightfully tender.

🔒 **BUY** Fall is the season for fresh pecans in shell, which have a moist texture and very sweet flavor. Look for evenly shaped nuts that do not rattle when you shake them. Shelled pecans are sold year round; choose plump, uniformly colored nuts.

📦 **STORE** Keep both pecans in the shell and shelled pecans (in a sealed container) in a cool, dry place. To enjoy them at their best, eat them within a few weeks of purchasing. Alternatively, store in an airtight plastic container in the fridge for 6 months, or in the freezer for a year.

⊙ **EAT** Pecans can be cracked open and eaten raw. Serve salted or spiced pecans with drinks. In cooking, use pecans, chopped or in complete halves, in cakes, pastries, confectionery, ice cream, and breads, as well as in savory dishes.

FLAVOR PAIRINGS Chicken, turkey, sweet potato, banana, cinnamon, maple syrup, chocolate.

CLASSIC RECIPES Pecan pie; Mexican pecan cake; New Orleans pralines; sandies.

Pecan shells have a distinctive pointed tip at one end.

TIGER NUTS

Despite its name, this is actually a small, edible tuber, borne by the Tigernut Sedge that is grown in southern Europe and parts of Africa. When dried, the brown, wrinkled "nuts," which are called *chufa* in Spain, have a mild, sweet, nutty flavor and a nutlike texture.

🔒 **BUY** Commercially processed tiger nuts, cleaned and dried, are available year round; they are sold both with their skins and without. Look for hard, unshriveled tiger nuts without any blemishes or holes. Ready-ground tiger nut "flour" is also available.

📦 **STORE** Keep dried tiger nuts in a covered container in a cool, dry place for up to a year.

⊙ **EAT** Dried tiger nuts need to be soaked for several hours to rehydrate before use; discard any that rise and float to the surface. In Ghana, tiger nuts are eaten raw or roasted, and are also used in desserts and to make non-alcoholic drinks. In Spain, too, the nuts are made into a beverage, called *horchata*, which is refreshing, sweet, and milky. The flour, which is gluten-free, can be used in baking.

FLAVOR PAIRINGS Lemon, cinnamon.

CLASSIC RECIPE *Horchata*.

Dried tiger nuts are wrinkled, but should not look shriveled.

GINKGO NUTS

Ginkgo nuts, which grow on the ginkgo tree, are much enjoyed in China, Japan, and Korea. Notoriously, the female fruit, which contains the edible nut, has a pungent, disagreeable smell. The nuts themselves smell pleasant and have a mild, nutty, slightly sweet flavor.

🔒 **BUY** Fresh ginkgo nuts are rarely available outside their countries of origin. They are usually sold dried, in shell or shelled, and also canned. Look for smooth nuts that are free from blemishes or marks.

📦 **STORE** Unshelled ginkgo nuts can be kept in a container in a cool, dark, dry place for several months. Shelled nuts are far more perishable and should be stored in a container in the fridge for 4–5 days.

⊙ **EAT** In China, roasted, salted ginkgo nuts are a popular snack. The unsalted nuts are added to sweet or savory soups, *congees*, and braised dishes in China, Japan, and Korea. The Japanese thread the nuts onto skewers and grill them over charcoal as a yakitori dish.

FLAVOR PAIRINGS Chicken, dried longan, ginger, pandan leaves, soy sauce.

CLASSIC RECIPES *Chawan mushi*; ginkgo barley dessert; ginkgo nut yakitori; *longan tong sui*.

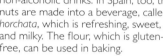

Inside the thin, brown skin are pale yellow kernels that turn a more intense yellow or a delicate shade of green when cooked.

PECAN PIE

This sweet, rich pie from the American South could also be made with brazil nuts or walnuts.

SERVES 6

9oz (250g) pie dough

9 tbsp butter

2 tbsp golden syrup, such as Lyle's (available in the imported-foods section of many well-stocked supermarkets)

⅓ cup packed light brown sugar

⅓ cup packed dark brown sugar

2 cups pecan halves

2 eggs, lightly beaten

1 Preheat the oven to 400°F (200°C). Roll out the pastry and use it to line an 8in (20cm) tart pan with a removable bottom. Refrigerate for about 10 minutes.

2 Prick the bottom of the pastry shell all over with a fork, then line with parchment paper and fill with pie weights or dry beans. Bake for 15 minutes, or until a very light golden brown. Lift out the beans and paper and then bake for another 5 minutes to crisp up the bottom of the shell. Set aside.

3 Turn the oven down to 325°F (160°C). Melt the butter with the syrup in a medium saucepan, then remove from the heat and stir in the brown sugars and nuts. Allow to cool. Stir in the beaten eggs.

4 Scrape the mixture into the tart shell, spreading it evenly. Bake for 30–40 minutes, or until the crust is golden and crisp; the filling should still be slightly soft. Leave to cool before serving.

WALNUTS

Growing in temperate regions around the world, the many species of walnut tree have long been valued for their delicious nuts. Walnuts may be picked when young ("green" or "wet"), but most are left on the tree to ripen.

BUY Fall is harvest season for walnuts, and this is the best time to enjoy them fresh. When buying nuts in the shell, check that they feel heavy and do not rattle when shaken. Walnuts are also available shelled, in halves or pieces, all year round.

STORE Keep shelled walnuts in a covered container in a cool, dry, dark place and use as soon as possible. Or, store in an airtight plastic container in the fridge for 6 months, or the freezer for a year. In shell, walnuts can be kept in a cool, dry place for up to 3 months.

EAT Add to cereal, salads, and snack mixes. Grind for sauces. Use in sweet and savory dishes, from soups and stuffings to breads, cakes, and pastries.

FLAVOR PAIRINGS Bananas, dried fruits, cream, blue cheese.

CLASSIC RECIPES Pickled walnuts; coffee and walnut cake; *fesanjoon*; *salsa di noci*; walnut bread; *tarator*.

Black walnut
The tough-shelled American black walnut is noted for its excellent flavor. As its texture is somewhat oily, it is a good choice for cakes and cookies.

Sorrento walnut
This Italian variety with a smooth shell has a pleasant flavor. It is much used in commercial confectionery, because the nut can easily be extracted whole from the shell.

Green or "wet" walnut
When young, the entire nut, including the skin that will become the shell, is edible, once pickled or preserved.

Pickled walnut
Unripe green nuts are too sour to eat fresh, so are normally pickled in a spiced vinegar (see recipe, right).

English walnut
Also known as the Persian or European walnut, this is widely cultivated, and is delicious in all kinds of sweet and savory cooking.

LOTUS NUTS

The edible seeds, or nuts, from the flowers of the exotic lotus plant have long been eaten in Asia. Today, China is the world's major producer. The nuts are usually sold dried and cored (to remove their bitter green germ), either with their brown membrane attached, or without it to reveal the pale nut. Their flavor is mild, sweet, and nutty.

BUY Lotus nuts are rarely available fresh, but are commonly found dried. They are also sold canned, crystallized, and as a sweetened paste.

STORE Store dried lotus nuts in a container in a cool, dry, dark place for up to a year.

EAT Rinse dried nuts before using. They are often soaked before cooking, or roasted. Use in sweet and savory dishes, such as soups and stews. The crystallized nuts are a popular snack in China, and the sweetened paste is used in pastries and desserts.

FLAVOR PAIRINGS Chicken, ginger, tangerine peel.

CLASSIC RECIPES Chinese mooncake; lotus seed soup; *congee*.

Lotus nuts should be creamy-colored, not discolored or yellowing.

CLASSIC RECIPE

PICKLED WALNUTS

In Britain, unripened (or "green"), immature walnuts have been preserved in spiced vinegar since the 17th century.

MAKES ABOUT 3LB (1.5KG)

1lb (450g) salt

2¼ lbs (1kg) shelled "green" walnuts

For the spiced vinegar

3½ cups malt vinegar

1 tbsp coriander seeds, crushed

12 allspice berries

2–3 red chiles, seeded if desired

½ cup muscovado, raw, or dark brown sugar

1 To make the brine, in a large bowl dissolve half of the salt in 2 cups hot water. Allow to cool (a brine should always be used cold to prevent bacterial growth).

2 Prick the walnuts all over with a silver or stainless-steel fork, then add to the brine. Make sure that they are submerged: weigh down with a plate if necessary. Leave for 5 days.

3 Make a fresh batch of brine as above with the remaining salt and another 2 cups hot water. Drain the walnuts, submerge in the new brine, and leave for another 7 days.

4 Drain the walnuts again and spread, in a single layer, on a baking sheet to dry for 2–3 days. Turn the nuts often and leave them to dry until they are uniformly black.

5 The day before you are due to pickle the walnuts, make the spiced vinegar. Combine the vinegar and spices in a nonreactive saucepan and bring to a boil. Add the sugar and stir to dissolve, then remove from the heat. Leave to infuse for 24 hours.

6 Strain the spiced vinegar into a clean nonreactive saucepan and bring to a boil to reheat. Pack the walnuts into hot, sterilized jars, pushing them down well, then cover with the hot, spiced vinegar. Cover the jars with vinegar-proof seals and label. Leave the jarred nuts for at least 3 months to mature before using.

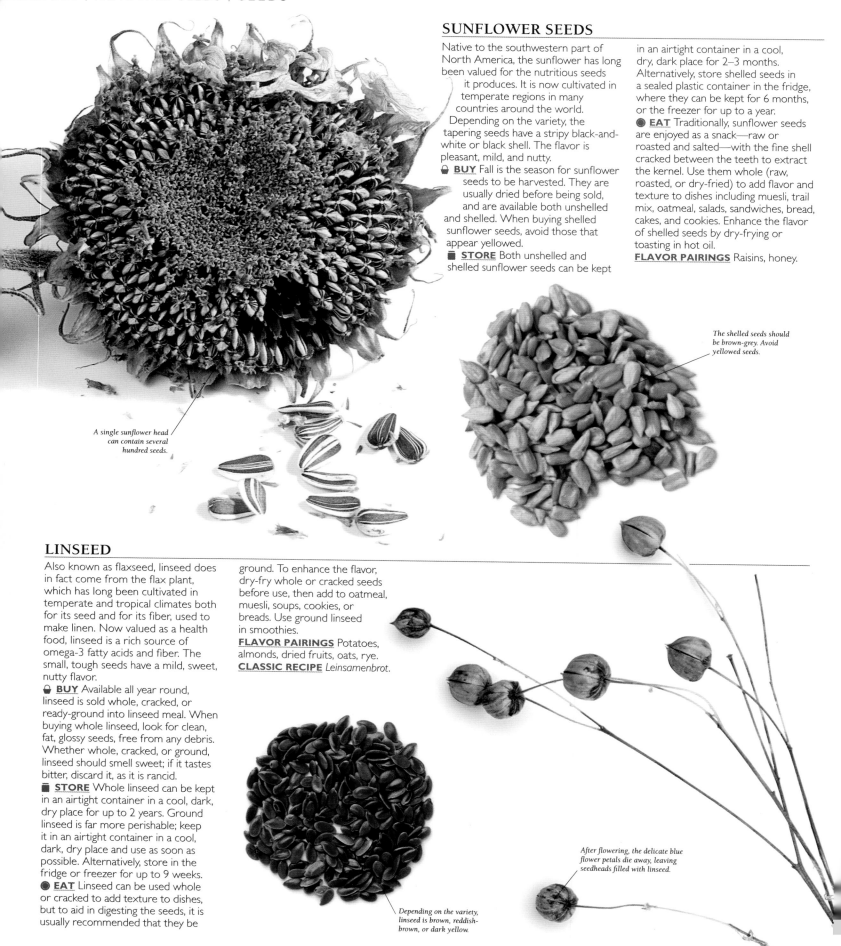

SUNFLOWER SEEDS

Native to the southwestern part of North America, the sunflower has long been valued for the nutritious seeds it produces. It is now cultivated in temperate regions in many countries around the world. Depending on the variety, the tapering seeds have a stripy black-and-white or black shell. The flavor is pleasant, mild, and nutty.

BUY Fall is the season for sunflower seeds to be harvested. They are usually dried before being sold, and are available both unshelled and shelled. When buying shelled sunflower seeds, avoid those that appear yellowed.

STORE Both unshelled and shelled sunflower seeds can be kept in an airtight container in a cool, dry, dark place for 2–3 months. Alternatively, store shelled seeds in a sealed plastic container in the fridge, where they can be kept for 6 months, or the freezer for up to a year.

EAT Traditionally, sunflower seeds are enjoyed as a snack—raw or roasted and salted—with the fine shell cracked between the teeth to extract the kernel. Use them whole (raw, roasted, or dry-fried) to add flavor and texture to dishes including muesli, trail mix, oatmeal, salads, sandwiches, bread, cakes, and cookies. Enhance the flavor of shelled seeds by dry-frying or toasting in hot oil.

FLAVOR PAIRINGS Raisins, honey.

A single sunflower head can contain several hundred seeds.

The shelled seeds should be brown-grey. Avoid yellowed seeds.

LINSEED

Also known as flaxseed, linseed does in fact come from the flax plant, which has long been cultivated in temperate and tropical climates both for its seed and for its fiber, used to make linen. Now valued as a health food, linseed is a rich source of omega-3 fatty acids and fiber. The small, tough seeds have a mild, sweet, nutty flavor.

BUY Available all year round, linseed is sold whole, cracked, or ready-ground into linseed meal. When buying whole linseed, look for clean, fat, glossy seeds, free from any debris. Whether whole, cracked, or ground, linseed should smell sweet; if it tastes bitter, discard it, as it is rancid.

STORE Whole linseed can be kept in an airtight container in a cool, dark, dry place for up to 2 years. Ground linseed is far more perishable; keep it in an airtight container in a cool, dark, dry place and use as soon as possible. Alternatively, store in the fridge or freezer for up to 9 weeks.

EAT Linseed can be used whole or cracked to add texture to dishes, but to aid in digesting the seeds, it is usually recommended that they be ground. To enhance the flavor, dry-fry whole or cracked seeds before use, then add to oatmeal, muesli, soups, cookies, or breads. Use ground linseed in smoothies.

FLAVOR PAIRINGS Potatoes, almonds, dried fruits, oats, rye.

CLASSIC RECIPE *Leinsamenbrot.*

Depending on the variety, linseed is brown, reddish-brown, or dark yellow.

After flowering, the delicate blue flower petals die away, leaving seedheads filled with linseed.

SESAME SEEDS

Native to Africa, the wild sesame plant has a venerable history of cultivation for its seeds. Today it is widely grown around the world in temperate and tropical regions, from Africa to Asia. Depending on the variety, the small seeds may be white, golden brown, or black, all with the same rich, nutty, earthy flavor.

BUY Sesame seeds are usually available already hulled. As they will deteriorate with age, check the use-by date on the pack. Sesame-seed pastes (Asian types and Middle Eastern tahini) are also available.

STORE The seeds can be kept in an airtight container in a cool, dark, dry place for up to 3 months. Or store in a sealed plastic container in the fridge for up to 6 months, or the freezer for up to a year.

EAT Dry-roasting and grinding enhance the flavor of sesame seeds. The seeds feature in sweet and savory dishes around the world, as well as in many classic seasoning mixes such as the Middle Eastern *za'atar* and Japanese seven spice powder. Use sesame seeds in rice and noodle dishes, and to coat foods before frying; sprinkle over salads and vegetables; and add to breads, cookies, pastries, and sweetmeats. Use sesame-seed paste to add richness to dips, sauces, and dressings, and sweetened paste in baking and confectionery.

FLAVOR PAIRINGS Chicken, fish, peanuts, vegetables, rice, noodles, honey, lemon.

CLASSIC RECIPES Bang-bang chicken; *goma-dofu*; *halva*; hummus; spinach with sesame dressing; tahini and parsley dip; shrimp on toast; *til laddoos*; *za'atar spice mix*.

Look for clean seeds, free of any debris.

LUPIN SEEDS

Also known as lupini beans, these are the seeds of certain varieties of the lupin plant, which grows in many temperate parts of the world including North and South America, the Mediterranean, the Middle East, and Australia. Lupin seeds have been eaten for centuries, with archaeological evidence of cultivation in Ancient Egypt and Ancient Greece. Being hard and bitter, the seeds require lengthy soaking before they are edible, although new "sweet" varieties have been developed. Each flat, yellow seed is encased in a thick skin, from which it is squeezed out, and has a nutty flavor and chewy texture.

BUY Lupin seeds are available in their dried form or ready-to-eat and vacuum-packed. When buying them dried, look for smooth, unblemished seeds.

STORE Keep dried lupin seeds in a sealed container in a cool, dry, dark place for 3–6 months.

EAT To prepare dried lupin seeds, first soak for 24 hours, then blanch in boiling water for 5 minutes, then soak again for 4–5 days in many changes of water (ready-to-eat seeds are a more convenient option). Roasted and salted lupin seeds are a popular snack in many countries around the world, including Lebanon and Italy, where they are traditionally eaten with beer.

FLAVOR PAIRINGS Olive oil, black pepper.

CLASSIC RECIPE *Tormus*.

Inside their thick skin, the seeds are yellow and chewy.

PUMPKIN SEEDS

Also known as *pepitas*, pumpkin seeds are found in the center of pumpkins. In Mexico, where pumpkin seeds have been eaten for thousands of years, the seeds are dried in the sun. Inside each thin, pale shell or husk is a tender green kernel with a delicately nutty flavor.

BUY Dried pumpkin seeds are available all year round, shelled and unshelled. Look for plump, unshriveled seeds. For fresh pumpkin seeds, you will have to buy a fresh pumpkin (traditionally harvested during the fall): scoop out the seeds, and separate them from the fibers.

STORE Fresh pumpkin seeds must be thoroughly dried before storage. Due to their high oil content, they can go rancid very quickly, so keep them in a tightly sealed, airtight container in a cool, dry place and use as soon as possible. Or, you can store them in a sealed plastic container in the fridge for a few weeks, or the freezer for up to 6 months.

EAT Dry-roasting and frying will enhance the flavor. Roasted fresh or dried, shelled or unshelled pumpkin seeds are often flavored with salt and spices to eat as a snack. Seeds are also used in cakes, bread, and cookies, or as a tasty garnish for salads and soups, in particular, pumpkin. In Mexican cooking, pumpkin seeds are ground and used to thicken and flavor sauces.

FLAVOR PAIRINGS Apricots, pumpkin, chile, cinnamon, ginger, maple syrup.

CLASSIC RECIPES *Camarones en pipian*; *papadzules*.

Popular as a snack or garnish, ready-hulled pumpkin seeds are widely available.

SPICES

CHILES | CITRUS
CORIANDER | ANISE
TURMERIC | NIGELLA
SUMAC | CLOVES
TAMARIND | GINGER

SPICE ESSENTIALS

Today, there is a growing awareness of and demand for authentic regional foods. Regional tradition, family tastes, and individual preferences determine the spices used, and even fairly standard mixtures will be adapted to the dish they are made for—masalas, *bumbus*, *rempahs*, and the like are infinitely variable. Complex flavors are built up in mixtures by using spices (or herbs) that complement each other. Some are used for their taste, others for their aroma. Some have souring properties; in others, the color is important. The moment at which spices are added to a dish makes a crucial difference. Whether they are first dry-roasted or not, spices will impart their flavor to a dish if they are added at the beginning of cooking; if sprinkled on toward the end of cooking, it is their aroma that will be emphasized in the finished dish.

Spices play *an important and defining part in many cuisines throughout the world, particularly in India, the Far East, and South America. Spices are added to curries, stews, marinades, and tandoori dishes whole, ground, or as pastes to add heat, flavor, and aroma.*

PREPARE

Many spices need some preparation before being added to a dish or used in a spice blend or paste. Bruising, cutting, and grinding serve to release the volatile oils and perfume of a spice. Large, bruised pieces of a spice are intended only for flavoring, and should be removed before a dish is served. Mild spices are sometimes cut into bite-sized pieces and eaten as part of the dish; otherwise, spices should be grated, finely sliced, or shredded.

DRY-ROAST Roasting whole spices in a dry frying pan is especially common in Indian cooking. The process concentrates the flavors and makes the spices easier to grind. Other dishes call for spices to be fried before the remaining ingredients are added. Frying brings out the flavor, which is imparted into the oil. The aroma of fried spices permeates a dish more fully than that of raw spices, but once a liquid is added, the amount of fragrance they release is reduced.

On the stovetop

1 *Heat a heavy pan until it feels hot when you hold your hand above the base. With the pan set over medium heat, toss in the spices. Stir them or shake the pan constantly.*

2 *Let the spices darken and smoke a little and they will soon give off a heady aroma. If they are changing color too quickly, lower the heat and make sure they do not burn.*

In the oven

Dry-roasting *a quantity of spices may be easier in an oven preheated to 475°F (450°C). Spread them on a baking sheet and cook until dark and aromatic. Cool before grinding.*

FRESH VERSUS GROUND Fresh spices that you grind or crush at home are always more aromatic than spices bought ready-ground. You will soon appreciate the difference if you take the trouble to grind, say, a teaspoon of coriander seeds and put them to one side for an hour or two. Grind another spoonful, smell the earlier batch and then the freshly ground seeds and you will find that some of the aroma of the first batch has already dissipated. Successfully making your own blend of spices gives a sense of achievement that nothing squeezed out of a tube or poured from a bottle can equal. In countries where such blends are used regularly, there is no such thing as an immutably fixed recipe.

FRY Prepare all the ingredients of a dish before frying its spices, as they will need to be added soon after frying. Some spices need to be fried for only a few seconds, others for up to a minute. All will darken, and some, such as cardamom pods, will puff up. Remove the pan from the heat to add the remaining ingredients and stir quickly to prevent them from burning in the oil.

1 *Pour a thin film of sunflower oil into a heavy frying pan set over medium heat, and wait to add the spices until you can see a faint haze rising from the pan.*

2 *Fry whole spices before ground ones. Spices should sizzle when they hit the hot oil and brown almost instantly. Watch them closely and stir them to prevent burning.*

GRATE Fresh spice roots and rhizomes, such as wasabi and horseradish, ginger, and its relatives, are often best grated rather than chopped. A Japanese *oroshigane*, designed specifically for grating wasabi and ginger, grates more finely than any Western grater. Although most spices are ground, it is easier to grate some of the larger ones. Use a nutmeg grater or the finest holes of a normal grater when grating whole nutmeg.

Grated galangal

A very sharp *Western grater will produce a pulp that is suitable for a variety of purposes, such as for extracting its juice.*

Grated dried ginger

Dried ginger, *turmeric, and zedoary are very hard and therefore best grated on a fine citrus grater or rasp.*

EXTRACT JUICE

Many Asian dishes call for the pure flavor of ginger juice, which can be quickly extracted from a fresh root.

Grate the ginger *or chop it finely in a food processor. Wrap up the shavings in a clean piece of muslin or a dish towel and squeeze the juice into a bowl.*

SLICE AND SHRED Some dishes require discs of fresh spices, while others call for spices to be shredded or chopped. The best technique for slicing and shredding spices such as ginger, galangal, or zedoary (white turmeric) is given below. Lemon grass should be cut into fine rings from the base, stopping where the texture becomes fibrous. Kaffir lime leaves should be shredded as fine as a needle if they are to be eaten.

1 *Peel away as much fresh rhizome or root as you need, cutting off any woody or dry bits.*

2 *Using a sharp knife, slice the root thinly across the grain into a series of fine disks.*

3 *Stack the disks, press down firmly with your fingers, and shred them into fine slivers.*

4 *Line up the slivers and cut across them. For a finer cut, mound and chop them as herbs.*

BLEND Some whole spices—such as allspice, cinnamon, and cloves—are aromatic, but most need to be crushed or ground to release their aroma. A blender can be used for large quantities, but most spices are too hard to grind evenly in a food processor. Some spices only need crushing, rather than pulverizing to a powder. A pestle and mortar allows you to see and control how much the spice is broken up—while enjoying its fragrance at the same time.

Using a pestle and mortar

Choose a mortar *that is deep, sturdy, and roughly textured, for many spices are very hard and it requires considerable force to grind them by hand.*

Using a rolling pin

Put the spice in a *plastic bag, spread out the seeds on a hard surface, then crush firmly with a rolling pin.*

Using a grinder

It is easier *to grind slightly larger quantities of spices in an electric coffee grinder. Keep the grinder specifically for spices to prevent mixing strong aromas.*

Making a spice paste

Crush garlic or ginger in a mortar, then work in ground spices and a little liquid, if needed, to make a smooth spice paste that can be used for Indian, Southeast Asian, and Mexican dishes.

SPICE MIXTURES A masala is a blend of spices; it may contain two or three, or even a dozen or more. It may be added to the dish, whole or ground, at different stages of cooking. For rice and some meat dishes, whole spices are traditional. The most common ground mixtures are the garam masalas (hot spices) used in northern Indian cooking. This mixture is best for meat and poultry dishes, especially those cooked in tomato or onion gravy, and is usually added toward the end of the cooking time to draw out the flavors of the other ingredients.

Garam masala *also makes a good flavoring for spiced bean or lentil soups. Extract 2 tablespoons seeds from black cardamom pods (discarding the pods), and break 1½ cinnamon sticks. Dry-roast with 4 tablespoons coriander seeds, 3 tablespoons cumin seeds, 2 tablespoons whole cloves, and 2 crumbled tejpat leaves over a medium heat—this will take 8–10 minutes. Let the spices cool, grind them to a powder, then sieve. The masala will keep in an airtight jar for 2–3 months.*

GALANGAL (ALPINIA SPECIES)

There are two main types of galangal: greater galangal (*A. galanga*), native to Java, and lesser galangal (*A. officinarum*), native to the coastal regions of southern China. Both are cultivated extensively throughout Southeast Asia, Indonesia, and India. Greater galangal is the type that is used in the kitchen, mainly in Southeast Asia. The aroma of greater galangal is mildly gingery and camphorous. Several plants with similar properties to lesser galangal are also referred to, confusingly, by this name. One of these is aromatic ginger. In Indonesia, pounded, dried aromatic ginger is added to various dishes; in China, it is mixed with salt and oil, and served with baked chicken; in Sri Lanka, it is roasted and ground for *biryanis* and curries. Fingerroot, also called Chinese ginger, *krachai*, and *temu kunci*, is another galangal-type plant that grows in Southeast Asia. As krachai, it is essential to some Thai curry pastes, and also used in soup.

◉ **BUY** Fresh greater galangal can be bought from Asian markets and some supermarkets. It may be identified by its local names: *kha* (Thailand), *lengkuas* (Malaysia), or *laos* (Indonesia). Dried slices and powdered galangal are often more widely available; galangal in brine can be substituted for fresh.

◉ **STORE** The fresh rhizome will keep for 2 weeks in the fridge, or can be frozen. Powdered galangal will keep for 2 months; dried slices keep their flavor for at least a year.

◉ **EAT** Like ginger, fresh galangal is easy to peel and grate or chop. It is always preferred to dried, but dried slices can be added to soups and stews; first soak them in hot water. Remove before eating, as they are too tough to be palatable. Throughout Southeast Asia, galangal is used fresh in curries and stews, in sambals, satays, soups, and sauces. In Thailand, it is an essential ingredient in some curry pastes, as it is in the *laksa* spices of Malaysian Nyonya cooking. In Thai cooking, it is often preferred where other Asian cuisines would use ginger, especially with fish and seafood. It is good with chicken and in many hot and sour soups, providing the key flavoring in *tom kha gai*, the popular chicken and coconut milk soup. Powdered galangal is used in spice blends throughout the Middle East and across North Africa to Morocco (in *ras el hanout*). Grated galangal and lime juice are used to make a popular tonic in Southeast Asia.

FLAVOR PAIRINGS Chicken, fish and in sauces for fish, seafood, chili, coconut milk, fennel, garlic, ginger, lemongrass, lemon, kaffir lime, shallots, tamarind.

CLASSIC RECIPES *Tom kha gai*; Thai curry pastes; *ras el hanout*.

Greater galangal root
The taste of greater galangal has a lemony sourness, with a flavor resembling ginger and cardamom mixed. It is used fresh in curries and stews.

The large rhizomes are knobby and light orange-brown, marked with dark rings.

The clusters of thin fingers are yellowish brown outside and yellow inside.

Fingerroot
(Boesenbergia pandurata/ Kaempferia pandurata)
The rhizome has a sweet aroma; a refreshing, lemony taste; and lingering warmth, somewhere between galangal and ginger. In the West, it is used fresh or in dried slices.

The dried slices of the greater galanghal rhizome are large, with a woody texture.

Aromatic ginger *(Kaempferia galanga)* The leaves of this wild plant, also known as the resurrection lily, kencur in Indonesia, cekur in Malaysia, and pro hom in Thailand, are served raw to accompany Thai fish curries, and in Malay salads.

Sliced dried greater galangal
Dried slices are good for flavoring soups and stews, and should be soaked in hot water for 30 minutes before use. They should be taken out before serving because they remain unpleasantly woody to chew.

BLACK CARDAMOM (AMOMUM AND AFRAMOMUM SPECIES)

The larger seeds of several species of *Amomum* and *Aframomum* are widely used in the regions where they are grown, and sometimes they are sold, ground, as cheap substitutes for green cardamom. The most important is Greater Indian or Nepal cardamom, *Amomum subulatum*, native to the eastern Himalayas. This particular variety, usually referred to as black cardamom, is never used as a substitute for green cardamom and has a distinct and separate role in Indian cooking. The seeds smell of tar and taste of pine, with a smoky, earthy, and astringent note. In color, the seeds are various shades of brown, and their taste is usually more camphorous than that of green cardamom.

BUY Black cardamom is best bought as whole pods; ensure they are not broken. The seeds inside should be sticky, not dry.

STORE Pods will keep for a year or more in an airtight jar. It is better to buy black cardamom as pods and grind them before use, to keep the flavor.

EAT Black cardamom is an important spice in *garam masala*, along with cloves, cinnamon, and black pepper. This hot spice mixture can be used either at the start of cooking or sprinkled over for a stronger effect toward the end. When pods are used whole in vegetable or meat stews they should be removed before serving, but crushed seeds will dissolve into the sauce. The flavor is intense, so use sparingly. Black cardamom is also used occasionally in confectionery and pickles.

FLAVOR PAIRINGS Meat and vegetable curries, yogurt, pilafs and other rice dishes, *ajowan*, green cardamom, cassia leaves, chiles, cinnamon, cloves, coriander seeds, cumin, nutmeg, pepper.

CLASSIC RECIPES *Garam masala*; tandoori spice mixtures.

Whole pods
Black cardamom has ribbed, often hairy fruits that are deep red when ripe. After drying, they turn a very dark brown.

Black cardamom ground powder
Whereas green cardamom is a "cooling" spice, black cardamom is a "heating" spice, and is an important ingredient in garam masala, and in rice and curry dishes.

Seeds
The seeds have a tarry smell and a taste of pine, with an astringent, smoky, earthy note. They are used to give depth to garam masala and tandoori-style spice mixtures.

Inside each seedpod are tiny, dark, sticky seeds; stickiness is a good sign of freshness.

WATTLE (ACACIA SPECIES)

Several hundred acacia species are native to Australia, but only a few have edible seeds. *A. victoriae* and *A. aneura*, the latter locally called the mulga tree, are two of those most regularly harvested for wattle seed. Highly nutritious, it has long provided food for indigenous Australians. New interest in bush foods has created a demand among food enthusiasts. When dried, roasted, and ground, the green, unripe seeds are transformed into a deep brown powder. The flavor has notes of coffee and roasted hazelnuts, with a hint of chocolate.

BUY Wattle seed is quite expensive because it is gathered from the wild and its preparation is labor intensive; this is still mostly done in the bush by Aboriginal women. The increased demand has also led to higher prices. Roasted, ground wattle is sold by some spice merchants and delicatessens.

STORE In an airtight container it should keep for up to two years.

EAT Wattle seed yields its flavor when infused in a hot liquid; do not allow to boil or the flavor will become bitter. The liquid can be strained and used alone, or the ground seed can be left in for its texture. Wattle seed can be used to flavor desserts, especially cream- or yogurt-based desserts such as mousses, ice creams, and cheesecakes, and in cream fillings for cakes. Try it in a sweet bread dough, or sprinkled into bread and butter pudding, a traditional British dessert. Wattle liquid is sometimes drunk as an alternative to coffee.

FLAVOR PAIRINGS Poultry, fish, yogurt, ice cream, chocolate, breads, pastries.

CLASSIC RECIPES Wattle ice cream; wattle-seed cheesecake.

The deep brown powder resembles ground coffee and has a rich, toasty aroma.

Ground greater galangal
The ground rhizome of greater galangal is sandy beige, with a sour aroma and a mild ginger flavor. This powdered form is used in many spice blends.

GRAINS OF PARADISE (AMOMUM MELEGUETA)

Grains of paradise are the tiny seeds of a perennial, reed-like plant with showy, trumpet-shaped flowers, indigenous to the humid tropical coast of West Africa. Among their other names are Guinea pepper, Melegueta pepper, and, less often, alligator pepper. Present-day production is still in the same region, with Ghana the main exporter. Grains of paradise taste pungently hot and peppery, with a fruity note; the aroma is similar, but fainter. The spice was originally brought to Europe via Saharan caravan routes in the 13th century, and was at that time appreciated as a replacement for true pepper and used to spice wine and beer. Grains of paradise are little used in Western cooking now, except in Scandinavian *akvavit*.

🔒 **BUY** Grains of paradise are stocked by spice merchants and can be bought from West Indian or African stores, or from health food stores.

📦 **STORE** Stored whole in an airtight container they keep their flavor for several years.

⬤ **EAT** Grind the seeds down into a fine, aromatic powder just before use and add at the last stage of cooking to braised lamb and vegetable dishes. Use the seeds in mulled wine. In West Africa, and to a lesser degree in the West Indies, grains of paradise are a much-used seasoning.

FLAVOR PAIRINGS Eggplant, lamb, potatoes, poultry, rice, squash, tomatoes, root vegetables, allspice, cinnamon, cloves, cumin, nutmeg.

CLASSIC RECIPES *Qâlat daqqa; ras el hanout.*

Whole seeds
Inside the seedhead, 60–100 red-brown seeds, the grains of paradise, are embedded in a white pulp. They are an essential ingredient in the Tunisian five-spice mixture qâlat daqqa.

Crushed seeds
Crushing breaks down the red-brown coats of the seeds to reveal the white flesh inside. Grains of paradise are related to cardamom, but their taste does not have that spice's camphor element.

Ground seeds
The seeds should be ground just before use, as they lose their flavor quickly. Pepper mixed with a little cardamom and ginger may be used as a substitute.

LEMON MYRTLE (BACKHOUSIA CITRIODORA)

The lemon myrtle tree is native to coastal Australian rainforests, mostly in Queensland. The trees have been introduced to southern Europe, the southern US, and South Africa, and are grown for their essential oil in China and Southeast Asia. Lemon myrtle has gained a place in the kitchen only in Australia, but it is becoming more widely appreciated. The aroma is refreshing and intensely lemony, like that of lemongrass and lemon verbena, and is more pronounced when the leaves are crushed. The taste is stronger still, more like lemon zest. The aftertaste is a lingering note of eucalyptus or camphor.

🔒 **BUY** Outside Australia, lemon myrtle leaves are usually only available dried or ground. The drying process intensifies the flavor. Whole, dried leaves and powder are available from herb or spice merchants, and some supermarkets. Buy the powder only in small quantities.

📦 **STORE** Dried leaves and powder can be stored in airtight containers in the dark for a few months.

⬤ **EAT** Lemon myrtle is versatile and can be used wherever lemongrass or lemon zest is called for, albeit more sparingly, as it is powerful. If cooked for too long, an unpleasant eucalyptus note can take over. It is therefore better in shortbread, cookies, and batters for things like pancakes than in longer-baked cakes. It is excellent for flavoring stir-fry dishes and fish cakes; with vinegar, sugar, basil, and olive oil it can make a dipping sauce for the cakes or a salad dressing. It gives a lift to mayonnaise, sauces, and marinades for chicken or seafood; combined with other spices it makes a good rub for chicken or fish to be barbecued or grilled. It also makes good vinegar, as well as a lemonade and an herbal tea.

FLAVOR PAIRINGS Chicken, pork, fish, seafood, yogurt, most fruit, rice, tea, *akudjura*, anise, basil, chiles, fennel, galangal, ginger, mountain pepper, parsley, pepper, thyme.

Lemon myrtle leaves are ground to produce a coarse, light green powder.

The leaves from which the powder is derived can be used whole, either fresh or dried.

ANNATTO (BIXA ORELLANA)

Annatto is the orange-red seed of a small, evergreen tree of the same name, native to tropical South America. In pre-Columbian times, the seeds were used as a colorant for food, fabrics, and body paint; in the West annatto (or *achiote*, its name in the Nahuatl language of Mexico) is still used as such in butter, cheese, and smoked fish. Brazil and the Philippines are the main producers, but it grows throughout Central America, the Caribbean, and in parts of Asia. The angular, red seeds have a faint flowery or peppermint scent, and a delicate, slightly peppery taste with a hint of bitterness. They impart an agreeably earthy taste to food.

BUY Available as seeds, whole or ground, from West Indian stores and spice merchants. Seeds should be a healthy rust-red; avoid dull, brownish ones. Powdered annatto is often mixed with cornstarch, and sometimes with other spices, such as cumin.

STORE Seeds and powder should be kept in an airtight jar out of the light. Seeds will last at least 3 years.

EAT The seeds are soaked in hot water to obtain a colored liquid for stews and rice. In the Caribbean, the seeds are fried in fat to color it a deep orange, and the fat is then used for cooking. Dried annatto seeds can also be ground for use. In Jamaica, annatto is combined with onion and chili in a sauce for saltfish and *ackee*. In the Philippines, ground annatto is added to soups and stews, mostly for color effect; it is an essential ingredient in *pipián*, a pork-and-chicken dish. In Mexico it goes into achiote paste—the Yucatán *recado rojo*—basis of the region's best-known dish, *pollo pibil* (marinated chicken wrapped in banana leaves and cooked in a pit oven).

FLAVOR PAIRINGS Beef, pork, poultry, fish (especially salt cod), egg dishes, okra, onions, peppers, beans and pulses, rice, squashes, sweet potatoes, tomatoes, most vegetables, allspice, chiles, citrus juice, cloves, cumin, epazote, garlic, oregano, paprika, peanuts.

CLASSIC RECIPES *Pipián*; *recado rojo*.

Annatto pod
Each orange-red pod contains about 50 seeds. The pods are harvested, split open, and macerated in water; the seeds are then dried for use as a spice.

Whole dried seeds
The seeds are mostly used as a food colorant for rice, stocks, and stews, by soaking ½ tsp seeds in 1 tbsp boiling water for 1 hour, or until the water is a deep golden color.

Ground seeds
The dried rust-red seeds are very hard and are most easily ground in an electric grinder. The powder is used in combination with other spices in many countries, to add color and flavor to recipes.

BARBERRY (BERBERIS VULGARIS)

Many species of the *Berberis* genus and of the closely related genus *Mahonia* grow wild in temperate zones of Europe, Asia, northern Africa, and North America. They are dense, spiny, perennial bushes with toothed leaves, and they all have edible berries—the *Berberis* berries some shade of red, the *Mahonia* ones blue. In Iran, the Caucasian republics, and countries farther east, barberries are still gathered from the wild, sun-dried, and stored for use in the kitchen. The small, oblong berries have a light aroma, reminiscent of currants, but with a tart note. The taste is agreeably sweet-tart, with an underlying sharpness that derives from malic acid. The Oregon grape of North America, *M. aquifolium*, is gathered in the wild and used in similar ways to the barberry.

BUY Dried barberries are somewhat difficult to buy outside their region of production, except from Iranian shops. The berries should be red rather than dark. Or buy a plant from a nursery, gather your own berries from July until late summer, and dry them.

STORE Dried berries will keep for several months. They retain their color and flavor best if stored in the freezer.

EAT Cooked: Barberries make a good finish for any dish with which you might otherwise use lemon juice: fresh berries strewn over lamb or mutton for the last minutes of roasting will burst and coat the meat with their tart juice. Crush dried berries in a mortar to use with herbs and spices to flavor meatballs, pâtés, and marinades, or mix with salt and rub on to lamb kebabs before grilling to give a tart piquancy. Fry gently in butter or oil, then sprinkle over rice dishes for a sour flavor and a splash of color, as they do in central Asia and Iran; there barberries also go into stuffings, stews, and meat dishes. In India, dried berries are added to desserts, rather like sour currants.

Preserved: Being rich in pectin they are easily made into jelly or jam. Or, preserve in syrup or vinegar to make a tart flavoring. In the past, the berries were also made into sweetmeats and comfits; the famous *confitures d'épine-vinette*, which are made in Rouen, are the last remnant of that tradition.

FLAVOR PAIRINGS Lamb, poultry, yogurt, almonds, rice, pistachios, bay, cardamom, cinnamon, coriander, cumin, dill, parsley, saffron.

Whole barberries
Whole, dried barberries have a soft texture and a pleasant, sourish flavor. Look for berries that are red rather than dark, as these may be older and will have less flavor.

MUSTARD (BRASSICA SPECIES)

Black mustard and white or yellow mustard are native to southern Europe and western Asia; brown mustard to India; white mustard has long been naturalized in Europe and North America. In medieval Europe, mustard was the one spice ordinary people could afford. The French started to add other ingredients in the 18th century, while the English refined the powder by removing the husks before grinding the kernels. Whole mustard seed has virtually no aroma, but when ground it smells pungent; cooking releases an acrid, earthy aroma. Mustard's pungent taste is determined by an enzyme, *myrosinase*, which is activated by water. English mustard powder is made with cold water, which develops its clean and pungent taste. To prepare blended mustards, the seeds are soaked in water, then mixed with an acidic liquid, such as vinegar, wine, or beer. French mustards, milder than English, are made in three forms: Bordeaux is brown, although made from white seed, and contains sugar and herbs, usually tarragon; Dijon, from brown

(but husked) mustard seed, is paler and stronger, made with white wine or verjuice; Meaux is quite hot, made from crushed and ground grains. In Germany, Bavarian mustard is of the Bordeaux type, but Düsseldorf mustard is a pungent version of Dijon. Zwolle, in Holland, makes a mustard flavored with dill that works well with *gravad lax*. Mild North American mustard is made from white mustard and colored with turmeric. The aromatic, mild Savora mustard is popular in South America. A yellow variety of *B. juncea* is used in Japan in cooking and as a condiment, made very hot. Field mustard, *B. campestris*, and rapeseed, *B. napus*, are used to produce mustard oil, as is brown mustard.

🔒 **BUY** White and brown mustard seeds are widely available. Black is hard to find; brown can be used instead but is less potent. English mustard powder and prepared mustards of all kinds are also easily obtainable.

▌ **STORE** All forms of mustard store well if they are kept scrupulously dry. Prepared

mustards are best stored at room temperature after opening; they will keep for 2–3 months.

● **EAT** In southern India, brown seeds are dry-roasted or heated in hot oil or *ghee* to bring out an attractive, nutty flavor for a *tadka* or *baghar* spice mix. In Bengal, ground raw seed is used in pastes for curries, especially fish in mustard sauce. The piquant flavor of a cooking oil made from brown mustard seed contributes to the distinctive taste of many Indian dishes. Powdered mustard flavors barbecue sauces, and works well with meat and root vegetables, added toward the end of cooking. Prepared mustards are mainly served as a condiment with meat casseroles, or with roasted or cold

meats. The various kinds are good in many cold sauces, from vinaigrette to mayonnaise, served with vegetable or fish dishes. They also go well with many cheese dishes. Sweet mustards, made with honey or brown sugar, make good glazes for chicken, ham, or pork, and can be a piquant addition to fruit salads. Fresh mustard shoots are used in salads, as in mustard and cress, and shredded leaves make a good garnish for root vegetables and tomato salads.

FLAVOR PAIRINGS Beef, rabbit, sausages, chicken, fish, seafood, strong cheese, cabbage, curries, *dal*.

CLASSIC RECIPES *Panch phoron*; sambhar powder.

MUSTARD VINAIGRETTE

The addition of mustard gives this dressing just the right amount of sharpness; use a good, flavorful olive oil for the best results.

MAKES ABOUT ½ CUP

2 tbsp white wine vinegar
1 tsp Dijon or coarse-grain mustard
6 tbsp extra virgin olive oil

1 Put the vinegar in a small bowl; add a pinch of salt and freshly ground black pepper, then whisk together. Now add the mustard and whisk again until combined.

2 Whisk in the olive oil. Let it rest for at least 15 minutes before use, to allow the flavors to blend. Whisk again just before using.

White or yellow mustard
(B. alba) Sandy-yellow European seeds are larger than the Asian variety used in Japan. In Western cooking, whole white seeds are used mainly as a pickling and preserving spice, and in marinades.

Black mustard *(B. nigra)*
Black seeds are larger than brown, and are oblong rather than round. When chewed, black have a forceful flavor, with the heat affecting the nose and eyes, as well as the mouth.

Brown mustard *(B. juncea)*
Brown seeds have a long-lasting pungency. They are slightly bitter, then hot and aromatic. They figure prominently in the cooking of southern India, where the seeds are known as rai.

CAPERS (CAPPARIS SPECIES)

The caper bush is a small shrub that grows wild around the Mediterranean, as far south as the Sahara and as far east as northern Iran, although it may have originated in western and central Asia. Capers are successfully cultivated in many countries with a similar climate—important producers are Cyprus, Malta, France, Italy, Spain, and California. Capers have a salty flavor with a hint of lemon. The quality depends on the place of origin, the preserving method, and size. Also available are caper berries, as well as lightly pickled leaves and shoots.

BUY Salting preserves taste and texture better than pickling. The intensely flavored, large Sicilian capers are always dry salted, as are top-quality small ones.

STORE Pickled capers keep for a long time provided they are covered by liquid, which should not be renewed or added to, least of all with vinegar.

EAT Rinse pickled or salted capers before use. When they are used in cooking, add toward the end: lengthy cooking tends to bring out an undesirable, bitter flavor. Most fish can be cooked or garnished with capers in a variety of ways. Salt cod is often accompanied by capers and green olives, a standard combination for fish dishes in Sicily and the Aeolian islands; in Spain, with fried fish, capers are combined with almonds, garlic, and parsley. They are also good in chicken or rabbit casseroles, and enhance many dishes of the fattier meats.

In Hungary and Austria, they flavor Liptauer cheese. Capers and caper berries can be eaten on their own, like olives, or as a relish with cold meats, smoked fish, and cheese.

FLAVOR PAIRINGS Fatty meats, poultry, fish, seafood, artichokes, eggplant, green beans, pickles, olives, potatoes, tomatoes.

CLASSIC RECIPES Tapenade; sauces *ravigote, rémoulade, tartare; salsa alla puttanesca;* English caper sauce.

Caper berries
The berries are the small, semi-mature fruit of the caper bush. They are usually preserved in vinegar, and their taste is similar to that of capers, but less intense.

Capers or caper buds
Caper buds are commonly pickled in vinegar or dry salted. Pickled capers (once the vinegar or salt is rinsed off) taste piquant, fresh, salty, and somewhat lemony.

CAPER BUTTER

A classic flavored butter, which is great to serve as an accompaniment to fish or barbecued meat.

MAKES ABOUT ½ CUP

8 tbsp (one stick) butter, softened

1 tbsp capers, rinsed if salted, chopped

juice of ½ lemon (optional)

1 Add the butter to a small bowl and, using a wooden spoon, beat it until creamy. Add the capers and continue beating until combined. Gradually beat in the lemon juice, if using.

2 Spoon the mixture onto a small sheet of parchment or wax paper and roll into a sausage shape, securing the edges. Refrigerate and leave to harden, then cut off slices as needed. Freeze for longer storage.

PAPRIKA (CAPSICUM ANNUUM SPECIES)

Spanish paprika or pimentón
The Denomination of Origin of pimentón de la Vera guarantees the consumer a hand-made, high-quality paprika, with its characteristic smoky aroma and taste. In Spain, paprika is used in sofrito, an onion mixture that forms the basis of many slow-cooked dishes.

Capsicums are native to the Americas and were first planted in Spain after the voyage of Columbus in 1492. It was the Spanish who first dried and ground the peppers to make *pimentón,* or paprika. Seeds later reached Turkey, and were planted there and throughout the Ottoman empire. The aroma of paprika tends to be delicate and restrained; caramel notes, fruitiness, or smokiness characterize some paprikas, while others have a nose-prickling, light heat. Hungarian cooks usually possess different grades of paprika and select the one best suited to the dish being prepared. Paprika paste and sauce are also produced in Hungary.

BUY Paprika is usually sold in sealed tins or bags. Hungarian and Balkan paprika is somewhat hotter than Spanish. Portuguese and Moroccan paprikas tend to resemble Spanish. Paprika from the US is mild. For Spanish *pimentón,* the peppers are dried over oak fires for a smoky flavor.

STORE All paprika should be kept in an airtight container and away from light, otherwise it will lose its vibrancy.

EAT Paprika should never be overheated because it becomes bitter. It is the predominant spice and coloring in Hungarian cooking. Fried gently with onion in lard, it forms the basis of traditional meat and poultry dishes, and it gives color and flavor to potato, rice, and noodle dishes, and many vegetables. Serbian cooks use paprika in similar ways. It also appears in Spanish rice and potato dishes, with fish, and in omelets, and is essential to romesco sauce. In Morocco, it is widely used in spice blends, in tagines, in *chermoula* for fish; in Turkey, it flavors soups, vegetables, and meat dishes, especially offal. In India, its principal use is as a red food colorant. Everywhere it is used to flavor sausages and other meat products.

FLAVOR PAIRINGS Beef, veal, chicken, duck, pork, white cheeses, pulses and vegetables, rice.

CLASSIC RECIPES Goulash; veal or chicken *paprikás;* duck or goose *pörkölt;* romesco sauce.

Paprika
Paprika may be sweet, bittersweet, or hot, depending on whether it is produced from mild or lightly pungent peppers, and also on the amount of ground seeds and veins included in the powder.

CHILES (CAPSICUM SPECIES)

Chiles (*C. frutescens, C. annuum,* and *C. chinense*) are the biggest spice crop in the world today: hundreds of different varieties are grown in all tropical regions and eaten daily by about a quarter of the global population. In their native region in the Americas, and throughout Asia and Africa, fresh and dried chiles, and chile products, are used extensively as a cheap means of pepping up the diet. India is the largest producer and consumer of chiles, each region using its local varieties. The most sophisticated use of chiles is found in Mexican cooking. Here, fresh and dried versions of a chile often have different names, and specific chiles are required for specific dishes; adding the wrong one can significantly affect the balance of flavors. Chiles come in many colors, shapes, and sizes: they can be as tiny as a young pea or as long as 12in (30cm). Many of them stimulate the appetite not only with pungency, but also with fruity, floral, smoky, nutty, tobacco, or licorice flavors, and they range from tingling to explosively hot. The bite of chiles is due to the presence of capsaicin in the seeds, white, fleshy parts, and skin. Capsaicin stimulates the digestive process and circulation, which induces perspiration and has a cooling effect on the body. The capsaicin content depends on the variety of chile and its degree of ripeness; removing seeds and veins will reduce the heat level. Just as the taste of green, immature chiles alters as they ripen and redden, so drying changes the flavors of chiles. Worldwide, dried chiles are used whole, as well as to produce chile flakes, chile oil, and ground chile. For chile powder, ground chile is blended with cumin, dried oregano, paprika, and garlic powder. Chile sauces and pastes are also made in most regions where chiles are grown.

🔒 **BUY** All fresh chiles should be shiny, smooth-skinned, and firm to the touch. Dried chiles vary in appearance according to the variety. A knowledgeable grocer will tell you the country of origin, the type, flavor characteristics, and heat level (rated on a scale of 1–10, with 10 being extremely hot). Good-quality ground chile smells fruity, earthy, and pungent and contains traces of natural oils that will stain the fingers slightly; a light orange color indicates the inclusion of a high proportion of seeds, which makes for a sharper taste. Thin, pungent sauces are labeled salsa picante or hot pepper sauce; some combine chiles with astringent ingredients such as limes or tamarind. Thick sauces may be mild or hot and are often sweetened; Indonesian sambals and Thai chile jam are among the hottest, the Chinese chile sauces are medium to hot.

📦 **STORE** Fresh chiles keep in the refrigerator for a week or more. Dried chiles can be stored almost indefinitely in an airtight container.

⬤ **EAT** In Mexico, large, fleshy poblanos are used as a vegetable, often stuffed; jalapeños and serranos are added to salsas, stuffings, and pickles; dried anchos and pasillas are often ground to thicken a sauce. In the North American southwest, Mexican chiles are used in Mexican-inspired dishes. West Indians tend to prefer hot chiles for marinades, relishes, and stews. In the Andean countries, chiles, called ají, are much used as a flavoring and as a condiment; a bowl of *uchu llajwa*—a fiery salsa of chiles and quillquiña (a local "cilantro")—is always on the table. Many Andean varieties have only local names; some are mild, some bitter, particularly the yellow ones, and some have rich flavors of raisin and prune. Chiles are also important in the cooking of Bahia in Brazil. Moderately hot chiles are used in Indonesian and Malaysian cooking, and more pungent varieties for Thai and Indian curries. Japanese santakas and hontakas resemble cayennes.

FLAVOR PAIRINGS Most spices, bay, cilantro, *rau ram*, coconut milk, lemon and lime.

CLASSIC RECIPES *Berbere*; chile powder; chili con carne; *harissa paste*; jerk seasoning; *kim chi; nam prik; pipián;* romesco sauce; *sambals.*

Red cherry bomb (*C. annuum*)
Cherry bomb chiles ripen green to bright red and are excellent for pickling, stuffing or roasting, and in salsas and salads.

Serrano (*C. annuum*)
This Mexican chile is mid-green, cylindrical, and crisp-textured, with a concentrated, fresh, grassy flavor and very pungent seeds and veins. It ripens to bright red and is commonly used in sauces.

Mirasol (*C. annuum*)
A popular Peruvian chile, Mirasol is also found in Mexico, where the dried form is known as guajillo. It is used green, yellow, or at its ripe, red-brown stage. Fruity and lively, Mirasol colors dishes well. It is good with meats, beans, and vegetables.

Rocoto (*C. pubescens*)
Native to the Andes, rocotos are plump and yellow to orange-red. They are used fresh in sauces, or as a vegetable, often stuffed with meat and cheese.

Cayenne (*C. annuum*)
The fruit of cayenne chile is slender and cylindrica and bright red when ripe. It is grown worldwide, and the flavor is tart, slightly smoky, and intensely pungent.

Korean *(C. annuum)*
This bright green, curved chile is related to the Thai chile. Fresh chiles are cooked in fish, meat, and vegetable stews, in stir-fries, or stuffed and fried.

Thai *(C. annuum)*
Used fresh and dried, this slender chile is bright red or green, with a lingering heat. Add whole to curries and stir-fries or chop for pastes and dips.

Jalapeño *(C. annuum)*
Jalapeños are green, some with dark patches, torpedo-shaped, and quite fat with crisp, thick flesh. Sometimes roasted and peeled, they have a light flavor and are medium—hot. Red and fully ripe they are sweeter and less hot. Also sold "en escabeche" (pickled), they are widely used as a table condiment.

Jamaican hot *(C. chinense)*
This West Indian chile is bright red and squat with thin flesh, and tastes sweet and very hot. It is used in salsas, pickles, and curries.

Scotch bonnet *(C. chinense)*
Yellow-green to orange-red, with a wrinkled top and flattened base, the Scotch bonnet chile is very hot and has a deep, fruity, smoky flavor. It is used in many Caribbean hot sauces and in jerk seasoning.

Poblanos are large, green, and triangular, with a ridge around the base of the stem.

Habanero *(C. chinense)*
Lantern-shaped, fruity, and mid-green ripening to yellow, orange, and red, habanero is mostly used in Yucatán, raw or roasted, to flavor beans and sauces. Roasted habaneros are blended with salt and lime juice to make a hot sauce.

Ají amarillo *(C. baccatum)*
Common in Peru, both fresh and dried, when it is called "cusqueno", this chile is hot with raisiny aromas. It is used with potatoes, guinea pig, ceviche, and other seafood dishes.

Poblano *(C. annuum)*
This chile is delicious roasted and peeled, then stuffed or fried. It pairs well with corn and tomatoes and has a rich flavor. The dried form is the ancho, which is the most popular dried chile in Mexico and the US.

CHILES (CONTINUED)

Guajillo (*C. annuum*)
This Mexican chile is maroon with brown tones, and long and slender, with a smooth skin. It has high acidity, which gives a tangy, pleasantly sharp taste. It is soaked and blended for enchilada sauces or crumbled in stews. It is also used to color food.

Chilaca (*C. annuum*)
The Mexican chilaca is thin, deep red, and shiny, with vertical ridges. The deep flavor has a hint of licorice. Roasted and peeled, they are used in vegetable dishes, with cheese, and in sauces, and are sometimes available pickled.

The Mexican cascabel is round and brown-red, with a smooth, translucent skin.

Choricero (*C. annuum*))
A favorite chile to use in the Spanish sausage chorizo, it lends a smoky spiciness to the cured pork sausage.

Cascabel (*C. annuum*)
This has a lightly acidic, smoky flavor, and is agreeably nutty after toasting. Moderately hot, it is toasted and blended with tomatoes or tomatillos to make a salsa, and crumbled in stews.

Chipotle (*C. annuum*)
This is the smoke-dried jalapeño. It is rust-red to coffee colored and wrinkled, and has a smoky, sweet, chocolate smell and taste. It is used whole to flavor soups and stews, and is also sold canned in a light pickle.

Guindilla (*C. annuum*)
Brick-red and smooth, this long, tapering Spanish chile is used in its dried form. Large pieces are soaked and added to a dish for extra piquancy; they should be removed before serving.

Kashmir (*C. annuum*)
This chile is grown in other parts of India as well as Kashmir, and is deep red in color, with sweet notes yet a distinct bite. In India it is known as lal mirch. It is also used to color food a distinctive, rich red.

Ancho (*C. annuum*)
This is the dried poblano chile. It is deep red-brown, wrinkled, fruity, and sweet, with rich flavors of tobacco, prune, and raisin, and slightly hot. Anchos are toasted and ground for sauces, or can be stuffed. They are also available as powder and blocks of paste.

Pasilla (*C. annuum*)
Pasilla is the dried chilaca, slender, wrinkled, and almost black. It has an astringent yet rich flavor with herbal notes that is complex and long lasting. Toasted and ground, it is used in table sauces or in cooked sauces for fish.

Pequin (*C. annuum*)
These chiles, also known as "bird peppers", are tiny and green, orange, or red, and are often used whole, to give a "finishing" flavor to a dish. They are fiercely hot and are used either fresh or dried.

Chile flakes
Produced from mild to moderately hot chiles, these are often used as a table condiment in Hungary, Turkey, and the Middle East; Korea and Japan use hotter flakes as a condiment.

Chile powder
This combination of ground chile, cumin, dried oregano, paprika, and garlic powder is used to flavor chili con carne and other southwestern US dishes.

Cayenne powder
Cayenne is the hottest of the ground chiles. It is also the most common, and is used in a variety of cuisines. The fruits are generally dried and ground, or pulped and baked into cakes, which are then ground and sifted to make the cayenne powder or pepper.

Yellow chile powder
The color of ground chiles ranges from yellow to red to mahogany. Yellow chile powder is used in South America; it can be mild or hot.

HARISSA

This fiery chile sauce is found throughout North Africa, but it is especially popular in Tunisia. It is usually made with dried chiles. Harissa is used as a cooking ingredient, and as a condiment with eggs, couscous, and tagines.

If you prefer to make harissa with fresh chiles, substitute the same quantity as dried, and omit the soaking in Step 1.

SERVES 4–6

3½oz (100g) dried chiles
2 garlic cloves, peeled
½ tsp salt
1 tsp caraway seeds, crushed
½ tsp ground cumin
olive oil

1 Break the chiles into pieces, discard the seeds and stems. Soak the flesh in almost-boiling water for about 30 minutes, until soft. Meanwhile, crush the garlic with the salt in a mortar and pestle.

2 Drain the chiles and crush them in the mortar, or in a small food processor. Add the caraway seeds and cumin, crushing to blend. Add 1–2 tbsp olive oil, or more, to lubricate the mixture as needed. Transfer the chile mixture to a small jar and cover with a layer of olive oil. Use at once, or screw on the lid and refrigerate for 3–4 weeks. Return to room temperature before using.

3 Harissa is usually thinned with more oil and lemon juice, water, or a few spoonsful of hot stock from the dish with which it is served.

CARAWAY SOUP

A really tasty twist on vegetable soup, and lovely served with crusty bread and butter. The recipe is easy and produces a thick soup, which may need to be thinned with a little water.

SERVES 4

| 2 tbsp butter |
| 1 tbsp olive oil |
| 1 onion, finely chopped |
| salt and freshly ground black pepper |
| 2 garlic cloves, finely chopped |
| 2 celery ribs, thinly diced |
| 2 carrots, cut into fine dice |
| 1–2 tsp caraway seeds, to taste |
| 3 medium russet or other floury baking potatoes, peeled and diced |
| 4 cups hot vegetable or chicken stock |
| Handful of curly parsley, finely chopped, for garnish (optional) |

1 Combine the butter and the oil in a large saucepan. Once the butter has melted, add the onion and a pinch of salt. Cook over low heat for about 5 minutes or until soft and translucent. Stir in the garlic, celery, and carrots and cook gently for about 10 minutes until the carrots begin to soften.

2 Stir in the caraway seeds to taste, then add the potatoes and stir. Season with pepper and a little more salt if needed. Pour in the hot stock and bring to a boil, then reduce the heat and simmer for 15–20 minutes until the potatoes are soft. Let cool for a few minutes.

3 Working in batches, puree the mixture in a blender or food processor until smooth; if too thick, add a little hot water. Return the soup to a clean pot and reheat over low heat; taste, and adjust the seasonings if needed. Just before serving, sprinkle with parsley.

CARAWAY (CARUM CARVI)

Caraway is cultivated in its native regions—Asia and northern and central Europe (Holland and Germany are the major producers)—as well as in Morocco, the US, and Canada. The Romans used this spice with vegetables and fish, medieval cooks used it for flavoring soups and bean or cabbage dishes. In 17th century England it was popular in bread, cakes, and baked fruit; coated with sugar the seeds made comfits. Today the essential oil flavors spirits such as *aquavit* and *kümmel*. Caraway seed has a pungent aroma that, like the flavor, is warm and bittersweet, sharply spicy, with a note of dried orange peel and a slight but lingering hint of anise. Young leaves, less pungent than the seeds, resemble dill in and appearance.

🔒 **BUY** Caraway seed can be bought ground, but is often used whole and is best bought that way: it is easy to grind or pound when needed. In the home garden, plants can be grown from seed.

🪣 **STORE** Seeds will keep for at least 6 months in an airtight jar; once ground they will lose strength quite quickly.

● **EAT** In central Europe, and especially in the Jewish cooking originating there, caraway is used to flavor brown or rye breads, biscuits, seedcakes, sausages, cabbage, soups, stews. It gives many southern German

Caraway seeds are curved with tapered ends, and are brown with light brown ridges.

and Austrian dishes their characteristic taste, be it pumpernickel bread or roast pork, coleslaw or sauerkraut, as well as flavoring French Munster cheese and *pain d'épices*. Caraway is also used in the cooking of North Africa, mostly in vegetable dishes and in spice blends, such as Tunisian *tabil* (a blend of caraway seed, coriander seed, garlic, and chili) and *harissa*. Morocco has a traditional caraway soup—as does Hungary, where caraway also figures prominently in *goulash*. Young leaves make an interesting addition to salads, soups, or fresh white cheese.

FLAVOR PAIRINGS Duck, goose, pork, breads, apples, cabbage, potatoes and other root vegetables, tomatoes.

CLASSIC RECIPES *Tabil; harissa.*

SAFFLOWER (CARTHAMUS TINCTORIUS)

The thistle-like safflower is an ancient crop, traditionally grown on small plots for local consumption, whether as medicine, dye, food colorant, or spice. Today it is grown in many parts of the world, mainly as an oilseed crop. Unscrupulous merchants sometimes pass it off to tourists as the much more expensive saffron, and indeed it is known as bastard or false saffron in some countries. Safflowers are the globe-shaped flowers of the plant, which are dried then crushed. It has little aroma, but smells herbaceous and somewhat leathery; the flavor is bitter and lightly pungent.

🔒 **BUY** Safflower is available from some spice merchants, and in countries where it is used it can be bought in markets. It may be sold as loose, dried petals or as compressed flower heads. In Turkey, where it is in common use, it may be sold as Turkish saffron.

🪣 **STORE** Keep in an airtight container. The flavor fades after 6–8 months.

● **EAT** Safflower will color rice, stews, and soups a light gold—it is often used in this way in India and in the Arab world—but it does not give the depth of color or complex flavors of saffron. Petals can be added straight to the dish or infused in warm water to obtain a coloring liquid. Portuguese cooks use safflower in seasoning pastes for fish stews and in the vinegar sauces that accompany fried fish. In Turkey it is used in cooking, but more frequently it garnishes meat and vegetable dishes.

FLAVOR PAIRINGS Fish, rice, root vegetables, chile, cilantro leaf, cumin, garlic, paprika, parsley.

When dried, safflowers are yellow to bright orange to brick-red in color.

CINNAMON
(CINNAMOMUM ZELANICUM)

True cinnamon is indigenous to Sri Lanka; by the late 18th century it had been planted in Java, India, and the Seychelles. Strips of dried cinnamon bark are rolled one into another to form long quills; the small inner pieces of bark (called featherings) along with bark shavings, not large enough to use in the rolled tubes, are mostly used to produce ground cinnamon. The spice has a warm, agreeably sweet, woody aroma that is delicate yet intense; the flavor is fragrant and warm with subtle hints of clove and citrus.

🔒 **BUY** There are many grades of cinnamon. Quills, or sticks, are classified as Continental, Mexican, or Hamburg, according to their thickness; the thin Continental quills have the finest flavor. Quills are available from spice merchants, delicatessens, and supermarkets. Ground cinnamon is widely available, but loses its flavor quite quickly so buy in small amounts.

🪣 **STORE** Cinnamon quills will keep their aroma for 2–3 years if stored in an airtight container.

● **EAT**. Cinnamon's subtle flavor is well suited to desserts and spiced breads and cakes. Use it in apple pie

CASSIA (CINNAMOMUM CASSIA)

Cassia is the dried bark of a species of laurel tree native to Assam and northern Burma. Most cassia is exported from southern China and Vietnam; the finest quality comes from northern Vietnam. As the bark dries it curls to make loose quills that are reddish-brown; it is often sold in pieces. The flavor is sweetish with a distinct pungency and an astringent edge. The dried unripe fruits, or buds, are also used as a spice. They have a warm, mellow aroma and their flavor is musky, sweet, and pungent, but less concentrated than that of the bark. Dried *tejpat* leaves (often called Indian bay leaves), from the related *C. tamala*, are used in the cooking of north India.

They have an immediate smell of spiced tea; a prolonged sniff reveals a warm, musky aroma of clove and cinnamon with citrus undertones.

🔒 **BUY** Bark, buds, and *tejpat* leaves can be bought from spice shops. Cassia and cinnamon are used interchangeably in many countries and labeling may be confused: in the US cassia is sold as cinnamon or cassia-cinnamon, and is preferred to true cinnamon because of its more pronounced aroma and flavor.

🗄 **STORE** Pieces or quills will keep for two years in an airtight container.

⬤ **EAT** Use in spice blends for baking and sweet dishes. Its pungency is suited to rich meats, such as duck or pork, and it goes well with squash, lentils, and beans. Cassia is an essential spice in China, where it is used to flavor braised dishes and meat sauces, and

Dried tejpat leaves are oval in shape with three long veins.

ground for five spice powder. In India it is found in curries and pilafs. Cassia buds are good in fruit compotes. *Tejpat* leaves are used in Indian *biryanis* and *kormas*, and in *garam masalas*.

FLAVOR PAIRINGS Meat and poultry, apples, plums, prunes, pulses, and root vegetables.

CLASSIC RECIPE Five-spice powder.

Cassia bark
The corky outer layer of bark is thicker and coarser than cinnamon, and is often left on when it is sold in pieces.

Ground cassia
Cassia's thick outer layer makes it difficult to grind so it may be better to buy small amounts of ground cassia as well as pieces and quills.

or with baked apples, with bananas fried in butter and flavored with rum, and in red wine used for poaching pears. It also makes an excellent flavoring for many meat and vegetable dishes in Middle Eastern and Indian cooking. Moroccan cooks use it widely in lamb or chicken *tagines*, in the stew to accompany *couscous*, and above all to flavor *b'stilla*, a pie of crisp, layered pastry filled with pigeon and almonds. The glorious Arab stew

of lamb with apricots, *mishmisheya*, uses cinnamon and other spices, and it plays a role in Iranian *khoresh* (stews that accompany rice). In India cinnamon is used in *masalas*, or spice mixtures, in chutneys and condiments, and in spiced pilafs. Mexico is the main importer of cinnamon, which is used to flavor coffee and chocolate drinks; cinnamon tea is popular throughout Central and South America. Once popular in Europe

for spicing ale, cinnamon, together with cloves, sugar, and sliced oranges, makes an excellent flavoring for mulled wine.

FLAVOR PAIRINGS Lamb, poultry, rice, chocolate, coffee, rice, almonds, apples, apricots, eggplants, bananas, pears, cardamom, cloves, coriander seed, cumin, ginger, nutmeg, tamarind.

CLASSIC RECIPES B'stilla; khoresh.

Ground cinnamon
The paler the color of ground cinnamon, the finer the quality. The powder is immediately aromatic, with the presence of eugenol in the essential oil giving it the note of clove.

Cinnamon quills
Dried cinnamon bark is rolled up to form long, slender smooth quills. They tend to hide their aromatic properties until broken or cooked in a liquid.

CINNAMON ROLLS

These sweetly spiced rolls are much lighter than you might imagine, and are incredibly addictive. Especially delicious served with hot chocolate!

MAKES 9

2 cups all-purpose flour, plus extra

3 tsp baking powder

salt

8 tbsp (1 stick) softened butter

1 cup whole milk

¼ cup granulated sugar

2 tsp ground cinnamon

3 tbsp confectioners' sugar, sieved

1 Preheat the oven to 400°F (200°C). Sift the flour and baking powder into a large bowl and mix in a pinch of salt. Add the 8 tbsp butter and rub it in, using your fingertips.

2 Pour in the milk and use a knife to pull the mixture together, then use floured hands to turn the dough out onto a floured work surface. Knead gently, then roll out into a rectangle about 16 x 10in (40 x 25cm).

3 Brush the dough with all of the melted butter, then sprinkle the sugar and cinnamon over the top, making sure it reaches the edges. Roll up the dough jellyroll fashion, and cut the roll crosswise into 1¼in (3cm) slices. Arrange cut-side down on a parchment-lined baking sheet, and bake for 15 minutes or until just golden and cooked through. Remove and cool on a wire rack.

4 Serve plain, or drizzle with icing. To make the icing, mix the confectioners' sugar with just enough water to be somewhat thick, but still fluid enough to fall from a spoon. Drizzle the icing over the rolls and leave to set.

CORIANDER (CORIANDRUM SATIVUM)

A few plants serve cooks as both herb and spice, and of these coriander is undoubtedly the most widely used in both its forms. As a spice crop, it is grown in Eastern Europe, India, the US, and Central America, as well as in its native habitat of western Asia and the Mediterranean. In all of these regions it is used extensively, sometimes in combination with the green herb (known in the US as cilantro, rather than coriander). Spherical Moroccan seeds are more commonly available than the oval Indian variety. Indian coriander has a sweeter flavor than Moroccan. Although coriander seeds and leaves smell and taste quite different, they complement each other in Indian and Mexican dishes.

BUY It is best to buy whole seeds and grind as needed.

STORE In an airtight container seeds can be kept for 9 months.

EAT Cooks use coriander in larger amounts than they do many other spices because its flavor is mild. In India, coriander forms the basis of many curry powders and masalas. Georgian *khmeli-suneli* and Iranian *advieh* mixtures usually include it, as do Middle Eastern *baharat* blends, and throughout the region coriander is a popular flavoring for vegetable dishes, stews, and sausages. In Europe and America

seeds serve as a pickling spice and give a pleasant, mild flavor to sweet–sour pickles and chutneys. French vegetable dishes *à la grecque* are flavored with coriander. It is a useful spice to add to marinades, to court-bouillon for fish, or to stock for soup.

FLAVOR PAIRINGS Chicken, pork and ham, fish, apples, citrus fruits, mushrooms, onions, pears, plums, potatoes, quinces, pulses.

CLASSIC RECIPES Harissa; *tabil*; *dukka*; most masalas.

Ground coriander
Ground coriander is a constituent of English sweet mixed spice for cakes and cookies. Its flavor combines well with those of fall fruits—apples, plums, pears, quinces— baked in pies or stewed in compotes.

Coriander seeds
Ripe seeds have a sweet, woody fragrance with peppery and floral notes; the taste is sweet, mellow, and warm, with a clear hint of orange peel.

Ground coriander
North African cooks use ground coriander in harissa, tabil, ras el hanout, and other spice mixtures. In Mexico, it is often paired with cumin.

CUMIN (CUMINUM CYMINUM)

Cumin is the seed of a small, herbaceous umbellifer, native to just one locality, the Nile valley of Egypt, but long cultivated in most hot regions —the eastern Mediterranean, North Africa, India, China, and the Americas. The smell of the oval seeds is strong

and heavy, spicy-sweet, with acrid but warm depth; the flavor is rich, slightly bitter, sharp, earthy, and warm, with a persistent pungency. Black cumin is an expensive variety grown in Kashmir, northern Pakistan, and Iran; it is used there and in the Gulf States.

BUY Cumin seeds are widely available, either whole or ground. Black cumin can be found in Indian shops, as can *dhana-jeera*, a blend of cumin and coriander seeds.

STORE Seeds will keep in an airtight jar for several months, but ground cumin has a very short shelf life.

EAT Use sparingly. For the best flavor, only grind seed as needed. Early Spanish

dishes combined cumin, saffron, and anise or cinnamon. Today cumin has diverse culinary uses. It is found in the merguez sausages of North Africa. It is added to pork sausages in Portugal, cheese in Holland, pickled cabbage in Germany, pretzels in Alsace, the tapas called Moorish kebabs (*pinchitos morunos*) in Spain, fish dishes in Lebanon, köfte in Turkey, and a pomegranate and walnut sauce in Syria. It is present in curry powders and masalas, and in commercial chili powders. Dry-roasted black cumin seeds go into pilafs and breads.

FLAVOR PAIRINGS Chicken, lamb, hard or pungent cheeses, eggplant, beans, bread,

cabbage, lentils, onions, potatoes, sauerkraut, squash.

CLASSIC RECIPES Iranian *advieh*; *baharat*; *berbere*; Cajun spice blend; *dukka*; *panch phoron*; *sambhar* powder; *zhug*.

Ground cumin
In all countries that like spicy food, cumin is used in breads, chutneys, relishes, savory spice mixes, and meat or vegetables stews. The combination of ground cumin and coriander gives much Indian food its characteristic pungent smell.

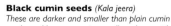

Black cumin seeds *(Kala jeera)*
These are darker and smaller than plain cumin seeds, and have a sweeter smell, and a complex, mellow flavor that lies somewhere between cumin and caraway.

Cumin seeds
The aroma of cumin is enhanced if the seeds are dry-roasted before they are ground, or fried in oil if used whole. Cumin is found in Moroccan couscous, in Tex-Mex chili con carne, and, more sparingly, in the spice mixes of Mexico itself.

KAFFIR LIME (CITRUS HYSTRIX)

Harvested from a shrubby, evergreen tree native to Southeast Asia, the leaves and rind of the kaffir lime have long imparted a clean, citrus flavor to the dishes of the region. Kaffir lime is now also grown in Florida, California, and Australia. The English name *kaffir* may originate in colonial usage or be a corruption of another word; some cooks prefer to call this spice by its Thai name, *makrut* lime. The upper side of the leaf is dark green and glossy, the underside lighter and matte. Leaves have an assertive and lingering aroma, and a citrus fragrance—not quite lemon, not quite lime.

BUY Fresh leaves and fruits are available from Asian markets and some supermarkets. Fruits should be firm and feel quite heavy for their size. You can also buy dried leaves and rind, which lack the intense aroma of the fresh fruit, as well as rind preserved in brine.

STORE Fresh leaves keep for weeks in a plastic bag in the fridge, or they can be frozen for up to a year. Store fruit in the fridge or in a cool room. In airtight containers, dried leaves and rind will keep for 6–8 months.

EAT If the leaves are to be eaten, rather than removed before serving, discard the central rib of the leaf and shred finely. To add a citrus flavor to a Western dish, use leaves in chicken casseroles, with braised or roasted fish, or in sauces to serve with chicken or fish. The thin rind is best removed from the fruit with a small-holed grater. Grated rind goes into curry pastes, larp, and fish cakes. Leaves and rind are used in fish and poultry dishes in Indonesia and Malaysia. If you buy rind in brine, wash it and scrape off the pith before use; soak shredded, dried rind briefly before using in slow-cooked dishes.

FLAVOR PAIRINGS Pork, poultry, fish, seafood, mushrooms, noodles, rice, green vegetables.

Fresh leaves
Leaves have an explosive fragrance, cleanly floral and citrus. They keep their flavor when cooked, and are responsible for the tangy, citrus taste of Thai soups, stir-fries, and curries.

Dried leaves should be green, not yellow; shred finely if they are going to be eaten.

Fresh fruit
The fruit is pear-shaped, bumpy, and lime green. What little juice it yields is sour and seldom used. The rind is slightly bitter with a strong citrus note; when grating the rind, try to avoid including the bitter pith.

CITRUS (CITRUS SPECIES)

Citrus fruits are universal providers of tartness in the kitchen. The Japanese use the peel of a small citron, called *yuzu*, which has an attractive, delicate aroma. The Chinese favour dried orange or tangerine peel; in Tunisia, bitter orange peel and fruit are used for pickling liquids.

BUY Dried yuzu peel is found in Japanese shops; Asian markets stock dried tangerine peel. Middle Eastern and Iranian shops have dried bitter orange peel, all forms of dried limes, and Moroccan preserved lemons.

STORE Stored in airtight containers, dried peel and fruits will keep indefinitely.

EAT Dried or fresh yuzu peel adds fragrance to Japanese soups, simmered dishes (*nabemono*), and aromatic yuzu-miso condiments. *Yubeshi*, a traditional sweet, is made by steaming yuzu shells filled with glutinous rice, soy sauce, and sweet syrup. Dried tangerine peel combines well with Sichuan peppercorns and star anise, along with dark soy sauce and rice wine. In the Gulf States, small, dried limes, often called *Omani* limes, are used in stews and pilafs. In Iran, dried limes are used to flavor stews, especially lamb stews.

FLAVOR PAIRINGS Poultry, lamb, rice, cardamom, cloves, allspice, pepper, ginger, cinnamon, cilantro.

CLASSIC RECIPES *Yubeshi*; Moroccan chicken tagine with lemon and olives.

Whole dried limes
These are pierced and added whole to stews; they soften in cooking and are served with the dish and squeezed to extract the juice. The Gulf States and Iran use them in fish and meat stews and pilafs.

Sliced dried peel
To dry your own tangerine or orange peel: after eating the flesh, remove all pith from the peel, put the peel on a rack, and leave to dry for 4–5 days. Tangerine peel is used in Sichuan and Hunan cooking, added to stir-fried dishes, or rich braises of pork or duck.

Preserved lemon peel
The chopped peel of salted lemons preserved in their juice is used to give a savory sharpness to Moroccan tagines; it combines particularly well with green olives in a renowned chicken dish. The salty juice is good in salad dressings.

TURMERIC (CURCUMA LONGA)

A member of the ginger family, turmeric is a robust perennial, native to southern Asia and appreciated there since antiquity as a flavoring, a dye, and a medicine. India is the main producer of turmeric, and more than 90 per cent of the crop is used domestically. Other producers include China, Haiti, Indonesia, Jamaica, Malaysia, Pakistan, Peru, Sri Lanka, and Vietnam. Fresh turmeric rhizome is crunchy; has gingery, citrus aromas; and an agreeably earthy flavor with citrus overtones. Dried turmeric has a complex, rich, woody aroma with floral, citrus, and ginger notes. The taste is slightly bitter and sour, moderately pungent, warm, and musky.

BUY Fresh turmeric is available from Asian markets. *Alleppey* and *Madras* are the best Indian grades of ground turmeric.

STORE Fresh turmeric will keep in the fridge for up to 2 weeks; it also freezes well. Dried turmeric keeps for 2 years in an airtight container.

EAT Turmeric binds and harmonizes the other spices with which it appears in many combinations. Fresh turmeric is used throughout Southeast Asia in spice pastes, and it goes into *laksas*, stews, and vegetable dishes. Juice extracted from crushed turmeric, flavors and colors rice dishes for festive meals in Indonesia and Malaysia. The fragrant leaves are used to wrap foods in Malaysia, and the shoots are eaten as a vegetable in Thailand. It occurs in North African tagines and stews, most notably in the Moroccan spice blend *ras el hanout*, and in *harira*, the national soup. In Iran, turmeric and dried limes flavor *gheimeh*, a rich stew-sauce that is spooned over rice. It is widely used in pickles and relishes of both Eastern and Western manufacture.

FLAVOR PAIRINGS Meat, poultry, fish, egg, eggplant, beans, lentils, rice, root vegetables, spinach.

CLASSIC RECIPES Masalas; curry powders and pastes; *ras el hanout*; *gheimeh*.

Fresh rhizome
Fresh turmeric should be firm and plump. The rhizomes are used sliced, chopped, or grated. Pared, sliced rhizome is used in pickles and relishes; it has a wonderful color and taste, and is also a preservative.

Dried ground turmeric
In India and the West Indies, ground turmeric combined with other spices is the basis of masalas, curry powders, and pastes. It imparts a warm flavor to vegetable and lentil dishes.

Whole dried rhizome
Dried rhizomes look like tough, yellow wood; they are almost impossible to grind at home, but can be grated. Turmeric stains fingers, utensils, and clothes, so care should be taken when using it.

ZEDOARY (CURCUMA SPECIES)

Native to subtropical, wet forest zones of Southeast Asia and Indonesia, zedoary was brought to Europe in the 6th century. During the Middle Ages, it became popular in the kitchen along with its close relation, galangal. Its culinary use has until recently been largely restricted to Southeast Asia, but recent interest in the food of this region has led to the availability of fresh zedoary elsewhere in the world. In Indonesia, it goes by the misleading name of *kencur*, which is also used for aromatic ginger (*Kaempferia galanga*). Fresh zedoary has a thin, brown skin and crisp, lemon-colored flesh. Its taste is pleasant and musky, similar to young ginger, with a hint of bitterness.

BUY Both fresh zedoary (often labeled as "white turmeric") and dried zedoary slices can be found in Asian markets. The spice is also available ground; the powder is usually colored reddish-brown artificially.

STORE Fresh zedoary will keep in the fridge for up to 2 weeks.

EAT Fresh, chopped zedoary, shallots, lemon grass, and cilantro make a good spice paste for cooking vegetables in coconut milk. In Thailand, peeled and shredded or finely sliced fresh zedoary is added to salads or raw vegetables to serve with *nam prik*; in Indonesia and India, fresh zedoary goes into pickles. The dried spice is used in the preparation of curries and condiments, and in dishes for which dried turmeric or ginger might be used. In Indonesia, young shoots are eaten, flower buds are used in salads; and the long, aromatic leaves wrap and flavor fish, as they do in Mumbai, where a fresh zedoary and vegetable soup is popular.

FLAVOR PAIRINGS Lamb, chicken, fish, chickpeas, curries, and stews, lentils, green vegetables, chiles, coconut milk, cilantro, garlic.

CLASSIC RECIPE Mumbai zedoary and vegetable soup.

Fresh rhizome (*C. zerumbet*)
Zedoary is increasingly available in fresh form. It is often combined with other fresh spices, or used as a crisp garnish. The taste is sometimes described as resembling green mango.

Crushed dried rhizome
Dried zedoary has a musky and agreeable aroma, with a hint of camphor. The flavor is pungent, resembling dried ginger, less acrid but rather bitter, and finishing on a citrus note.

SAFFRON (CROCUS SATIVUS)

Saffron consists of the dried stigmas of the saffron crocus. Native to the Mediterranean and western Asia, it was used by ancient civilizations as a dye, and to color and flavor food and wine. Spain is the main producer. It takes about 80,000 crocus flowers, the stigmas picked by hand, to produce 1lb (450g) of saffron. No wonder it is the most expensive spice in the world. The best saffron is deep red, called *coupe* for Spanish and Kashmiri saffron, *sargol* for Iranian. Some thicker, yellow threads from the style of the flower are included in the next grade: *Mancha* if Spanish or Kashmiri, *poshal*, or *kayam* if Iranian. Good-quality saffron is also produced in Greece and Italy. Lesser grades are often brownish with scruffy threads. Saffron's smell is unmistakable: rich, pungent, musky, floral, and tenacious. The taste is delicate yet penetrating, warm, earthy, musky, and lingering.

BUY Turmeric, marigold petals, and safflower are often passed off as saffron by unscrupulous merchants. None has saffron's penetrating aroma, so smell before buying.

STORE Threads will last for 2–3 years if kept airtight.

EAT Saffron gives the characteristic flavor for many Mediterranean fish soups and stews, such as Provençal *bouillabaisse* and Catalan *zarzuela*. It enhances a mussel and potato stew, or a fish baked in white wine. Saffron rice is excellent as a Valencian paella, *risotto alla Milanese*, an Iranian *polo*, a Moghul *biryani*, or a simple vegetable pilaf. In Sweden, saffron buns and cakes are made for the festival of light on St. Lucia's Day. In Britain, Cornish saffron cakes and breads were once traditional. Saffron ice cream, whether in the European style, Middle Eastern with *mastic*, or Indian *kulfi* is also worth a try.

FLAVOR PAIRINGS Chicken, game, fish, eggs, asparagus, carrots, leeks, mushrooms, squash, spinach.

CLASSIC RECIPES Risotto alla milanese; bouillabaisse; zarzuela; rouille; Swedish saffron buns.

Whole threads
For most dishes, saffron threads are infused in liquid. If an infusion is added in the early stages of cooking it will impart more color; added later it contributes aroma. Avoid overuse as the taste can become bitter and medicinal.

Ground threads
Ground saffron is easily adulterated with cheap and inferior spices. If a recipe does not call for liquid, grind the threads and stir in. If they are not quite dry, dry-roast lightly before grinding.

CLASSIC RECIPE

SAFFRON RICE

This beautifully colored rice is subtly scented with saffron. It is especially good served with chicken dishes.

SERVES 4

1 ½ cups white basmati rice or Thai jasmine rice, rinsed under cold water

½ tsp saffron threads

pinch of salt

1 Add the rice to a medium-size saucepan. In a large liquid measuring cup or other heatproof container, combine 3 cups of boiling water with the saffron, stirring to dissolve. Pour the saffron water over the rice, add a pinch of salt and stir, bring to a boil, then reduce to a simmer. Cover the pan and cook the rice over low heat for 12–15 minutes or until the liquid has been absorbed. Remove from the heat and leave the lid on the pan for 5–10 minutes to allow the rice to continue to steam.

2 When ready to serve, fluff the rice with a fork and serve immediately. Add a squeeze of lemon juice if you wish.

LEMONGRASS (CYMBOPOGON CITRATUS)

A showy, tropical grass with fibrous, sharp-edged leaves, lemongrass flourishes in temperate climates if it is overwintered indoors. The bulbous base imparts an elusive aromatic and lemon fragrance to the cooking of Southeast Asia. Previously hard to find outside that region, fresh lemongrass is now widely available, thanks to the increased appreciation of Thai, Malaysian, Vietnamese, and Indonesian food. It is cultivated in Australia, Brazil, Mexico, West Africa, and in Florida and California. The flavor of lemongrass is refreshingly tart, clean, and citrus-like with peppery notes.

BUY Fresh lemongrass can be found at farmers' markets and supermarkets. Buy firm stalks; they should not be wrinkled or dry. Freeze-dried lemongrass keeps its aroma quite well, but air-dried lemongrass loses its volatile oils; grated lemon rind gives more flavor than dried lemongrass. Lemongrass purée is available, but lacks flavor.

STORE Fresh lemongrass will keep for 2–3 weeks in the fridge if wrapped in plastic. It freezes well for up to 6 months. Freeze-dried lemongrass has a long shelf life if kept airtight.

EAT Pounded with other spices and herbs, lemongrass goes into pastes to flavor curries, stews, and stir-fried dishes. It is a key ingredient in the *Nonya* cooking of Singapore and the southern part of the Malay Peninsula. It is used in Thai larp, curries, and soups; in Vietnamese salads and spring rolls; in Indonesian *bumbus* (spice blends) for chicken and pork. Sri Lankan cooks use it in combination with coconut. If you grow the plant, the upper part of the leaves makes a pleasant, refreshing tea.

FLAVOR PAIRINGS Beef, chicken, pork, fish and seafood, noodles, most vegetables, basil, chiles, cinnamon, cloves, coconut milk, cilantro, galangal, ginger, turmeric.

CLASSIC RECIPES Thai larp; Vietnamese salads; Indonesian *bumbus*.

Whole fresh stalks
In Western cooking, lemongrass is added to stock for poaching fish or chicken. Steep a few chopped stalks in a vinaigrette for 24 hours; or use it, alone or with ginger or fennel seeds, to poach peaches or pears.

Bruised stalks
Bruising releases the lemongrass's volatile oils. If it is to be used whole in a stew or curry, remove the outer layers and bruise the stalk; take it out before serving.

Sliced lemongrass
If the lemongrass is intended to be eaten in a soup or salad, discard the top end of the stalk and slice the rest into fine rings, starting from the softer, bottom end.

CARDAMOM (ELETTARIA CARDAMOMUM)

Cardamom is the fruit of a large, perennial bush that grows wild in the rainforests of the Western Ghats (also known as the Cardamom Hills) in southern India; a closely related variety grows in Sri Lanka. Both are cultivated in their regions of origin, as well as in Tanzania, Vietnam, Papua New Guinea, and Guatemala, which has become the main exporter. Green pods from Kerala traditionally set the standards of quality and price, but Guatemalan cardamom is nearly as good. The aroma of cardamom is strong but mellow and penetrating. The taste is lemony and flowery, with a note of camphor or eucalyptus; it is pungent and smoky, with a bittersweet note, yet also clean and fresh.

BUY Cardamom is best bought as pods, which should be green and hard.

STORE Pods will keep for a year or more in an airtight jar.

EAT Cardamom enhances both sweet and savory flavors. Hulled seeds can be either lightly bruised and fried, or toasted and ground, before being added to a dish. In India and Lebanon, Syria, the Gulf States, and Ethiopia, cardamom is one of the essential components in many spice mixes. It goes into sweetmeats, pastries, puddings, and ice creams (*kulfi*), and is used to flavor tea; Arab countries use it in coffee. Scandinavia is the biggest importer in Europe; there and in Germany and Russia, cardamom is used in spiced pastries and bread.

FLAVOR PAIRINGS Apples, oranges, pears, sweet potatoes, pulses.

CLASSIC RECIPES *Baharat*; *berbere*; *dals*; masalas; Indian rice pudding (*kheer*); *zhug*.

Look for hard, plump, and green pods, with dark brown or black seeds that feel sticky.

LICORICE (GLYCYRRHIZA SPECIES)

Licorice has been cultivated in Europe for about 1,000 years; in China at least twice as long. It is still used medicinally, as well as to flavor tobacco and toothpaste, and to make sweets, but the roots are also dried to be used as a spice. The aroma of licorice is sweet, warm, and medicinal; the taste is very sweet, earthy, and anise-like, with a lingering, bitter, salty aftertaste.

BUY Dried licorice roots can be bought from spice merchants; powder is most readily available from Chinese shops. Licorice plants are easily grown from seed or root cuttings. Roots can be dug up in fall; drying them takes several months.

STORE Roots keep almost indefinitely if they are quite dry; they can be sliced or ground as needed. Powder should be kept airtight.

EAT Licorice should be used sparingly, or its bitterness may come through too strongly. Asian spiced stocks or marinades often contain licorice along with other spices. In the form of drinks such as *sambuca* and *pastis* the flavor enters a variety of dishes, both sweet and savory. In the West, licorice is a flavoring for sweets and ice cream. In Turkey, fresh roots are eaten and powder is used in baking.

FLAVOR PAIRINGS Cassia, cloves, cilantro, fennel, ginger, Sichuan pepper, star anise, ice cream.

CLASSIC RECIPES *Ras el hanout*; Chinese five spice powder.

Shaped extract
Extract of licorice is hard, black, and glossy, and is molded into sticks, discs, and other shapes. Sticks are popular in Asia for chewing. The English use the extract in multi-colored licorice candies, as well as lozenges, called Pontefract cakes.

Dried roots
Roots are dried and usually crushed to a pulp, which manufacturers boil and reduce to produce extract of licorice. The Dutch extrude this into black, salty licorice called drop, in a range of shapes.

ASAFOETIDA (FERULA SPECIES)

Asafoetida is a dried, resinous gum obtained from three species of *Ferula*, or giant fennel, a tall, fetid-smelling, perennial umbellifer native to the dry regions of Iran and Afghanistan, where it is also cultivated. It came to India via the Moghul empire and has remained a popular spice there. Asafoetida is available either as "tears," small individual pieces, or "lumps," consisting of tears processed into a uniform mass. Solid asafoetida has little smell, but crushing releases the sulphur compounds responsible for the odor. Powdered asafoetida has a strong, unpleasant smell, reminiscent of pickled garlic and as pervasive as that of truffles. The taste is bitter, musky, and acrid—nasty when sampled alone, but becoming pleasantly onion-like when the spice is briefly fried in hot oil.

🔒 **BUY** In India, asafoetida is sold in a wide range of qualities; the lighter, water-soluble *hing* is preferred to dark, oil-soluble *hingra*. In the West, it is bought in solid or powdered form.

📦 **STORE** In an airtight container (which also contains the smell), solid asafoetida keeps for several years, while the powdered form lasts for about a year.

⊙ **EAT** Asafoetida should be used sparingly. A tiny amount enhances the flavor of a dish or spice mix, such as sambhar powder. In western and southern India, asafoetida flavors pulse and vegetable dishes, soups, pickles, relishes, and sauces. Brahmin and Jain sects use it as a substitute for garlic or onions, which are forbidden in their diet. It is good in many fish dishes. In Afghanistan, it is used, with salt, to cure meat. Try rubbing a piece on a grill or griddle before cooking meat.

FLAVOR PAIRINGS Meat, fresh or salted fish, grains, pulses, most vegetables.

CLASSIC RECIPES Sambhar powder; *chat masala*.

Whole lumps and tears
Solid asafoetida, which is available as lumps or tears, is prepared for use by grinding it with an absorbent powder such as rice flour. Only a small piece is needed for an individual dish. It can be used where garlic would be appropriate.

Ground tears
Asafoetida is most widely available as a powder, mixed with a starch or gum arabic to keep it from lumping. Brown powder is coarse and strong; yellow powder (with added turmeric) is more mellow.

KOKAM (GARCINIA INDICA)

Kokam is the fruit of an evergreen tree that is related to the mangosteen. It is native to India and grows almost exclusively in the tropical rainforests along the Malabar (Malwani) coast. The small, round, sticky fruits are dried whole or split. The rind is also dried, and has a leathery appearance. Kokam has a mildly fruity, balsamic smell; a sweet-sour, tannic, astringent taste, often with a salty edge; and a lingering, sweetish aftertaste of dried fruit.

🔒 **BUY** Dried rind and kokam paste can be bought from Indian stores and spice merchants. The deeper the skin color, the better the kokam. Kokam is often labeled black mangosteen.

📦 **STORE** In an airtight jar, dried rind and paste will keep for up to a year.

⊙ **EAT** In India, kokam is used as a souring agent, milder than tamarind. Whole fruits or slices may be added to flavor a dish and removed before eating. Dried fruit or rind are usually soaked in water, and the liquid used for cooking pulses or vegetables. For *kokam saar*, the liquid is flavored with grated ginger, chopped onion, and chiles, cumin, or cilantro, and served both as an appetizer and a cooling accompaniment to fiery, coconut-based fish curries. In Kerala, kokam is known as "fish tamarind." With coconut milk, and with or without jaggery, kokam makes *sol kadhi*, a fragrant beverage.

FLAVOR PAIRINGS Fish, okra, plantain, potatoes, squash, lentils.

CLASSIC RECIPES *Kokam saar*; *sol kadhi*.

The dried fruits contain hard seeds: remove the fruits before eating a dish that is flavored with them and beware of any seeds left behind.

STAR ANISE (ILLICIUM VERUM)

Certainly the prettiest spice, star anise is native to southern China and Vietnam, where it has a long history of medicinal and culinary use. It is the fruit of a Chinese evergreen magnolia tree, which now also grows in India, Japan, and the Philippines. The aroma is fennel- and anise-like—star anise and anise both contain essential oil with anethole. Star anise also has licorice and warm notes. It has a pungent and sweet flavor with a mildly numbing effect, and an agreeable, fresh aftertaste.

CLASSIC RECIPE

STAR ANISE COOKIES

These are melt-in-the-mouth cookies, with the warm hit of licorice from the star anise lingering after each bite. Use fresh star anise, with plenty of flavor and aroma.

MAKES 18–20 COOKIES

8 star anise seeds, removed from pods and finely ground in a spice grinder or with a mortar and pestle

1 cup self-rising flour

1 tsp baking powder

¼ cup light brown sugar

4 tbsp honey

7 tbsp butter, melted and cooled slightly

1 Preheat the oven to 375°F (190°C). Put the finely ground star anise into a bowl (if there are still lumps, sieve to remove them), and add the flour, baking powder, and brown sugar; mix together. Now stir in the honey, followed by the melted butter; mix well with a wooden spoon.

2 Lightly grease a baking sheet or line with parchment paper. Scoop up a heaping teaspoon of the mixture and drop it onto the baking sheet, pressing it down gently with your hand. Make sure there is at least 2in (5cm) between each cookie, as they will spread a little during baking.

3 Bake for 10–15 minutes or until just beginning to turn golden. The cookies may still be a little soft, but they will firm up as they cool. Leave on the baking sheet to cool for 5 minutes, then transfer to a wire rack to cool completely. The cookies are delicious either by themselves or served with a glass of dessert wine.

BUY Star anise is best bought whole or in pieces.

STORE Star anise, either whole or in pieces, will last for 1 year if kept out of bright light in an airtight container.

EAT In Chinese cooking, star anise is used in soups and stocks, in marinades for steamed chicken and pork, and in "red-cooked" chicken, duck, and pork—the meat is turned a red-brown color by braising in a dark broth flavored with spices and soy sauce. Star anise also colors and flavors marbled tea eggs. It is the main ingredient in Chinese five spice powder. Vietnamese cooks also use it in simmered dishes, in stocks, and in *pho* (beef and noodle soup). The flavor of star anise can be detected in some of the cooking of Kerala in southern India; in some dishes of northern India it may be used as a cheaper substitute for anise. Western cooks use star anise to flavor fish and seafood, in syrups for poaching figs and pears, and to spice tropical fruits. It is also used in Western cooking to flavor drinks such as pastis and anisette, and in chewing gum and confectionery. In addition to flavoring fish and seafood and some fruit dishes, it enhances the sweetness of leeks, pumpkin, and root vegetables.

FLAVOR PAIRINGS Chicken (in stock for poaching), oxtail, pork, fish and seafood (in broth for court-bouillon), figs, tropical fruits, leeks, pumpkin, root vegetables, cassia, chile, cinnamon, coriander seed, fennel seed, garlic, ginger, lemongrass, lime peel, Sichuan pepper, soy sauce, dried tangerine peel.

CLASSIC RECIPES Chinese five spice powder; Vietnamese *pho*.

Whole pods
Used whole, star anise, shaped like irregular, eight-pointed stars, make a decorative addition to a dish.

Broken pods
The dried pods are easily broken into pieces when only a little is needed. Star anise is potent, so use it sparingly. Old European recipes indicate that the spice was used to flavor syrups, cordials, and preserves.

Ground pods
For the best flavor, the pods and seeds should be ground in a mortar or electric grinder and used immediately. Alternatively, buy ground spice in small quantities.

JUNIPER (JUNIPERUS COMMUNIS)

Juniper is a prickly, evergreen shrub or small tree that grows in the northern hemisphere, especially on chalky, hilly sites. It is a member of the cypress family, the only one with edible fruit. The aroma of the small, purple-black, smooth berries is pleasantly woody, bittersweet, and like gin—juniper's use as a flavoring for gin and other spirits dates back to at least the 17th century. The taste is clean and refreshing, sweetish with a slight burning effect, and a hint of pine and resin.

BUY Berries are always sold whole and usually dried. Juniper berries growing in southerly latitudes have more flavor; if you come across them in the wild, on vacation in Tuscany perhaps, it is well worth picking them.

STORE Dried berries will keep for several months in an airtight jar.

EAT Easily crushed in a mortar, the berries impart a mild, but pungent, persistent flavor that can benefit many dishes, both savory and sweet. Crush or grind just before use to keep their flavor. Juniper is a natural foil for game and for fatty foods. Use in brines and marinades, in stuffings and pâtés, and in sauces for meats. Scandinavians add juniper to marinades for pickled beef and elk, and to red-wine marinades for roast pork. In northern France, juniper appears in venison dishes and pâtés; in Belgium with veal kidneys flamed in gin; in Alsace and Germany with sauerkraut. Famed British culinary writer Elizabeth David's spiced beef recipe includes juniper in the dry salting mixture.

FLAVOR PAIRINGS Beef, pork, game, goose, lamb, venison, apples, celery, caraway, garlic, marjoram, pepper, rosemary, savory, thyme.

CLASSIC RECIPES Sauerkraut; spiced beef.

Fresh berries are soft and bruise easily, so it is better to buy whole, dried berries.

AMCHOOR (MANGIFERA INDICA)

Native to India and Southeast Asia, the big, evergreen mango tree is now widely cultivated for its fruit. Every part of the tree is utilized in some way —bark, resin, leaves, flowers, seeds. The fruits are eaten fresh: both green (unripe) and ripe mangoes are made into chutneys and pickles; in India, thin slices of green mango are also sun-dried. *Amchoor* is made from unripe fruit and is produced in India. It has a pleasant, sweet-sour aroma of dried fruit and a tart, but also a sweetish, fruity flavor.

BUY Amchoor is available from Indian and some Asian markets, usually as a powder. It may be labeled "mango powder." It is also sold as dried slices.

STORE Slices can be stored for 3–4 months; the ground spice will keep for up to a year in an airtight jar.

EAT Amchoor is used in north Indian vegetarian cooking to give a tang of tropical fruit to vegetable stews and soups, potato *pakoras*, and *samosas*. It is good with stir-fried vegetables, in stuffings for breads and pastries, and in marinades used to tenderize poultry, meat, and fish. It is also an important ingredient in the preparation of meats to be grilled in the tandoor. Amchoor is essential to *chat masala*, a fresh-tasting, astringent spice blend from the Punjab, used for vegetable and pulse dishes, and for fruit salads. It is also much used as a sourish flavoring in *dals* and chutneys. In the West Indies, the chutneys have been adapted to incorporate local ingredients.
FLAVOR PAIRINGS Eggplant, cauliflower, okra, pulses, potatoes.
CLASSIC RECIPE *Chat masala*.

Amchoor powder
The lumpy amchoor powder is easily crushed and provides acidity in a dish without adding moisture: 1 tbsp has the acidity of 3 tbsp of lemon juice.

The finely ground powder has a slightly fibrous texture, and should be sandy-beige.

Sliced dried fruit
Dried slices are normally light brown and look like rough-textured wood. They are often used for pickles: if added to curries, they should be removed before serving.

CHAT MASALA

The amchoor adds a tart and slightly sour flavor to this masala spice mix; use it in small quantities sprinkled over fruit and vegetable salads.

1 tbsp coriander seeds
2 tsp cumin seeds
2 tsp fennel seeds
5 cardamom pods, seeds only
5 small dried red chile peppers, each cut into pieces, stems and seeds discarded
1 tbsp amchoor (mango powder, available at Indian markets or specialty spice shops)
1 tbsp garam masala
1 tsp ground ginger
1 tsp asafoetida powder (available at Indian markets or specialty spice shops)

1 In a small dry frying pan, warm the coriander, cumin, fennel, and cardamom seeds over low heat, stirring, until fragrant. Put them in a spice grinder or pound in a mortar and pestle.

2 Place the chiles in the dry skillet and heat them for about 2 minutes, stirring, being careful not to burn them. Leave to cool slightly, so they crisp up a bit, then add to the spice grinder and pulse once or twice.

3 Now add the armchoor, garam masala, ginger, and asafoetida to the grinder. Grind or pound into a well blended powder. Store in an airtight container for up to 2 months.

CURRY LEAVES (MURRAYA KOENIGII)

Curry leaves come from a small, deciduous tree that grows wild in the foothills of the Himalayas, and in India, northern Thailand, and Sri Lanka. The tree is cultivated in southern India and northern Australia. When bruised, fresh leaves are intensely aromatic, giving off a musky, spicy odor with a citrus note. The taste is warm and pleasant, lemony and faintly bitter. Fresh leaves impart a delicate, spicy flavor to curries without the heat often also associated with those dishes.

BUY Fresh curry leaves can be bought in Indian and other Asian stores, where they may be labeled *meetha neem* or *kari* (or *kadhi) patta*.

STORE Store fresh leaves in an airtight plastic bag in the freezer; they will keep for a week in the fridge.

EAT Leaves can be used in cooking and either eaten or removed before serving. They are used in long-simmered meat stews, and in the fish curries of Kerala and Chennai (Madras); Sri Lankan curry mixtures also include them. Quickly shallow-fried with mustard seeds, *asafoetida*, or onion, curry leaves may be used as a flavoring at the start of cooking; or at the end, as in the basic *bagaar* or *tadka* that goes over most lentil dishes.
FLAVOR PAIRINGS Lamb, fish and seafood, lentils, rice, most vegetables, cardamom, chiles, coconut, cilantro, cumin, fenugreek seed, garlic.
CLASSIC RECIPES Coconut *chatni*; *chat masala*.

Fresh leaves
These are used extensively in South Indian cooking and in Gujarat vegetarian dishes, much as cilantro is in the north, and in chutneys (notably coconut chatni), relishes, and marinades for seafood.

Strip fresh curry leaves from the stalk just before they are added to a dish.

POPPY (PAPAVER SOMNIFERUM)

The opium poppy—*Papaver somniferum* means "sleep-inducing poppy"—is a plant of great antiquity, native from the eastern Mediterranean to central Asia. It has been cultivated since earliest times for opium, a narcotic latex that oozes from the unripe seed pods if they are cut, and for its ripe seeds. Neither the seeds nor the dried pods from which they are harvested have narcotic properties. Poppy seeds may be slate blue, mid-brown, or creamy-white. The mid-brown are common in Turkey and the Middle East; the blue-gray seeds are most used in Europe, and the creamy-white seeds in India. The aroma of dark seeds is lightly nutty and sweet; the flavor is strong and somewhat almondlike.

White seeds are lighter and more mellow in flavor. The aroma and flavor of seeds are enhanced by dry-roasting or baking.

BUY Blue poppy seeds are available from supermarkets; the white can be bought from spice merchants or Indian markets, and the brown in Middle Eastern stores. The seeds tend to go rancid quickly because of their high oil content, so buy in small amounts and use quickly.

STORE Store in an airtight container, or in the freezer if you intend to keep them longer than a few months.

EAT Sprinkle over or incorporate into breads, bagels, pretzels, and cakes. Use, with or without other spices, in dressings for noodles or to garnish vegetables. Grind to a paste with honey or sugar, to fill strudels and other pastries. In Turkey, roasted, ground seeds are made into halva or desserts with syrup and nuts. They are used extensively in Bengali cooking in *shuktas* (bitter vegetable stews) and to coat crusty, dry-textured vegetables.

FLAVOR PAIRINGS Eggplants, green beans, breads and pastries, cauliflower, zucchini, potatoes.

CLASSIC RECIPES *Suktas*; poppy-seed cake.

Dark seeds
The flavor of dark poppy seeds is stronger than that of white. The blue-gray seeds are commonly used in Europe, added to breads and cakes. They do not grind easily, but dry-roasting followed by processing in a coffee grinder can help to break them down.

White seeds
White poppy seeds are commonly used in India, where they are roasted and ground, then combined with spices to flavor and thicken kormas, curries, and gravies.

NIGELLA (NIGELLA SATIVA)

Nigella is the botanical name of love-in-a-mist, the pretty garden plant with pale blue flowers and feathery foliage. The species grown for its seed is a close but less decorative relative, native to western Asia and southern Europe, where it grows wild and in cultivation. India is the largest producer of nigella and a large consumer. The small, matte-black seeds are often misnamed and sold as black onion seed. Nigella does not have a strong aroma; when rubbed it is herbaceous, somewhat like a mild oregano. The taste is nutty, earthy, peppery, rather bitter, dry, and quite penetrating; the texture is crunchy.

BUY Nigella is stocked by spice merchants and by Indian and Middle Eastern supermarkets. Buy whole seeds because they keep better; ground seeds may be adulterated.

STORE In an airtight container they will keep their flavor for 2 years.

EAT Sprinkle nigella on flatbreads, rolls, and savory pastries, alone or with sesame or cumin. It is good with roast potatoes and other root vegetables. Indian cooks usually dry-roast or fry the seeds to develop their flavor before sprinkling them over vegetarian dishes and salads. In Bengal, it is combined with mustard seeds, cumin, fennel, and fenugreek in the local spice mixture, *panch phoron*, which gives a distinctive taste to pulses and vegetable dishes. Elsewhere in India, nigella is used in pilafs, kormas, and curries, and in pickles. In Iran, it is a popular pickling spice used for fruit and vegetables. Ground with coriander and cumin it adds depth to a Middle Eastern potato or mixed vegetable omelet.

FLAVOR PAIRINGS Breads, pulses, rice, green and root vegetables, allspice, cardamom, cinnamon.

CLASSIC RECIPE *Panch phoron.*

Seeds are black and teardrop-shaped; it is better to buy the seeds and grind as needed.

NUTMEG (MYRISTICA FRAGRANS)

This spreading, evergreen tree, native to the Banda islands of Indonesia, often called the Spice Islands, produces fruit that yields two distinct spices, nutmeg and mace. Grenada now grows almost a third of the world's crop. To produce nutmeg, the fruit of the tree is split open to reveal the hard-shelled seed. The lacy aril that clings to the shell is mace; the kernel within the shell is nutmeg. Both spices have a similar rich, fresh, and warm aroma; nutmeg smells sweet but is more camphorous and pinelike than mace. The taste of both is warm and highly aromatic, but nutmeg has hints of clove and a deeper, bittersweet, woody flavor.

🔒 **BUY** Nutmeg is best bought whole.

📦 **STORE** In an airtight container it keeps almost indefinitely and is easily ground or grated as required. Once ground, nutmeg tends to lose its flavor rather quickly.

⬤ **EAT** You can use nutmeg in both sweet and savory dishes. It goes well in stews and in most egg and cheese dishes. The Dutch add nutmeg lavishly to white cabbage, cauliflower, vegetable purées, meat stews, and fruit puddings; the Italians add rather more subtle quantities to mixed vegetable dishes, spinach, veal, and fillings or sauces for pasta. In France, it is used with pepper and cloves in slow-cooked stews and ragoûts. In India it is added, sparingly, to Moghul dishes. Together with mace, the Arabs have long used it in delicately flavored mutton and lamb dishes; in North Africa, both are found in traditional spice mixtures. Half-ripe nutmeg, pricked all over (as is done with green walnuts) and soaked before being boiled twice in syrup, was once a popular sweetmeat from Malaysia.

FLAVOR PAIRINGS Chicken, veal, lamb, fish and seafood chowders, cheese and cheese dishes, egg dishes, milk dishes, cabbage, carrots, onion, potato, pumpkin pie, spinach, sweet potato, cardamom, cinnamon, cloves, coriander, cumin, rose, geranium, ginger, mace, pepper, rosebuds.

CLASSIC RECIPES Quatre épices; ras el hanout; Tunisian five spices.

Nutmeg kernels
Nutmeg kernels are best whole and only grated when needed. Banda and Penang nutmeg and mace are considered superior to the West Indian ones.

Nutmeg seeds
Nutmeg seeds may be bought intact, with the kernel—the nutmeg—still inside its hard shell. This shell is stripped from the kernel and discarded.

Grated nutmeg
Grated nutmeg is widely used in Europe, in both sweet and savory dishes. It adds flavor to honey cakes, rich fruit cakes, fruit desserts, and fruit punch.

MACE (MYRISTICA FRAGRANS)

This spice from the apricotlike fruit of *Myristica fragrans* is the thin, lacy covering or aril clinging to the hard seed shell, the kernel of which is the spice nutmeg. After the aril is removed from the seed it is pressed flat and dried, then stored in the dark. The resulting mace pieces are called "blades." Mace has the rich and warm aroma of nutmeg, but the smell is stronger and shows a lively, floral character with notes of pepper and clove. The taste of mace is warm, aromatic, delicate, and subtle with some lemony sweetness, yet it finishes with a potent bitterness.

🔒 **BUY** Ground mace is more commonly available than blades, but the latter are worth seeking out.

📦 **STORE** Mace blades keep almost indefinitely in an airtight container and can be ground in a coffee grinder. Ground mace keeps its flavor better than many other ground spices.

⬤ **EAT** Mace and nutmeg can be used interchangeably; however, mace gives a lighter flavoring and will preserve the delicate color of a dish. Mace gives a lift to béchamel and onion sauces, clear soups, shellfish stock, potted meat, cheese soufflés, chocolate drinks, and cream cheese desserts.

FLAVOR PAIRINGS Chicken, veal, lamb, pâtés and terrines, fish and seafood chowders, cheese and cheese dishes, egg dishes, milk dishes, cabbage, carrots, onion, potato, pumpkin pie, spinach, sweet potato, cardamom, cinnamon, cloves, coriander, cumin, rose geranium, ginger, nutmeg, paprika, pepper, rosebuds, thyme.

CLASSIC RECIPE Pickling spice.

Mace blades
Whole "blades," or pieces, of mace can be used to flavor soups or stews, but should be removed before serving. Nutmeg and mace have a similar taste and aroma; nutmeg is more widely used since it is cheaper.

The orange-yellow blades are brittle, yet exude oil when pressed with the fingertips.

Ground mace
Ground mace keeps its flavor reasonably well. The mild masala blend, aromatic garam masala, which is dominated by cardamom, is made with cardamom, mace, cinnamon, black peppercorns, and cloves.

ANISE (PIMPINELLA ANISUM)

This delicate plant, native to the Middle East and eastern Mediterranean, is now widely established throughout Europe, Asia, and North America. Called anise or aniseed, it is cultivated for its seeds, but young leaves are also used as an herb. The small, oval seeds vary in color from pale brown to green-gray, with lighter-colored ridges. The aroma and taste are sweet, licorice-like, warm, and fruity; Indian anise can have a hint of bitterness. The leaves have the same fragrant, sweet, licorice notes, with mild peppery undertones. The essential oil distilled from anise flavors aperitifs and liqueurs such as *ouzo*, *pastis*, and *anisette*.

🔒 **BUY** Anise seeds are best bought whole, and ground just before use. Alternatively, plants are available from some herb nurseries.

▣ **STORE** In an airtight container seeds will retain their flavor for at least 2 years. To dry anise you have grown yourself, put the seedheads in paper bags and hang in a well-ventilated place.

● **EAT** In Europe, anise is mostly used to flavor cakes, such as Catalan dried fig and almond cakes, and an Italian fig and dried fruit "salami"; also breads, particularly rye bread; biscuits; and sweet fruit dishes. It is added to Scandinavian pork stews and root vegetable dishes. The Portuguese add a handful of anise to the water when boiling chestnuts to impart a delicate fragrance. Around the Mediterranean, anise often flavors fish stews. In the Middle East and India, anise is mostly used in breads and savory foods; in Morocco, *krachel*, or sweet rolls, are made with anise and fennel. In Iran, a spice blend for pickling vegetables includes anise. The spice is also valued for its digestive properties: along with betel leaves, nuts, and other spices, it is offered in the traditional *paan* at the end of a meal. Fresh anise leaves can be added to salads; they also make a good garnish for carrots, beets, parsnips, and fish soups.

FLAVOR PAIRINGS Pork, fish and shellfish, apples, chestnuts, figs, pumpkins, root vegetables, *ajowan*, allspice, cardamom, cinnamon, cloves, cumin, fennel, garlic, nigella, nutmeg, pepper, star anise, nuts.

CLASSIC RECIPES Moroccan *krachel*; Lebanese fritters and spiced custards; Iranian pickling spice blend.

Whole seeds
The seeds are more subtly flavored than fennel or star anise. Indian cooks dry-roast the seeds to enhance the aroma before using them in vegetable or fish curries, or they can be quickly fried in hot oil as a garnish for lentils.

Check that there is no more than a minimum of stalks and husks when buying seeds.

Ground seeds
The aroma of ground anise dissipates quickly, so grind seeds as needed. In Morocco and Tunisia, anise flavors bread; in Lebanon, it goes into fritters and spiced custard.

CUBEB (PIPER CUBEBA)

Cubebs, also known as Java pepper and tailed pepper, are the fruit of a tropical vine of the pepper family native to Java and other Indonesian islands. They were cultivated in Java from the 16th century, and for 200 years were a popular substitute for black pepper in Europe. Now scarcely known in the West, there is a revival of interest in them among spice aficionados. Slightly larger than peppercorns, cubebs have a warm, pleasant aroma, lightly peppery but also allspice-like, with a whiff of eucalypt and turpentine. When raw, the flavor is strongly pine-like, pungent, and glowing with a lingering, bitter note, but cooking brings out the allspice flavor.

🔒 **BUY** Cubebs are not easy to find, except from some spice merchants. Buy sparingly; although they keep their aromatic properties well, they are only used in small amounts.

▣ **STORE** If kept airtight, seeds will stay fresh for 2 years.

● **EAT** Cubebs are used in Indonesian cuisine, in meat and vegetable dishes, and to a lesser extent in Sri Lanka. They were traded from the 7th century by Arab merchants, and their role in Arab cooking persists in the Moroccan spice mixture *ras el hanout*.

FLAVOR PAIRINGS Lamb, cardamom, cinnamon, sage.

CLASSIC RECIPES *Ras el hanout*; North African lamb and mutton tagines.

Cubebs are furrowed and wrinkled, and have a short tail. Buy whole and grind as needed.

PEPPER (PIPER NIGRUM)

The history of the spice trade is essentially about the quest for pepper, and it remains, in volume and value, the world's most important spice; India, Indonesia, Brazil, Malaysia, and Vietnam are the main producers. Pepper has different characteristics in different places of origin, and is therefore classified according to where it is grown. Black pepper of the best quality is Indian *Malabar*; *Tellicherry* is the grade with the largest berries. The best white pepper is considered to be *Muntok* from Indonesia. Black pepper has a fine, fruity, pungent fragrance with warm, woody, and lemony notes. The taste is hot and biting with a clean, penetrating aftertaste. White pepper is less aromatic, and can smell musty, but it has a sharp pungency with a sweetish afternote. Red or pink peppercorns, which are fully ripe fruits, have a delicate, almost sweet, fruity taste; the inner core provides a moderate, lingering heat. Both red and green are available packed in brine or vinegar. Green (unripe) peppercorns are not overpoweringly hot, with a light taste. The long pepper species originated in India and Indonesia. The spikes of minute fruits are harvested and sun-dried.

🔒 **BUY** Black and white pepper rapidly lose their aroma when ground, so it is best to buy whole berries and grind in a pepper mill or crush in a mortar, as needed. Sun-drying is preferable for pepper than being dried at high temperatures in artificial heat, when some of the volatile oils are lost.

▣ **STORE** In airtight containers, peppercorns will keep for up to a year. Keep fresh green and red pepper berries in the fridge.

● **EAT** Pepper is neither sweet nor savory, merely pungent. Although mostly used in savory foods, it can be used with fruits and in some sweet breads and cakes. It brings out the flavor of other spices and retains its own flavor well during cooking. The aroma of black pepper can be detected in foods all around the world, flavoring cooking liquids, stocks, salad dressings, sauces, spice mixtures, and marinades. Ground black pepper flavors rich stews and curries, and is used to season simple buttered vegetables and smoked fish. Rinse brined peppercorns before using.

Red peppercorns
Red or pink peppercorns are fully ripe fruits, usually available preserved in brine or vinegar. The inner core provides a moderate, lingering heat. The outer skin is removed, and they are dried to produce white peppercorns.

ALLSPICE (PIMENTA DIOICA)

Allspice is native to the West Indies and tropical Central America. Columbus found it growing in the Caribbean islands and thought he had found the pepper he was looking for, hence allspice's Spanish name *pimienta* (pepper), which was anglicized as pimento. The name was later altered to Jamaica pepper because most of the crop, and certainly the best quality, comes from that island. Allspice has a pleasantly warm, fragrant aroma. The name reflects the pungent taste, which resembles a peppery compound of cloves, cinnamon, and nutmeg, or mace. Most of the flavor is in the shell rather than the seeds.

BUY Buy whole berries in preference to ground, as ground allspice loses its flavor quickly. It can be bought whole or ground.

STORE Berries crush easily, and if kept airtight will last almost indefinitely.

EAT Long before the discovery of the Americas, the people of the islands used allspice to preserve meat and fish. The Spaniards learned from them and used allspice in *escabeches* and other preserving liquids. In the Middle East, allspice is used to season roasted meats. It is used in pilafs and in some Indian curries. In Europe, allspice is used whole as a pickling or mulling spice. Most of the world's crop goes to the food industry for use in commercial ketchups and other sauces, as well as sausages, meat pies, Scandinavian pickled herrings, and sauerkraut.

FLAVOR PAIRINGS Eggplant, most fruit, squash, root vegetables.

CLASSIC RECIPES *Escabeches*; pilafs; Indian curries.

Whole dried berries
In Jamaica, allspice is still an important ingredient in jerk seasoning pastes that are rubbed on chicken, meat, or fish for barbecuing. It is also used extensively, crushed rather than ground, in breakfast breads, soups, stews, and curries.

Ground berries
In Europe, ground allspice is used to give a gentle, warm flavor to cakes, puddings, jams, and fruit pies. It also enhances the flavor of pineapple, plums, blackcurrants, and apples.

CLASSIC RECIPE

PEPPERCORN SAUCE

This rich, creamy sauce is delicious as an accompaniment to pan-fried filet mignon or sirloin steak. Use whole black or green peppercorns, or a combination of the two.

SERVES 2

2 tbsp butter

1–1 ½ tsp black or green peppercorns to taste, coarsely crushed in a pestle and mortar, leaving some peppercorns whole

1 tbsp brandy

½ cup heavy whipping cream

salt

1 Add the butter to the frying pan in which you have just cooked the steak; if not cooking steak, use a small frying pan. When the butter has melted and is just beginning to bubble, add the peppercorns and cook for 1 minute, then add the brandy and cook for 1–2 minutes until the alcohol evaporates.

2 Stir in the cream and simmer for 2–4 minutes over low heat to blend flavors and thicken slightly. Taste and season with salt, if needed. Spoon the sauce over the steak to serve.

Rub butter mixed with crushed green pepper and ginger under chicken skin before baking; green pepper is also excellent for steak au poivre. Red pepper can be used in similar ways. In France, *mignonette* pepper, a mix of black pepper, for aroma, and white, for strength, is popular.

FLAVOR PAIRINGS Meat, fish and seafood, most vegetables, basil, cardamom, cinnamon, cloves, coconut milk, cilantro, cumin, garlic, ginger, lemon, lime, nutmeg, parsley, rosemary, thyme.

CLASSIC RECIPES Baharat; berbere; garam masala; ras el hanout; quatre épices; steak au poivre.

Long peppers resemble gray-black catkins in appearance, and are generally used whole.

Long black pepper
(P. longum and P. retrofactum)
Long pepper is mostly used in Asia, East Africa, and North Africa in slow-cooked dishes and pickles. It smells sweetly fragrant, and initially resembles black pepper in taste, but has a biting, numbing aftertaste.

Crushed black pepper
Peppercorns can be crushed in a mortar, and pressed into steaks or fish to be grilled or baked. They are also added to spice mixtures and marinades in Latin America and southern Asia.

Green peppercorns
These have a light aroma and an agreeable, fresh pungency. They combine beautifully with sweeter spices, such as cinnamon, ginger, bay, fennel seed, and lemon grass, to flavor pork, chicken, and seafood. Green berries are fermented and dried to produce black peppercorns.

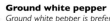

Ground white pepper
Ground white pepper is preferable to black in pale sauces and cream soups, to preserve their appearance. White pepper contains less essential oil than black because the oil, present in the hull, is removed in cleaning; that also explains why white has less aroma.

SUMAC (RHUS CORIARIA)

Sumac is the fruit of a decorative, bushy shrub that grows wild around the Mediterranean, especially in Sicily, where it is also widely cultivated. It is found also in parts of the Middle East, notably in Turkey (Anatolia) and in its native Iran. The berries are picked just before they are fully ripe, dried in the sun, and crushed to a brick-red or red-brown powder. Sumac is only slightly aromatic; the taste is pleasantly tart, fruity, and astringent.

BUY Outside the growing regions, sumac is normally only available as coarse or fine powder.

STORE In an airtight container, ground sumac keeps for several months. Whole berries can be kept for a year.

● EAT Sumac has little taste of its own, but brings out the flavors of the food to which it is added, much as salt does. Rub ground sumac on to food before cooking: the Syrians and Lebanese use it on fish, the Iraqis and Turks on vegetables, the Iranians and Georgians on kebabs. In Turkish and Iranian kebab houses, a small bowl of ground sumac is usually on the table alongside a bowl of chile flakes. Sumac is also used in chicken or vegetable casseroles, in stews, and in stuffings for chicken. With sliced raw onion it is used as an appetizer.

Mix ground sumac into yogurt with fresh herbs to make a dipping sauce or side dish.

FLAVOR PAIRINGS Chicken, lamb, fish and seafood, eggplants, chickpeas, lentils, onion, pine nuts yogurt.

CLASSIC RECIPES Fattoush; za'atar.

Ground berries
Ground sumac is often sprinkled on flatbreads; it provides the tart element in the Lebanese bread salad, fattoush, and is an essential part of the spice and herb blend za'atar.

Whole berries
If the berries are used whole they should be soaked in water for 20–30 minutes, then squeezed out well to extract all the juice. The latter is used for marinades and salad dressings, in meat and vegetable dishes, and to make a refreshing drink.

MAHLAB (PRUNUS MAHALEB)

This agreeable spice, little known outside the Middle East, comes from a sour cherry tree that grows wild throughout the region and in southern Europe. The tree bears small, thin-fleshed, black cherries; the soft, beige kernels from the cherry stones are dried to yield the spice. Mahlab is sweetly perfumed and floral with hints of almond and cherry. It has a mouthwatering flavor that is nutty with a soft, almond sweetness, but then finishes with a bitter aftertaste.

BUY Mahlab is best bought whole and ground as needed: once ground, it loses its flavor quite quickly. Spice merchants and Middle Eastern or Greek markets are the best sources.

STORE Store whole mahlab in an airtight container, where it will keep for a few months.

● EAT In Greece, Cyprus, Turkey, and the neighboring Arab countries, from Syria to Saudi Arabia, ground mahlab is primarily used in baking, especially in breads and pastries for festive occasions. A pungent note of mahlab spices the braided Greek Easter bread, tsoureki; Armenian sweet rolls called *chorek*; Arab *ma'amool*, little pastries stuffed with

nuts or dates baked by Lebanese Christians for their Easter celebrations; and Turkish *kandil* rings, made for the five religious feast nights each year when the mosques are illuminated. It is also used as a flavoring for sweetmeats.

FLAVOR PAIRINGS Almonds, apricots, dates, pistachio nuts, rose water, walnuts, anise, cinnamon, cloves, mastic, nigella, nutmeg, poppy seed, sesame.

CLASSIC RECIPES Tsoureki; chorek; ma'amool; kandil rings.

Ground mahlab should be pale cream in color: if it is dark or turning yellow, it is too old.

Ground kernels
Try adding a little ground mahlab to spiced or fruit breads or pastry.

Whole kernels
Beige mahlab kernels are creamy white inside, with a soft and chewy texture. Mahlab is best ground in a coffee grinder. If that proves difficult, add a little salt or sugar, according to the recipe, to help break down the mahlab.

MASTIC (PRUNUS MAHALEB)

Mastic is a resin yielded by an evergreen tree native to the Greek island of Chios; most of the crop is exported to Turkey and the Arab states. The tree has many veins, rich in mastic, just beneath the bark. When the gnarled trunks are cut, the sticky resin oozes out; in contact with the air the resin hardens into oval or oblong "tears" that are semitransparent, with a light, golden color. The dried tears have a brittle texture, but when chewed they take on the consistency of chewing gum. Mastic has a light, pine aroma; the taste is pleasantly mineral-like, lightly bitter, and mouth-cleansing.

BUY Mastic is expensive, but you need only a small amount at a time. It is available from Greek and Middle Eastern stores and spice merchants.

STORE Keep in a cool place.

EAT Mastic is powdered so that it blends evenly into a dish. The main use is in baking, desserts, and sweetmeats. Greeks use mastic to flavor festive breads, especially the Easter bread *tsoureki*, and Cypriots in their Easter cheese pastries, *flaounes*. With sugar and rose or orange flower water, mastic is used to flavor milk puddings, dried fruit and nut fillings for pastries, Turkish delight, and preserves. Mastic soup, mastic stew, and a mastic sweetmeat are made in Izmir.

FLAVOR PAIRINGS Fresh cheese, almonds, apricots, dates, pistachio nuts, walnuts, allspice, cardamom.

CLASSIC RECIPES *Tsoureki; flaounes.*

The mastic resin hardens into "tears," which are powdered before use in cooking.

PINK PEPPER (SCHINUS TEREBINTHIFOLIUS)

Pink pepper is the fruit of the Brazilian pepper tree, native not just to Brazil but Argentina and Paraguay as well. The tree has been introduced in many places as an ornamental or shade tree and now grows in almost every temperate zone in the world; Réunion is the only place where pink pepper is commercially cultivated. The aroma of the crushed berries is pleasantly fruity, with a clear note of pine. The taste is fruity, resinous, and sweetly aromatic, similar to juniper but not as strong. Pink pepper has none of the heat of true black pepper.

BUY Dried pink pepper is sold by spice merchants and supermarkets—freeze-dried berries have the best color and flavor. It is also available pickled in brine or vinegar, bottled or canned.

STORE Keep pink peppercorns whole in an airtight container and crush or grind them as needed.

EAT Pickling softens the berries and they can be crushed easily. Dried berries have a brittle, papery outer shell enclosing a hard seed. Use in small amounts—not, for example, in the quantity needed to prepare a pepper steak. Pink pepper is mostly recommended for fish or poultry, but goes well with game and other rich foods in the same way as juniper. Pink pepper makes quite delicate sauces to accompany such varied ingredients as lobster, veal escalopes, and pork.

FLAVOR PAIRINGS Poultry, veal, game, pork, rich and fatty meats, fish and shellfish, chervil, fennel, galangal, kaffir lime leaves, lemongrass, mint.

CLASSIC RECIPE Pink peppercorn sauce to accompany fish or poultry.

The berries are easily crushed with a mortar and pestle or under the blade of a knife.

ROSE (ROSA SPECIES)

Western cooks seldom think of roses as a flavoring ingredient, but throughout the Arab world, Turkey, and Iran, and as far east as northern India, dried rosebuds or petals and rosewater distilled from them are consumed in a variety of ways. Turkey and Bulgaria are the biggest producers of attar of roses (the essential oil) and rosewater. Only intensely fragrant roses are used, such as the highly perfumed damask rose, *R. damascena*, produced in the Balkans, Turkey, and the Middle East. Most of the flowers are processed to make rosewater but you can also buy the wonderfully scented, pink, dried buds.

BUY Rosewater and rose oil are available from Middle Eastern, Indian, Iranian, and Turkish supermarkets. Some stores sell dried rosebuds.

STORE Dried buds can be stored in an airtight container for up to a year.

EAT Infuse fresh or dried petals in syrups to make desserts and drinks, or put petals into a jar of sugar to give it a delicate rose scent that will flavor creams and cakes. In India, powdered buds are used in marinades and in delicately flavored kormas. In Bengal and the Punjab rosewater features prominently in desserts such as *gulab jamun and rasgulla*, in sweet lassi, and in kheer (a rice pudding). In Morocco rosebuds are a constituent of ras el hanout. Tunisian cooks seem to appreciate rosebuds most of all, using them in spice blends for a wide range of dishes. A *bharat* of ground cinnamon and rosebuds is used with black pepper to flavor roast meats, stews using fruits such as quinces, and couscous with fish or lamb.

FLAVOR PAIRINGS Poultry, lamb, fish, apples, apricots, chestnuts, quinces, rice, desserts, and pastries.

CLASSIC RECIPES *Ras el hanout; bharat; gulab jamun;* sweet lassi.

Dried rosebuds keep their scent and should be ground as needed in an electric grinder.

AKUDJURA (SOLANUM SPECIES)

Akudjura, *S. centrale*, is the name of an edible member of a group of wild tomatoes, native to the deserts, or "bush," of western and central Australia. There is, as yet, no cultivation of the bush tomato—what is available has been gathered in the wild. Their aroma suggests baked caramel and chocolate. The taste is of tamarillo, and tomato, with a bitterish, lingering aftertaste that is refreshing.

🔒 **BUY** Bush tomatoes are sold whole and, more frequently, ground to an orange-brown powder, called akudjura.

📦 **STORE** The ground powder keeps in an airtight container for 2–3 months.

⬤ **EAT** Akudjura must be soaked for 20–30 minutes before use in cooking, and suits both sweet and savory dishes. Use it in place of sun-dried tomato or sweet paprika, and to flavor tomato-based sauces and meat stews, particularly goulash. It is sprinkled on salads, soups, egg dishes, and steamed vegetables. In Australia it is used whole in casseroles

and in an interesting version of damper, the traditional breadlike "bush tucker." The powder goes into cookies, chutneys, dressings, relishes, and salsas. A mixture of akudjura, wattle, and mountain pepper is used the same way as Cajun blackening spice, especially for fish; in other mixtures akudjura is used for barbecuing and marinating meat, especially lean kangaroo meat.

FLAVOR PAIRINGS Lean meats, fish, cheese dishes, apples, onions, peppers, potatoes, lemon myrtle.

CLASSIC RECIPES Bush tucker.

The brown dried bush tomato has a chewy texture.

CLOVES (SYZYIUM AROMATICUM)

The clove tree is a small, tropical evergreen with fragrant leaves. Its crimson flowers seldom develop, and unopened flower buds constitute the spice. Native to the Moluccas, volcanic islands now part of Indonesia, cloves reached Europe overland through Alexandria in Roman times. Now, Madagascar, Zanzibar, and Pemba Island are the main exporters; Indonesia uses nearly all its vast production itself. The aroma of cloves is assertive and warm, with notes of pepper and camphor. The taste is fruity but also sharp, hot, and bitter; it leaves a numbing sensation in the mouth.

Whole cloves
Good-quality cloves should be clean and intact. They should exude a small amount of oil if pressed with a fingernail. Use sparingly, since they easily overpower other spices.

🔒 **BUY** Whole cloves vary greatly in size and appearance. Ground cloves should be dark brown.

📦 **STORE** Whole cloves will keep in an airtight jar for a year. The powder loses its strength quite quickly.

⬤ **EAT** Cloves are equally good in sweet and savory dishes, and go into baked goods, desserts, syrups, and preserves almost everywhere. In Europe, cloves are used as a pickling or mulling spice. The Dutch use them liberally in cheese, the British in apple pies. In Germany they are found in spiced breads. In the Middle East and North Africa cloves go into spice blends used to flavor meat dishes or rice, often with cinnamon and cardamom.

FLAVOR PAIRINGS Ham, pork, apples, beets, red cabbage, carrots, onions, oranges, squash, chocolate.

CLASSIC RECIPES *Quatre épices*; five spice powder; *garam masala*.

Ground cloves
Cloves must be ground in an electric grinder. In India they are essential to garam masala, in China to five spice powder, and in France to quatre épices.

AJOWAN (TRACHYSPERMUM AMMI)

Ajowan, native to southern India, is a small, annual umbellifer closely related to caraway and cumin. The seeds, which are green or brown and resemble celery seeds, are a popular spice throughout India; the plant is also grown and used in Pakistan, Afghanistan, Iran, and Egypt. The taste is hot and bitter; cooking mellows the flavor to resemble that of thyme or oregano, but it is stronger and with a peppery note. If chewed on their own, ajowan seeds numb the tongue.

🔒 **BUY** Ajowan can be bought from Indian supermarkets, where it may also be called ajwain or carom.

📦 **STORE** The seeds will keep indefinitely in an airtight jar.

⬤ **EAT** Ajowan should be used judiciously; too much will make a dish taste bitter. Just before use, bruise or crush whole seeds, or grind in a mortar, to release their flavor. Ajowan has a natural affinity with starchy foods and in south Asia is used in breads (paratha), savory pastries (pakora), and fried snacks (especially those made with chickpea flour). It is also used to

flavor pickles and root vegetables. It is often cooked with pulses and is an ingredient in some curry mixes. In northern India, ajowan is fried in ghee with other spices before being added to a dish. Probably its best-known use in the West is in the flavoring of the popular snack Bombay mix. With lemon juice and garlic it makes an excellent rub for fish fillets; leave the fish to marinate for an hour or two before frying.

FLAVOR PAIRINGS Fish, green beans, pulses, root vegetables, cardamom, cinnamon, cloves, cumin, fennel seed, garlic, ginger, pepper, turmeric.

CLASSIC RECIPES *Berbere; chat masala.*

Ground seeds
Ajowan seeds are often used whole or crushed. Do not grind until needed. In Gujarat it is used in batters for bhajis and pakoras, and with chile and cilantro to flavor pudlas, or pancakes.

MOUNTAIN PEPPER (TASMANNIA LANCEOLATA)

Mountain pepper comes from a genus of small trees, native to the uplands of Tasmania, Victoria, and New South Wales. Early colonists there soon discovered that the ground berries could be used as a condiment. All parts of the tree are aromatic. The leaves have a warm, woody aroma with a citrus note; the taste is similar, with a kick that recalls Sichuan pepper rather than black pepper. Fresh berries initially taste of sweet fruit, followed by an intensely pungent bite that leaves a numb sensation in the mouth. Berries are more potent than leaves, and dried leaves are stronger than true pepper. The leaves and berries of a related tree, *T. stipitata*, are sold as Dorrigo pepper, named for the Dorrigo mountains where it grows.

🔒 **BUY** In Australia, fresh and dried whole leaves and berries are available. Elsewhere dried, ground leaf, and berries preserved in brine are more commonly found. Buy both leaf and berries in small quantities, since they are used sparingly and the flavor diminishes once they are ground.

📦 **STORE** Fresh leaves and berries will keep for several weeks if kept in a sealed plastic bag in the refrigerator. Store dried leaves and berries in an airtight container.

⬤ **EAT** The berries are very potent. Add a few crushed or whole berries to long-cooked meat stews and hearty bean dishes or mixed vegetable soups; prolonged cooking dissipates their

sharpness and pungency somewhat and allows the flavor of the pepper to permeate the dish. Or try them in a classic French sauce *poivrade*, which is good with beef and rich, well-flavored game—in particular hare or venison. In Australia, mountain pepper is often combined with other bush spices, such as wattle and lemon myrtle; a mixture of ground leaf, lemon myrtle, and thyme is good in marinades or as a dry rub for lamb.

FLAVOR PAIRINGS Game meats, beef, lamb, pulses, squash, root vegetables, bay, garlic, juniper, lemon myrtle, marjoram and oregano, mustard.

CLASSIC RECIPE *Sauce poivrade.*

Dried berries can be ground in a peppermill and are often sold crushed.

TAMARIND (TAMARINDUS INDICA)

Tamarind is obtained from the beanlike pods of the tamarind tree, native to eastern Africa, probably Madagascar, which makes it the only important spice of African origin. The tall, evergreen trees with their handsome crowns were already growing in India in prehistoric times. The pods contain a dark brown, sticky, and very fibrous pulp, which is extracted and pressed into flat cakes; these often include the shiny, black seeds. Further processing results in tamarind paste and concentrate. Tamarind has little smell, and a sourish but also sweet and fruity taste. The spice has long been exported—principally from India—for the manufacture of such condiments as Worcestershire sauce.

Whole seeds *The seeds are small, ridged ovals, grayish-green to reddish-brown. When crushed, they have a strong, rather crude smell of thyme.*

BUY From Indian stores and spice merchants, tamarind is available as a dried block, with or without seeds, as a thick, fairly dry paste, or as a more liquid, brown-black concentrate. Supermarkets usually have concentrate or paste. Occasionally, fresh leaves, slices of dried pulp, and dried powdered tamarind can be found.

STORE In all processed forms tamarind keeps almost indefinitely.

EAT Try using it with salt as a rub for fish or meat before cooking, or with soy sauce and ginger in a marinade for pork or lamb. In India and Southeast Asia tamarind is used as an acidulant (much as the West uses lemon and lime) in curries, sambhars, chutneys, marinades, preserves, pickles, and sherbets. With raw sugar and chiles it is simmered to a syrupy dipping sauce for fish. In Indonesia it is used in sauces, both savory and sweet, and for marinades. On Java, especially, it is preferred to lemon for the island's sweet-sour dishes. In India ground

seeds are used in cakes. In Iran stuffed vegetables are baked in a rich tamarind stock. In the Middle East a lemonade-like drink made from tamarind syrup is popular; Central America and the West Indies also have canned tamarind drinks, which are consumed on their own or in tropical fruit punch, or made into milk shakes with ice cream. Jamaica uses tamarind in stews and with rice; in Costa Rica it is used to make a sour sauce. In Thailand, Vietnam, the Philippines, Jamaica, and Cuba tamarind pulp is also used as a sweetmeat, dusted with sugar or candied.

FLAVOR PAIRINGS Chicken, lamb, pork, fish and shellfish, cabbage, lentils, mushrooms, peanuts, most vegetables, *asafoetida*, chile, cilantro, cumin, galangal, garlic, ginger, mustard, shrimp paste, soy sauce, (brown or palm) sugar, turmeric.

CLASSIC RECIPES Goan vindaloo; Thai tom yom soup.

Whole pods
Unripe pods are used in Vietnam and Thailand in tart soups and stews. In the regions where tamarind grows, especially Thailand and the Philippines, young leaves and flowers are used in curries and chutneys.

Block
Indian supermarkets and spice merchants generally sell tamarind as a dried block. To use, soak a small piece, about the equivalent of 1 tbsp, for 10–15 minutes in a little hot water. Stir to loosen the pulp, squeeze out, and sieve to remove fiber and, if they are present, seeds.

Concentrate
Concentrate has a "cooked" smell reminiscent of molasses, and a sharp, acid taste. To use, stir 1–2 tsp into a little water.

Leaves and seeds
When substituting mountain pepper for true pepper, use half the amount of ground leaf as you would true pepper, and even less if you are using the berries. Dried leaves are stronger than fresh.

Paste
Adding prepared tamarind to dishes moderates the heating effect of fiery chiles and hot spices. Tamarind gives many hot South Indian dishes, such as Goan vindaloo and Gujarati vegetable stews, their characteristic sourness. It goes into Thai tom yom soup and Chinese hot-and-sour soup.

CLASSIC RECIPE

VANILLA ICE CREAM

Nothing beats creamy homemade vanilla ice cream. This is delicious served with fresh berries, macaroons, biscotti, or other cookies crumbled into the bottom of the serving glass.

SERVES 4

| 1 vanilla bean |
| 1¼ cups whole milk |
| 3 egg yolks |
| ½ cup superfine sugar |
| 1¼ cups heavy whipping cream |

1 Split the vanilla bean lengthwise with the tip of a sharp knife. Scrape out the seeds. Put seeds, pod, and milk into a heavy saucepan. Heat gently to a simmer; do not boil. Remove from the heat, cover, and set aside for 30 minutes to infuse the milk. Remove the pod.

2 Beat the egg yolks and sugar in a large bowl. Stir in the infused milk, then return the mixture to the saucepan.

3 Cook over low heat, stirring constantly, until the mixture thickens slightly and just coats the back of a spoon. Do not boil or the custard will curdle.

4 Pour the mixture through a sieve into a bowl. Cover and refrigerate until thoroughly chilled.

5 Whip the cream until very soft peaks form, and fold into the cold custard.

6 To freeze using an ice cream maker, churn according to manufacturer's instructions. (This usually takes 20–30 minutes.) Transfer to a freezer-safe container and freeze until needed. To freeze the ice cream without a machine, pour the mixture into a freezer-safe container and freeze for at least 3–4 hours, then whisk to break up any ice crystals. Freeze for another 2 hours and repeat the process; freeze until ready to use.

7 To serve the ice cream, remove it from the freezer 10–20 minutes prior to scooping. Machine-churned ice cream will keep for up to 1 month in the freezer; manually-frozen ice cream is best served within 1 week, to prevent ice crystals from forming.

FENUGREEK (TRIGONELLA FOENUM-GRAECUM)

Native to western Asia and southeastern Europe, fenugreek is prized in Middle Eastern and Indian cooking, but has yet to capture the imagination of Western cooks. The aroma of the raw seeds forms the overriding smell of some curry powders. Their taste is celerylike and bitter; the texture is floury. Fresh leaves (methi) are grassy and mildly pungent with astringent tones; in the dried leaves there is a note of hay.

 BUY Seeds and leaves are available from Iranian and Indian supermarkets.

STORE In an airtight container, seeds and dried leaves will keep their flavor for a year or more. Store fresh leaves in the refrigerator; use within 3 days.

 EAT Fenugreek is widely used by vegetarians in India. It goes well with lentils and with fish, and is much used in *dals* and fish curries in southern India, and in local breads. Seeds are used in pickles and chutney, and traditional spice blends. In Ethiopia, fenugreek is a constituent of berbere spice mixture. In Turkey and Armenia, ground fenugreek is combined with chile and garlic and rubbed on to *pastirma*, or dried beef. In Yemen, seeds are used in *hilbeh*, a potent dip. Fenugreek adds bitterness to Bengali vegetable stews, or *shuktas*. Leaves are added to the Iranian lamb stew, *ghormeh sabzi*.

FLAVOR PAIRINGS Green and root vegetables, tomatoes.

Fresh leaves
Fresh leaves are used in India as a vegetable, cooked with potatoes, spinach, or rice. They are also chopped and added to the dough for naans and chapattis.

Roast and grind seeds when needed, as ground fenugreek loses its flavor quickly.

Whole seeds
Brief dry-roasting or frying mellows the flavor and gives the seeds a nutty, burned-sugar, or maple-syrup taste, but do not heat for too long or the bitterness is intensified. Use immediately after roasting.

VANILLA (VANILLA PLANIFOLIA)

Vanilla is the fruit of a perennial, climbing orchid, native to Central America. Tribes ruled by the Aztecs had fairly sophisticated methods of fermenting the beanlike fruits to extract vanillin crystals. Fresh vanilla beans have no aroma or taste. After fermentation, they develop a rich, mellow, intensely perfumed aroma with hints of licorice or tobacco matched by a delicate, sweetly fruity or creamy flavor. There may also be hints of raisin or prune, or smoky, spicy notes. Today vanilla is exported from Mexico, Réunion, Madagascar, Tahiti, and Indonesia.

The tiny, sticky, black seeds inside the pod can be removed with the point of a knife.

Whole dried pods
Good vanilla pods are deep brown or black, long and narrow, somewhat wrinkled, moist, waxy, supple, and immediately fragrant.

 BUY Vanilla is expensive because its production is labor-intensive. The best beans have a light, white frosting of vanillin crystals. You are more likely to get good-quality beans from a spice merchant than a supermarket. When buying vanilla extract, look for bottles labeled "natural vanilla extract," with an indication of alcohol content, usually about 35 percent by volume.

STORE Stored in a dark, airtight container, vanilla will keep for 2 years.

 EAT Use whole or split beans to flavor creams, custards, ice cream, and sugar; a whole vanilla bean that has been infused in a syrup or cream can be rinsed, dried, and reused. Add a bean when poaching fruit or lay cut beans over fruit before baking. Use vanilla extract to flavor cakes and tarts. Vanilla goes well with seafood, particularly lobster, scallops, and mussels, and chicken. It enhances the taste of root vegetables and in Mexico is used with black beans.

FLAVOR PAIRINGS Fish, milk, eggs, apples, melon, peaches, pears, rhubarb, strawberries.

CLASSIC RECIPE Vanilla ice cream.

Vanilla extract
Made by macerating beans in alcohol, vanilla extract has a sweet aroma and a delicate taste. Avoid synthetic vanilla, derived from pulp waste, which has a cloying smell and a disagreeable, bitter aftertaste.

SICHUAN PEPPER AND SANSHO
(ZANTHOXYLUM SIMULANS AND Z. PIPERITUM)

These spices, one traditional to the cooking of Sichuan province in China, the other to Japan, are both the dried fruits of prickly ash trees. Also called flower pepper and Japanese pepper, the spices should not be confused with black and white peppercorns harvested from the Piper nigrum vine. Sichuan pepper is very fragrant, woody, somewhat pungent, with notes of citrus peel. Sansho is tangy and quite sharp. Both have a numbing or tingling effect in the mouth. Sansho leaves, called kinome, have a minty-basil aroma and a refreshing, mild flavor.

⚱ **BUY** Sichuan pepper is sold whole or ground by Asian supermarkets and spice merchants. Sansho is available as a powder from the same sources. Leaves are not found easily outside Japan.

▤ **STORE** Store berries and powder in an airtight container. Sansho leaves keep for a few days in a plastic bag in the fridge.

◉ **EAT** Sichuan pepper is traditionally used to flavor Himalayan yak, beef, and pork dishes, as well as the vegetable dumpling momo. Sansho is used as a table condiment in Japan, and is also an ingredient of seven spice blend, shichimi togarashi, which flavors udon (wheat noodles), soups, nabemono (one-pot dishes), and yakitori.

FLAVOR PAIRINGS Black beans, chiles, citrus, garlic, ginger, sesame oil and seeds, soy sauce, star anise.

CLASSIC RECIPES Sichuan pepper: five spice powder; Chinese spiced salt. Sansho: seven spice blend.

Whole Sichuan pepper
To dry roast, heat for 3–4 minutes to release the aromatic oils. They smoke as they get hot, so watch carefully and discard blackened berries. Cool, then grind.

Remove the bitter seeds from whole berries before using.

Ground Sichuan pepper
Ground berries are used as a condiment. Sichuan pepper is used with poultry and meat to be roasted, broiled, or fried, and also with stir-fried vegetables. It is also good with green beans, mushrooms, and eggplant. Grind berries a little at a time, since the flavor soon dissipates.

AROMATIC LEAVES (VARIOUS SPECIES)

The aromatic leaves of a variety of trees are used as flavorings in many parts of the world. They are often described, somewhat misleadingly, as being rather like bay leaves. While the way they are used may be similar, their aromatic properties are very different. The fresh, soft leaves of hoja santa, which grows in Central America and Texas, have a lightly pungent, musky aroma and flavor, with a hint of mint and anise; dried leaves have a warm, anise-fennel aroma with a citrus note. The lightly spicy leaves of lá lót are used in Thailand and Vietnam. Native to Malaysia and Indonesia, the salam tree, a relative of the clove tree, has lemony, aromatic leaves.

The avocado is cultivated for its wonderful fruit; the glossy, scented leaves, with their light hazelnut-anise or licorice flavor, come as a bonus.

⚱ **BUY** Fresh and dried hoja santa leaves are sold in Latin supermarkets, as are dried avocado leaves. Fresh lá lót leaves can be found in Southeast Asian stores; dried salam in Indonesian stores. Most dried aromatic leaves are available via mail order or the internet.

▤ **STORE** Dried leaves hold their flavor quite well; freeze fresh leaves between sheets of plastic wrap.

◉ **EAT** The aromatic leaves included here are used in similar ways: to wrap food and added to soups, vegetable and meat dishes, and stir-fries.

FLAVOR PAIRINGS Ginger, chiles, garlic, lemongrass, paprika, galangal.

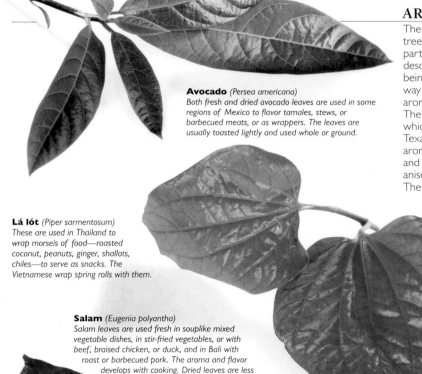

Avocado *(Persea americana)*
Both fresh and dried avocado leaves are used in some regions of Mexico to flavor tamales, stews, or barbecued meats, or as wrappers. The leaves are usually toasted lightly and used whole or ground.

Lá lót *(Piper sarmentosum)*
These are used in Thailand to wrap morsels of food—roasted coconut, peanuts, ginger, shallots, chiles—to serve as snacks. The Vietnamese wrap spring rolls with them.

Salam *(Eugenia polyantha)*
Salam leaves are used fresh in souplike mixed vegetable dishes, in stir-fried vegetables, or with beef, braised chicken, or duck, and in Bali with roast or barbecued pork. The aroma and flavor develops with cooking. Dried leaves are less fragrant than fresh.

The leaves of lá lót are large, glossy and heart-shaped.

Hoja santa *(Piper auritum)*
These leaves feature in Mexican cooking, particularly in Veracruz and Oaxaca. They are used to wrap fish or chicken to be steamed or baked; to line or layer casseroles of fish or chicken; and as a flavoring for tamales. They are also used with other herbs in green mole sauces.

Use colourful and aromatic spices to infuse your food with anything from a subtle spiciness to a dramatic kick.

GINGER CAKE

It's worth making this deliciously moist cake a few days before you want to serve it: as the days go by, it will mature in flavor.

MAKES ONE 10IN (25CM) CAKE, TO SERVE 8–10

| 1 cup Lyle's Golden Syrup* or corn syrup |
| 1 cup dark molasses |
| 15 tbsp (2 sticks) butter |
| 1⅔ cup superfine sugar |
| 2¼ cups all-purpose flour, sifted |
| 1–2 tsp ground ginger, to taste |
| 1 tsp apple- or pumpkin pie spice blend, or ground cinnamon |
| 1 tsp baking soda |
| 2 large eggs, lightly beaten |
| ¾ cup boiling water |

1 Preheat the oven to 350 F (180 C). Grease and line a 10in- (25cm-) round cake pan with parchment paper. Put the syrup, molasses, butter, and sugar in a large saucepan. Cook over low heat until the sugar has dissolved, then increase the heat to medium and continue to cook, stirring occasionally until the mixture reaches a boil. Remove from the heat.

2 Combine the flour, ginger, spice blend, and baking soda in a large bowl and scrape in the syrup mixture. Mix well with a wooden spoon.

3 Beat in the eggs, then mix in the boiling water until well blended.

4 Scrape the batter into the prepared pan and bake for 45–50 minutes, or until the cake springs back when pressed lightly in the center. Leave in the pan to cool on a wire rack before unmolding. Cut into wedges to serve.

*Available in the imported-foods section of many well-stocked supermarkets.

GRATING FRESH GINGER

This is a simple way to prepare shreds of fresh ginger, which can be time-consuming to cut with a knife.

1 Peel the ginger rhizome with a knife. **2** Using a grater with coarse blades, grate the peeled rhizome at an angle. **3** The finely shredded ginger should be used soon after grating, or it will lose its flavor.

FRESH GINGER (ZINGIBER OFFICINALE)

Ginger is a rhizome of a lush plant that resembles bamboo. It has been an important spice for more than 3,000 years, and is cultivated in China, India, and northern Australia. Fresh ginger has a rich and warm aroma with a refreshing, woody note and citrus undertones. The flavor is hot and tangy. The Japanese and Koreans use the buds and shoots of mioga ginger, *Z. mioga*, which have a delicate, crunchy texture. A wild ginger, *Nicolaia elatior*, known as ginger flower or torch ginger, is used in Thailand and Malaysia.

🔒 **BUY** Ginger is available fresh, chopped, and preserved, and frozen as a paste. *Hajikami shoga* are pickled ginger shoots. *Gari, beni-shoga*, and *hajikami shoga* are all available in packs or jars from Asian shops, as is pickled and fresh mioga; ginger flower buds are mainly found in Asia.

📦 **STORE** Fresh ginger can be kept in the refrigerator or a cool place for 10 days.

⬤ **EAT** In China ginger is common with fish and seafood, meat, poultry, and vegetables, particularly cabbages and greens, and it goes into soups, sauces, and marinades. In Japan freshly grated ginger and its juice are used in tempura dipping sauce, in dressings, and with grilled and fried foods. In India, ginger goes into chutneys and relishes, marinades for meat and fish, and into salads. Sliced mioga is used to flavor soups, tofu, salads, vinegared dishes, and pickles.

FLAVOR PAIRINGS Chiles, coconut, garlic, lime, scallions.

CLASSIC RECIPE Chinese stir-fries.

Whole fresh rhizome
Ginger is used in savory dishes throughout Asia. Peel the rhizome, then grate, slice, or shred; or use large, unpeeled slices and discard before eating.

Fresh ginger rhizomes should be hard, unwrinkled, plump, and heavy.

Sliced rhizome
Familiar to sushi lovers, gari is finely sliced rhizome that is pickled in sweet vinegar.

Shredded rhizome
Beni-shoga is preserved in salt, then vinegar. This vivid red pickle offers a sharp contrast in color and taste when served with seafood.

Crystallized ginger
To make this lightly pungent sweetmeat, knobs of young ginger are cooked in a thick syrup, air dried, and rolled in sugar.

DRIED GINGER (ZINGIBER OFFICINALE)

The Assyrians and Babylonians used dried ginger in cooking, as did the Egyptians, Greeks, and Romans. Middle Eastern and European dishes developed using dried ginger rather than fresh because that was the form in which it came via the ancient caravan routes. Today India is the main exporter of dried ginger. Whole, dried rhizomes are less aromatic than fresh, but once bruised or powdered they are warm and peppery with light, lemony notes. The taste is fiery and penetrating.

🔒 **BUY** Dried ginger can be bought as pieces of rhizome, slices, and powder; rhizomes are hard to grind. The quality and flavor of dried ginger vary greatly according to its origin, with Jamaican considered the best for its delicate aroma and fine-textured powder.

📦 **STORE** If kept airtight, rhizomes will last for 2 years, and ground for 1 year.

⬤ **EAT** In Asia dried ginger is used in many pungent spice mixtures. Fruits marry well with ginger, and it is good for spicing jams. In Arab countries dried ginger is used with other spices in tagines, couscous, and slow-cooked meat dishes with fruit. It flavors ginger beer and wine, and soft drinks.

FLAVOR PAIRINGS Squash, carrots, dried fruits, bananas, pears, pineapple, oranges, nuts, cinnamon, cloves.

CLASSIC RECIPES Berbere; five spice powder; pickling spice; *quatre épices*; *ras el hanout*; gingerbread.

Dried rhizome pieces
Dried, pale-beige rhizomes release a warm aroma when bruised. Whole pieces are most used in pickling spices.

Ground ginger
In the West, ground ginger is essential to many breads, cakes, and pastries. Dried ginger has a different taste to fresh, and the one should not be substituted for the other.

DAIRY & EGGS

EGGS | MILK | CREAM
YOGURT | BUTTER
FRESH CHEESES
BLUE CHEESES
SOFT WHITE CHEESES
HARD CHEESES

DAIRY AND EGG ESSENTIALS

Dairy and eggs are core ingredients in many cuisines around the world. Often taken for granted, these are wonderfully versatile foodstuffs that can be used in many different ways. It is hard to imagine cooking without the possibility of using eggs, butter, cream, milk, or yogurt. Delicately flavored, all these ingredients add texture and a mild but distinctive richness to a diverse range of dishes. They are ingredients that are both consumed and enjoyed in their own right, but also play an essential part in both savory and sweet dishes, such as fresh pasta, pastries, cakes, dips, and classic sauces. In the case of both eggs and dairy, one bird and one animal dominate production. Although we use eggs from different birds, it is the hen's egg that is the most widely produced and consumed around the world, with the term "egg" generally taken to mean "hen's egg." Similarly, in the world of dairy, "milk" is usually assumed to mean cow's milk, with cows providing the majority of milk consumed internationally.

Dairy products *are essential for baking: butter will help produce perfect melting cookies, and freshly whipped cream makes the ideal, luxurious accompaniment.*

BUY

There is a multitude of different dairy ingredients available, but it is worth knowing what to look for when buying them.

Milk and yogurt Always look at the sell-by date on both these products and buy well before that date. You can buy organic products if you prefer, and choose from whole, 2 per cent, 1 per cent, or skim milk. Yogurt can be bought with varying fat contents, flavored, and smooth or set, depending on your preference.

Cheese Make sure cheese is well wrapped and has no sign of a cracked rind or discoloration. If you can, smell it to see if it has an odor that is not characteristic of the type of cheese.

Eggs Choose between organic and free-range. Check the sell-by date and make sure none are cracked or broken before buying.

STORE

To get the very best from dairy products, they need to be stored in sealed containers to prevent them from absorbing other flavors, and kept at the appropriate temperatures.

Milk, cream, and butter Store milk in the refrigerator or freeze it while it is still fresh—do not wait until it reaches its use-by date. (Milk expands when frozen, so empty a little milk out of the container before freezing it.) Creams with a higher fat content, such as whipping cream, will freeze more successfully than lower-fat versions, such as light cream. Milk and cream can be frozen for up to a month. Keep butter in the refrigerator or freeze it, well wrapped, for up to eight months.

Yogurt Store in the refrigerator or freeze it for up to three months. Defrost frozen milk, cream, butter, and yogurt in the refrigerator.

Eggs Store in a cool, dry place, ideally the fridge, and consume before the use-by date. Bring back to room temperature before use.

Store cheese *in the fridge, well wrapped in wax paper or foil to keep it fresh.*

HOW TO STORE CHEESE Primarily, cheese should be kept cool. It was traditionally stored in the cellar or pantry, but today, since most homes no longer have such storage spaces, the fridge is used instead. However, refrigerators are, in fact, too cold and too dry to provide the ideal atmosphere for storing cheese, but there are positive measures you can take to store your cheese as well as possible. Cheese should be stored wrapped, both to prevent its aromas from tainting other foods and to prevent it from becoming tainted by other strong odors. Wrap it thoroughly, since any exposed parts will quickly dry out and deteriorate. Ideally, use wax paper, since this retains humidity and allows the cheese to breathe; aluminum foil is the second-best option. Avoid plastic wrap, since this causes the cheese to sweat and creates a tainted taste; if you bought your cheese wrapped in plastic, rewrap it in wax paper or foil before storing. Place the wrapped cheese in a plastic container with a close-fitting lid, then store this in the refrigerator—if possible, in the warmest part farthest from the freezer.

PREPARE

Unless you are cooking eggs in their shells to produce soft- or hard-boiled eggs, most recipes call for some initial preparation or the knowledge of a few simple techniques. They are often basic but essential, such as separating the yolk and white, and beating and whisking. This initial preparation pays dividends later on, since it can affect the texture of the finished dish.

SEPARATE EGGS Many recipes call for eggs that have been separated, which means they have been divided into yolks and whites.

1 *Hold the egg over a sturdy bowl and crack it lightly and cleanly on the edge. Holding both pieces of the egg shell in your hands, let the egg white fall into the bowl below.*

2 *Taking care not to puncture the yolk on a sharp piece of shell, pass it into the other half of the egg shell, letting any remaining egg white drop into the bowl.*

WHISK EGG WHITES
Whisked egg whites are used to add lightness to dishes such as soufflés, cakes, and meringues. The action of whisking incorporates air into the egg whites so that they thicken and increase substantially in volume. For best results, use a large, roomy metal bowl and a balloon whisk.

1 *First, ensure your egg white has no trace of yolk and is at room temperature. Place it in a large bowl that is dry and free of grease.*

2 *As you whisk, the translucent egg white will turn an opaque white and will begin to expand and fill the space in the bowl.*

3 *To test for the desired consistency, lift up the whisk, bringing up a little of the whisked egg with it. If it stands up in soft peaks, it is ready.*

WHIP CREAM
Heavy cream and whipping cream are the best for whipping, because a fat content of 30 per cent is needed, and both are high in fat. Whipped cream is often used to fill or decorate cakes and desserts, or to accompany fruit. Recipes will state if the cream should be whipped to light or stiff stage.

1 *Pour cold cream into a large bowl that is chilled or placed on ice. Whisk the cream using a handheld whisk or an electric mixer.*

2 *Keep whisking around the bowl in a circular motion; as air is beaten into the cream it will thicken in texture, forming a light, fluffy mass.*

3 *Once the cream has reached the soft peak stage, take care not to overwhip it or the fat in the cream will begin to form butter.*

COOK

Since many dairy products are often used as ingredients rather than as dishes in their own right—with the exception of cheese—individual recipes will dictate how the varying foods should be incorporated and cooked in each case.

BOIL EGGS A simple, fat-free way of cooking eggs is to boil them. Depending on your preference, eggs can be soft-boiled—so that they have a runny yolk within a set white, or they can be cooked longer until hard-boiled—when both the yolk and white are firm.

CLARIFIED BUTTER This is butter that has been treated to remove its water content and milk solids. It is valued for its rich flavor and as a cooking fat, since it has a higher burning point than ordinary butter.

To clarify butter, *place it in a heavy-bottomed saucepan and heat it gently so that it melts but does not brown. Skim off any scum then carefully pour away the clear golden-yellow liquid; leave behind the milky layer below and discard. The cooled clarified butter can be stored in the refrigerator for several weeks.*

To soft-boil *an egg, lower it into a pan of cold water, heat the water to boiling point, then cook at a simmer for 3 more minutes.*

To hard-boil *an egg, lower it into a pan of cold water, heat to boiling point, then cook at a simmer for 7 more minutes.*

EGGS

Bird eggs have long been an important food in many cultures. A versatile ingredient with a mild flavor, eggs are used extensively in baking, in batters and sauces, and also as the main ingredient in dishes such as omelets.

🔒 **BUY** Eggs are sold graded according to weight, from small to large. Terms used to describe how the laying birds are reared can be confusing: "farm fresh" and "barn" eggs have been laid by birds kept indoors in large industrial units with little space to move around; "free range" means the birds have an outside area to enjoy; "organic" means the birds are kept free range and fed on an organic diet. Always check shells are free from any cracks; any eggs with cracks in their shells should be discarded.

📦 **STORE** Eggs in their shells should be kept at an even temperature below 68°F (20°C), preferably in the fridge.

The shells are porous, and eggs can become tainted by strong-smelling foods nearby. To avoid this, store them in a covered container. For certain recipes, such as poaching, fresh eggs are required. To test for freshness, place in water. A fresh egg will sink to the bottom, as eggs become lighter with age. For some recipes it is advised to bring the eggs to room temperature before cooking with them. Egg whites freeze well, but egg yolks need stabilizing with the addition of either a little salt or sugar before freezing in order to retain their texture.

⚫ **EAT** Boil, fry, poach, and scramble. Eggs are suitable for both savory and sweet dishes, used whole or separated into yolks and whites. Yolks are a key ingredient in custard and emulsified sauces like mayonnaise or Hollandaise. Egg whites can be whisked, trapping air into them, and used to create dishes such as soufflés, meringues, and cakes.

FLAVOR PAIRINGS Cheese and cream, bread, rice, most kinds of herbs and peppery salads, tomatoes, peppers, asparagus, spinach, kale, onions, potatoes, oily fish such as tuna and salmon, sausages and cured meats

(particularly pork-derived), many kinds of spices especially those used in Spanish, Mexican, Middle Eastern, and Indian cuisine.

CLASSIC RECIPES Eggs Benedict; Chinese egg drop soup; eggnog; egg mayonnaise; meringue.

Quail
These tiny, fragile, delicately-flavored eggs are a luxury. Serve in canapés, hard-boiled with celery salt, or as miniature Scotch eggs.

Shells are speckled dark-brown, and the eggs have a high yolk-to-white ratio.

Hen
A versatile food with a delicate flavor, hen eggs are the most widely consumed eggs of any bird worldwide. Poach, boil, fry, or scramble, use in egg drop soup, meringues, Spanish tortilla, soufflés and zabaglione.

Ostrich
An average ostrich egg weighs around 3lb 3oz (1.5kg), equivalent to 24 hen eggs, and has a delicate flavor. Boil, fry, poach, or scramble, bearing in mind their large size means longer cooking times.

CLASSIC RECIPE

EGGS BENEDICT

The smooth buttery sauce makes a truly indulgent breakfast or brunch.

SERVES 4

8 large eggs

4 English muffins

butter, for spreading

8 slices Canadian bacon, heated

1 recipe Hollandaise sauce, (see page 373)

1 Fill 2 large saucepans with boiling water to a depth of 2in (5cm). When tiny bubbles appear at the bottom of the pan, crack 4 eggs into each pan.

2 Leave the pans on the heat for 1 minute, then remove and let the eggs sit in the hot water for exactly 6 minutes. Remove the eggs, and blot dry with paper towels.

3 Meanwhile, preheat the broiler on its highest setting; split each muffin in half and toast the cut sides, watching carefully to avoid burning them.

4 Butter each muffin half and place 2 on each plate, cut-side up. Top with a slice of Canadian bacon, and then with a poached egg. Drizzle with warm Hollandaise and serve at once.

Duck
Larger than hen eggs and thicker-shelled, duck eggs contain large yolks and watery whites, giving them a rich flavor. Use in baking, such as sponge cake, or for Chinese tea eggs.

Gull eggs have pretty, mottled blue-green shells.

Gull
The eggs of the black-headed gull are a rare, British spring delicacy, harvested by licensed collectors. They have a faint fishy flavor. Hard-boil and serve with celery salt.

Goose
A seasonal delicacy of late spring to summer, these large eggs have a strong flavor. Scramble, fry, poach, and boil, or use them to make an intensely rich sponge cake.

Thousand year
A Chinese preserved food made by coating duck eggs in a quicklime paste and storing for 3 months. Yolks are gray-green with an amber-colored white, and a distinctive, salty flavor. Clean, peel, and slice into congee.

Salted
A Chinese preserved food, made by soaking duck eggs in brine or coating them in a salted charcoal paste. They have a rich, salty flavor. Clean, peel and use in congee, soups, dumplings, and moon cakes.

Preserving quicklime creates an appearance of large grey pebbles.

FOLDED OMELET

This iconic French egg dish is a quick meal and can be flavored with many different ingredients.

SERVES 1

10in (25cm) non-stick frying pan (measured across the top)

3 eggs

salt and freshly ground black pepper

1 to 2 tbsp butter, to taste

1 In a bowl, gently beat the eggs with a fork until the yolks and whites are well blended. Season to taste.

2 Melt the butter in the frying pan over high heat until foaming but not brown. Pour in the beaten eggs and shake the pan to distribute evenly.

3 Working quickly, stir the eggs with a table fork, keeping the rounded side of the fork flat. Stop stirring after 20–30 seconds, or when the eggs are set but still soft.

4 Using the fork, fold the side of the omelet nearest you halfway over itself, as if folding a letter. Grasp the handle of the pan from underneath, and lift the pan to a 45-degree angle. Sharply tap the top of the handle closest to the pan, to ease the omelet over the folded portion. Use the fork to fully "close the letter."

5 Tilt the pan so the omelet will slide onto a warm serving plate. Serve at once.

CREME PATISSIERE

This sweet pastry cream is a rich and custard-like filling for fruit tarts and cream puffs.

MAKES ABOUT 1¼ CUPS

1¼ cups whole milk
2 egg yolks
¼ cup superfine or granulated sugar
3 tbsp all-purpose flour
3 tbsp cornstarch
¼ tsp pure vanilla extract

1 Pour the milk into a saucepan and heat it to the simmering point; do not let it boil.

2 Beat the egg yolks and sugar in a bowl, mix in the flour and cornstarch, then add the hot milk, and mix well.

3 Return the mixture to the pan and slowly bring it to a boil, stirring constantly, until it becomes smooth and lump-free. Once the mixture reaches the boiling point, immediately reduce the heat, and simmer, stirring for 1–2 minutes, to cook the flour.

4 Allow the mixture to cool a bit, then stir in the vanilla extract. Use at once, or cover and refrigerate until needed.

MILK

In most countries today, "milk" will usually mean "cow's milk," although in many parts of the world milk is produced by other dairy animals, including goats and sheep, especially in southern Europe; water buffalo, which are widespread in Asia; camels, common in the Middle East and North Africa; yaks in parts of China and Tibet. Traditionally valued as a useful source of nutrients, protein, and calcium, milk contains water, protein, fat, sugar, and minerals. All milk is opaque, but varies in color, from bright white to buttery cream. In industrialized countries, where milk is mass-produced, dairy cattle, such as Friesian or Holstein, have been bred to produce large quantities of milk, which is then processed, often homogenized (to disperse the fat evenly), pasteurized to eliminate bacteria, and widely distributed. If milk hasn't been homogenized, it will separate into two layers, the fat globules at the top and the watery content at the bottom.

■ **STORE** Milk is highly perishable and can turn sour very quickly, so it should be stored in the refrigerator after purchase and used as soon as possible. It can be frozen (though it will expand), but should still be used within a month.

● **EAT** Milk is an enormously versatile foodstuff. Most varieties can be drunk, turned into yogurt and cheese, and used as a common ingredient in cooking. Drink it on its own, in a milkshake, or added to tea, coffee, or hot chocolate. In cooking, use it in sauces, soups, batters, and desserts. Care should be taken when heating up milk due to its tendency to boil over very rapidly. One of the characteristics of heated milk is the development of a "skin," created by the proteins in milk. As it also curdles very easily when heated, some recipes suggest adding it to a flour base to prevent curdling.

CLASSIC RECIPES Béchamel sauce; *crème pâtissière*; *crème anglaise*; *dulce de leche*; Yorkshire pudding; pork cooked in milk (Italy's *maiale al latte*).

Whole milk
Also known as "full-fat milk," this cow's milk contains about 3.5 percent fat. With a creamy texture and flavor, it is ideal in béchamel sauce, custard, and baked rice pudding. It is also used as the base of Indian desserts like gulab jamun.

Reduced-fat milk
Also known as "semi-skim milk," this cow's milk has a reduced fat content, typically about 2 percent. Although thinner than whole milk, it tastes quite similar. Add it to tea, coffee, or hot chocolate. Use it in batters, desserts, sauces, and soups.

Skim milk
As its name implies, this cow's milk has been skimmed of nearly all its fat, leaving 0.1–0.3 percent. It is a watery liquid with a less creamy flavor than reduced fat milk. Use it as a low-fat alternative to milk, with cereals, and in drinks.

Jersey cow's milk
The milk from Jersey cows has an especially high fat content of 5 percent. Its buttery, yellow color and rich, creamy flavor is quite distinctive. It is ideal for recipes where a rich, full, milk flavor is required, such as rice pudding, or béchamel sauce.

Buttermilk
Although it was originally produced as a by-product of butter making, most buttermilk today is made by fermenting low-fat milk. It has a thicker texture than milk and a mild, slightly sour flavor. Use it in baking; it is excellent for scones or soda bread.

UHT milk
Ultra-high-temperature (UHT) milk has been heated up to 280°F (138°C) for 1–2 seconds. The process produces "long-life" milk that can be kept without refrigeration, as long as it is bought sealed. UHT milk has a distinctive, cooked taste.

Sheep's milk
Bright white, with a rich, nutty flavor, sheep's milk is high in fats and proteins. Used as an alternative to cow's milk, it is popular for making yogurt and cheeses, such as feta, Pecorino, and Roquefort.

Buffalo's milk
Produced by water buffalo, this brilliant-white milk is high in proteins, calcium, and lactose. With a rich, full flavor, it is ideal for drinks, such as chai, and cheeses, including paneer and mozzarella.

Goat's milk
Bright white, with a faintly nutty taste, this milk is naturally homogenous. Valued by people with an allergy to cow's milk, goat's milk is both drunk and used in cooking instead of cow's milk.

Ymer
A Danish dairy product, ymer is made from skimmed cow's milk to which live bacterial cultures have been added. The resulting strained yogurt has a thick texture and mild, sour flavor. Eat with cereal and fruit, or use it in dressings and sauces.

Condensed milk
With a sugar content of 50 percent, condensed milk has been sweetened and heat treated for a long shelf life. If bought sealed, it can be kept for years without refrigeration. Its sweet taste makes it ideal for fudge and desserts such as banoffee pie.

Filmjölk
A Swedish dairy product, this sour milk has a pleasant, mild, sour flavor. Containing 3 percent fat, it is valued for its high nutrients and calcium. Drink it as it is, pour it over cereal and fresh fruit, or use it for dressings with a gentle, sour flavor.

Evaporated milk
Heat treated to evaporate about 50 percent of its water content, this thick, cream-colored milk has a rich, creamy, cooked flavor. Use it in beverages, sweet sauces, such as chocolate fudge sauce, and desserts, such as Ecuador's tres leches cake.

DULCE DE LECHE

An indulgent, caramelized milk dessert that is very popular in Latin America.

SERVES 8

3 quarts (3 liters) whole milk

3 cups granulated sugar

3 tbsp white wine vinegar

vanilla ice cream, fresh fruit or fruit compote, and wafer cups (optional), to serve

1 Bring the milk and sugar to a boil in a large heavy saucepan. Reduce to a simmer and stir in the vinegar; which will cause the milk and sugar to separate.

2 Simmer for about 3 hours, stirring occasionally, until the liquid evaporates, leaving an almost solid toffee. Cool completely and scrape into a bowl. Use at once, or cover and refrigerate.

3 Serve this thick, custard-like sauce with vanilla ice cream, fresh fruit, such as sliced bananas, or fruit compotes. Any leftovers can be stirred into slightly softened vanilla ice cream and refrozen; then served in wafer cups or small bowls.

CRÈME ANGLAISE

A classic, rich French custard sauce, made from egg yolks and milk, and traditionally flavored with vanilla. Serve with desserts.

MAKES ABOUT 1¼ CUPS

1¼ cups whole milk

1 vanilla bean, split lengthwise

3 egg yolks

3 tbsp superfine or granulated sugar

1 tsp pure vanilla extract (optional)

1 Heat the milk and vanilla bean in a saucepan until nearly boiling. Remove the pan from the heat and leave for 10 minutes, to allow the flavor of the vanilla to infuse the milk. Use the tip of a small sharp knife to scrape the vanilla seeds into the milk. Remove the pod, rinse it, and let it dry completely; then store in an airtight container for future use.

2 Meanwhile, beat the yolks with the sugar in a bowl. Whisk in the hot milk, then return the mixture to the pan.

3 Place the pan over medium–low heat and simmer, stirring constantly with a wooden spoon until the sauce is just thick enough to coat the back of the spoon. Do not allow the sauce to boil once the egg yolks are added, or the sauce will curdle.

4 Strain the sauce through a sieve into a bowl and serve as needed. If using vanilla extract, add it at this point. If serving cold, stir occasionally to avoid a skin from forming. Cover with plastic wrap, pressing the plastic directly onto the surface of the sauce, and refrigerate for up to 2 days.

PANNACOTTA WITH STRAWBERRY PURÉE

Strawberries are just one of the seasonal fruits that complement this creamy Italian dessert.

SERVES 4

1 ⅛ tsp unflavored gelatin (about ½ envelope)

1 ¼ cups heavy whipping cream

3–4 tbsp superfine or granulated sugar

1 tsp vanilla extract

3 cups whole fresh strawberries, hulled, plus extras for garnish

1 Lightly oil 4 x 6oz (175g) molds, custard cups, or ramekins and set aside. Pour 2 tbsp water into a small heatproof bowl, sprinkle the gelatin over the top, and leave to stand for 3–5 minutes, or until it softens and becomes spongy. Quarter-fill a saucepan with water, bring to a boil, then remove the pan from the heat. Carefully set the bowl of gelatin in the pan of hot water, and leave until it has completely dissolved, shaking the bowl occasionally.

2 Combine the cream and 2 tbsp sugar in another pan over medium heat, and slowly bring to a simmer, stirring until the sugar has dissolved. Turn off the heat, and stir in the vanilla, then whisk in the gelatin until completely incorporated. Strain the vanilla-flavored cream into a liquid measuring cup; then fill the prepared molds and leave to cool completely. Cover with plastic and refrigerate for at least 3 hours until set.

3 Meanwhile, place the berries in a blender or food processor and blend to make a purée. Stir in 1–2 tbsp sugar, then cover and set aside.

4 To serve, quickly dip the bottom of each mold in hot water. Working with one mold at a time, place a serving plate on top and invert, giving a gentle shake. Lift and remove the mold, and set aside. Spoon the purée around each panna cotta and garnish with whole strawberries.

CREAM

Long considered a luxury, cream comes from the richest part of cow's milk, the milkfat, or "butterfat," which is much thicker and fuller than milk itself. Its basic color, "cream," comes in many shades, from white to golden yellow. In texture, it is thick and creamy smooth, with a mild, rich taste. Traditionally, in the days before milk was homogenized, cream was created by setting milk aside to stand, allowing the milkfat to rise to the surface naturally, from where it could be skimmed off. This time-consuming process "ripened" the cream, resulting in a slightly sour taste. Today, cream is usually separated from milk mechanically through the use of centrifugal force, a very quick process that results in "fresh" cream, without any trace of sourness to its flavor. Cream is now mass-produced in dairy countries worldwide, including Europe, the US, UK, and Australia.

■ **STORE** Cream should be stored in the refrigerator and used within a few days of purchase before it spoils. High-fat creams, such as heavy or whipping cream, may be successfully frozen, but low-fat varieties, such as light cream, do not freeze well.

● **EAT** Cream is a versatile ingredient, used in both sweet and savory dishes. High-fat creams can be heated without

them separating, making them ideal for hot dishes, such as sauces. Often cream is simply served as an accompaniment to desserts, both hot and cold. In savory cooking, use it to thicken and enrich sauces, braised dishes, stews, casseroles, and curries, and fillings in tarts and flans. Cream is also widely used in desserts: ideal in profiteroles, trifles, pannacotta, crème brûlée, and ice cream. Its smooth texture and mild flavor also make it a popular cocktail ingredient.

CLASSIC RECIPES Crème brûlée; *syllabub*; pannacotta; vanilla ice cream.

Light cream
With a fat content of 18 percent, this is a thin-textured cream, ideal for pouring. Its low-fat content makes it unsuitable for either whipping or boiling, as it will curdle. Especially in Great Britain, this is also known as "single cream."

Heavy cream
A rich cream, with a minimum fat content of 36-38 percent, heavy cream has a thick texture and full flavor. It is valued in cooking, as its high-fat content means that it can be boiled without separating, and also whipped until fluffy. Add to sauces, use in sweet and savory flans and tarts, or serve as a thick pouring cream with desserts.

Whipping cream
With a fat content of 30 percent, this cream can be transformed by whipping with a whisk into a light, fluffy consistency. Use it whipped and to decorate desserts, such as pies, pastries, trifles, and cakes; use it unwhipped, as a light-textured pouring cream, with fruit salad, poached fruits, sweet tarts, chocolate cakes, tarts, and fruit pies.

Sour cream
Made by adding a lactic bacteria to light cream, this thick-textured, white cream has a sour tang and a medium-fat content of 12–20 percent. It is ideal for sweet and savory dishes. Use it in dips, canapés, casseroles, or cheesecake; serve with baked potatoes. Its mild, sour taste contrasts well with chili con carne, guacamole, or lentil soup. As it curdles when cooked, always add it at the end.

Crème fraîche
A French dairy product made by adding a lactic bacteria to cow's cream, this is a thick-textured cream with a distinctive, slightly sour tang. Its high-fat content of 38 percent allows it to be boiled without curdling, making it more versatile than sour cream. Use it in sauces, casseroles, savory flans, and salad dressings; serve with desserts, such as baked puddings, chocolate cakes, and fruits.

CRÈME BRÛLÉE

This popular French dessert consists of a baked custard, topped with a fine, crisp layer of caramelized sugar.

SERVES 6

2 cups heavy whipping cream

1 vanilla bean, split in half lengthwise

5 egg yolks

¼ cup superfine sugar

12 tbsp granulated or raw sugar

1 Preheat the oven to 275°F (140°C). Place the cream in a saucepan and add the vanilla bean. Heat the cream over low heat until just simmering, then set aside to infuse for 1 hour.

2 Whisk the egg yolks and superfine sugar together. Lift the vanilla bean from the cream, and, scrape the seeds into the cream. Whisk the cream into the egg mixture, then strain through a sieve. Pour the mixture into 6 ramekins or custard cups, and place in a roasting pan. Add enough boiling water to the pan to reach halfway up the sides of the ramekins. Bake for 40 minutes, until just set. Once cooled, refrigerate until fully chilled.

3 Before serving, sprinkle 2 tbsp of the granulated sugar over each custard. Place the ramekins under a broiler and cook just until the sugar melts and caramelizes. Let cool and harden, then serve at once or refrigerate for up to 1 hour.

Clotted cream
A traditional delicacy from Britain's West Country, clotted cream is a rich, thick-textured, and slightly sweet treat, varying from pale to golden cream. Made by heating cow's cream, it has a high-fat content of 55–60 percent. Qashtah and kaymak are similar products from the Middle East, served with pastries, preserves, and honey. Eat clotted cream with scones and jam, or serve with desserts.

Perfectly suited for baking, French butter is beautifully subtle in flavor, with a rich, creamy texture.

YOGURT

A versatile, nourishing milk food, with a smooth texture and mildly sour flavor, yogurt is consumed in many parts of the world. It is made by adding lactic-acid-producing bacterial cultures to heated milk, then setting it aside in a warm place to ferment. The process thickens the milk, while the acid adds a distinctive sour tang. Different bacterial cultures produce different flavors, varying from mild to sharp. Traditionally, yogurt has been made from the milk of various dairy animals, including cows, sheep, goats, and buffaloes. A highly nutritious food, rich in calcium, it is now widely produced. In addition to the plain, unflavored, or "natural" variety, yogurt is available in many sweetened and flavored versions. Historically, it has been regarded as an aid to digestion. "Live" yogurt, particularly, is today viewed as beneficial, containing living and "friendly" bacteria, such as probiotics, thought to promote healthy digestion.
■ **STORE** Yogurt should be stored covered in the fridge after purchase. It can be frozen, but should be used within 3 months of freezing.
● **EAT** Eat yogurt just as it is, or sweetened with sugar or honey. Cool and refreshing, it is widely used in appetizing drinks, such as *ayran* or *lassi*. Its mild flavor also makes it an ideal base for dips, and it goes well with cucumber, eggplant, and herbs such as

mint. It is also useful for marinades, as it has tenderizing properties. If cooked, cow's milk yogurt will curdle very easily when brought to a boil. To stop it from splitting when boiled, simply stir in some cornstarch mixed with a little water (allow 1 tsp cornstarch mixed with 1 tbsp water to 1lb (450g) yogurt). Another traditional way of stabilizing yogurt in a cooked dish is to whisk in egg yolks. Add yogurt to smoothies; serve with fruit and desserts; use in dips, sauces, dressings, and marinades; stir into soups just before serving.
CLASSIC RECIPES *raita; lassi; shrikhand; ayran; tzatziki; mast-o mooseer.*

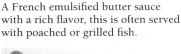

Cow's yogurt
Made from cow's milk, this common yogurt has a mild, slightly sour flavor. As it curdles easily when heated, be sure to stabilize it first (see left). Eat on its own, or with cereal and desserts; use as a base for refreshing dips and drinks, such as lassi; serve as a cooling relish with rich, spicy curries.

Natural yogurt
As its name suggests, this is simply plain, unflavored yogurt, made from cow's, goat's, sheep's, or buffalo's milk. It has a smooth, thickish texture and mild, sour tang. A versatile ingredient, it is ideal for both sweet and savory dishes. Eat as it is, or sweeten with honey, sugar, or fruit. Use it to thicken and enrich smoothies and dressings; as a tenderizing marinade, or as a base for dips.

Strained yogurt
Some yogurts, such as Greek, are strained through a cloth, usually muslin, to remove excess moisture, resulting in a thick, creamy texture and a mild, full flavor, with a fat content of 8–10 percent. Labne, a Middle Eastern variety, ranges in texture from creamy to thick—like a soft cheese. Eat with honey, fruit, or bread, or mix with egg yolks to make a topping for moussaka.

LASSI

A traditional Indian beverage, this yogurt drink is valued for its cooling, refreshing properties, ideal for drinking in a hot climate. It can be made either salted or sweet, depending on your preference.

SERVES 4

1 tsp cumin seeds
1 lb (450g) plain yogurt
¼–½ tsp salt
ice cubes, to serve

1 In a small, dry skillet, cook the cumin seeds over medium-low heat, stirring constantly, until fragrant. Leave to cool and grind finely with a mortar and pestle.

2 Place the yogurt, ¾ cup water, salt to taste, and ground cumin in a blender; and blend until thoroughly mixed and frothy. Alternatively, use a hand mixer to blend together.

3 Pour the lassi into 4 glasses; add ice cubes to taste, and serve at once.

Goat's yogurt
Made from goat's milk, this bright white yogurt has a refreshing, distinctive, slightly nutty flavor. Eat it with honey, sugar, or fruit; use it in salads, smoothies, dips, and dressings for salad or pasta.

Sheep's yogurt
This white yogurt has a sharp tang and creamy texture. Eat it sweetened with honey, sugar, or fruit; use it to flavor salad dressings, or as a base for drinks and dips, such as ayran or tzatziki.

Skyr
A traditional Icelandic dairy product, skyr is made from skim milk to which live bacterial cultures have been added; the resulting yogurt is then strained. Nowadays, cow's, rather than sheep's, milk is used. Skyr has a thick, smooth texture and mild, sour tang. Eat with fresh fruit, sugar, or honey.

Kashk
An Iranian dairy product, kashk is made from dried buttermilk. Traditionally dried in the sun and rolled up to form balls, or crushed into a powder, it has a distinctive sour flavor. The Jordanian variety is called jameed. Use it to thicken and flavor soups and stews, sauces, and dips.

BUTTER

A soft, creamy spread, ideal on bread, butter has been common dairy fare since ancient times. It is made by churning cream until the milkfat, or "butterfat," within the cream binds together to form a smooth, yellow mass containing at least 80 percent fat, with a subtle yet distinctive, creamy flavor. For centuries, butter was made by hand, using a churn. Now most butter is mass-produced in creameries, with the cream churned in large vats, then kneaded to improve its texture. The majority of butter produced worldwide is made from cow's milk, characterized by a creamy flavor and a smooth texture. In color, it varies from pale cream to a deep, rich yellow, depending on the breed of cow and method of production. The standard cow's milk butter, now used in many parts of the world, including North America, Britain, and Australia, is known as "sweet cream butter." Made from pasteurized cream, it is yellow, with a mild but full flavor.

BEURRE BLANC

A French emulsified butter sauce with a rich flavor, this is often served with poached or grilled fish.

MAKES ABOUT 1 CUP

2 shallots, finely chopped
4 tbsp dry white wine
3 tbsp white wine vinegar
14 tbsp (1¾ sticks) unsalted or slightly salted butter, chilled and cut into ½in (1cm) dice
salt and freshly ground white pepper
fresh lemon juice, to season

1 Place the shallots, wine, and vinegar in a saucepan and bring to a boil.

2 Lower the heat and cook for about 2 minutes until 1 tbsp of liquid remains. It should have a syrupy consistency.

3 Over low heat, add 2 tbsp of cold water, then gradually whisk in the butter until melted and emulsified. Season with salt, white pepper, and a squeeze of lemon juice. Usually served unstrained, beurre blanc can be strained for a smoother sauce.

The butter more traditionally used in Continental Europe is lactic cow's milk butter, made from cream that has soured slightly by the addition of lactic-acid bacteria. Also known as "ripened," "cultured," or "cultured cream" butter, it is usually pale in color, with a subtle, creamy flavor. Both sweet cream butter and lactic cow's milk butter can be used as either a spread or cooking fat.

■ **STORE** Butter softens and melts as it warms. To keep it fresh, it should be stored in the fridge, where it becomes firm. Wrap it well (in its own wrapper, wax paper, or plastic wrap) to delay rancidity, and to prevent it becoming tainted by flavors in the atmosphere. Wrapped well, butter can also be frozen and kept for up to 8 months. One way of extending the shelf life of butter is to "clarify" it: first, gently melt the butter, skimming off the whey foam that forms on the surface, while letting the milk solids sink to the bottom; then strain the rich golden liquid through muslin or a fine sieve to remove any remaining sediment.

● **EAT** Spread butter on bread, toast, buns or crumpets. Use it in baking, too. As a highly versatile cooking fat, butter adds its distinctive flavor to many dishes, from cakes and puff pastry to omelets and pancakes.

CLASSIC RECIPE

BUTTERSCOTCH DESSERT SAUCE

Rich and buttery, this sauce is a big hit with children.

MAKES ABOUT 1¼ CUPS

6 tbsp butter, cut into pieces

¾ cup light brown sugar

1 cup heavy whipping cream

1 Melt the butter in a small saucepan. Stir in the sugar and cook over low heat, stirring occasionally, until the sugar dissolves.

2 Pour in the cream and stir until well blended and glossy. Increase the heat and boil gently, whisking, for 2 minutes, or until slightly thickened. Remove from the heat and allow to cool. Serve warm or cold.

When shallow-frying with butter, take care not to let it burn, as it has a lower burning point than oil. A useful tip when frying with butter is to add a little oil to the butter to prevent it from burning so easily. In cooking, it is ideal for baking cakes, cookies, scones, and pastries; for making icing or flavored butters, and enriching mashed potatoes, sauces, or cooked vegetables.

CLASSIC RECIPES

Beurre noisette; beurre blanc; garlic butter; croissants; brandy butter; butterscotch dessert sauce; hollandaise sauce.

Unsalted
Free from salt, "sweet," or unsalted, butter has a mild, slightly sweet flavor. It is ideal for baking, as its use allows total control over the salt content. Use as a spread or as a cooking fat, excellent in pastry and cakes.

Salted
Traditionally added to preserve butter, salt is now added for taste. Flavored with 1–2 percent salt, this butter has a subtle, salty taste. Use it as a spread or cooking fat, ideal for sweet and savory dishes, from cakes to omelets.

A soft texture is a hallmark of France's famous beurre d'Isigny.

Beurre d'Isigny
Protected by an Appellation D'Origine Contrôlée, this French lactic butter is produced traditionally in northern France. It is golden-colored, with a subtle, creamy flavor. Use in baking, in hollandaise sauce, or as the base for flavored butters.

Goat butter
Made from churned goat's milk, this pale butter has a subtle but distinctive, slightly nutty flavor and a smooth, soft texture. Use as a spread or cooking fat.

Ghee
A traditional Indian dairy product, ghee is made by clarifying and cooking butter to remove its excess water content. Once solidified, the resultant smooth, creamy yellow paste has a rich, nutty flavor. Ghee can be stored at room temperature for several weeks and has a far higher burning point than butter, making it a useful cooking fat. Use in curries, lentil dishes, Indian desserts; or spread on Indian breads, such as rotis.

CLASSIC RECIPE

HOLLANDAISE SAUCE

A quick version of a versatile sauce.

MAKES ABOUT 1 CUP

1 tbsp white wine vinegar

juice of ½ lemon

3 large egg yolks

sprinkle of salt and freshly ground white pepper

12 tbsp (1½ sticks) butter, cut into pieces

1 Put the vinegar and lemon juice in a small saucepan. Bring to a boil and remove from the heat.

2 Meanwhile, place the egg yolks in a food processor or blender, season with a little salt and pepper, and process for 1 minute. With the motor running, slowly add the vinegar and lemon juice mixture.

3 Put the butter in the same saucepan and warm over low heat until melted. When the butter begins to foam, remove from the heat. With the motor of the food processor still running, gradually add the butter to form a thick emulsion. Serve immediately.

Beurre d'Echiré
Protected by an Appellation D'Origine Contrôlée, this French lactic butter is produced traditionally from cows grazed within a 12 mile distance of the village of Echiré, in the Deux-Sèvres region of France. Made in small quantities, this butter is valued for its distinctive, delicate flavor and soft texture. Use as a spread or as a cooking fat, excellent for making puff pastry.

FRESH CHEESES

Ready to eat within a few days, or even hours, of being made, fresh cheeses are so young that most barely have time to develop any more than a whisper of the milk's potential flavor. This does not mean they are bland. On the contrary, subtle flavors can be coaxed from the milk: the sweet, grassy notes of cow's milk; the aromatic, herbaceous character of goat's milk; the richness of ewe's milk; or the leathery, earthy undertones of buffalo's milk. Fresh cheeses are easy to recognize because they are very white, usually shiny, and have no rind. Beyond these defining characteristics, however, there is much variety among them, particularly in terms of texture, which ranges from soft, crumbly, spreadable, or creamy to firm and sliceable.

🔒 **BUY** With the highest moisture content of all types of cheese, they have a very short shelf life, unless they have been pickled in brine or oil. If possible before buying, check that they have a fresh aroma and appearance.

🗄 **STORE** Keep tightly covered in the fridge and use as soon as possible after purchase.

⬤ **EAT** Fresh: They are the basis of many spreads and cocktail dips, and a wide variety of desserts. Cheeses decorated, rolled, or dusted in ash, herbs, or spices are superb additions to a cheeseboard. **Cooked:** Fresh cheeses can be baked in a dish or broiled. They tend to fall apart or split in sauces and become tough if broiled for too long.

FLAVOR PAIRINGS Fresh and dried fruits, Mediterranean vegetables such as tomatoes, spinach, olives.

CLASSIC RECIPES Boreks; *insalata tricolore*; Greek salad; spinach and ricotta ravioli; pizza and calzone; *mozzarella en carozza; melanzane alla Parmigiana*; smoked salmon and cream cheese bagels; *mattar paneer; liptauer; topfennockerl*; tiramisu; cannoli; *coeur à la crème*.

Gjetost
The color of French mustard and the texture of fudge, this is not to everyone's taste, but Norwegians love its sweet caramel and peanut-butter flavors, and its unique aromatic, goaty taste.

If you find the taste of feta too salty, simply soak in cold water or milk for 10–15 minutes.

Boursin
Rich Normandy milk and cream make this a moist yet creamy, sweet, and very rich cheese with a touch of acidity. It simply melts in the mouth like ice cream.

Boursin may be made with a carefully balanced mix of garlic and herbs, or rolled in fiery, cracked pepper.

Beyaz Peynir
Depending on the area, producer, season, and milk used to make it, this feta-like cheese can vary from strong to mild, salty to very salty, and hard to soft. It plays a major role in Turkish cuisine.

When frying, do not use any oil, since this seals the cheese and the crunchy caramel crust will not form as easily.

Halloumi
To make this Cypriot cheese the curds are kneaded by hand to remove excess whey, which produces a firm, dense texture that is easy to cut. It is the kneading that gives halloumi its unique ability to keep its shape and not melt when cooked.

Crescenza

This delicate, moist Italian cheese derives its name from the Latin carsenza, meaning "flat bread," because when it is kept in a warm place the cheese ferments, swelling up like rising bread and bursting through its thin rind.

The coating of toasted oats enhances the flavor and adds a pleasant texture.

Caboc

A traditional Scottish cheese made from cream-enriched milk that has curdled naturally without rennet, this is very rich, smooth, and buttery. It has a nutty taste but slightly sharp finish like soured cream.

Feta PDO

Consumed at every meal in Greece, this popular cheese is firm yet easily crumbled. If made with goat's milk, it is very white, with a fresh taste that hints of wild herbs; ivory-white ewe's-milk feta is slightly richer and creamier. Feta does not melt completely when baked or broiled.

Cream cheese

Mild and velvety-smooth cream cheese has a fresh lemony zing, making it perfect to spread on bagels, toast, or your favorite cracker. It has one of the highest fat contents of all cheese, which is why it tastes so good. Low-fat versions may contain whey powder, giving them a slightly grainy feel.

Innes Button may be coated with herbs, ash, pink peppercorns, or chopped nuts.

Innes Button

This tiny, unpasteurized British goat cheese is soft and almost mousselike, melting in the mouth to release its lemony freshness with hints of walnuts and white wine on the finish. Spread on bread, or broil.

Fromage Frais

As the name implies this is a very fresh and therefore very simple cheese. After draining, the soft curd is shaped, salted, and served. Fromage Blanc is similar but smoother.

CLASSIC RECIPE

BOREKS

These cigar-shaped cheese pastries from Turkey are seen on Middle Eastern menus all over the world.

MAKES 24

4 tbsp butter, melted

8 fresh or thawed frozen sheets of filo dough

1 ½ cups finely crumbled feta cheese

1 tsp dried mint or 1 tbsp chopped fresh mint

pinch of grated nutmeg

freshly ground black pepper

1 Preheat the oven to 350°F (180°C). Combine the feta, mint, and nutmeg, and season with pepper. Brush a large baking sheet with some of the butter and set aside.

2 Lay the filo sheets on top of each other and cut into three long strips, each 4 in (10 cm) wide. Keep the dough covered with plastic wrap.

3 Working with one strip of dough at a time, brush with butter.

4 Place a heaping teaspoon of the cheese mixture at one end of a dough strip. Roll into a cylinder, stopping after rolling up about one-third; then fold in the long sides of the dough to enclose the filling completely, and finish rolling. Make sure the ends are tightly sealed. Arrange the pastries seam-side down and about 1 in (2.5 cm) apart on the prepared baking sheet. Keep the formed pastries covered with plastic wrap as you work.

5 Bake for 10–12 minutes, or until crisp and golden. Serve hot or warm.

FRESH CHEESES (CONTINUED)

INSALATA TRICOLORE

Named for the three colors of the Italian flag, the main ingredients of this salad are always buffalo mozzarella, tomatoes, and basil.

SERVES 4

1 firm but ripe avocado
juice of ½ lemon
4 firm but ripe tomatoes, thinly sliced
8oz (250g) drained fresh buffalo mozzarella, thinly sliced
12 fresh basil leaves, torn
4 small handfuls wild arugula
olive oil
coarse sea salt
freshly ground black pepper

1 Halve the avocado and remove the pit, then peel and slice. Toss with the lemon juice immediately to prevent browning.

2 Arrange the tomatoes, mozzarella, and avocado attractively in rings on 4 small salad plates, halving any larger slices of cheese. Scatter the torn basil leaves over the top.

3 Put a small handful of arugula in the center of each ring. Drizzle all over with olive oil and sprinkle with coarse sea salt. Add a good grinding of black pepper and serve immediately.

Tupí
An ancient Catalan shepherd's recipe, this spread is made from fresh and cured cheeses, blended with olive oil and brandy or liqueur. It is a strangely compulsive cheese, with the texture of oatmeal, a very strong pungent flavor, and a slightly fetid aroma. It is not a cheese for the faint-hearted.

Paneer
An integral part of numerous Indian dishes, this is one of the few cheeses indigenous to the Indian subcontinent, where most milk is used to make yogurt or ice cream. Similar in texture to feta but not as crumbly, it is only lightly salted. Lemon juice, not rennet, is used to curdle the milk for paneer, so it is suitable for vegetarians.

Queso blanco
Simply meaning "white cheese," this is popular throughout Mexico and Latin America. It is like a cross between salty cottage cheese and mozzarella, with a buttery, mild flavor and firm, elastic texture. Use to top spicy dishes such as enchiladas and empanadas.

Mozzarella di Bufala PDO
Mozzarella is made around the world and varies from lush, juicy, pure white balls to yellow, rubbery blocks of cow's milk, suitable for family pizzas. But none can match mozzarella di bufala PDO, made with milk from the handsome water buffalo of Campania.

Labane
Throughout the Middle East, this deliciously rich and velvety smooth cheese is made in many households by draining thick, full-fat yogurt overnight in a cloth. It is traditionally eaten at breakfast, or served with olive oil, fresh local herbs, pine nuts, and pitta bread.

Pant-Ys-Gawn
Named after the family farm in Wales where it was first made, this goat's-milk cheese is available with or without fresh herbs. It is smooth and creamy in texture and refreshing with a mild, goaty finish. Spread it thickly on crusty bread.

Sussex Slipcote
The name derives from an Old English word meaning a "little" (slip) piece of "cottage" (cote) cheese. It is very moist and almost mousselike, with a lemony fresh tang that finishes with sweet notes typical of ewe's milk. Best spread on bread or crackers, it is also a good addition to a baked potato or other baked vegetable dish.

This garlic-and-herb variety is perfect for crumbling generously over a warm baked potato.

Mascarpone
Known to have been a favorite of Napoleon, this smooth and wickedly rich Italian cheese is made by heating cream and allowing it to separate or curdle naturally, at which point the whey is drained off. The sweet, lemony taste and buttery aroma make it ideal for use in desserts and a perfect partner for tart fruits. Mascarpone is a key ingredient in the famous Italian dessert, tiramisu.

Ricotta
Unlike other cheeses, this is named after the cheesemaking process: in Italian, ricotta means "cooked twice" because the cheese is made by reheating the whey left over from making hard cheeses. Milky, with a touch of acidity, it has a delicate lemony aroma. Some ricotta is pressed and salted or smoked. Use in baked pasta dishes, and creamy desserts.

AGED FRESH CHEESES

As the name suggests, these are fresh cheeses that are aged in caves or cellars. Molds and yeasts grow on the rinds, and the cheeses lose moisture and shrink, causing the rinds to wrinkle. Like all cheeses, each develops its own individual character. Varying in shape, from small rounds and pyramids, to cones, bells, and logs, the cheeses are often covered in herbs, spices, or ash, or wrapped in vine or chestnut leaves, over which the molds grow. Mostly goat cheeses, they are moist, creamy, and aromatic when young, gradually becoming more crumbly in texture and nutty tasting, then turning dense, flaky, and brittle with a sharp flavor as they mature. When made with cow's, or ewe's milk, the cheeses are typically softer and sweeter.

BUY The best-known aged fresh cheeses are made in the Loire in France—you see them in small, straw-lined wooden boxes on rickety tables in French markets—but they are increasingly being produced around the world. They are sold at varying stages of ripeness, depending on the taste and preference of the purchaser: the best way to buy is from a good cheesemonger and take their advice.

STORE Aged fresh cheeses are sold ready to eat, so it is best to enjoy them the same day you buy them or the next. Keep in an airtight container in a cool, moist place or the fridge.

EAT Fresh: No cheeseboard is truly complete without one of these attractive, rustic-looking cheeses.
Cooked: Slice, drizzle with olive oil, and broil or bake on rounds of crisp baguette. An aged fresh cheese, such as Crottin de Chavignol, is wonderfully nutty and aromatic prepared this way.
FLAVOR PAIRINGS Crusty or fruity bread, peppery salad leaves such as arugula, celery, endive, dried fruit, walnuts.
CLASSIC RECIPE Chévre salad.

The edible crust is made up of rosemary, thyme, juniper berries, and small, pungent chiles.

Fleur de Maquis
The name of this unusual ewe's-milk cheese, which means "flower of the maquis", refers to the Corsican landscape. The crunchy, aromatic crust is a perfect partner for the tender cheese and the overall taste is rather honeyed.

Holy Goat La Luna
From Australia, this very creamy, hand-made goat cheese has deliciously complex, lingering nutty flavors. Made in a ring shape, a barrel shape, or a small "baby," it is sometimes wrapped in chestnut leaves.

As aging progresses, the chestnut leaves dry and the cheese softens.

Bouton-de-Culotte

The smallest of the French cheeses, whose name means "pants button," this is traditionally made in the late summer and stored through fall for winter use, when it is hard enough to be grated into the pungent local cheese, fromage fort.

Banon AOC

Sold rustically wrapped in chestnut leaves and bound with raffia, the flavor of this French goat cheese is mild and lactic at first, changing to slightly nutty and then developing a distinct goaty tang.

Chabichou du Poitou AOC

The attractive, wrinkled white rind dusted with gray, yellow, and blue molds conceals a French cheese with a firm to almost brittle texture and nutty-to-strong goaty flavor that intensifies as it ages and dries out.

Pérail

This French cheese has a less assertive flavor than most ewe's-milk cheeses, probably because of its rather short aging period. But it is still identifiably nutty, with a smooth texture and tender rind. Try it with dried figs and new season's walnuts.

The paprika coating on the rind gives a hot, peppery bite.

Boulette d'Avesnes

Made in France with the fresh curds of Maroilles cheese, mashed with herbs and spices, this is spicy and sharp. A shot of gin will bring out the unusual combination of flavors.

Crottin de Chavignol AOC

This is the classic Loire goat cheese sold across the world. Known for its pungent taste, it can be eaten at various stages: when young it is tender in texture, becoming harder, crumbly, and sharp as it ages.

AGED FRESH CHEESES (CONTINUED)

The coating of ground, locally grown pecans adds a crunchy texture and nutty flavor.

Pecan Chèvre
This creamy goat cheese from Georgia in the United States is fairly strong, with a tart bite to the rind as it ages. It is best served young—ideal with ripe peaches.

The distinctive rind is covered in gray and black molds.

Monte Enebro
The flavor of this Spanish artisan goat cheese matures over time from a light citric creaminess to an assertive, pungent bite. Add it to a beet salad, or deep-fry in tempura batter and serve with orange-blossom honey.

Pouligny Saint Pierre is nicknamed "the Pyramid" and "the Eiffel Tower" because of its shape.

Pouligny Saint-Pierre AOC
Moist, soft, and crumbly, the flavor of this French goat cheese changes with age from citrussy to nutty to pungent and goaty. Like all aged fresh cheeses it is superb for a cheeseboard or broiled.

Saint-Marcellin
This pale and creamy cheese has been made in homes and small farms in the Dauphiné region of France for centuries. Traditionally produced from goat's milk, today all but a handful are made from cow's milk. It is superb when baked.

The interior is firm to creamy, almost liquid, with a light, subtle lemony freshness and a nutty aroma.

Rocamadour AOC
With a tender and creamy rind and interior, this French goat cheese tastes mild and slightly milky, but has a delicious sweet and nutty aftertaste. Serve it with fresh, ripe figs.

Wabash Cannonball
This firm and slightly dry North American goat cheese from Indiana has a goaty flavor with a lemony tang. The ash-dusted rind lends a pleasant muskiness and the finish is rich and buttermilky. It is ideal with dried fruit and sparkling wine.

Bleu des Causses is similar to Roquefort but made with cow's milk rather than ewe's.

BLUE CHEESES

Unlike their white counterparts, blue molds grow inside a cheese: in ideal damp, cool conditions, they can enter through cracks in the rind. Today, however, the mold is typically added to the milk in powder form, and then after a few weeks the young cheese is pierced to allow air to enter and the mold to turn blue. The blue molds create an array of wonderful cheeses offering extraordinary variety in flavor and texture. All blue cheeses have a spicy, slightly metallic tang and often taste saltier than other cheeses, but individually they range from creamy and mellow, to sweet and herbaceous, to dense and buttery, and to luscious and gooey. Most European blues are wrapped in foil, ensuring their rinds remain damp and sticky and to slow down the development of too much mold on the surface. Their moist interiors develop wide, uneven streaks and pockets of blue. Traditional British blues have dry, rough, crusty, orange-brown rinds, often splashed with blue and gray molds. They develop a dense, more compact texture and when pierced grow thinner, longer streaks that look like shattered porcelain when cut. There are also blues with soft-white rinds, but the blue molds must be injected into the young cheeses because they are too creamy and dense for the mold to spread naturally.

🔒 **BUY** The rind of foil-wrapped blues should be moist but not overly wet and soggy. Crusty rinds should generally be dry and uncracked; some may be slightly sticky.

📦 **STORE** If you have a large chunk it is best stored in a cool, airy cheese "safe." Otherwise, wrap in wax paper and keep in an airtight container in the fridge.

⊙ **EAT** Fresh: A blue cheese is essential on any cheeseboard and good with walnut bread. A drizzle of honey brings out the subtlety of the cheese. With the exception of the soft-white or brie-style blues, it can add another dimension to salads: try it crumbled over flageolet (kidney) beans, walnuts, and peppery arugula dressed with honeyed vinaigrette. **Cooked:** Stir small amounts into a creamy sauce to serve with broiled steak. Toss with hot pasta and pine nuts, or use in a stuffing for pasta shapes. Flavor soups, soufflés, and savory mousses. Crumble over pizza. **FLAVOR PAIRINGS** Walnuts, honey, peppery salad leaves such as arugula and watercress, celery, endive, pears. **CLASSIC RECIPES** Blue cheese dressing; Stilton and celery soup; galettes au Roquefort.

Barkham Blue
The buttery consistency of Channel Islands milk, which colors the interior deep yellow, characterizes this excellent cow's milk cheese that looks as good as it tastes. It is a blue for anyone who usually avoids blue cheese.

Beenleigh Blue
One of a very few British blue cheeses made from ewe's milk, this is rich, sweet, and slightly crumbly, with hints of burned caramel. The rough exterior has a slight stickiness. Use in a salad or serve on its own.

Gippsland Blue
This was the first artisan Australian blue. Rich and creamy, it is at its best from late fall to early summer, when it develops a soft and sticky texture that is punctuated with steely blue veins.

Bleu des Causses AOC
Aged longer than most blues, in natural caves in the limestone plateaux of the Causses, the flavor of this French cow's-milk cheese differs depending on the season in which it is produced. Ivory-yellow summer cheeses are milder than the stronger tasting, white winter cheeses.

Bleu d'Auvergne AOC
Named after the province in France in which it originated, this has a very sharp, engaging flavor and makes a delicious addition to salad dressings, hot pasta dishes, or salads of endive, nuts, and raw mushrooms.

BLUE CHEESES (CONTINUED)

Fourme d'Ambert AOC
One of the oldest cheeses in France, this has a very pronounced flavor, with a well-rounded, spicy tang. The texture is creamy, bold, and rich, while the aroma gives a hint of the cellar in which it is aged. Try it with a sweet Sauternes or Banyuls.

Danablu or Danish Blue
Invented in Denmark in the early 20th century, this is now popular worldwide. With deep purple-blue streaks, it has a smooth yet crumbly, moist texture, and a full flavor with a sharp, salty, almost metallic blue bite and creamy finish.

Cabrales DOP
This very strong, artisan cheese, heavily streaked with blue veins, is matured in the mold-rich caves of the isolated Picos de Europa mountains in Spain. Although the cheese's aroma is a touch fetid, a smooth creaminess comes through.

Cashel Blue
One of Ireland's best-loved cheeses, this cow's-milk blue is soft and silky. The medium flavor has a gentle buzz from the mold veining. It is great melted into colcannon, or crumbled into salads or a smooth celery soup.

Blue Monday is the only blue cheese in the world produced in squares, instead of cylinders.

Blue Monday
Soft and creamy, this cube-shaped Scottish blue cheese has a surprisingly mild spicy flavor with a kick of malt and chocolate.

Dorset Blue Vinny
Once upon a time, every self-respecting Dorset farmhouse made this cheese—an excellent use for milk left over from making butter. As it is unpasteurized and the butterfat content of the milk varies according to the time of year, this British cheese is sometimes crumbly and sometimes creamy. It is nutty but not too strong. Try with traditional Dorset crackers and sweet cider.

Dolcelatte

Meaning "sweet milk," this has a luscious, melting-ice-cream feel to it. It was created for those who find the more traditional blues too robust and spicy and prefer softer, milder flavors. Made only in factories, it may also be labeled Gorgonzola Dolcelatte. At its best melted over pasta.

Bleu de Gex Haut-Jura AOC

This unusually dense, almost hard, blue cheese is produced in small French dairies using milk from cows grazing the pastures of the Jura mountains. The soft interior has a speckled blue appearance and a slightly bitter, savory flavor.

Cornish Blue

With a creamy texture like Gorgonzola and thick streaks of blue, this English cheese is surprisingly mild and sweet, becoming spicier and tangier as it ages. It is perfect for pepping up—but not overpowering—risottos, sauces, and appetizers, and goes beautifully with fruit.

Serve as the locals do, with boiled potatoes and a fruity, regional red wine.

Roquefort AOC

This famous French ewe's-milk blue is one of the world's finest cheeses. There are only seven producers in the world, each using the same basic process, yet each achieves a cheese with its own distinct and individual character. When fully aged, the flavor is spicy, strong, and mouth-watering. Sadly, some Roquefort is consumed too young, when there is barely a hint of blue and no bite, and the texture is crumbly rather than cohesive.

BLUE CHEESES (CONTINUED)

Buffalo Blue
Milk from a British herd of water buffalo is used to make this cheese. Paler than a cow's-milk cheese and creamier, it has an earthy taste, while the streaks of purple-blue mold give it a tang and slightly salty finish.

Meredith Blue
The first Australian ewe's-milk blue, this is hand-made and matured in old shipping containers next to the dairy. Since ewe's milk is highly seasonal, the cheese is at its best in early spring, when the soft ivory interior texture develops dark pockets of salty blue molds.

Stilton PDO
Stilton was named after the place where it was made famous (the Bell Inn in Stilton), rather than where it was first made (the nearby town of Melton Mowbray). It is one of a handful of British cheeses granted Protected Designation of Origin (PDO) status by the European Commission. Stilton is sharp and aggressive when eaten too young, but mellows out to a rich, buttery taste with hints of cocoa on the finish, and sometimes a touch of walnuts.

Shropshire Blue
Despite its name, this was actually first created in Scotland. Based on the recipe for Stilton, it is milder but equally creamy, and its streaks of blue stand out against the orange interior. There is a hint of caramel sweetness behind its spicy tang. Crumble into salads, or melt into soups.

The uneven and erratically spread streaks and patches of blue mold impart a spicy flavor to the rich, creamy cheese.

Gorgonzola DOP
Thought to be the first blue cheese, with an origin steeped in folklore and legend, everything about Italian Gorgonzola is sexy: its rustic yet elegant appearance, its melt-in-the-mouth texture, its musky aroma, and its sweet, spicy tang. Today, it can only be made by approved producers, with cow's milk (usually pasteurized) from designated areas in Italy. Toss into salads, or add to sauces and dips.

Cambozola

Also called Bavaria Blu and Bresse Bleu, this German cheese is a fusion of Camembert and Gorgonzola. Considerably milder than both, it has a very rich, creamy taste and subtle spicy finish. A perfect cheese for the cheeseboard.

Rogue River Blue

With great depth of flavor, this blue from Oregon is firm, yet moist and smooth in the mouth. It is less salty than many blues, and is creamy and sweet with a spicy finish. It is superb with desserts such as poached pears or calvados soufflé.

Rogue River Blue is wrapped in grape leaves and soaked in pear brandy.

The interior should be straw yellow, not brown or dull, and the rind rough and crusty with the pierced holes quite visible.

BLUE CHEESE DRESSING

An American favorite to accompany anything from steak to green salad. Use a blue cheese that crumbles easily, such as Gorgonzola, Rogue River Blue, or Roquefort, and avoid blues with a soft white rind like Cambozola.

MAKES ABOUT 2 CUPS

1 cup mayonnaise
½ cup sour cream
3 tbsp milk
1 tbsp cider vinegar
1 small garlic clove, crushed through a press
1 cup crumbled blue cheese
salt and freshly ground black pepper

1 Combine all the ingredients, except salt and pepper, in a bowl. Using a balloon whisk, or a handheld electric mixer, beat together until fairly smooth but still with some tiny lumps of cheese visible. Season to taste with salt and pepper.

2 Cover and refrigerate, preferably overnight, to allow the flavors to develop. Refrigerate any unused dressing for up to 1 week.

Maytag Blue

Despite high demand, this North American cow's-milk blue is still produced by hand, as it was when it was first made in 1941. Although cave-aged, it always remains white on the outside. The flavor is enigmatic: initially creamy and steely blue, it yields to a lemon-tartlike sweet—sourness on the finish. It is perfect for salads, melted on to steak, or baked into fruit-based desserts.

*The more **blue–black veins** of mold that run through a blue cheese, the tangier and sharper the flavor.*

SOFT WHITE CHEESES

Typical characteristics of this type of cheese are a white crust; a texture that is slightly chalky when young, becoming soft and creamy when mature, almost runny, and a subtle-to-distinct aroma of mushrooms. Cheeses made with ewe's milk have a subtle sweetness, while those made with goat's milk taste of almonds or even marzipan. Factory-made varieties tend to have a thick, velvety rind that seems more like a wrapping than an integral part of the cheese. In contrast, artisan examples grow a thinner white crust that can be stained with reddish pigments or yellow-gray blotches of mold. The coat protects the cheese from drying out and speeds up the ripening process, which is why these are sometimes called mold-ripened cheeses.

BUY They are best eaten within a few days of purchase as refrigeration will dry them out. If the rind beneath the wrapping looks wet and sticky, the chances are that the cheese is too ripe.

STORE Keep in the original paper or wax paper rather than plastic wrap, which prevents the cheese from breathing. Ideally, store large pieces and whole cheeses in a pantry; otherwise, keep in the fridge. Don't be alarmed by any edible white mold that grows down the cut surface—this just tells you the cheese is alive and merely trying to protect its soft interior from drying out.

EAT Fresh: These wonderful cheeses are at their very best when served at room temperature with crusty bread and a glass of wine.

Cooked: Bake small, whole cheeses for about 15 minutes, then scoop out the molten interior with chunks of bread or raw vegetables. Or cut off the rind and then broil on bread or a croissant, perhaps layered with roasted peppers or sweet chutney.

FLAVOR PAIRINGS Fresh and dried fruits, nuts, celery, carrots.

CLASSIC RECIPE Camembert en boîte.

Green Peppercorn Chèvre
Firm and crumbly, this goat cheese made in New York state has a lemony freshness that is perfectly accented by the green peppercorn flavor. The finish is delicate and clean. Ideal with a summer salad of fresh greens and ripe tomatoes.

Camembert de Normandie AOC
One of the most famous French cheeses, this comes packed in a wooden box. By its AOC status, it must be made with raw milk. The flavor is fruity, with a slight aroma of mushrooms and mold. Locals prefer it when the heart is white and not yet creamy.

Coeur de Neufchâtel AOC
As its name suggests, this French cheese is heart shaped, although it can also be found as a small cylinder or brick, when it is simply called Neufchâtel. The interior is firm but slightly grainy, with a subtle milk taste and salty tang. Locals like to melt it on warm bread to eat for breakfast.

Lucullus
Produced in Normandy and named after a famous Roman general and gourmet, this has a wickedly rich, luxurious feel in the mouth and a nutty flavor. Eat on crackers or crusty bread. The high cream content means it is more stable than other soft white cheese, so it will keep longer in the fridge.

Brie de Melun AOC
Unlike other Bries, the coagulation of the curd relies mainly on lactic fermentation rather than rennet. This French cheese can be sold young, when it is lemony fresh, or fully mature, when it has a very fruity flavor and a strong scent of fermentation.

The white rind is covered in fine, dried strands of summer grasses, herbs, and meadow flowers.

Pithiviers

This French cow's-milk cheese is soft with a slight fragrance of meadow flowers and mushrooms, exuding a tangy flavor.

Brie de Meaux AOC

Made in the region of Ile-de-France, Le Roi des Fromages ("The King of Cheeses") can trace its history back to Emperor Charlemagne. Today, it is enjoyed the world over. It is probably the strongest of all the soft white cheeses and becomes more intense with age. If it smells strongly of ammonia, then it will deliver a vicious bite.

At its peak, Brie has a glossy, soft interior that oozes irresistibly toward you, and a characteristic savory and mushroom taste.

CAMEMBERT EN BOÎTE

Baking cheese in its own package is a great innovation; but you will need cheese that comes in a wooden box rather than cardboard. The vermouth and thyme add delicious aromas.

SERVES 2–4

| 1 8-to 9-ounce (250g) wheel of Camembert in its wooden box |
| 1 garlic clove, halved |
| 2 tsp white vermouth or dry white wine |
| 1 tsp olive oil |
| 2 tsp chopped fresh thyme |
| freshly ground black pepper |
| French bread, heated |

1 Preheat the oven to 400°F (200°C). Unwrap the cheese and rub the surface with the garlic; discard the garlic. Return the cheese (unwrapped) to the box. Set it on a baking sheet.

2 Make small holes all over the top of the cheese with a skewer. Carefully drizzle with the vermouth and oil, spreading them out with a spoon.

3 Sprinkle with the thyme and season with pepper. Replace the lid of the box. Bake for 25 minutes, or until the cheese is soft and melted in the center.

4 Remove the lid, set the open box on a heatproof plate, and place in the center of the table. Serve immediately with chunks of warm, crusty French bread for dipping (eat the crust, too).

SOFT WHITE CHEESES (CONTINUED)

Gaperon
Traditionally in the Auvergne, France, the number of Gaperons hanging in the kitchen was an indication of a farmer's wealth. An unusual cheese in both texture and shape, it is made with skimmed milk and mixed with garlic and peppercorns.

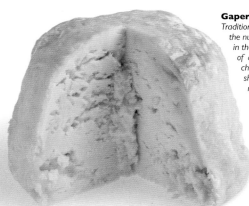

Reminiscent of Brie, Sharpham is best matched with a red wine produced on the same estate.

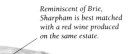

The moist interior becomes almost runny just beneath the rind.

Sharpham
Made in Devon, England, this is firm and slightly grainy when young but gradually softens from the outside in as it ripens. The flavor is slightly salty and creamy with some mushroom character on the finish.

Flower Marie
Made in East Sussex, England, the sweetness of ewe's milk gives this artisan cheese a caramel subtlety, while the soft rind has a mushroomy taste and aroma. Spread on a chunk of fresh, crusty bread.

Capricorn Goat
Eaten young, this cheese from Somerset, England, has a slight nutty flavor; however, as it ripens, it develops a salty sweetness and becomes softer and creamier. Slice and broil on roast vegetables or simply savor with a glass of white wine or pale ale.

Brillat-Savarin
Named after a renowned 18th-century gourmand, this triple-cream French cow's milk cheese has a fat content of 75 percent for every 3½oz (100g). When young, it has no rind and a texture like thick crème fraîche; if eaten once it has developed its thin, white coat, the texture becomes luscious, creamy, and soft.

Little Wallop
This English goat's-milk cheese is washed in Somerset cider brandy and wrapped in vine leaves. When young, it exudes a mild, creamy freshness, which later matures into a nutty, distinctly goaty complexity with a hint of yeast and fermenting apples from the cider. It will grace any cheeseboard.

The curds are sprinkled with black vine ash before the rind starts to grow. When the cheese matures, the rind is unpalatably peppery hot.

Woodside Edith
Taking its name from the Frenchwoman who provided the original recipe, this Australian goat's milk cheese is deliciously nutty when young. It ages gracefully as the chalky center gradually breaks down to a smooth, clotted texture. It is ideal on a cheeseboard.

Gratte-Paille
The white rind of this triple-cream French cheese bears the imprint of the straw mats on which it is ripened. When young, the richness is delicious with strawberries. With age, it develops a slightly aggressive, lingering tang and is best enjoyed on its own.

Chaource AOC
The creamy texture and milky, fruity flavor, with a faint aroma of mushrooms, becomes sharper and salty as this French cheese ages. When mature, it matches well with its local wine, Champagne.

Ragstone
Ragstone Ridge in Kent, England, lends its name to this English goat's-milk cheese. It is creamy yet light on the tongue, with a hint of mushroomy notes and a lemony tang. Since it slices easily into rings, it is ideal for broiling and baking, to be served warm and oozy on a bed of leaves.

Constant Bliss
This is a rarity, because soft raw-milk cheeses are typically unavailable in the US. Made in Vermont, it has a salty, buttery, almost popcornlike flavor. With age, it becomes soft and rich, but not runny.

SEMI-SOFT CHEESES

Semi-soft cheeses vary in appearance and texture more than any other cheese type, but they can be divided into two broad styles: dry rind and washed rind. Dry-rind cheeses are typically washed in brine once or twice and range from springy, mild, sweet, and nutty with barely formed rinds to rubbery, floral, and pungent with thick, leathery rinds. Washed-rind cheeses are dipped frequently in baths of brine and as a result they have wet, sticky, pale orange to russet-red rinds; the more they are washed, the softer, stickier, and smellier the rind. The cheeses are softer than the dry-rind style and have a pungent, savory, smoky, even meaty taste and aroma. The texture of both tends to be grainy, with a softening just under the rind when the cheese is young, becoming soft, supple, or even runny with age. The washed-rind type includes those cheeses known as Trappist or monastery-style.

🔒 **BUY** Once cut, semi-soft cheeses do not continue to ripen, so buy them when they have reached the degree of ripeness you prefer and eat promptly.

🗄 **STORE** Dry-rind cheese keep well in the fridge, but those with washed rinds will dry out and become bitter if kept too cold for too long.

⬤ **EAT** Fresh: Mild semi-soft cheeses such as Edam or Havarti are classic breakfast cheeses, while the stronger varieties are essential on any cheeseboard. **Cooked:** Dry-rind cheeses are superb when broiled

because their rubbery texture stretches but holds its shape; conversely, for this reason, they do not work well in sauces. Washed-rind cheeses, however, melt superbly in sauces. When they are baked whole, they become sweeter and more savory, which makes them an amazing appetizer.

FLAVOR PAIRINGS Sweet-pickled onions and cornichons, sweet chutneys, dried fruit.

CLASSIC RECIPES *Raclette; fonduta.*

Caciotta
Made throughout Italy, using every type of milk, Caciotta is sold as a fresh cheese or semi-soft. Mild and sweet when made using cow's milk, it is intense, buttery, and mushroomy when made with ewe's or goat's milk, or a mix.

Havarti
Probably Denmark's most famous cheese, Havarti is sweet, mellow, and very creamy. Some contain caraway seeds. This great snacking cheese is ideal for open-faced sandwiches, slicing and broiling, or in salads.

Azeitão DOP
This rustic-looking ewe's-milk cheese hails from Portugal. It has a very delicate, sweet, slightly acidic taste, with fatty spice on the finish. Cut open the top, scoop out the runny cheese, dollop into mini pastry shells, and sprinkle with oregano to serve with an apéritif, or eat with nutty bread.

Azeitão is molded in cloth before being washed in brine.

Epoisses de Bourgogne AOC
This great French washed-rind cheese was created in the 16th century. Young Epoisses Frais is firm, moist, and slightly grainy with a mild savory tang, while Epoisses Affiné has an intense flavor, a pungent spicy aroma, and a velvety texture. Cooking brings out its sweeter side.

Torta Extremeñas
Lush Spanish tortas, with their near liquid interiors, have a distinctive earthy flavor. There are three versions from Extremadura: Torta de Barros (pictured), Torta del Casar, and Torta La Serena. It is delicious served warm from the oven, with breadsticks for scooping out the interior.

Ardrahan
One of Ireland's best-loved washed-rind cheeses, this is supple, dense, and creamy, with a sweet—savory taste that intensifies with age. It melts superbly.

Jarlsberg is recognizable by its large, round holes and lemon-yellow color.

Jarlsberg
Norwegian Jarlsberg was modeled on Emmental but is more supple, sweeter, and less nutty. It is a very versatile cheese—great in sandwiches and salads, or melted like raclette and served with crudités.

Chimay à la Bière
This is made by Cistercian monks in Belgium, who also make the Chimay Trappist beer in which it is washed. The firm, leathery rind has a heady aroma of hops, while the creamy, supple interior is fruity, with a distinct taste of toasted hops. A superb melting cheese.

The attractive sticky rind gives the cheese a smoky-bacon tang.

Edam has a thin rind beneath the distinctive red waxed coat.

Carré de l'Est
As its name suggests (it means "square of the east"), this French washed-rind cheese is square in shape. Soft and grainy when young, it becomes almost liquid when mature. It has a pleasantly salty flavor.

Edam
Familiar the world over, Edam has a smooth, supple, elastic texture and sweet, buttery flavor, becoming more flavorsome and firmer with age. It is equally at home as a snack, in sandwiches, broiled, grated, or served at breakfast with chocolate and eggs, as they do in the Netherlands.

Fontina PDO
This exceptional Italian cheese has a sticky washed rind and a supple interior with a mild, nutty flavor. It is famously used in a fonduta, a dish in which the cheese is whipped with eggs and cream.

Chevrotin
Washed-rind French Chevrotin is similar to Reblochon, except that it is made with goat's milk. Chevrotin des Aravis AOC (pictured) has a subtle, aromatic goaty flavor. Creamy, sweet farmhouse Chevrotin des Bauges AOC has a thick, rustic rind and a smooth, melting interior with small, irregular eyes.

SEMI-SOFT CHEESES (CONTINUED)

The rind is washed regularly with brine and finally with the local brandy, marc de Bourgogne.

Ami du Chambertin
Created in France in 1950 to accompany the famous wine, Gevrey-Chambertin, made close by, this has a powerful meaty, pungent taste and a creamy texture.

Tomme de Savoie
The many cheeses or "tommes" of Savoie range in flavor from mild and milky to nutty with a savory tang, and have a herbaceous or farmyard aroma. Some are flavored with herbs or spices.

Langres AOC
This strong-smelling French cheese tastes a little spicy when young. The texture changes with age, starting grainy and becoming very creamy, sticky, and melt in the mouth.

Livarot's nickname, "the Colonel," comes from the five strips of sedge grass, or tape, around the cheese: they resemble the stripes on military uniforms that denote rank.

Livarot AOC
One of the ancient cheeses of Normandy, a good Livarot should have a firm, slightly sticky rind, a strong, very pungent aroma, and a savory, spicy flavor.

Reblochon de Savoie AOC
When young, this supple French cheese has the sweetness of stolen fruit; as it matures it is no longer sweet but tastes of freshly pickled walnuts with a hint of mountain flowers. It is traditionally served with crusty pain de campagne, local charcuterie, and pickled gherkins.

Monterey Jack
Known colloquially as "Jack," this is one of the best-loved North American cheeses. When young it is very mild, with a lactic taste and is sometimes flavored with spices, pimientoes, or jalapeños peppers.

A band of spruce bark encircles the cheese inside its round box.

Mont d'Or AOC
Made in the mountains that lie on the French–Swiss border, this has the most voluptuous texture of almost any cheese and can be spooned straight from the box in which it is sold. Just roll back the thick rind and enjoy the sweet, earthy flavor.

Palet de Bourgogne
The rind of this strongly scented Burgundian cheese is washed every two days with brine and marc de Bourgogne. Smooth and creamy, it has a flavor that is not unlike Epoisses and Ami du Chambertin, but not as powerful or penetrating.

Munster AOC
When properly matured, this washed-rind cheese from Alsace and Lorraine has a strong, penetrating farmyardy smell and the flavor of rich milk. There is also a version flavored with cumin.

The dark line was once soot from wood fires, separating curds from morning and evening milking. Today, wood ash is used.

Pont-l'Evêque AOC
This washed-rind Normandy cheese is one of the oldest French cheeses recorded. When young, it has a lingering, sweet taste; older cheeses have a stronger, more meaty or savory flavor.

Morbier AOC
Made by the cheesemakers of Comté, this washed-rind French cheese has a soft and delicate texture, a rather pronounced flavor, and a mild, milky aroma. The more it ages, the sweeter and stronger the taste.

Gubbeen
This washed-rind farmhouse cheese made in Ireland is smooth and creamy and has gentle herb and floral notes with a meaty finish. It melts well for pizzas and omelets.

The supple texture makes it perfect for broiling, snacking, and Mexican-style dishes.

Saint-Nectaire AOC
One of the great cheeses of France. At maturity, the thick rind gives off a subtle, slightly pungent aroma of the farmyard, straw, and mushrooms, while the soft, supple interior has a pronounced taste of nuts, milk, and lush pastures. Eat with crusty bread.

SEMI-SOFT CHEESES (CONTINUED)

Tetilla DO
This popular cheese from northwestern Spain is ready to eat after only seven days, when the interior is sweet, clean, buttery, and unctuous; with maturity, Tetilla becomes firmer and more resilient, with a slight acidity on the finish. Delicious served at the end of a meal, with quince paste or a sharp apple purée.

The distinctive shape of Tetilla gives it its name, which means "small breast" in Spanish.

Milleens
Probably Ireland's first modern artisan cheese, this has an inviting soft texture that becomes unctuously runny. The flavor is full-bodied and complex, with farmyardy aromas. Serve with good bread, preferably Irish soda.

Stinking Bishop
Named after an old variety of pear used to make the perry (pear cider) in which the cheese is washed, the English cheese Stinking Bishop is milder than the name suggests. It is rich and meaty, with a hint of sweetness, and has an almost runny, supple texture.

Taleggio PDO
Made in an area of Italy famous for other great cheeses, Taleggio is soft and voluptuous, almost liquid. Eat with fruit, or use in dishes such as pasta and risotto; take care to heat slowly, stirring well, or it will form into a clump rather than melt.

The crust is a little gritty, so cut it off before eating or cooking.

Torta de Cañarejal
Made with ewe's milk and thistle rennet, which gives it its typical slightly bitter finish, this artisan cheese is the creamiest of all the Spanish tortas and is very aromatic, with soft, earthy flavors.

Scoop out the silky interior with a spoon or breadsticks. Or melt on a broiled steak and serve it with caramelized onions.

Raclette
The leathery, washed rind of this well-known mountain cheese made in both France and Switzerland encases a smooth, supple interior with a rich, fruity—savory flavor. Traditionally, a large wheel of cheese is cut in half and placed in front of an open fire. As the cut surface bubbles, the cheese is scraped on to bowls of piping-hot potato.

Provolone
An Italian pasta filata, or "stretched curd" cheese, this was traditionally the cheese of the poor because just a little piece gave a lot of flavor. The dolce variety, which is mild, sweet, and milky, can be broiled when young; use aged Dolce or the denser, more strongly flavored provolone piccante in risottos.

Bourrée
From Vermont, this North American washed-rind cheese has a relatively mild and floral aroma. The texture is smooth, rich, and somewhat sticky on the palate, with a peanutlike flavor that grows more intense as it finishes. It is best served simply with some chutney.

CLASSIC RECIPE

RACLETTE

Like fondue, this is a traditional Swiss/French dish. The name comes from the French *racler*, "to scrape". Tabletop electric raclette grills are available online and at many cookware stores.

SERVES 4

20–24 small waxy potatoes, scrubbed

1lb (400g) sliced raclette cheese (about 20 slices)

about 28 thin slices mixed charcuterie (e.g., salami, garlic sausage, prosciutto, and baked ham)

accompaniments: cornichons, sliced or pickled shallots, cherry tomatoes, and a lightly dressed green salad

French bread and butter (optional)

1 Cook the potatoes in lightly salted boiling water for 15–20 minutes, or until tender; drain and return to the pan (or put into a heatproof dish). Cover to keep warm.

2 While the potatoes are cooking, arrange the cheese slices on one platter, the charcuterie on another. Place these on the table with the accompaniments.

3 Set the table with a coupelle (raclette cheese pan). Put the raclette grill in the center of the table and turn it on. Put the covered pan or dish of potatoes on top of the grill to keep warm.

4 To serve, set a slice of cheese on a coupelle and place it under the grill. Meanwhile, put one or two potatoes and some of the accompaniments on your dinner plate. When the cheese has melted, slide it over the potatoes and eat with the meats and accompaniments.

5 If you don't have a raclette grill, put all the potatoes in a shallow flameproof dish, lay the cheese slices over them, and place under a low broiler until the cheese has melted. Serve with the accompaniments.

HARD CHEESES

All traditional cheesemaking countries produce hard cheeses made from cow's, goat's, or ewe's milks. There are two basic types: pressed, uncooked cheeses, which are eaten when they are still mild and springy, and cooked, pressed cheeses, which are heated before they are compressed and shaped. Hard cheeses vary greatly in appearance, in shape from drums or tall cylinders to large wheels or barrels, and with rinds ranging from smooth and polished to rough and pockmarked. When they are young, hard cheeses may be creamy and flexible, and slightly sharp or buttery sweet in flavor. With age, they dry out and become dense; the taste intensifies and grows more complex.

BUY Once cut, hard cheeses will dry out even when tightly wrapped, so buy big rather than small chunks and use as soon as possible. Very hard grating cheeses like Parmesan are best bought in smallish pieces and used within a few days, or they will start to lose their wonderful flavor.

STORE Wrap firmly in plastic wrap (if possible leave the rind uncovered, especially if it is covered in obvious mold, or its aroma may taint the flavor) and store in the fridge.

EAT Fresh: The most versatile of any cheese type, hard cheeses can be used in salads, dips, dressings, and sandwiches. They are also essential on any cheeseboard. **Cooked:** Hard cheeses such as Gruyère and Beaufort become stretchy when heated, making them perfect for broiling or fondues rather than in sauces. Other hard cheeses melt completely, while those that are very hard, such as Parmigiano-Reggiano, simply dissolve, which makes both of these latter types excellent for sauces, soups, quiches, and gratins.

FLAVOR PAIRINGS Dried and fresh fruit, fruit cheeses, nuts.

CLASSIC RECIPES Cheese soufflé; cheese straws; cheese sauce; Swiss cheese fondue; Welsh rarebit; *gnocchi alla romana*; macaroni cheese; *gougère*; plowman's lunch; *pommes dauphinoise*; cauliflower *gratin*.

Beaufort AOC

One of the great cheeses of the world, Beaufort is made in the French Alps. Cheese produced in the lush summer pastures is known as Beaufort d'alpage; paler winter cheese is called Beaufort d'hiver. Young Beaufort is firm but melts in the mouth and has a full-bodied, complex, savory—fruity flavor. Best served simply, as part of a cheeseboard.

Caerphilly

Welsh Caerphilly is crumbly with a mild, lemony, fresh taste; with age, it becomes softer, creamier, and more complex. It can be used in sweet or savory dishes, especially Welsh rarebit.

Appenzeller
This is made in the hilly pre-Alps of Switzerland. At six months, the cheese has nutty notes and a distinct spicy finish, but it develops a more intense, rich flavor with age. Appenzeller is popular for breakfast when young; for cheeseboards when aged.

The aromatic rind comes from washing with a secret blend of cider, white wine, herbs, and spices.

Allgäuer Bergkäse
This dense German Alpine cheese is like a little Gruyère with very small holes. It has a sweet, buttery taste, becoming more intense and slightly salty. Perfect with charcuterie and dark bread, especially at breakfast.

Berkswell
This modern British classic was created using traditional artisan methods and modern ideas, including draining the curd in a plastic colander. giving the rind a knobbled appearance. It has a slightly oily texture and a sweet, nutty taste with a surprisingly tangy finale.

Comté AOC
Made for over eight centuries in huge wheels, this is still one of France's most popular cheeses. Matured for 4–18 months, it ranges in taste from melted butter and hazelnuts to peppery. Its superb melting quality means Comté is found in numerous French dishes, from quiches and tarts to sauces and salads.

Garrotxa
Made just north of Barcelona, this is one of the new generation of Spanish artisan cheeses. It is firm and dense yet lightly supple, with a subtle goaty flavor that hints of walnuts. Garrotxa is ideal for tapas or at the end of a meal, served with walnuts.

CLASSIC RECIPE

CHEESE SOUFFLÉ

Soufflés are not challenging at all, and are actually quite easy. Once you master this soufflé, there are many options beyond the basic cheese version.

SERVES 4

1 tbsp freshly grated Parmesan

3 tbsp butter, plus extra for greasing the soufflé dish

3 tbsp all-purpose flour

1 cup whole milk, heated

salt and freshly ground pepper

1 cup shredded Cheddar or Gruyère cheese

½ tsp Dijon mustard

4 large eggs, separated, plus 1 large egg white, at room temperature

1 Preheat the oven to 375°F (190°C). Butter the bottom and sides of a 6-cup soufflé dish, and dust evenly with the Parmesan cheese.

2 Melt the butter in a saucepan over medium heat. Whisk in the flour and cook, stirring, for 1 to 2 minutes. Gradually whisk in the milk and bring to a boil, whisking constantly, until thickened and smooth.

3 Remove the pan from the heat. Stir in the cheese and mustard and season with salt and pepper. Add the egg yolks to the cheese mixture one at a time, stirring each until blended before adding the next.

4 In a large, clean bowl, beat the egg whites until stiff peaks form. (The whites should still be glossy; do not overbeat.) Stir about one-fourth of the whites into the cheese mixture, then fold in the remaining whites.

5 Pour the cheese mixture into the prepared soufflé dish and sprinkle the Parmesan over the top. Place the dish on the hot baking sheet in the oven and bake for 25–30 minutes, or until the soufflé is puffed and golden brown on top. Serve at once.

The bloomy protective rind on whole cheese rounds increases in color, density, and depth of flavor as the cheese matures.

CHEESE STRAWS

A popular 18th-century appetizer, these crunchy fingers were later served as a savory after a formal dinner or as a supper snack.

MAKES ABOUT 45

1 cup all-purpose flour
½ tsp celery salt
large pinch of cayenne pepper
4 tbsp butter, cut in small pieces
¾ cup shredded sharp Cheddar cheese (or other flavorful semi-hard cheese)
1 egg, beaten

1 Preheat the oven to 350°F (180°C).

2 Put the flour in a bowl and stir in the celery salt and cayenne. Add the butter and rub in with your fingertips until the mixture resembles coarse crumbs. Stir in the cheese.

3 Mix in enough of the beaten egg to bind to a stiff dough. On a lightly floured work surface, gently knead the dough into a smooth ball free from cracks; then roll into a rectangle about ¼ in (5 mm) thick. Trim away and reserve any ragged edges.

4 Cut the rectangle into strips about 4 in (10 cm) wide, and then crosswise into ½ in (1 cm) strips. Using a metal spatula, carefully transfer the strips on to lightly greased baking sheets, placing about 1 inch apart. Roll out the trimmings into another triangle and cut more strips.

5 Bake for about 15 minutes, or until lightly golden and cooked through. Leave to cool on the baking sheets for about 5 minutes before serving, or transfer to a wire rack to cool completely and store in an airtight container.

HARD CHEESES (CONTINUED)

Castelmagno PDO
The center of this Italian cheese is very crumbly. It is delicate in flavor when young, becoming strong and very savory when mature. Castelmagno is served locally drizzled with wild honey.

Cheshire
One of England's oldest cheeses, this was originally produced from cows that grazed on the salt marshes of Cheshire. It has a very fine, crumbly texture and savory, salty tang that lingers in the mouth. It is available white, but is usually a pale orange, colored with annatto. Broil, bake, or crumble into soups and salads.

Gouda
Young cheeses are supple with a sweet, fruity taste, but when matured for a minimum of 18 months, Gouda becomes deeply colored and almost brittle and granular in texture. Each bite reveals more of its complex character, while the feel in the mouth is rich and smooth. The strong taste of aged gouda lends itself to hot dishes, from gratins to tarts and pasta, as well as to the cheeseboard.

Cheddar

Originating in Southwest England, authentic farmhouse Cheddar is firm but yielding, with an earthy and savory aroma. Young cheeses are mild and almost buttery; with maturity the taste intensifies and the texture becomes harder. Often used in sandwiches, it is also superb in sauces, melted over baked potatoes, grated over vegetable dishes, and broiled.

Dry Jack

The hardest of the Monterey Jacks, this was created in the US in the 1930s as an alternative to Parmesan. It has a grainy, brittle texture and a deep, full-bodied tang that is sweet and nutty. Great for sauces and soufflés, or grated on pasta, tacos, and enchiladas.

Gruyère AOC

Switzerland's most popular cheese is firm and dense when young, with a nutty flavor; at eight months, it has a wonderful complexity that is rich, nutty, and earthy. It is essential for fondue, and ideal for pasta, salads, vegetables, and sauces.

Graviera DOC

This Greek cheese is roughly based on Swiss Gruyère. In Crete, it is made using mainly ewe's milk and is sweet and fruity with a delicate fragrance and burnt-caramel finish. Graviera from Naxos, made primarily with cow's milk, is richer, creamier, and more nutty. This classic table cheese can also be baked in cheese pastries.

The fine, compact texture of Cantal is a result of the curd being milled and then dry-salted.

CLASSIC RECIPE

CHEESE SAUCE

A basic cheese sauce is a cook's classic mainstay for serving with fish, vegetables, or pasta.

MAKES ABOUT I CUP

| 1 ½ tbsp butter |
| 1 ½ tbsp all-purpose flour |
| 1 cup milk, heated |
| ½ tsp Dijon mustard (optional) |
| ½ to ¾ cup shredded sharp Cheddar cheese or other flavorful semi-hard cheese |
| salt and freshly ground black pepper |

1 Melt the butter in a small heavy or nonstick saucepan. Stir in the flour and cook, stirring, for 1 minute.

2 Remove from the heat and gradually stir in the milk until smooth. Return to the heat, bring to a boil, and cook for 2 minutes, stirring all the time, until thick, smooth, and glossy.

3 Stir in the mustard, if using, and cheese to taste. Season with salt and pepper. Use as required.

Cantal AOC

One of France's oldest cheeses, Cantal is the only one that uses a process similar to Cheddar making. A young cheese has a mild, nutty, and milky flavor; a well-ripened Cantal is very strong, sharp, and intense.

HARD CHEESES (CONTINUED)

Queso Majorero DOP

This exceptional Spanish cheese varies from creamy fresh with a subtle, aromatic goaty flavor to a more robust, almondy sweetness. It is traditionally grated into vegetable soups or summer salads.

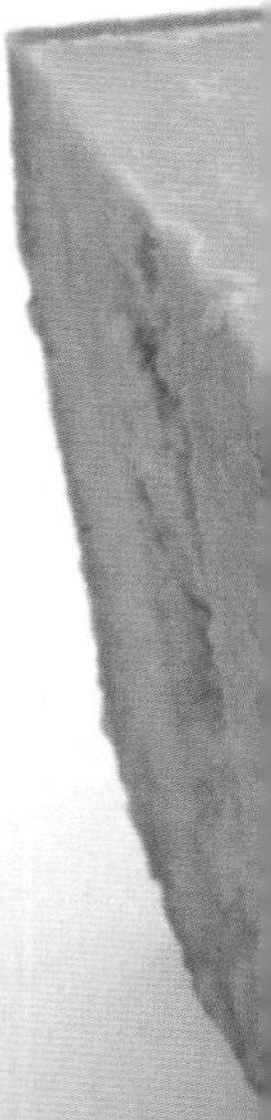

Lincolnshire Poacher

This much loved, modern farmhouse English cheese created in the 1980s is similar to Cheddar. Hard and chewy, lively and complex, it offers a full taste experience. Eat with bread or crackers, grill, or bake with onions, bacon, and potatoes for a gratin.

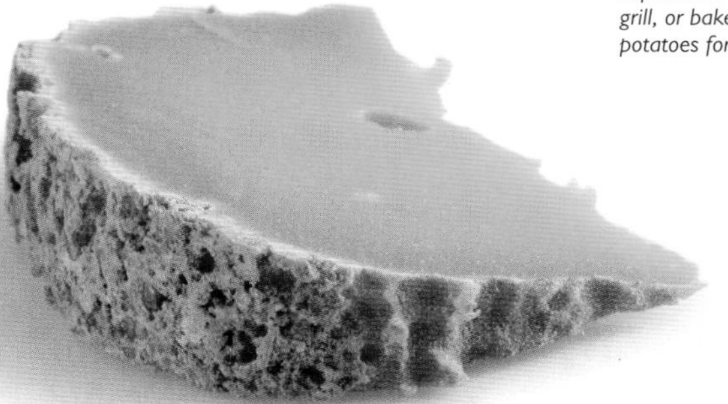

Ibérico

Imprinted with the marks of its woven-basket mould, Ibérico, like many traditional Spanish cheeses, is made from a blend of milks, with each adding its own flavors: creamy and mellow from cow's milk, sweet and nutty from ewe's, and herbaceous notes from goat's. It is both an excellent tapas and a grating cheese.

Mimolette

This cheese originated in the Netherlands, but has also long been made in northern France. It is produced using the same methods as Edam. As it ripens, it becomes brittle in texture and the flavor develops intensity. Eat as an appetizer, or crumbled into sauces.

Lancashire is made by a unique method of combining the curd of two or three consecutive days, which gives it a mottled appearance.

Lancashire

When young it is called "Creamy" Lancashire and is moist and crumbly, almost like scrambled eggs, and melts very quickly. Aged "Tasty" Lancashire is stronger and drier with an even more crumbly texture.

The distinctive texture of Manchego is firm and dry, yet rich and creamy, almost oily.

Manchego DOC

Manchego takes its name from the vast, dry plateau of La Mancha, south of Madrid. The thick, sweet, aromatic milk from the sheep that graze there is what makes this cheese unique. It has an unmistakable richness reminiscent of Brazil nuts and caramel, with a slightly salty finish.

Grana Padano PDO

Created in the 12th century by Cistercian monks and very similar to Parmesan, this hard cheese is now made in numerous dairies in the Padana Valley in Italy. The thick, polished rind protects the brittle interior that has a long, sweet, fruity taste and fragrance with hints of dried fruits. Grate over pasta dishes, or use in ravioli.

Pecorino Romano PDO

Considered essential for the rations of the Roman legions in 100 BC, this firm, compact cheese is crumbly and crunchy and has the sweetness typical of ewe's milk, with a characteristic salty tang. It is ideal for grating over pasta and risottos.

Pondhopper

The traditional methods of Dutch and Italian cheesemaking have been combined to make this unique goat's-milk cheese from Oregon. Washed in ale, it has a smooth, creamy, supple feel, with a hoppy aroma and taste. Pondhopper is natural partner for dried cherry and walnut bread, and a nutty ale.

Mahón DO

Mahón comes from the Balearic island of Menorca and its rind is rubbed with a mix of butter, paprika, and olive oil. Young cheeses are supple, buttery, and mild, but when aged are hard and slightly granular, not unlike Parmesan. Mahón is traditionally served as an appetizer, drizzled with olive oil and topped with a sprig of fresh rosemary.

Pecorino Sardo PDO

From Sardinia, dolce is a young, elastic, white ewe's-milk cheese with buttery and floral notes, while maturo is more intense, and full of pleasant pungent and salty flavors. Pecorino Sardo is a basic ingredient in a local dish called culingiones, a sort of ravioli with ricotta and herbs.

CLASSIC RECIPE

SWISS CHEESE FONDUE

The name of this well-loved Swiss peasant dish comes from the French word *fondue*, meaning "melted."

SERVES 4

1 garlic clove
1 ½ cups dry white wine
2 cups shredded Gruyère cheese
2 cups shredded Emmental cheese
2 tbsp kirsch
2 tbsp water
2 tbsp cornstarch
pinch of grated nutmeg
French bread, to serve

1 Cut the garlic clove in half and rub around the inside of a heavy-bottomed saucepan; discard the garlic.

2 Add the wine to the pan and heat until gently bubbling. Gradually add the cheeses, stirring all the time until melted.

3 In a small bowl, mix the kirsch and water with the cornstarch until blended; stir into the cheese mixture. Stir over low heat until smooth and barely bubbling at the edges. Season with nutmet.

4 Light the heat source under the fondue pot. When the pot is warm, pour in the warm fondue. (If you do not have a fondue pot, set the saucepan on a small rack over a candle, or on a small electric warming tray, to keep the fondue fluid.) Serve with cubes of French bread for dipping with fondue forks.

HARD CHEESES (CONTINUED)

Swaledale Goat PDO
From North Yorkshire, this firm English cheese has a sweet taste with traces of the salty brine in which it is soaked and a mild goat flavor. It develops a natural brown rind, or is waxed at three days old for a slightly softer texture. Choose for subtle flavor in soufflés and tarts.

São Jorge DOP
The abundant grass and salty pastures of Madeira allow this cheese to gain a strong, spicy flavor, a clean bouquet, and a hard but crumbly texture. It is likened to a cross between Cheddar and Gouda, with some small holes. Ideal for fondue, São Jorge also makes a fine addition to a cheeseboard, with pears and muscat grapes.

Handcrafted wooden molds give Oštiepok its unusual shape.

Red Leicester
Made in a similar way to Cheddar, this has a sweet, mellow nuttiness that strengthens as it matures. Serve on toast or in tarts, or use to add color and flavor to a cheeseboard.

This distinctively colored cheese is dense, waxy, and smooth.

Oštiepok PGI
A traditional ewe's-milk cheese from Slovakia, this is very similar to the Polish Oszczypek. Being naturally smoked, the cheese has a smoky, slightly salty taste with a caramel finish from the milk. Often served as a table cheese, it also complements cured meats and sausages.

Pleasant Ridge Reserve
A hand-made Alpine-style cheese from Wisconsin, this is only produced during the peak pasture season from spring to fall. The flavor varies from very fruity and sweet when young to slightly sour and savory as it matures. It is a great melting cheese.

San Joaquin Gold
This California original was inspired by Swiss-mountain cheeses. It is full-flavored with a crumbly texture. As it ages, the complex flavors of nuts and grass rise to the palate.

San Joaquin Gold is made in huge 30 lb (13.6 kg) wheels.

Sbrinz is superb grated into pasta and soups.

Sbrinz AOC
Although it is very hard and grainy, Swiss Sbrinz is less crumbly than Parmesan because it is made with whole milk. It has a distinct aroma from the flowery meadows, with spicy, slightly salty undercurrents, and is superb grated into pasta and soups.

Roncal DOP
A ewe's-milk cheese from the Spanish side of the Pyrenees, Roncal is dense with a smooth rind that bears the imprint of the cloth wrapping. With age, there can be hints of dried fruit, a growing piquancy, and a lingering aftertaste.

Wensleydale
Immortalized by the cartoon characters Wallace and Gromit, Wensleydale is one of Britain's oldest cheeses. It has a dense yet flaky texture, and a subtle wild-honey flavor balanced by refreshing acidity. In Yorkshire, they like to pair the cheese with a slice of apple pie.

Ossau-Iraty PDO
The name refers to the valley of Ossau, in Béarn, and the forests of Iraty, in the Basque country, and encompasses a number of wonderful ewe's-milk cheeses with a long, lingering, rich, and somewhat nutty taste. Eat in traditional fashion with the local black cherry jam, called itxassou.

Winchester Super Aged Gouda
Made in California by a cheesemaker from the Netherlands, this is dense and gives a crunch in the mouth. When mature the sweet, buttery flavor becomes sharp and assertive. A classic cheeseboard cheese.

WELSH RAREBIT

Sometimes called Welsh Rabbit, this is a British version of Swiss cheese fondue, served over toast. When topped with a poached egg, it is called Buck Rarebit.

SERVES 4

| 1 tbsp butter |
| 1 tbsp all-purpose flour |
| pinch of cayenne pepper |
| ¼ cup beer, stout, or milk |
| ½ tsp English mustard powder |
| 2 cups shredded or crumbled Brish cheese such as Caerphilly, Lancashire, Wensleydale, Cheshire, or any other slightly crumbly cheese |
| salt and freshly ground black pepper |
| 4 slices bread, toasted |

1 Position the oven rack about 6 inches from the heat source and preheat the broiler to high. Melt the butter in a saucepan. Stir in the flour and cayenne and cook for 1 minute, stirring. Remove from the heat and whisk in the beer.

2 Return to the heat and bring to a boil, whisking until thick. Stir in the mustard and cheese until melted and smooth. Season with salt and pepper to taste.

3 Arrange the toast in one or more flameproof gratin dishes, or on a broiler pan. Spoon the cheese mixture on top of the toast to cover evenly; broil for 3 to 4 minutes, or until the cheese mixture is golden brown and bubbling. Serve hot.

FLAVOUR-ADDED CHEESES

With their bright colors, the vast array of flavor-added cheeses stands out on deli counters across the world. They may seem very modern, but, in fact, they have a long history: smoked cheeses have existed since people learned to make hard cheeses and stored them in the eaves above their wood fires; in the 16th century Dutch cheesemakers were quick to incorporate the exotic spices brought back from the East Indies into Edam and Gouda, producing a tantalizing mélange of flavors. Today, most flavor-added cheeses are well-known hard or semi-soft cheeses combined with fruit, spices, or herbs. There are four distinct types. Natural-smoked cheeses have a golden-brown to caramel-colored rind but the internal color is not affected. Traditional-style cheeses (based on the original Dutch method, where the ingredients are matured with the fresh curds) absorb and intensify the aroma and essence of the added ingredients. Rind-flavored cheeses have various ingredients, such as vine leaves, grape-must, or toasted hops pressed into the rind. Re-formed cheeses, which constitute the majority of flavor-added cheeses, are created by breaking up a young cheese, blending it with added ingredients, and then re-forming it.

BUY The flavor added should complement rather than overpower the cheese, so find a retailer who encourages you to taste before buying.

STORE Keep in an airtight container in the fridge.

EAT Fresh: Flavor-added cheeses with garlic or herbs, or those that are smoked, work well in sandwiches and salads. Those flavored with dried fruit are typically served in place of dessert. Cooked: Traditional-style semi-soft or hard flavor-added cheeses behave like their unflavored counterparts when cooked and can add character to basics like baked potatoes or pasta dishes—natural-smoked cheeses work especially well for this.

Wensleydale with cranberries
To make this cheese, young Wensleydale is broken up and mixed with cranberries, then re-formed. The original cheese is hard, but after flavoring, re-forming, and pressing, the result is softer, almost spreadable.

Calcagno
Made in Sardinia and Sicily from ewe's milk, black peppercorns are added to the fresh curd before the cheese is drained, salted, and aged. With maturity, it becomes saltier and more pungent and the sheep flavor more distinct. Serve a younger cheese with roasted peppers, and use older cheese for grating over pasta or vegetable dishes.

San Simón da Costa
The distinctive copper-colored rind of this Spanish cheese is the result of gentle smoking over birch wood. The smokiness blends with the buttery aroma and taste, while the overall flavor is mild with some salt. A good melting cheese, it works well in rice, pasta, and vegetable dishes, or added to salads.

Idiazábal DOP
A great example of a natural-smoked cheese, this was traditionally stored in the rafters of Basque shepherds' huts, where the young cheeses would absorb the smoke from the wood fires. Today, they are cold smoked with beech wood. Hard and chewy, Idiazábal has a wonderful smoky-bacon taste. In the Basque region of Spain, it is added to squid risotto.

Pecorino Tartufo
Slivers of black truffles are added to the fresh ewe's-milk curd so the essence from the truffles is absorbed into the fat globules as they mature together. The result is a wonderful balance of sweetness from the ewe's milk with the earthy, nutty character of the truffles.

Karikaas Vintage Leyden (Leiden)
Flavored with cumin, this traditional-style Leyden made in New Zealand is a pale sunshine yellow, firm yet supple, sweet, spicy, and with a hint of curry. At two years old, it is drier, sharper, and caramel sweet.

Leyden is great melted over potatoes, or matched with strong, spicy cured meats.

Formaggio Ubriaco
Ubriaco ("drunken") is so-named because the young cheeses are matured in barrels of crushed grape skins and seeds left over from winemaking. The creamy richness of the cheese marries well with the distinct flavor and aroma of the wine. Superb with polenta and mushrooms.

Yarg Cornish cheese
Probably the best-known British example of a rind-flavored cheese, mild, crumbly Yarg is wrapped in interwoven nettle leaves. With age, the nettles start to break down the rind, making it very soft and creamy, and they impart a delicate, slightly mushroomy aroma and subtle vegetal flavor to the cheese. Crumble over crostinis, baguettes, baked potatoes, pasta, and grains.

Nagelkaas
Made all over the Netherlands, this traditional Gouda-style cheese is flavored with cloves and cumin. Despite being made from skimmed milk, it has a firm, creamy texture and pronounced hot, spicy, aromatic taste. It becomes a deep yellow with age. Use sparingly in salads and hot dishes.

FRUITS

ORCHARD | STONE
BERRIES | BUSH FRUITS
CITRUS | TROPICAL

FRUIT ESSENTIALS

Of all the food we eat, fruit is perhaps the most beautiful. However, when it comes to the practicalities of shopping, looks can deceive. A lot of fruit has been developed to meet the convenience of the market rather than to please the palate: as a result, complex flavor is often sacrificed for good looks and long shelf life. A bright red apple can disappoint with floury, dry flesh. A large, luscious strawberry too often is watery and dull. A pretty, blushing apricot may be tasteless and woolly. Smell, touch, and a practiced eye can help you buy the best. The heady fragrance of a ripe Charentais melon, for instance, is unmistakable. Ripe papayas turn yellow. Purple figs and muscat grapes are at their best when almost overripe.

BUY

If you can, gently feel the fruit before you buy to check for ripeness: many fruits, especially stone fruits, should feel firm but not hard, and when fully ripe will give slightly to gentle pressure. Sweet, juicy fruit should feel heavy for their size, and all fruit should look fresh, firm, unblemished, and enticing (unless they are passionfruit, when wrinkles are a sign of intense flavor). If the fruit has leaves or stalks, make sure they are green and fresh looking. Try to buy seasonal and local fruit; anything that has been transported thousands of miles by air or sea is often picked underripe in order to survive the journey, and will never taste as good as when freshly picked and at the height of its season. Preservation by freezing, bottling, and drying, however, enables us to also enjoy these healthy and delicious foods throughout the year.

DISCOLORATION The flesh of some fruit, such as apples, pears, and bananas, quickly oxidizes and turns brown when sliced and exposed to air. To prevent this unsightly discoloration, rub or brush all surfaces of the exposed fruit with the cut surface of a citrus fruit such as a lemon, lime, or orange. Or dip the fruit into a bowl containing acidulated water (cold water and lemon juice).

Force unripe fruits to ripen *by putting them in a paper bag with already ripe fruits. Close the bag loosely, allowing some air in, and set aside at room temperature and out of direct sunlight. Be sure to keep the bag and its contents dry at all times.*

STORE AND RIPEN

Ripe fruit spoils quickly, so handle it with care and as little as possible, and try not to buy more than you can use within a few days. Fruit is usually stored at the bottom of the refrigerator or in a cool pantry, but it is at its best if brought to room temperature before eating. Some fruit, such as bananas, should never be stored at cold temperatures. "Ripe" means "mature," but not all fruits ripen after picking. Apricots, nectarines, cherries, and berries, for example, may change color and soften, but they will not necessarily become sweeter or juicier. To speed up the ripening/softening process of fruits such as apples, pears, mangoes, and pineapples, try one of these tricks.

On a windowsill Spread out the fruit on a dry, shady windowsill or flat tray, making sure they are not touching each other (to prevent mold spread). Keep them out of the sun or they will shrivel and dry out. Once soft, transfer to the fridge.

In a bowl Most fruits emit natural ethylene gas as they ripen, which, as a by-product of ripening, encourages further ripening. Storing fruit together, in a bowl or a paper bag, speeds up the process as the ripe fruits ripen the unripe ones.

Speed ripen If you want to accelerate the ripening process still further, place an apple or banana (both give off very high concentrations of ethylene gas) inside the bag with the fruit. Check the fruit daily to be sure they do not overripen and remove any that look ready. Once soft, store the fruit in the refrigerator if not intending to eat it immediately.

FRUITS THAT IMPROVE WITH RIPENING AFTER PICKING
• Apples • Pears • Plums • Most Sweet melons • Kiwis • Mangoes • Pineapples • Papaya • Passionfruit • Bananas •

FRUITS THAT DETERIORATE AFTER PICKING
• Apricots • Peaches • Nectarines • Cherries • Grapes • Olives • Soft berries • Currants • Rhubarb • Citrus fruits • Watermelons

PREPARE

Most fruits are simple to prepare—just wash them and they're ready to eat—while others may hide their delicious flesh under tough skins. To serve with desserts, some fruits are excellent puréed.

PUREE Soft fruits, such as berries, can be puréed fresh, but other fruits will need to be braised or poached first to soften them ready for mashing. Wash all fruit before puréeing and peel those that need their skins removed. Take out any pits, too.

1 *Place the fresh or cooked fruit in a blender, and pulse a few times to break down the flesh.*

2 *Press the pulp through a sieve to remove pits and seeds. Sweeten, if necessary, and chill.*

COOK

Fruit is at its most delicious when fresh and ripe, but cooking fruit allows you to alter the texture of the flesh and also to add complementary flavors. Cooking also makes good use of overripe fruit.

POACH A great method for stone fruits, choose firm fruits that are not too ripe, since they will hold their shape better during cooking. You can flavor the cooking syrup with lemon, orange, or spices, or poach them in fruit juice or red wine with added sugar.

1 *To simmering sugar syrup add pitted fruit, either halved or sliced. Make sure the fruits are completely submerged in the syrup.*

2 *Poach for 10–15 minutes, or until tender. Remove the fruit with a slotted spoon. Boil the syrup to reduce, strain, and serve with the fruit.*

BROIL Fruit is made up of water and sugar, and the process of grilling it concentrates the flavors by reducing the water and caramelizing the natural sugars. Citrus fruits soften and turn from tart to sweet after grilling. And tropical fruits, such as pineapple and bananas, are excellent grilled in slices or threaded onto skewers to make fruit kebabs.

***Halve citrus fruits**, dot with butter, sprinkle with sugar, or drizzle with honey. Place on a grill or under a broiler until soft and caramelized.*

***Slice a pineapple** into even rounds and coat with butter and sugar or honey on both sides. Grill or broil until soft and caramelized.*

DEEP-FRY Use firm fruit, especially tropical ones such as pineapple, mango, and papaya for this method of cooking. The best way to do this is to dip the fruit pieces in batter first—for crisp, light fritters use an Asian tempura batter recipe. Drying the fruit well before coating will both help the batter adhere and keep the fruit juicy.

1 *Peel and cut the fruit into even pieces. Dip the fruit in batter using tongs or your fingers. Coat the fruit completely.*

2 *Deep-fry in oil heated to 375°F (190°C) for 3–5 minutes until they are crisp and golden. Drain on paper towels and sprinkle with sugar.*

BAKE

Baking enhances the natural sweetness of fruit. Slow-baking in a low oven is the best way of treating hard fruit such as apples and pears, since it softens and cooks the fruit through, while maximizing the flavor.

1 *To bake whole apples, start by removing the cores from the fruit, taking care also to remove any residual seeds and membranes that may remain in the cavity.*

2 *Stuff the apples with dried fruit and nuts. Score around the sides, to allow the fruit to expand during baking. Place on a baking sheet, top with a pat of butter, and bake at 400°F (200°C) for 45 minutes.*

3 *Once cooked, remove from the oven. Serve the apples with their cooking juices, a sugar syrup, or a spoonful of heavy cream or ice cream.*

PRESERVE

Fruits naturally decay over time, but effective preserving techniques have been developed to slow down the decaying process so that we can continue to enjoy fruits for longer in different ways.

Whether you are heating, adding sugar or alcohol, drying, freezing, or a using a combination of some of these methods, the process of preserving fruit at home is an enjoyable and rewarding one.

MAKE JAM Use fruit that is perfectly ripe, but not overripe. Blemished fruit is usually past its best and will not make good jam. Some fruits, such as cherries and strawberries, do not contain sufficient pectin (a natural setting agent) to set properly on their own and need added pectin to aid setting. Most jam consists of equal weights of fruit and sugar, but the exact quantities vary from recipe to recipe. Store homemade jam for up to a year.

Put the fruit and sugar in a preserving pan or large saucepan. Simmer over low heat until the sugar has dissolved. Boil rapidly to 220°F (105°C): the length of time will depend on the fruit and the recipe you are using.

Use the flake test for setting by putting some of the jam in a bowl and letting it cool slightly. Scoop some of the jam out with a wooden spoon. If the last of the jam falls back into the bowl in a flake, rather than a stream, it is set.

Use the wrinkle test as an alternative test for set. Spoon some of the jam onto a chilled saucer. Once it has cooled slightly, use your finger to push the jam across the saucer. If it is set, it will wrinkle slightly as you push it.

MAKE JELLY Jelly is made from the strained juice of cooked fruit. It is easy to make, and useful to have in the pantry for both savory and sweet dishes. Store for up to one year. Making jelly is almost identical to making jam and the equipment is much the same, aside from the use of a nylon sieve or a jelly bag. This must be scalded with boiling water before use. Fruits high in pectin, such as black currants, red currants, and gooseberries are best for jelly making. Others, such as blackberries, are best combined with a high-pectin fruit such as apples or made using sugar with pectin.

1 In a saucepan, cook the fruit slowly. This helps to extract the natural pectin in the fruit. Use the back of a wooden spoon to squash the fruit to a pulp once it is soft enough.

2 Ladle the fruit pulp into a nylon sieve or a suspended jelly bag and leave to drip overnight into a bowl. Don't squeeze the fruit against the sieve or bag or the jelly will be cloudy.

3 Boil the juice with sugar until the setting point is reached. Skim but do not stir. Transfer to sterilized jars as soon as possible; if left to stand, the jelly can start to set in the pan.

BOTTLE Bottling fruit has remained popular over the decades, and is an excellent way of preserving a glut of fruit. Choose just-ripe, unblemished fruit, and use preserving jars with matching lids, close-fitting seals, and wide necks. Once filled, store the bottled fruit in a cool, dark place for 10–12 months.

1 Rinse the fruit, remove any pits, and keep whole or cut into quarters or slices—you'll need to pack the fruit into sterilized jars or bottles as tightly as possible without damaging it.

2 Place the jars in a deep, paper-lined baking pan. Fill the jars right up to the neck with sugar syrup and seal loosely. Tap the jars to remove any air bubbles and top them off with syrup again.

3 Remove any plastic seals before securing the lids of the jars. Place the pan in a 300°F (150°C) oven for the time appropriate to the fruit and recipe. Reseal properly once removed and cooled.

PRESERVE IN ALCOHOL All fruits can be preserved in alcohol. Vary your choice of fruit and spirit. Try cherries in brandy, clementines with rum and spices, or plums with port, for example. Use just-ripe fruit in good condition.

1 *Wash and dry the fruit, and pack it tightly in wide-mouthed, sterilized preserving jars, without bruising or damaging the fruit.*

2 *Pour sugar into the jar (enough to fill a third of the jar) and pour the alcohol over the top so that the alcohol covers the fruit completely.*

3 *Seal the jar and tap it and turn it to release any air bubbles. Top off with alcohol and reseal. Leave the sugar to dissolve, turning the jar occasionally to help the process.*

4 *Store in a cool, dark place and allow the sugar to dissolve completely and the fruit to absorb the alcohol and mature—this can take 2–3 months, depending on the fruit.*

DRY You can dry fruit such as apples, figs, stone fruits, pears, and bananas in a domestic oven at a very low temperature (120°F/50–60°C) for 8–24 hours, depending on the oven and the fruit.

1 *Core the fruit (if necessary) and remove any stones from stone fruit. Slice thinly and evenly. Heat the oven to a very low temperature.*

2 *Lay the fruit on a slatted trays and dry in the oven until the texture resembles chamois leather. Cool and store in sterilized sealed jars.*

FREEZE Freezing is an excellent and easy way to preserve fruit at its best. Wash and thoroughly dry fruit first, although strawberries and raspberries should be rinsed only if absolutely necessary. Avoid fruit that is bruised or damaged. There are three main methods of freezing fruit: open/dry freeze (see below), sugar freeze, and syrup freeze. Some fruit may also require a brief blanching in water or syrup first. You can also freeze puréed fruit and juice. A good trick is to freeze small amounts in ice cube trays. Frozen fruit will keep well for 8–10 months.

1 *Spread the fruit evenly and in one layer on a baking sheet. Place the sheet in the freezer and allow the fruit to freeze until solid.*

2 *Once frozen, pack into freezer bags or rigid boxes (the fruit will now stay separate and not stick together), label, and return to the freezer.*

MAKE CANDIED PEEL

Candied fruits are also known as crystallized fruits. Some fruits such as citrus slices and peel, physalis, and pineapple give better results than others.

Make candied citrus peel *by putting equal quantities of peel to granulated sugar in a pan and covering with water. Bring to a boil, then simmer over low heat until the peel is translucent. Place the peel pieces on a tray to dry out, then dip them into superfine sugar to coat. Place the candied peel in a sterilized jar, seal and strore in a cool, dark place.*

FROST This is a pretty technique that you can use on grapes and red currants for decorative effect. The fruit will not last a great deal longer than fresh fruit, but will preserve its freshness for a few days.

1 *Leave the fruit on the stalk. Beat one or two egg whites lightly. Dip the fruit into the egg white or brush it onto the fruit with a pastry brush.*

2 *Use a teaspoon to cover the fruit superfine sugar, or roll the fruit in the sugar, so that the fruit is frosted all over. Leave to dry.*

APPLES

Grown in temperate climates around the world, the many varieties of apple range in color from green to red, yellow, and russet; in taste from sour to sweet; and in texture from crisp to soft. Most apples can be eaten both fresh and cooked.

BUY Apples are generally harvested in the fall, but can ripen between late summer and midwinter, depending on the variety. Choose unblemished fruit with firm, unwrinkled skin. There should be a faint aroma around the stem—try pressing this area lightly with your finger. Color has little to do with flavor: sometimes vivid, waxy skins conceal woolly, tasteless flesh.

STORE Apples can be kept in open bags at the bottom of the refrigerator for several weeks; transfer to the fruit bowl as needed. For bulk fruit and long-term storage, wrap individually in newspaper and store in a cool, dark, airy place; or peel and core, then dry. Apples can also be frozen.

EAT Since they contain tannin, apples will discolor once cut. Prevent this by rubbing with lemon or placing in a bowl of water acidulated with lemon juice. **Fresh:** Eat whole at room temperature. Peel, or keep the skin on for added color, then slice or dice for salads. **Cooked:** Slice or chop for tarts, pies, or fritters, or poach and purée for sauces. Core and bake whole. **Preserved:** Bottle in syrup; make into chutney or apple butter; or dry in rings.

FLAVOR PAIRINGS Pork, goose, black pudding, cheese, celery, red cabbage, blackberries, raisins, nuts, cinnamon, cloves, nutmeg, vanilla, cider, Calvados.

CLASSIC RECIPES Apple strudel; apple sauce; *tarte Tatin*; baked apples; apple pie; Waldorf salad; *pandowdy; apfeltorte;* apple snow; apple trifle; *tarte normande;* apple fritters.

Danziger Kantapfel
An old Dutch—German variety, this has a nice balance of sweet and tart flavors, which makes it a good all-arounder.

The shiny red skin and sweet aroma give this its other name of "strawberry apple."

Belle de Boskoop
From Holland, this fine heirloom apple has crisp, aromatic flesh. Being slightly tart in flavor it is excellent both for eating and for applesauce and strudel.

Cox's Orange Pippin
This scented, mottled yellow-green apple with an orange-red flush has crisp and juicy flesh. Its superb flavor has made it one of Britain's favorite dessert apples.

Annurca
Widely grown in southern Italy, this apple has crisp flesh and a fine, aromatic flavor. It is ideal for both eating and cooking.

PREPARING APPLES

The thin skin peels off easily and, once the core is removed, apples can be used whole or cut into quarters, slices, or cubes.

1 *Peel the apple with a vegetable peeler or small, sharp knife. To use whole, cut out the core with an apple corer.* **2** *Alternatively, cut the peeled apple into quarters and remove the core with a small knife.*

Braeburn
Supermarket-friendly Braeburn originated in New Zealand. It has medium firm, juicy flesh and a balanced flavor. Enjoy it fresh or use in crumbles, cobblers, and pies.

Annurca is a medium—small apple with a flattish shape.

Discovery
The bright red skin with a touch of green, and the crisp, juicy, and slightly acidic flesh make this one of the most appealing of English apples. Before eating fresh, chill this apple slightly to bring out the flavor.

Select fruit with smooth, shiny skin that shows no signs of bruising.

Belle de Boskoop is a large apple with rough russeted skin.

Elstar
Sweet and slightly crunchy, this medium-sized Dutch apple is a cross between Ingrid Marie and Golden Delicious. It is a popular, easy-eating apple with a honeyed flavor, good to eat whole and in fruit salads.

Elstar has marbled red skin with red and yellow highlights.

Aroma
A Swedish-bred apple with a good, rich, fruity flavor and melting, juicy flesh, this is suitable for both eating raw and baking. The skin is predominantly red flushed and smooth.

APPLE STRUDEL

There are many different fillings for this traditional Central-European pastry, but apple remains a favorite. Filo is a convenient substitute for strudel pastry.

SERVES 4–6

1¼lb (600g) cooking apples, peeled, cored, and cut into medium—small chunks

finely grated zest and juice of 1 lemon

6 tbsp granulated sugar

2 tsp ground cinnamon

½ cup dark raisins

6 sheets filo pastry (keep covered with a clean, damp cloth to prevent the sheets from drying out)

4 tbsp butter, melted

2 tbsp dry bread crumbs

confectioners' sugar, to dust

1 Preheat the oven to 400°F (200°C). Butter a large baking sheet.

2 Mix together the apples, lemon zest and juice, sugar, cinnamon, and raisins. Set aside.

3 Lay a clean kitchen towel on a work surface and place a sheet of filo pastry on top, with one of the longer sides closest to you. Brush with melted butter, then cover with another sheet of filo, placing it over half of the first sheet, so you are increasing the length of the strudel. Brush this sheet with butter. Repeat with the remaining sheets.

4 Sprinkle the bread crumbs over the long pastry sheet, leaving a 2in (5cm) border around the edges.

5 Arrange the apple mixture down the middle of the filo, then roll up away from you like a jellyroll, using the towel to help. Tuck in the ends of the pastry to encase the filling.

6 Brush with melted butter. Carefully lift on to the baking sheet, seam-side down.

7 Bake for 30–40 minutes, or until golden brown and crisp. Loosen the strudel with a metal spatula, then carefully slide on to a serving plate. Dust with confectioners' sugar. Serve hot or cold, with whipped cream.

APPLE SAUCE

The flavor of apples contrasts well with rich meats. A family favorite, this sauce goes well with roast pork.

SERVES 4

1 lb (450g) tart apples, such as Granny Smith

2 tbsp granulated sugar, or more to taste

juice of ½ lemon

½ cinnamon stick

pinch of salt

2 tbsp butter, cut into pieces

1 Peel, core, and coarsely chop the apples, and place in a heavy saucepan with ½ cup of water, the sugar, lemon, cinnamon, and salt. Cover and cook over medium heat, shaking the pan occasionally, for 12–15 minutes, or until the apples are tender, but not dried out. Remove the cinnamon stick. Taste, stirring in more sugar, if needed.

2 Take the pan off the heat and, using a fork, beat in the butter. If desired, press the apples through a coarse sieve, or put into a blender or food processor to make a smoother sauce. Serve warm. This sauce keeps well, covered, in the refrigerator for up to 3 days. Reheat before serving.

APPLES (CONTINUED)

Gala
This widely grown, colorful apple originated in New Zealand. It has a sweet, pleasant flavor that can sometimes verge on the bland, but it is a good fruit to use in salads, pies, and cakes.

Granny Smith
Originally Australian, this fairly large apple has glossy, luminous green skin (that turns yellow in some climates), firm, crunchy flesh, and an intensely sharp flavor that adds interest to fruit salads.

Gloster
The Gloster is large and heart-shaped with an almost solid crimson color. The lightly textured and crisp flesh is refreshing, which makes it a good choice as a dessert apple.

The Gloster is attractive, with a dark-red flush and crisp, sweet flesh.

Grasten
Also known as Gravenstein, this superb heritage variety has a sharp and aromatic flavor. Enjoy it fresh or make it into apple sauce during its brief season.

Chinese Fuji
The same variety as the Kent Fuji, this squat-shaped apple is refreshing, sweet, and crisp. They keep best in the refrigerator, and are good for eating and for apple sauce.

The skin of the Chinese Fuji is yellow-green with pink-red streaks.

Kent Fuji
This apple has the same honeyed sweetness of Golden Delicious, and crisp, firm, quite juicy flesh. The Fuji variety grows in Japan, New Zealand, Brazil, the US, and Europe.

Ida Red
The large, round, slightly flattened fruit is a good keeper, and the firm, dry flesh produces a lovely fluffy, pink-tinged apple sauce. It is good for baked apple and for apple sauce.

The skin of the Ida Red should be waxy and dark crimson.

The color of Golden Delicious ranges from pale green to yellow-gold.

The skin of the Grasten has attractive red and yellow-green streaks.

Golden Delicious
A popular supermarket variety, the thin-skinned fruit is crisp, sugary, and mild. They are best kept chilled for eating fresh, but are also good baked.

TARTE TATIN

At the Tatin sisters' restaurant in the Loire Valley, they created this upside-down apple tart on a pastry base. Use apples that keep their shape, such as Golden Delicious.

SERVES 4–6

2lb (900g) apples

juice of ½ lemon

¾ cup sugar

11 tbsp (1 stick plus 3 tbsp) unsalted butter

1 sheet of cold, prepared sweet shortcrust pastry, pie dough, or puff pastry (enough for a 9–10in (23cm) pie

1 Preheat the oven to 400°F (200°C).

2 Peel, core, and quarter the apples. Sprinkle with lemon juice and set aside.

3 Gently melt the sugar in a 12in (30cm) cast-iron frying pan or other shallow flameproof pan. When the sugar starts to caramelize, add the butter and cook until it looks like crunchy crumbs of toffee. Take the pan off the heat.

4 Add the apples to the pan, packing the apples closely together, overlapping, if necessary.

5 Place over medium–low heat and cook for 15–20 minutes. The butter–sugar mix will become thick and syrupy as it bubbles up around the apples. Do not stir or move the apples. Set aside to cool.

6 If needed, roll out the pastry into a circle large enough to cover the pan. Lay the sheet of pastry over the cooled apples. Trim neatly and push the edges down the inside of the pan to enclose the apples.

7 Bake for 20–30 minutes, until the crust is crisp and golden brown and the apple filling is bubbly-hot.

8 Cool in the pan for 5–10 minutes. Place a heatproof serving plate over the pan and carefully invert the tart onto the platter, using oven gloves to protect your hands and arms. Cut into wedges and serve warm or at room temperature.

APPLES (CONTINUED)

Jonathan
A good, medium-sized, all-purpose apple popular in North America. It has tough but smooth crimson skin brushed with green. The spicy tang makes it a good baking apple, but it is also a crisp addition to salads.

Pinova
A modern German apple, called Piñata in the US, Pinova has an attractive, large, oval shape with striped red and yellow skin. Use in strudel or serve with cheese.

The flesh of the Pinova is crisp and juicy, with a tart–sweet flavor.

Pink Lady
A pretty eating apple with a strong pink blush, tender skin, crisp and firm flesh, and well-balanced flavor.

Reinette du Canada
This medium-sized fruit has a dull, yellow-green russet coat and white flesh. The flesh is crisp and dry with a sweet-sharp flavor. Use in pies or eat fresh.

Red Delicious
This large, heart-shaped crimson apple has shiny, rather tough skin and sweet, crumbly flesh. It is best kept chilled and eaten fresh.

Reine des Reinettes
This large, well-flavored, and aromatic French variety has slightly rough yellow skin streaked with russet. It is the definitive choice for apple tarts.

Bramley
The most famous British cooking apple, the Bramley is green-yellow, particularly large, and irregular in shape. It cooks quickly to a frothy pulp and is the top choice in the UK for apple sauce and apple pie.

Reineta
These large, wide Spanish apples have russet skin and an excellent balance of juice and flavor that makes them ideal for eating as well as baking and poaching.

Pink Pearl
This conical apple, with crisp, juicy pink flesh and a sweet–tart flavor, can be enjoyed as a dessert or snack.

As its name implies, Pink Pearl has a pretty, pearly pink appearance.

Ingrid Marie
This variety is related to Cox's Orange Pippin, and is a popular apple in northern Europe, particularly for baking and cooking.

The skin of the Ingrid Marie apple has crimson flushes with russet streaks.

SPICED BAKED APPLE WITH WALNUTS

Serve this traditional British family-style dessert with crème fraîche, custard, or heavy cream.

SERVES 4

4 large apples, such as Golden Delicious or Bramley
¾ cup coarsely chopped walnuts
1 tbsp dark raisins
1 tbsp brown sugar
½ tsp ground cinnamon
2 tbsp butter, softened

1 Preheat the oven to 350°F (180°C).

2 Clean the apples with a damp cloth, and remove the cores with either an apple corer, grapefruit spoon, or a sharp knife. Make a horizontal cut in the skin around the middle of each apple. Place in a shallow, lightly buttered baking dish.

3 Mix the walnuts, raisins, sugar, and cinnamon with the butter.

4 Stuff each apple cavity with some of the mixture, and add ½in (1cm) water to the dish.

5 Bake for 30 minutes, or until the flesh is tender when pierced with the tip of a knife. When slightly cooled, carefully remove the apples from the baking dish, transfer them to serving plates, and serve warm.

PEARS

Pears are primarily grown in the temperate zones of Europe, Australia, New Zealand, the Americas, and South Africa. They are related to the apple but have a longer neck and more bulbous shape. Their fine, granular, white flesh is soft, juicy, and perfumed. Pears ripen from the inside out and pass from rock-hard to woolly and unpleasant very quickly, so once they are perfectly ripe, they should be eaten as soon as possible.

🔒 **BUY** Traditionally harvested in late fall, pears generally have a shorter season than apples. Since they ripen quickly once picked, most are taken from the tree underripe. When ripe, the stalk end should yield gently if pressed. Never buy pears that are too soft or bruised, and always handle with care, since they damage easily.

▤ **STORE** Ripen hard fruit in a paper bag at room temperature. Once ripe, keep in open bags at the bottom of the fridge, but serve at room temperature. Freeze peeled, halved pears in a syrup.

● **EAT** When preparing pears, brush the cut surface with lemon juice to prevent browning, or place in a bowl of water acidulated in lemon juice.

Fresh: Peel if wished, then eat whole; or quarter or slice for fruit salad. Use up overripe fruit in sauces and smoothies. **Cooked:** Pears that are slightly underripe work best. Peel, chop, or slice, and poach or bake for desserts and pies. Peel, leaving on the stalk, to bake whole. **Preserved:** Bottle in syrup or alcohol, make fruit butter, or use in chutneys and pickles.
FLAVOR PAIRINGS Game, blue cheese, Parmesan cheese, arugula, watercress, lemon, walnuts, almonds, cinnamon, ginger, butterscotch, chocolate, vanilla, tarragon, balsamic vinegar, red wine.
CLASSIC RECIPES *Poires Belle Hélène*; pears in red wine; braised red cabbage with pears; *pato con peras; piquechagne*.

Conference
You can identify this pear by its long, thin shape and russeting on the skin, which turns from green to yellow as the fruit ripens. Sweet, creamy, and juicy, it is perfect for fruit salads as well as poaching, baking, or bottling.

Beurré Bosc is recognizable by its dark green-yellow russeted skin.

Beurré Bosc
Recognizable by its long, tapered neck and lengthy stalk, this has aromatic, crisp, and sweetly spicy flesh, and holds its shape well when poached or baked.

The Seckel is a small, chubby russet pear.

Seckel
With a grainy texture and delicious, spicy flavor, this is best eaten fresh with cheese and nuts, but is also good for pickling or making pear butter.

The firm skin and globular form conceal the delicate flesh of one of the finest dessert pears.

Beurré Hardy
This French variety is an all-purpose fruit with rough bronze, russet skin. The ripe, pink-tinged flesh is tender and sweet with a buttery texture.

Red Sensation
Similar to Red Williams (Bartlett), this dual-purpose pear ripens in late summer. It is juicy with a smooth texture and tender, bright red skin.

Abate Fetel
Large, elongated, and rounded at the bottom, the Abate Fetel has juicy, sweet white flesh with a good crunch, which makes it a great all-around pear.

The freckled russet and lemon-yellow skin of this variety is tender enough to eat.

Doyenné du Comice
Considered to be the best-flavored dessert pear, the creamy-pink flesh of this variety is juicy, with a melting texture and spicy flavor. Serve fresh as a special dessert.

The Doyenné du Comice is plump and rather stubby in shape.

Anjou
A lopsided pear with a wide girth and a striking yellow to lime green skin, this has tender, aromatic flesh that is full of sweet juice. It is good to eat both fresh and poached with spices.

CLASSIC RECIPE

POIRES BELLE HÉLÈNE

This famous 19th-century French dessert is an inspired combination of poached pears, vanilla ice cream, and warm chocolate sauce.

SERVES 8

| 1 cup granulated sugar |
| 1 long, thin strip lemon rind |
| a few drops of vanilla extract |
| 8 firm, ripe pears, peeled, halved, and cored |
| 10oz (300g) semisweet chocolate, in pieces |
| 4 tbsp unsalted butter, cut into pieces |
| ½ cup heavy whipping cream |
| 1 quart (1 liter) vanilla ice cream |
| 1 cup toasted, slivered almonds |

1 Place the sugar in a wide, heavy saucepan with the lemon rind and 1 quart (1.2 liters) water. Heat gently, stirring, until the sugar has dissolved, then bring to a boil and simmer for 1 minute. Remove from the heat and add the vanilla extract.

2 Place the pear halves, cut-side down, in the pan, preferably in a single layer. Cover and simmer very gently over low heat for 15–20 minutes, or until tender.

3 Transfer the pears to a wide bowl and cover with the syrup. Leave to cool, then cover and refrigerate.

4 Combine the chocolate with ½ cup water in a heatproof bowl. Set the bowl over a saucepan containing 1 inch (2.5cm) of hot but not boiling water. (Do not let the water touch the bottom of the bowl.) Stir the chocolate until melted and smooth, then stir in the butter and cream. Remove the pan from the stove; keep warm over the hot water.

5 To serve, place scoops of vanilla ice cream in individual serving dishes. Arrange 2 pear halves on top of the ice cream so they lean in and touch at the top. Drizzle the pears with the warm chocolate sauce, and sprinkle with almonds. Serve at once.

PEARS (CONTINUED)

Red Williams
Red Williams are part of the Williams family, known as Bartlett in North America, differing only in color from the green-gold norm. All varieties have a classic waisted shape, grainy texture, and sweet, musky flavor, which makes them a good choice for both eating and cooking.

The skin is green-gold with speckles and russet patches.

Williams' Bon Chrétien
This is the original Williams variety bred in the UK about 1770. In the US, it is called Bartlett, after the importer, as are all other Williams varieties. The squat bell-shaped fruit is tender, juicy, and slightly musky, and is particularly good for preserving.

Passe Crassane
A late-winter pear common in southern Europe, this is big and broad, with russeted, greenish-yellow skin. Although juicy and sweet, the texture can be slightly coarse, which makes it best suited for cooking.

CLASSIC RECIPE

PEARS IN RED WINE

Pears poached in red wine is a simple but classic French dessert. Serve with whipped cream, perhaps flavored with pear brandy.

SERVES 4

4 large, firm pears, such as Bosc or Conference

juice of 1 lemon

1 bottle (750ml) dry red wine, such as Cabernet Sauvignon

⅔ cup granulated sugar

1 small stick cinnamon

1 Preheat the oven to 300°F (150°C). Peel the pears and, working from the bottom, remove the cores, keeping the pears whole with the stems attached. Sprinkle with the lemon juice to prevent browning and set aside.

2 Put the wine, sugar, and cinnamon in a small flameproof casserole dish. Bring to a simmer, stirring to dissolve the sugar. Add the pears in a single layer if possible, cover, and transfer to the oven. Cook for 2 hours, gently turning the pears halfway through the cooking time so they are evenly tinted red from the wine.

3 Remove from the oven and leave the pears to cool in the poaching liquid, then use a slotted spoon to transfer them to a serving dish.

4 Set the casserole dish over high heat and boil the cooking liquid until it is syrupy. Remove the cinnamon stick and spoon the syrup over the pears. Allow to cool, then refrigerate until well chilled before serving.

ASIAN PEARS

Native to China, Japan, and Korea, Asian pear trees are cultivated throughout East Asia as well as in the cool, humid, and temperate regions of Australia, India, New Zealand, and the US. They are often called nashi, Japanese pear, Korean pear, or apple pear. There are two main cultivars: round "red pears" with pale green to yellow or bronze skin, and pear-shaped "green pears" with yellow-green skin. All have a crisp texture, white flesh, delicate flavor, and abundant sweet juice.

BUY The season generally stretches from early summer to early fall. Asian pears ripen on the tree and are firm with a sweet aroma when they are picked ready to eat. The skin damages easily so most fruit is individually wrapped to prevent spots and bruising. Avoid any pears that look soft, wrinkled, or marked.

STORE Asian pears are best stored in a loosely closed paper bag in the refrigerator. Most will keep for up to 3 months.

EAT As with other types of pear, cut surfaces need to be brushed with lemon juice to prevent browning.
Fresh: Peel, if desired, then discard seeds and any hard flesh. Eat whole, slightly refrigerated; or slice thinly or cut into wedges for fruit and savory salads. Chop or juice for marinades. In Japan, they are eaten with a sprinkling of salt. **Cooked:** Finely chop or juice to sweeten Asian sauces and dishes. Poach in spiced syrup.
Preserved: Add to jelly or jam. Preserve in syrup.
FLAVOR PAIRINGS Beef, papaya, mango, lime, chile, soy, ginger, cardamom, star anise, rice vinegar, honey.
CLASSIC RECIPES *Yukhoe; bulgogi.*

Nijisseiki
Sometimes called 20th Century, this variety of "green pear" is highly popular in Japan and the US. The fruit is pale green and very juicy, ideal for fruit or savory salads.

Hosui
Meaning "water of abundance," this is a fairly large, round, golden-brown "red pear" with juicy, sweet flesh. Similar in appearance, although smaller, is the sweet, full-flavored Kosui, whose name means "water of happiness" in Japanese.

Hosui is best used in salads or eaten fresh as a snack fruit.

Shinseiki
This round, pale Japanese variety of "green pear" has mild and creamy-white flesh. Enjoy it fresh or poached.

PRICKLY PEAR

Sometimes known as "Indian figs" or "cactus pear," barrel-shaped prickly pears are the fruit of a type of cactus, and are native to Central America and the Southern United States but grow in many other regions of the world. As the name suggests, the skin is covered in tiny, sharp, hairlike prickles. They ripen from green to yellow to a deep apricot-pink color. The orange-pink flesh has a melonlike texture, and a sweet, scented flavor. The small, crunchy seeds can be eaten raw, but become hard when cooked.

BUY Choose unblemished fruit. When collected in the winter months, the prickles are usually mechanically removed before the fruits are sold commercially, but the fruit must still be peeled with care, since it may contain invisible needles that can become embedded in your hands.

STORE Store carefully wrapped in a cool place. Freeze the puréed pulp or slices in syrup.

EAT Fresh: Slice or cut into chunks and eat fresh. Add to fruit salads and ice cream. Sieve pulp for soft drinks. **Cooked:** Stew for compotes and sauces. Add the pulp to sauces and cake fillings. **Preserved:** Use in jams, marmalade, and jellies. Candy for decorative additions to cakes and desserts.

FLAVOR PAIRINGS: Proscuitto, yogurt, lime, lemon, mango, passion fruit, cream, ginger.

CLASSIC RECIPES: Prickly pear jam; prickly pear jelly.

Resembling fluorescent hand grenades, prickly pears must be handled almost as carefully.

MEDLAR

The small brown fruit, the size of a golf ball, is open at the end opposite the stalk, like a cup, revealing five pointed internal sections. The trees grow wild in temperate areas, or can be found in private gardens, but are rarely cultivated commercially. In 1990, a rare species with red fruit was found in North America. The ripe fruit are hard, green, and acidic, and the fruit is actually eaten when overripe and half-rotted. The process is known as "bletting," and occurs either naturally with frost, or by storing them in an airy place for several weeks.

BUY By late fall or early winter, the brown skin should be wrinkled and russetted. When ripe, the pulp is opaque, sticky, and sugar-sweet with a touch of astringency. It should be soft enough to remove with a spoon.

STORE To speed up the rotting or "bletting" process, whole unripe medlars can be frozen to break up the cell structure, then left to "decay" at room temperature.

EAT Fresh: Eat raw. Peel back the skin and suck or scrape out the flesh, or halve and spoon it out. **Cooked:** Add the pulp to a rich meat sauce. **Preserved:** Make jelly or curd.

FLAVOR PAIRINGS: Meat, game, cheese, spices, wine.

CLASSIC RECIPES: Medlar jelly; medlar cheese (curd).

The shriveled brown fruit has exposed seed boxes at the end opposite the stalk.

QUINCE

The golden-yellow fruit is found in most temperate zones, but is particularly associated with the Middle East, Greece, France, and Spain. Quinces can resemble in size and shape both lumpy apples and fat pears. The fresh fruit is hard and granular and unpleasantly sour to eat raw, but when cooked it becomes soft, with a distinctive flavor and beautiful red-gold hues. Once peeled, drop the pieces into a mixture of lemon and water to prevent browning.

BUY They are most likely to be found in the fall, on sale in small specialty grocers and markets. Although the golden yellow skin is tough, it is extremely fragrant. Look for fruit of uniform color with no brown patches. Unripe fruit has a downy skin but this becomes smooth as the fruit ripens. Remaining spots can be rubbed off.

STORE Store in a bowl in a cool, dry place for up to a week. Keep apart from other foods, since the aroma is heavenly but penetrating. If necessary, store wrapped in paper towels in the fridge for up to two weeks. Wash before cooking. To freeze, peel, core, slice, and poach in light syrup.

EAT **Cooked:** Peel, core, and chop for sauces and meat dishes, tarts, pies, and crumbles. Purée for mousses and fruit creams. **Preserved:** Make into jams and jellies or a thick, jellied paste.

FLAVOR PAIRINGS: Pork, lamb, chicken, game, cheese, apples, pears, ginger, cloves, cinnamon.

CLASSIC RECIPES: Lamb and quince tagine; Persian stuffed quinces; quince cheese.

The yellow quince may look misshapen, but it has a wonderful, honeyed fragrance.

QUINCE CHEESE

Known as membrillo in Spain, this thick fruit purée is often served with a sheep's milk cheese, such as Manchego.

MAKES ABOUT 3LB (1.25 KG)

2¼lb (1kg) quinces

2lb (900g) granulated sugar

freshly squeezed juice of 3 lemons

1 Peel and core the quinces, then cut into 2in (4cm) chunks. Put in a saucepan and add enough water to cover. Bring to a boil; reduce the heat and simmer, partially covered, for 30 minutes, or until the quinces are soft. If the water evaporates, add more. Alternatively, wrap the chunks in foil and bake in a preheated 350°F (180°C) oven for about 1 hour, until they are soft.

2 Mash the quinces coarsely, and press through a fine sieve or food mill to make a smooth purée.

3 Put the purée in a heavy saucepan with the sugar and lemon juice. Simmer over low heat for 20 minutes, stirring frequently, until the sugar dissolves.

4 Increase the heat to medium and cook, stirring frequently, until the purée is very thick. It will darken slightly. Watch carefully, as it can stick to the pan and burn.

5 Pack the quince "cheese" into hot sterilized jars, seal, and label as directed by the canning jar maker.

The oval apricot-colored fruit bruises easily when ripe.

LOQUAT

Also known as the Japanese medlar, the loquat is one of the few subtropical fruits that belong to the apple and pear family. It is native to China and South Japan but is now cultivated in many other places such as Hawaii, Florida, Spain, and Brazil. They do best in temperate climates or in cooler elevations in the tropics. They look like small apricots, with pale orange, downy skin and similar colored flesh that contains a few large, flat, inedible seeds. The fruit is juicy and luscious, with a pleasantly tart flavor.

BUY They are briefly in season in late spring, but spoil quickly after picking and are very fragile, so care must be taken in handling and transportation. Look for tender, richly colored fruit with a few brown spots—these indicate ripeness. Since loquats keep longer on the vine, they are sometimes marketed with stems and leaves.

STORE Loquats have a short shelf life, so should be eaten or used soon after purchase. Refrigerate only if very ripe. Rinse carefully before use. Freeze in syrup without stem, blossom end, or seeds.

EAT Fresh: Cut across and remove the seeds. Spoon out the flesh. Peel if wished. Quarter and add to fruit salad, ice cream, and cake fillings.
Cooked: Poach in syrup. Chop and add to sauces.
Preserved: Chop or purée for jellies, jams, and liqueurs. Candy or dry.
FLAVOR PAIRINGS: Poultry, shrimp, goat's cheese, vanilla ice cream, apples, pears, oranges, peaches, lemon, lime, ginger, spirits.
CLASSIC RECIPES: Exotic fruit salad; loquat jam; Chinese chicken with loquats.

FIGS

Figs grow widely in Mediterranean climates and are exported, in particular, from France, Greece, Turkey, and Brazil. Small and squat, they vary in color from purple-black to golden yellow, lime, and pale green. Color, however, makes little difference to taste; the flavor depends more on where they were grown and the degree of ripeness. When ripe, all have honeyed, succulent flesh that ranges in color from pale to deep pink, and is studded with tiny, edible seeds.

BUY Ripe figs are picked in the summer and fall, but are very delicate and do not travel well. They should be unblemished, feel heavy in the hand, and just yield without pressing. The aroma should be faint and delicate. A few beads of sugar juice around the stem indicate ripeness.

STORE Ripe figs should be eaten as soon as possible, but can be stored in the refrigerator for a day; serve at room temperature. Keep underripe figs at room temperature until the skin softens. Figs can be frozen and used for cooked preparations.

EAT Fresh: Eat whole. Peel or discard the skin if it seems tough. Halve, quarter, or cut into wedges almost to the base and press gently up into a flower shape. Add to salads. Stuff for sweetmeats. **Cooked:** Poach whole or halved in syrup. Bake or stew for sauces and sweet or savory dishes. **Preserved:** Bottle or make into jam. Dry fruit.
FLAVOR PAIRINGS: Cured meat, salad, yogurt, cream, cheese, fruit, nuts, anise, marzipan, fortified wine.
CLASSIC RECIPES: Proscuitto and figs; duck with figs; fig tart; fig jam.

CLASSIC RECIPE

BAKED FIGS WITH CINNAMON AND HONEY

A simple-to-prepare, but stylish end to a meal. Serve warm or at room temperature with heavy cream.

SERVES 4

6 firm but ripe figs

2 tbsp honey

2 tbsp brandy or rum

ground cinnamon

1 Preheat the oven to 350°F (180°C). Cut the figs in half lengthwise and place, cut-side up, in a shallow baking dish.

2 Drizzle the figs with the honey and brandy, and sprinkle each with a generous pinch of cinnamon.

3 Bake for 20 minutes, or until the figs are heated through and soft, but still hold their shape. Check them after 10 minutes, as the figs may vary slightly in ripeness.

When ripe, white figs look plump and pale green.

White figs
"White" figs cover a range of varieties but they are, in fact, typically light green in color, with strawberry-pink flesh that makes them perfect for both eating fresh and preserving.

Brown Turkey
Typically this fig has meaty, soft, red flesh and purplish-brown skin. It has a very good flavor and is best eaten fresh.

Yellow fig
This includes a range of yellow-green varieties with flesh that ranges from pale amber to green-yellow and deep red. The pulp is full of seeds that are actually tiny individual fruits.

Black Mission
This famous variety has thin, black-purple skin and watermelon-pink flesh loaded with minute edible seeds. It has a rich, sweet flavor and also dries well.

PLUMS

Plums are widely cultivated in temperate zones. There are many varieties, with flesh of orange-red, orange-yellow, or golden-green, and purple, red, green, or yellow skin. The types differ in sweetness, tartness, and amount of juice, so some are more suitable for eating fresh than for cooking, although many can be used for both. European varieties tend to be smaller and firmer than plums of Asian origin. Pluots are a plum—apricot hybrid, with plum as the dominant parent. Mainly grown in California, they are extremely sweet, juicy, and fragrant.

BUY Buy in midsummer to early fall for immediate use, if possible. They should be firm, yet give slightly when pressed, and have a slight bloom. They should never feel squishy. Avoid hard, wrinkled, or shriveled plums and those with brown patches.

STORE Ripe plums can be kept for several days in an open paper bag in the crisper of the refrigerator. Soften fruit that is slightly underripe in a paper bag at room temperature. Freeze in syrup, or as a purée.

EAT Cut along the seam and twist the two halves to open the fruit. **Fresh:** Eat as a snack or add to salads. **Cooked:** Leave the skin on for dishes in which they need to keep their shape. Purée for soufflés, mousses, and sauces. Poach or bake in syrup. Use in pies, tarts, crumbles, batter desserts, and quick breads. Enclose in pastry for dumplings. Add to stews. Halve and broil. **Preserved:** Bottle in syrup or brandy. Make into preserves. Dry (as prunes).

FLAVOR PAIRINGS Lamb, duck, pork, ham, goose, almonds, spices, mascarpone, brandy.

CLASSIC RECIPES Plum jam; plum dumplings; plum and mascarpone tart; potato gnocchi stuffed with plums; damson cheese; *tarte aux mirabelles; pflaumenkuchen; tzimmes; karcho.*

Guide your knife down the natural crease to cut the fruit in half before removing the stone.

Santa Rosa
A particularly large, round plum, this has firm, shiny, dark red-purple skin and a pleasantly tart flavor. Eat fresh, or use in crumbles and cobblers.

Flavor Rich
A Pluot with black skin, crunchy amber flesh, and a medium-sweet taste, this cooks well in tarts and sauces, but is also good to eat fresh.

Greengages are oval and green-yellow or acid green, with a dusty white bloom.

Greengage
Distinctively sweet and fragrant, greengages are best eaten fresh, although they also make excellent jam and tarts.

Victoria
The classic British dessert plum, this has an all-too-short summer season. Large, oval, and pinkish-yellow, Victorias are luscious fresh but also superb for cooking and preserving.

Sloe
These are wild plums, the small, black fruits of the blackthorn, a wild hedgerow bush. They are too sour to eat but make good jam and homemade sloe gin.

Damson
Small, dark blue damsons have a large stone and spicy-tart flavor that makes them superb for jam. Their midsummer season is very short, so buy when you see them.

Coe's Golden Drop
An old English variety, this has clear yellow skin and flesh and a sweet, melting flavor.

Flavor Queen
A large, green-yellow Pluot, Flavor Queen has sweet, juicy flesh and tender skin. Eat fresh or use in salsas and cakes.

Mirabelle
Small and round, the Mirabelle is an enchanting yellow with a pink blush, often speckled with reddish dots. Intensely sweet, it is mainly used in tarts, preserves, and eaux-de-vie.

PLUM JAM

Most plum varieties make delicious jam. Properly sealed jars can be stored in a cool, dark place for up to a year, but must be refrigerated after opening.

MAKES ABOUT 11 CUPS

3lbs (1.5kg) firm but ripe plums

3lbs (1.5kg) granulated or superfine sugar

1 Halve the plums and remove the stones. (If the fruit is too hard to remove them easily, you can cook with the stones intact and let them loosen naturally. Use a slotted spoon to scoop them out when the jam is boiling.)

2 Put the fruit in a large heavy-bottomed pot or preserving pan. The pan should be no more than half full to ensure sufficient space for rapid boiling. Add 2 cups water and bring to a boil. Reduce the heat and simmer gently for about 30 minutes, or until soft. The exact time will depend on the ripeness of the fruit.

3 Add the sugar and stir until it has dissolved completely, then bring back to a boil. Boil constantly and rapidly for 15–20 minutes, or until the setting point is reached.

4 Remove from the heat and skim any foam from the surface of the jam. Let the jam stand for about 5 minutes, then ladle it into warmed sterilized jars, cover, and seal.

APRICOTS

Apricots are cultivated in the warmer temperate regions of the world. The top producers are Turkey, Iran, and Italy, but Australia, Chile, South Africa, and California also have important export crops. Typically, the small, dimpled fruit has golden-orange, velvety skin flushed with deep pink; honey-sweet, slightly tangy juice; and a delicious fragrance when ripe. The kernel of the stone is used to flavor jams, cookies, and Amaretto liqueur.

BUY Once harvested, between May and September, apricots will not ripen any further. However, when fully ripe they are also fragile and bruise easily, which is why many apricots are picked underripe. As a result, what you buy may be woolly, dry, or just plain disappointing. Select plump, smooth, slightly soft apricots with a rich color. Reject pale, dull, or greenish fruit.

STORE Apricots can be kept at room temperature for a few days (if hard they might soften but they won't ripen further) or store in an open paper bag at the bottom of the refrigerator. Freeze, peeled and stoned, in syrup.

EAT Use the natural line in the fruit to cut in half and twist apart. **Fresh:** Eat as a snack. Add to fruit salads or a fruit plate. **Cooked:** Halve and use in tarts and pastries. Poach in syrup or wine. Halve, stuff, and bake for desserts. Purée for sweet and savory sauces. Add to rice and couscous dishes, stews, roasts, and stuffings. **Preserved:** Make jam and conserves. Bottle in syrup or liqueur. Dry.

FLAVOR PAIRINGS Lamb, pork, poultry, ham, yogurt, cream, custard, oranges, almonds, rice, ginger, vanilla, sweet white wine.

CLASSIC RECIPES Apricot and almond tart; apricot jam and jelly; apricot ice cream; spiced apricots; apricot leather.

APRICOT AND ALMOND TART

When apricots are not in season, make this popular European dessert with fresh peaches or nectarines. Serve warm with crème fraîche or whipped cream.

SERVES 4–6

9oz (250g) cold pie dough or puff pastry

2 tbsp apricot jam

1lb (500g) fresh apricots, halved and stoned

¼ cup slivered almonds

3 tbsp Amaretto liqueur

3 tbsp demerara (raw) sugar

2 tbsp cold butter

1 Preheat the oven to 425°F (220°C).

2 Roll out the pastry into a rectangle about 12 x 9in (30 x 23cm). Trim the edges with a sharp knife. Place on a lightly greased baking sheet.

3 Spread the jam over the pastry to within ¾in (2cm) of the edges.

4 Gently press the apricot halves, cut side up, on the pastry in rows, leaving a ½in (1cm) margin all around the outside.

5 Scatter the almonds over the apricots. Sprinkle with the Amaretto and then the sugar. Place a dot of butter in each apricot cavity.

6 Bake for 10 minutes, then reduce the heat to 400°F (200°C). Bake for another 20 minutes, or until the pastry and apricots are glazed and golden brown.

Patterson apricots are plump, well shaped, and soft to the touch when ripe.

Patterson
A popular, widely grown variety, Patterson scores highly in terms of durability and shelf life. It is an excellent choice for baking and cooking.

The skin of the fruit looks like soft, golden suede lightly speckled with pink.

Royal Blenheim
A delicate, exquisite heritage variety, Royal Blenheim has a musky perfume and soft, downy skin. It is a rare find, so if you are lucky savor it fresh.

Goldstrike
This large, meaty apricot has an attractive orange color with a red blush. You can eat these fresh or make into delicious jam.

Although the stone is large, the size of the fruit means there is still plenty of flesh to enjoy.

Take advantage of abundant trays of blushed, plump peaches – a sweet scent is a tell-tale sign of ripeness.

PEACHES AND NECTARINES

These classic summer fruits are grown worldwide in Mediterranean-type climates. Peaches usually have a downy skin, whereas nectarines, which are a variety of peach, are smooth-skinned with a generally sharper flavor. The leading export countries for both fruits are Spain, Italy, France, and the US. Freestone fruit has flesh that separates easily from the stone or pit; clingstone types have flesh that "clings" more to the pit. Fragrant white-flesh peaches and nectarines are low in acid and best for eating fresh, while yellow-fleshed fruit are ideal for baking and cooking.

BUY Select by touch, but handle carefully: when ripe, the fruit should yield to gentle pressure and have a sweet fragrance. Look for fruit with unblemished skin. Avoid any that is extremely hard or has a dull color, and fruit with very soft, wrinkled, bruised, or punctured skin.

STORE Keep at room temperature for a couple of days, or in an open paper bag at the bottom of the refrigerator for up to a week. Both peaches and nectarines are suitable for freezing.

EAT Fresh: Wash and eat at room temperature, whole or halved (cut down the natural seam and twist in opposite directions to separate). Peel peaches, if wished, then section or slice for fruit salads and desserts; dice for salsas; purée for ice cream, sorbet, cold soups, and sauces. **Cooked:** Slice and sauté, or halve, stuff, and bake for hot desserts. Halve and broil to serve with savory dishes. **Preserved:** Bottle in syrup or alcohol; make jams and jellies; use underripe fruit for chutney; dry.

FLAVOR PAIRINGS Beef, duck, sour cream, yogurt, passion fruit, mangoes, berries, lime, mint, almonds, cinnamon, ginger, nutmeg, chiles, Champagne, sherry, Amaretto.

CLASSIC RECIPES Peach Melba; *pêches cardinal*; peaches stuffed with macaroons; nectarine salsa; Bellini.

PEELING PEACHES

A quick blanch in boiling water will loosen the downy skin, and it will slip off easily. Nectarines are usually not peeled because their skin is smooth and thin.

1 With a small, sharp knife, cut a small cross in the skin on the base of the fruit. **2** Immerse the fruit in boiling water for 30 seconds. **3** Remove from the water and pull off the skin with your fingers.

CLASSIC RECIPE

PEACH MELBA

According to legend, the opera singer Dame Nellie Melba lent her name to this truly great dessert that was created in her honor by Escoffier.

SERVES 4

1 ½ cups fresh raspberries

1–2 tbsp superfine or granulated sugar

1 tsp fresh lemon juice

2 large, ripe peaches (or 4 small ones)

1 pint (500ml) vanilla ice cream

toasted, slivered almonds, to serve

1 Press the raspberries through a nylon sieve to remove the seeds, then place in a small nonreactive saucepan.

2 Set the pan over very low heat to gently warm the purée, then stir in the sugar with a wooden spoon. When dissolved, remove from the heat and stir in the lemon juice.

3 Allow to cool, then scrape into a container, cover tightly, and refrigerate for at least 1–2 hours, or overnight.

4 Shortly before serving, peel and halve the peaches, and remove the pits.

5 Divide the ice cream among 4 chilled serving dishes and top each with a peach half. Spoon over some of the Melba (raspberry) sauce over the top and sprinkle with almonds.

PEACHES

Donut
So named because it is shaped like a doughnut with a sunken middle, this peach has a mildly sweet flavor with a hint of almonds. Eat fresh, or use in salsas, or halve and broil.

Red Haven
A midseason, freestone peach, Red Haven has firm, yellow flesh and a rich, juicy flavor. It's a good all-arounder and a popular choice for pies and jam.

Red Baron
Large and richly colored, this freestone peach has firm yet juicy yellow flesh. Its fine flavor makes it an all-around winner, to be enjoyed both fresh and cooked.

Use the natural crease as a guide when cutting the fruit in half.

Rich Lady
This variety is part of the early-season "Lady" family of freestone yellow-flesh peaches, which are all known for their beautiful color and delicious taste. Eat fresh and use in desserts and ice cream.

Pêche de Vigne

Only found for a few brief weeks in the Rhône Valley in France, this small peach with a thick, grayish down on the skin develops deep pink-red flesh as it ripens fully. It has the most exquisite flavor, so reserve for a special dessert.

The beautiful, fragrant red flesh tastes like a cross between white peaches and raspberries.

NECTARINES

In this freestone variety, the large pit comes away easily from the flesh.

Flavortop

This is an excellent firm, sweet nectarine with yellow flesh. Popular in the US, it is ideal for both eating and cooking.

Babcock

A small to medium-sized peach, this has fuzz-free, blushed skin. The white flesh is tender, juicy, and tangy sweet. Eat fresh or use to make a perfect Bellini.

Arctic Glo

A white-fleshed nectarine with a unique sweetly tart flavor, Arctic Glo is best eaten fresh as a snack or dessert.

Some white-fleshed fruit has a pretty pink blush when cut open.

Calanda

This large, firm, and deliciously sweet Spanish peach is hand-wrapped in waxed paper bags as the fruit matures on the tree. It is superb for both desserts and cooking.

The golden flesh of Calanda peaches matches the color of the skin.

Snow Pearl

Round in shape with warmly colored skin, this nectarine has firm, white flesh that clings around the pit. It is a good choice for pies and baking.

Choose cherries that are plump and firm, with shiny, rather than bloomy, skins.

CHERRIES

Native to western Asia, cherries are now cultivated in temperate regions worldwide. There are two main types: plump sweet cherries (best eaten raw, although they can be cooked), which may be either firm and crisp or soft and juicy, and the usually smaller sour cherries (often inedible raw but delicious cooked), which range from almost sweet to bitter and tart. In addition, there are sweet—sour hybrids. Cherries can vary in color from pale creamy-yellow to deep red and black.

🔒 **BUY** Best bought on the stalk in summer, cherries should look plump, firm, and shiny. Pliant green stems are an indication of freshness. Avoid fruit that is too soft, bruised, or split, or that looks dry and withered. Sour cherries have a very short midsummer season.

🗄 **STORE** Keep (unwashed and on the stem) in an open paper bag in the bottom of the refrigerator for a few days. For longer storage, open freeze whole, or freeze without pits in syrup.

⦿ **EAT Fresh:** Eat sweet cherries or hybrids at room temperature; add to fruit salads; decorate cakes and desserts. **Cooked:** Use cherries in cakes, pies, compotes, soups, and sweet or savory sauces. **Preserved:** Make jam; preserve in brandy or syrup; pickle or candy/crystallize; dry.

FLAVOR PAIRINGS Duck, game, almonds, sweet spices, chocolate, citrus, brandy, grappa.

CLASSIC RECIPES Cherry pie; Black Forest cake; *canard Montmorency; clafoutis;* cherry soup; cherries jubilee.

Rainier
A pretty fruit with golden skin, pink blush, and yellow flesh, Rainier is a juicy and rich sweet cherry. It is expensive to buy because it is delicate and easily bruised so needs to be handled carefully.

Stella is a plump cherry that is almost square in shape.

Stella
This sweet variety, which may be dark red or purple-black, has a pure, gentle flavor. Like the soft-fleshed Bing cherry, popular in North America, you can eat them fresh or use in pies, sauces, or clafoutis.

Morello
The shiny red or black Morello is tangy and sour with dark juice. It is inedible raw, but very juicy and full of flavor when preserved in brandy or syrup, or made into jam or a cold soup.

Montmorency
Bright red, sour Montmorency has clear juice and a fresh, tart flavor that is brought out by cooking in sauces, in cold soups, or with duck.

Barbados cherry
Also widely known as acerola, this small fruit resembles a cherry although it is not related. Refreshingly juicy and pleasantly acidic, Barbados cherries are often used in preserves and cakes.

CHERRY PIE

Cherry pie is an all-American favorite that can be made with either sweet or sour cherries. This double-crust version uses sweet Bing cherries.

SERVES 6

For the pastry

5 tbsp cold butter, cut into pieces

5 tbsp lard, cut into pieces

2 cups all-purpose flour, sifted with a pinch of salt

milk and superfine or granulated sugar, to glaze

For the filling

3 tbsp demerara (raw) sugar

1½lbs (750g) Bing cherries, pitted

1 tbsp cornstarch

½ tsp ground cinnamon

2 drops almond extract

1 tbsp fresh lemon juice

1 egg white, lightly beaten with 1 tbsp water

2 tbsp cold butter, cut into pieces

1 Preheat the oven to 400°F (200°C). Make the pastry by rubbing the butter and lard into the flour until the mixture resembles coarse crumbs; then work in 2–3 tbsp ice water until the mixture just holds together. Wrap in plastic and refrigerate for 30 minutes.

2 In a saucepan, dissolve the demerara sugar in 1 cup (300ml) water, then boil rapidly for 3–4 minutes to make a syrup. Stir the cherries into the syrup and cook just until the mixture reaches a boil. Drain the cherries and allow to cool.

3 In a bowl, gently mix together the cherries, cornstarch, cinnamon, almond extract, and lemon juice.

4 Roll out two-thirds of the pastry on a well-floured surface and use to line a 9in (23cm) round greased pie plate. Brush the entire pastry with the egg-white mixture to prevent a soggy crust. Spoon in the cherry mixture and dot with the butter.

5 Roll out the remaining pastry and lay it over the cherries. Trim the pastry so it hangs about ¾in (2cm) over the edge of the pan. Moisten the edges of the pastry, then press together lightly and fold under to seal. Crimp the edge decoratively. Cut several small vents in the top crust so steam can escape. Brush with milk and dust with the sugar.

6 Place the pie plate on a baking sheet (to catch any drips) and bake for 30–40 minutes, or until the crust is golden brown. Cool on a wire rack before serving warm or at room temperature.

GRAPES

These sun-loving fruit are grown in most warm, temperate climates. The showpiece of the grape family is table or dessert grapes, which are cultivated primarily in Spain, South Africa, Chile, Australia, and California. They are larger and sweeter than wine grapes, although a few varieties are used for both purposes. Table grapes may be either seedless or seeded. The leaves from the grapevines are also used in the kitchen, particularly in the cuisines of the eastern Mediterranean.

BUY Traditionally harvested in the summer and fall (unless hothouse grown), the best are transported in bunches in individual wrapping and should still have their dusty "bloom." A slight ring of bruising around the stalk indicates loss of freshness. White grapes should have an amber tinge; uniformly bright green ones will be acidic. Black varieties should not show any green. Avoid wrinkled grapes or those with brown spots.

STORE Grapes are very delicate and bruise easily, so keep handling to a minimum. Store unwashed bunches carefully on several layers of paper towels or in an open paper bag in the refrigerator for up to 5 days. Grapes can be frozen in syrup.

EAT Fresh: Use in both savory and fruit salads; press for juice; or eat at room temperature, particularly with soft or rich cheeses. **Cooked:** Peel and seed as preferred. Sauté for cream and wine sauces; add to poultry stuffings; use in tarts and puddings. **Preserved:** Make jams and jellies or bottle in syrup.
FLAVOR PAIRINGS Poultry, liver, game, fish, cheese, walnuts, brandy.
CLASSIC RECIPES Sole *Véronique*; grape tart; *fazan po kavkazki*; duck liver with grapes; *bavaroise aux raisins; codornices con uvas.*

Ribier
A popular large, seeded variety, this has crisp, jet-black skin and juicy flesh with a mild flavor. A bunch of these is a perfect complement to a cheeseboard.

Choose triangular bunches laden with plump grapes of equal size.

Grapes that have been carefully transported retain their dusty "bloom."

Concord
The oldest North American grape variety, this has medium to large, blue-black fruit. Eat fresh or use for making deeply colored jam, jelly, and juice, as well as wine.

Italia
This well-known seeded variety of the muscat type of grape has a delicious flowery flavor, juicy flesh, and thin skin. Halve and seed for fruit salads.

Muscat Rosada
Also called Moscatel Rosada and Muscat Rosa, this is a gourmet grape with a rich, musky flavor. It has crisp skin and juicy flesh that contains seeds. Reserve for a special fruit dessert or to eat fresh.

OLIVES

Spain is the world's largest producer of table olives, which are cultivated in all Mediterranean-type climates. There are hundreds of varieties, with myriad flavors, textures, and ratio of pit to flesh. All olives are green at first and turn black when fully ripe—some varieties are best picked green, others when black. When first picked, olives are very bitter and must be cured in brine, salt, oil, or water, or by other means before they are edible. The final taste will also depend on any oil, herbs, and spices used in their marinade.

BUY For the best flavor buy olives still with their pits—loose or in jars, or cans—since pitted olives can be mushy. In general, look for plump, shiny olives, although small, shriveled ones can also be delicious, depending on variety.

STORE Loose olives or those in salt or brine should be used within 2–3 days. Olives covered in olive oil can be kept in a cool, dark place for several months. If mold appears, rinse and cover with fresh oil.

EAT Fresh: Serve as a snack or appetizer. Add to salads, or chop finely for a spread. **Cooked:** Pit and add to casseroles, sauces, or bread dough.

FLAVOR PAIRINGS Fish, meat, poultry, cheese, pasta, sweet peppers, tomatoes, garlic, preserved lemons, oranges, herbs, spices.

CLASSIC RECIPES Tapenade; *salade niçoise; pissaladière; pasta puttanesca; olive focaccia; pato con aceitunas a la sevillana; olive salad.*

TAPENADE

Spread this Provençal olive paste on bread or use as a dip for crudités or a basting for grilled fish and chicken.

SERVES 8

2 cups drained Kalamata black olives, pitted

2 garlic cloves, coarsely chopped

2 tbsp capers, rinsed and drained

1 x 2oz (50g) can flat anchovy fillets, drained and coarsely chopped

¼ cup canned tuna fish (optional)

1 tbsp fresh lemon juice

1 tbsp brandy

½ cup olive oil, or to taste

freshly ground black pepper

1 Combine the olives, garlic, capers, anchovies, tuna (if used), lemon juice, and brandy in a food processor. With the machine running, gradually add the oil until the desired consistency is reached. Season to taste with pepper.

2 Or, pound the olives, garlic, capers, anchovies, and tuna (if using) into a paste with a mortar and pestle, gradually adding the lemon juice, brandy, and olive oil to taste. Season with pepper.

Tanche
From Nyons in Provence, these have a delicious, rich flavor that is ideal for traditional dishes of the region such as salade niçoise.

Tanche olives are small, plump, and dull black.

Picholine
Dusky green Picholine have a surprising amount of crisp, nutty flesh. They make tempting appetizers, but are also good in chicken and fish stews.

Manzanilla
Large, khaki-colored, silky olives from Seville, Manzanillas are often sold stuffed with pimiento. Either whole or stuffed, they are the perfect martini olive.

Taggiasca
Cured in brine with aromatic herbs, these tiny, black Ligurian olives have a rich, fruity taste and are just right to nibble with drinks.

Arbequina
Serve these tiny, nutty brown Spanish olives with an aperitif such as chilled fino sherry or as part of a tapas selection.

Stuffed green olives
Small green olives are often sold pitted and stuffed with pimiento, almond, anchovy, capers, onion, lemon, or celery.

Niçoise-Coquillos
With their delicate, nutty flavor, these very small, purple-black olives from southern France are well suited to Provençal dishes such as pissaladière.

Kalamata
Greek Kalamata olives are large, almond-shaped, and dark purple with a rich, fruity flavor. They are superb for both the table and cooking.

Dry salt-cured olives
Drying or salt-curing works best for black olives, producing shriveled olives that are full of flavor. Serve as snacks, bake in bread, or use for tapenade.

PEACH PALM FRUIT

Also known as pejibaye palm, the wild peach palm is native to the tropical rainforests of Central and South America. It is cultivated in countries such as Brazil, Venezuela, and Panama and is particularly important economically in Costa Rica. The small, lantern-shaped fruit gets its name from its peachlike red, orange, and yellow colors. When cooked, the fruit has a nutty flavor with the dry texture of cooked yam. A flour made from the fruit is used in confectionery and bread.

BUY Occasionally, the fresh fruit can be found in specialty stores outside the countries of origin. Otherwise, buy it preserved in jars or cans.

STORE Undamaged, raw fruit will keep in good condition in the refrigerator for several weeks. Fruit that has been roughly handled and bruised will begin to ferment in a few days.

EAT Peach palm fruit cannot be consumed raw. **Cooked:** Wash, cut open to remove the seed, and peel. Boil in salted water for several hours and serve with a dressing. Use in stews, compotes, and jellies. Roast for a snack or use to stuff poultry. Purée for soup. **Preserved:** Preserve in brine or syrup. The fruit is also fermented to make home-made wine.

FLAVOR PAIRINGS Soured cream, mayonnaise, butter, lime, honey, salt.

CLASSIC RECIPE Cream of peach palm soup.

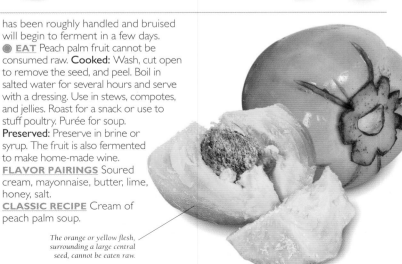

The orange or yellow flesh, surrounding a large central seed, cannot be eaten raw.

DATES

This fruit of the handsome date palm is cultivated in hot, dry climates where there is a source of water. Varieties of dates differ in color, shape, size, and sweetness. There are three main types, classified by their moisture content: soft (e.g., Medjool), semi-soft (e.g., Deglet Noor), and dry (e.g., Thoory).

BUY Fresh dates are usually best from November to January; they should look plump, smooth, and glossy. Dates that have been dried or partially dried will have slightly wrinkled skins, but should still look moist with an even color. Whether sold on the stem or in boxes, they should smell of honey. Avoid shriveled or blemished fruit.

STORE Fresh dates will keep in an airtight container in the refrigerator for a week. Store tightly wrapped dried dates at room temperature for a few weeks, or for several months in the refrigerator. Do not freeze dates unless you are sure of their freshness: they are often frozen in their country of origin, then thawed before being sold.

EAT Fresh: If wished, squeeze the date out of its papery skin. Eat as a snack, stuff the cavity, or chop and add to salads and compotes. **Cooked:** Pit and chop for stuffings and for rice and couscous dishes. Add to desserts, cakes, cookies, tea breads, and savory stews. **Preserved:** Make chutney, jams, and syrups.

FLAVOR PAIRINGS Poultry, lamb, bacon, cheese, cream cheese, crème fraîche, yogurt, lemons, oranges, nuts, marzipan, chocolate.

CLASSIC RECIPES Stuffed dates; date and walnut loaf; chicken tagine; *khoshaf*; fried dates.

The brown-red Thoory date has a bluish bloom on its dry skin.

Thoory
Originally from Algeria, this date is firm, chewy, and nutty, as well as being highly nutritious (which is why it is sometimes called the "bread date"). Great for snacks, it is also good for baking and cooking.

When fresh, the flesh of golden Barhi dates is crunchy, sweet, and slightly astringent.

Medjool
Large, crinkled, purple-brown Medjool dates are soft, fleshy, and sticky— sweet. Eat as a sweetmeat.

Barhi
This round date has a rich flavor and crisp texture. As the fruit ripens it darkens, softens, and wrinkles to become deliciously moist. It is popular fresh in the Middle East and perfect for nibbling.

Deglet Noor
This large, slightly winkled, golden-brown date has translucent flesh and a sweet, mild flavor. It is much used for cooking and baking.

CLASSIC RECIPE

STUFFED DATES

These simple but exotic Middle Eastern sweetmeats are delicious with coffee after dinner.

MAKES 12

12 Medjool dates

1 cup ground almonds

2 tbsp superfine sugar

1 tbsp rose or orange-flower water

granulated sugar, for coating (optional)

1 Make a small slit down the side of each date and remove the pit.

2 Put the almonds, superfine sugar, and flower water in a food processor. Process until well blended and the mixture starts to come together. Scrape into a bowl and knead until the mixture forms a paste. Alternatively, use a mortar and pestle to pound the ingredients into a paste.

3 Stuff each date with a small ball of almond paste and press the sides together to enclose the filling partially.

4 Use a small knife to score the surface of the exposed almond paste decoratively. If desired, roll the dates in granulated sugar to coat.

COCONUT

Coconut palms flourish on tropical seashores. The top commercial export countries are Indonesia, the Philippines, and Sri Lanka. Outside the countries of origin, the coconut is usually sold husked to reveal the hard shell in its hairy coat. Inside, lining the shell, is a thick layer of dense, candylike white flesh. The coconut also contains thin, sweetish "water" or juice, which makes a pleasant drink.

BUY Choose a coconut that feels heavy for its size. To make sure it is fresh, hold it to your ear and shake it: you should be able to hear the juice sloshing around inside. Without juice, the coconut will be rancid inside. The fibrous shell should be dry with no cracks, dampness or mold, particularly around the "eyes."

STORE Whole coconuts can be kept in a cool, dry place for a week. Grated fresh coconut will keep for 2 weeks in a closed container in the refrigerator; immerse larger chunks in water or coconut juice and cover tightly. Freeze shredded or chopped.

EAT Fresh: Chunks of fresh coconut make a good snack. Add grated coconut to breakfast cereal, salads, cold puddings, and ice cream. **Cooked:** Grate for curries, cookies, cakes, and desserts, or infuse in liquid to make coconut milk and cream. **Preserved:** Make jam. Dry sliced or diced coconut.

FLAVOR PAIRINGS Chicken, shellfish, yogurt, chiles, rice, bananas, citrus fruits, tropical fruits, cherries, vanilla, curry spices, jaggery.

CLASSIC RECIPES Coconut cream pie; ambrosia; coconut rice; coconut cookies; *flan de coco*; coconut jam.

PREPARING A COCONUT

The coconut "water" or juice needs to be drained out before the shell is broken open.

1 Hold a thick metal skewer or screwdriver against each "eye" and bang in with a hammer. Drain out the juice. **2** Use the hammer to tap the coconut all around its circumference. When a crack appears, break the coconut in half. **3** Wrap the halves in a thick dish towel and break into pieces with the hammer. **4** Trim the brown skin off the flesh, then grate on a hand grater or in a food processor.

The coconut shell is covered with bristly brown fibers and has three weak spots, or "eyes," on one side.

BLUEBERRIES

Blueberries are native to the woods, forests, and heaths of the tundra and temperate regions of the far northern hemisphere. They are commercially grown around the world, particularly in Maine and Michigan, as well as in Canada, Poland, Hungary, Australia, New Zealand, South Africa, and South America. The cultivated "high-bush" berries are large and even in size, but have a less distinctive taste than the smaller "wild" berries, most of which are harvested from semi-managed, scrubby low-bush plants. The bilberry is a close relative.

BUY Cultivated blueberries are available year-round but are at their best between July and September. Avoid any containers with juice stains, since they may contain mushy, possibly moldy fruit. Don't buy damaged, squashed, or shriveled berries.

STORE Handle blueberries carefully. They can be kept in the refrigerator for several days. Or freeze (do not wash blueberries before freezing, since this toughens the skins).

EAT Fresh: Serve as a snack or dessert, alone, or in a fruit salad. Purée for smoothies and cold soups; press for juice. **Cooked:** Bake in pies and tarts, crumbles, cobblers, cakes, and muffins. Stew for sweet and savory sauces, compotes, or cheesecake toppings. **Preserved:** Make into jam, jelly, or relish; bottle in syrup; or dry.
FLAVOR PAIRINGS Game, cream, sour cream, yogurt, lemon, lime, almonds, mint, cinnamon, allspice, chocolate.
CLASSIC RECIPES Blueberry muffins; blueberry pie; blueberry pancakes; blueberry cheesecake; blueberry buckle; *tarte à la cannelle*.

Huckleberries are related to blueberries, but are smaller, darker, and juicier.

Blueberry
Small, plump, and round, blueberries are sweet and mild with a tart edge and a firm texture. While delicious raw, their flavor is enhanced when cooked.

The blue-black skin has a distinctive silvery bloom.

Huckleberry
Found wild in North America, huckleberries have crunchy seeds and a sweet—tart taste. Use in pies and tarts, as well as in sauces for meat.

CLASSIC RECIPE

BLUEBERRY MUFFINS

Serve these North American favorites, freshly baked and still slightly warm, for breakfast or brunch.

MAKES 12

2¼ cups all-purpose flour

1 heaping tbsp baking powder

½ tsp salt

½ tsp grated fresh nutmeg

½ tsp ground cinnamon

3 tbsp granulated sugar

1 cup milk, at room temperature

3 eggs, lightly beaten

9 tbsp unsalted butter, melted and cooled

1½ cups fresh blueberries

1 Preheat the oven to 400°F (200°C). Line a 12-cup muffin pan with paper liners, or butter the pan.

2 Sift the flour, baking powder, salt, nutmeg, and cinnamon into a bowl. Stir in the sugar.

3 In another bowl, lightly whisk the milk and eggs into the melted butter. Add to the flour mixture and fold together lightly so the ingredients are just combined: the batter should be fairly wet and lumpy. Take care not to overmix. Fold in the blueberries.

4 Divide the batter equally among the paper muffin cups. Bake for about 20 minutes, or until the muffins are firm, risen, and golden brown. A skewer inserted into the center of a muffin should not show any evidence of uncooked batter.

5 Remove from the pan; cool on a wire rack. Serve warm or at room temperature.

CLOUDBERRIES

Found in peaty bogs and marshes of the northern parts of Scandinavia, Siberia, and Canada up toward the North Pole, the cloudberry is laboriously collected from the wild by hand. The unique, delicious tangy—sweet flavor of these soft, juicy berries is particularly prized in Scandinavia and by the Sami and Inuit peoples. In North America, the fruit is also called the baked-apple berry.

BUY The berries are picked in late summer, but as they are so difficult to transport they are rarely found outside their native regions.

STORE Handle very gently. Keep in the refrigerator and eat as soon as possible. For longer storage, freeze them.

EAT Fresh: Rinse carefully, if desired, then enjoy for dessert with a little sugar. **Cooked:** Add to desserts and fruit soups. Stew for a sweet sauce. **Preserved:** Make into jam and liqueur.
FLAVOR PAIRINGS Soft cheese, ice cream, venison.
CLASSIC RECIPES Cloudberry jam; cloudberry pancakes.

Cloudberries look like golden raspberries.

CRANBERRIES

Native to northern temperate regions, cranberries are commercially cultivated in North America. The waxy berries have a mouth-puckering sour taste and a hard, crunchy texture when raw. Their color ranges alluringly from bright light red to dark crimson red. The similarly vibrant red lingonberries, which are often called "cranberries" in Scandinavia, are a close relative. They too make excellent relish and juice.

BUY They are best at their peak in winter, when shiny and red. Avoid bags containing squashed or shriveled fruit.
STORE Keep in a closed plastic bag in the refrigerator for up to 2 weeks. Or freeze and use without thawing.
EAT Because they are so astringent, cranberries need generous sweetening. **Fresh:** Grind for a relish; press for juice. **Cooked:** Stew for sauces and desserts.

Add to tarts, pies, muffins, cakes, and parfaits, as well as pâtés and stuffings for poultry and meat. **Preserved:** Make jelly; dry; or bottle in syrup.
FLAVOR PAIRINGS Turkey, goose, ham, oily fish, apples, oranges, nuts, red wine, Cognac, cinnamon.
CLASSIC RECIPES Cranberry jelly; cranberry sauce; cranberry and orange relish.

CLASSIC RECIPE

CRANBERRY JELLY

This tart, fruity, preserve is perfect with Christmas roast turkey and also complements any cold meat.

MAKES ABOUT 2 CUPS

4 cups fresh or frozen cranberries

2¼ cups granulated sugar

1 Put the cranberries and 1½ cups water in a saucepan. Bring to a boil, then reduce the heat to low and simmer until the berries are tender, about 10 minutes.

2 Pour the mixture into a fine sieve set over a bowl and press the cranberries through the sieve with a large spoon. Discard the pulp. Return the purée and juice to the saucepan and bring to a boil. Stir in the sugar until dissolved.

3 Simmer for 10 minutes, then place a spoonful on a saucer in the refrigerator to test that the jelly has thickened and reached the setting point. Ladle into sterilized jars and refrigerate. (For longer storage, seal the lids in a hot water bath, according to canning instructions.) Store the sealed jars for up to 1 year; once opened, refrigerate for up to 3 weeks.

Choose firm, brightly colored cranberries of uniform size.

BLACKBERRIES

Blackberries or brambles grow wild throughout the cooler and more temperate parts of the world in both hemispheres. The fruit is cultivated widely in Oregon, Mexico, Chile, Serbia, and other countries in Eastern Europe. There are many hybrids and cultivars, including the loganberry, youngberry, and olallieberry, and close relatives such as the dewberry. Thornless commercial varieties now make picking a lot easier. When picked, the berries come off the plant with the solid center (receptacle) attached, and do not ripen further.

BUY In late summer and early autumn, the ripe drupelets (the round globules that make up each berry) should be firm and juicy with a good color. Do not buy berries that look green, damaged, or shriveled, and avoid punnets stained with juice, since this is a sign the fruit is past its best.
STORE It is best to eat blackberries

as soon as possible after picking or purchase, although they can be kept in the fridge for 1–2 days: pat the fragile berries with paper towels to remove any moisture and store in a closed paper bag. They are also well suited to freezing.
EAT Fresh: The flavor is best at room temperature. Eat as a snack or dessert; blend for sauces, cold desserts, and smoothies; or juice. **Cooked:** Use in hot desserts, crumbles, pies, and tarts. **Preserved:** Make into jelly or flavored vinegar; or bottle in syrup.
FLAVOR PAIRINGS Poultry, game, sweet cream, sour cream, apples, soft fruit, hazelnuts, almonds, oats, honey, vanilla, cinnamon.
CLASSIC RECIPES Blackberry and apple pie; summer pudding; blackberry jelly; blackberry jam.

Blackberry
Cultivated blackberries, such as the popular Loch Ness variety, should look firm, plump, and glossy. Although most are midnight-black, it is also possible to find red blackberries.

Wild blackberry
Gather blackberries from the wild early in the season: the first wild fruits are the best, while later berries are smaller and tougher. Use to make jams and jellies.

Wild blackberries are less fleshy than cultivated berries and have more seeds.

Boysenberry
A blackberry—raspberry—loganberry hybrid, this yields beautiful wine-colored fruit. The berries are softer and larger than blackberries, with smaller seeds, and make delicious ice cream.

Choose fragrant, dark blueberries with a white bloom. The bloom protects the growing berries from the sun, and is a sign of freshness.

RASPBERRIES

Raspberries are cultivated in moist, temperate regions of the world. Most often a deep red—although white, golden-amber, and other colors are also grown—each richly hued, slightly triangular berry is really a small cluster of velvety, slightly hairy drupelets. When ripe, the fruit comes away easily from the solid white center or "hull" that remains on the stem. Tart black raspberries (called Black Caps) are common in the eastern part of North America; they are good for juice. There are also many raspberry hybrids.

🔒 **BUY** Different varieties crop at different times, but raspberries are at their best in summer and early fall. Look for firm, dry berries with a good color. Avoid containers stained with juice, since this is a sign the fruit is past its best. Do not buy berries that look damaged or shriveled or that have specks of mold.

📦 **STORE** If possible, use on the day of purchase. Raspberries are fragile, so handle carefully. Pat with paper towels to remove any moisture, then store in a closed paper bag in the refrigerator for 1–2 days. You can open freeze, freeze in syrup (the berries will lose some of their delicate texture), or as a purée.

● **EAT** Fresh: Eat as a snack or dessert at room temperature. Blend for sauces, cold and iced desserts, and smoothies. **Cooked:** Use in hot desserts, crumbles, pies, and tarts. **Preserved:** Bottle in syrup or make into juice, flavored vinegar, and preserves.
FLAVOR PAIRINGS Poultry, game, sweet cream, sour cream, peaches, other berries, hazelnuts, almonds, oats, honey, vanilla, cinnamon, red wine.
CLASSIC RECIPES Rote grütze; raspberry jam; raspberry coulis (Melba sauce); summer pudding; English trifle.

ROTE GRUTZE

From northern Germany, this red fruit compote makes a delicious, not-too-sweet dessert.

SERVES 4

1½ cups cherries, pitted

1½ cups strawberries, hulled and quartered, if large

1 cup raspberries

1 cup red currants

¾ cup blackberries

¼ cup superfine sugar

2 tbsp cornstarch

1 Place all the fruit in a saucepan with ½ cup water and bring slowly to a boil; then reduce the heat to a simmer.

2 Combine the sugar and cornstarch with 2 tbsp cold water to form a smooth paste. Gradually stir the cornstarch paste into the fruit. Cook gently, stirring, until the mixture begins to thicken.

3 Allow to cool, then spoon the mixture into individual dishes. Chill well and serve with whipped cream.

Raspberries are made up of dozens of tiny drupelets, each one bursting with juice.

Raspberry
Soft and delicate, raspberries have an intense, slightly sharp, perfumed flavor. When ripe, they are full of juice that can stain hands and clothes.

Loganberry
A blackberry-raspberry cross, this elongated, glossy, dark red berry can be tart if not absolutely ripe. Loganberries have a short summer season so make the most of them then in pies and preserves.

The large, richly colored berries can be too sharp in flavor to eat fresh.

STRAWBERRIES

Plump and juicy strawberries are grown in all temperate regions. The many hybrids vary in size and in color, from scarlet to pinkish-orange, and the shape can be conical, globular, oval, or heart shaped. The flesh grows around a firm, pale hull and the surface of the berry is covered with tiny seeds. Wild strawberries are found in woods and shady pastures, and are commercially grown to a much lesser degree.

🔒 **BUY** Strawberries are usually sold in plastic baskets, sometimes loose at the height of the summer season. They do not ripen further after picking. Choose firm, juicy, fragrant berries; the leaf calyx should be bright and fresh looking. Avoid containers stained with juice, since this indicates the fruit is mushy.

📦 **STORE** Ripe strawberries are highly perishable, so use as soon as possible. Discard moldy or squashed berries, then cover loosely and keep at the bottom of the refrigerator. Freeze as purée.

● **EAT** Fresh: Eat as a dessert. Dip in melted chocolate. Top cheesecakes and tarts. Purée for coulis, cold and iced desserts, and milk shakes. **Cooked:** Use in pie fillings. **Preserved:** Bottle in syrup; make jam; or flavor vinegar.
FLAVOR PAIRINGS Cream, ice cream, curd cheese, cucumber, oranges, rhubarb, almonds, vanilla, rosewater, chocolate, black pepper.
CLASSIC RECIPES Strawberry jam; strawberry semifreddo; strawberry shortcake; strawberry ice cream; fraisier; strawberries in Marsala; strawberry and rhubarb pie.

STRAWBERRY JAM

Strawberries make a classic, much loved jam. Use organic berries with a sweet, full flavor.

MAKES ABOUT 8 CUPS

3lbs (1.5kg) strawberries

3lbs (1.5kg) granulated sugar

freshly squeezed juice of 4 lemons

1 In a large ceramic or glass bowl, make a layer of the strawberries; sprinkle with some of the sugar and lemon juice. Repeat until all the ingredients have been used. Cover with plastic wrap; leave to macerate for 24 hours in a cool place.

2 Scrape the contents of the bowl into a preserving pan or large saucepan and slowly bring to a boil. Simmer over low heat for 5 minutes. Remove from the heat, cover, and let stand for 48 hours.

3 Return the pan to the heat and bring the mixture back to a boil. Skim off any scum from the surface, then boil until the jam reaches the setting point.

4 Remove from the heat. Ladle into hot, sterilized jars and seal.

Chandler
This large, firm variety has a typically flat, wedge shape. It is a good all-purpose strawberry with a brilliant glossy color and excellent berry flavor.

Albion
A modern California variety with a long growing season, Albion is an extra-large, dark red conical berry with a lush, very sweet taste. It makes quite an impact in desserts and cakes.

Elsanta
One of the most popular commercial varieties in the UK, Elsanta has glossy good looks but muted flavor. It is a useful berry for cold desserts such as puddings and mousses.

The berries look like red spinning tops with a bright green hull.

Mieze Schindler
A classic German variety, the berries are plump and heart shaped, and have a delicious, full-fruit flavor. Enjoy them fresh, make into jam, or use in Rote Grütze.

The wild strawberry is small in size but big in flavor.

Wild strawberry
Also known as fraises des bois, these are found both in the wild and cultivated (when they are often called Alpine strawberries). The tiny, fragile red or white fruit has an exquisite fragrant taste. Use in tarts or as a special dessert.

STRAWBERRY SEMIFREDDO

This is Italian berry ice cream with a twist—texture and sweetness are added by crushed meringues.

SERVES 6–8

Vegetable oil, to brush

3 cups strawberries, hulled, plus extra strawberries and red currants for garnish

1 cup heavy whipping cream

½ cup confectioners' sugar, sifted

4oz (115g) crisp meringue cookies or shells, coarsely crushed

3 tbsp raspberry-flavoured liqueur

For the coulis

3 cups strawberries, hulled

¼ to ½ cup confectioners' sugar, sifted

1–2 tsp lemon juice, brandy, grappa, or balsamic vinegar

1 Very lightly brush an 8in (20cm) round springform pan with vegetable oil and line the bottom with parchment paper. Set aside.

2 Purée the strawberries in a blender or food processor. Whip the cream in a bowl with the confectioners' sugar just until it holds its shape. Fold the strawberry purée into the whipped cream, then fold in the crushed meringues and liqueur. Scrape the mixture into the prepared pan, smooth the top, and cover with plastic wrap. Freeze for at least 6 hours or overnight.

3 Meanwhile, make the coulis. Purée the strawberries in a blender or food processor, then press them through a fine sieve to remove the seeds. Stir ¼ cup confectioners' sugar into the purée. Taste for sweetness and add more sugar if needed. Flavor with the lemon juice, brandy, grappa, or vinegar.

4 Just before serving, remove the semifreddo from the pan; peel away the parchment. Using a warmed knife, cut in to wedges. Spoon the coulis on to individual plates and top with a wedge of semifreddo. Garnish with whole strawberries and red currants.

SEA BUCKTHORN BERRIES

Native to northern temperate regions of Asia and Europe, the thorny sea buckthorn is being increasingly grown in North America and China for the nutritional and medicinal properties of its berries. Initially very acidic, the bright orange, glossy, and plump oval berries become soft, juicy, and rich in oils once "bletted," or exposed to winter frost. Although some thornless varieties have been cultivated, the wild berries have to be shaken off the tree. In Scandinavia, a special tool is used to press the juice out of the berries while they are still on the branch.

BUY The berries are mostly sold in a ready-processed form such as juice, syrup, tea, purée, or powder.

STORE Keep fresh berries in a cool, dry place but use as soon as possible.

EAT **Fresh:** Rinse and eat sugared, or press for juice and sweeten. Add to ice cream, desserts, and sauces. Dried berries in powdered form can be added to yogurt and cereals. **Cooked:** Add to oatmeal and hot desserts. **Preserved:** Make jam or jelly. Sea buckthorn berries are used to flavor schnapps.

FLAVOR PAIRINGS Cream, ice cream, apple juice, oats.

CLASSIC RECIPE Sea buckthorn ice cream.

The slender branches of the deciduous shrub are covered with garlands of brightly colored berries in fall.

ROSE HIP

These are the glossy, bright orange-red seedpods of the rose that appear after the flower petals have fallen in fall. Rose hips have a fruity, spicy flavor not unlike cranberries.

BUY Rose hips are not cultivated commercially and must be gathered from the garden or the wild. Collect or forage plump hips after the first frost, preferably from wild roses or the rugosa rose (do not use from any plants that have been treated with pesticide). Rose hips are edible when ripe. Avoid those that are overripe, soft, or wrinkly.

STORE Keep in sealed plastic bags in the refrigerator for up to 2 weeks, or freeze whole.

EAT Rose hips are enormously rich in vitamin C. They contain extremely hairy seeds that are irritating to the intestines; remove before eating. **Fresh:** Scoop out the pulp. **Cooked:** Purée for sauces, desserts, fruit leathers, and candy. **Preserved:** Use for syrups, cordials, and jellies. Dry for fruit tea.

FLAVOR PAIRINGS Turkey, game, apple, nuts, honey.

CLASSIC RECIPES Rose hip jelly; rose hip syrup.

When ripe, rose hips will be fully colored and just yield to the touch.

MULBERRIES

Mulberries are the fruit of trees that grow in the temperate regions of the world. Black mulberries are a luscious purple-black and have a delicious sweet, musky flavor; the large, swollen berries contain a copious amount of finger-staining juice. White mulberries are milder and less distinctive in taste; however, when dried they develop a richer flavor and a crunchy texture. Red mulberries, similar in characteristics to black, are also prized.

🔒 **BUY** In late summer, the fruit must be allowed to ripen fully before it can be gathered: the berries are usually allowed to fall to the ground. It is unlikely you will find a supply in the supermarket, but if you know someone with a tree, pick out plump, firm specimens.

📦 **STORE** Use as soon as possible. They will only last a day or two in the fridge before they start to ferment or get moldy. Mulberries can be frozen.
● **EAT** Fresh: Savor as a dessert at room temperature, press for juice, or purée for drinks and cocktails. **Cooked:** Use in pies, desserts, sorbets, and ice cream. **Preserved:** Make into jam or jelly. Use to flavor vinegar or vodka; or dry.
FLAVOR PAIRINGS Poultry, lamb, game, cream, pears, citrus fruits.
CLASSIC RECIPES Summer pudding; roast lamb with mulberry sauce; mulberry jelly; mulberry ice cream.

The eye-catching berries are soft and juicy, which makes them popular with birds.

Ripe mulberries are extremely fragile so handle carefully.

ROWANBERRIES

During the late summer and fall, these astringent, vivid scarlet or orange berries appear, growing in clusters, on the rowan or mountain ash, a tree found in both rural and urban areas of cool, temperate regions throughout Europe and northern Asia. The berries are rich in vitamin C but toxic when raw.

🔒 **BUY** Rowanberries are not sold commercially, so need to be collected or foraged after the first frosts (which help to reduce their bitterness). You will need to pick them fast before the birds strip them from the trees.

📦 **STORE** The berries can be kept in a closed paper bag or container at the bottom of the refrigerator for a few days. For longer storage, freeze them: freezing also helps cut down the bitter taste.
● **EAT** When raw the fruit is toxic, but this is eliminated by cooking. **Cooked:** Use in sauces, pies, and crumbles **Preserved:** Make jelly or preserves. Use in country wines and liqueurs.
FLAVOR PAIRINGS Lamb, mutton, venison, poultry, hedgerow fruits.

ELDERBERRIES

The elder tree grows in temperate regions of both the northern and southern hemispheres. Its fruit appears in flat, wide clusters after the flowers in late summer. The small, purple-black berries are fragile and burst easily when picked. Their taste is tart and the pulp is seedy. Elderberries are not a significant commercial crop, although Austria is the world's leading elderberry-producing country. If picking them yourself from the wild, gather from trees growing away from the road to avoid contamination from pollution.

🔒 **BUY** If you find them in a market, look for shiny, black berries.

📦 **STORE** They can be kept in a container in a cool, dry place but should be used as soon as possible after picking. They can be frozen.

● **EAT** Elderberries are unsuitable to eat raw. **Cooked:** Use as a pie filling and in crumbles and desserts. Include in fruit soups and compotes. Stew for sauces. **Preserved:** Make into country wine and cordial, jelly, and jam; use to flavor vinegar; or dry whole berries.
FLAVOR PAIRINGS Game, crab apple, hedgerow fruits, strawberries, lemon, walnuts, cinnamon, allspice, nutmeg, cloves.
CLASSIC RECIPES Elderberry soup; elderberry jam or jelly; elderberry wine or cordial.

Rinse briefly, then gently strip the berries off the stalk using a fork.

CURRANTS

Currant bushes thrive best in cool, moist, temperate climates and are grown in northern Europe, Asia, North America, Australia, and New Zealand. The berries grow in clusters, like tiny, shiny bunches of grapes, and span the color spectrum from black to red to white. They should be juicy and soft with a number of edible seeds. The acidity of the fruit, however, means they are usually more suitable for cooking than eating raw.

🔒 **BUY** In midsummer, buy currants in containers that protect them from damage. Freshly picked currants should have a fragrant aroma, and look tight, bright, and shiny. Avoid containers stained with juice or fruit that looks mushy, withered, or dusty.

🗄 **STORE** Use on the day of purchase, if possible. Keep covered in the refrigerator for a couple of days, preferably in a single layer. Open-freeze or purée and freeze. Rinse before use. If necessary, pinch off the calyx tops.

⬤ **EAT** Fresh: Strip the berries from the stalks by running a fork down the cluster. Eat sugared as a dessert or frost for cake decoration.
Cooked: Use whole or purée for sauces and savory stews. Poach for fruit soups, warm desserts, crumbles, pies, fools, creams, and ices.
Preserved: Bottle in syrup or turn into homemade wine and liqueur. Preserve as jam, jelly, syrup, or chutney.
FLAVOR PAIRINGS Duck, game, lamb, ham, soft cheese, lemon, pears, peaches, mint, cinnamon.
CLASSIC RECIPES Red currant jelly; black currant jam; summer pudding; crème de cassis.

Red currants
The shiny crimson berries are slightly smaller and more fragile than blackcurrants and have a tangy kick. They make good jelly, syrup, and a pretty decoration for cakes and desserts.

These small, round, purple-black berries are full of juice.

White currants
These translucent, delicate berries have a pearl-like, pinkish blush. They are a bit smaller and sweeter than redcurrants, and can be served fresh or used for preserves. They can also be frosted with egg white and sugar.

Black currants
These have an intense, tart flavor, and are a classic choice for pies, sauces, and jam. Fragrant leaves are used to flavor ice cream.

GOOSEBERRIES

Gooseberries grow in cool, moist temperate climates such as northern Europe, Asia, and parts of Australia and New Zealand. The berries are oval or round, and vary in size. The small edible seeds inside are coated in a slippery pulp. Gooseberries are divided into two types: cooking and dessert. They do not ripen after picking.

🔒 **BUY** Gooseberries have a short season, from early cooking varieties in late spring to softer, dessert varieties in midsummer. Choose berries that are fleshy, firm, and glossy, and avoid any that are dull, wrinkled, or split. Buy cooking berries slightly unripe but not rock-hard.

🗄 **STORE** Ideally, use fruit on the day of purchase or picking. Keep cooking gooseberries in a closed bag in the refrigerator for a week; dessert fruit for 2 or 3 days. Pluck and clean before use. Open-freeze, freeze in syrup, or as a purée.

⬤ **EAT** Cooked: Poach and/or purée cooking berries for fools, creams, mousses, and ices, as well as crumbles and tarts. Use in savory sauces and stuffings. Preserved: Bottle in syrup. Use in preserves and country wine.
FLAVOR PAIRINGS Pork, mackerel, Camembert, cream, lemon, cinnamon, cloves, dill, fennel, elderflower, honey.
CLASSIC RECIPES Gooseberry sauce; gooseberry jam; gooseberry pie; gooseberry fool.

Dessert gooseberries are usually red, but can also be pink, yellow, white, or green.

Dessert gooseberries
These should be yielding but not squishy, and smell sweet. Eat at room temperature. The skin is generally smooth.

Cooking gooseberries
Sour cooking gooseberries are typically lime-green with thick, veined skin covered in small hairs.

RHUBARB

Rhubarb grows wild along parts of the Volga River, where it is native. Today, it is cultivated outside in cool temperate climates around the world and in hothouses, where it is forced for year-round production. Different varieties offer a range of sizes and colors, but all have rhubarb's tangy flavor, caused mostly by oxalic acid in the long leaf stalks, which are the only edible part of the plant (the green leaves are poisonous).

BUY The best seasonal rhubarb shows up early in midspring, and there may be a second crop in July. Look for stalks that are glossy and firm, and inspect both cut ends for freshness of the cuts. Hothouse rhubarb is generally sweeter and more highly colored than outdoor-grown stalks.

STORE Rhubarb stalks will keep well in the refrigerator for a week, wrapped in moist paper towels inside a plastic bag so they do not dry out.

EAT Some types of rhubarb are stringy and need to be thinly peeled. **Fresh:** In moderation (because of the oxalic acid that renders iron unusable in the body if eaten in quantity), fresh rhubarb stalks have an irresistible sweet–sour flavor. **Cooked:** Stew, bake, or roast. Aside from its many sweet uses, in pies, creamy desserts, and jams, rhubarb makes a fine sauce to accompany oily fish or pork.

FLAVOR PAIRINGS Strawberries, citrus fruits, plums, cinnamon, brown sugar, ginger.

CLASSIC RECIPES Strawberry-rhubarb pie; rhubarb crumble; *khoresh;* rhubarb fool; *rabarberkage.*

PHYSALLIS

Also known as Cape gooseberries, the shiny, golden-orange fruits are encased in a papery, gauzelike husk that looks a bit like an inflated Chinese lantern. They are juicy, with tiny seeds, and have a lively sweet–tart taste. The size of a cherry, physallis are grown commercially in both temperate and tropical regions of South Africa, South America, Australia, New Zealand, and India.

BUY The fruit should look firm and waxy with no bruising. Ripe fruit will have straw-colored husks. The berries should have a mild, sweet scent.

STORE Inside their husks, the berries will keep in a cool place for a week or two. Wash before use. Open-freeze without the husks.

EAT **Fresh:** Eat raw at room temperature. Dip in chocolate or fondant for petit fours. **Cooked:** Poach for desserts, sauces, and ice cream. Add to cakes and tarts. **Preserved:** Use for preserves. Bottle in syrup.

FLAVOR PAIRINGS White fish, scallops, yogurt, exotic fruit, nuts, tarragon, chocolate, orange liqueur.

CLASSIC RECIPES Physallis jam; petit fours.

Light, papery husks enclose the small, round, golden-orange fruits.

The green leaves of the rhubarb plant are poisonous.

"Canada Red"
This variety produces long, meaty stalks that show a fine balance of sweetness and sourness.

"Cherry Red"
Also known as "Cherry" and cultivated in California, this variety has long, thin stalks that are bright cherry-red. It has a tart flavor and tender texture, and grows vigorously.

ORANGE

The senior member of the citrus family is the orange, which is commercially grown in Mediterranean and subtropical regions worldwide, especially in Spain, the US, Brazil, China, and Mexico. There are many varieties of orange: size and thickness of skin can vary; taste can range from sharp to sweet; flavor intensity can differ; and they may or may not contain seeds. The tough, bitter peel of all oranges is highly scented and contains aromatic essential oils. Another type of orange is the mandarin, which is a name generally applied to all small, orange-colored citrus fruit with loose skin and fibrous strands of orange pith. Mandarins are smaller and flatter than oranges, generally less acidic in flavor, and easily separated into segments. Within the mandarin family is a group known as tangerines, although exact terminology can be bewildering. In the UK, a tangerine tends to be a particular small, tangy fruit with seeds and a pebbly skin. In the US, however, the term tangerine is often used more generally instead of mandarin to refer to small citrus fruits, including satsumas and clementines (featured on page 451).

⬛ **BUY** Winter oranges are generally better than summer fruit for juice and flavor. Look for skins that are bright, taut, and glossy. Fruit should feel heavy for its size, and should smell aromatic. Avoid any oranges that look dry or moldy, or have brown marks. Unwaxed fruit is the best choice if you want to use the peel or zest.

⬛ **STORE** Keep in a cool place, or uncovered in the fridge, for up to 2 weeks; use before the skins shrivel. Smaller oranges will not keep as long as large ones. For longer storage, you can freeze peeled segments and slices, or whole Seville oranges.

⬛ **EAT** Fresh: Peel and segment or slice flesh to add to sweet and savory salads and compotes. Squeeze the juice for drinks, jellies, and sorbets. **Cooked:** Poach the fruit whole (peeled). Use the grated zest and juice to flavor casseroles, sauces, cakes, and cookies. **Preserved:** Make marmalade. Bottle in syrup or alcohol. Candy, or dry the peel.

FLAVOR PAIRINGS Beef, duck, ham, scallops, tomatoes, beets, black olives, nuts, cloves, cinnamon, ginger, chocolate, soy sauce, Marsala.

CLASSIC RECIPES Marmalade; *sauce bigarade; sauce maltaise;* caramelized oranges; crêpes Suzette; *pastel de naranja y almendras; canard à l'orange;* fennel and orange salad.

Sour and full of seeds, bitter oranges are best used for preserves and cooking.

Bitter oranges
Unlike sweet oranges, bitter varieties such as the Seville are unpleasant to eat raw. However, they are the classic marmalade orange because of their acidity, thick peel, and numerous seeds, which help the preserve to set. The Seville has a very short, early season.

Valencia
The world's leading commercial variety, this has a long growing season, easy-to-peel, thin skin, and a refreshing sharp—sweet flavor. It is first class for both eating and juicing.

Jaffa
The nearly seedless Jaffa has pale, thick skin that is easily removed. The flesh is sweet, crisp, and juicy, with an intense orange flavor. It is excellent to eat and to use for candied peel dipped in chocolate.

The Jaffa is a good winter orange with bright orange-colored flesh.

The rough, thin skin is flushed with red, hinting at the fabulous color of the flesh beneath.

This has a distinctive bulge at the apex end that contains a baby fruit or "navel."

Navel orange
Second only to the Valencia in commercial importance, the deliciously sweet navel orange is seedless with a thick skin. These oranges are at their best in winter and excellent for eating, juicing, and cooking.

The juicy flesh of the Valencia is mostly seed free.

Blood oranges
These small oranges have richly hued flesh that yields dazzling ruby-colored juice—essential for sauce maltaise and sorbets.

CLASSIC RECIPE

MARMALADE

Bitter oranges such as Seville are essential for a good marmalade.

MAKES ABOUT 20 CUPS

3lb (1.5kg) Seville oranges, rinsed well

juice of 2 lemons

6½lb (3kg) granulated sugar, warmed in a very low oven

1 Use a vegetable peeler or a thin knife to peel the oranges without removing any of the white pith beneath. Cut the peel into thin or medium strips, as preferred; set aside.

2 Halve the oranges and squeeze the juice. Set aside. Also reserve the seeds.

3 Chop the remaining membranes and white pith coarsely and tie in a muslin bag with the seeds. Put this into a heavy-bottomed pot or preserving pan with the shredded peel.

4 Strain the orange and lemon juices into the pan. Add 3 quarts (3.5 liters) water. Slowly bring to a boil over low heat, then simmer uncovered for about 2 hours, or until the peel is soft and the liquid has reduced by about half.

5 Remove the muslin bag with a slotted spoon and discard. Add the warmed sugar to the pan and stir until it has dissolved. Increase the heat and boil the marmalade rapidly for 15–20 minutes, or until setting point is reached.

6 Skim off any foam from the surface and leave to stand, off the heat, for 10–20 minutes. Stir the marmalade once, then ladle into warmed sterilized jars, cover, and seal.

CLEMENTINE

Cultivated in Mediterranean and subtropical regions around the world, including Spain, Morocco, Mexico, and Australia, clementines are among the smallest of the mandarin citrus family. They look like bright orange golf balls, with thin, shiny skin, a delicate membrane, and hardly any seeds. The juice has a sweet, elusive fragrance with a tangy edge.

BUY Available during the winter, choose fruit that is firm and heavy for its size, without soft spots or wrinkled skin. Clementines in good condition should smell fresh and fragrant.

STORE Keep in a cool place, or uncovered in the refrigerator, for up to a week; use before the skins shrivel. Or freeze in segments.

EAT Fresh: Peel for a snack or add to salads. Juice for smoothies and sorbets. **Cooked:** Lightly sauté or broil segments as a side dish. **Preserved:** Use in marmalade. Bottle whole in syrup or liqueur. Crystallize segments as candied fruit.

FLAVOR PAIRINGS Shellfish, pork, chicken, duck, spinach, carrots, peppers, salad leaves, almonds, cilantro, chocolate, meringues, Grand Marnier.

CLASSIC RECIPES Three-fruit marmalade; clementine sorbet.

At Christmas time, clementines are often sold with the stalks and leaves attached.

SATSUMA

Satsumas are part of the extensive family of mandarin oranges. Originally developed in Japan several centuries ago, they are typically slightly flat in shape with an easy-peel, smooth, thick skin; delicate, sweet flavor; and few seeds. Like other citrus fruits, they are widely grown in Mediterranean and subtropical regions worldwide, with China the largest producer.

BUY Widely available in the winter months, when they are generally better for juice and flavor. The skin should be bright and glossy. Fruit should feel heavy for its size, and smell aromatic. Avoid any fruits that look dry, damaged, or moldy.

STORE Keep in a cool place for a week, or uncovered in the refrigerator for up to 2 weeks; use before the skins shrivel. Both the juice and segments can be frozen.

EAT Fresh: Peel and eat as a snack or dessert, or add to salads. Use the zest and juice in sorbets, sauces, salsas, desserts, and cocktails. **Cooked:** Lightly sauté or broil segments for a side dish, or bake whole in cakes. **Preserved:** Bottle segments in syrup or alcohol, or use in marmalade.

FLAVOR PAIRINGS Shellfish, pork, chicken, duck, salad leaves, spinach, carrot, peppers, cilantro, almonds, meringues, chocolate, Grand Marnier.

CLASSIC RECIPE
Three-fruit marmalade.

The loose skin makes satsumas easy to peel, so they are a good snack for children.

GRAPEFRUIT

Cultivated in Mediterranean and subtropical regions of countries such as the US, South Africa, and Israel, this fruit is so-called because of the way it grows on its evergreen tree in clusters like outsize yellow grapes. Grapefruit has a squat, round shape with skin that differs in thickness according to variety, and bitter pith and membrane. The juicy flesh ranges from pale yellow to pink or deep red; rosier-hued varieties tend to taste sweeter.

● **BUY** The season typically runs from late fall to spring. Choose fruit with a good aroma whose skin is smooth and free from marks or blemishes, and that feels firm and heavy, with no soft spots. A spongy, soft skin can indicate a lack of juice and flesh. A greenish tinge, however, does not mean the fruit is unripe.

■ **STORE** In common with all citrus fruits, grapefruit ripens on the tree and does not continue to develop after picking. It can be kept for a few days at room temperature or for up to 2 weeks, uncovered, in the fridge. The juice and segments can be frozen.

● **EAT** Fresh: Halve or segment to eat alone or in salads. Squeeze the juice for drinks and sorbet. **Cooked:** Grill halves. Add the juice to sauces. **Preserved:** Use in marmalade. Candy the peel.
FLAVOR PAIRINGS Chicken, ham, smoked meats, shrimp, avocado, spinach, lemon, mint, ginger, nutmeg, coconut, honey, brown sugar, cherry brandy.
CLASSIC RECIPE Grapefruit marmalade.

White grapefruit
White-grapefruit varieties such as Marsh are notable for tender and generally extremely juicy, pale yellow flesh. The fruit tends to have thin, pale yellow skin, a narrow layer of pith, and few seeds. It makes excellent grapefruit marmalade.

Pink grapefruit
Pink-grapefruit varieties such as the popular Pink Marsh tend to be smaller than white grapefruit, and often have a longer shelf life. Add them to a fruit compote or a savory salad.

The pale, coral-colored flesh has no seeds and is full of sweet juice.

The smooth, thin skin has a reddish tinge.

Red grapefruit
The brightly colored flesh of varieties such as Ruby Red and Rio Red is juicy, tart—sweet, and almost seedless. Use in compotes and salads and for juice.

TWO WAYS OF PREPARING GRAPEFRUIT

Take segments from whole, peeled fruit, or cut the fruit in half and loosen the segments for easy removal to eat.

1 *With a sharp knife, cut a small slice of peel from the top and base of the grapefruit.* **2** *Hold the fruit upright on the flat base and slice off the peel from the sides, cutting straight down and around the contour of the fruit, and taking off as much white pith as possible.* **3** *To remove each segment, cut down one side close to the dividing membrane. Then cut on the other side of the segment to free it from the other membrane.*

1 *Cut the grapefruit across in half.* **2** *Using a small, curved, serrated knife (a grapefruit knife) or paring knife, cut around the outside of the flesh in each half to separate it from the pith. To loosen each segment cut close along the membranes on either side.*

LEMON

Brightly colored lemons flourish in frost-free Mediterranean-climate regions such as in southern California, Sicily, Greece, and Spain. The size and shape of the fruit varies, as does the skin, which can be thick or thin, smooth or bumpy. Smooth-skinned lemons tend to have more juice; the thick skin of other varieties is best for zesting, candying, and preserving. Sour lemon juice enhances the flavors of other foods and also acts as a preservative.

BUY At their best in winter, lemons should be glossy, strongly colored, and firm and feel heavy for their size. Avoid shriveled fruit or any with patches of mold. Buy unwaxed fruit if you are intending to zest or use the peel.

STORE Whole fruit can be kept in the fridge for 2 weeks; use at room temperature for maximum juice. Wrap cut pieces in plastic wrap, refrigerate, and use as soon as possible. Lemons can be frozen whole or in slices and segments; freeze juice in ice cube trays.

EAT Fresh: Squeeze the juice for dressings, marinades, and drinks. Cooked: Add the juice to tarts, pies, soups, savouries, and emulsion sauces. Grate the zest for baking and desserts. Add pith-free peel to casseroles. Preserved: Chop for marmalade and preserves. Pickle whole or sectioned fruit. Candy peel.

FLAVOR PAIRINGS Chicken, veal, fish, shellfish, eggs, butter, artichokes, garlic, olives, cream, sage, tarragon, coriander seeds, capers, olive oil, gin.

CLASSIC RECIPES Lemon sorbet; *avgolemono;* lemonade; *tarte au citron;* scaloppine with lemon; lemon meringue pie; *citrons givrés.*

Amalfi
Also known as the Sorrento lemon, this fruit of exceptional aroma and flavor is protected under European legislation. The bumpy skin is highly scented and the flesh sweet—tangy. It yields the best juice for limoncello.

The oval citron looks misshapen because it is rather lumpy.

Citron pulp is dry and seedy and usually discarded along with the thick layer of white pith.

Citron
Available in early fall, the Citron has little juice, but the peel is valued for its fragrance in pickles, preserves, confectionery, and Asian teas.

Eureka
This widely grown smooth-skinned, "oblong" lemon, with a small nipple at one end, is juicy with a full flavor, which makes it a good all-arounder.

Meyer
A California lemon—mandarin cross, the Meyer is low enough in acidity to eat raw, so the delicious juice needs little or no sweetening.

Femminello
The most important lemon "family" in Italy, these are typically "oblong" in shape with finely pitted skin and plenty of juice. Use for all aspects of cooking and juicing.

LIME

Limes flourish in hot, wet tropical regions worldwide. Normally round, with thin, smooth, bright green or yellowish-green skin, limes have a distinctive tangy juice that varies in its degree of sourness. Two of the most widely known types are the Tahiti or Persian lime and the sharper Mexican or Key lime. Like that of lemons, the juice of limes has a flavor-enhancing and preservative effect on other food.

🔒 **BUY** Look for glossy, firm, plump fruit year-round. Avoid limes with brown patches or ones that look very yellowish. Choose fruits that feel heavy for their size, since this indicates juice content. The skin is thinner than lemons, so handle the fruit carefully.

🗄 **STORE** Limes can be kept whole for 2 weeks in the refrigerator, but bring to room temperature before use. Once cut, wrap in plastic wrap, refrigerate, and use the next day. Freeze whole fruit or slices and segments; freeze juice in ice cube trays.

⬤ **EAT** Fresh: Squeeze the juice for dressings, marinades, drinks, and cocktails. **Cooked:** Use the juice and zest in desserts, pies, and baked goods. **Preserved:** Make into pickles, chutneys, jams, jellies, and marmalade. Dry for Middle Eastern dishes.

FLAVOR PAIRINGS Poultry, fish, shellfish, tomatoes, avocado, lemon, mango, papaya, melon, spices, chile, Tabasco, rum, tequila, mint.

CLASSIC RECIPES *Ceviche*; Key lime pie; lime pickle; margaritas.

Tahiti lime
Also called the Persian lime, this is large, green, and seedless. The pale, fine-grained pulp has a sharp flavor. It's a great choice for zesting, salsas, and marinades.

The lightly pitted, acid-green skin is shiny and vibrant.

Looking like stubby fingers, these may be green when ripe or purple.

Finger lime
This Australian citrus fruit is not a true lime but provides similar pleasantly sour juice. When lightly crushed, the tiny juice sacs pop open to give a refreshing burst of juice. Wonderful squeezed on to oysters or fish.

Honey pomelo
A seedless Chinese citrus variety, this is mild and succulent, with pale flesh and a honeyed fragrance. The goose-pimpled skin can be candied or added to marmalade.

OTHER CITRUS

The extensive citrus family takes in all fruit with segments of flesh made up of small sacs of juice; a layer of white pith; and a scented, oily, and bitter skin that can be used for zest. Like the more familiar members of the family, such as orange and lemon, other citrus vary in degree of acidity or sweetness and in seed content. The hybrids and new varieties developed expand the range and quality of citrus-fruit choice.

🔒 **BUY** The main citrus season, with tropical exceptions, generally runs from late fall to spring. All citrus fruit should have a good aroma and feel firm and heavy; the skin should be smooth and free from blemishes, marks, and soft spots. Spongy skin can indicate a lack of juice and flesh. A greenish tinge, however, does not necessarily mean the fruit is unripe.

🗄 **STORE** All citrus fruits ripen on the tree and do not continue to develop after picking. Keep for a few days at room temperature or store for 2 weeks, uncovered, in the fridge. Both the juice and segments can be frozen.

FLAVOR PAIRINGS Shellfish, smoked fish, poultry, ham, pork, endive, frisée, celery, spinach, plain chocolate, cloves, cardamom.

Minneola
The juicy, seedless flesh of this mandarin—grapefruit hybrid has an intense, sharp flavor, making the fruit refreshing to eat as a snack and also to use in salads and desserts.

Murcott
Sometimes called a honey tangerine, the Murcott is a variety of tangor, which is a mandarin—orange hybrid. The abundant juice yielded is seriously sweet, which makes it a luxurious drink for breakfast.

The glossy, smooth skin is so thin and fragile that the fruit needs to be clipped off rather than pulled from the tree.

Ugli™
A Jamaican cross between a tangerine, Seville orange, and grapefruit, the Ugli™ has greenish skin that is thick and bumpy, but easy to peel. Its pale flesh is refreshingly sweet. Eat fresh, use the juice for salad dressings, and candy the peel.

The bright orange Minneola has a distinctive bulge at the stalk end.

The flesh has a sweetness and aroma that gives the fruit its name.

CLASSIC RECIPE

SPICED KUMQUATS

You can serve this modern classic either with creamy desserts or with savory meats such as duck, pork, or ham. The compote keeps well for several weeks in the refrigerator.

SERVES 4–6

1 lb (450g) kumquats
⅔ cup granulated sugar
1 small cinnamon stick
4 cloves
2 cardamom pods
1 star anise

1 Cut the kumquats in half and discard the seeds.

2 Place in a heavy-bottomed saucepan with the sugar, spices, and ½ cup water. Bring to a boil, then reduce the heat and simmer very gently, uncovered, for 20–30 minutes, or until tender.

3 Remove from the heat and leave to cool, then refrigerate. If desired, remove the spices before serving.

The thin skin of the kumquat is soft and pulpy and completely edible.

Kumquat
Although not a true citrus, the kumquat is used in similar ways in the kitchen. The cute little bitter sweet fruit contains a burst of juice in the skin, but the pulp has a mouth-puckering sourness by contrast. Eat fresh or use for preserves.

Red pomelo
Sometimes called the shaddock, this is the ancestor of the grapefruit, with a thick, spongy skin and bright red pulp. Sweeter and less acidic than grapefruit, it is delicious in salads and salsas, but make sure to remove all the pith and membrane.

Choose heavy but hollow-sounding watermelons for maximum sweetness, freshness, and ripeness.

SWEET MELON

Sweet or dessert melons are cultivated in hot, sunny regions around the world. The top melon-producing countries are China, Turkey, Iran, and the US. Melons vary in both color and shape, and range in size from single portions to those large enough to feed a crowd. The two main types are summer melons, which include those with a raised cross-hatched pattern or netting on the rind, and winter melons, which have a smooth or finely ridged yellow rind and pale flesh. In all sweet melons, the juicy flesh encloses a central cavity filled with pointed seeds.

BUY Press the end opposite the stem: if the melon is ripe, this should yield readily. The melon should also feel heavy for its size and give off a pleasant aroma through the skin. If it smells too musky it may be overripe. The rind should be thick and unblemished.

STORE If you need to ripen a melon further, keep it at room temperature. Ripe melons are best kept in a cool, airy place, but can be stored in the refrigerator, wrapped in plastic wrap, for up to a week. Open-freeze balls or cubes, or freeze in syrup.

EAT Fresh: Remove seeds and eat halved, or in balls, chunks, or wedges. Note that chilling most melons makes them more refreshing but diminishes the flavor. Add to fruit salads, salsas, sorbets, and chilled soups. **Cooked:** Briefly sauté in savory dishes. **Preserved:** Make into jam.

FLAVOR PAIRINGS Poultry, smoked or cured meats, seafood, cheese, tropical fruit, raspberries, cucumber, coconut milk, ginger, pepper, mint.

CLASSIC RECIPES Melon and prosciutto; chilled melon soup.

Crenshaw
An exceptionally large summer melon, this has a pointed stem end, smooth, lightly ribbed skin, and seductively spicy, salmon-pink flesh. Eat as a dessert on its own or with vanilla ice cream.

Ambrosia
The Ambrosia is a highly perfumed, hybrid cantaloupe with pale, netted skin and a relatively small seed cavity. Serve it fresh or in a fruit salad.

The peach-colored flesh of the Ambrosia is extremely sweet.

Canary
This is a large winter melon with a slightly corrugated, bright yellow rind and refreshing, crisp, green-white flesh. The aroma is strong and pleasing. Serve it on its own or as part of a festive fruit platter.

Charentais
The green ribs on the netted rind of this round summer melon make it look as if it comes ready sectioned. With its tender, apricot-orange flesh and its heady and delicious fragrance, this is a gorgeous dessert melon.

The vivid orange flesh is juicy, sweet, and fragrant.

The seed cavity is large compared with the amount of seeds it contains.

Galia
A honeydew-cantaloupe cross, the Galia is small and spherical with a raised pattern of fine netting. The creamy, light green flesh is spicy-sweet with a lovely aroma. Eat as a dessert.

The soft, juicy flesh is at its best when eaten chilled.

The rind typically shows the lacy pattern of the netting.

Cantaloupe
Also known as muskmelon and netted melon, this summer melon has a rind covered with a pattern of raised netting. The pale orange flesh is sweet and juicy. Serve for a breakfast treat.

CLASSIC RECIPE

MELON AND PROSCIUTTO

For this popular Italian summer appetizer, use a perfectly ripe melon and paper-thin slices of ham.

SERVES 4

1 medium-size ripe, sweet melon, such as cantaloupe or honeydew

3–4oz (100g) thinly sliced prosciutto, such as Parma ham

1 Cut the melon into four quarters and remove the seeds. Use a sharp knife to slice the flesh away from the rind.

2 Wrap the prosciutto around the melon, or serve the two ingredients alongside each other on individual plates. The melon is best served at room temperature.

SWEET MELON (CONTINUED)

Honeydew
The best known winter melon, Honeydew has a smooth, pale yellow or yellow-green rind and ivory-colored flesh. It is the classic choice for melon boat appetizers.

The pale, juicy flesh surrounds a cavity filled with large, oval seeds.

The juicy, sweet flesh of the ogen melon has a green tint.

Ogen
The ogen has a yellow-green, lightly netted skin with striped sections. Sweet and aromatic, it can be enjoyed on its own or paired with cured meats.

Piel de Sapo has a distinctive oval shape like a football.

Piel de Sapo
This popular Spanish variety has a thick, rough-ridged, dark green skin and crisp, pale, refreshing flesh. Eat it on its own or serve with smoked ham.

WATERMELON

Watermelons are grown in both tropical and subtropical regions. The main producing countries are China, Turkey, Iran, the US, and Brazil. The fruit can be either round or elongated; some have dark green skin, others have pale green skin streaked with darker green. The sweet, melting, thirst-quenching flesh is usually deep pink-red but can also be yellow or white. It is the only melon to have seeds scattered throughout the flesh, although seedless varieties are now common.

BUY Watermelons should be firm and evenly colored, and feel heavy. They should not sound hollow when tapped. The side where the melon has rested should be yellowish, not white or green. If buying wedges, avoid any with faded flesh or white streaks.

STORE Wrap slices and refrigerate for up to 2 days. Uncut watermelon can be stored in a cool place for up to 2 weeks.

EAT Fresh: Serve chilled in wedges. Add to a fruit platter. Cube for salads. **Preserved**: Pickle chunks or the rind. Make into jam. Roast and salt the seeds.

FLAVOR PAIRINGS Chicken, shrimp, crab, feta cheese, beets, melon, apple, berries, lime, chiles, ginger, mint.

CLASSIC RECIPES Watermelon salsa; watermelon rind pickles; Greek watermelon and feta salad; watermelon granita.

Sugar Baby
This small "icebox" variety of watermelon
has a round shape, dark green skin,
and supersweet red flesh. It makes
a fabulous sorbet.

The vivid, juicy
flesh is scattered
with black seeds.

Charleston Gray
Large, commercially popular, oval fruit with
a light greenish-gray skin and crisp red
flesh. Excellent for all purposes.

KIWI

Although Chinese in origin, it was New Zealand that put kiwi fruit on the commercial map. They are now grown in other temperate countries such as Italy, Australia, California, and Chile. Sometimes called Chinese gooseberries, the fruit is small and egg-shaped, with a fuzzy, dull brown skin. When peeled, the flesh underneath is brilliant translucent green, tangy, and succulent, with a halo of minute black seeds around the central core.

🔒 **BUY** Kiwi fruit are at their best in the winter months; choose firm, plump, unwrinkled, and unblemished fruits that give slightly when squeezed.

📦 **STORE** To ripen, store kiwi fruit at room temperature for a few days or put in a paper bag. Keep ripe fruit in an open bag in the refrigerator for about 10 days. Freeze peeled fruit in sugar syrup.

⬤ **EAT** Raw: Halve and spoon out for a snack at room temperature. Peel and slice for fruit salads or to decorate cakes, pavlovas, and pastries. Use as a garnish for meat and fish. Dice for use in salsas. Purée for smoothies, coulis, sorbets, and marinades.
Cooked: Not suitable.
Preserved: Peel and chop for use in preserves.

FLAVOR PAIRINGS Steak, chicken, guinea fowl, squid, salmon, swordfish, chiles, oranges, strawberries, tropical fruit.
CLASSIC RECIPES Fruit salad; kiwi salsa.

Zespri Gold
A New Zealand original, the smooth bronze skin covers succulent golden flesh with a central ring of tiny seeds. The taste is deliciously exotic.

Fuzzy Hayward
A popular variety shaped like a flattened barrel. The black seeds make a striking starburst pattern around the white core. Eat fresh or use in salads and salsas.

The thin, rough, and hairy skin of Fuzzy Hayward is inedible.

SAPODILLA

The sapodilla is found in the wild from southern Mexico to Nicaragua, but is now cultivated in other areas, including Southeast Asia. The egg-shaped fruits have rough, russet skin and translucent flesh with a smooth, creamy texture and luscious, fruity taste. Avoid eating the shiny black seeds, since they have a hooked end that is dangerous to swallow.

🔒 **BUY** At its peak in November, the fruit must be perfectly ripe: when unripe it is hard, grainy, and astringent. It should be slightly firm when lightly pressed, but not totally soft. Unripe fruit has a greenish tinge. Avoid any that are overripe, since the flavor will have deteriorated.

📦 **STORE** If the unpeeled skin does not smell fragrant and is still hard, leave it at room temperature to ripen for up to a week. Ripe fruit can be kept in the fridge for a few days. Freeze whole fruit, then half thaw and serve like sorbet.

⬤ **EAT** Fresh: Slice down or across, peel and cut in wedges or scoop out with a spoon, either chilled or at room temperature. Remove the seeds. Eat as a snack or dessert. Purée and mix with mayonnaise or vinaigrette. Mash and use in custards, creams, mousses, and milk shakes.
Cooked: Unsuitable for cooking.
Preserved: Use the pulp for jam or boil down for syrup.

FLAVOR PAIRINGS Chicken, fish, cream, tropical fruit, berries, lemon, lime, coconut, rum.
CLASSIC RECIPES Exotic fruit salad; sapodilla ice cream.

Remove the shiny, hooked, black seeds before eating.

MANGO

Mangoes have been cultivated in India since ancient times, and are now grown in other tropical regions such as China, Mexico, and Brazil. The color ranges from mottled green to yellow and red, and the size and shape varies as well. Generally they have a slight ridge on one side and a "beak" at one end. The flesh is usually neon-orange and surrounds a large, hairy, flat stone.

BUY Color is not a good indication of ripeness. Choose fruit that gives slightly all over when gently squeezed and has a perfumed aroma at the stem end. Avoid mushy looking fruit with blemishes, black spots, or wrinkles.

STORE If unripe, ripen in a warm place or in a paper bag. Once ripe, store in the refrigerator, but try and eat as soon as possible. Open-freeze slices or freeze purée. Freeze purée.

EAT Fresh: Eat at room temperature, peeled and stoned. Slice or chop for salads and cakes. Purée for juices, smoothies, and sorbets. Purée or chop for salsas, sauces, mousses, and creams. **Cooked:** Heat destroys the flavor, so only warm gently at the most. **Preserved:** Slice and bottle in syrup. Cut into strips for drying (see dried fruit). Use unripe green mangoes in Indian pickles and chutney. Dried mango powder is also used as an Indian spice.

FLAVOR PAIRINGS Chicken, smoked meats, fish, shellfish, green salads, lime, lemon, exotic fruit, vanilla ice cream, sweet sticky rice, chiles, rum.

CLASSIC RECIPES Mango salsa; mango sorbet; mango chutney.

Kent
A popular cultivated large oval variety originating in Florida, Kent mangoes have thin greenish-yellow skin with a red blush. The flesh is soft with a rich, sweet flavor. Good for a succulent snack.

Alphonso
The dark green "king of mangoes" has a brief summer season. The buttery flesh has a saffron hue, the aroma is heady, and the sweetness is enhanced by a dash of tartness. Eat as an exquisite dessert.

Ataulfo
Sometimes called Champagne mango, this popular Mexican summer variety is golden yellow with a slightly oblong shape. The silky flesh is deep yellow and has a rich spicy-sweet flavor. It makes a delectable fruit salad.

Kensington Pride
The most widely grown variety in Australia, the fruit has deep-orange, soft, and juicy flesh under yellow skin with an orange-red blush. Eat fresh or use for salads and salsas.

MANGO CHUTNEY

British empire-builders picked up a taste for this Indian chutney and brought the recipe back home with them. It is usually served with curry, but it also goes well with cheese. Traditional, chutney is made with unripe green mangoes, but these can be hard to find, so this recipe uses firm, semi-ripe mangoes instead, which results in a fairly sweet chutney with a light color.

MAKES ABOUT 5½LB (2.5 KG) CHUTNEY

2 cups granulated sugar
2 cups cider vinegar
4½lb (2kg) semi-ripe mangoes, peeled, seeded, and cut into cubes
4oz fresh ginger, peeled and finely grated
4oz red chile peppers, seeded and cut into very thin strips
½ cup dark raisins
2 tsp salt

1 Put the sugar and vinegar in a flameproof casserole dish or large saucepan. Cook over low heat, stirring, until the sugar dissolves.

2 Add the mango, ginger, chiles, raisins, and salt.

3 Bring the mixture to a boil, stirring frequently.

4 Reduce the heat to low and simmer for 1 hour, stirring occasionally, until the mixture is thick.

5 Cool and pour into sterilized jars. Seal according to the canning manufacturer's directions. The chutney will keep for up to 1 year when stored in a cool, drak place.

This medium-sized fruit has a medium-thick yellow to orange-colored skin.

PINEAPPLE

Pineapples are cultivated in tropical and subtropical climates such as Thailand, the Philippines, Brazil, and Costa Rica. The rough, bumpy skin of the fruit is divided into dozens of lozenges, which makes it resemble an enlarged pinecone topped with a gray-green plume of spiked leaves. The firm, rich yellow to pale cream flesh is juicy and sweet with an astringent finish.

PREPARING PINEAPPLE

When slicing off the skin, cut thickly so you take the brown "eyes," too. Any remaining eyes can be nicked out with a knife point.

1 *Cut off both ends of the pineapple. Stand it upright on its base, and slice off the skin all around the fruit, cutting from the top down and following the contour of the pineapple.* **2** *Cut lengthwise in half and then into quarters.* **3** *Slice away the fibrous core from the center of each quarter.* **4** *Slice across the quarters.*

🔒 **BUY** Pineapples are only harvested when ripe (when buying whole fruit, neither the skin color nor the size is any indication of ripeness). For optimum flavor, choose fruit that smells sweet and feels solid and firm, with a crown of stiff, glossy leaves. Avoid fruit that looks dull or bruised, with withered leaves.

📦 **STORE** Eat as soon as possible. Do not keep whole fruit in the refrigerator; however, peeled, sliced, or cubed pineapple can be refrigerated, in an airtight container or wrapped in plastic wrap, for up to 3 days. Pineapple slices and chunks freeze well.

⬤ **EAT** **Fresh:** Peel and slice or cube for fruit salads, salsas, pastries, and desserts. Juice for marinades, drinks, and smoothies. **Cooked:** Sauté slices; fry as fritters; or broil on skewers. Bake in cakes. **Preserved:** Use in jam, pickles, chutneys, and preserves. Dry slices or crystallize. Bottle in syrup.

FLAVOR PAIRINGS Pork, ham, chicken, duck, fish, shellfish, cottage cheese, coconut, ginger, allspice, cinnamon, black pepper, Cointreau, rum, kirsch.

CLASSIC RECIPES Sweet and sour pork; Hawaiian shrimp salad; pineapple upside-down cake; ambrosia; pineapple cheesecake.

If you can easily pull out one of the inner leaves, the pineapple is ripe and ready for eating.

Pineapple
Varieties of pineapple differ slightly in size, shape, and color—some have a golden shell when ripe, others are dark green or reddish— as well as in their degree of sweetness. All can be eaten fresh or used in salads and desserts.

Baby pineapple
These are miniature versions of the larger fruit but with a rounder shape, brighter color, and an edible, tender, and sweet inner core. Ideal for two, so save for a special dessert or breakfast.

PAPAYA

Also called pawpaw, the papaya grows in tropical or subtropical regions such as Hawaii and South Africa. It can vary in size, shape, and color, but typically is an elongated pear shape with thin, shiny, yellow-green skin and vivid pink or orange flesh that is musky-sweet and succulent. The fruit and its leaves contain an enzyme called papain that is used as a meat tenderizer.

🔒 **BUY** Papaya are in season all year round. Choose a papaya that feels heavy for its size and has smooth skin with no pitting or cracking. Ripe fruit will have a sweet aroma and be soft enough to hold an impression when gently squeezed (but handle carefully to avoid bruising).

📦 **STORE** Keep slightly unripe fruit at room temperature until soft and yellow. If ripe, store in a closed paper bag in the refrigerator. Papaya flesh can be frozen in sugar syrup.

⬤ **EAT** **Fresh:** Use in salads, desserts, and salsas. Press for juice.

Cooked: When unripe, steam as a vegetable, dice for soup, or stuff and bake as a savory dish.
Preserved: Bottle in syrup; make preserves and pickles; dry; or candy/crystallize.
FLAVOR PAIRINGS Meat, smoked meats, avocado, chiles, lime, lemon, other tropical fruits, coconut, ginger.
CLASSIC RECIPES Thai green papaya salad; papaya salsa.

Mexican papaya
This jumbo-sized fruit has yellow, orange, or pink flesh that is firm and juicy if not quite as intense in flavor as Hawaiian papaya, the type common in supermarkets. Eat fresh or use for sauces and smoothies.

The crunchy seeds in the cavity of the fruit are edible although usually not eaten.

Hawaiian papaya
A smooth-skinned variety with a shallow seed cavity, Sunrise has very sweet flesh. It is part of a group of papayas called "solo," because they are a suitable size for one person.

POMEGRANATE

Native to Iran, pomegranates are grown in Mediterranean-type climates around the world. Inside the leathery, burnished skin, with its calyx end strikingly shaped like a crown, the fruit is composed of cavities filled with many kernels (called arils). Unless the variety is seedless, each kernel consists of a small, crunchy or softish seed covered with brilliant ruby-red or white jelly. The jelly has a delicate sweetly tart flavor and a juicy texture. The suedelike pith lining the skin and the dividing membrane is very bitter.

BUY Pomegranates are in season from late fall to the winter months. Select by weight, not color, choosing glossy fruit that feels heavy for its size. Avoid any that look dry or damaged.

STORE Whole fruit can be kept in the refrigerator for a few weeks. Scooped-out pulp can be refrigerated for a few days or frozen to be used for juice.

EAT Fresh: Use in salads, salsas, dressings, and cold and iced desserts. Press for juice. **Cooked:** Add juice or pulp to desserts, as well as soups, stews, and sauces. **Preserved:** Make molasses, syrup, and cordials.

FLAVOR PAIRINGS Shrimp, lamb, chicken, duck, pheasant, eggplant, figs, almonds, pistachios, couscous, rice, orange-flower water.

CLASSIC RECIPES *Faisinjan*; Persian chicken and rice; pomegranate soup; pomegranate molasses; pomegranate jelly; grenadine.

PREPARING POMEGRANATE

By scoring the skin and then breaking the fruit apart, the kernels will not be punctured and leak their sweetly tart juice.

1 *Cut off the top of the pomegranate.* **2** *Score the skin into quarters, then break the fruit apart with your hands.* **3** *Use your fingers or a spoon to remove the kernels from the surrounding membrane.*

Wonderful
A leading California variety with a signature crimson color, this has abundant juice, a sweet flavor, and glowing red arils. It is a top choice for both eating and juicing.

Bedana
This medium—large Indian fruit has light-colored arils. Since they are very sweet, juicy, and seedless, Bedana pomegranates are excellent for eating fresh.

PASSION FRUIT

The passion fruit, also known as granadilla, is cultivated in temperate to subtropical areas such as in Brazil, Ecuador, Kenya, and Australia. There are two main types: purple and yellow. The purple varieties can be either round or slightly oval, and the dimpled, leathery skin cracks like parchment when the fruit is ripe (except in the case of the purple Panama fruit, pictured below right). Inside the membranous lining are gelatinous, yellow-gray arils shaped like tiny teardrops filled with crunchy seeds. The juice is a heavenly taste of the tropics. Yellow varieties, which are grown in hotter regions such as Hawaii and Fiji, tend to be larger than purple types, with thick, smooth skin.

BUY Select fruit that is heavy for its size, and avoid any that is overly hard. Purple passion fruit should turn brown, brittle, and dented as it ripens, and smell fragrant. If very heavily wrinkled, however, it may have dried out. Yellow passion fruit is ripe when the skin just starts to wrinkle.

STORE Passion fruit can be ripened at room temperature. Store ripe fruit in an open paper bag in the refrigerator. Whole fruit can be frozen in a plastic bag, or the pulp in ice-cube trays.

EAT Fresh: Halve and spoon out the pulp for fruit salads and desserts. Strain the pulp to yield juice for dressings, ices, mousses, drinks, and smoothies. **Cooked:** Use the juice for soufflés and sauces. **Preserved:** Make the juice into a fruit curd or jelly, or syrup.

FLAVOR PAIRINGS Tuna, venison, game birds, cream, yogurt, custard, oranges, kiwi fruit, strawberries, bananas, peaches, brown sugar, rum.

CLASSIC RECIPES Passion fruit soufflé; Pavlova.

PREPARING PASSION FRUIT

Everything inside a passion fruit is edible—all the fragrant juicy pulp and the tiny, crunchy seeds.

1 With a sharp knife, cut the fruit in half, cutting across the center. **2** Using a small spoon, scrape all around the edge of each half to release the pulp from the membrane. Scoop out the pulp.

Dents on the skin are a sign the fruit is ready to eat.

Purple passion fruit
Typically the size of a lime. Smooth purple passion fruit are unripe. Once wrinkled, the round, purple-brown fruit contains masses of scented, juicy capsules with tiny, crunchy seeds. Eat fresh or use as a fragrant flavoring.

Sweet granadilla
This member of the passion fruit family has a brittle orange rind and long stem. The sweet, delicate flavor of the gray, jellylike pulp and black seeds makes them a pleasure to eat fresh.

Panama
This large variety of purple passion fruit is an exception to the rule, in that it is sweet before the smooth, dark red shell wrinkles. It lends itself equally to desserts or snacks.

The jellylike arils packed inside the fruit are sweet and juicy.

BANANA

Thousands of different varieties of banana are grown in the tropics. Fruit from the large plantations in Central America tends to bland, mealy uniformity, whereas varieties from places such as the Canary Islands are smaller, sweeter, and more curved. As the banana ripens, the leathery, easy-to-peel skin turns from green to yellow. Cooking bananas or plantains are larger and flatter, with firm flesh that is always eaten cooked.

BUY Buy according to requirements and personal preference at different stages of ripeness, from quite green to blackish-yellow. Brown speckles indicate softness; when dark all over, the banana is generally too ripe to eat, but it can still be used for cooking. As plantains ripen, their flesh becomes darker and sweeter, and the skin develops black spots.

STORE Ripen bananas at room temperature. Do not store in the refrigerator or freezer. Keep plantains in a cool pantry for up to a week.

EAT Fresh: Peel and slice bananas for fruit and savory salads; purée for smoothies. **Cooked:** Bake or fry whole, or slice for fritters; purée or chop for cakes and breads. Boil hard green plantains; fry and broil those that are yellow semi-ripe; and mash, curry, or deep-fry ripe black fruit. **Preserved:** Use bananas in jam and chutney, or dry banana slices.

FLAVOR PAIRINGS Chicken, trout, cream, yogurt, custard, orange, lime, coconut, walnuts, chocolate, coffee, ginger, brown sugar, liqueurs, rum.

CLASSIC RECIPES Banana bread; banana split; chicken Maryland; banana ice cream; *bananes flambées*; banoffee pie; *arroz a la cubana*; *plátanos fritos*.

The skin is smooth but blemishes easily unless handled with care.

Yellow banana

The standard supermarket bunch has large, curved yellow fruit that is thick skinned and robust, making it easy to ship. The creamy-white flesh is consistently sweet, if somewhat floury. These are good all-arounders for both eating and baking.

Select fruit of even size and color with a few dark spots, which indicate ripeness.

The small size gives these fruit their other name of baby bananas.

Plantain

The leading commercial variety of plantain, Maricongo, is large and angled, and the green skin turns yellow with dark splotches to brownish-black as it ripens. Use as you would a potato.

Lady Finger

Tiny bananas with creamy flesh and a very sweet flavor, these make perfect mini-snacks or can be used whole for fritters.

Red banana

Sweeter, shorter, and plumper than the average banana, this delicate type has red wine-colored skin and creamy purple-pink flesh.

The leathery skin of the plantain must be peeled off or cut away before the fruit is cooked.

CLASSIC RECIPE

BANANA BREAD

A very popular tea-time loaf with Anglo-Jamaican roots, this is moist and keeps well. Serve it sliced, with or without butter.

MAKES I LOAF

9 tbsp unsalted butter, at room temperature

¾ cup packed light brown sugar

I large egg

I tsp pure vanilla extract

I ¼ cups all-purpose flour

I tbsp baking powder

½ tsp salt

½ tsp freshly grated nutmeg

I lb (500g) ripe bananas, mashed

¾ cup raisins, tossed in I tsp flour

¼ cup chopped walnuts

1 Preheat the oven to 350°F (180°C). Butter a 1-quart (1-liter) capacity loaf pan.

2 Cream the butter and sugar together with an electric mixer until light and fluffy. Add the egg and vanilla extract and beat into the mixture.

3 Sift the flour, baking powder, salt, and nutmeg into another bowl. Add this in batches to the creamed mixture, alternating with batches of mashed banana, beating well by hand after each addition. When thoroughly blended, mix in the floured raisins and the walnuts.

4 Scrape the mixture into the loaf pan. Bake for about 1 hour, or until a skewer inserted into the loaf comes out clean. Cool in the pan for 5–10 minutes, then transfer to a wire rack.

PERSIMMON

This eye-catching fruit is cultivated in Mediterranean and subtropical climates. There are two types: the Japanese or Oriental persimmon (kaki) and the smaller American persimmon, which is grown in gardens. The many varieties of Japanese persimmon offer a range of shapes, sizes, and colors, but many look like large, waxy, amber tomatoes. The silky-smooth flesh is usually bright orange. When ripe, most varieties have a sweet, honeyed taste.

BUY In season in late fall and winter, choose fruit with rich color, glossy skin, and no blemishes. They should look swollen, as if just about to burst. The leaves should be intact.

STORE Ripen in a paper bag. Ripe fruit can be kept in the refrigerator for a short time, but eat as soon as possible. Or freeze whole or as purée.

EAT Fresh: Cut off the top and spoon out the pulp, or add to fruit salads. Blend for smoothies. Use in sauces and cold and iced desserts. **Cooked:** Poach unripe fruit. Add to cakes, breads, and muffins. **Preserved:** Dry; or purée for preserves.

FLAVOR PAIRINGS Ham, pork, game, lime, crème fraîche, yogurt, *fromage frais*, walnuts, ginger, cinnamon, allspice, nutmeg, honey.

CLASSIC RECIPES Persimmon pudding; persimmon ice cream.

Both the skin and seeds of the Sharon Fruit are edible.

Sharon Fruit
Sliced and eaten when firm like an apple, this Israeli variety has a sweet, datelike texture and is ideal for avocado and fruit salads.

Fuyu is a flat, squat variety with firm flesh.

Fuyu
Although seemingly unripe, when pale and hard this variety is actually ready to eat. Its sweetness and "crunchy" texture make it particularly good for salads.

Rojo Brillante
This large Spanish persimmon has an oblong shape and highly colored skin. When ripe, it is meltingly soft. Serve fresh or use in desserts.

Hachiya
A large, heart-shaped fruit with a papery, pale-green calyx, Hachiya must be almost mushy before it can be eaten. It is then deliciously sweet, and excellent for desserts.

Fully ripe fruit are very soft and pulpy, so handle with care.

ACKEE

Ackee or akee is native to West Africa, but has been adopted as Jamaica's national fruit. The pear-shaped fruits are picked when they are fully ripe: bright red and split open in a "yawn" or "smile" to reveal their creamy-yellow pulp or curd and large black seeds. Only the ripe curd can be eaten; underripe curd and other parts are toxic. Although slightly sweet, ackee curd is most commonly treated as a vegetable because it picks up the taste of other ingredients in a dish.

🔒 **BUY** Outside Jamaica, fresh, vacuum-packed ackee can sometimes be found in the summer months; otherwise buy canned ackee.

🗃 **STORE** Follow the instructions on the label.

◉ **EAT** Cooked: Boil and purée for patties. Use in soups and stews. Fry in oil.

FLAVOR PAIRINGS Bacon, salt pork, salt cod, butter, chiles, peppers, garlic, tomatoes, curry spices.

CLASSIC RECIPES Ackee and saltfish; ackee patties.

As ackee ripens it turns from green to greenish-yellow to red and then splits open along the seams.

PEPINO

Sometimes called a "tree melon" or "melon pear," this beautiful heart-shaped fruit is native to temperate Andean areas and cultivated in Chile, New Zealand, and Australia. The pale yellow flesh is aromatic and mildly sweet with a slight tartness. Some varieties have abundant seeds, while others are seedless.

🔒 **BUY** Select pepino with a deep yellow or gold base color, since this indicates the fruit is fully ripe; avoid any with greenish undertones. The fruit should be firm yet still somewhat pliant when gently squeezed by hand (they are delicate and have to be handled and transported with care).

🗃 **STORE** Ripen at room temperature for a few days if necessary. If ripe, pepino can be kept unwrapped in the bottom of the refrigerator for up to a week, or cubed and frozen in sugar syrup.

◉ **EAT** Fresh: Peel and slice to eat alone or add to fruit salads. Dice for salsas and cake fillings. Cooked: Poach slices for desserts. Preserved: Bottle in syrup or make into chutney.

FLAVOR PAIRINGS Prosciutto, shrimp, scallops, vanilla ice cream, other tropical fruits, honey.

CLASSIC RECIPES Exotic fruit salad; Spanish gazpacho.

Pepino typically has shiny gold skin streaked with violet.

RED MOMBIN

The red mombin—or Spanish plum or *jocote*, among many of its colloquial names—is native to tropical North and South America, but it also grows in the Philippines, where it is known as *siniguelas*. The flesh of the deep red to yellow, oval fruits is juicy and fragrant with a spicy, sweetly tart flavor.

🔒 **BUY** Choose hard, underripe, greenish fruit for chutney; otherwise, look for well-colored, glossy, soft fruit.

🗃 **STORE** Red mombin is fragile and needs to be handled carefully. Ripen at room temperature; keep ripe fruit in a paper bag in the bottom of the fridge. They are not suitable for freezing.

◉ **EAT** Fresh: When ripe, eat out of hand. Purée for sorbets and ice cream. Press the juice for cocktails. Salt underripe fruit for snacks, or make into a tart green salsa. Cooked: Simmer in curries and stews. Poach for desserts. Preserved: Make conserves, chutney, and pickles; use in syrups and cordials; dry; bottle in syrup.

FLAVOR PAIRINGS Chiles, raisins, ginger, cinnamon, curry spices, brown sugar, rose water, rum.

Red mombins are the size of large olives, with a big, fibrous seed in the center.

DRAGON FRUIT

The cacti that bear this small fruit, also known as pitaya, are native to Central America, but the fruit is cultivated also in the West Indies, Southeast Asia, and other tropical regions. Dragon fruit has a striking appearance with its fleshy scales and skin color, which may be a fluorescent shocking pink or golden yellow. The spongy, juicy flesh, which ranges from deep pink to pearl white, is studded with tiny black seeds and tastes mild and slightly sweet.

BUY Dragon fruit is generally available in the fall. If ripe and ready to eat, the fruit should yield slightly when gently squeezed.

STORE Keep in the bottom of the fridge, but eat as soon as possible after purchase. It is not suitable for freezing.

EAT Dragon fruit should not be cooked. **Fresh:** For the best flavor, eat chilled. Halve and scoop out the flesh. Add to fruit salads. Press the juice for drinks, cocktails, and sorbets.

FLAVOR PAIRINGS Other tropical fruits, lime, lemon, coconut, sugar, ginger.

The small edible seeds are pleasantly crunchy.

Pink dragon fruit
The thick scales give this fruit the look of a crimson artichoke. Its flesh, which can be pink or white, is sweet and refreshing. Enjoy fresh or juiced.

Yellow dragon fruit
Looking like mini-pineapple crossed with banana, this type of dragon fruit tastes similar to the pink variety, whether eaten fresh or juiced.

RAMBUTAN

A close relative of the lychee, the rambutan is cultivated throughout Southeast Asia as well as tropical Honduras and Australia. As with the lychee, the shell of the rambutan is brittle and the white flesh covers a smooth, dark pit. The taste is similarly aromatic and sweet, although with a slight sharpness.

BUY Rambutan are at their best in summer. Choose fruit with lively, curly "hairs." Do not buy if they look flat, tired, and brown. The fruit is fragile, so handle with care.

STORE Rambutans can be kept in the lower part of the refrigerator for several days in an open paper bag, but should be eaten as soon as possible after purchase. Freeze unpeeled.

EAT Fresh: Eat as a snack, or use in fruit salads. Purée flesh for drinks, smoothies, and ice cream. **Cooked:** Poach for desserts. **Preserved:** Bottle in syrup. Add to jams and jellies.

FLAVOR PAIRINGS Pork, duck, cream, chiles, avocado, other tropical fruits, coconut, vanilla, ginger.

LYCHEE AND LONGAN

Lychees, or litchis, and longans are closely related tropical fruits native to China and Southeast Asia. The heart-shaped lychee is slightly larger than the longan. Both have similar juicy, sweet, translucent flesh, with the lychee's more richly flavored.

BUY The fruits are at their best in summer. Choose lychees with a good red or pink color (greenish fruit are underripe; brownish fruit will taste unpleasant). Avoid any fruits that look shriveled. Buy in small amounts, since the fruits can soon dry out.

STORE Keep in an open paper bag in the lower part of the refrigerator, but eat as soon as possible after purchase. Unpeeled fruit can be frozen.

EAT Fresh: Shell and eat as a snack. Use for salads or ice cream. Purée flesh for juice, smoothies, cocktails, and dressings. **Cooked:** Poach for desserts. Use to finish sweet-and-sour and stir-fried dishes. **Preserved:** Dry whole. Bottle the pitted pulp in syrup. Add to jams and jellies.

FLAVOR PAIRINGS Pork, duck, seafood, vanilla ice cream, chiles, avocado, other tropical fruits, raspberries, coconut, ginger, rose water.

Longan
This has a rough brown shell and juicy flesh surrounding a large seed that is jet black with a white eye-shaped mark.

Lychee
Inside the brittle, scaly, red shell is pearly white pulp enclosing a large, shiny brown seed. The pulp has a delicate, sweet, clean flavor that works well in both sweet and savory dishes.

The "hairs" on the fruit should be lively and curly, not flat, tired, or brown.

FEIJOA

Although sometimes known as the pineapple guava, the feijoa is in fact unrelated to these fruits. Native to South America, it is cultivated in warm, temperate regions. The bumpy, lime-green, barrel-shaped fruit looks like a tiny, plump avocado. Inside the thin, leathery skin, the sweetly tart, grainy flesh surrounds a jellylike pulp packed with tiny, slippery, edible seeds.

🔒 **BUY** A ripe feijoa will give slightly to the touch and its perfumed aroma will be heady.

📦 **STORE** Handle carefully, since feijoa are prone to bruising. Ripen in a paper bag at room temperature. If ripe, they can be kept in the refrigerator for a few days. Puréed fruit can be frozen.

⊙ **EAT** Fresh: Halve and scoop out the flesh to eat as it is, or add to fruit salads and salsas. **Cooked:** Use the pulp for crumbles, pancake fillings, and pies. Poach for compotes. Purée for sauces. **Preserved:** Make into jelly, chutney, or relish; bottle in syrup.
FLAVOR PAIRINGS Roast meat, prosciutto, cream, chiles, salad greens, lime, other tropical fruits, honey, mint, ginger, hazelnuts.
CLASSIC RECIPES Feijoa jelly; feijoa pancakes; feijoa salsa.

When ripe, the jellied inner section of the feijoa is clear, not white.

STAR FRUIT

Also called carambola, the pretty star fruit is widely grown in tropical and subtropical regions. The cylindrical, yellow-green fruit has thick, waxy skin with five sharp ribs that look like raised fins. The crisp, juicy flesh is citruslike, differing in sweetness according to variety and how ripe the fruit is.

🔒 **BUY** Select shiny, even colored, firm fruit without blemishes. Star fruit is green when unripe, turning to pale yellow and then rich gold as it ripens. When ripe the aroma should be fruity. Once soft, it will quickly lose flavor. Buy unripe green fruit, which will be more acidic, for cooking as a vegetable.

📦 **STORE** Keep at room temperature until the fragrance develops. Ripe fruit can be kept in a closed paper bag in the refrigerator for a few days. Or freeze.

⊙ **EAT** Trim off any traces of brown along the top of the ridges since this will taste bitter. **Fresh:** Include in fruit salads. Use as a garnish. Extract the juice for drinks. **Cooked:** Poach or purée for cakes and desserts. Use the

syrup for sauces. In Asia, unripe fruit is used as a vegetable. **Preserved:** Make into jam, chutney, and pickle. Slice and preserve in sugar as candied fruit.
FLAVOR PAIRINGS Poultry, shrimp, avocado, red peppers, other tropical fruits, lime, coconut, lemongrass, nutmeg, vanilla, honey, rum, salt.

GUAVA

The guava thrives in tropical and subtropical conditions. There are many varieties, but the most common is pear shaped with thin, yellow-green skin and juicy, tartly sweet flesh. At the outside edge, the flesh tends to be somewhat granular; the sweetest, softest pulp is at the core amid the array of small, hard but edible seeds.

🔒 **BUY** Choose unblemished fruit. When ripe, a guava will have an intense floral fragrance; it will be firm but will give slightly when squeezed gently (handle with care since the fruit bruises easily). Underripe fruit is popular in Asian countries for salads and snacks.

📦 **STORE** Ripen in a warm room until the fragrance develops. Ripe guavas can be kept in an open paper bag in the refrigerator for a few days. Freeze peeled fruit in syrup.

⊙ **EAT** Fresh: Add to sweet and savory salads. Purée for sauces, smoothies, pancake fillings, sorbets, and ice cream. **Cooked:** Poach or bake for desserts, compotes, and savory dishes. Use in pies. **Preserved:** Make jelly, jam, or "butter." Bottle in syrup.
FLAVOR PAIRINGS Pork, pheasant, duck, seafood, chicken, cream cheese, apple, pear, lime, chiles, other tropical fruits, lemon, coconut, ginger, honey.
CLASSIC RECIPES Guava and apple pie; guava jelly; guava butter.

The juicy flesh of the guava is a vivid salmon-pink.

The star fruit is so-called because when cut across, a section or slice is decoratively star-shaped.

TAMARILLO

The tamarillo or tree tomato is grown in many tropical and subtropical countries, particularly New Zealand. The small, egg-shaped fruits have pointed ends and a thin green stem. The milder, yellow variety is suitable for preserving. The attractive flushed flesh has swirls of dark edible seeds, and a tangy, sweet-sour taste.

🔒 **BUY** Available in the fall, select fruit that is heavy for its size, richly colored, and slightly soft to the touch. Unripe fruit will have a greenish tinge. When ripe, they should smell like a mix of tomatoes and apricots. Only eat when fully ripe.

🗄 **STORE** Ripen at room temperature until fragrant. Store ripe fruit in a plastic bag in the refrigerator for up to a week. Dry-freeze peeled fruit.

⬤ **EAT Fresh:** Cut in half, sprinkle with sugar, refrigerate overnight, and scoop out the chilled pulp the next day. Add to ice cream. **Cooked:** Peel and stew for savory sauces and relishes. Bake or broil for desserts and compotes **Preserved:** Use for chutney and preserves.

FLAVOR PAIRINGS: Roast meats, chicken, fish, cream, kiwis, oranges, brown sugar, curry spices.

CLASSIC RECIPES: Tamarillo ice cream; tamarillo chutney.

The tough, bitter skin of the tamarillo is inedible. This dark red variety is best eaten fresh.

CHERIMOYA

Closely related to the custard apple and the soursop, the cherimoya has green smooth skin with a pattern of grooved indentations like enlarged fingerprints. They are large, juicy, and scented with slightly grainy flesh, a mellow, sweet-sour flavor, and dark, beanlike seeds, and are commercially grown in subtropical regions such as Brazil, California, Australia, and Spain.

🔒 **BUY** Usually available in the winter months; choose fruits without dark spots. They should be slightly firm. If they feel very soft, they will be overripe and have a poor texture.

🗄 **STORE** Handle carefully, since the fruit is fragile. Ripen at room temperature in a paper bag. Wrap ripe fruit in plastic wrap and store in the fridge for a few days. Freeze purée.

⬤ **EAT Fresh:** Scoop out the flesh. Add to fruit salads, ices, and desserts. Blend for drinks. **Cooked:** Pulp or purée for savory dishes and stir-fries. **Preserved:** Use in jam and preserves.

FLAVOR PAIRINGS: Pork, chicken, citrus, yogurt, cinnamon, ginger.

CLASSIC RECIPES: Cherimoya sorbet; cherimoya sauce.

Fino de Jete Campa
A variety widely grown in Spain and New Zealand, it has very white flesh but is somewhat lacking in perfume. Use in sorbets and smoothies.

Libby
A popular variety with a conical shape and indented skin that looks like beaten metal. The sweet, strong flavor makes it superb to eat fresh.

DURIAN

About the size of a soccer ball, the durian is famous for its delicious flavor and nauseating, pervasive aroma. The woody shell is hard and spiked, and the pulp is divided into segments containing sweet, rich, yellow-white flesh with the texture of creamy custard. The few seeds are the size of chestnuts. The main export countries are Thailand, Malaysia, and Indonesia.

🔒 **BUY** Eat very fresh in their summer season. Avoid split or damaged fruit, as it means the fruit is overripe; the smell will also be overpowering. When ripe, the fruit will be a dull yellow-green, and the flesh yellow-white.

🗄 **STORE** Store for as short a time as possible, and keep separate from other foods. Freeze slightly overripe flesh in plastic bags.

⬤ **EAT Fresh:** Split open the shell and scoop out the pulp surrounding the seeds. Purée for shakes and smoothies.

Cooked: Add to cakes. Cook the unripe fruit as a vegetable. **Preserved:** Use in jam. Sugar and salt for snacks and sweetmeats. Roast the seeds. Preserve as paste to flavor desserts.

FLAVOR PAIRINGS: Milk, cream, coconut, tropical fruit, curry spices, chiles, glutinous rice.

CLASSIC RECIPES: Durian jam; durian ice cream.

The thorny shell must be cracked open to reveal the creamy pulp.

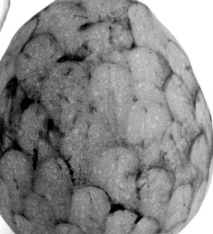

Custard apple
Closely related to the cherimoya, these are heart-shaped with thick, overlapping raised green petals, rather like a large pine cone. Brown patches develop as the fruit ripens. The custardlike flesh contains shiny black seeds. Enjoy fresh or use in pies, pancakes, stir-fries, and savory sauces.

MAMMEE APPLE

Native to the Caribbean, the tree (sometimes known as mamey or mamey apple, but not to be confused with the mamey sapote) was introduced into West Africa, Southeast Asia, Hawaii, and Florida. The round, orange-size fruit has brown russeted skin.

🔒 **BUY** When unripe, the fruit is hard and heavy, but the flesh slightly softens when fully ripe. Look for evenly colored fruit.

📦 **STORE** Ripen hard fruit at room temperature. Refrigerate ripe fruit for a day or two. Freeze the pulp.

⦿ **EAT Fresh:** Halve and seed and eat raw. Peel, chunk, and add to salads. Purée for ice cream. Juice for drinks. **Cooked:** Peel and stew for desserts, sauces, pies, and compotes. **Preserved:** Make into jam and preserves. Make into wine. Distill the flowers for liqueur.
FLAVOR PAIRINGS: Milk, cream, yogurt, tropical fruit, lime, lemon.
CLASSIC RECIPES: Fruit salad; jam;

The flesh is apricot-colored with a pleasing fragrance. The large pit should be discarded.

MANGOSTEEN

Inside the thick shell of the purple fruit, the pith contains juicy, perfumed arils of sweet flesh. It is grown commercially in Thailand, Vietnam, Central America, and Australia.

🔒 **BUY** In its summer season, look for fruit with a deep color. To test if the fruit is ripe, squeeze gently. The fruit is also available canned.

📦 **STORE** Store at room temperature until ripe, then refrigerate.

⦿ **EAT Fresh:** Cut off the top and serve in the half shell. Remove white flesh from the pith and eat raw. Juice for drinks or sorbet. **Cooked:** Unsuitable. **Preserved:** Add unripe fruit to preserves.
FLAVOR PAIRINGS: Tropical fruit, coconut, strawberries, lemongrass.
CLASSIC RECIPES: Exotic fruit salad; mangosteen sorbet.

The small, purple fruit has a prominent calyx that remains attached to the stalk.

GUANABANA/SOURSOP

At its best, this large, pear-shaped fruit is soft and abundantly juicy, but it can be quite acid, which gives the fruit its alternative name of soursop. It is cultivated in tropical regions such as the West Indies, Central America, India, and Southeast Asia.

🔒 **BUY** Look for green or yellow-green fruit. If yellow, they are overripe. Avoid any with black blotches. Guanabana is frequently found canned.

📦 **STORE** Keep in the fridge but use ripe fruit as soon as possible, as they rapidly ferment and become inedible. Freeze sweetened purée.

⦿ **EAT Fresh:** Juice for drinks and smoothies. Add the pulp to fruit salad, and purée for ice cream and creamy desserts. **Cooked:** Immature guanabana can be roasted and fried as vegetables. **Preserved:** Guanabana is frequently found canned.
FLAVOR PAIRINGS: Tropical fruit, cream, condensed milk, cinnamon, vanilla, nutmeg.
CLASSIC RECIPES: Soursop ice cream; soursop custard; soursop juice.

The thin, leathery skin is dotted with soft spines. The seeds in the fibrous white flesh are toxic.

ACHACHA

Related to the mangosteen, achacha means "honey kiss." Originating in the tropical Amazon basin, they are now under commercial cultivation in North Queensland, Australia. The fruit look like tiny orange golf balls. Inside, the pure white flesh is refreshingly juicy, with a good sweet-tangy balance. Discard the central seed.

🔒 **BUY** The Australian season runs from December to February. Look for firm, brightly colored fruit with no blemishes.

📦 **STORE** Once harvested, the fruit does not ripen further, so will keep well in a cool place without refrigeration. Freeze whole.

⦿ **EAT Fresh:** Pinch and pop open the skin and eat the flesh as a snack or dessert. Add to fruit salads. Use the pulp in sauces, ices, sorbets, and dressings.
Cooked: Not suitable.
Preserved: The washed skins can be used to make a refreshing drink.
FLAVOR PAIRINGS: Yogurt, lime, berries, pistachios, honey, mint, rosewater, rum.
CLASSIC RECIPES: Exotic fruit salad; achacha frozen yogurt.

Inside the orange fruit, the white flesh is juicy and sorbetlike.

MUSK CUCUMBER

Also known as cassabanana, this is widely grown in tropical Cuba, Puerto Rico, and Mexico. The herbaceous perennial vines produce large, oval-shaped fruit. The thick, hard shell varies in color from orange-red to violet-black. The refreshing, yellow-orange flesh is firm, sweet, and highly aromatic. The pulp in the center is softer and contains numerous flat oval seeds running in rows along the length of the fruit.

🔒 **BUY** The fruit should look glossy and smooth when ripe.

📦 **STORE** The summer fruit will remain in good condition for several months if kept dry and out of the sun.

⦿ **EAT Fresh:** Peel and eat as a dessert. Add to a fruit salad. **Cooked:** Chop the immature fruit as a vegetable for soups and stews. **Preserved:** Make into jam or chutney.
FLAVOR PAIRINGS: Lime, coconut, cinnamon, star anise, ginger, mint.
CLASSIC RECIPES: Exotic fruit salad; musk cucumber jam.

The torpedo-shaped fruit can grow to the size of loofahs.

DRIED AND CANDIED FRUITS

Drying is one of the oldest methods of preserving food. When applied to fruit, the process intensifies the taste of the natural sugar, especially if the fruit is sun-dried. Candied fruits are preserved in sugar syrup. When the fruit has an extra coating of granular sugar it is called crystallized.

🔒 **BUY** Look for plump, unblemished, supple dried fruit; avoid any that appears hard and leathery. Dried fruit is sometimes treated with sulfur dioxide to help preserve it further, or may contain extra sugar, oil, flavorings, and additives. This will be indicated on the label. When buying candied fruit make sure it looks soft and moist.

📦 **STORE** Once a package or pot is open, place it in an airtight container and store in a dry, cool place: dried fruit for up to 6 months, and candied fruit for up to a year.

EAT Some dried fruit may need to be soaked in water or other liquid before use, while others are ready to eat. Enjoy dried fruit as a snack or add to cereal. Use in cooking both sweet and savory dishes, in stuffings, cakes, breads, cookies, and pies. Use candied peel in cakes and desserts or eat crystallized fruits as after-dinner sweetmeats. Candied cherries are used in cakes and as a decoration for desserts.

FLAVOR PAIRINGS Poultry, pork, lamb, fresh citrus, yogurt, custard, oats, honey, seeds, spices, liqueurs.

CLASSIC RECIPES Prune and Armagnac tart; Christmas cake; mincemeat pies; *birnenbrot; far Breton;* Dundee cake; lamb tagine with apricot and prunes; cock-a-leekie soup.

Chopped mixed peel is sweet and aromatic.

Dried cherry
Sour cherries have a marvelous tart but fruity flavor that makes them irresistible for snacking. Use sweet cherries in desserts and pies, but go easy on the sugar.

Candied citrus peel
A mix of orange, lemon, and citron makes the best candied peel. Available diced or in strips, use it in cakes, cookies, and Christmas cake.

Dried blueberry
Nutritious, sweetly tart blueberries are slightly chewy when dried. Use in cereals, cakes, muffins, trail mix, and salads for added flavor and color.

Dried cranberry
When dried, cranberries are sweeter than fresh but still have a slightly sour taste. Fruity and chewy, they are versatile and can be added to cakes, cookies, muffins, desserts, granola, or savory stuffings.

Dried banana
Creamy-golden chips, often coated with sugar or honey, are delightfully crisp. The longer brown and sticky slices are good to use in tea breads, soufflés, stews, and winter fruit salads. Add crunchy slices to granola, or eat as a snack.

Add dried coconut shavings to cereals and granola.

Dried coconut
Available both sweetened and unsweetened, coconut shavings (chips) and shredded (desiccated) coconut should look fresh and white. Use them in baking, cooking, or anything that requires a taste of coconut.

Dried mango
The orange-hued slices, strips, and "cheeks" have a vibrant flavor and chewy texture. Use in cakes, tea breads, chutney, and jam.

Dried apple
Tender, with a sharply sweet flavor, apple rings and wedges work well in compotes and casseroles, particularly those made with pork. Add dried apple chips to granola.

Dried apricot
Neon orange-gold, soft, and supple, ready-to-eat dried apricots can be used in compotes, or with ham, chicken, duck, and rice dishes. They do not require soaking before use. The best come from Turkey. Use in stews and casseroles as well as sweet dishes.

Unsulfured dried apricots are darker in color, with a more intense flavor.

Dried fig
Purple Mission figs have an intense, sweet flavor. Stuff them for sweetmeats or use in baking, desserts, and compotes, and with poultry and game. Calimyrna, made from the California version of the Smyrna fig, are golden, plump, and full of fiber—a great choice for baking and cooking.

DRIED AND CANDIED FRUITS (CONTINUED)

Dried strawberry
Add these sweet little berries
to cereals, muffins, cakes,
and snack bars.

Dried papaya
The pretty pink strips or cubes
are usually sugared; sugar-free dried
fruit is chewier but has a more intense
taste. Dried papaya makes a good
addition to cakes and muffins.

Dried peach
Use the large, sweet, wrinkled,
and chewy halves whole or
chopped in compotes,
desserts, cakes, and
casseroles. Soak in wine or
orange juice for extra flavor.

Raisins may be brown,
black, or white,
depending on the
variety of grape
that is dried.

Dried pears are usually
sold in halves.

Raisin
Use raisins in rice and couscous dishes,
salads, cakes, desserts, and chutney.
Dried, seedless red Flame grapes are
very sweet and a good snack choice.
The larger black Monukka raisins
have great depth of flavor.

Dried pear
Delicately sweet, with a slightly chewy
texture, they can be eaten as a snack, and
make a delicious addition to compotes,
desserts, cakes, and casseroles. Purée for
sauces to go with pork and venison.

Prune
Wrinkled, black, ready-to-eat
prunes (which are dried plums)
are soft and tender; others may
need to be soaked before use.
Agen prunes are among the finest.
Add prunes to savory dishes,
desserts, and compotes.

Dried goji berry
These deep red Himalayan berries are reputedly very healthy. Tasting like a sweet cross between a cranberry and cherry, they are a good addition to granola, snack mix, and yogurt.

Dried pineapple rings sometimes have added color and sweetening.

Add diced, dried papaya to a home-made snack mix.

Dried pineapple
The pale yellow dried fruit, which comes in chunks, rings, or diced, has a sweet, fragrant flavor that is wonderful in cakes and desserts.

Candied citron peel
The thick, aromatic peel of this citrus fruit is moist and sticky. Use it in cakes, marmalades, and jam.

Dried currant
Seedless Zante (Black Corinth) currants are small and dark, with a slightly sharp taste. They are an essential component of Christmas cakes and desserts.

CLASSIC RECIPE

PRUNE AND ARMAGNAC TART

Sweet Agen prunes and rich vanilla custard are elegantly presented in this delicious French tart.

SERVES 6

8oz (200g) Agen or other pitted prunes

6–7 tbsp Armagnac or brandy

1 cup heavy whipping cream

2 tbsp superfine or granulated sugar

1 vanilla bean, split lengthwise

2 large egg yolks

For the pastry

1¼ cups all-purpose flour

1 tbsp confectioners' sugar

pinch of salt

5 tbsp unsalted butter, softened

1 large egg yolk

1 Pour enough Armagnac over the prunes to just cover and leave to macerate for several hours.

2 To make the pastry, sift the flour, confectioners' sugar, and salt into a bowl. Add the butter and rub in with your fingertips until the mixture resembles coarse meal. Mix in the egg yolk and 1–2 tbsp cold water to form a dough. Wrap in plasttic wrap; leave in the fridge for at least 30 minutes, or overnight.

3 Preheat the oven to 350°F (180°C) with a baking sheet inside. Roll out the pastry and use to line a greased 9in (23cm) fluted tart pan with a removable bottom. Prick the base with a fork, line with parchment paper, and fill with pie weights or dry beans.

4 Set the pan on the hot baking sheet and bake blind for 20–25 minutes, or until the pastry is crisp and lightly browned. Remove from the oven, keeping the pan on the baking sheet, and carefully lift out the parchment paper and weights. Set aside.

5 Combine the cream and sugar in a saucepan. Scrape in the seeds from the vanilla bean; add the pod. Bring to a boil, then simmer gently, stirring occasionally, until reduced by one-third. Leave to cool, then discard the vanilla pod and whisk in the egg yolks. Pour the mixture through a fine sieve to remove any cooked egg.

6 Arrange the drained prunes on the bottom of the pastry shell. Pour in the custard; it is fine if some of the prunes peep through. Bake for 35–40 minutes, or until the custard is golden brown and puffy, but still looks a little wobbly in the center. Remove from the oven and cool on a wire rack. Cut into wedges.

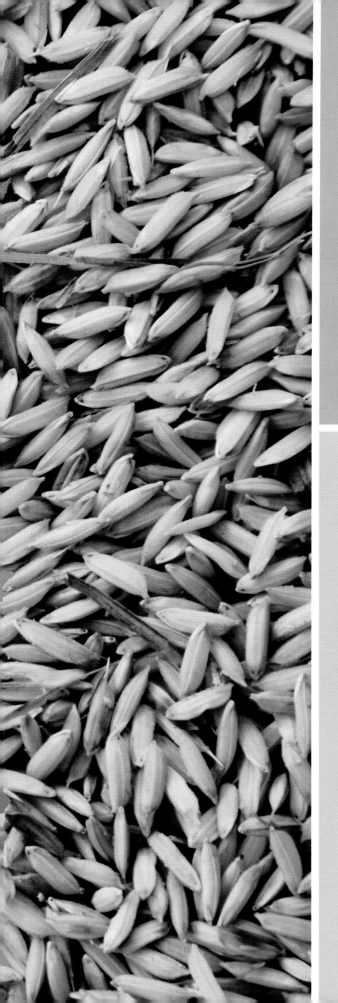

GRAINS, RICE, PASTA, & NOODLES

BARLEY | RYE | QUINOA
WHEAT | WILD RICE
FRESH PASTA | DRIED
PASTA | COUSCOUS
RICE NOODLES
WHEAT NOODLES

GRAINS, RICE, PASTA, AND NOODLE ESSENTIALS

Grains, rice, pasta, and noodles are the energy-giving, starchy, staple foods that have made the world go round for thousands of years. Whether whole grains or further processed products such as rice sticks, couscous, and flour, these foods are a valuable source of nutritious fiber and complex carbohydrates. They are inexpensive, abundant, and, compared to fresh ingredients, have a long storage life that makes them a most practical foundation for everyday meals. Even a small selection in the pantry (ideally kept in airtight containers) will allow you to produce recipes from cuisines the world over—and that is by no means restricted to savory dishes.

BUY

Grains It is hard to determine the quality of grains by sight, but do check the package for the sell-by date before buying.

Rice Buy packages of grains that complement the style of dish you are cooking, such as basmati to accompany curries, jasmine for Thai dishes, Arborio or Carnaroli for risottos, or paella rice for Spanish paella dishes. Choose packages that are not expired and contain unbroken grains.

Pasta Decide whether or not you wish to cook fresh or dried pasta and if you prefer a flavored or wheat-free variety. Pasta comes in myriad shapes: some are better suited to meat, tomato, or cream sauces or casseroles. Choose the pasta shape that is most appropriate for the dish you are cooking.

Noodles Again, noodles are available in many forms for a variety of dishes. Buy noodles that are unbroken and are suitable for the dish you are cooking.

STORE

Check the packages for any specific storage instructions and sell-by dates, but generally all grains, rice, dried pasta, and noodles should be stored in airtight containers in a cool, dry place out of direct sunlight. Stored in this way, all these dried goods can be kept for up to a year without any deterioration to their condition.

STORING FRESH PASTA AND NOODLES
Ideally, fresh pasta and noodles should be eaten on the day they are made or purchased. If they must be stored, they can be kept in the refrigerator for 2–3 days in a sealed container. They can also be frozen in a sealed container for up to 1 month.

Pasta
Dried pasta, such as tagliatelle, is ideal to keep in the pantry as a basis for quick, easy, filling dishes with a simple sauce.

Rice
Keep different varieties of rice in the pantry to form the basis of meals such as paella and risotto, and as a ready accompaniment to stews and curries.

Rice mixtures *Rice is the ideal accompaniment to many cooked dishes, but it can also be used very successfully as a dish in its own right. Mix grains to add texture and flavor, such as the nutty wild rice here combined with long-grain rice.*

PREPARE

Flour is a versatile powder made from ground grains. A wide variety of dishes can be made using flour as its main ingredient, from cakes, cookies, pastry, and pancakes to pasta, bread, and pizza dough. There are many varieties available that are intended for specific use, such as bread flour for bread, tipo 00 for pasta, self-rising and all-purpose for cakes, cookies, pastry, and sauces, and those that offer nutritional benefits, including whole wheat, rye, amaranth, and barley, or gluten-free types such as quinoa and buckwheat, for those with intolerances.

MAKE PIZZA DOUGH

Making pizza at home is satisfying and surprisingly straightforward. The trick to achieving a finish as good as that of your local pizza parlor is to make sure the oven is as hot as possible, and preheat the baking sheets before placing the crusts on them.

Ingredients

4 cups bread flour, plus extra for dusting
a pinch of salt
1 x ¼oz (7g) envelope quick-rising active
*   dry yeast*
1½ cups warm water
¼ cup olive oil

1 *Sift the flour into a mixing bowl, stir in the salt and yeast. Make a well in the center and pour in the warm water, then the olive oil, stirring with a wooden spoon to incorporate the liquid and form a soft dough. Alternatively, use a electric mixer fitted with a dough hook.*

2 *Turn out the dough on to a lightly floured work surface, then knead it using the heel of your hand for about 10 minutes, or until it becomes soft, smooth, and pliable.*

3 *Return the dough to the bowl, then cover it with a clean kitchen towel or plastic wrap and set aside in a warm place until the dough has almost doubled in size—this should take 30–45 minutes. Meanwhile, prepare your preferred toppings.*

MAKE PASTA
Fresh pasta—a simple combination of flour, eggs, and salt—is very easy to make at home. You can use a rolling pin to stretch the pasta, but a hand-cranked pasta machine will make light work of producing long thin sheets of dough, while also giving it a professional finish.

Ingredients

4 cups Italian tipo 00 flour or all-purpose flour,
*   plus extra for dusting*
large pinch of salt
4 large eggs

1 *Pile the flour onto a clean work surface and make a well in the center. Sprinkle with salt then break in the eggs. Using a fork, or your fingers, gradually incorporate the flour into the egg, bringing the flour in from the sides of the pile a little at a time to form a dough.*

2 *Once the flour has all been incorporated, clean the work surface and dust it with flour. Knead the dough using the heel of your hand for about 10 minutes, or until the dough is smooth and elastic. Leave the dough to rest for around 30 minutes before continuing.*

3 *Roll out pieces of dough to ovals about 1in (2.5cm) thick. Set the machine to its widest setting and crank a piece of dough through several times until smooth. Adjust to the next setting and repeat two or three times. Continue to do this on each setting until the pasta is the desired thickness, then cut into shapes.*

MAKE BREAD DOUGH

The way in which you combine the ingredients of your dough is important to the success of your bread, so use these tips to perfect your technique.

Mix the ingredients thoroughly, as quickly as possible, to make a soft, sticky dough. Dig right down to the bottom of the bowl and squeeze the dough through your fingers to make sure all the flour is mixed with the liquid.

Scrape any dough from your fingers back into the bowl, then cover with a cloth to keep the dough moist. Leave it for 10 minutes before starting to knead.

KNEAD The key to kneading is to concentrate on mixing the dough evenly.

Before starting to knead, wash and dry a glass bowl, then rub the inside and your hands with a little oil. Set aside. Uncover the dough, put it on a lightly floured work surface and fold it in half toward you.

With one hand, hold the fold in place, while with the heel of the other hand gently but firmly press down and away to seal and stretch it.

Repeat the folding, pressing, and rotating 10–12 times, stopping before the dough sticks to the surface. Place the dough in the oiled bowl, seam-side down, cover with a cloth, and leave to rest for 10 minutes.

Repeat the kneading procedure twice at 10-minute intervals. Each kneading will require less oil. The dough will change from its lumpen start to a silken and elastic finish.

SHAPE After the initial rise, you need to divide the dough into smaller pieces according to what you want to use it for—be it small loaves or rolls.

Weigh your dough and divide it up accurately into pieces. Larger loaves take longer to bake than smaller loaves, so taking this extra precaution will ensure even baking.

Lightly flour your work surface before shaping. This will slightly dry the outside of the dough to encourage a good crust to form during baking.

MAKE WHITE BREAD Try this recipe at least twice: once you get into the habit of baking bread at home you'll find it fits easily into your lifestyle and the inferior flavor of store-bought loaves simply doesn't compare.

Ingredients
½oz (15g) fresh yeast (dissolved in 1¼ cups lukewarm water), or 1 x ¼oz (7g) envelope quick-rising active dry yeast
4 cups bread flour, plus extra for dusting
2 tsp fine sea salt
oil, for greasing

1 Sift the flour and salt into a mixing bowl. Pour the yeast liquid (or dry yeast) into the bowl and stir. Work the mixture into a dough with your hands, kneading until it comes away cleanly away from the sides of the bowl.

2 Turn the dough out onto a lightly dusted work surface. Knead until the dough is smooth and firm, not sticky. Return the dough to the bowl, cover with a clean kitchen towel and leave in a warm place.

3 Once the dough has doubled in size—this should take about 1–2 hours—remove from the bowl and return to a lightly dusted work surface. Punch the dough down and knead well to punch the air out of the risen dough.

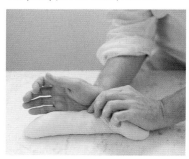

4 Cut the dough in half and use your hands to shape each piece into a rounded rectangle. Grease a loaf pan and ease both pieces of dough into it side by side. Cover with a kitchen towel and leave to rise for about 30 minutes.

5 Bake in the center of a 425°F (220°C) oven for 15 minutes. Reduce the heat to 375°F (190°C) and bake for another 30 minutes. To check doneness, rap the base with your knuckle. The loaf should sound hollow.

WHOLE WHEAT BREAD

Ingredients
½oz (15g) fresh yeast (dissolved in 1¼ cups lukewarm water), or 1 x ¼oz (7g) envelope quick-rising active dry yeast
2 cups bread flour, plus extra for dusting
2 cups whole wheat flour
2 tsp fine sea salt
oil, for greasing

To make, use the same method given for white bread, opposite.

The two types of flour used in this recipe give the bread a lighter, moister texture than regular whole wheat bread. If you prefer a denser, heavier whole wheat loaf, use 4 cups whole wheat flour and omit the bread flour.

COOK

The success, or otherwise, of grain, rice, pasta, and noodle dishes is all in the cooking. These are ingredients that most home cooks use time and time again, but even with so much practice, many people still find they can get the method or timing wrong and end up with over- or undercooked food. With a bit of know-how, however, you can soon start to make these staples stars.

COOK RICE This open-pan boiling technique uses five or six times as much water as rice and results in light, distinct grains. It works well for long-grain white rice and is the preferred method for all whole-grain varieties, the only difference being that you add whole-grain rices to cold water and once at a boil cook for 18-25 minutes, depending on the individual variety.

Ingredients
1 lb 2oz (500g) long-grain rice
3 quarts water

1 Bring a large saucepan of water to a rolling boil. Add the rice and, once it has returned to a simmer, cook for 12–15 minutes, or until the rice is tender but still has some "bite."

2 Drain the rice in a colander, cover with a clean kitchen towel and leave to steam dry for 10 minutes. Fluff up the grains with a fork before serving.

COOK RICE BY ABSORPTION This technique, popular in Asia, is best suited to white rice. Measure the liquid accurately—it should be 1¼ times the volume of rice—and choose a heavy-bottomed saucepan with a tight-fitting lid. Remember that it should be large enough to allow the rice to triple in volume during cooking.

1 Put the rice in a large saucepan, pour in the cold water or stock and bring to a boil over medium heat. Stir the rice once only, then simmer, uncovered, for 10–12 minutes, until all the liquid has been absorbed.

Ingredients
1lb 2oz (500g) long-grain white rice
2½ cups water or stock

2 Remove the pan from the heat, lay a clean, folded kitchen towel over the rim and top with a tight-fitting lid. Return the pan to a very low heat and leave the rice for 10 minutes.

3 Remove the pan from the heat once more and leave the rice undisturbed for 5 minutes before removing the lid and kitchen towel. It is now ready to serve.

COOK PASTA AL DENTE

Al dente, which translates from the Italian as "to the tooth," describes the consistency of perfectly cooked pasta—cooked through, but still slightly firm when you bite into it. Overcooked pasta will be sloppy and waterlogged, so take care to check the pasta toward the end of the recommended cooking time.

1 *Bring large pan of salted water to a boil and gently pour in the pasta.*

2 *Boil uncovered, following the recommended cooking time on the package, or until "al dente" when tasted.*

3 *Drain the pasta through a colander, shake the colander so that the pasta does not stick together, and serve immediately.*

MAKE SOFT POLENTA

Polenta is a staple food of Northern Italy and has not always been made with cornmeal, although that is most common today. It is very similar to the grits dishes of the Southern US, mamaliga of Romania, and mealie-pap of South Africa, all of which are also derived from corn. Instant or precooked polenta is a quick-cooking alternative to traditional stoneground cornmeal, but fails to match the latter's superior flavor and texture. It is common, although not essential, to stir flavorings such as butter, black pepper, and grated Parmesan cheese, or cubed semi-soft cheeses such as Fontina, into a creamy batch of soft polenta before serving.

Ingredients
4 cups water
1 tsp coarse sea salt
1 cup stone-ground polenta (cornmeal)

1 *Bring the water to a simmer in a heavy-bottomed saucepan, adding the salt. Once bubbling, gradually sprinkle in the polenta while stirring the mixture continuously with a whisk.*

2 *Turn the heat down (the polenta will still bubble) and cook, stirring frequently, for 35-40 minutes, or until the mixture is thick, creamy, and comes away from the sides of the pan.*

COOK COUSCOUS

Couscous is a mixture of fine and coarse semolina. It is traditionally steamed using a laborious rubbing technique to keep the grains separate, but with modern manufacturing techniques come easier and quicker ways of preparing it. It is normally enriched with oil or butter and seasoning before serving.

Ingredients
1¾ cups water
1¾ cups couscous
1 tbsp olive oil or 3 tbsp butter, diced
1 tsp salt and freshly ground black pepper

1 *Boil the water in a kettle. Put the couscous in a large heatproof bowl and pour the water over it. Cover with plastic wrap and leave to stand for 5 minutes. Fluff up the grains with a fork.*

2 *Recover with plastic wrap and leave to stand for another 5 minutes. Add the olive oil or butter and salt and pepper and fluff up the grains to coat and separate. Serve immediately.*

Steam couscous *by placing it in a bowl, sprinkling it with water, and leaving it for 5 minutes. Then transfer to a muslin-lined steamer and steam for 15–20 minutes.*

BOIL NOODLES

Noodles made from wheat and buckwheat need to be boiled before use, whereas most rice noodles and those based on starches such as mung bean or sweet potato flour need only to be soaked in warm or just-boiled water. If you are using very wide dried rice noodles, boil them briefly until tender. Fresh rice noodles don't need cooking, only reheating. Once prepared, all noodles need to be kept moist if you don't intend to serve them immediately, otherwise they will harden or set together.

1 *In a large saucepan of boiling water, cook the noodles for 2-6 minutes, referring to the package instructions for your particular variety. They are ready as soon as they are soft and pliable.*

2 *Drain the noodles in a sieve and refresh them under cold running water before draining thoroughly. Toss the noodles gently with oil to stop them from sticking and serve immediately.*

BARLEY

Versatile barley grows in hot and cold climates and is grown extensively in North America, Europe, and Russia. One of the oldest-known staple foods, it looks similar to wheat, but tends to be plumper and sweeter tasting. Barley is a good source of fiber and selenium. Its modest gluten content means it is often overlooked as a source of bread flour, however, its rich, honeyed flavor readily compensates for this. Pot barley has only the indigestible part of the husk removed, so retains its bran layer; semi-pearled barley removes some of this layer; pearl barley has most or all of the bran layer removed by polishing.

🔒 **BUY** Packages vary in the amount of bran retained, which affects the fiber content and cooking time, so try to look at the grains before you buy.

📦 **STORE** Barley is particularly prone to infestation and is best stored in airtight containers in a cool, dark, dry place, or in the refrigerator.

⬤ **EAT** A handful of pot or pearled barley adds substance, texture, and sweetness to soups and stews. The grains make a chewy pilaf or side dish when boiled in stock; cooking them in water provides a hearty base for salads, while cooking in milk is a fine alternative to hot oat cereals and rice puddings.

FLAVOR PAIRINGS Apples, beef, beer, blackberries, cabbage, carrots, celery, duck, lamb, lemon, mushrooms, onions, parsley, thyme.

CLASSIC RECIPES Barley bread; *orzotto* (Italian barley risotto); Scotch broth; iced barley tea; lemon barley water.

Cracked grit
This is made from grains of pot or semi-pearled barley that have been chopped into two or three pieces, exposing the starchy endosperm and making them stickier when boiled. Cracked barley cooks quicker than whole grains, without sacrificing the fiber content, and makes a delicious wholegrain porridge. Barley grits are grains that have been crushed and ground and sometimes pre-toasted.

Unlike other grains, the bran layer is retained on pot barley.

Pot barley
Sometimes called Scotch or whole barley, these grains have a rugged, pleasantly chewy texture and a good balance of sweetness and toastiness. Boiling can take as long as 75 minutes, which makes pot barley best for slow-cooked stews and soups.

Beremeal
A smoky-flavored speciality of the Scottish Highlands and Islands, this flour is stoneground from grains dried in a kiln fired by their own husks. Traditionally used in bannocks, a quick, scone-like bread, it also works well in crackers. Its strong taste can be tempered with wheat or oat flour.

Pearl barley
Two main types are available. White, powdery-looking grains are fully pearled with a sweet, bland flavor and take just 20–25 minutes to cook. In contrast, beige pearled barley retains some of its nutty-tasting bran around the endosperm, and can require 10–15 minutes more simmering.

AMARANTH

The amaranth plant produces edible leafy greens similar to spinach, as well as tiny, gluten-free seeds, and grows easily in challenging climates where better-known grains, such as rice and wheat, struggle. It is highly nutritious and an excellent source of vegetable protein, fiber, iron, and calcium. India, China, the USA, and Bolivia are all common sources of amaranth.

BUY If buying amaranth flour, choose a store with a high turnover of stock, as it turns bitter within a few months of grinding.

STORE Decant amaranth grains and flour into airtight containers and store in a cool, dark, dry place, or in the refrigerator. The shelf life will vary according to the time of processing, so observe the use-by dates on the package; the flour will turn bitter over time. For longer storage, amaranth flour can be kept, tightly sealed, for up to 6 months in the freezer.

EAT For a simple, starchy base to stews, boil whole amaranth grains in three times their volume of salted water for 20–25 minutes. Alternatively, cook for a further 5 minutes for a porridge consistency and stir in chopped fresh or dried fruit. The popped grains can be added to cereal mixes, doughs, and used as crumb coatings. Or stir them into cinnamon-scented rice pudding about 15 minutes before the end of cooking. Amaranth flour can be added to pastry, batter, and dough mixes, but for a puffy or light texture, combine it with a gluten-containing flour such as wheat, rye, or barley.

FLAVOR PAIRINGS Beans, cheese, chicken, chile, chocolate, coconut, corn, zucchini, honey, milk, squash, tomato.
CLASSIC RECIPES Flatbreads/tortillas; *mole*; *atole* (gruel); *alegria* (candy).

Whole
The diminutive size of these woodsy-tasting seeds makes it difficult to see their flying-saucer shape. When boiled, the tiny equatorial ring uncurls, helping create a sticky, spongy mass; brief toasting helps the grains stay more distinct. Baking the whole seeds in dough mixtures gives a pleasing, gritty texture.

Flour
Lends a malty, herbaceous flavor to baked goods and hot drinks. The grain is usually grown to organic standards, then stoneground to retain its high fiber content.

QUINOA

Pronounced "keen-wah," this astringent-tasting native of South America is not a member of the cereal grass family, but an herb seed of the broad-leaved goosefoot family. The plant's leaves can also be eaten, prepared like spinach. Quinoa's fairly high protein and fat contents make it a sustaining choice for meals; it is also rich in calcium and iron. Commercially grown in countries including the USA, Bolivia, Peru, China, and the UK, quinoa can also thrive in inhospitable climates. Various colors, including gold, black, and red, are available.

BUY It is not possible to gauge by sight, but packs of quinoa are cleaned to varying degrees. Modern processors are quite effective at removing the bitter-tasting saponin dust that naturally coats the seeds, but always rinse them thoroughly before cooking.

STORE The seeds can be stored in an airtight container in a cool, dark place for more than a year, while the flour should be kept in the fridge or freezer and used within 4 months.

EAT Quinoa has a pearlescent, springy texture and a grassy, slightly bitter flavor. It is a good alternative to rice, and is quicker to cook.

FLAVOR PAIRINGS Apple, beef, black beans, chicken, chile, cilantro, corn, grapes, nuts, orange, shrimp, squash, sweet potato.
CLASSIC RECIPES Pilafs; porridge; salads; soup; vegetable stews.

Flour
A nutritious addition to all sweet and savory baked goods, but as it is gluten free it needs to be combined with a rising agent such as baking powder. Mix with wheat flour to help give it a sweeter flavor.

When cooked, the grains' equatorial bands uncurl, giving each bead a little crunchy tail.

Whole
Providing it is well rinsed, quinoa has a neutral flavor that welcomes the flavors with which it is combined. If not, it can taste bitter, due to residual dust from the seeds' natural saponin coating, which is removed during processing. A good alternative to rice, or excellent added to stuffings and in salads.

These quick-cooking flakes are ideal for making speedy porridge.

Flakes
The seeds are steamed and rolled into flakes for faster cooking. They can be worked into multigrain doughs and batters, or used as a coating in place of breadcrumbs when frying.

BUCKWHEAT GALETTES

Although "galette" often refers to a free-form pie or tart, it can also describe a savory buckwheat crêpe. These are popular in Brittany, in northwest France, where the local cuisine is defined by rich, rustic flavors.

SERVES 4

½ cup buckwheat flour

½ cup all-purpose flour

2 eggs, beaten

1 cup whole milk

sunflower or canola oil, for frying, plus extra for greasing the pan

2 small red onions, thinly sliced

8oz (200g) smoked ham, chopped

1 tsp fresh thyme leaves

4oz (115g) Brie, cut into small pieces

½ cup crème fraîche

1 Sift the flours into a large mixing bowl, make a well in the center and add the eggs. Gradually beat the eggs into the flour using a wooden spoon, then add the milk and ½ cup water to make a smooth batter. Cover and leave to stand for 2 hours.

2 Heat the oil in a frying pan, add the onions and cook gently until softened. Stir in the ham and thyme, then remove the pan from the heat and set aside.

3 Preheat the oven to 300°F (150°C). Heat a crêpe pan or small frying pan and grease it lightly. Spoon in 2 tbsp of the batter and swirl the pan so it coats the bottom. Cook for about 1 minute, or until lightly browned underneath, then flip over and cook for another minute, or until browned on the other side. Make 7 more crêpes in this way, regreasing the pan as necessary.

4 Stir the Brie and crème fraîche into the ham mixture and divide the mix among the 8 crêpes. Roll or fold up the filled crêpes and place them in a baking dish. Just before serving, bake the crêpes or galettes for 10 minutes, or until heated through.

BUCKWHEAT

A favorite of cold-climate Eastern European, Russian, and Japanese cuisines, hearty buckwheat is native to Manchuria and Siberia. Today, it is grown in areas as disparate as China, Canada, and Australia. The seeds are distinctively brown and triangular and, despite the name, are not part of the wheat family: instead, the plant is related to rhubarb and sorrel.

🔒 BUY Look for pale-colored, speckled flour: a dark gray-brown color can indicate old age rather than a high fiber content. Buckwheat can be found in a wide range of gluten-free convenience foods, including pasta and breakfast cereals.

📦 STORE Whether sold in cellophane or paper bags, buckwheat is best transferred to a robust, airtight container for storage in a dry, dark pantry. Observe the use-by date on the package, since its shelf life is determined by the time of processing. It is worth keeping buckwheat flour in the refrigerator (up to 3 months) or freezer (up to 6 months), providing it is well sealed to keep moisture out.

● EAT The grains are easily toasted in a little fat before adding stock or water and boiling to make a simple pilaf-style side dish that can be flavored with herbs and other ingredients. Left to go cold, that mixture is also a fine base for a salad. For a wintry risotto, add a few tablespoons of buckwheat to the rice as you cook it. A portion of buckwheat flour is a good addition to pancake batters and pasta doughs, lending a tangy flavor to common wheat. Buckwheat crêpes made exclusively from buckwheat flour have a stronger flavor and brittle texture.

FLAVOR PAIRINGS Bacon, chicken, cream, cucumber, cottage cheese, egg, fish, ginger, mushrooms, onions, parsley, rice, soy sauce.

CLASSIC RECIPES Blinis; Breton crêpes or galetes; soba noodles; *kasha*; pierogi; polenta.

Buckwheat flour
In Japan, buckwheat flour is made into a savory warm cereal that is served with a soy-based sauce. For baked goods, it works well mixed with wheat or corn flour in a ratio of 1:3 or 1:4.

Freshly ground buckwheat flour has a talcum-powderlike quality that becomes darker, earthier, and stronger as the product ages.

Kasha
Kashka groats are sometimes labeled "roasted buckwheat" on the packet. Add a couple of tablespoons to a wintry risotto along with the rice for a deeper, more complex flavor.

. These brown, preroasted groats do not need toasting to enhance their meaty flavor before boiling.

Whole
Greeny-brown raw buckwheat groats are considered whole grains even though their inedible, dark brown seed coat (hull) has been removed. If you want to sprout buckwheat, buy the dark brown seeds specified as suitable for sprouting. Use the woodsy tasting grains in pilaf-style accompaniments and stuffings.

BLINIS

These little yeasted pancakes are delicious served with smoked fish, sour cream, or crème fraîche, and a sprinkling of chives or dill.

MAKES 25

3 cups whole milk

1 x ¼oz (7g) envelope active dry yeast

1 cup buckwheat flour

1 cup bread flour

3 eggs, separated

1 tsp superfine or granulated sugar

1 tbsp melted butter, plus extra for frying

1 In either a small saucepan or a microwave-safe liquid measuring cup, heat half the milk until lukewarm. Add the yeast and whisk to combine.

2 Mix together half of each flour in a mixing bowl and make a well in the center. Add the egg yolks, sugar, and a pinch of salt, then pour in the warm yeasty milk and mix until smooth and well blended. Cover and set aside in a warm place for about 1 hour or until the mixture has doubled in bulk.

3 Beat the remaining flours, milk, and the melted butter into the batter then cover and leave to rise again, for a minimum of 1 hour, but preferably overnight in the refrigerator. When you are ready to cook the blini, whisk the egg whites in a clean bowl until stiff peaks form; then fold them into the risen batter.

4 Heat a large, heavy-bottomed frying pan or griddle over medium heat. When thoroughly hot, grease lightly with butter and pour spoonfuls of batter onto the pan or griddle, making blini about 2–3in (5–8cm) diameter. Cook until small bubbles appear on the surface, then flip and cook on the other side until golden brown. Keep the blini warm in a low oven while you cook the remaining batter.

CORN

Grown and eaten extensively in the Americas, corn (or maize) is also a staple food crop of areas as disparate as Africa, Romania, northern Italy, and Malaysia. There are five main families of corn plant, with hundreds of varieties and several colors within each. The term sweet corn is commonly used to distinguish the vegetable crop from the grain varieties, but it is not the only type of corn that can be eaten fresh. Corn is entirely free of gluten and rich in essential fatty acids, complex carbohydrates, vitamin A, potassium, and magnesium.

BUY Choose the right corn for its intended usage, as varieties vary greatly.

STORE Dried corn kernels can be stored in an airtight container for several years with no compromise to quality. Hulled and degermed cornmeal, including most polenta brands, can be kept in a cool, dry pantry for a year or so, preferably in an airtight container; however, stoneground, whole-grain cornmeal is best tightly wrapped and stored in the freezer for no more than 6 months.

EAT Corn tastes light, sweet, and vegetal. Taking advantage of its creamy texture, many cultures grind and boil it to a rib-sticking, oatmeal-like mush that may be served plain alongside barbecued meats, flavored with herbs and cheese, or sweetened to create a comforting pudding. Baked goods made from corn flours/meals tend to need a high proportion of fat, eggs, or cream to give a moist texture; they also dry out quickly, so they are best eaten right after cooking.

FLAVOR PAIRINGS Beans, beef, bacon, chicken, chile, cheese, coconut, cilantro, lime, milk, mushrooms, pork, pumpkin, rabbit, tomatoes.

CLASSIC RECIPES Cornbread; corn cakes; polenta; succotash; tamales; tortillas.

Masa harina
This Mexican flour is ground from dried posole or hominy and is used for tortillas and tamales. It also makes an excellent cake flour.

Yellow polenta is the best known, but white polenta is favored in and around Venice.

Grits
Hard, dried corn kernels that have been crushed then sifted to separate out the floury meal. Stoneground grits have the best flavor, since they include the nutritious endosperm that commercial steel-roller mills remove to lengthen the shelf life. Cook grits with liquid to produce oatmeal-like mush and flavor with savory or sweet ingredients. Quick-cook or instant grits are also available.

Polenta
Stoneground varieties have a superior flavor and a satisfying, chewy texture, but a lengthy cooking time (30–45 minutes). Polenta can be boiled to produce a warm cereal, or be left to set then cut into slabs and fried or broiled. Use it in baked goods, too, but instant or quick-cook varieties have a grittier, crunchy texture that is less appealing in cakes. Northern Italians traditionally use polenta bramata—polenta mixed with buckwheat flour.

Popcorn
Available in several different colors, popcorn is a special hard variety of corn with a tough hull and endosperm. When heat is applied, the moisture inside the kernel turns to steam, causing it to explode.

Posole/pozole
Traditional to Mexico, this is flint or field corn that has been soaked and cooked in a calcium-hydroxide solution, making it easier to digest and its nutrients more readily absorbed. Thanks to the removal of the pointed germ at the bottom of each kernel, the grains splay out when cooked to look like a flower. It is mainly used for soup-stews of the same name.

Cornmeal
Compared to other flour products, cornmeal is coarsely ground and can be purchased in white, blue, and yellow varieties. It is used in baked goods and also for crumb coatings.

CORNBREAD

This sweet, rich-tasting golden bread gets a little spice from added chiles. Best served warm, fresh from the oven.

SERVES 6

butter, for greasing

1½ cups yellow cornmeal or polenta (not instant polenta)

¾ cup all-purpose flour

½ cup granulated sugar

2 tsp baking powder

2 cups buttermilk

2 eggs

4 fresh red chiles, seeded and thinly sliced

1 Preheat the oven to 375°F (190°C) and generously grease an 8–10in- (20–25cm-) round baking pan.

2 Stir together the cornmeal, flour, sugar, and baking powder in a mixing bowl and make a well in the center. Pour the buttermilk into a liquid measuring cup, then gently whisk in the eggs and chiles. Pour the mixture into the well in the dry ingredients and stir until the mixture is evenly moistened and just comes together. Do not overmix.

3 Pour the batter into the prepared pan; bake at the center of the oven for 30–40 minutes, or until the cornbread is firm and golden on the outside and a skewer inserted in to the center comes out clean.

MILLET

Millet is widely grown in Asia, Africa, the US, and Europe, yet it is under-appreciated as a culinary ingredient and often dismissed as a food of the rural poor. Its light, mild flavor is versatile; the small, bead-like grains are quick to cook; and millet rehydrates well, so that small quantities readily satisfy the appetite. The hardy plants also mature much faster than other grain crops, offering practical advantages for farmers.

STORE Millet grains will keep for many years in a dark place without attracting infestation, but the flour easily turns bitter so should be stored in an airtight container and used as quickly as possible. (Grinding your own is worth considering.)

EAT Thanks to its neutral, alkaline flavor, millet is one of the most satisfying alternatives to rice. In the recipes of many rural areas, it was a forerunner to cornmeal.

FLAVOR PAIRINGS Beans, chicken, chile, cilantro, cream, eggs, salmon, sesame, soy sauce, spinach.

CLASSIC RECIPES *Congee;* milk puddings; pilafs; porridge.

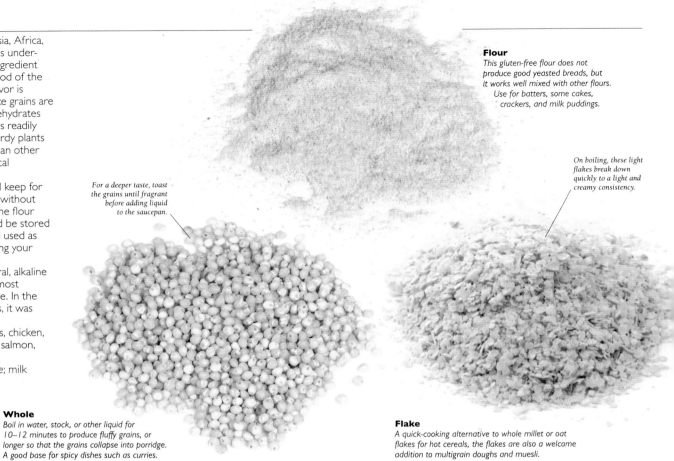

Flour
This gluten-free flour does not produce good yeasted breads, but it works well mixed with other flours. Use for batters, some cakes, crackers, and milk puddings.

On boiling, these light flakes break down quickly to a light and creamy consistency.

For a deeper taste, toast the grains until fragrant before adding liquid to the saucepan.

Whole
Boil in water, stock, or other liquid for 10–12 minutes to produce fluffy grains, or longer so that the grains collapse into porridge. A good base for spicy dishes such as curries.

Flake
A quick-cooking alternative to whole millet or oat flakes for hot cereals, the flakes are also a welcome addition to multigrain doughs and muesli.

OATS AND OATMEAL

A beloved grain of cold climates, oats are at their most flavorful when allowed to grow slowly. This allows the grain steadily to become plumper, optimizing the moisture and fat content. Oats are high in soluble fiber (proven to lower cholesterol levels) as well as insoluble fiber (good for digestive health), and help to regulate blood-sugar levels. They also contain useful levels of B vitamins and calcium.

STORE Whole oats can be stored in airtight containers in a cool, dark place for up to a year; oat bran (because it does not contain the endosperm) will last even longer.

Oatmeal and rolled oats are best used within 3 months.

EAT The sweet, creamy flavor of oats makes them ideal for desserts and baking; toasting and frying them adds a nutty flavor to savory dishes.

FLAVOR PAIRINGS Apricots, berries, butter, cabbage, cream, ham, herring, lamb, nuts, onion, peaches, thyme, rye, sausages, syrups.

CLASSIC RECIPES Oatmeal cookies; fruit crisps; herring in oatmeal; muesli; *laverbread;* oatcakes; porridge.

Medium oatmeal
A favorite choice for porridge and skirlie in Scotland, and the most versatile variety to have on hand for baking. It also gives a good, even coating to fried fish.

Use in place of barley in meat stews for distinct yet creamy-textured grains.

Coarse oatmeal
In addition to making a pleasingly chewy porridge, coarse oatmeal is suitable for thickening soups, stews, and minced-meat mixtures. It can also be sprinkled over dishes to be gratinéed, in place of breadcrumbs.

Fine oatmeal
Use for recipes such as pancakes, pastry, milk puddings, and gravies, where a smooth or floury texture is desired.

Rolled oats
Invented in the US, whole oats or pieces of oat grain are softened by steam-cooking, then rolled into flakes. Porridge, cookies, and muesli are typical uses, and they are a popular, flavorful addition to bread doughs, including Scandinavian crispbreads.

Whole oats/oat groats
They can take 75 minutes to cook, so tend to be used in slow cooking. They are a delicious addition to meat stews, root vegetables, and greens; the grains maintain their shape, yet become tender and creamy. Precooked whole oats can be baked into coarse-grain bread doughs.

Cooks to porridge consistency in just 5 minutes, and has the health benefits of whole grains.

On boiling, these flakes break down quickly to a smooth, velvety consistency.

Quick or instant oats
A highly refined version of rolled oats designed to produce hot breakfast cereal very quickly.

Oat bran
A concentrated source of soluble fiber (good for reducing cholesterol levels), oat bran can be used in cereals, muffins, cakes, and bread.

Pinhead oatmeal
Whole kernels cut into a few pieces, exposing the starchy endosperm of the grain. It has a pleasingly coarse texture that is good for rough oatcakes and adds crunchiness to fried fish. It is also a favorite with haggis manufacturers.

OATCAKES

These rustic crackers are good with soft cheeses, sardines, peanut butter, or marmalade.

MAKES 12

1 cup oat flour, plus extra for dusting

½ cup rolled oats (old fashioned oatmeal)

½ tsp salt

2 tbsp butter, plus extra for greasing

1 First, boil some water in a kettle. Combine the oat flour, rolled oats, and salt in a large mixing bowl. Cut the butter into small dice and work it into the dry ingredients.

2 Make a well in the center of the mixture and carefully pour in about 1 tbsp of boiling water. Stir until the mixture comes together to form a dough, adding more hot water, in very small amounts, as necessary.

3 Dust a work surface lightly with the oat flour and roll out the dough to a thickness of ⅛–¼in (3–5mm). Leave to rest for 5–10 minutes while you preheat the oven to 300°F (150°C) and lightly grease a baking sheet.

4 Using a 3in- (7.5cm-) round cookie cutter, cut discs from the dough. Use a metal spatula to transfer the discs to the prepared baking sheet. Continue to re-roll the scraps and cut out more discs until you have used all of the dough.

5 Bake the oatcakes for 30 minutes, or until the edges are starting to brown. Leave to cool on the baking sheet. The oatcakes can be stored in an airtight container for up to 5 days.

RYE CRISPBREADS

These earthy crispbreads have a long life, so they are ideal for having on hand to serve with cheese, smoked fish, or butter and jam.

MAKES 2

1¼ cups rye flour, plus extra for dusting
½ cup oat flour
1 tsp salt
1 tsp from a cake of compressed yeast

1 In a mixing bowl, combine the rye flour, oat flour, and salt. Crumble the yeast into a liquid measuring cup and add ¾ cup lukewarm water. Whisk until the yeast dissolves. Stir the yeast mixture into the dry ingredients to make a smooth but sticky paste. Cover with plastic wrap or a kitchen towel and set aside to rise in a warm place for 3 hours.

2 Line 3 large baking sheets with parchment paper. Once the dough is nicely puffed, divide it between 2 of the sheet pans, spreading it out evenly. Dust the surface generously with the extra rye flour, then roll out the dough on the pans to a thickness of ¼in (5mm). Cover as before and leave to rise for another hour, until the dough has doubled in bulk.

3 Preheat the oven to 400°F (200°C). Cut each sheet of dough into a 12in (30cm) circle, and cut a 1¾in (4cm) hole in the center of each. Peel away the excess dough and re-roll the trimmings to make additional crispbreads of any shape you like, arranging them on the third baking sheet. Use the rounded end of a wooden spoon handle to make dimples all over the surface of the crispbreads.

4 Bake for 40 minutes for the large rounds (and less for the smaller pieces), or until the crispbreads are dry and crisp at the edges. Remove from the oven and leave to cool before storing in an airtight container for up to 5 days. To serve, have guests break off pieces from the large rounds.

WHEAT

It is more accurate to describe wheat as a family of grains, rather than a single variety. It is grown throughout the world because of the high esteem in which it is held nutritionally and culinarily. However, the health benefits of wheat are dependent on the degree of processing the grain has had: 100 percent whole-wheat products are high in fiber, protein, B vitamins, iron, and folic acid, whereas highly refined white flour has had its most nutritious parts, the germ and bran, removed.

STORE Whole grains should be stored in an airtight container in a cool, dark place for no more than 1 year; cracked wheat can be kept for up to 6 months; rolled flakes for 3 months. Wheatgerm turns rancid quickly so must be stored in the refrigerator and used within two weeks. Observe the use-by dates on any packages of flour: their shelf life varies with the date and method of processing, but usually they must be used within 6 months.

EAT Perhaps the most versatile grain, wheat has a mild, sweet flavor, and its high gluten content allows it to be used in a wide range of recipes, from rustic breads to fine pastries.

FLAVOR PAIRINGS Cheese, cream, fruit, garlic, ham, herbs, honey, mushrooms, poultry, sweet spices, tomatoes.

CLASSIC RECIPES Bread; couscous; pancakes; pasta; pastry; porridge; minestrone soup; *tabbouleh*; bran muffins.

Whole
Sometimes called wheat berries, whole grains take around 2 hours to reach tenderness in boiling water. They are most suited to slow-cooked dishes and recipes that require prior cooking, such as salads.

Whole grains have had the inedible outer husk removed, but retain the nutritious bran layer.

RYE

The hardy rye plant grows well in damp climates and temperatures close to freezing, so it is a favorite crop of Russia, Eastern Europe, the UK, and Scandinavia. It is thought to promote satiety better than many other grains, thanks to its high fiber content and water-binding capacity.

STORE Check the use-by dates carefully, as rye easily becomes musty. Stoneground dark rye flour should be stored in the fridge or freezer and used within 6 months, or within 2 months if stored in a cupboard. Factory-milled, light rye flour can be kept in a cool, dry cupboard for a year or so.

EAT Rye has a strident, darkly fruity flavor that doesn't always appeal to the uninitiated. Most commonly it is made into breads (and alcohol), and there are many Scandinavian, German, and Eastern European recipes that make use of leftover rye bread, including dumplings, sauces, and soups.

FLAVOR PAIRINGS Cauliflower, cheese, cinnamon, crab, cream, fennel, ham, honey, oats, orange, shrimp, raisins, sauerkraut, smoked salmon.

CLASSIC RECIPES Pumpernickel bread; Dutch honey/breakfast cake; crispbreads.

Rolled
Whole grains are steamed and, once softened, rolled into flakes. Add them to muesli mixtures, bread or cracker doughs, or cook them like porridge oats.

A distinct leathery texture and strong flavor mean rolled rye is best mixed with milder, softer grains.

Flour
This has sufficient gluten to make cakes and bread rise, but is often mixed with wheat flour to boost the texture, and temper its strong, fruity flavor. Dark and light rye flours have the same cooking qualities, but the latter is milder and paler, due to the removal of bran and germ during processing.

Whole rye grains are plump, dark, and aromatic berries.

Whole
Whole rye grains need to boil for an hour to reach tenderness. They can be added to soups and stews, used in stuffings or hearty salads, or sprouted and added to bread doughs.

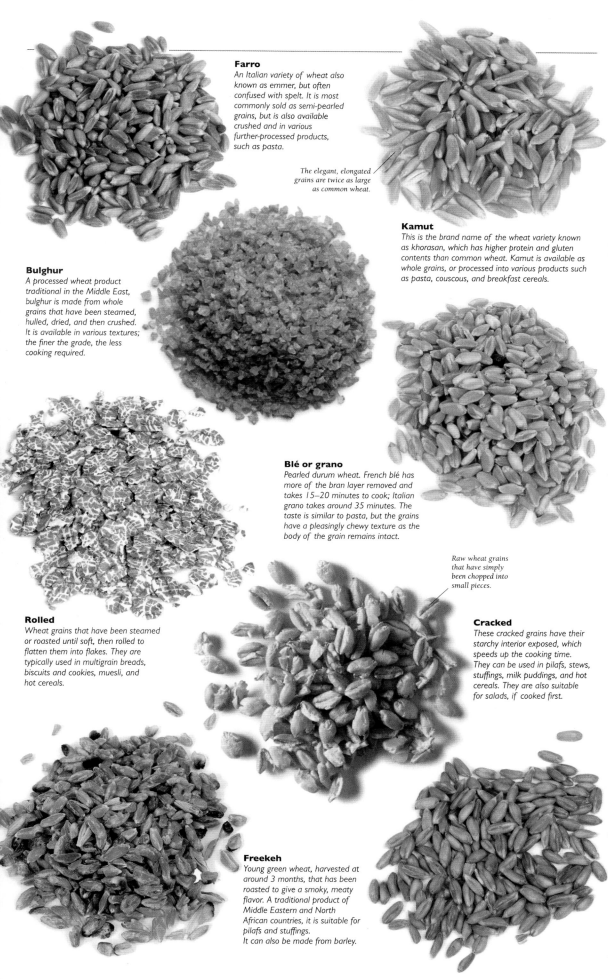

Farro
An Italian variety of wheat also known as emmer, but often confused with spelt. It is most commonly sold as semi-pearled grains, but is also available crushed and in various further-processed products, such as pasta.

The elegant, elongated grains are twice as large as common wheat.

Kamut
This is the brand name of the wheat variety known as khorasan, which has higher protein and gluten contents than common wheat. Kamut is available as whole grains, or processed into various products such as pasta, couscous, and breakfast cereals.

Bulghur
A processed wheat product traditional in the Middle East, bulghur is made from whole grains that have been steamed, hulled, dried, and then crushed. It is available in various textures; the finer the grade, the less cooking required.

Blé or grano
Pearled durum wheat. French blé has more of the bran layer removed and takes 15–20 minutes to cook; Italian grano takes around 35 minutes. The taste is similar to pasta, but the grains have a pleasingly chewy texture as the body of the grain remains intact.

Raw wheat grains that have simply been chopped into small pieces.

Rolled
Wheat grains that have been steamed or roasted until soft, then rolled to flatten them into flakes. They are typically used in multigrain breads, biscuits and cookies, muesli, and hot cereals.

Cracked
These cracked grains have their starchy interior exposed, which speeds up the cooking time. They can be used in pilafs, stews, stuffings, milk puddings, and hot cereals. They are also suitable for salads, if cooked first.

Freekeh
Young green wheat, harvested at around 3 months, that has been roasted to give a smoky, meaty flavor. A traditional product of Middle Eastern and North African countries, it is suitable for pilafs and stuffings. It can also be made from barley.

TABBOULEH

A traditional Lebanese salad, often served as part of a mezze (appetizer) selection, with cabbage, lettuce, or grape leaves used as scoops.

SERVES 4

¼ cup bulghur wheat

6 plum tomatoes

6 scallions, finely sliced

14oz (400g) flat-leaf parsley

2½oz (75g) mint, stems discarded

½ tsp ground cumin

¼ tsp ground cinnamon

juice of 1 large lemon

6 tbsp olive oil, or more to taste

salt and freshly ground black pepper

white cabbage, lettuce, or fresh grape leaves, to serve

1 Put the bulghur in a bowl, cover with cold water, and shake the bowl gently to agitate the grains. Drain well in a fine sieve, then repeat two more times or until the water runs clear. Spread the bulghur over the bottom of a wide salad bowl and set aside.

2 Finely dice the tomatoes and spread them and their juices over the bulgur. Sprinkle the scallions over the top.

3 Trim away the coarse bottoms of the parsley stems, leaving about ¾–1in (2–2.5cm) of stem on each sprig. Slice the leaves and stems very thinly and add to the bulghur. Slice the mint leaves just as thinly and add them to the bowl. Leave the salad to stand for 30 minutes.

4 Sprinkle the cumin and cinnamon over the salad, then add the lemon juice and oil and toss gently to mix. Season to taste with salt and plenty of pepper, and serve with the leaves for scooping up the salad.

Spelt
This ancient wheat variety has had a recent resurgence in popularity as an alternative to common wheat. It is available as white and whole wheat flours, and also as chewy grains for soups, pilafs, and risotto.

Take advantage of the wide variety of artisan breads that use different grains and flours as their base.

FLATBREAD

A simple, flattened yeast bread that can be cooked in a frying pan.

MAKES 8

¾ cup bread flour, plus extra for dusting

¼oz (7g) envelope quick-rising active dry yeast

2 tsp salt

3 tbsp olive oil, plus extra for greasing

1 Combine the flour, yeast, and salt in a bowl. Make a well in the center, add 1 cup of lukewarm water and the oil, and stir to make a soft dough. Turn out on to a lightly floured work surface and knead for about 10 minutes. Place in a lightly oiled bowl, turn to coat the dough with oil, then cover tightly with plastic wrap. Leave to stand in a warm place for 45 minutes, until nearly doubled in bulk.

2 Briefly knead the dough again on a lightly floured work surface. Cut into 8 equal pieces. Flatten each piece into a round about ½in (1cm) thick. Use a rolling pin to make them a little thinner. Place on floured baking sheets, cover with plastic wrap, and set aside for 10 minutes, until puffy.

3 Heat a large frying pan over medium heat. Working with one at a time, add a flatbread to the hot pan. Cook for 3 minutes, or until the underside is browned. Turn over and cook for 2 minutes to brown the other side. Transfer to a wire rack to cool slightly. Repeat with remaining flatbreads. Serve warm.

Wheatgerm
The nutritious heart of the grain, which, once processed, tends to be eaten as a health supplement rather than a food. It can be added to hot and cold cereals, breads, and other baked goods, but benefits from prior toasting to bring out its nutty flavor.

WHEAT (CONTINUED)

Whole wheat flour
More nutritious than refined white flour because it contains the grain's bran and germ. It adds not only a nutty flavor, but a denser texture, to baked goods. When making cakes or cookies, use finely milled whole wheat flour, or sift to remove any coarse particles before use.

Wheat bran
Milled from the husk of the grain, this ingredient is particularly high in fiber and is often recommended as a supplement for digestive health. Stir it into breakfast cereals or muffin batters.

Self-rising flour
This is plain flour that has had rising agents such as sodium bicarbonate and monocalcium phosphate blended into it during manufacture. It is used for baking and recipes that require a light texture. A good substitute is to add a little baking powder to plain flour.

Tipo 00
Also known as farina 00 and doppio zero, this Italian flour is milled from durum wheat and used for making fresh pasta, gnocchi, and cakes.

Strong flour
"Strong" indicates that the flour, whether plain or whole wheat, is high in protein and therefore gluten, which makes it ideal for bread making.

Harina especial para freír
A flour from southern Spain that is made particularly for frying. It helps gives a crisp, grease-free finish to deep-fried fish and seafood.

Pastry flour
Although some manufacturers sell cake and pastry flour as one and the same, true pastry flour produces a stronger dough. It is preferred for pastries such as puff and choux that need to maintain their structure after baking.

Fine milling gives a talcum-powder-like consistency to this speciality flour.

SHORTBREAD

Rich, buttery, Scottish cookies that can be enjoyed with tea or alongside creamy and fruity desserts.

MAKES 12

8oz (2 sticks) plus 2 tbsp (250g) butter, plus extra for greasing

½ cup superfine or granulated sugar, plus extra for sprinkling

2 cups all-purpose flour, sifted, plus extra for dusting

⅓ cup rice flour or cornstarch, or a mixture of the two

1 Beat together the butter and sugar until the mixture is pale, light, and creamy. Gradually add the flours, beating just until the mixture comes together as a dough.

2 Turn the mixture on to a lightly floured work surface and knead lightly to form a smooth ball. Roll out the dough to a thickness of ⅛ –¼in (3–5mm) and cut into circles or other desired shapes. Prick the surface of each with a fork.

3 Transfer the shapes to a greased, floured baking sheet and refrigerate for 15 minutes. Preheat the oven to 300°F (150°C).

4 Bake in the lower half of the oven for 12–15 minutes, until pale golden. Remove and sprinkle with the extra sugar. Let cool on the baking sheet for 5 minutes to firm up, then transfer to a wire rack to cool completely.

RICE

Although native to Asia, rice is now grown on every continent, and while the ever-increasing variety of packages on store shelves may seem confusing, it is still tiny compared to the thousands available at local level. Rice has always been considered a premium staple food and its production processes—in some regions involving extensive irrigation of dry areas, or harvesting on steep hillsides—mean it is likely to become more so with the challenges of climate change. Prices have risen sharply in recent years.

🔒 **BUY** Choose clear packages of unbroken grains. In ready-made mixes, wild rice grains may be broken or pierced, so they cook at a similar rate to the other ingredients in the pack.

📦 **STORE** Wholegrain and polished rices will keep in a cool, dry cupboard for over two years; fragrant varieties become less aromatic, though. Ground rice and rice flour can be stored for over a year in an airtight container.

⬤ **EAT** Rice needs to be cooked with care as textures vary greatly.

FLAVOR PAIRINGS Beans, cheese, herbs, lentils, milk, onions, spices, soy sauce, yogurt.

CLASSIC RECIPES *Biryani*; paella; *pilau*; rice pudding; risotto; sushi.

Brown short grain varieties are also available and are ideal for long, slow cooking.

Short grain
There are many types of short grain rice, including varieties of risotto, sticky, and pudding rices. They are united by their plump middles and starchy textures.

Pearled and polished rice grains have a lustrous, bright white appearance that is particularly admired in the Middle East.

Pearled and polished
All white rice has been pearled or polished. Usually the process involves removing the fibrous bran and germ layers, then brushing or rubbing the rice, and perhaps coating it with glucose, mineral oil, or talc.

RISOTTO BALLS

Crispy on the outside but soft and creamy on the inside, these tasty rice balls make an unusual side dish, or they can be eaten hot or cold as a party nibble with a tomato or sweet chili dipping sauce.

SERVES 4–6

1 cup Arborio or other risotto rice

1 vegetable bouillon cube

½ cup shredded Gruyère cheese

2 tbsp prepared pesto

½ cup dried bread crumbs

oil, for frying

basil leaves, to garnish (optional)

1 Place the rice and bouillon cube in a saucepan and pour in 3 cups of water. Place over high heat and bring to a boil. Cover and reduce the heat to low; simmer for 15 minutes, or until the rice is just tender.

2 Drain the rice thoroughly, then stir in the cheese and pesto, and set aside to cool.

3 Using dampened hands, divide the rice mixture and roll it into walnut-sized balls. Roll in the breadcrumbs to coat well.

4 Heat about ½in (1cm) oil in a frying pan. Working in batches if necessary, fry the balls for 5–10 minutes, or until crisp and golden on the outside. (Alternatively, the balls can be deep-fried for 2–3 minutes, or until golden.) Drain on paper towels and garnish with basil leaves.

WILD RICE

Despite the name, most wild rice is commercially cultivated in areas of North America including California, Minnesota, and Canada. After harvesting, the long, green seeds of this aquatic grass (Zizania aquatica) are cured and parched, which turns them dark brown or black and intensifies their flavor.

🔒 **BUY** Choose clear packages of unbroken grains. In ready-made mixes the grains of wild rice may be broken or pierced so that they cook at a similar rate to the other ingredients in the pack.

📦 **STORE** Wild rice will last up to a year in an airtight container kept in a cool, dark, dry place.

⬤ **EAT** The intense grassy, tea-like flavour of wild rice means a little goes along way. Whole grains take 45–50 minutes to boil and are cooked when they have split lengthwise, revealing their fluffy, white interior. Do not presoak wild rice in an effort to reduce cooking time.

FLAVOR PAIRINGS Asparagus, bacon, celery, eggs, game, mango, maple syrup, mushrooms, nuts, potato, poultry, pumpkin, salmon, shellfish.

CLASSIC RECIPES: Pancakes, popped rice, stuffings.

Wild rice
Although they look elegant, these long, dark grains are too spiky to eat when undercooked. Boil until the skins split and they will have a pleasing, chewy texture.

RICE (CONTINUED)

BASIC PILAF

A simple, savory accompaniment to chicken, fish, and vegetable dishes. The secret to fluffy rice is to rinse the grains of excess starch, then boil without stirring, and leave to steam briefly off the heat before serving.

SERVES 4

1 cup long grain white rice
1½ tbsp unsalted butter or 1 tbsp olive oil
1 onion, finely chopped
1 garlic clove, finely chopped
1½ cups chicken or vegetable stock, heated
salt and freshly ground black pepper

1 Put the rice in a sieve; rinse under cold water until the water runs clear. Drain.

2 Heat the butter in a saucepan over medium heat and cook the onion and garlic, stirring occasionally, for 5 minutes or until soft and translucent. Add the rice and stir well to coat with the butter. Pour in the hot stock and bring to a boil.

3 Cover the pan and reduce the heat to low. Cook for 15 minutes, then remove the pan from the heat and leave to sit, without lifting the lid, for 5 minutes, until excess liquid is absorbed.

4 Fluff up with a fork; season to taste.

Paella rice
Various Spanish rices can be used to make the classic dish paella, including the Denomination of Origin rices from Calasparra and Valencia. You may find packages labeled Bomba, which is the main rice variety.

Slender grains are about four or five times as long as they are wide.

White long grain
Simple long grain rice is the most versatile variety to have in the kitchen for side dishes, thanks to an unobtrusive, sweet flavor that marries well with most cuisines.

Thai jasmine rice is available as white or brown grains, which have a nutty flavor.

Thai jasmine rice
A slightly sticky long grain variety also known as Thai fragrant rice because of its delicious aroma. It is commonly used to accompany Thai and Chinese savory dishes.

Red rice
Specialty crops of the French Camargue, Piedmont, in Italy, the Sacramento Valley in the US, and Bhutan. Only the grain coat is red: the interior is white. Colored wholegrain and paler semipearled varieties are available. It is good for buffet salads and side dishes.

Thai black sticky rice
These dark purple grains with a fruity, grassy aroma are most commonly served as a sweet breakfast cereal, a dumplinglike snack, or a pudding flavored with coconut milk and palm sugar.

Nuttier in flavor than white rice and the grains won't stick together when cooked.

Brown rice
Wholegrain rice with a nutritious, brown-colored bran coat. Most varieties are available in this form, from short grain, Italian, risotto-style rices, to long grain and fragrant ones such as basmati. The bran coating lengthens the cooking time; it is good for side dishes, salads, pilafs, and stuffings.

The grains cling together readily, so it is perfect for eating with chopsticks.

White sticky rice
Also known as glutinous or sweet rice, these tend to be short grain varieties, such as sushi rices. The grains become sticky on cooking so they adhere when lightly pressed together. Thai white sticky rice is best cooked by steaming so that the grains remain distinct; when boiled, it becomes mushy.

Puffed rice
Familiar from breakfast cereals, this requires a more complicated manufacturing process than popcorn. Sweetened short grain rice is cooked under pressure, and the steam that builds inside the grains causes them to expand. Usually used in sweet snacks, though it also appears in some Asian savory mixtures.

The crispy texture makes it ideal for use in baking children's sweets.

Rice flour
Bland, gluten-free rice flour can be ground from any rice variety. Most common is glutinous rice flour, used in Asia to make dumplings, crêpes, cakes, and sweets, and brown rice flour, which is good for cakes, breads, and cookies for people on special diets.

Basmati rice
Grown in the Himalayan foothills of India and Pakistan, this long grain rice is matured prior to sale to reduce its moisture content and enhance its fragrance and flavor. Recommended for Indian and Iranian dishes.

Flaked rice
A popular ingredient for desserts and sweet snacks in Asia, this rice is part-cooked to soften it before being rolled into flakes.

Ground rice
Slightly grittier than rice flour, ground rice is made from white rice and can be used in baking or for milk puddings.

The coarse texture helps give a crisp finish to pastries and cookies such as shortbread.

The seed coat removed from wholegrain rice during milling is processed into rice bran and germ.

Rice bran and rice germ
These health-food products offer vitamins, minerals, essential fatty acids, and fiber. Hardly delicious, rice bran is best added to breakfast cereals and baked goods, but it might also be stirred into soups and stews to help thicken them. The oil extracted from the rice bran and germ can be used for frying and studies show it is useful in reducing blood cholesterol.

CLASSIC RECIPE
RICE PUDDING
Enriched with butter, this traditional British milk pudding can be eaten simply as it is, or with some seasonal stewed fruit or a dab of jam.

SERVES 4

2 cups whole milk

2 tbsp granulated sugar

½ vanilla bean, split lengthwise

1 tbsp butter, diced, plus extra for greasing

¼ cup short grain white rice or Arborio rice

freshly grated nutmeg, for sprinkling

1 Preheat the oven to 250°F (130°C). In a small saucepan, gently heat the milk, sugar, and vanilla bean, stirring so that the sugar dissolves.

2 Meanwhile, lightly grease a 3- to 4-cup baking dish with butter and sprinkle the rice over the bottom. Pour in the hot milk mixture, and carefully remove the vanilla bean. Sprinkle in the nutmeg, then dot with the butter.

3 Bake for 3 hours, stirring every 30 minutes or so, until the rice pudding is soft and creamy with a golden-brown color. Serve hot or cold.

DRIED PASTA

Fresh is not necessarily best when it comes to pasta: some sauces are better suited to dried pasta shapes, and a quality brand will be superior to the products of cheap fresh-pasta manufacturers. Dried durum wheat pasta is a simple mix of flour and water extruded by machine and cut into tiny, short, or long shapes. It tastes nutty compared to dried egg pasta, which is also made with durum wheat and by law must contain 5.5 percent egg solids. The egg gives the pasta a richer color and flavor, but should not by definition be considered superior to plain durum wheat pasta.

BUY A rough texture is a positive attribute, indicating that it has been made in small batches, shaped and cut by bronze dyes, and that sauces will cling well to it. Long dried pasta shapes such as spaghetti should be slightly flexible when bent. Dried egg pasta should have an appealing golden color.

STORE Dried pasta can be stored in a dry place in an airtight container or sealed pack for at least a year.

EAT Boil for slightly less than the manufacturer's recommended cooking time, then drain quickly and finish cooking in the sauce. Or boil until *al dente* (tender, but with some bite) then drain thoroughly, toss with dressing, and serve at room temperature as part of a salad.

FLAVOR PAIRINGS Broccoli, broths, butter, chicken, chile, cream, garlic, eggs, onions, pepper, seafood, tomatoes, white wine.

CLASSIC RECIPES Macaroni cheese; fettuccine alfredo; orecchiette with broccoli.

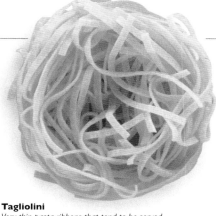

Tagliolini
Very thin pasta ribbons that tend to be served with broths or very liquid sauces. They are available fresh and dried, and cook quickly. Look out for the green-colored version, often cooked with plain tagliolini.

Corn pasta
To cater for special diets, pasta is made from an increasing number of non-traditional grains including quinoa, brown rice, and multigrains. Gluten-free corn is one of the most successful of these alternative grains because its neutral flavor and golden color are easy substitutes for dried durum wheat pasta.

Filini
Wiry pasta strands most commonly used to make elegant soups more substantial. The name means "little cat's whiskers," but while some filini pasta is short cut, it can also be kept long. Being so thin, filini is quick to cook. It is available in dried egg pasta and wholewheat versions, as well as fresh.

Fusilli (shown) and spaghetti are easily available, or you can buy shapes such as macaroni and penne.

Orecchiette
This Puglian speciality can be found sold dried or fresh (which is eggless), and is sometimes colored. The bowl shape of orecchiette (meaning "little ear") is ideal for vegetables or chunky sauces as the ingredients sit neatly inside. It can also be used for salads.

Vermicelli
Vermicelli is very fine durum wheat pasta similar to spaghetti in shape but thinner and quicker to cook (5 to 6 minutes). It has many different regional names in Italy, and the same type of pasta is used in other cuisines including Greek, Spanish, Mexican, and Persian. In Naples it is traditionally layered with a mixture of shellfish, Vegetables, and olives and baked with a breadcrumb topping, or tossed with a sauce of tuna and anchovies. Cut vermicelli is sold in short pieces ready to add to broth for soup making.

Spaghetti
Long, thin, and round, spaghetti (which means "lengths of cord") is the best-known pasta shape in the world, probably because it is one of the oldest and most versatile—used with everything from simple garlic, chile, and olive oil to creamy ham sauces. Spaghetti is normally 10in (25cm) long and 1/16in (1.5mm) thick, but can be longer. It is readily available in different colors, and made with alternative flours.

Fusilli
Pasta spirals of all kinds are enduringly popular. Although fusilli, which hails from Campania, is mass-produced on a wide scale, it was traditionally a fresh, eggless variety made by hand. It is a favorite shape for colored pasta and multigrain combinations. It works just as well in salads and pasta bakes as it does with chunky vegetable or creamy sauces.

Orzo

Orzo is the Italian word for barley, although this is not made from barley flour but durum wheat. Use it for soups, as a side dish, or in place of white rice. Flavored varieties are also available. Greece has its own version of orzo called kritharaki, which is used in baked dishes and soups.

Pasta made from durum wheat is shaped to look like barley grains.

Macaroni

In southern Italy, macaroni is the word for pasta; however, elsewhere it is usually applied to smooth or ridged short pasta tubes. Maccheroni leccesi means pasta in the style of Lecce, in Puglia. Use for macaroni and cheese and other baked dishes, such as timbales.

Farfalle

Simple tomato sauce or cheese and ham are the classic matches for this northern Italian shape that is likened to bow-ties or butterflies. However, farfalle also works well in pasta salads and oven-baked dishes. The small version, farfalline, is used in soups.

Tagliatelle

Often sold dried in clusters or nests, tagliatelli is popular with cream sauces for ham or salmon.

Dried lasagna

When buying, check the package to see if the pasta needs boiling before baking or can be used without prior cooking. Some varieties have curly edges for a decorative finish and to help trap chunks of meat or vegetables.

MACARONI CHEESE

A creamy, comforting supper with a mustard kick. Serve with a crisp salad or steamed vegetables.

SERVES 6–8

1 lb (500g) elbow macaroni or other dried pasta

4 tbsp butter, plus extra for greasing

¼ cup all-purpose flour

2 cups whole milk

1 tsp English mustard powder, such as Colman's

freshly grated nutmeg, to taste

salt and freshly ground black pepper

1½ cups shredded Cheddar cheese

½ cup shredded Gruyère cheese

½ cup finely grated Parmesan cheese

¾ cup fresh white bread crumbs

1 Cook the pasta in a pot of salted boiling water for 7–8 minutes, or 2 minutes less than the package directs. Drain in a colander, rinse under cold water, and set aside to fully drain.

2 Preheat the oven to 375°F (190°C) and grease a 13 x 9in (30 x 20cm) baking dish. Melt the butter in a saucepan, add the flour, and whisk to blend. Cook for 1–2 minutes, then reduce the heat and add the milk gradually, whisking well. Stir in the mustard and nutmeg, salt, and pepper. Bring to a boil, stirring, and simmer for 5 minutes, until the sauce thickens and becomes glossy.

3 Add all but 2 tbsp of the Cheddar and all of the Gruyère, and stir until melted and smooth. Gently stir in the macaroni. Scrape into the baking dish.

4 Toss the remaining 2 tbsp Cheddar with the Parmesan and bread crumbs and sprinkle over the top. Bake for 15–20 minutes. Remove the dish from the oven and move the oven rack 6–8 inches from the heat source. Preheat the broiler, then broil 3–5 minutes, until bubbly-hot and golden. Let cool 5–10 minutes before serving.

DRIED PASTA (CONTINUED)

Penne
Pasta quills are versatile and easy to cook. Penne lisce has smooth sides while penne rigate is ribbed; small and very large versions are also available. Classically paired with tomato and chile sauces, penne is also good for salads and pasta bakes.

Penne rigate have ribbed sides and angle-cut ends.

Large, chunky pasta tubes with ridges on the outside.

Linguine
A flattened, long, thin version of spaghetti that works well as a wholemeal pasta. Serve with seafood (especially clams (vongole), or prawns), pesto, and green beans, creamy tomato sauces, or simple combinations of olive oil, lemon, and herbs.

Conchiglie
Pasta shells are available in small, medium, and large sizes. The small are used for soups, the large for stuffing, and the medium for serving with chunky or thin sauces, or in salads or pasta bakes.

Rigatoni
These large pasta tubes originated in Rome. Satisfying to eat, they can hold very chunky sauces of meat and vegetables, but are equally good with smooth cream or cheese sauces. The shape is also ideal for pasta bakes.

Trofie
A speciality of Liguria, these chewy handmade spirals with tapered ends look a little like worms. They are traditionally served with pesto, which originates from the same region. They are correctly made from tipo 00 flour and water.

Fettuccine
Central Italy's answer to tagliatelle, these medium-width pasta ribbons are rolled slightly thicker than the tagliatelle of the north but work with similar sauces.

FRESH PASTA

Fresh egg pasta is unlike other pastas because it is made with softer tipo 00 flour rather than durum wheat semolina. Sometimes oil is added for easier handling. Italy's Emilia-Romagna region is the center of commercial production, but good-quality, fresh egg pasta is made by specialists around the world, as well as in the home. More unusual is fresh durum wheat pasta (*pasta di semola fresca*) which is usually handmade and comes mostly from the south of Italy, especially Puglia and Sardinia. It takes several minutes longer to cook than fresh egg pasta.

BUY When choosing long shapes, buy those sold in nests to protect them during transport, often dusted with semolina flour to prevent sticking.

STORE Freshly made pasta keeps up to 3 days in the refrigerator and 3 months in the freezer. Bought fresh, pasta will keep for a week or two—see the package's use-by date.

EAT Fresh egg pasta is malleable and can be produced in a wide range of shapes, whereas *pasta di semola fresca* tends to be made in short shapes, such as *fusilli* and *orecchiette*.

FLAVOR PAIRINGS Basil, beans, beef, cheese, garlic, olives, oregano, tomato, red wine, walnuts.

CLASSIC RECIPES *Pappardelle with hare sauce; trofie with Genovese pesto; lasagna.*

Black ink pasta
Known as nero di seppia or nero di calamaro, this pasta colored with the ink sacs of squid or cuttlefish tends to have a fishy flavor, which means it is best matched with seafood or vegetable sauces. Usually sold in long, thin shapes, such as spaghetti and linguine.

Flavored pasta
There are many novelty versions of flavored pasta, including red wine and chocolate, but the most enduring are green (made by adding spinach purée to the dough) and red (adding tomato purée). Although the taste of these pastas is rarely strong, it is worth making sure the sauce contains complementary flavors.

Pappardelle
These long, ¾–1½in- (2–3cm-) wide pasta ribbons from the Veneto and Tuscany are usually served with chunky meat sauces. Dried pappardelle is also available; both varieties have wavy or straight edges.

These pasta ribbons are of medium width.

Lasagna sheets
Fresh lasagna sheets are made with eggs, whereas dried lasagna tends to be eggless. Lasagna verdi is green and colored with spinach. These fresh sheets can be casually piled on plates with other ingredients and served as "open lasagna."

Tagliatelle
Originally from the Emilia-Romagna region of Italy, these pasta ribbons work with heavy and creamy sauces, although Bologonese sauce is the classic partner. Tagliatelle is often sold in nests.

FILLED PASTA

Good-quality filled pasta seems luxurious but in fact the recipes are frugal: Piedmont's *agnolotti*, for example, derives from leftover meat and available local greens. Names, shapes, and fillings vary throughout Italy, so classification can be confusing.

🔒 **BUY** Choose plump, well-sealed pasta parcels—tears and gaps cause leakages during cooking.

📦 **STORE** Fresh pasta should be cooked on the day of purchase but may keep for a day or two if kept dry in the refrigerator. When buying vacuum packed pasta, check the use-by date.

⬤ **EAT** Good stuffed pasta needs no more than a little melted butter, or some herbs and cheese.

FLAVOR PAIRINGS Artichoke, asparagus, beef, gorgonzola, mushrooms, Parmesan, pumpkin, ricotta, spinach, veal, walnuts.

CLASSIC RECIPES Ravioli with sage butter; tortellini in broth (in *brodo*); tortellini with ham and peas; *pansôti* with walnut sauce.

Cappelletti
This pasta is a favorite for the Christmas dinner table in central Italy. The shape is modelled on hats worn in the Middle Ages. Traditional stuffings are mixed meats or cheese.

Lunette
This semi-circular shape is said to resemble "little moons". Cheese stuffings are the traditional favourite, but you may also find them flavored with truffles, or with mixtures such as broccoli and almond.

Ravioli
Pasta parcels with serrated edges; usually square but may be round. Raviolini are tiny parcels used for soups; ravioloni are giant versions. Serve with sauces or simply with olive oil or butter.

Girasole
Large, round parcels with scalloped edges that mimic sunflowers ("girasole" is Italian for sunflower). Their size works well with chunky, braised meat fillings.

Tortellini
This shape is based on Venus's navel and should be delicate. Cheese, meat, or vegetables are classic fillings, and the pasta is served in broth, or with cream sauce or ragù. The larger tortelloni have stuffings based on vegetables or ricotta.

CLASSIC RECIPE

LASAGNE AL FORNO

The perfect dish for family meals or for casual entertaining.

SERVES 6

1 tbsp olive oil
1 large onion, chopped
2 celery ribs, chopped
2 small carrots, chopped
2oz (50g) pancetta, diced
1lb (500g) ground beef
1 x 14½oz (400g) can diced tomatoes
1 tsp dried oregano
4 tbsp butter
⅓ cup all-purpose flour
2 cups whole milk
salt and freshly ground black pepper
¾ cup ricotta cheese
12oz (350g) lasagna noodles or sheets, cooked and drained
½ cup Parmesan cheese, grated

1 To make the ragù, heat the oil in a large saucepan and add the onion, celery, carrots, and pancetta. Cook for 5 minutes, stirring occasionally, until just beginning to brown. Add the ground beef and cook until browned, stirring and breaking it up with a wooden spoon. Add the tomatoes and their juices, the oregano, and ½ cup of water. Bring to a boil, then reduce the heat and simmer uncovered, to reduce moisture for 40 minutes.

2 Meanwhile, to make the béchamel sauce, melt the butter in a small saucepan and stir in the flour. Cook over low heat, stirring, for 1 minute. Remove the pan from the heat and gradually whisk in the milk. Return to the heat and cook, stirring constantly, until the sauce thickens. Season to taste with salt and black pepper, then stir in the ricotta.

3 Preheat the oven to 375°F (190°C). Spread a little of the béchamel sauce over the bottom of a 9 x 13in (20 x 30cm) baking dish. Arrange a layer of noodles on top, then add one third of the ragù, spreading it into an even layer. Drizzle with 1–2 spoonfuls of the béchamel sauce and top with another layer of noodles.

4 Repeat until all the pasta and ragù have been used, and top with a thick layer of béchamel sauce. Sprinkle with Parmesan and bake for 45 minutes, or until bubbly-hot at the edges. Let stand 10 minutes before serving.

Dried pasta comes in different shapes that suit different dishes. Conchiglie shells, for example, are great for capturing sauces.

COUSCOUS WITH PINE NUTS AND ALMONDS

A tasty alternative to rice; serve hot as a side dish or cold as a salad. Good with grilled meats, chicken, or fish.

SERVES 4–6

| 1 ½ cups couscous |
| 1 red bell pepper, seeded and chopped |
| 1 cup dark raisins |
| 1 cup chopped dried apricots |
| ½ cucumber, seeded and diced |
| 12 kalamata or other black olives, pitted |
| ½ cup slivered almonds, lightly toasted |
| ½ cup pine nuts, lightly toasted |
| ¼ cup light olive oil |
| juice of ½ lemon |
| 1 tbsp chopped mint |
| salt and freshly ground black pepper |

1 Put the couscous in a bowl and pour over enough boiling water to cover it by about 1in (2.5cm). Cover and set aside for 15 minutes, or until the couscous has absorbed all the water, then fluff the grains up lightly with a fork.

2 Stir in the bell pepper, raisins, apricots, cucumber, olives, almonds, and pine nuts.

3 Whisk together the olive oil and lemon juice until blended. Stir in the mint. Season to taste with salt and pepper and stir into the couscous. Serve at once while warm, or leave to cool.

COUSCOUS

Couscous is often mistakenly called a grain because of its granular shape but, in fact, it is a processed pastalike product. As with pasta, it is most commonly manufactured from durum wheat semolina, however, it can be made from a variety of grains, and still is in rural North Africa, from where it originates.

STORE In dark, dry conditions, preferably an airtight box, couscous will keep for at least 12 months (often Berber people will make enough to last an entire year) but you should also refer to the use-by date on the package. Whole wheat varieties will turn rancid slightly quicker because they contain the germ of the grain—your nose will tell you when they are past their best,

EAT Couscous's sandy texture is something people tend to love or loathe, so you might want to gauge interest before serving it to guests. The larger grains of Israeli couscous and fregola have a more substantial mouth feel and a pleasant toasted flavor. North African couscous is prepared by rehydrating or steaming, however, Israeli couscous and fregola need to be boiled for around 6–8 minutes.

FLAVOR PAIRINGS Almonds, eggplants, cilantro, cumin, lamb, lemon, olives, poultry, raisins, sesame, squash.
CLASSIC RECIPES Couscous cake, couscous royale, *couscous alla trapanese*, fregola with clams, jeweled couscous

Barley couscous
Most common in Tunisia, but also traditional in some parts of Morocco, this couscous has a richer, more honeyed flavor than couscous made from wheat, but it is prepared and cooked in the same way.

Wheat couscous
Outside North Africa, whole wheat and fine couscous are the most widely available varieties. Both are made from semolina—the hard, central part of the durum wheat grain and a by-product of grinding it into flour. Fine couscous is lighter in texture but slightly blander than whole wheat couscous.

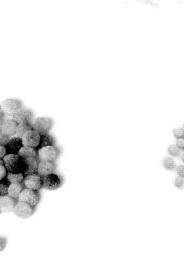

Fregola
A large, Sardinian version of couscous, traditional to homes on the south side of the island and typically served with shellfish. It is made from semolina and water and, like Israeli couscous, roasted during manufacture, although fregola arguably has the better flavor.

Israeli couscous
Sometimes called giant couscous, these pearl-like balls of pasta are made from durum wheat and roasted during manufacture so that they are not as sticky as North African couscous and have a chewier texture. White and whole wheat versions are available.

RICE NOODLES

These opaque noodles made from rice flour and water have a more delicate taste and texture than their wheat-based cousins, resulting in a lighter eating experience. They can be chewy or very soft, but that is down to the accuracy of the cook.

BUY Fresh rice noodles are superior to dried only if they are purchased from a reputable store with a high turnover, and eaten on the day of purchase.

STORE Fresh rice noodles should be kept well wrapped in plastic in the refrigerator, where they will last for a week, although their texture deteriorates quickly. Dried rice noodles can be kept in a dry pantry for years without compromise.

EAT Fresh rice noodles are already cooked and need only reheating to serve. Few rice noodle recipes demand boiling—instead, the noodles are rehydrated by soaking in hot or cold water, depending on the variety, then drained and combined with other ingredients.

FLAVOR PAIRINGS Beef, chile, coconut, eggs, garlic, ginger, lamb, oyster sauce, peanuts, poultry, sesame, shellfish, soy sauce, spices, scallions.

CLASSIC RECIPES Shanghai pork noodles; Vietnamese beef noodle soup (pho); pad thai; spring rolls.

Rice sticks
These dried flat noodles vary in width from a couple of millimeters to about half an inch. They are best known for their use in pad thai and their robust texture makes them ideal for stir-fries.

Fine rice noodles
Usually manufactured in Thailand or Vietnam, these thin, straight versions of flat rice sticks are suitable for soups and stir-fries.

Rice vermicelli
Very thin and wriggly dried noodles sold in brittle skeins and used throughout much of Asia. They are used to add bulk and texture to dishes, yet the effect is light, as when featured in spring rolls or salads. Rice vermicelli can also be deep-fried, which makes them puff up and turn crisp.

Brown udon rice noodles
The most common varieties of brown rice noodle are Thai brown rice vermicelli and Japanese brown rice udon. Check the ingredients list on the package, since the udon may be made with a proportion of wheat flour—adding the brown rice flour gives a noodle of darker color, more distinctive flavor, and firmer texture than plain wheat or rice noodles.

WHEAT NOODLES

Wheat is second to rice in Asia, but in cold-climate areas such as northern China it is the predominant grain and noodles made from it play a major role in the local cuisine. From there, they have spread in popularity to other parts of Asia and the world: wheat noodles feature in many of the world's best-known noodle dishes, from chicken noodle soup to commercial instant noodle products.

STORE Fresh noodles are best used on the day of making or purchase, but will last in the refrigerator for a week. Dried noodles, kept well wrapped in a dry cupboard, will last several years, though ideally would be consumed within two.

EAT Boil them and serve with matching sauce, or add to soups and stir-fries. In Japan and Korea especially, certain noodles and recipes are considered appropriate for summer (rather than winter) dining, and are even served cold.

FLAVOR PAIRINGS Beef, cashew nuts, chile, green peppers, miso, onion, oyster sauce, pork, poultry, spinach, star anise.

CLASSIC RECIPES Chow mein; eggflower noodle soup; spicy Sichuan noodles; curry udon; Indian vermicelli pudding.

Chinese egg noodles
Can be purchased dried or fresh, round or flat, in a variety of thicknesses. Color ranges from tan to golden. Egg noodles are more sustaining and springy textured than eggless or rice noodles, and are most famously used in chicken chow mein; however, they appear in dishes across China and countries such as the Philippines, Thailand, Vietnam, and Malaysia.

Indian vermicelli
Also known as seviya, sev, and sevian, these fine wheat noodles are sold plain and pretoasted, as the first step of many recipes is to fry them until brown in ghee. They are used in savory dishes in India, Pakistan, and Malaysia, but are most commonly used for lightly spiced milk puddings.

Udon
These rugged, white wheat-flour noodles from southern Japan are pleasingly plump with rounded or square-cut edges. They can be purchased fresh or dried, and are popular served in warming broths and thick curry (katsu) sauces.

Chinese wheat noodles
These eggless wheat noodles with an unobtrusive flavor are robust and versatile. They hail from northern China, and are available fresh or dried. Choose them for stir-fries and hearty soups.

Kishimen
From Japan's Nagoya region, these wide, flat noodles are like a slippery, chewy version of Italian fettuccine. They are served cold with dipping sauce, swimming in hot broth with fish cake and tofu, or with stir-fries.

Somen
These thin Japanese wheat noodles are particularly associated with summer time and usually served cold with a dipping sauce, or sometimes iced. Look out for flavored varieties (citrus, green tea, plum) in speciality shops and restaurants.

Ramen
Japan's take on the Chinese wheat noodle is filling fast food and popular in street stalls, served in brothy dishes with greens, scallion, and proteins such as roast pork, egg, and fishcake. Instant ramen noodles are the basis of various convenience products.

OTHER NOODLES

Staple foods such as noodles have traditionally been made from the inexpensive starches available in each region. In areas not conducive to the production of wheat or rice, other ingredients such as tubers and legumes have provided a satisfying solution.

BUY Some packages are confusingly labeled—look to the ingredients list to clarify which noodles you are buying.

STORE Dried noodles will last in a dry, dark cupboard, ideally well wrapped in plastic or stored in an airtight container, for years, though do refer to the use-by date on the package. Fresh soba noodles should be consumed within a few days of making.

EAT Aside from the nutritional benefits of eating a wide range of foods high in complex carbohydrates, these noodles offer an enticing variety of textures and flavors, from elegantly crisp to rustically rubbery.

FLAVOR PAIRINGS Beef, broccoli, crab, cucumber, green beans, mushrooms, shrimp, seaweed, sesame, soy sauce, scallion.

CLASSIC RECIPES Spring rolls; Korean beef; noodle and vegetable stir-fry (*chap chae*); Thai seafood and glass noodle salad; soba with dipping sauce; bird's nest noodles.

Soba
Japanese noodles made exclusively from earthy-tasting buckwheat, or a mixture of buckwheat and wheat flours. Dried versions are most common, but some specialist stores sell fresh soba.

Bean thread noodles
Light vermicelli-style noodles also known as cellophane, glass, and jelly noodles thanks to the transparent appearance and gelatinous texture they acquire once rehydrated. They are made from mung bean and tapioca starches, and are especially good for salads.

Green tea noodles
An appealing green variety of soba, colored and flavored with green tea powder, giving a slightly vegetal taste. Usually enjoyed cold in salads or with a simple dipping sauce.

Naengmyun
Made from a mix of buckwheat and sweet potato flours, these very thin Korean noodles are delightfully elastic and can be eaten hot or cold. They are traditionally cut into shorter lengths with a pair of scissors at the table.

OILS, VINEGARS, & FLAVORINGS

OLIVE OILS | NUT OILS
WINE VINEGARS
SUGAR | SYRUP
HONEY | SOY SAUCE
MISO | PASTES | SALT

OLIVE OILS

Olive oil is unique among vegetable oils in that it is simply the fresh juice of the olive with the water removed. The fruits are crushed and mixed, then the oil is separated out centrifugally into solid vegetal particles and water. The traditional method of making olive oil, using grindstones and a hydraulic press, is still in use in a few places today. Oil meeting the complex legal requirements for virgin and extra virgin status is bottled. This is the best olive oil; it has an excellent flavor and good nutritional value. Olive oil is produced in all countries around the Mediterranean basin and those in the northern and southern hemisphere that have a similar climate of hot summers and mild winters. These include US (California), China, Argentina, Chile, Australia, New Zealand, and South Africa. The largest producer is Spain, which accounts for more than half the world's olive oil production. Italy and Greece are ranked in second and third place. Olive oil is available in a wide range of flavors; each producing region has its own olive varieties, micro-climates and methods for cultivating

and processing the fruit, and so the results vary. Delicate olive oils are fruity with low levels of bitterness and pepper; medium have a well-balanced flavor; while strong oils are robust and intense with bitter, peppery elements. The oil can be either a varietal oil made from a single olive variety, or a varietal blend made from a blend of more than one variety of olive. Some oils are filtered, others are allowed to settle naturally. The texture of unfiltered oil is thicker, but there is no detectable difference in flavor. Filtered oil lasts a little longer than unfiltered but has less nutritional value.

🔒 **BUY** The best oils are processed at temperatures below 80°F (27°C). Labels stating the oil is "cold-pressed" mean it has been processed below this temperature by a traditional extraction system using a hydraulic press. "Cold extraction" signifies it has been produced by continuous centrifugation. Some oils are labeled "first-pressed," which is meaningless as almost all olive oils come from a single pressing. Both heat and light are detrimental to olive oil, so choose oils packaged in dark glass or cans and avoid those that have been displayed in a window or under strong lights.

📦 **STORE** Store in a cool, dark place for 12–18 months and use within 3 months of opening. It is best not to store oil in the fridge as it will solidify. This will not harm it; however, it soon liquifies when returned to room temperature.

⬤ **EAT** Olive oil can be used in all culinary applications from grilling and frying to roasting and baking. Extra virgin olive oil is also a flavoring ingredient, which can be served as a condiment or a dip. Use in soups, sauces, and stews and to finish grilled meats and vegetables. It is a good base for bastes and marinades, and can be used in sweet dishes, bread, and cakes.

DELICATE EXTRA VIRGIN OLIVE OILS

Manzanillo varietal oil
Originally from Jaen in Andalucia, this variety produces a delicate oil with notes of tomato, grass, and herbs. Use in most culinary applications, except the most delicate, such as salads.

Taggiasca varietal oil
This oil is imbued with the flavor of light apples and nuts and has gentle bitterness and pepper tones. Use this Italian from Liguria with fish, cooked vegetables, and salads.

Lake Garda varietal blend
The typical regional blend uses Casaliva olives with Leccino. Most are nutty with meadow-sweet herbal tones and light bitterness and pepper. Use with oily fish, chicken dishes, and salads.

Arbequina varietal oil
Delicate herbaceous tones with a definite nutty element and light pepper. Originally from Catalonia in northern Spain, but now found around the world, this is a good all around oil for cooking and baking.

La Tanche varietal oil
Flavors of apples and pears predominate in this sweet oil from northern Provence, in the south of France. There is little bitterness or pepper tones. Ideal for use in sauces and in baking.

Olivastra varietal oil
With complex tones of apples, herbs, and nuts with light bitterness and pepper, this oil is more delicate than other oils from Tuscany, in Italy. It is suitable for use in most culinary applications.

Middle Eastern varietal blend
Oils from the eastern Mediterranean tend to be delicate in character, with light herby flavors with apples and nuts. Use for general cooking, where a strong flavor is not required, and in baking.

Hojiblanca varietal blend
Definite flavor of flowers and tropical fruits in this Spanish oil from Andalucia. Use to finish traditional cold soups, such as gazpacho, to dress light salads, and in desserts with oranges and other fruits.

Cailletier varietal oil
A sweet oil from the Nice area of Provence, France. It has little bitterness or pepper tones. The apple, nut, and cut-salad tones go well with pasta and steamed vegetables, or use for mayonnaise.

MEDIUM-STYLE EXTRA VIRGIN OLIVE OILS

Tonda Iblea oil
This Sicilian oil tastes of vine tomatoes, with herbaceous tones with medium bitterness and pepper. Use as a dip or with salads, chicken, lamb, or vegetables dishes, such as the local caponata.

Andalucian varietal blend
Blended Picudo, Hojiblanca, and Picual olives give a fruity oil with lemon, tropical fruit, and almond flavors, a little bitterness and medium pepper. Use in local Spanish dishes, salads, and desserts.

Portuguese varietal blend
The best Portuguese oils have complex fruity flavors with well-balanced bitterness and pepper; others are more rustic with a flavor reminiscent of table olives. Use in most culinary applications.

Koroneiki varietal blend
This widespread Greek variety is a very herbaceous oil with a fruity taste and a well-balanced bitterness and pepper. Serve as a dip or use in salads, grilled meat dishes, and with vegetables.

Sicilian varietal blend
A blend of Cerasuolo, Biancolilla, and Nocellara del Belice olives gives a fruity oil with tomato flavors, often with herbs and citrus. The bitterness and pepper varies. Use as a dip and with pasta.

Vallée des Baux varietal blend
Five or six local French varieties produce an oil with flavors of apples, pears, and oranges, a touch of herbs and nuts, and a well-balanced bitterness and pepper. Use as a dip and a versatile cooking oil.

Leccino varietal oil
Originally from central Italy, this olive is now grown in other regions and the southern hemisphere. The oils have milky almond tones, light bitterness, and strong pepper. Use in most culinary applications.

VINAIGRETTE

Known widely as French dressing because of its country of origin, the recipe sometimes includes a teaspoon or so of Dijon mustard, or a little of minced shallot, garlic, or fresh herbs.

MAKES ABOUT I CUP

3 tbsp red wine vinegar

salt and freshly ground black pepper

⅔ cup olive oil

1 Combine the vinegar, salt, and pepper in a bowl.

2 Gradually add the oil in a thin stream, whisking constantly.

3 Taste the seasoning before serving, adding more salt and pepper, if needed. Store freshly made vinaigrette in a sealed container and keep refrigerated.

STRONG EXTRA VIRGIN OLIVE OILS

Picual varietal oil
Originally from Jaen, Andalucia, this olive can be found across the Southern Hemisphere. Strong with bitter pepper tones and often tomato, grass, and herb flavors. Good for dipping and salads.

Coratina varietal oil
This southern Italian variety from Puglia produces a very aggressive oil with a flavor of bitter herbs and almonds and some strong pepper. Use with robust salads and barbecued meats.

Frantoio varietal oil
This variety, grown worldwide, gives backbone to Tuscan oils. The oils have strong woody flavors, with watercress, and raw artichoke. Bitter and peppery, they are good as dipping oils.

Puglian varietal blend
Coratina olives are often blended with the milder Ogliarola olive. The result is nutty with a strong peppery punch. Use in salads and serve with the robust vegetable-based cuisine of southern Italy.

Tuscan varietal blend
Typically, Tuscan oils use blends of Frantoio, Moraiolo, and Leccino olives to produce strongly fruity oils with plenty of bitterness and pepper. Use with pasta and in traditional regional dishes.

South African blend
European olives grow side by side in South Africa and other southern-hemisphere growing regions. These blended olives produce strong oils with grassy apple tones with bitter almonds and pepper.

NUT OILS

The best nut oil is extracted mechanically after the nuts have been crushed and the pulp has been gently roasted to bring out their flavor. Uncooked nut oil is virtually tasteless, so it is most often used in cosmetics and wood preserving. Nut oils retain the flavor of the nuts from which they are pressed, and so the better the quality of the nuts used, the better the quality of the resultant oil. The main country for mechanical production of nut oil is France. Elsewhere, nut oils are produced by refining with solvents, but these have a lesser flavor.

🔒 **BUY** Check the bottle's sell-by date, since nut oil has a short shelf life.

📦 **STORE** Keep bottles well sealed, in a cool, dark place for up to 6 months.

⚫ **EAT** Use in salad dressings and mayonnaise, to flavor grilled or roasted meats, fish, cooked vegetables, and in baking bread and cakes. Nut oils are generally not suitable for use in cooking at high temperatures, with a few exceptions, such as peanut oil.

Almond oil
This oil has a delicate flavor of sweet almonds. Use to dress grilled fish, steamed green beans and broccoli, or in confectionery and baking, in particular in almond pastries and tarts.

Pistachio oil
A strong-flavored oil that has the distinctive aroma and taste of pistachio nuts. Often used in Greek and Middle Eastern pastries made with filo pastry, and with steamed vegetables.

Walnut oil
Rich, toasty aroma and taste, traditionally used in French salad dressings. Drizzle over cooked vegetables and use in stir-fry dishes. It is high in polyunsaturates, so refrigerate after opening.

Pine nut oil
Lightly nutty oil with a subtle, slightly sweet flavor. It is best used uncooked, in salad dressings, drizzled over cooked meat, and for finishing pasta dishes. It is ideal in pesto instead of olive oil.

Hazelnut oil
The strong aroma of hazelnuts and a subtle taste make this oil a good choice for use in dressings and desserts. Use in cold dishes only, as it can give a bitter tone when heated.

Macadamia oil
Chefs like this oil for its stability—it can be used when cooking at high temperatures—and for its versatility. It has a delicate, milky, nutty flavor—and is good for use in baking.

RED PALM OIL

From the fruit of the tropical palm of Asia and Africa, this unrefined oil gets its color from its high beta-carotene content. This is destroyed at high temperatures, leaving the oil white. Refined palm oil and coconut palm oil are virtually tasteless.

🔒 **BUY** The colored oil has the most flavor. African oils tend to be more viscous than South American ones.

📦 **STORE** Unlike most seed oils it is also high in saturated fatty acids and so it does not keep well.

⚫ **EAT** Popular in Southeast Asian, Caribbean, and African cooking.

Red palm oil
Strong and distinctive flavor. Traditionally used in Caribbean and West African soups and stews. It is also used to dress vegetables.

ARGAN OIL

This oil comes from the kernel of the fruit of the argan tree, which is indigenous to southwestern Morocco. The kernels are extracted from the hard shells, roasted, then ground into a powder that is mixed with water. The nut-flavored oil used to be extracted by hand, but now extraction is by mechanical equipment similar to that used in making olive oil.

🔒 **BUY** Pure organic oil is the best choice in the kitchen.

📦 **STORE** Store in a cool, dark place for a year or more. After opening, use within 3 months.

⚫ **EAT** Suitable for use as a cooking medium at high temperatures and as a flavoring ingredient in its own right.

Argan oil
Lightly toasty and nutty flavor reminiscent of hazelnuts, it is used in North African tagines. Use in salad dressings and culinary applications where you might use nut oil.

AVOCADO OIL

Avocado oil is produced from the pulp of the avocado fruit without the use of chemical solvents. Water is added to the fruit, the mixture is crushed to a paste and the oil is then extracted in a centrifuge. The main areas of production are US (California), Australia, New Zealand, and Chile.

🔒 **BUY** The flavor varies widely, so taste before you buy. Choose strong herbal tones for dressings and marinades, lighter oils for cooking.

📦 **STORE** Store in a cool, dark place for a year or more. After opening, use within 3 months.

⚫ **EAT** Suitable for use as a cooking medium at all temperatures and as a flavoring ingredient in its own right.

Avocado oil
Thick, velvety texture plus a full and fruity flavor with vegetal and herbal tones. Use in salad dressings and sauces as well as in marinades, grills, stews, and also as a dipping oil.

SEED OILS

Oil is obtained from the cells of plant seeds by a complicated chemical process using solvents, and is then refined to remove any unpleasant aromas and flavors. The resulting oil has little or no flavor but is stable at high temperatures. Seed oils were developed in the second half of the 20th century for their nutritional value; most are rich in polyunsaturated fatty acids, which are considered beneficial against heart disease. Sometimes seed oils are obtained solely by mechanical squeezing or pressing. These oils have their own aromas and flavors. Cold-pressed oils, which are rich in monounsaturated fatty acids, are stable and can withstand high temperature; however, oils with a high level of polyunsaturated fatty acids are not so stable.

BUY Choose cold-pressed seed oils for their flavor or nutritional value. Some cold-pressed seed oils are labeled "extra virgin," but this has no legal meaning in relation to seed oils.

STORE Both refined and cold-pressed seed oils should be stored, firmly sealed, in a cool, dark place. Unopened like this, the oils will last a year or more. After opening, use refined oils within 4 to 6 months, while cold-pressed oils must be stored in the fridge and used within 2 or 3 months. Seed oils high in polyunsaturated fatty-acids should also be stored in the fridge and used within a few weeks.

EAT Use as a cooking medium at all temperatures, including deep-fat frying. All except cold-pressed seed oils with a high polyunsaturated fatty acid content will not break down until they reach 437°F (225°C). Use as the base for dressings and sauces, such as mayonnaise.

Corn oil
With a very light, oily flavor, this oil is used in most culinary applications. It is a good frying oil and also a common ingredient in margarine.

Soy oil
Extracted from soy beans, this oil has a very light, oily flavor. It is used in most culinary applications, particularly in Asia, as well as in salads and for making margarine.

Canola or grapeseed oil
Available as refined and cold pressed, the latter has a definite but mild flavor of brassicas or asparagus. Both are stable and can be used at high temperatures and in all culinary applications.

Sunflower oil
Available in refined and cold-pressed versions, the former has a light, oily taste, the latter a strong, earthy flavor. Use in most culinary applications, including cooking at high temperatures.

Safflower oil
A member of the sunflower family, it is also very light in flavor and can be used in just the same way as sunflower oil. It is an important ingredient in diet mayonnaise and salad dressings.

Pumpkin seed oil
The refined oil has little aroma and is sweetish. Cold-pressed versions are not stable. Popularly used in Austria to finish dishes, such as Styrian pumpkin soup, roast pork, and salads.

Sesame oil
The refined version has a lightly nutty and earthy flavor. However, if the seeds are roasted before processing, the oil has a strong, toasty aroma and flavor. Both are widely used in Chinese cooking.

Mustard oil
Obtained from black and brown mustard seeds, this oil has a distinctive aroma and a light flavor with a little heat. It can be used in Indian cooking in place of ghee, or in savory biscuits or bread.

Peanut Oil
The refined oil is almost tasteless and is used when no flavor is required. Cold-pressed versions are popular in India and China, they have a distinct peanut flavor.

Grapeseed oil
Available in both refined and cold-pressed versions, this oil has a delicate flavor and is widely used in French cooking and salad dressings. It is highly stable, so good for high-temperature cooking.

Rice bran oil
Extracted from the bran and germ of rice kernels, this oil has a mild, nutty flavor and is highly stable. Used in Asia for deep frying and high-temperature crispy cooking.

Cold-pressed flaxseed oil
Also known as linseed oil, this has a distinctive woody flavor. It is used mainly in uncooked dishes for its nutritional value. It is not suitable for cooking, being unstable at higher temperatures.

FLAVORED OILS

The best flavored oils are made by crushing the chosen fruit or herb with olives and processing in the usual manner. In southern Italy these oils are known as *Agrumato* oils. Other regions producing good quality, flavored olive oils are northern Spain and California. Flavored oils are also made by infusing the chosen flavoring in ordinary olive oil or in a refined vegetable oil. This should be done commercially with specially treated flavorings, because if this is done at home there can be problems with bacteria from the flavoring multiplying in the oil and causing illness. Some flavored oils are made with herb or fruit extracts or essences; however the latter do not usually have such a good flavor.

🛒 **BUY** Check the label to see which kind of oil has been used as the base for the product, since this may affect the overall flavor. Take particular care when buying truffle oils and buy the best you can afford—smell the oil carefully on opening as the strong, truffle aroma can mask a rancid oil base. If in doubt, take it back to the shop.

🗄 **STORE** Store in a cool, dark place for up to 6 months and use within 2 or 3 months of opening. There is no need to refrigerate, as the oil will start to solidify.

⦿ **EAT** Use in most culinary applications to add extra flavor to many dishes, especially when the particular flavoring is not at hand. Keep a selection through the winter when fresh herbs are not always available. Do not use these oils for high temperature cooking.

Tarragon oil
This oil has a strong flavor of tarragon with a spicy ginger note. Use in vinaigrette mixed with walnut oil, or serve drizzled over chicken dishes, steamed carrots, or artichokes.

Orange oil
The strong orange aroma and flavor adds a new dimension to marinades. Also use in dressings for green beans, seared scallops, and grilled pork chops, or use to flavor biscuits and cakes.

White truffle oil
Strong flavors of earthy, woody truffles. Made with white truffles, which is the more pungent varietiy. Serve with simple pasta dishes and drizzle over grilled dishes, stews, and casseroles.

Basil oil
The herbal aroma is reminiscent of pesto sauce. This oil is excellent drizzled over grilled chicken breasts and cooked veal cutlets. Also use to dress simple tomato and potato salads.

Rosemary oil
Strong flavor of rosemary with spicy tones. Particularly good with lamb and in potato dishes. Use to make savory biscuits with oatmeal or cheese and Italian focaccia bread.

Black truffle oil
A distinctive flavor of earthy, woody truffles, but black truffles are less pungent than white. In Italy, chefs fry eggs in the oil over low heat until just set, then serve on brioche with the cooking oil.

Garlic oil
Earthy, garlic flavor. Use in all culinary applications except when cooking at very hot temperatures. Good for dressings, marinades, and in potato dishes, such as dauphinois and galette.

Citrus fruit oil
Strong, zesty flavors of the specific citrus fruit. Available using lemon, orange, and tangerine. Use with pasta, in marinades, to dress vegetable dishes and salads, and in cakes and biscuits.

Chile oil
There are many different types of chile oil, but they are all quite pungent with spicy tones. Serve with pizzas and pasta dishes, and add to soups and stews for a little extra piquancy.

VERJUICE

This is unfermented fruit juice, taken from unripe fruit, such as grapes and crab apples. The name comes from the French *vert jus* or "green juice." It was a popular condiment in medieval times when it was used as lemon juice is today—to add piquancy to a dish or to prevent oxidation of fruits, such as apples and pears. With the arrival of lemons in Europe and elsewhere, the use of verjuice has almost completely died out. Though it is widely used in Iran and Lebanon, where it is known as *abghooreh* and *hosrum* respectively, and used in certain condiments, such as Dijon mustard. It is now making a comeback as a general flavoring, using

grapes thinned from the vines in the early stages of development, particularly from vineyards in South Africa and Australia. The flavor and degree of sourness of the verjuice depends on the grape varieties used and the maturity of the picked fruit.

🛒 **BUY** Red verjuice has a stronger flavor and piquancy than yellow.

🗄 **STORE** Keep in a cool, dark place and refrigerate after opening.

⦿ **EAT** Use as a condiment to dress fish and seafood dishes, and as a flavoring in a wide variety of sweet and savory dishes. Unlike vinegar and lemon juice, verjuice can be used successfully in conjunction with wine.

Verjuice
Fruity with delicate sourness. Use to deglaze the pan when making sauces, add to stews and casseroles, or combine it with nut oils to give an acidic tang to salad dressings.

WINE VINEGARS

White wine vinegar
Delicately sour with fruity undertones. Use in dressings for delicate salads, to make mayonnaise and to deglaze the pan when making cream sauces for steaks, pork fillets, and veal cutlets.

Wine vinegar has a long history, though its origin is unknown. It is the result of a naturally occurring double fermentation. In the first fermentation, yeasts convert the sugar in sweet liquids into alcohol. In the second fermentation, bacteria sour the liquid by converting the alcohol to acetic acid. In wine-producing countries, grapes and wine form the base, but elsewhere, apples, cider, or other fruits and their wines, such as blackcurrant, elderberry, plum, and apricot, are used. In the tropics, vinegar is made using dates or coconut liquor. The very best wine vinegar is produced from good-quality wine under controlled conditions in a long, slow, and natural process. A specially bred starter culture of pure vinegar-producing bacteria is added to the wine, which is then left at ambient temperatures to turn into vinegar. Some vinegars are then matured in wooden barrels to intensify their flavor before being bottled and sealed. Wine vinegar is also made in an industrial process in an acetator. The wine is placed in huge vats with a starter culture and warm air is filtered through the liquid to raise the temperature to 86°F (30°C), which speeds up the bacterial process. When the vinegar has developed the required level of acetic acid it is drawn off, filtered, pasteurized, and bottled. More wine is added to the vat for the next batch. In North America, acid levels can range between 5 and 7.5 percent.

🔒 **BUY** Each vinegar has its own particular flavor and is rarely interchangeable in recipes, so buy a selection of various wine vinegars from which to choose.

📦 **STORE** Wine vinegar will last almost indefinitely if well sealed. Naturally produced wine vinegar that has not been pasteurized or heavily filtered may grow a "vinegar mother" or cluster of vinegar-producing bacteria. Just remove them or use to make your own vinegar at home. Flavored wine vinegar may not keep as long, but it can usually be stored for 2 to 3 years.

● **EAT** Use as a seasoning and as a flavoring in salad dressings and mayonnaise, in hot sauces, pot roasts, stews and in chocolate dishes. Very often vinegar will serve more than one purpose in a dish: it acts as a preservative in pickles and chutneys and as an effective tenderizer in marinades. Use nonreactive pans if cooking with vinegar and use vinegar-proof lids for pickle and chutney jars.

Red wine vinegar
Robust, fruity flavors with a good depth of acidity. Used in most culinary applications, including meat stews and casseroles, it is also the French vinegar of choice when making vinaigrette.

Mature red wine vinegar
Made using the classic red wines of Bordeaux, Rioja, and Barolo, it has harmonious, mellow flavors that retain elements of the base wines. Show off in dressings and when finishing dishes.

FLAVORED WINE VINEGARS

The best flavored vinegar is made by infusing the flavoring in white wine vinegar. Others are made by adding essences or extracts. If this is done carefully it can make a pleasant vinegar, which is cheaper, though infusions generally taste better.

🔒 **BUY** If "natural ingredients" appears on the label, it usually means that it was made by adding essences or extracts.

📦 **STORE** Keep cool and away from light. Any herbs, fruit, or spices in the bottle can fade. Store for up to a year if unopened, and use within 3 months once opened.

● **EAT** These add an extra dimension to salads, marinades, and sauces, particularly if the featured flavoring is not available fresh.

Champagne vinegar
Made from the ice-plug of wine at the top of the champagne bottle when the sediment is removed by freezing. A smooth, delicate flavor with fruity tones. Use in a dressing for warm goose liver salad.

Sherry vinegar
This is matured for a number of years in a series of wooden barrels. It is full of dried fruit flavors and makes an aromatic dressing for robust salads. Use to marinate pork loin for pot roasting.

Honey vinegar
Wine vinegar mixed with honey, but sometimes honey is diluted with water to produce a pure honey-based vinegar. Sweet with a sour aftertaste. Use as a dip for fish goujons or to pickle cucumber.

Fruit vinegar
These taste strongly of the featured fruit, such as raspberries, blackberries, and cherries. Some are made from fruit wine rather than by infusion. Serve sliced avocado with raspberry vinegar and oil.

Muscat vinegar
This vinegar has a strong aroma and flavor of the sweet muscat grapes with which it is made. It has a light acidity. It is particularly good used in seafood dressings, desserts, and fruit sauces.

Apple and cider vinegar
These vinegars are made from apple juice fermented to make apple wine or cider. Both taste strongly of apples. Use as wine vinegar. Cider vinegar is said to be beneficial for arthritis.

Tarragon vinegar
Tarragon vinegar, like other herb vinegars, tastes of the featured herb. Other flavorings used include dill, oregano, thyme, mixed herbs, garlic, and shallots. Use in dressings and marinades.

Pickling vinegar
Special blends of pickling spices are infused in vinegar specifically for use in pickle making; they are usually malt based. Lager eddike is a special pickling vinegar used widely in Denmark.

BALSAMIC VINEGARS

Balsamic vinegar is made from fruit juice that has been concentrated by cooking down; this is generally grape juice, but apple, elderberry, plum, and quince are also sometimes used. The flavors can be quite complex. However, some balsamic vinegars may also have other ingredients in them. Others are made using a mix of concentrated grape must and ordinary wine vinegar, plus caramel and preservatives. Some of these are hardly aged at all, and taste of little more than burned sugar. The most famous version is made in Modena, in Italy, where the best of all is the Traditional Balsamic Vinegar of Modena. This is made from the juice of local grapes, that are cooked over a fire until it is reduced by a third. The very sweet liquid is then decanted into small wooden casks and laced with a little old vinegar as a starter. The vinegar is matured in a series of barrels, rather like a solera system. Each barrel is made from different wood; the type is not specified in the regulations and the producers can choose their own combinations. The most popular woods used include chestnut, cherry, oak, and mulberry. The different woods add their own dimensions to both the color and flavor of the final vinegar. The first

traditional balsamic vinegar to be released from the system must be at least 12 years old. More can be released at 20 years. Plain Balsamic Vinegar of Modena is less costly. The best are made from a mixture of concentrated grape juice and aged wine vinegar, which is matured in a short series of barrels for anything up to 8 or 10 years.

🔒 **BUY** With the exception of Traditional Balsamic Vinegar of Modena, which is well labeled, the price and the list of ingredients are the only indications of which method has been used to make the vinegar. The best do not include caramel or preservatives. If both grape and aged wine vinegar are used, they should be in that order. Be prepared to pay more for a good balsamic vinegar.

🗄 **STORE** Store in a cool, dark cupboard after opening, where it will keep for a very long time.

⬤ **EAT** Use as a condiment and to give added depth and flavor to both sweet and savory cooking. Traditional Balsamic Vinegar of Modena is expensive but only a few drops are needed. The acetic-acid level is very low so balsamic vinegar cannot be used as a preservative.

Traditional Balsamic Vinegar of Modena
Thick, syrupy texture and a sweet taste with complex molasses and dried-fruit flavors. Use to add depth to savory dishes, or drizzle over aged Parmesan cheese, ice cream, and fruit desserts.

Balsamic Vinegar of Modena
The best examples have a rich, fruity flavor that is good in dressings, savory sauces, and desserts. Decorate serving plates with drizzled, intensely flavored vinegar; boil until thick, cool, then use.

Corinthian vinegar
Grapes grown in the Peloponnese on the Greek mainland are dried on the vine before the juice is used. Intense fruity flavor with a clean aftertaste. Serve as a dip, mixed with extra virgin olive oil.

White balsamic vinegar
Very light flavor with just a touch of fruit, white balsamic vinegar is usually the cheapest balsamic vinegar that does not contain caramel. Use to dress a cucumber salad or fish carpaccio.

GRAIN VINEGARS

Grain vinegars are made from grains that are cooked to release their starch; this is then converted into sugar to make a sweet liquid, that is fermented to make a light alcohol. This is in turn converted into vinegar, either in barrels or in an acetator, as for wine vinegar. In northern Europe, fermented malt from barley is a common base for vinegar, which produces a strong, sour vinegar with a malty taste. In China and Japan rice is the more usual base, though sorghum, wheat, barley, and rice bran may also be used. These vinegars are milder than European versions and many have their own distinctive, complex flavors.

🔒 **BUY** Avoid vinegar with added sugar. For preserving, choose one with a minimum acetic-acid level of 5 per cent. Avoid "non-brewed condiment": it is not real vinegar but a cheap mix of water, acetic acid, and caramel.

🗄 **STORE** Grain vinegar will last almost indefinitely if well sealed. It does not need to be refrigerated.

⬤ **EAT** Widely used in general cooking, particularly in the East where it is added to savory dishes, including marinades, dips, stir-fries, and stews. Each vinegar has its own particular flavor and is rarely interchangeable in recipes. Avoid using aluminium pans when cooking with it, and make sure lids are vinegarproof when bottling pickles and chutneys.

Chinese white rice vinegar
The higher acetic-acid content in this vinegar gives it a milder, less acidic flavor and a taste that's similar to white wine or malt vinegar. Use in sweet—sour dishes and as a condiment.

Chinese red rice vinegar
Widely used in Chinese cooking, the sweet—sour flavor of this rice vinegar makes it ideal for dipping also for use in soups, seafood, and noodle dishes.

Shanxi aged sorghum vinegar
This speciality of northern China has a sweet—sour mellow taste. It is used in much of the region's cooking; in dishes, such as sweet and sour meatballs, and eggplant with chili.

Chinese black rice vinegar
Made from glutinous rice and salt, this vinegar has a mellow, slightly smoky flavor. Traditionally used as a dipping sauce and in braised dishes, or as balsamic vinegar. Chinkiang is considered the best.

Japanese rice vinegar
Similar to Chinese red rice vinegar but milder in flavor. Mix with salt and sugar to make sushi vinegar, with lemon juice and soy sauce to make ponszu sauce. Add to tempura batter for a crispy effect.

Malt vinegar
Strong, acetic, sour flavor with a hint of caramel. Traditional European accompaniment to fish and chips, tripe, beets, and other vegetables. Use for pickles, chutney, and in sauces and stews.

SUGARS

Sugar is sucrose; it is extracted from the crushed juice of sugar cane grown in the tropics, or from sugar beet grown in more temperate climates. Sugar cane juice can either be processed in such a way as to retain its natural color and flavor, or it can be refined to remove them. Sugar-beet juice is always refined since the taste of unrefined sugar-beet is not pleasant. Another, rarer source of sugar is sweet sorghum, and in Southeast Asia, palm sugar is extracted from the sap of the date palm tree. Dry white sugar is refined to be almost 100 per cent sucrose. As well as removing the impurities from the sugar, refining also removes any flavor other than that of sweetness. Most brown sugar is dry white sugar, that has had some molasses, sugar syrup, or caramel color added to it. Light brown soft sugar has less color added to it than dark brown soft sugar and so it also has a lighter flavor. "Raw" sugars are extracted from unrefined sugar-cane juice; they are moist in texture and have a distinctive taste that derives from the natural residues that remain in the sugar.

🔒 **BUY** Choose the right sugar for the job: light-colored sugars are more delicate in flavor and are the most suitable for baking and for making sweet sauces. Darker sugars have a stronger flavor and are good for savory dishes and pickles. Choose brown sugars that are moist, not hard. Moist brown sugars that are not colored white sugars are usually labeled "unrefined cane sugar."

📦 **STORE** If protected from moisture, dry sugar will not deteriorate and can be stored for a year or more. If it does absorb water it will form lumps and harden, but this can be reversed by pulverizing. Moist sugar should be protected from drying out since otherwise it will harden into a solid block. This can be reversed by placing the sugar in a bowl with a damp towel over the top.

⬤ **EAT** Use to sweeten everything from drinks and desserts to jams and baked goods. It is also the base for many sweets and confectionery. Sugar can be used as a seasoning in savory dishes, such as stews and steamed vegetables. Moist, dark-brown sugars add depth and flavor to cakes and cookies as well as to marinades, stews, and chutneys. When dissolving sugar in water, start over a low heat, stirring gently all the time, then turn up the heat once the sugar has fully dispersed.

CLASSIC RECIPE

CARAMEL SAUCE

Caramel has been used as a flavoring since sugar was first crystallized. This sauce appears in 19th-century European cookbooks as a topping for ice cream and other desserts.

MAKES ABOUT 1 CUP

| 1¼ cups superfine or granulated sugar |
| 4 tbsp water |
| 4 tbsp salted butter, cut into pieces |
| ⅔ cup heavy whipping cream |

1 Mix together the sugar and water in a deep-sided, heavy-bottomed saucepan. Cook over low heat, stirring constantly, until the sugar has completely dissolved. Continue cooking for 4-5 minutes without stirring, until the resulting caramel becomes a rich amber color.

2 Remove the pan from the heat and whisk in the butter and the cream. Place the pan over low heat and gently bring to a boil, stirring constantly, until the sauce is smooth. Cool for a few minutes before serving warm.

Sichuan rice bran vinegar
The strong, acetic taste from this rice bran, wheat, and rice-based vinegar matches the robust flavors of Sichuan cuisine. It is particularly good in sweet-and-sour dishes and also for dipping.

Japanese brown rice vinegar
Made exclusively from wholegrain glutinous rice, with the bran and germ intact, this vinegar has a mellow taste. It is renowned for its medicinal properties and is more often served as a tonic.

Confectioner's sugar
Also known as powdered sugar or icing sugar, this fine, refined sugar often has a small amount of corn starch added to prevent caking. Use for icing cakes and in delicate sweets, such as fondants.

Muscovado sugar
The dark and light versions of this unrefined, moist sugar have more or less intense caramel, spicy, and bitter flavors. Use dark in fruit cakes and savory dishes; light in biscuits and crumbles.

Caster sugar
This is a finer version of refined granulated sugar and is the best choice when baking cakes, scones, and light biscuits. If this is not on hand, grind granulated sugar in a blender until fine.

Jaggery sugar
Blocks or cones of unrefined sugar evaporated from cane or palm juice. It has a rich, almost mineral flavor. Widely used in Indian cooking as a flavor enhancer in place of salt.

Granulated sugar
A refined sugar that is used in general cooking and to sweeten hot drinks. It is the best choice when making sweets and confectionery. It is also available in a golden unrefined version.

Demerara sugar
Originally from Guyana, this is a coarse crystal sugar traditionally used to sweeten coffee and for baking rich fruit cakes. It is available in refined, colored, and unrefined versions.

Barbados sugar
An unrefined, slightly moist muscovado sugar that is made from sugar cane grown specifically in Barbados. It is quite strong in flavor. Use in rich fruit cakes, fruit puddings, and chutneys.

Molasses sugar
With around 2 per cent natural cane molasses, this raw sugar has a spicy, bitter—sweet character. Use in dark chocolate and ginger cakes, and also in rich Christmas cakes and Christmas puddings.

The darker the color of honey, the richer and more robust the flavor. Comb honey is a delicacy that comes straight from the hive.

HONEYCOMB

Sometimes called sponge candy or hokey pokey, this recipe appeared in North America in the 19th century.

2½ cups superfine or granulated sugar

1 cup water

4 tbsp golden syrup (such as Lyle's)* or light corn syrup

2 tsp baking soda, sifted for lumps

1 Line a baking sheet with oiled parchment paper and set aside. Combine the sugar, water, and syrup in a deep, heavy-bottomed saucepan. Cook over medium heat, stirring constantly, until sugar dissolves.

2 Bring to a boil, cover, and boil 3 minutes. Uncover and boil without stirring until the temperature reaches 290°F (145°C) on a candy thermometer and the mixture turns golden.

3 Remove from the heat. Stir in the baking soda just until incorporated. The mixture will bubble vigorously and pull away from the sides of the pan.

4 Quickly pour it onto the prepared sheet. Do not pat or spread it. You do not want the bubbles to deflate.

5 Leave uncovered until it is room temperature, completely set, and easily breaks into bite-sized pieces. Store in an airtight container.

*available in the imported foods section of many well-stocked supermarkets

SUGAR SYRUP

The most common sugar syrups are those made from a by-product of the sugar-refining process. This substance is itself refined to give various strengths of syrup. Sugar-syrup bases may be derived from sugar cane, sugar beet, or sorghum. (The latter is not considered to be as good as the former two.) Some cane syrups are made by simply boiling down sugar-cane juice so that it evaporates and thickens. Corn syrup is a sugar syrup that is produced by treating corn starch with enzymes.

🔒 **BUY** The darker the color of the syrup, the stronger and more bitter the flavor is likely to be.

📦 **STORE** Syrups may crystallize during storage but the crystals will dissolve with gentle heating. Corn syrup should not be stored for more than 4 to 6 months, since it is prone to mold and fermentation.

⏺ **EAT** Eat on bread or drizzle over cereal. Use as a flavoring as well as a sweetener, to enhance the flavor of cakes and desserts, and to add a deeper richness to savory dishes. It can be easier to mix a thick syrup into a cake or biscuit mixture if it is heated gently first.

Golden syrup
This British syrup has a light caramel taste and a runny consistency. It is the main ingredient in classic treacle tart, British flapjacks, and steamed ginger pudding.

Blackstrap molasses
The unrefined syrup that remains after sugar-cane juice has been boiled three times to remove white sugar crystals. It is bittersweet with a distinctive flavor. Use in baked beans and ginger bread.

Black treacle
This is a quite thick, though still runny, British syrup with a strong flavor that is similar to but lighter than that of molasses. Use in rich sauces, to make treacle toffee, and in baking ginger cakes.

Corn syrup
Available in both light and dark varieties, corn syrups have a similar flavor to cane syrups and can be used in just the same way. Use as golden syrup to make cakes, desserts, and sweetmeats.

FRUIT SYRUP

These syrups are made by evaporating fruit juice or tree sap to produce syrups that taste like their base fruits. Some are used immediately, others are matured for a year or two in order to concentrate the flavor. They are often known by different names, according to the region from which they originate.

🔒 **BUY** Read the label carefully. Good-quality fruit syrups and *vincotto* do not need any additives to preserve them. Check to see that maple syrup is not flavored with corn or cane syrup.

📦 **STORE** Store in a cool, dark place for up to a year and use fairly quickly after opening.

⏺ **EAT** Use as a flavoring and sweetener in both sweet and savory dishes.

Grape molasses
Thick, honey-like consistency with a rich, dark flavor of warm grapes. In Turkey it is known as pekmez. Spread on bread or use it in sweet sauces to pour over puddings and ice cream.

Vincotto
This southern Italian syrup is made from grapes dried on the vines, pressed, then boiled and aged in oak barrels. It is runny with rich dried-fruit tones. Use to add sweet richness to savory sauces.

Date syrup
This thick, viscous syrup tastes strongly of dates. It is sweet with light bitterness and a touch of acidity. Paired with tahini paste, it is used in the popular Middle Eastern dish dibis w'rashi.

Pomegranate syrup
Thick texture with a tangy sweet-sour flavor. Thicker versions are labeled pomegranate molasses. It is popular in Iraq and the eastern Mediterranean in sweet and savory dishes.

Maple syrup
This is a runny syrup from the sap of the maple tree. It has a distinctive lightly woody and earthy taste. The darker the syrup, the richer the taste. It is traditionally served on pancakes and waffles.

SOFIA LARRINUA-CRAXTON Consultant on South American ingredients. Sofia is Mexican by birth and lives in London, working as a cooking teacher, consultant, writer, and broadcaster specializing in Mexican cuisine and world street food. She is the author of *The Mexican Mama's Kitchen* and *The Tomato Book* (DK).

JENNY LINFORD Author of the Dairy, Nuts, and Seeds chapter. Jenny is a food writer and member of The Guild of Food Writers, as well as the author of 15 books including *Food Lovers' London* and DK's *Great British Cheeses*. She founded Gastro-Soho Tours in 1994, offering personal guided tours of London's food shops.

CHRISTINE MCFADDEN Consultant on the Vegetables and Fruit chapters. A food writer with an extensive knowledge of global cuisines and ingredients, Christine has written 16 books, including *Pepper, The Farm Shop Cookbook,* and *Cool Green Leaves and Red Hot Peppers*, all three shortlisted for international food media awards.

MARIE-PIERRE MOINE Consultant on French ingredients. Marie-Pierre was brought up in Paris, and lives and works in London. She is the author of DK's *Provence Cookery School* and *The Cook's Herb Garden,* and of many books on French cooking and food. She writes a monthly food column for *House & Garden* magazine.

JENNI MUIR Author of the Grains, Rice, Pasta, and Noodles chapter. Jenni learned to make soba noodles with a soba noodle master in Tokyo. She is the editor of *Time Out Eating & Drinking Guide*, and works with chefs and other food experts to produce cookbooks and culinary websites, as well as contributing on a freelance basis to newspapers and magazines.

LYNNE MULLINS Consultant on Southeast Asian and Australian ingredients. Lynne is an award-winning food writer who has traveled extensively to master her culinary skills. She is the author of 7 cookbooks, writes a weekly food column in *The Sydney Morning Herald* and the *Newcastle Herald*, and also appears regularly on Australian radio and television.

JILL NORMAN Author of the Herbs and Spices chapters. An award-winning author and food and wine publisher, Jill is one of the most influential food writers of recent times. She is the author of DK's *Herb & Spice, The Classic Herb Cookbook, The Complete Book of Spices,* and *The New Penguin Cookery Book*; her work is published in many languages throughout the world.

HELEN YUET LING PANG Consultant on Chinese ingredients. Helen is the author of food and travel blog World Foodie Guide, shortlisted for the Guild of Food Writers 2009 New Media Award. She is enthusiastic about all cuisines, particularly Chinese, and enjoys traveling to eat and photograph food.

JUDY RIDGWAY Author of the Oils, Vinegars, and Flavorings chapter. Judy is an olive oil expert, consultant, author, and broadcaster specializing in all aspects of taste and flavor. She has written four books on olive oil, including *Best Olive Oil Buys Round the World*, and more than 60 books on food and wine.

MARIA JOSE SEVILLA Consultant on Spanish ingredients. Maria is a food writer, broadcaster, and the Chief Executive of Foods and Wines from Spain at the Spanish Embassy in London.

AUTHORS AND EXPERTS

KIMIKO BARBER Consultant on Japanese ingredients. Kimiko was born in Kobe, Japan, and is the author of DK's *Sushi* and many other publications on Japanese cuisine. She regularly writes for the *Weekend Financial Times* on food and travel. She has contributed to BBC Radio 4's *Food Programme*, and has taught in various culinary schools.

JEFF COX Author of the Vegetable chapter. Jeff has been writing about vegetable gardening for 40 years. He is a former editor of *Organic Gardening* magazine and has written 18 books on food, wine, and gardening.

NICHOLA FLETCHER Author of the Meat chapter. Regarded as one of the world's leading authorities on meat, Nichola has written seven books on the subject. She gives workshops to cooks and chefs, and also leads tutored meat tastings. Nichola is an award-winning food historian; she lives in Scotland.

OLIVIA GRECO Consultant on Italian ingredients. Olivia worked as a head chef in Tuscany, also researching all aspects of Italian and other cuisines, and later taught at the Italian Cooking School in Tuscany. After years of travel, she is based in London where she teaches and cooks for cooking schools and private clients.

TRINE HAHNEMANN Consultant on Scandinavian ingredients. Described as "Denmark's answer to Nigella Lawson" by *The Daily Telegraph*, Trine is a chef, food writer, and cookbook author.

JULIET HARBUTT Author of the Cheese chapter. Juliet regularly judges cheese competitions around the world, as well as promoting artisan cheese through writing, training, and consultancy. She created the British Cheese Awards in 1994 and the Great British Cheese Festival in 2000, and wrote *The World Cheese Book*, published by DK in 2009.

ANISSA HELOU Consultant on Middle Eastern and North African ingredients. Anissa is a food writer, journalist, and broadcaster, whose books include *Lebanese Cuisine* and *Mediterranean Street Food*. She has her own cooking school in London.

CLARISSA HYMAN Author of the Fruit chapter. Clarissa is an award-winning food and travel writer, twice recipient of the prestigious Glenfiddich Food Writer of the Year Award. She contributes to a wide range of newspapers and magazines and has written three books on food, travel, culture, and cooking: *The Spanish Kitchen*, *The Jewish Kitchen,* and *Cucina Siciliana*.

C.J. JACKSON Author of the Fish chapter. C.J. is Director of the Billingsgate Seafood Training School, a charity situated above the famous London fish market. She runs the school and both teaches and demonstrates on some courses. She writes for the BBC's *Good Food* magazine and is author of *The Billingsgate Market Cookbook* and co-author of *Leith's Fish Bible*.

CORNELIA KLAEGER Consultant on German ingredients. A home economist, ingredients expert, and food writer, Cornelia also translates from English, adapts, and produces cookbooks for international publishers. Cornelia lives in Munich, Germany.

Adelaide or Alaska, we can also take the opportunity to look at our own traditional recipes with fresh eyes, and perhaps give them a modern twist with a new ingredient.

Alongside this expansive global mindset is a deepening concern for the environment, responsible animal husbandry, and a fair return for food producers. Worldwide food scares of the last two decades have made many people think deeply about the provenance of their food, particularly meat and poultry. Responsible cooks are becoming increasingly aware of depleted fish stocks and the importance of sustainable fishing. In the Western world, those who are able are increasingly opting for locally produced food, in a well-intentioned attempt to support farmers and artisan producers, and reduce food miles. Growing-your-own and making-your-own are becoming key parts of the food culture. School gardens and land set aside for community food production are on the rise in urban areas from Cuba to Australia, and in many parts of the US and Europe. The last five years have seen a renaissance in bread-making, cheese-making, pickling, and preserving in countries where these traditional skills are not necessarily a feature of everyday life.

As this complex and exciting food culture unfolds, the home cook's need for practical information has never been greater. *The Cook's Book of Ingredients* more than meets this need. It takes you on a fascinating journey, opens your eyes to the vast global pantry, and provides you with all you need to know to choose the best ingredients. The book is a superior resource that delivers on every level, enabling you to shop with authority and cook with confidence.

Christine McFadden

Had this book been produced twenty years ago, it would have been a slim volume with fewer photographs. Missing would be some of the exotica that long-haul travel has made commonplace, along with the melting pot of foods emerging from our increasingly multicultural society. Fewer pages would be devoted to the wealth of fresh produce that modern harvesting and refrigerated transportation systems have made possible. The book would also be lacking some of the in-depth knowledge and culinary expertise that the internet makes so speedily accessible.

In the 80s and 90s, supermarkets ruled the roost; decades later they remain the essential one-stop shop for many of us in the West. That said, our growing passion for food has been matched by a significant rise in delicatessens, butchers, fishmongers, greengrocers, farm shops, and farmers' markets. Their shelves are packed with produce, much of it in season and locally grown, opening up yet more choices. Mail-order food companies are increasing, too. We can order every imaginable ingredient, from exotic spices and heirloom beans to *foie gras* and oven-ready squirrel, by e-mail or phone—though this rather misses the sensory pleasure of looking, touching, and smelling to evaluate what is on offer.

The time has never been better for the curious cook. Every day the pantry grows, with foods that were previously geographically or culturally isolated now being shared at tables around the world. With this unprecedented abundance, we can return from our travels, inspired by the food we have eaten, and create the same dishes at home—from an aromatic Thai curry or spicy Mexican mole to Spanish paella or Hungarian goulash. Whether we live in Dallas or Dijon,

Every page of this book reveals an ingredient that simply must be tried, or a new piece of information about a familiar ingredient. Space is devoted to lesser-known regional items, with foods such as beremeal and biltong given the same attention as chicken and cheese. For every ingredient, there is a short introduction describing provenance and seasonality, together with insider information on how to assess quality and freshness, and clear explanations of how best to prepare and cook the ingredient. Following this are recommendations for flavor pairings with compatible ingredients that will open the mind of even the most accomplished cook.

The book includes more than 200 classic recipes, distinctly regional but well known the world over, chosen to showcase a particular ingredient and to help you explore its flavors further. These are classic recipes from around the world in which the ingredient is star.

This colossal culinary encyclopedia has been produced by a team of expert food writers, chefs, and connoisseurs, backed by worldwide regional consultants. Photographers have traveled the globe to far-flung food markets, from Barcelona's Boqueria to San Francisco's Ferry Plaza to Tokyo's Tsukiji in search of the very best ingredients to illustrate the book. Their work is shown in 2,500-plus photographs of a complete spectrum of foods: fish and shellfish; meat, poultry, and game; vegetables; herbs; spices; dairy and eggs; fruits; nuts and seeds; grains; rice; pasta; and noodles, oils, vinegars, and flavorings.

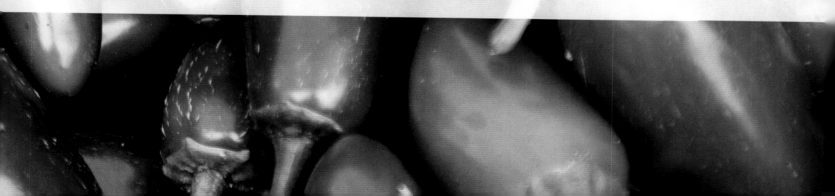

INTRODUCTION

In the past twenty years, food lovers and cooks the world over have witnessed the phenomenal growth of a vast global market. It is as if a seemingly constant and burgeoning stream of produce is there for the asking—exotic fruit and heirloom vegetables, rare-breed meat and poultry, remarkable fish and seafood, artisan cheeses and cured meats, rare spices and herbs, authentic sauces and flavorings. The list goes on and more keeps coming, sometimes making us feel like excited children in a candy store.

Since good cooking is about good ingredients, we need the knowledge necessary for making informed choices. We need to be able to recognize quality—ingredients that are the best of their kind, produced with care and pride. We need to know when food is in prime condition, how to store it, ripen it, prepare it, cook it, or preserve it in the most appropriate way. Regardless of where we live, if we are to make the most of this rich global market, we need to be aware that everyday ingredients in one part of the world may seem unusual or exotic in another. If we don't recognize ingredients or know what to do with them, we are likely to pass over items that could enrich our culinary repertoire. *The Cook's Book of Ingredients* provides the in-depth information you need to do all this and more. It will fascinate and inform beginners and experienced cooks, professional chefs, passionate foodies, and even the mildly curious whose interest has been kindled by the sheer wealth of produce available.

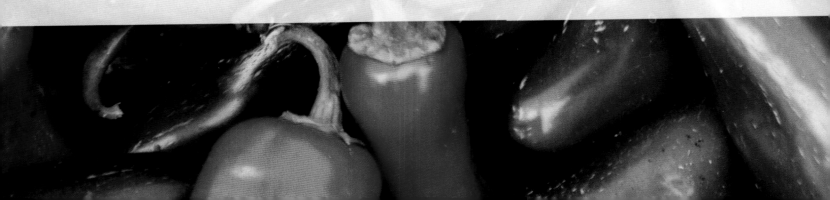

HONEY

Honey bees gather nectar from the flowers and plants in their vicinity and carry it back to the hive, where it is mixed with enzymes and stored. Water evaporation and enzyme action then turn the nectar into honey. It is produced everywhere from the tropics to the wilds of Siberia, although the hotter the weather, the longer the bees are able to gather nectar. The flavor of honey varies according to the type of plants the bees have visited. Mono-floral honeys are produced from the nectar of only one flower species, and these taste specifically of the plant from which the nectar has been taken. Other honeys are made using blends of nectars, and "honeydew" is made from the secretions of insects feeding on the sap of New Zealand black and red beech trees. Clear or liquid honey is made by removing the wax cappings from the honeycomb and extracting the honey. Most honeys will eventually naturally crystallize into a set honey. Honey is made up of a mixture of fructose and glucose sugar; the higher the glucose percentage, the faster the honey will crystallize. Whipped or creamed honey is produced through a commercial process and can be spread at room temperature.

BUY The darker the honey, the more robust the flavor is likely to be. Cloudy honey is not a sign of an old or inferior product, but that it has either not been filtered or is starting to

crystallize. Only honey labeled "pure" is entirely honey, not honey blended with other sweeteners. If you prefer a mono-floral honey, look for the name of the flower on the label.

STORE Stored at room temperature unopened and out of direct sunlight, honey will last for many years.

EAT Honey can be eaten spread on bread or drizzled on to cereal. It may also be used in cooking to replace sugar, but it is sweeter, so less is needed. It will dissolve in hot or cold liquids even if it is set. Honey attracts water, so it is good for baking since it keeps cakes moist longer. Set honey can be made runny again by standing the jar in hot water for an hour or so.

Comb honey
Honey-filled beeswax combs are taken directly from the hive and sold in their original state. Spread on bread and biscuits. Bits of wax remain in the honey so it is unsuitable for cooking.

Beech honeydew
Produced from aphid secretions on beech trees, this honey is thick in texture and does not crystallize easily. The flavor is strong and earthy. It is ideal for serving with bread or fruit.

Lavender honey
French, Spanish, and some English lavender honeys are produced from the nectar of the flower, but others are infusions. Both have a lavender flavor. Use in cakes and biscuits, or to sweeten drinks.

Rosemary honey
The flavor is reminiscent of the herbal aromas of Provence. Found in Spain and France, Rosemary honey is used in both sweet and savory dishes, also in sauces and marinades for pork and lamb.

Heather honey
Found in the UK and Scandinavia, this is an intensely flavored honey with a light resin aroma. The texture may be waxy, firm, or slightly crunchy. Serve on cereal, or use to make shortbread.

Clover honey
Sweet, flowery-flavored honey with a touch of grassiness. It is found mainly in North America and New Zealand. Useful in most culinary applications, and good for sweetening biscuits and pastries.

Wild thyme honey
A distinctive honey with a flavor that has the aromas of the herb. It is renowned in New Zealand and Greece, where it is served with thick natural yogurt. It does not crystallize easily.

Lime blossom (aka Linden) honey
Mild with typical fragrance of lime blossom, this honey is found across Europe and in China. Used to sweeten and add a minty flavor to drinks. The lime tree is also known as the linden tree.

Chestnut honey
This is a runny, intense honey that does not set. Originating in Italy and the south of France, it has a spicy, leathery flavor. Often served with Italian pecorino cheese, and excellent with fresh figs.

Eucalyptus honey
Distinctive medium-strength Australian honey. Its color varies depending on the variety of eucalyptus visited by the bees. It is excellent in barbecue sauces for veal and lamb.

Leatherwood honey
Said to taste of the rainforests, this unique, buttery-textured Tasmanian honey has a piquant aroma and complex flavor. Its buttery, spreadable texture is perfect for use with bread.

Manuka honey
The nectar of the manuka plant or New Zealand tea tree yields a rich, dark honey with an aromatic flavor. It is widely used across New Zealand to add flavor to cakes and desserts.

Orange blossom honey
Mild honey from Spain, Mexico, and Florida and California in the US. It often has a light citrus taste, but it is much sweeter than many other honeys. Use in most culinary applications.

SOY SAUCES

Soy sauce is an Asian speciality made from soy beans usually mixed with roasted grains, such as wheat, rice, or barley. This mixture is fermented for several months before being strained and bottled. It comes in light and dark versions, the darker version being aged for a longer period. *Tamari* is a Japanese soy sauce that is made only from fermented soy beans; no grains are in the mix. Japanese white soy sauce reverses the usual ratio of wheat and soy bean, using 80 per cent or more wheat. They all taste salty. Sweet soy sauce is a speciality of Indonesia.

🔒 **BUY** Always check the label to ensure you are not buying synthetically manufactured soy sauce, which is produced in just a few days from combining corn syrup, caramel coloring, salt and water.

🗄 **STORE** Store unopened at room temperature away from direct heat and light for up to 6 months. Once opened, soy sauce keeps its flavor better if it is stored in the fridge.

⬤ **EAT** A small amount of soy sauce acts as a salt substitute and brings out the flavors of the other ingredients. Use as a marinade and as a flavoring; light soy sauces in stir-frying and dark soy sauces in stews. It is also good as a dipping sauce.

Sweet soy sauce
Known as kecap manis *in Indonesia, sweet soy sauce is sweetened with palm sugar and sometimes flavored with garlic and anise. The thick sauce is good for dipping and for stir-fries, noodles, or rice.*

Tamari soy sauce
This Japanese soy sauce is thick, though still runny in texture, with a rich, savory, and mildly salty. Use as dipping sauce, and to season and flavor all types of savory Japanese food.

Chinese light soy sauce
This variety of soy sauce has a thin pouring texture and a tastes salty, with complex tones of vanilla, citrus, and mature yeasts. Use as a condiment, a dipping sauce, and in stir-fries.

Chinese dark soy sauce
A darker version, that is aged longer and has molasses added to produce a thick and syrupy texture with a rich, mellow flavor. Use in cooking and to flavor Chinese "red" stews.

FISH SAUCES

Dried, salted, and fermented fish or fish extracts are used in a number of Asian sauces. Chinese oyster sauce used to be made from salted oysters, but is now produced by boiling oyster extract with a mix of seasonings. Thai and Vietnamese fish sauces are prepared by layering anchovies and other small fish in sea salt in barrels or earthenware pots and leaving the mixture to ferment for up to a year. Some fish sauces smell very strong upon opening, but once they are cooked their pungency softens to attractive flavors, that blend well with other cooking ingredients.

Thai fish (Nam pla) sauce
Known as nam pla in Thailand, this sauce is clear with no sediment and has an intensely fishy aroma that is not too strong on the palate. Use in Thai salad dressings, stews, and curries.

Worcestershire sauce
Based on an Indian recipe, anchovies, tamarind, soy, garlic, and spices are matured together. A smooth sauce with tangy flavors. Use in traditional cookery and in a Bloody Mary.

XO sauce
A relatively new sauce (invented in the 1980s), made from dried scallops, oil, chiles, and garlic, it has a chunky, oily texture and a salty, spicy taste. Use to enhance seafood and vegetable dishes.

Oyster sauce
This rich, savory sauce is made by cooking oysters but it does not taste very fishy. Use to flavor Chinese meat and vegetable dishes, such as beef in oyster sauce or red stewed eggplants.

BARBECUE SAUCE

The popularity of outdoor cooking in North America led to the development of this sauce. Use barbecue sauce as a marinade, a baste, or a dipping sauce.

MAKES ABOUT 3 CUPS

1 ½ tbsp vegetable oil
1 onion, finely chopped
2 garlic cloves, finely chopped
½ cup ketchup
½ cup packed dark brown sugar
¼ cup cider vinegar
juice and finely grated zest of 2 lemons
2 tbsp Worcestershire sauce
1 ½ tbsp chili sauce
1 tbsp Dijon mustard
freshly ground black pepper, to taste

1 Warm the oil in a saucepan over low heat. Stir in the onion and garlic and cook until soft and lightly browned.

2 Stir in the ketchup, sugar, vinegar, lemon juice and zest, Worcestershire, chili sauce, mustard, and pepper and bring to a boil. Reduce the heat and simmer for 10-15 minutes, stirring occasionally, until the sauce thickens. Leave to cool completely before using.

🔒 **BUY** Check the labels and avoid any sauces that contain MSG; it is not a necessary ingredient. Neither should they need to include corn-starch thickening or caramel.

🗄 **STORE** Store in a dark place away from direct heat, as fish sauces may start to ferment if the surrounding temperature gets too high. Once opened, keep in the fridge for 3 to 6 months.

⬤ **EAT** Use in small quantities to add saltiness to Asian cooking and bring out the flavor of other ingredients; in larger quantities for flavoring. They are rarely used as dipping sauces.

VEGETABLE SAUCES

Some vegetable sauces, such as North American tomato ketchup and English mushroom ketchup, are made by cooking the chosen vegetable with salt, vinegar, and a variety of spices until the consistency thickens and the flavors have combined. The sauce is then strained, puréed, and bottled. Other vegetable sauces, such as Tabasco pepper sauce and the various Chinese soy bean sauces, are made by mashing, salting, and fermenting the chosen vegetable in wooden barrels. The higher the temperature at which the fermentation takes place, the darker in color the resulting sauce will be. The fermenting beans may be matured for a few months, or for some years. Chinese bean sauces are mixed with rice wine and sugar and a variety of other ingredients, depending on the producer and the traditions of the region in which they are made. Chile-based sauces, made from fresh and preserved peppers, are popular throughout the world. Traditional versions can be found in the Caribbean, in Mexico, and across South America, China, and Thailand, as well as in Spain, Portugal, and the US.

🔒 **BUY** Check the labels and avoid any sauces that contain long lists of additives. Choose tomato sauces for sweetness, and chile-based sauces for piquancy.

📦 **STORE** Store in a dark place away from heat, as vegetable sauces may discolor or start to ferment if the surrounding temperature gets too high. Once opened, keep in the fridge for 3 to 6 months. Chile-based sauces keep for longer.

⦿ **EAT** Serve either as a condiment or use to spice up other dishes, such as stir-fries, soups, and stews. Sauces make good glazes for barbecued, grilled and roasted meats. Use also as a dipping sauce on their own or mixed with soy sauce and other ingredients. Some sauces, including Tabasco and hoisin, are strong so need to be used sparingly.

Tabasco sauce
Matured red peppers are blended with vinegar to produce a sauce with a strong chile flavor and a salty, sour tone. Use to spice up soups, sauces, and stews, and in Bloody Mary cocktails.

Tomato ketchup
This tomato-based condiment has a thick consistency that runs on shaking and a sweet and tangy flavor with a hint of spice. Serve with hamburgers and grills, and use in sauces.

Mushroom ketchup
Probably English in origin, this thin but pungently mushroom-flavored sauce was traditionally served with roast meats and game. Use instead of Worcestershire sauce on Welsh rarebit.

Yellow bean sauce
Made from fermented soy beans, this sauce has a thick, glossy texture and tastes salty. It is widely used in Chinese cooking, especially in pork, chicken, and vegetable stir-fries.

Black bean sauce
Delicately or strongly flavored sauce, depending on the amount of chile added to it. Use in stir-fry and steamed dishes, particularly with beef and chicken. Add it toward the end of cooking.

Chinese chile sauce
This sauce comes in varying strengths of piquancy, often with sweet undertones. It is usually quite thick in texture. Good for dipping, or stir-frying. Use the stronger versions in Sichuan cuisine.

Hoisin sauce
Based on soy, with garlic, chile, and other spices, hoisin is thick and smooth with a strong, balanced mixture of garlic and salty, spicy flavors. Use in sauces, to glaze meats for roasting, and as a dip.

MISO

This is a traditional Japanese seasoning paste made from soy beans mixed with cereals, such as rice, barley, wheat, or rye, and then fermented.
A special yeast mold is used to start the fermentation. The longer the process the stronger, darker, and more pungent the flavor. Once fermented, the mixture is ground to a thick paste. The most common Japanese miso is rice based. It comes in various colors and textures, depending on the ingredients used and the length of the fermentation process. In China very similar products are known simply as bean paste. Miso is said to be a healthy substitute for salt since it contains mineral trace elements such as zinc, manganese, and copper, as well as enzymes and vitamin B12.

🔒 **BUY** As a general guide, light-colored miso tends to be lighter and sweeter in flavor; darker miso is stronger and more mature in flavor. Check the labels and avoid sauces containing MSG.

📦 **STORE** Keep in the fridge in a tightly sealed container. Except for very light miso pastes, most will keep for a year or more. If you prefer, you can freeze it for a longer storage life.

⦿ **EAT** Very widely used in Japanese cooking, particularly in soups, dressings, and sauces. It is also used as a glaze, and in marinades, stir-fries, and stews.

Barley and soy miso
Made from fermented barley grains and soy beans, this relatively thick, dark miso has a strong, salty flavor and is quite rich. Use for seasoning rich soups, stews, and sauces.

Rice and soy miso
Usually has a smooth and slightly runny texture and delicate, fruity, nutty flavors. Lighter "white miso" is sweet in flavor; darker "red miso" is stronger. Use in soups, stews, and marinades.

Wheat and soy miso
This medium-strength miso tastes savory and salty. Use it in vegetable and meat dishes or dilute it with a little water to serve as a dip with raw fish dishes or fried bean curd.

VEGETABLE PASTES

Simple vegetable pastes are made by crushing the chosen fresh ingredient and then bottling it for later use, but some are also concentrated by cooking before bottling. Vegetable pastes may also be flavored in a variety of ways, depending on the country of origin. Sometimes the chosen vegetable is preserved first by drying, fermenting, or curing.

BUY Check the sell-by dates on fresh vegetable pastes, since they do not have a long shelf life. If buying sun-dried tomato paste, tomatoes should be dried in the sun, rather than being dried in a dehydrator, for better flavor.

STORE After opening, store fresh pastes in the fridge and use within a week or so. Concentrated pastes, such as *tahini* and tomato paste, will last in the fridge for a year or more. Some pastes also have preservatives added to give them a longer shelf life.

EAT Fresh pastes are used in general cooking and flavoring throughout the world and make useful convenience foods. Concentrated pastes can be used as they are or they can be thinned and served as dips or added to pasta sauces.

Tomato purée
Intense tomato flavor. Use generally in soups, stews, and sauces. In southern Italy, tomatoes are dried before they are crushed in order to give them a sweeter, more fruity flavor.

Tamarind paste
A key ingredient in Indian, Thai, and Chinese food, tamarind paste has a fruity flavor with a tangy sourness. It can be used in place of lemon or vinegar in both sweet and savory dishes.

Chinese chile paste
This strong chile paste is flavored with garlic and soy beans and has a chunky texture and tastes spicy. Use it to give piquancy to stir-fry meat, poultry, and vegetable dishes and Chinese stews.

Green olive paste
This green paste has the lightly bitter taste of unripe olives. Ripe olives are used to make black olive paste, which has a stronger, deeper taste. Serve both as spreads, or use in pasta dishes.

Achiote paste
A distinctively flavored paste made from crushed achiote or annatto seeds mixed with vinegar, garlic, and spices. It is widely used in meat and rice dishes in Mexico and across Central America.

Garlic paste
This paste offers a strong flavor of garlic. Similar pastes of crushed onion and ginger root are also available. Use in place of the fresh product in any recipe that calls for crushed garlic.

Tahini paste
Very thick, smooth paste from the Middle East made from crushed sesame seeds. Mix with ground chickpeas to make hummus, or thin with lemon juice to eat with falafel and local dishes.

Harissa paste
A fiery chile paste with a distinctive spicy taste that is widely used in North Africa. It is flavored with garlic and coriander, and sometimes caraway. Use as a rub on barbecue meats or in chile con carne.

Sambal ulek paste
In this Southeast Asian paste, chiles are mixed with salt and lime, lemon juice, or vinegar. It is very strong and hot with a tangy aftertaste. Serve as a relish, or use to pep up savory dishes.

FISH PASTES

The two most common types of fish paste are made from cured anchovies in Europe, and from fermented and dried shrimps and other small fish in Asia, southern China, Thailand, Cambodia, Vietnam, Malaysia, and the Philippines. There are many different versions available, depending on the type of fish or shellfish used, and the length of time they are fermented. They are all strong in flavor, but the ones that are fermented the longest, such as those from Cambodia, are very pungent indeed. Some of the longest-fermenting pastes are dried into blocks.

BUY Check the label to see that the paste is pure fish or shellfish with no other additives. Avoid *surimi* products; these are made from pulverized fish of various kinds and synthetically flavored.

STORE Fish paste keeps well out of the fridge. Stronger dried Asian pastes should be put in an airtight container to prevent the flavors being taken up by ingredients stored alongside them.

EAT Use as a seasoning and as a flavoring in both European and Asian dishes. Use a knife to take flakes off solid-block pastes. Most Asian fish pastes have a very strong flavor, so use them sparingly.

Anchovy paste
Intense anchovy flavor. Spread on toast or use to enhance the flavor of meat pâtés or fish sauces. Butter, herbs, and spices are added to make the spreadable English invention, Gentleman's Relish.

Asian shrimp paste
Very pungent aroma and strong fishy taste. Use to add a further dimension and an authentic taste to well-flavored Asian dishes. Use in green and red curries, and fish and vegetable stir-fries.

SALTS

Salt is made up of crystals of sodium chloride. Most table salt is a refined type of rock salt, that is mined underground, milled into very small grains and treated to ensure that it pours easily. Some brands have added iodine for those who prefer it. Less common is sea salt, sometimes known as *gros sel* or "cooking salt", which is obtained by the evaporation of salt from sea water. The crystals are usually larger and may have a light flavor of their own, due to minor impurities, that remain in the salt. In some regions traditional methods are used to prepare the salt; sea water is channelled into open pans and allowed to evaporate naturally in the heat of the sun. Salt may also be flavored with other ingredients, such as mixed spices, celery, or garlic. Some sea salt is cold smoked (smoked with wood chippings at cold temperatures).

🔒 **BUY** Choose rock salt crystals or pickling salt for food preservation. Sea salt is unsuitable for food preservation because of the minerals it contains.

Avoid table salt or iodized salt for pickles since they can cause clouding of the liquid or darkening of the food.

📦 **STORE** The storage life for salt is indefinite; however, it should be kept in an airtight container since it will take up moisture from the air and become lumpy. If this happens, dry in the oven and break up the lumps. Iodized salt may turn yellow, but this is harmless.

⬤ **EAT** Use as a condiment, seasoning, and a food preservative.

Table salt
The ultimate all-purpose salt in the kitchen. It has a straightforward salty flavor that makes it perfect for use at the table as a seasoning and across the board in all types of general cooking.

Rock salt crystals
This commonest form of salt tastes plain and salty. It is mined rather than evaporated from sea water. The best choice for use in a salt grinder and for pickling onions, cucumbers, or walnuts.

Black salt
The color of this lava salt is due to various impurities that give it a distinctive smoky, bitter taste. It is an important ingredient in chat masala spice mix, which is used in many Indian curries.

Celery salt
This has a strong flavor of celery from the ground celery seeds that are mixed with the table salt. Use to season soups, stews, and other dishes that call for fresh celery when it is not available.

Maldon sea salt
Made in Maldon, Essex, UK for over two hundred years, this salt is famous for its lack of bitterness. It is often the chef's first choice for seasoning, due to its distinctive, clean, fresh flavor.

Himalayan rock salt
This is the name given to rock salt from Pakistan. It contains trace elements, which give it a strong mineral flavor and a touch of sulfur. Its pretty color looks good on the table. Use as other salts.

Murray River pink salt
This Australian speciality is produced in the Murray Darling Basin. The peach-colored flakes taste sweetish, and slightly floral. Use sprinkled over sweeter foods, in salad dressings, and in baking.

Fleur de Sel sea salt
This is the purest form of sea salt, derived from the top layer of salt formed in salt pans. The Guérande area of France is famous for it. Use sparingly, as it has a sharp, pure, salty flavor.

Garlic salt
This has a concentrated garlic taste from the powdered dried garlic that is mixed with the table salt. Use it to season soups, stews, and other dishes when fresh garlic is not available.

Sel épicé
Spiced salt has a mixed herb and spice flavor, depending on the added ingredients chosen by the producer. Used widely in French cooking, particularly in salad dressings, soups, and stews.

Smoked sea salt
Salty and lightly smoky. Use to add interest to simple dishes where the unusual flavor will be allowed to come through, such as chilled soups, white sauces, and grilled fish or chicken.

INDEX

Recipe names in *italics*

RECIPE INDEX

THANK YOU

Dorling Kindersley would like to thank the following suppliers who kindly helped us with sourcing ingredients for the making of this book.

FISH

THE FISH SOCIETY
Unit 1, Coopers Place,
Wormley, Surrey GU8 5TG
01428 687768
www.thefishsociety.co.uk

BILLINGSGATE MARKET
Billingsgate seafood training school
Office 30 Billingsgate Market,
Trafalgar Way,
London E14 5ST
020 7517 3548
www.billingsgate-market.org.uk

MEAT

F. DRURY AND SONS LTD
The Abattoir
Tockenham,
Wootton Bassett,
Wiltshire SN4 7PF
01793 840 841
www.fdruryandsons.co.uk

M. MOEN & SONS
24 The Pavement
Clapham Common
London SW4 OJA
020 7622 1624
www.moen.co.uk

RAMSAY OF CARLUKE
22 Mount Stewart Street
Carluke,
Scotland ML8 5ED
01555 772277
www.ramsayofcarluke.co.uk

TAJ STORES
112 Brick Lane
London E1 6RL
020 7247 3844
www.tajstores.co.uk

GERMAN DELI
3 Park Street
London SE1 9AB
020 7250 1322/020 7703 6674
www.germandeli.co.uk

DAYLESFORD ORGANIC
44b Pimlico Road
London SW1W 8LP
020 7881 8060
www.daylesfordorganic.com

DRINGS BUTCHERS
22 Royal Hill, London SE10 8RT
020 8858 4032

HARRODS
87–135 Brompton Road
London SW1X 7XL
0207 730 1234
www.harrods.com

VEGETABLES, HERBS FRUITS, AND SPICES

SKY SPROUTS
Gosworthy Cottage
Higher Plymouth Road
Totnes, Devon
01364 72404,
www.skysprouts.com

PANZERS DELICATESSEN
13–19 Circus Road,
St. Johns Wood, London NW8 6PB
020 7722 1496
www.panzers.co.uk

THE SPICE SHOP
1 Blenheim Crescent,
London W11 2EE
0207 221 4448
www.thespiceshop.co.uk

DAIRY

SCANDINAVIAN KITCHEN
Great Titchfield Street
London W1W 7PP
020 7580 7161
www.scandinaviankitchen.co.uk

GALLERIA RESTAURANT
17 New Cavendish Street
London W1G 9UA
020 7224 1692
www.galleriarestaurant.co.uk

TRAY GOURMET
240 Fulham Road
Chelsea,
London SW10 9NA
0207 352 7676
www.traygourmet.com

LA FROMAGERIE
2–6 Moxon Street,
Marylebone
London W1U 4EW
020 7935 0341
www.lafromagerie.co.uk

GASTRONOMICA
45 Tachbrook Street
London SW1V 2LZ
0207 233 6656
www.gastronomica.myzen.co.uk

OILS

VALLECOPA
1 Southside Farm Cottages,
Warkworth, Northumberland NE65 OYD
07748 562760
www.vallecoppa.com

MEDITERRANEAN DIRECT
66 Joseph Wilson Business Park
Whitstable, Kent CT5 3PS
www.mediterraneandirect.co.uk

GARDA OLIVE OIL
020 8673 4439
www.gardaoliveoil.com

THE LITTLE ITALIAN SHOP
33 Bell Street,
St. Andrews
Fife KY16 9UR
01334 478 396
www.thelittleitalianshop.co.uk

OIL AND MORE
Nutrition Gateway Ltd.
PO Box 34, Wrexham LL14 5YG
01691 772 407
www.oilandmore.co.uk

KING'S FINE FOOD
Unit 2, Mill Farm Business Park
Hounslow, Middlesex TW4 5PY
020 8894 1111
www.kingsfinefood.co.uk

OLLY OILS
Shropshire Mill,
Eaton-upon-Tern,
Shropshire TF9 2BX
0845 680 3579
www.ollyoils.com

WILD WOOD GROVES
www.wildwoodgroves.com

ODYSEA
020 7608 1841
www.odysea.com

BELLA PUGLIA
www.bellapuglia.co.uk

EQUAL EXCHANGE
122 Commercial Street
Edinburgh EH6 6JA
00 44 131 554 59
www.equalexchange.co.uk

OLIVES ET AL
North Dorset Business Park,
Sturminster Newton,
Dorset DT10 2GA
01258 474300
www.olivesetal.co.uk

THE ITALIAN OLIVE OIL COMPANY
Park Farm
Hever Lane,
Hever
Kent TN8 7ET
01342 850992
www.oliveoil4u.co.uk

THE FRESH OLIVE COMPANY
7 Barretts Green Road,
London NW10 7AE
020 8838 1912
www.fresholive.com

MISCELLANEOUS

BIEN MANGER
04 66 42 90 80
www.bienmanger.com

HARVEY NICHOLS
109–125 Knightsbridge
London SW1X 7RJ
0845 604 1888
www.harveynichols.com

OCADO
0845 399 1122
www.ocado.com

GOODNESS DIRECT
South March, Daventry
Northants NN11 4PH
0871 871 6611
www.goodnessdirect.com

JAPAN CENTRE
020 3405 1151
www.japancentre.com

CASA MEXICO
1 Winkley Street
Bethnal Green
London E2 6PY
www.casamexico.co.uk

GREEN LIFE DIRECT
11 The Paddocks
Totnes Industrial Park
Burke Road
Devon TD9 5XT
01803 868733
www.greenlife.co.uk

BUY WHOLEFOODS ONLINE
0800 0431 455
www.buywholefoodsonline.co.uk

ACKNOWLEDGMENTS

DORLING KINDERSLEY WOULD LIKE TO THANK

Recipe Writing Heather Whinney, Carolyn Humphries

Ingredients Sourcing Betsey Clendenen, Caroline Allis

Recipe Testing Katy Greenwood, Lisa Harrison

Home Economist Tina Asher

Art Direction Kat Mead

Photography Assistance Alastair King

Design Mandy Earey, Joanne Mitchell, Sunita Gahir, Caroline Hewitson

Additional Editorial Assistance Salima Hirani

Proofreading Helen Armitage

Indexing Hilary Bird

SPECIAL THANKS ALSO GO TO

Everyone at Billingsgate Seafood training school
Eduard Soley, Manel Bosh, Roqueta Fish SA, Loredana Della Fonte, Elisa Vecchia, Marcello Alinari
Alistair Blair from the Fish Society
Gary and Richard from Moens butchers
John Fletcher for help with the Meat chapter
Ryan Farr for his butchery skills
Brett Kellett from Sky Sprouts
John and Kathy from Panzers Greengrocers
Oliver Driscoll from Vallecopa Oils
Barry Cotgrave from Mediterranean Direct
Jeffery Benson from Garda Olive Oil
Raffaele from The Little Italian Shop
Colin Boag from Bella Puglia Oils
Jo Busck from Equal Exchange
Tamsyn Goodager from Olives et al
Robert from The Italian Olive Oil Company
Laurance Lesbats from The Fresh Olive Company
Andrew Ramsay from Ramsay of Carluke
Jamal from Taj Stores
Jana from German Deli
Michael and Galia from Daylesford Organics
John from Drings Butchers
Nicolas from Très Gourmet
Bronte Blomhoj from Scandinavian Kitchen
Ali Bidarbakht from Galleria Restaurant
Patricia Michelson from La Fromagerie
Susan from The Spice Shop
June McCarry from Waller Road

PICTURE CREDITS

The publisher would like to thank the following for their kind permission to reproduce their photographs:

(Key: a-above; b-below/bottom; c-center; l-left; r-right; t-top)

8-9 Photolibrary: John Warburton-Lee Photography. 12-13 Photolibrary: Fresh Food Images / Maximilian Stock Ltd. 28-29 Getty Images: Rick Price (b). 34 Getty Images: MIXA (cl). 34-35 iStockphoto.com: grandriver (b). 41 fotolia: Le Do (tr). 43 Alamy Images: Art of Food (cra); Image Source (cb). Getty Images: Koki Iino (cla). 44-45 Photolibrary: Tsuneo Nakamura (t). 45-47 Alamy Images: Bon Appetit (b). 50 Alamy Images: Foodcollection.com (cl). 53 Dreamstime.com: Foodmaniac (t). 56-57 fotolia: Roman Ponomarev (c). 57 Dreamstime.com: Deepcameo (crb). 62-63 Alamy Images: Bon Appetit (r). 74 fotolia: Reika (t). 86-87 Dreamstime.com: Mpemberton (t). 97 iStockphoto.com: WEKWEK (tl). 98 Getty Images: Jonathan Kantor Studio (bl). 100-101 Getty Images: Image Source. 122-123 Getty Images: Image Source. 180-181 Corbis: AgStock Images. 192 iStockphoto.com: vtupinamba (br). Photolibrary: Foodcollection.com (bl); Fotosearch Value (tr); MIXA Co Ltd (tl). 199 Alamy Images: Rob Walls (bl). 204 Photolibrary: Maximilian Stock Ltd (t). 206-207 Getty Images: Beverly Logan. 208 iStockphoto.com: Suzifoo (tr). 216-217 Corbis: Christina Simons. 222 Getty Images: Brian Summers. 231 Alamy Images: Teubner Foodfoto (tl). Baker Creek Heirloom Seed Co: (c). 234-235 Getty Images: Paul Poplis. 238 Alamy Images: CuboImages srl (br). 241 Photolibrary: Maximilian Stock Ltd (bl). 242-243 iStockphoto.com: dirkr (c). 245 Science Photo Library: Ed Young / AGStockUSA (tl). 247 fotolia: Maceo (br). 248-249 Corbis: Owen Franken. 250 Purcell Mountain Farms: (bl). 253 Purcell Mountain Farms: (tr). 256 fotolia: Shariff Che'Lah (tl). 257 Getty Images: Visual Cuisines (bl). 260 fotolia: peter bauwens (cl). 264-265 fotolia: Elena Schweitzer (bc). 272-273 Corbis: Hein van den Heuvel. 276 Alamy Images: Arco Images GmbH (b). Getty Images: Doable / A. collection (cr). 280-281 Corbis: Matilda Lindeblad / Johnér Images. 286 Alamy Images: amana images inc (br). 288 fotolia: ott (tl). 295 Dreamstime.com: Paylessimages (tr). 303 Alamy Images: Westend61 (br). 310 Corbis: Photolibrary. 322 fotolia: Shariff Che'Lah (br). Photolibrary: Kidd Geoff (bl). 326-327 Getty Images: Michael Rosenfeld. 354-355 fotolia: Bell (b). 371 Corbis: Sudres / photocuisine. 386-387 Photolibrary: John Warburton-Lee Photography. 416 Alamy Images: VG Stock (br); WILDLIFE GmbH (tr). 417 The National Fruit Collection at Brogdale: (br). 420 Alamy Images: Bon Appetit (tl). 424 Photolibrary: Riou Riou (crb). 433 Scope: J Guillard (tl). 436 fotolia: Unclesam (cr). 438 Alamy Images: Bon Appetit (tc). fotolia: Alexander Bedoya (br). 440 Dreamstime.com: Ksenia Krylova (br). 444 Photolibrary: Sue Atkinson / Fresh Food Images (b). 447 fotolia: sil (cl). 450 Alamy Images: Keith Leighton (tl). 453 Alamy Images: Nigel Cattlin (cr). 454 StockFood.com: Peter Rees (clb). 454-455 Getty Images: Image Source (tc). 462 Photolibrary: Dinodia Dinodia (bl). 469 Dreamstime.com: Vinicius Tupinamba (b). iStockphoto.com: microgen (tl). 473 Achacha Fruit Group: (br). Alamy Images: Flavio Coelho (bl). 478-479 Getty Images: Martin Harvey. 492-493 Corbis: Lars Ternblad / Johnér Images. 508-509 Getty Images: Franck Bichon.

All other images © Dorling Kindersley

For further information see: www.dkimages.com